Lecture Notes in Computer Science　　　9404

Commenced Publication in 1973
Founding and Former Series Editors:
Gerhard Goos, Juris Hartmanis, and Jan van Leeuwen

More information about this series at http://www.springer.com/series/7410

Herbert Bos · Fabian Monrose
Gregory Blanc (Eds.)

Research in Attacks, Intrusions, and Defenses

18th International Symposium, RAID 2015
Kyoto, Japan, November 2–4, 2015
Proceedings

 Springer

Editors
Herbert Bos
Computer Science Department
Vrije Universiteit Amsterdam
Amsterdam
The Netherlands

Gregory Blanc
Télécom SudParis
Université Paris-Saclay
Evry
France

Fabian Monrose
University of North Carolina at Chapel Hill
Chapel-Hill, NC
USA

ISSN 0302-9743   ISSN 1611-3349   (electronic)
Lecture Notes in Computer Science
ISBN 978-3-319-26361-8   ISBN 978-3-319-26362-5   (eBook)
DOI 10.1007/978-3-319-26362-5

Library of Congress Control Number: 2015953803

LNCS Sublibrary: SL4 – Security and Cryptology

Springer Cham Heidelberg New York Dordrecht London

Printed on acid-free paper

Springer International Publishing AG Switzerland is part of Springer Science+Business Media
(www.springer.com)

Foreword

Welcome to the proceedings of the 18th International Symposium on Research in Attacks, Intrusions and Defenses (RAID). Over the past 18 years, RAID has established itself as a highly influential venue with a prime focus on attacks and defenses. We believe that this year was no different, and that the conference once again offered a great program in this increasingly important field of research.

We had a large number of submissions, with 119 papers that met the anonymity and formatting guidelines, considerably more than in previous years. Interestingly, authors from European-, US-, and Asian-based institutions each accounted for about one third of the submissions. In terms of the accepted papers, the balance shifted slightly in favor of EU- and US-based authors, but not by much.

The Program Committee (PC) selected 28 papers, representing an acceptance rate of 23.5 %. The papers were reviewed using a double-blind reviewing process, ensuring that the reviewers were unaware of the authors or their affiliations until after the selection was finalized. All papers that were on-topic and met the formatting requirements received at least three reviews and the final selection was made during an in-person meeting in Washington DC in August. We thank the authors of both accepted and rejected papers for submitting their papers to RAID.

As always, the bulk of the meeting was spent discussing papers where the reviews from the PC were not in agreement. The task at hand was not only to identify those papers that were ready for publication, but to also identify promising work that could be improved before the camera-ready deadline. Out of the 28 selected papers, several were assigned shepherds to ensure that the camera-ready version addressed all the reviewers' concerns and suggested improvements. In many cases, these papers received several rounds of additional feedback by their shepherds.

In selecting PC members, we strived to introduce new talent to the RAID conference. Similar to the year before, our goal was to form a PC that included researchers who had not served on the RAID PC more than once in the past few years, and also had a proven track record in terms of top-tier publications. We also made a deliberate attempt to introduce a number of younger researchers, while balancing that with more senior members in the field. Our hope was that in doing so, the younger researchers would gain invaluable experience by serving on the PC, and could help shape the direction of future RAID conferences.

It goes without saying that we are indebted to the RAID 2015 PC for selflessly dedicating their time to the process of selecting papers and providing detailed feedback to authors. Serving as a PC member is a hard task, and we believe the recognition for these efforts is often overlooked. For this reason, and to encourage PC members to write critical, yet constructive, reviews, we decided to award an "Outstanding Reviewer" prize to Manos Antonakakis (Georgia Tech) and Konrad Rieck (University of Göttingen). The procedure was that we encouraged PC members to rate each other's reviews. While many reviewers received positive ratings, Konrad and Manos edged out all others with their thoughtful and very helpful reviews and we congratulate them with their well-deserved awards!

There are so many other people we need to thank. First, we would like to thank the general chair, Youki Kadobayashi, and his team for the wonderful organization. Until one has been closely involved with a conference, it is hard to appreciate everything that the local arrangements chair has to do, and this conference was no exception. We are very grateful to Kazuya Okada for the job well done. A massive thanks is also owed to Gregory Blanc for handling the publications and making sure that every paper conformed to the format required by Springer, and to Giorgos Vasiliadis for being such a good publicity chair that we had even more submissions than last year. In addition to RAID's main conference, we had a very interesting poster session organized by Sanjay Rawat. The poster session included posters from many of the accepted papers as well as posters that were selected by the poster chair. Finally, we thank the very active and helpful Steering Committee.

We hope that you enjoyed RAID conference as much as we enjoyed putting the event together. A great set of papers, covering a wide range of topics, this is what makes RAID truly special.

Finally, none of this would be possible without the generous support by our sponsors: Deloitte Tohmatsu Risk Services, Farsight, TAPAD, NTT Communications and Asterisk Research. We are also grateful to Tateishi Science and Technology Foundation for their generous support. We greatly appreciate their help and their continued commitment to a healthy research community in security.

September 2015

Herbert Bos
Fabian Monrose

Organization

Organizing Committee

General Chair
Youki Kadobayashi   Nara Institute of Science and Technology, Japan

Local Arrangements Chair
Kazuya Okada   Nara Institute of Science and Technology, Japan

Program Committee Chair
Herbert Bos   Vrije Universiteit Amsterdam, The Netherlands

Program Committee Co-chair
Fabian Monrose   University of North Carolina at Chapel Hill, USA

Poster Chair
Sanjay Rawat   Vrije Universiteit Amsterdam, The Netherlands

Publication Chair
Gregory Blanc   Télécom SudParis, Université Paris-Saclay, France

Publicity Chair
Giorgos Vasiliadis   FORTH, Greece

Program Committee

Manos Antonakakis	Georgia Institute of Technology, USA
Elias Athanasopoulos	FORTH, Greece
Herbert Bos	Vrije Universiteit Amsterdam, The Netherlands
Gabriela Ciocarlie	SRI International, USA
Lucas Davi	Intel CRI-SC at TU Darmstadt, Germany
Tudor Dumitras	University of Maryland, USA
Petros Efstathopoulos	Symantec Research Labs, USA
William Enck	North Carolina State University, USA
Bryan Ford	EPFL, Switzerland
Aurélien Francillon	Eurécom, France
Flavio Garcia	University of Birmingham, UK
Chris Kanich	University of Illinois at Chicago, USA

Christopher Kruegel	UC Santa Barbara, USA
Andrea Lanzi	University of Milan, Italy
Corrado Leita	LastLine Inc., USA
Brian Levine	University of Massachusetts Amherst, USA
Fabian Monrose	University of North Carolina at Chapel Hill, USA
Zachary Peterson	California Polytechnic State University, San Luis Obispo, USA
Georgios Portokalidis	Stevens Institute of Technology, USA
Niels Provos	Google Inc., USA
Konrad Rieck	University of Göttingen, Germany
William Robertson	Northeastern University, USA
Christian Rossow	Saarland University, Germany
Andrei Sabelfeld	Chalmers University of Technology, Sweden
Stelios Sidiroglou-Douskos	MIT, USA
Patrick Traynor	University of Florida, USA
XiaoFeng Wang	Indiana University, USA
Dongyan Xu	Purdue University, USA

External Reviewers

Benjamin Andow	North Carolina State University, USA
Orlando Arias	University of Central Florida, USA
Daniel Arp	University of Göttingen, Germany
Andrei Bacs	Vrije Universiteit Amsterdam, The Netherlands
Musard Balliu	Chalmers University of Technology, Sweden
Henry Carter	Georgia Institute of Technology, USA
Tom Chothia	University of Birmingham, UK
Andrei Costin	Eurécom, France
Dimitrios Damopoulos	Stevens Institute of Technology, USA
Hamid Ebadi	Chalmers University of Technology, Sweden
Gurchetan Grewal	University of Birmingham, UK
Per Hallgren	Chalmers University of Technology, Sweden
Daniel Hausknecht	Chalmers University of Technology, Sweden
Panagiotis Ilias	FORTH, Greece
Kangkook Jee	NEC Laboratories America, USA
Jill Jermyn	Columbia University, USA
Lazaros Koromilas	FORTH, Greece
Christopher Liebchen	Technische Universität Darmstadt, Germany
Sergio Maffeis	Imperial College London, UK
Adwait Nadkarni	North Carolina State University, USA
Susanta Nanda	Symantec Research Labs, USA
Martin Ochoa	Singapore University of Technology and Design, Singapore
Mihai Ordean	University of Birmingham, UK
Panagiotis Papadopoulos	FORTH, Greece
Thanasis Petsas	FORTH, Greece

Andreea Radu   University of Birmingham, UK
Moheeb Abu Rajab   Google Inc., USA
Bradley Reaves   University of Florida, USA
Raphaël Rieu-Helft   Imperial College London, UK
Merve Sahin   Eurécom, France
Brendan Saltaformaggio   Purdue University, USA
Nolen Scaife   University of Florida, USA
Daniel Schoepe   Chalmers University of Technology, Sweden
Alexander Sjösten   Chalmers University of Technology, Sweden
Kevin Z. Snow   University of North Carolina at Chapel Hill, USA
Dean Sullivan   University of Central Florida, USA
Adrian Tang   Columbia University, USA
Sam Thomas   University of Birmingham, UK
Steeve Van Acker   Chalmers University of Technology, Sweden
Giorgos Vasiliadis   FORTH, Greece
Victor van der Veen   Vrije Universiteit Amsterdam, The Netherlands
Andrew M. White   University of North Carolina at Chapel Hill, USA
Fabian Yamaguchi   University of Göttingen, Germany
Vinod Yegneswaran   SRI International, USA
Man-Ki Yoon   University of Illinois at Urbana-Champaign, USA

Steering Committee

Marc Dacier (Chair)   Qatar Foundation/Qatar Computing Research
                             Institute, Qatar
Davide Balzarotti   Eurécom, France
Hervé Debar   Télécom SudParis, Université Paris-Saclay, France
Deborah Frincke   DoD Research, USA
Ming-Yuh Huang   Northwest Security Institute, USA
Somesh Jha   University of Wisconsin, USA
Erland Jonsson   Chalmers University of Technology, Sweden
Engin Kirda   Northeastern University, USA
Christopher Kruegel   UC Santa Barbara, USA
Wenke Lee   Georgia Institute of Technology, USA
Richard Lippmann   MIT Lincoln Laboratory, USA
Ludovic Mé   CentraleSupélec, France
Robin Sommer   ICSI/LBNL, USA
Angelos Stavrou   George Mason University, USA
Alfonso Valdes   SRI International, USA
Giovanni Vigna   UC Santa Barbara, USA
Andreas Wespi   IBM Research, Switzerland
S. Felix Wu   UC Davis, USA
Diego Zamboni   CFEngine AS, Mexico

Sponsors

Deloitte Tohmatsu Risk Services Co., Ltd. (Gold level)
Farsight Security, Inc. (Silver level)
Tapad Inc. (Silver level)
NTT Communications Corporation (Bronze level)
Asterisk Research, Inc. (Bronze level)

Contents

Hardware

Ensemble Learning for Low-Level Hardware-Supported Malware Detection   3
  Khaled N. Khasawneh, Meltem Ozsoy, Caleb Donovick,
  Nael Abu-Ghazaleh, and Dmitry Ponomarev

Physical-Layer Detection of Hardware Keyloggers   26
  Ryan M. Gerdes and Saptarshi Mallick

Reverse Engineering Intel Last-Level Cache Complex Addressing
Using Performance Counters   48
  Clémentine Maurice, Nicolas Le Scouarnec, Christoph Neumann,
  Olivier Heen, and Aurélien Francillon

Hardware-Assisted Fine-Grained Code-Reuse Attack Detection   66
  Pinghai Yuan, Qingkai Zeng, and Xuhua Ding

Networks

Haetae: Scaling the Performance of Network Intrusion Detection
with Many-Core Processors   89
  Jaehyun Nam, Muhammad Jamshed, Byungkwon Choi, Dongsu Han,
  and KyoungSoo Park

Demystifying the IP Blackspace   111
  Quentin Jacquemart, Pierre-Antoine Vervier, Guillaume Urvoy-Keller,
  and Ernst Biersack

Providing Dynamic Control to Passive Network Security Monitoring   133
  Johanna Amann and Robin Sommer

Hardening

Probabilistic Inference on Integrity for Access Behavior Based
Malware Detection   155
  Weixuan Mao, Zhongmin Cai, Don Towsley, and Xiaohong Guan

Counteracting Data-Only Malware with Code Pointer Examination   177
  Thomas Kittel, Sebastian Vogl, Julian Kirsch, and Claudia Eckert

Xede: Practical Exploit Early Detection   198
  Meining Nie, Purui Su, Qi Li, Zhi Wang, Lingyun Ying, Jinlong Hu,
  and Dengguo Feng

Attack Detection I

Preventing Exploits in Microsoft Office Documents Through Content
Randomization   225
   Charles Smutz and Angelos Stavrou

Improving Accuracy of Static Integer Overflow Detection in Binary   247
   Yang Zhang, Xiaoshan Sun, Yi Deng, Liang Cheng, Shuke Zeng,
   Yu Fu, and Dengguo Feng

A Formal Framework for Program Anomaly Detection   270
   Xiaokui Shu, Danfeng (Daphne) Yao, and Barbara G. Ryder

Web and Net

jÄk: Using Dynamic Analysis to Crawl and Test Modern
Web Applications   295
   Giancarlo Pellegrino, Constantin Tschürtz, Eric Bodden,
   and Christian Rossow

WYSISNWIV: What You Scan Is Not What I Visit   317
   Qilang Yang, Dimitrios Damopoulos, and Georgios Portokalidis

SDN Rootkits: Subverting Network Operating Systems
of Software-Defined Networks   339
   Christian Röpke and Thorsten Holz

Android

AppSpear: Bytecode Decrypting and DEX Reassembling for Packed
Android Malware   359
   Wenbo Yang, Yuanyuan Zhang, Juanru Li, Junliang Shu, Bodong Li,
   Wenjun Hu, and Dawu Gu

HELDROID: Dissecting and Detecting Mobile Ransomware   382
   Nicoló Andronio, Stefano Zanero, and Federico Maggi

Continuous Authentication on Mobile Devices Using Power Consumption,
Touch Gestures and Physical Movement of Users   405
   Rahul Murmuria, Angelos Stavrou, Daniel Barbará, and Dan Fleck

Privacy

Privacy Risk Assessment on Online Photos   427
   Haitao Xu, Haining Wang, and Angelos Stavrou

Contents   XIII

Privacy is Not an Option: Attacking the IPv6 Privacy Extension.   448
Johanna Ullrich and Edgar Weippl

Evaluating Solutions

Evaluation of Intrusion Detection Systems in Virtualized Environments
Using Attack Injection.   471
*Aleksandar Milenkoski, Bryan D. Payne, Nuno Antunes, Marco Vieira,
Samuel Kounev, Alberto Avritzer, and Matthias Luft*

Security Analysis of PHP Bytecode Protection Mechanisms.   493
Dario Weißer, Johannes Dahse, and Thorsten Holz

Radmin: Early Detection of Application-Level Resource Exhaustion
and Starvation Attacks.   515
Mohamed Elsabagh, Daniel Barbará, Dan Fleck, and Angelos Stavrou

Towards Automatic Inference of Kernel Object Semantics
from Binary Code.   538
Junyuan Zeng and Zhiqiang Lin

Attack Detection II

BOTWATCHER: Transparent and Generic Botnet Tracking.   565
*Thomas Barabosch, Adrian Dombeck, Khaled Yakdan,
and Elmar Gerhards-Padilla*

Elite: Automatic Orchestration of Elastic Detection Services
to Secure Cloud Hosting   588
*Yangyi Chen, Vincent Bindschaedler, XiaoFeng Wang, Stefan Berger,
and Dimitrios Pendarakis*

AmpPot: Monitoring and Defending Against Amplification DDoS Attacks. . .   615
*Lukas Krämer, Johannes Krupp, Daisuke Makita, Tomomi Nishizoe,
Takashi Koide, Katsunari Yoshioka, and Christian Rossow*

Author Index   637

Hardware

Ensemble Learning for Low-Level Hardware-Supported Malware Detection

Khaled N. Khasawneh[1], Meltem Ozsoy[2], Caleb Donovick[3],
Nael Abu-Ghazaleh[1(✉)], and Dmitry Ponomarev[3]

[1] University of California, Riverside, CA, USA
{kkhas001,naelag}@ucr.edu
[2] Intel Corporation, Santa Clara, CA, USA
meltem.ozsoy@intel.com
[3] Binghamton University, Binghamton, NY, USA
{cdonovi1,dima}@cs.binghamton.edu

Abstract. Recent work demonstrated hardware-based online malware detection using only low-level features. This detector is envisioned as a first line of defense that prioritizes the application of more expensive and more accurate software detectors. Critical to such a framework is the detection performance of the hardware detector. In this paper, we explore the use of both specialized detectors and ensemble learning techniques to improve performance of the hardware detector. The proposed detectors reduce the false positive rate by more than half compared to a single detector, while increasing the detection rate. We also contribute approximate metrics to quantify the detection overhead, and show that the proposed detectors achieve more than 11x reduction in overhead compared to a software only detector (1.87x compared to prior work), while improving detection time. Finally, we characterize the hardware complexity by extending an open core and synthesizing it on an FPGA platform, showing that the overhead is minimal.

1 Introduction

Malware continues to be a significant threat to computing systems at all scales. For example, AV TEST reports that 220,000 new malicious programs are registered to be examined every day and around 220 million total malware signatures are available in their malware zoo in the first quarter of 2014 [2]. Moreover, detection is becoming more difficult due to the increasing use of metamorphic and polymorphic malware [37]. Zero-day exploits also defy signature based static analysis since their signatures have not been yet encountered in the wild. This necessitates the use of dynamic detection techniques [9] that can detect the malicious behavior during execution, often based on the detection of anomalies, rather than signatures [4,16]. However, the complexity and difficulty of continuous dynamic monitoring have traditionally limited its use.

This research was partially supported by the US National Science Foundation grants CNS-1018496 and CNS-1422401.

© Springer International Publishing Switzerland 2015
H. Bos et al. (Eds.): RAID 2015, LNCS 9404, pp. 3–25, 2015.
DOI: 10.1007/978-3-319-26362-5_1

Recent work has shown that malware can be differentiated from normal programs by classifying anomalies in low-level feature spaces such as hardware events collected by performance counters on modern CPUs [3,6]. We call such features *sub-semantic* because they do not rely on a semantic model of the monitored program. In recent work, a classifier trained using supervised learning to differentiate malware from normal programs while the programs run was introduced [23]. To tolerate false positives, this system is envisioned as a first step in malware detection to prioritize which processes should be dynamically monitored using a more sophisticated but more expensive second level of protection.

The objective of this paper is to improve the classification accuracy of sub-semantic malware detection, allowing us to detect malware more successfully while reducing the burden on the second level of protection in response to false positives. We base our study on a recent malware data set [21]; more details are presented in Sect. 2. We pursue improved detection using two approaches. First, we explore, in Sect. 3, whether specialized detectors, each tuned to a specific type of malware, can more successfully classify that type of malware. We find that this is indeed the case, and identify the features that perform best for each specialized detector. Second, in Sect. 4, we explore how to combine multiple detectors, whether general or specialized, to improve the overall performance of the detection. We also evaluate the performance of the ensemble detectors in both offline and online detection.

To quantify the performance advantage from the improved detection, we develop metrics that translate detection performance to expected overhead in terms of the second level detector (Sect. 5). We discover that the detection performance of the online detection is substantially improved, reducing the false positives by over half for our best configurations, while also significantly improving the detection rate. This advantage translates to over 11x reduction in overhead of the two-level detection framework. We analyze the implications on the hardware complexity of the different configurations in Sect. 6. We compare this approach to related work in Sect. 7.

This paper makes the following contributions:

- We characterize how specialized detectors trained for specific malware types perform compared to a general detector and show that specialization has significant performance advantages.
- We use ensemble learning to improve the performance of the hardware detector. However, combining specialized detectors is a non-classical application of ensemble learning, which requires new approaches. We also explore combining general detectors (with different features) as well as specialized and general detectors.
- We evaluate the hardware complexity of the proposed designs by extending the AO486 open core. We propose and evaluate some hardware optimizations.
- We define metrics for the two-level detection framework that translate detection performance to expected reduction in overhead, and time to detection.

2   Approach and Evaluation Methodology

Demme et al. [6] showed that malware programs can be classified effectively by the use of offline machine learning model applied to low-level features; in this case, the features were the performance counters of a modern ARM processor collected periodically. Subsequently, Ozsoy et al. [23] explored a number of low-level features, not only those available through performance counters, and built an *online* hardware-supported, low-complexity, malware detector. Such low-level features are called *sub-semantic* since they do not require knowledge of the semantics of the executing program. The online detection problem uses a time-series window based averaging to detect transient malware behavior. As detection is implemented in hardware, simple machine learning algorithms are used to avoid the overhead of complex algorithms. This work demonstrated that sub-semantic features can be used to detect malware in real-time (i.e., not only after the fact).

The goal of this work is to improve the effectiveness of online hardware-supported malware detection. Better machine learning classifiers can identify more malware with fewer false positives, substantially improving the performance of the malware detection system. To improve detection, we explore using specialized detectors for different malware types. We show that such specialized detectors are more effective than general detectors in classifying their malware type. Furthermore, we study different approaches for ensemble learning: combining the decisions of multiple detectors to achieve better classification. In this section, we overview the approach, and present the methodology and experimental details.

2.1   Programs Used for This Study

We collected samples of malware and normal programs to use in the training, cross validation and testing of our detectors. Since the malware programs that we use are Windows-based, we only used Windows programs for the regular program set. This set contains the SPEC 2006 benchmarks [12], Windows system binaries, and many popular applications such as Acrobat Reader, Notepad++, and Winrar. In total 554 programs were collected as the non-malware component of the data.

Our malware programs were collected from the MalwareDB malware set [21]. We selected only malware programs that were found between 2011–2014. The malware data sets have a total of 3,690 malware programs among them.

The group of regular and malware programs were all executed within a virtual machine running a 32-bit Windows 7 with the firewall and security services for Windows disabled, so that malware could perform its intended functionality. Moreover, we used the Pin instrumentation tool [5] to gather the dynamic traces of programs as they were executed. Each trace was collected for a duration of 5,000 system calls or 15 million committed instructions, whichever is first.

The malware data set consists of five types of malware: Backdoors, Password Stealers (PWS), Rogues, Trojans, and Worms. The malware groups and the

Table 1. Data set breakdown

	Total	Traning	Testing	Cross validation
Backdoor	815	489	163	163
Rogue	685	411	137	137
PWS	558	335	111	111
Trojan	1123	673	225	225
Worm	473	283	95	95
Regular	554	332	111	111

regular programs were divided into three sets; training (60 %), testing (20 %) and cross-validation (20 %). Table 1 shows the content of these sets.

We note that both the number of programs and the duration of the profiling of each program is limited by the computational overhead; since we are collecting dynamic profiling information through Pin [5] within a virtual machine, collection requires several weeks of execution on a small cluster, and produces several terabytes of compressed profiling data. Training and testing is also extremely computationally intensive. This dataset is sufficiently large to establish the feasibility and provide a reasonable evaluation of the proposed approach.

2.2 Feature Selection

There are numerous features present at the architecture/hardware level that could be used. We use the same features as Ozsoy et al. [23], to enable direct comparison of ensemble learning against a single detector. For completeness, we describe the rationale behind these features:

– **Instruction mix features**: these are features that are derived from the types and/or frequencies of executed opcodes. We considered four features based on opcodes. Feature INS1 tracks the frequency of opcode occurrence in each of the x86 instruction categories. INS3 is a binary version of INS1 that tracks the presence of opcodes in each category. The top 35 opcodes with the largest difference (delta) in frequency between malware and regular programs were aggregated and used as feature (INS2). Finally, INS4 is a binary version of INS2 indicating opcode presence for the 35 largest difference opcodes.
– **Memory reference patterns**: these are features based on memory addresses used by the program. The first feature we consider in this group is MEM1, which keeps track of the memory reference distance in quantized bins (i.e., creates a histogram of the memory reference distance). The second feature we consider (MEM2) is a simpler form of MEM1 that tracks the presence of a load/store in each of the distance bins.
– **Architectural events**: features based on architectural events such as cache misses and branch predictions. The features collected were: total number

of memory reads, memory writes, unaligned memory accesses, immediate branches and taken branches. This feature is called ARCH in the remainder of the paper.

The features were collected once every 10,000 committed instructions of the program, consistent with the methodology used by earlier works that use this approach [6,23]. These prior studies demonstrated that classification at this frequency effectively balances complexity and detection accuracy for offline [6] and online [23] detection. For each program we maintained a sequence of these feature vectors collected every 10 K instructions, labeled as either malware or normal.

3 Characterizing Performance of Specialized Detectors

In this section, we introduce the idea of *specialized detectors*: those that are trained to identify a single type of malware. First, we explore whether such detectors can outperform *general detectors*, which are detectors trained to classify any type of malware. If indeed they outperform general detectors, we then explore how to use such detectors to improve the overall detection of the system.

We separate our malware sets into types based on Microsoft Malware Protection Center classification [19]. We use logistic regression for all our experiments because of the ease of hardware implementation [13]. In particular, the collected feature data for programs and malware is used to train logistic regression detectors. We pick the threshold for the output of the detector, which is used to separate a malware from a regular program, such that it maximizes the sum of the sensitivity and specificity. For each detector in this paper, we present the threshold value used.

Training General Detectors. A general detector should be able to detect all types of malware programs. Therefore, a general detector is trained using a data set that encompasses all types of malware programs, against another set with regular programs. We trained seven general detectors, one for each of the feature vectors we considered.

Training Specialized Detectors. The specialized detectors are designed to detect a specific type of malware relative to the regular programs. Therefore, the specialized detectors were trained only with malware that matches the detector type, as well as regular programs, so that it would have a better model for detecting the type of malware it is specialized for. For example, the Backdoors detector is trained to classify Backdoors from regular programs only. We chose this approach rather than also attempting to classify malware types from each other because false positives among malware types are not important for our goals. Moreover, types of malware may share features that regular programs do not have and thus classifying them from each other makes classification against regular programs less effective.

Each specialized detector was trained using a data set that includes regular programs and the malware type that the specialized detector is built for. On the other hand, the general detectors were trained using all the training data sets that we used for the specialized detectors combined plus the regular programs. In experiments that evaluate specialized detectors, the testing set (used for all detectors in such experiments including general detectors) consists only of normal programs and the specialized detector malware type. The reasoning for this choice is that we do not care about the performance of the specialized detector on other types of malware; if included these malware types would add noise to the results.

3.1   Specialized Detectors: Is There an Opportunity?

Next, we investigate whether specialized detectors outperform general detectors when tested against the malware type they were trained for. Intuitively, each malware type has different behavior allowing a specialized detector to more effectively carry out classification. Moreover, the detectors in this section were evaluated using the offline detection approach explained in Sect. 4.3.

General Vs. Specialized Detectors. We built specialized detectors for five types of malware which are Backdoor, PWS, Rogue, Trojan and Worm. Each of the seven general detectors' performance was compared against the performance of each specialized detectors in detecting the specific malware type for which the specialized detector was trained. Moreover, each comparison between specialized and general detectors used the same testing set for both of the detectors. The testing set includes regular programs and the malware type that the specialized detector was designed for.

Figures 1a, b show the Receiver Operating Characteristic (ROC) curves separated by type of malware using the general detector and the specialized detectors which were built using MEM1 features vector. Table 2 shows the Area Under the Curve (AUC) values for the ROC curves that resulted from all the comparisons between the general and specialized detectors in each feature vector. The ROC curves represent the classification rate (Sensitivity) as a function of false positives (100-Specificity) for different threshold values between 0 and 1. We found that in the majority of the comparisons, the specialized detectors indeed perform better than or equal to the general detector.

There were some cases where the general detector outperforms the specialized detectors for some features. We believe this behavior occurs because the general detector is trained using a larger data set than the specialized detector (it includes the other malware types). There are only a limited number of cases where the generalized detector outperforms the specialized ones for a specific feature. In most of these cases, the detection performance is poor, indicating that the feature is not particularly useful for classifying the given malware type.

Estimating the opportunity from deploying specialized detectors compared to general detectors is important since it gives an intuition of the best performance that could be reached using the specialized detectors. Thus, we compared the performance of the best performing general detector against the best specialized detector for each type of malware. Figure 2a shows the ROC curves of the INS4 general

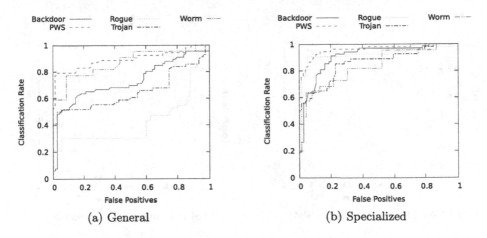

(a) General   (b) Specialized

Fig. 1. MEM1 detectors performance

Table 2. AUC values for all general and specialized detectors

		Backdoor	PWS	Rogue	Trojan	Worm
INS1	General	0.713	0.909	0.949	0.715	0.705
	Specialized	0.715	0.892	0.962	0.727	0.819
INS2	General	0.905	0.946	0.993	0.768	0.810
	Specialized	0.895	0.954	0.976	0.782	0.984
INS3	General	0.837	0.909	0.924	0.527	0.761
	Specialized	0.840	0.888	0.991	0.808	0.852
INS4	General	0.866	0.868	0.914	0.788	0.830
	Specialized	0.891	0.941	0.993	0.798	0.869
MEM1	General	0.729	0.893	0.424	0.650	0.868
	Specialized	0.868	0.961	0.921	0.867	0.871
MEM2	General	0.833	0.947	0.761	0.866	0.903
	Specialized	0.843	0.979	0.931	0.868	0.871
ARCH	General	0.702	0.919	0.965	0.763	0.602
	Specialized	0.686	0.942	0.970	0.795	0.560

detector (best performing general detector) while Fig. 2b shows the ROC curves for the best specialized detectors. In most cases, the specialized detectors outperform the general detector, sometimes significantly. Table 3 demonstrates this observation by showing that the average improvement opportunity using the AUC values is about 0.0904, improving the AUC by more than 10 %. Although the improvement may appear to be modest, it has a substantial impact on performance. For example, the improvement in Rogue detection, 8 % in the AUC, translates to a 4x reduction in overhead according to the work metric we define in Sect. 5.2).

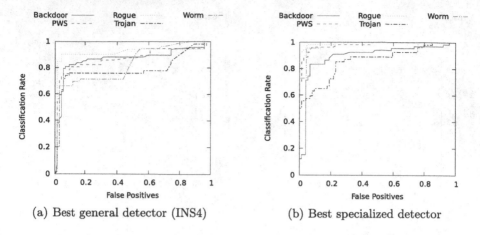

(a) Best general detector (INS4)   (b) Best specialized detector

Fig. 2. Opportunity size: best specialized vs. best general detector

Table 3. Improvement opportunity: area under curve

	General	Specialized	Difference
Backdoor	0.8662	0.8956	0.0294
PWS	0.8684	0.9795	0.1111
Rogue	0.9149	0.9937	0.0788
Trojan	0.7887	0.8676	0.0789
Worm	0.8305	0.9842	0.1537
Average	0.8537	0.9441	0.0904

These results make it clear that specialized detectors are more successful than general detectors in classifying malware. However, it is not clear why different features are more successful in detecting different classes of malware, or indeed why classification is at all possible in this subsemantic feature space. To attempt to answer this question, we examined the weights in the Θ vector of the logistic regression ARCH feature specialized detector for Rogue and Worm respectively. This feature obtains 0.97 AUC for Rogue but only 0.56 for Worm (see Table 2). We find that the Rogue classifier discovered that the number of branches in Rogue where significantly less than normal programs while the number of misaligned memory addresses were significantly higher. In contrast, Worm weights were very low for all ARCH vector elements, indicating that Worms behaved similar to normal programs in terms of all architectural features. Explaining the fundamental reasons behind these differences in behavior is a topic of future research.

4 Malware Detection Using Ensemble Learning

Starting from a set of general detectors (one per feature) and a set of specialized detectors, our next goal is to explore how to compose these detectors to improve overall detection; such composite detectors are called ensemble detectors [8]. A decision function is used to combined the results of the base detectors into a final decision. Figure 3 illustrates the combined detector components and overall operation.

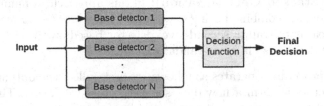

Fig. 3. Combined detector

The general technique of combining multiple detectors is called *ensemble learning*; the classic type considers combining multiple independent detectors which are trained to classify the same phenomena [8]. For example, for malware detection, all the general detectors were designed to detect any type of malware. Thus, ensemble learning techniques apply to the problem of combining their decisions directly.

On the other hand, for the specialized detectors, each detector is trained to classify a different phenomena (different type of malware); they are each answering a different classification question. Given that we do not know if a program contains malware, let alone the malware type, it is not clear how specialized detectors can be used as part of an overall detection solution. In particular, its unclear whether common ensemble learning techniques, which assume detectors that classify the same phenomena, would successfully combine the different specialized detectors.

In order to solve this problem, we evaluated different decision functions to combine the specialized detectors. We focused on combining techniques which use all the detectors independently in parallel to obtain the final output from the decision function. Since all the detectors are running in parallel, this approach speeds up the computation.

4.1 Decision Functions

We evaluated the following decision functions.

- **Or'ing:** If any of the detectors detects that a given input is a malware then the final detection result is a malware. This approach is likely to improve sensitivity, but result in a high number of false positives (reduce selectivity).

- **High Confidence:** This decision function is an improved version of the or'ing decision function. In particular, the difference is that we select the specialized detector thresholds so that their output will be malware only when they are highly confident that the input is a malware program. Intuitively, specialized detectors are likely to have high confidence only when they encounter the malware type they are trained for.
- **Majority Voting:** The final decision is the decision of the majority of the detectors. Thus, if most of them agreed that the program is a malware the final decision will be that it is a malware program.
- **Stacking (Stacked Generalization):** In this approach, a number of first-level detectors are combined using a second-level detector (*meta-learner*) [33]). The key idea, is to train a second-level detector based on the output of first-level (base) detectors via cross-validation.

The stacking procedure operates as follows: we first collect the output of each of the base detectors to form a new data set using cross-validation. The collected data set would have every base detector decision for each instance in the cross-validation data set as well as the true classification (malware or regular program). In this step, it is critical to ensure that the base detectors are formed using a batch of the training data set that is different from the one used to form the new data set. The second step is to treat the new data set as a new problem, and employ a learning algorithm to solve it.

4.2   Ensemble Detectors

To aid with the selection of the base detectors to use within the ensemble detectors, we compare the set of general detectors to each other. Figure 4 shows the ROC graph that compares all the general detectors. We used a testing data set that includes the testing sets of all types of malware plus the regular programs testing set. The best performing general detectors use the INS4 feature vector; we used it as the baseline.

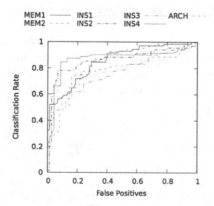

Fig. 4. General detectors comparison

We tested different decision functions and applied to them different selections of base detectors. An ROC curve based on a cross-validation data set was generated for each base detector to enable identification of the best threshold values for the base detectors. Subsequently, the closest point on the ROC curve to the upper left corner of the graph, which represents the maximum Sensitivity+Specificity, was selected since the sensitivity and specificity are equally important. However, for the High confidence decision function, the goal is to minimize the false positives. Therefore, we selected the highest sensitivity value achieving less than 3 % false positive rate. Since the output of logistic regression classifier is a probability between 0 and 1, the threshold value is a fraction in this range.

The cross-validation data set used for the general detectors includes all types of malware as well as regular programs. However, for the specialized detector, it only includes the type of malware the specialized detector designed for and regular programs. We consider the following combinations of base detectors:

- *General ensemble* detector: combines only general detectors using classical ensemble learning. General ensemble detectors work best when diverse features are selected. Therefore, we use the best detector from each feature group (INS, MEM, and ARCH), which are INS4, MEM2, and ARCH respectively. Table 4 shows the threshold values for the selected base detectors which achieves the best detection (highest sum of sensitivity and specificity). Furthermore, the best threshold value is 0.781 for the stacking second-level detector.
- *Specialized ensemble* detector: combines multiple specialized detectors. For each malware type, we used the best specialized detector. Thus, we selected the specialized detectors trained using MEM1 features vector for Trojans, MEM2 for PWS, INS4 for Rogue, and INS2 for both Backdoor and Worms. The selected threshold values of the selected detectors are shown in Table 5. In addition, the threshold value for the stacking second-level detector is 0.751.

Table 4. General ensemble base detectors threshold values

	INS4	MEM2	ARCH
Best threshold	0.812	0.599	0.668
High confidence threshold	0.893	0.927	0.885

Table 5. Specialized ensemble base detectors threshold values

	Backdoor	PWS	Rogue	Trojan	Worm
Best threshold	0.765	0.777	0.707	0.562	0.818
High confidence threshold	0.879	0.89	0.886	0.902	0.867

Table 6. Mixed ensemble base detectors threshold values

	INS4	Rogue	Worm
Best threshold	0.812	0.707	0.844
High confidence threshold	0.893	0.886	0.884

– *Mixed ensemble* detector: combines one or more high performing specialized detectors with one general detector. The general detector allows the detection of other malware types unaccounted for by the base specialized detectors. In addition, this approach allows us to control the complexity of the ensemble (number of detectors) while taking advantage of the best specialized detectors. In our experiments, we used two specialized detectors for Worms and Rogue built using INS4 features vector because they performed significantly better than the general detector for detecting their type. The threshold values of the base detectors are shown in Table 6. The threshold value for the stacking second-level detector is 0.5.

4.3   Offline Detection Effectiveness

As discussed in Sect. 2.2, each program is represented as multiple feature instances collected as the program executes. To evaluate the offline detection of a detector, a decision for each vector in a program is made. If most of the decisions of that program records are malware, then the program is detected as malware. Otherwise, the program is detected as regular program.

Table 7 shows the sensitivity, specificity and accuracy for the different ensemble detectors using different combining decision functions. Also, it presents the work and time advantage, which represent the reduction in work and time to achieve the same detection performance as a software detector; these metrics are defined in Sect. 5.2. The specialized ensemble detector using stacking decision function outperforms all the other detectors with 95.8 % sensitivity and only 4 % false positive, which translates to 24x work advantage and 12.2x time advantage. The high confidence OR function also performs very well. This performance represents a substantial improvement over the baseline detector.

The Or'ing decision function results in poor specificity for most ensembles, since it results in a false positive whenever any detector encounters one. Majority voting was used only for general ensembles as it makes no sense to vote when the detectors are voting on different questions. Majority voting performed reasonably well for the general ensemble.

For the general ensemble detector, Stacking performs the best, slightly improving performance relative to the baseline detector. The majority voting was almost as accurate as stacking but results in more false positives. The mixed ensemble detector did not perform well; with stacking, it was able to significantly improve specificity but at low sensitivity.

Table 7. Offline detection with different combining decision functions

	Decision function	Sensitivity	Specificity	Accuracy	Work advantage	Time advantage
Best general	–	82.4%	89.3%	85.1%	7.7	3.5
General ensemble	Or'ing	99.1%	13.3%	65.0%	1.1	1.1
	High confidence	80.7%	92.0%	85.1%	10.1	3.7
	Majority voting	83.3%	92.1%	86.7%	10.5	4.1
	Stacking	80.7%	96.0%	86.8%	20.1	4.3
Specialized ensemble	Or'ing	100%	5%	51.3%	1.1	1.1
	High confidence	94.4%	94.7%	94.5%	17.8	9.2
	Stacking	95.8%	96.0%	95.9%	24	12.2
Mixed ensemble	Or'ing	84.2%	70.6%	78.8%	2.9	2.2
	High confidence	83.3%	81.3%	82.5%	4.5	2.8
	Stacking	80.7%	96.0%	86.7%	20.2	4.3

4.4 Online Detection Effectiveness

The results thus far have investigated the detection success offline: i.e., given the full trace of program execution. In this section, we present a moving window approach to allow real-time classification of the malware. In particular, the features are collected for each 10,000 committed instructions, and classified using the detector. We keep track of the decision of the detector using an approximation of Exponential Moving Weighted Average. If during a window of time of 32 consecutive decisions, the decision of the detector reflects malware with an average that crosses a preset threshold, we classify the program as malware.

We evaluate candidate detectors in the online detection scenario. The performance as expected is slightly worse for online detection than offline detection, which benefits from the full program execution history. The overall accuracy, sensitivity, and specificity all decreased slightly with online detection. The result of the online detection performance are in Table 8.

5 Two-Level Framework Performance

One of the issues of using a low-level detector such as the ensemble detector we are trying to implement, lacking the sophistication of a rich-semantic detector, is that false positives are difficult to eliminate. Thus, using the low-level detector on

Table 8. Online detection performance

	Sensitivity	Specificity	Accuracy
Best general	84.2 %	86.6 %	85.1 %
General ensemble (*Stacking*)	77.1 %	94.6 %	84.1 %
Specialized ensemble (*Stacking*)	92.9 %	92.0 %	92.3 %
Mixed ensemble (*Stacking*)	85.5 %	90.1 %	87.4 %

its own would result in a system where legitimate programs are sometimes identified as malware, substantially interfering with the operation of the system. Thus, we propose to use the low-level detector as the first level of a two-level detection (TLD) system. The low-level detector is always on, identifying processes that are likely to be malware to prioritize the second level. The second level could consist of a more sophisticated semantic detector, or even a protection mechanism, such as a Control Flow Integrity (CFI) monitor [39] or a Software Fault Isolation (SFI) [31] monitor, that prevents a suspicious process from overstepping its boundaries. The first level thus serves to prioritize the operation of the second level so that the available resources are directed at processes that are suspicious, rather than applied arbitrarily to all processes.

In this section, we analyze this model and derive approximate metrics to measure its performance advantage relative to a system consisting of a software protection only. Essentially, we want to evaluate how improvements in detection translate to run-time capabilities of the detection system. Without loss of generality, we assume that the second level consists of a software detector that can perfectly classify malware from normal programs, but the model can be adapted to consider other scenarios as well.

The first level uses sub-semantic features of the running programs to classify them. This classification may be binary (suspicious or not suspicious) or more continuous, providing a classification confidence value. In this analysis, we assume binary classification: if the hardware detector flags a program to be suspicious it will be added to a priority work list. The software detector scans processes in the high priority list first. A detector providing a suspicion index can provide more effective operation since the index can serve as the software monitoring priority.

5.1   Assumptions and Basic Models

In general, in machine learning the percentage of positive instances correctly classified as positives is called the Sensitivity (S). The percentage of correctly classified negative instances is called the Specificity (C). Applied to our system, S is a fraction of malware identified as such, while C is a fraction of regular programs identified correctly. Conversely, the misclassified malware is referred to as *False Negatives* - *FN*, while the misclassified normal programs are referred as

False Positives -FP. For a classification algorithm to be effective, it is important to have high values of S and C.

We assume a discrete system where the arrival rate of processes is N with a fraction m of those being malware. We also assume that the effort that the system allocates to the software scanner is sufficient to scan a fraction e of the arriving processes (e ranges from 0 to 1). Note that we derive these metrics for a continuous system for convenience of derivation. Assuming a system with large N this approach should not affect the derived expected values.

In the base case a software scanner/detector scans a set of running programs that are equally likely to be malware. Thus, given a detection effort budget e, a corresponding fraction of the arriving programs can be covered. Increasing the detection budget will allow the scanner to evaluate more processes. Since every process has an equal probability of being malware, increasing the effort increases the detection percentage proportionately. Thus, the detection effectiveness (expected fraction of detected malware) is simply e.

Clearly, this is a first-order model in that they use simple average values for critical parameters such as the effort necessary to monitor a processes. However, we believe the metrics are simple and useful indicators to approximately quantify the computational performance advantage obtained in a TLD system as the detection performance changes.

5.2   Metrics to Assess Relative Performance of TLD

In contrast to the baseline model, the TLD works as follows. The hardware detector informs the system of suspected malware, which is used to create a priority list consisting of these processes. The size of this suspect list, $s_{suspect}$, as a fraction of the total number of processes is:

$$s_{suspect} = S \cdot m + (1 - C) \cdot (1 - m) \tag{1}$$

Intuitively, the suspect list size is the fraction of programs predicted to be malware. It consists of the fraction of malware that were successfully predicted to be malware $(S \cdot m)$ and the fraction of normal programs erroneously predicted to be malware $(1 - C) \cdot (1 - m)$.

Work Advantage. Consider a case where the scanning effort e is limited to be no more than the size of the priority list. In this range, the advantage of the TLD can be derived as follows. Lets assume that the effort is $k \cdot s_{suspect}$ where k is some fraction between 0 and 1 inclusive. The expected fraction of detected malware for the baseline case is simply the effort, which is $k \cdot s_{suspect}$. In contrast, we know that S of the malware can be expected to be in the $s_{suspect}$ list and the success rate of the TLD is $k \cdot S$. Therefore, the advantage, W_{tld}, in detection rate for the combined detector in this range is:

$$W_{tld} = \frac{k \cdot S}{k \cdot s_{suspect}} = \frac{S}{S \cdot m + (1 - C) \cdot (1 - m)} \tag{2}$$

The advantage of the TLD is that the expected ratio of malware in the suspect list is higher than that in the general process list under the following conditions. It is interesting to note that when $S + C = 1$, the advantage is 1 (i.e., both systems are the same); to get an advantage, $S + C$ must be greater than 1. For example, for small m, if $S = C = 0.75$, the advantage is 3 (the proposed system finds malware with one third of the effort of the baseline). If $S = C = 0.85$ (in the range that our sub-semantic features are obtaining), the advantage grows to over 5.

Note that with a perfect hardware predictor ($S = 1$, $C = 1$), the advantage in the limit is $\frac{1}{m}$; thus, the highest advantage is during "peace-time" when m approaches 0. Under such a scenario, the advantage tends to $\frac{S}{1-C}$. However, as m increases, for imperfect detectors, the size of the priority list is affected in two ways: it gets larger because more malware processes are predicted to be malware (true positives), but it also gets smaller, because less processes are normal, and therefore less are erroneously predicted to be malware (false positives). For a scenario with a high level of attack (m tending to 1) there is no advantage to the system as all processes are malware and a priority list, even with perfect detection, does not improve on arbitrary scanning.

Detection Success Given a Finite Effort. In this metric, we assume a finite amount of work, and compute the expected fraction of detected malware. Given enough resources to scan a fraction a of arriving processes, we attempt to determine the probability of detecting a particular infection.

We assume a strategy where the baseline detector scans the processes in arbitrary order (as before) while the TLD scans the suspect list first, and then, if there are additional resources, it scans the remaining processes in arbitrary order.

When $e <= s_{suspect}$, analysis similar to that above shows the detection advantage to be ($\frac{S}{s_{suspect}}$). When $e >= s_{suspect}$, then the detection probability can be computed as follows.

$$D_{tld} = S + (1 - S) \cdot \frac{e \cdot N - N \cdot s_{suspect}}{N \cdot (1 - s_{suspect})}. \tag{3}$$

The first part of the expression (S) means that if the suspect list is scanned, the probability of detecting a particular infection is S (that it is classified correctly and therefore is in the suspect list). However, if the malware is misclassified ($1 - S$), malware could be detected if it is picked to be scanned given the remaining effort. The expression simplifies to:

$$D_{tld} = S + \frac{(1 - S) \cdot (e - s_{suspect})}{1 - s_{suspect}} \tag{4}$$

Note that the advantage in detection can be obtained by dividing D_{tld} by $D_{baseline}$ which is simply e.

Time to Detection. Finally, we derive the expected time to detect a malware given an effort sufficient to scan all programs. In the baseline, the expected value of the time to detect for a given malware is $\frac{1}{2}$ of the scan time. In contrast, with the TLD, the expected detection time is:

$$T_{tld} = S \cdot \frac{s_{suspect}}{2} + (1 - S) \cdot (s_{suspect} + \frac{(1 - s_{suspect})}{2}), \tag{5}$$

The first part of the expression accounts for S of the malware which are correctly classified as malware. For these programs, the average detection time is half of the size of the suspect list. The remaining $(1 - S)$ malware which are misclassified have a detection time equal to the time to scan the suspect list (since that is scanned first), followed by half the time to scan the remaining processes. Simplifying the equation, we obtain:

$$T_{tld} = S \cdot \frac{s_{suspect}}{2} + (1 - S) \cdot (\frac{(1 + s_{suspect})}{2}), \tag{6}$$

Recalling that $T_{baseline} = \frac{1}{2}$, the advantage in detection time, which is the ratio $\frac{T_{tld}}{T_{baseline}}$ is:

$$T_{advantage} = S \cdot s_{suspect} + (1 - S) \cdot (1 + s_{suspect}), \tag{7}$$

substituting for $s_{suspect}$ and simplifying, we obtain:

$$T_{advantage} = \frac{1}{1 - (1 - m)(C + S - 1)} \tag{8}$$

The advantage again favors the TLD only when the sum of C and S exceeds 1 (the area above the 45 degree line in the ROC graph. Moreover, the advantage is higher when m is small (peace-time) and lower when m grows. When m tends to 0, if $C + S = 1.5$, malware is detected in half the time on average. If the detection is better (say $C + S = 1.8$), malware can be detected 5 times faster on average. We will use these metrics to evaluate the success of the TLD based on the Sensitivity and Specificity derived from the hardware classifiers that we implemented.

5.3 Evaluating Two Level Detection Overhead

Next, we use the metrics introduced in this section to analyze the performance and the time-to-detect advantage of the TLD systems based on the different hardware detectors we investigated. We selected the work and time advantage from these metrics to evaluate our detectors as a TLD systems; the first stage (hardware detector) will report the suspected malware programs to the second stage to be examined.

The time and work advantages for the online detectors are depicted in Fig. 5 as the percentage of malware processes increases. The specialized ensemble detector reduced the average time of detection to 1/6.6 of the heavy-software only detector that is 2x faster than single general detector when the fraction of malware programs is low. This advantage was at 1/3.1 when malware intensity increased to the point where 20 % of the programs are malware ($m = 0.2$). In addition, the specialized ensemble detector has the best average time-to-detection. The amount of work required for detection is improved by 11x by the specialized ensemble detector compared to using heavy-software detector only (1.87x compared to the best single detector). Although the general ensemble detector had a 14x improvement due to the reduction in the number of false positives, its detection rate is significantly lower than that of the specialized ensemble due to its lower sensitivity.

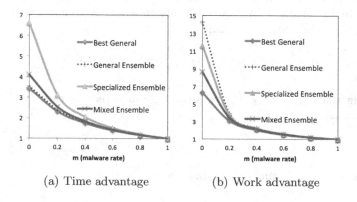

(a) Time advantage   (b) Work advantage

Fig. 5. Time and work advantage as a function of malware rate

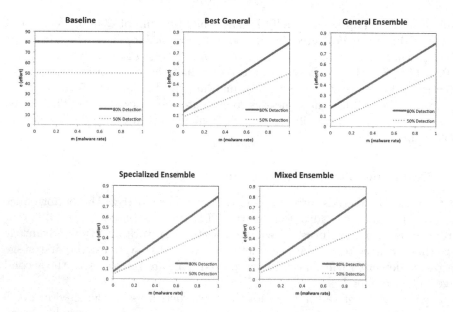

Fig. 6. Detection performance as a function of effort and malware rate

In Fig. 6, we show the effort required by the online detectors to achieve 50 % and 80 % detection rate for the different detectors. Note that the effort increases with the percentage of malware. However, under common circumstances when the incidence of malware is low, the advantage of effective detection is most important. We see this for the specialized ensemble detector which is able to detect 80 % of the malware while scanning less than 10 % of the programs.

6   Hardware Implementation

In this section, we describe the hardware implementation of the ensemble detectors. During the execution of the program, instruction categories are collected at the feature collection unit (FCU), after the features are sent to prediction unit (PU) to create the prediction for 10 K periods of committed instructions and finally online detection unit (ODU) creates a continuous signal with a value every 10,000 instructions for the executing program during runtime.

The FCU is implemented as an observer of the Reorder Buffer (ROB). ROB is a processor structure that keeps track of all in-flight instructions in their program order. The feature collection implementation differs with the type of feature. For example, for INS4, each ROB entry is augmented with instruction category information (6 bits). The feature vector used for classification is a bit vector with a bit for every instruction category. It is updated with each committed instruction by setting the corresponding category to 1.

We use logistic regression to implement the detectors due to its simplicity. The PU consists of different logistic regression units, one for each detector.

For the last part of the detection module, we use two counters in order to keep track of the malware and normal behavior. These counters are incremented at every 10 K instructions accordingly and subtracted from each other to make the final decision.

The ensemble detector requires a minimal hardware investment. Taking up only 2.88 % of logic cells on the core and using only 1.53 % of the power. While the detector may be lightweight in terms of physical resources, the implementation required a 9.83 % slow down of frequency. However, while this may seem high, the vast majority of this overhead comes from collecting the MEM feature vectors; when we do not collect this feature, the reduction in frequency was under 2 %. If feature collection was pipelined over two cycles this cost be significantly reduced or eliminated. Moreover, we could use detectors that use simpler features to avoid using the MEM feature.

7   Related Work

Malware detection at the sub-semantic level was explored by several studies. Bilar et al. use the frequency of opcodes that a specific program uses [3]. Others use sequence signatures of the opcodes [28,34]. Runwal et al. use similarity graphs of opcode sequences [27]. However, these works used offline analysis. In addition, Demme et al. use features based on performance counters [6] but did not explore online detection.

Ensemble learning can combine multiple base detectors to take a final decision for the improved accuracy [32]. The different base detectors are trained to solve the same problem. In contrast to traditional machine learning approaches that use the training data to learn one hypothesis, our ensemble approach learns a set of hypotheses and combines them.

Ensemble learning is attractive because of its generalization ability which is much powerful than using one learner [7]. In order for an ensemble detector to work, the base detectors have to be diverse; if the detectors are highly correlated, there is little additional value from combining them [26]. In this paper, the diversity is based on different features (general ensemble detector), data sets (mixed ensemble detector), or both (specialized ensemble detector).

The proposed specialized ensemble detector in this paper combines multiple specialized detectors and dynamically collects sub-semantic features to perform online detection. Researchers built ensemble malware detectors [1,10,11,14,17, 18,20,22,24,25,29,30,35,36,38], based on combining general detectors. Moreover, most of them used off-line analysis [1,10,14,25,29,30,35,36]. A few used dynamic analysis [11,20,24] and some used both static and dynamic analysis [17,18,22]. None of these works uses sub-semantic features or is targeted towards hardware implementation (which requires simpler machine learning algorithms). Specialized detectors were previously proposed [15] for use in malware classification (i.e., labeling malware). Labeling is used to classify collected malware using offline analysis. This is quite a different application of specialized detectors than the one we introduce in this paper.

8   Concluding Remarks

We build on Ozsoy et al. [23] work that uses low level features to provide a first line of defense to detect suspicious processes. This detector then prioritizes the effort of a heavy weight software detector to look only at programs that are deemed suspicious, forming a two-level detector (TLD). In this paper, we seek to improve the detection performance through ensemble learning to increase the efficiency of the TLD.

We start by evaluating whether specialized detectors can be more effectively classify one given class of malware. We found out that this is almost true for the features and malware types we considered. We then examined different ways of combining general and specialized detectors. We found that ensemble learning by combining general detectors provided limited advantage over a single general detector. However, combining specialized detectors can significantly improve the sensitivity, specificity, and accuracy of the detector.

We develop metrics to evaluate the performance advantage from better detection in the context of a TLD. Ensemble learning provides more than 11x reduction in the detection overhead with the specialized ensemble detector. This represents 1.87x improvement in performance (overhead) with respect to Ozsoy et al. [23]

work previously introduced single detector. We implemented the proposed detector as part of an open core to study the hardware overhead. The hardware overhead was minimal: around 2.88 % increase in area, 9.83 % reduction in cycle time, and less than 1.35 % increase in power. We believe that minor optimizations to the MEM feature collection circuitry could alleviate most of the cycle time reduction.

Acknowledgements. The authors would like to thank the anonymous reviewers and especially the shepherd for this paper, Tudor Dumitras, for their valuable feedback and suggestions, which significantly improved the paper.

References

1. Aung, Z., Zaw, W.: Permission-based android malware detection. Int. J. Sci. Technol. Res. **2**(3), 228–234 (2013)
2. Malware Statistics (2014). http://www.av-test.org/en/statistics/malware/
3. Bilar, D.: Opcode as predictor for malware. Int. J. Electron. Secur. Digit. Forensic **1**, 156–168 (2007)
4. Christodorescu, M., Jha, S., Seshia, S.A., Song, D., Bryant, R.E.: Semantics-aware malware detection. In: Proceedings of the IEEE Symposium on Security and Privacy (SP), pp. 32–46 (2005)
5. Luk, C., Cohn, R., Muth, R., Patil, H., Klauser, A., Lowney, G., Wallace, S., Reddi, V., Hazelwood, K.: Pin: building customized program analysis tools with dynamic instrumentation. In: Proceedings of the PLDI (2005)
6. Demme, J., Maycock, M., Schmitz, J., Tang, A., Waksman, A., Sethumadhavan, S., Stolfo, S.: On the feasibility of online malware detection with performance counters. In: Proceedings of the International Symposium on Computer Architecture (ISCA) (2013)
7. Dietterich, T.G.: Machine learning research: four current directions. AI Magazine **18**, 97–136 (1997)
8. Dietterich, T.G.: Ensemble methods in machine learning. In: Kittler, J., Roli, F. (eds.) MCS 2000. LNCS, vol. 1857, pp. 1–15. Springer, Heidelberg (2000)
9. Egele, M., Scholte, T., Kirda, E., Kruegel, C.: A survey on automated dynamic malware-analysis techniques and tools. ACM Comput. Surv. **44**(2), 6:1–6:42 (2008)
10. Eskandari, M., Hashemi, S.: Metamorphic malware detection using control flow graph mining. Int. J. Comput. Sci. Netw. Secur. **11**(12), 1–6 (2011)
11. Folino, G., Pizzuti, C., Spezzano, G.: GP ensemble for distributed intrusion detection systems. In: Singh, S., Singh, M., Apte, C., Perner, P. (eds.) ICAPR 2005. LNCS, vol. 3686, pp. 54–62. Springer, Heidelberg (2005)
12. Henning, J.L.: Spec cpu2006 benchmark descriptions. ACM SIGARCH Comput. Archit. News **34**(4), 1–17 (2006)
13. Hosmer Jr., D.W., Lemeshow, S.: Applied Logistic Regression. Wiley, New York (2004)
14. Hou, S., Chen, L., Tas, E., Demihovskiy, I., Ye, Y.: Cluster-oriented ensemble classifiers for intelligent malware detection. In: 2015 IEEE International Conference on Semantic Computing (ICSC), pp. 189–196. IEEE (2015)
15. Kolter, J.Z., Maloof, M.A.: Learning to detect and classify malicious executables in the wild. J. Mach. Learn. Res. **7**, 2721–2744 (2006)

16. Kruegel, C., Robertson, W., Vigna, G.: Detecting kernel-level rootkits through binary analysis. In: Proceedings Annual Computer Security Applications Conference (ACSAC), pp. 91–100 (2004)
17. Liu, J.-C., Song, J.-F., Miao, Q.-G., Cao, Y., Quan, Y.-N.: An ensemble cost-sensitive one-class learning framework for malware detection. Int. J. Pattern Recogn. Artif. Intell. **29**, 1550018 (2012)
18. Lu, Y.-B., Din, S.-C., Zheng, C.-F., Gao, B.-J.: Using multi-feature and classifier ensembles to improve malware detection. J. CCIT **39**(2), 57–72 (2010)
19. How Microsoft antimalware products identify malware and unwanted software. www.microsoft.com/security/portal/mmpc/shared/objectivecriteria.aspx
20. Natani, P., Vidyarthi, D.: Malware detection using API function frequency with ensemble based classifier. In: Thampi, S.M., Atrey, P.K., Fan, C.-I., Perez, G.M. (eds.) SSCC 2013. CCIS, vol. 377, pp. 378–388. Springer, Heidelberg (2013)
21. Malwaredb Website (2015). www.malwaredb.malekal.com. Accessed May 2015
22. Ozdemir, M., Sogukpinar, I.: An android malware detection architecture based on ensemble learning. Trans. Mach. Learn. Artif. Intell. **2**(3), 90–106 (2014)
23. Ozsoy, M., Donovick, C., Gorelik, I., Abu-Ghazaleh, N., Ponomarev, D.: Malware aware processors: a framework for efficient online malware detection. In: Proceedings of the International Symposium on High Performance Computer Architecture (HPCA) (2015)
24. Peddabachigari, S., Abraham, A., Grosan, C., Thomas, J.: Modeling intrusion detection system using hybrid intelligent systems. J. Netw. Comput. Appl. **30**(1), 114–132 (2007)
25. Perdisci, R., Gu, G., Lee, W.: Using an ensemble of one-class svm classifiers to harden payload-based anomaly detection systems. In: Proceedings of the IEEE International Conference on Data Mining (ICDM) (2006)
26. Quinlan, J.R.: Simplifying decision trees. Int. J. Man-Mach. Stud. **27**(3), 221–234 (1987)
27. Runwal, N., Low, R.M., Stamp, M.: Opcode graph similarity and metamorphic detection. J. Comput. Virol. **8**(1–2), 37–52 (2012)
28. Santos, I., Brezo, F., Nieves, J., Penya, Y.K., Sanz, B., Laorden, C., Bringas, P.G.: Idea: opcode-sequence-based malware detection. In: Massacci, F., Wallach, D., Zannone, N. (eds.) ESSoS 2010. LNCS, vol. 5965, pp. 35–43. Springer, Heidelberg (2010)
29. Shahzad, R.K., Lavesson, N.: Veto-based malware detection. In: Proceedings of the IEEE International Conference on Availability, Reliability and Security (ARES), pp. 47–54 (2012)
30. Sheen, S., Anitha, R., Sirisha, P.: Malware detection by pruning of parallel ensembles using harmony search. Pattern Recogn. Lett. **34**(14), 1679–1686 (2013)
31. Wahbe, R., Lucco, S., Anderson, T., Graham, S.: Efficient software-based fault isolation. In: ACM SIGOPS Symposium on Operating Systems Principles (SOSP), pp. 203–216. ACM Press, New York (1993)
32. Witten, I.H., Frank, E.: Data Mining: Practical Machine Learning Tools and Techniques. Morgan Kaufmann Series in Data Management Systems, 2nd edn. Morgan Kaufmann Publishers Inc., San Francisco (2005)
33. Wolpert, D.H.: Stacked generalization. Neural Netw. **5**, 241–259 (1992)
34. Yan, G., Brown, N., Kong, D.: Exploring discriminatory features for automated malware classification. In: Rieck, K., Stewin, P., Seifert, J.-P. (eds.) DIMVA 2013. LNCS, vol. 7967, pp. 41–61. Springer, Heidelberg (2013)

35. Ye, Y., Chen, L., Wang, D., Li, T., Jiang, Q., Zhao, M.: Sbmds: an interpretable string based malware detection system using svm ensemble with bagging. J. Comput. Virol. **5**(4), 283–293 (2009)
36. Yerima, S.Y., Sezer, S., Muttik, I.: High accuracy android malware detection using ensemble learning. IET Inf. Secur. (2015)
37. You, I., Yim, K.: Malware obfuscation techniques: a brief survey. In: Proceedings of the International Conference on Broadband, Wireless Computing, Communication and Applications, pp. 297–300 (2010)
38. Zhang, B., Yin, J., Hao, J., Zhang, D., Wang, S.: Malicious codes detection based on ensemble learning. In: Xiao, B., Yang, L.T., Ma, J., Muller-Schloer, C., Hua, Y. (eds.) ATC 2007. LNCS, vol. 4610, pp. 468–477. Springer, Heidelberg (2007)
39. Zhang, M., Sekar, R.: Control flow integrity for cots binaries. In: Proceedings of the 22nd Usenix Security Symposium (2013)

Physical-Layer Detection
of Hardware Keyloggers

Ryan M. Gerdes$^{(\boxtimes)}$ and Saptarshi Mallick

Utah State University, Logan, UT 84322, USA
ryan.gerdes@usu.edu, saptarshi.mallick@aggiemail.usu.edu

Abstract. This work examines the general problem of detecting the
presence of hardware keyloggers (HKLs), and specifically focuses on
HKLs that are self-powered and take measures, such as passively tapping
the keyboard line, to avoid detection. The work is inspired by the *observer
effect*, which maintains that the act of observation impacts the observed.
First, a model for HKLs is proposed, and experimentally validated, that
explains how attaching a HKL necessarily affects the electrical characteristics of the system it is attached to. The model then motivates the
selection of features that can be used for detection. A comparison framework is put forth that is sensitive enough to identify the minute changes
in these features caused by HKLs. Experimental work carried out on
a custom keylogger designed to conceal its presence, at the expense of
reliability, shows that it is possible to detect stealthy and evasive keyloggers by observing as few as five keystrokes. Optimal attack strategies
are devised to evade detection by the proposed approach and countermeasures evaluated that show detection is still possible. Environmental
effects on detection performance are also examined and accounted for.

Keywords: Physical layer identification · Device fingerprinting ·
Keyloggers · Hardware keylogger

1 Introduction

A hardware keylogger (HKL) is a device, situated between the analog interfaces
of a computer and its keyboard, that recovers the keystrokes transmitted by a
keyboard through the sampling of the electrical impulses transmitted by the keyboard. These devices represent a real and persistent public threat, as evidenced
by the discovery that keylogger-like devices inside point-of-sale terminals at 63
stores were used to steal customer credit card information [34]. When installed
on public computers, HKLs enable identify theft on a wide scale and allow an
attacker to acquire credentials that may be used to gain access to other systems
and services (as a Cal State student did to perpetrate voting fraud [1]). On private computers the surreptitious installation of HKLs makes it possible for an
attacker to bypass full disk encryption. These devices are inexpensive and readily
available (the authors found keyloggers for $30–$400, depending on the features,
such as keystroke capacity, point of attachment, size, and wireless transmission

© Springer International Publishing Switzerland 2015
H. Bos et al. (Eds.): RAID 2015, LNCS 9404, pp. 26–47, 2015.
DOI: 10.1007/978-3-319-26362-5_2

of recorded keystrokes, from eight manufacturers). Alternatively, the knowledge required to build an efficient HKL can be obtained in an undergraduate micro-controllers course or instructions can be procured for free online.

The most popular countermeasure against HKLs is simple visual inspection [35]; however, this is impractical for large organizations [3] and is complicated by the fact that keyloggers are increasingly unobtrusive. Indeed, HKLs are available for embedding inside keyboards [18], inside laptops [19], and as PCI cards [20] for the expressed purpose of avoiding casual visual detection. Existing non-visual methods [24] are also only capable of detecting certain types of HKL.

To enable the detection of stealthy and evasive hardware keyloggers we pro-pose an approach based on the *observer effect*, which states that the act of observing must perforce impact the phenomenon being observed [28]. Specifi-cally, the mere fact that an attacker connects a piece of equipment (the HKL) to measure the output of a keyboard affects the output of the keyboard. The mechanism by which this occurs is known as *loading*, a well known problem encountered, for example, when attempting to measure the voltage of a high resistance circuit [25]. For this work we examined a HKL especially designed for stealth and evasion and found that it impacted keyboard signaling to a measur-able and detectable degree. In fact, we conjecture that any HKL that recovers keystrokes via direct measurement of the wired keyboard/PC communication channel, even those hidden within a keyboard or PC, should be discoverable using our method.

Within the broader context of the security literature, our work falls into the category of physical layer identification (PLI), also known as device finger-printing. In PLI hardware and manufacturing inconsistencies that cause minute and unique variations in the signaling behavior of devices are utilized for iden-tification and monitoring purposes [8]. The approach outlined below utilizes PLI techniques for keylogger detection by having the host computer fingerprint the keyboard and compare the fingerprint to baseline fingerprints, which were acquired in the absence of a keylogger, to determine whether a keylogger has been attached.

1.1 Related Work

Countermeasures for HKLs generally fall into one of four categories: avoidance, detection, exhaustion, and obfuscation.

An avoidance strategy involves giving the PC input using another method, such as an onscreen keyboard, whenever sensitive information is called for [35]. This method tends to be tedious, cannot be used while others are nearby, and is potentially vulnerable to screen capture, though methods have been proposed to counter the latter threat [29].

Resource exhaustion, wherein spurious keystrokes and commands are received from/sent to the keyboard so as fill/overwrite its memory, was sug-gested in [14,24]. While severely resource-constrained HKLs, e.g. a self-powered HKL that wirelessly transmits keystrokes, may be uniquely vulnerable to this type of countermeasure, exhaustion is generally an impractical strategy as HKLs can have GBs of memory while the clock of the keyboard is on the order of ten KHz (the author of [24] gives 109 min to fill 64 KB at $\approx$10 keystrokes per second).

Obfuscation refers to the encryption of keystrokes before they are transmitted (the keyboard and PC sharing a secret key) or hiding keystrokes in a continuous flood of random keystrokes (perhaps the PC and keyboard share the seed of a common pseudo-random number generator). The authors are unaware of either technique being used in practice.

Current, non-visual, HKL detection methods rely upon changes in timing or deviations in power caused by the keylogger drawing power from the bus [24]. These methods, however, are only effective against inline keyloggers; i.e. those that are connected in serial with the keyboard/computer and actively intercept and then recreate the signals from the keyboard. Stealthy and eva- sive keyloggers—i.e. ones that are self-powered, hidden within the keyboard or connectors, and passively tap the keyboard by being connected in parallel with it—are undetectable using these approaches.

The possibility of using PLI to detect taps on lines—i.e. eavesdroppers on wired communications—was first suggested in [13]. Ours is the first work to directly confirm this conjecture, though in [10] it was demonstrated that changes to the communication medium (in that case increasing the length of the Ethernet cable) leads to a perceptible shift in a device's fingerprint. The reader is referred to [5, 7, 12] for an overview of PLI techniques, issues, and results.

1.2 Paper Structure

In the next section we describe the types of keyloggers and set forth a threat model that characterizes the type of keyloger we hope to detect. We then explain the workings of the PS/2 protocol to the extent necessary to understand the operation of keyloggers. A first-order model that explains how a HKL indu- bitably affects the system it is connected to concludes the section. In Sect. 3, our architecture for detecting keyloggers is introduced. We then leverage the model set forth in the previous section to select features to detect the presence of a HKL. The methods used for the extraction and comparison of features are also discussed. Experimental validation of the detection methodology is described in Sect. 4. Details of the keylogger designed to test our approach are given and experimental procedures discussed. Section 5 considers feature stability due to changes in the environment and examines the extent to which attacker coun- termeasures could be employed to evade detection. We conclude with further avenues of research.

2 Theory of Detection

The types and characteristics of HKL are discussed and a threat model is cho- sen that maximizes an attacker's chances of remaining undetected. The PS/2 protocol and physical layer are described to understand how they are leveraged by HKL designers. The effects a HKL has on transient and steady-state line voltages are examined through the use of a first-order model.

2.1   Threat Model and Assumptions

Hardware keyloggers may be divided into *active* and *passive* types, either of which may be self-powered or use the resources of the host PC for power. The active type, sometimes known as inline, sits between (in series with) the keyboard and host PC and intercepts and regenerates the signaling of the keyboard/PC. According to [24] these are the most common commercial type of keylogger. A passive HKL, on the other hand, sits aside (in parallel with) the keyboard/PC and simply observes the state of the line connecting the two to recover keystrokes. For the purposes of this work, we consider a HKL *stealthy* if it does not draw upon the host PC for power and *evasive* if it takes measures against a detection methodology to avoid discovery. The keylogger we studied (modeled on a commercial HKL design [17] and discussed in Sect. 4.1) was passive and stealthy; evasive variants are considered in Sects. 5.2 and 5.3.

While all of the HKLs we are aware of are based on microcontrollers (uC), in some circumstances, such as when a special form-factor is called for or in an attempt reduce energy consumption, an attacker might design an application-specific integrated circuit (ASIC) HKL. Without loss of generality, as ASICs and uCs use the same transistor-level technology for interfacing purposes, our keyloggers were constructed using a uC. This simplified development and testing significantly as uCs are commonly equipped with enough features (general-purpose input/output [GPIO] ports, memory, samplers, converters, and computation abilities) to allow for a flexible HKL design.

Given the success of previous PLI work in identifying wired devices [11], we chose not to examine active devices as it was thought that they would be easily discoverable. In fact, a sophisticated PLI approach is probably unnecessary to detect these devices due to the fact the signals they generate are based on GPIO ports that do not attempt to reproduce exactly the analog signaling of the keyboard. This is because GPIO ports know only two outputs, which correspond to the logic high and low voltage levels of the microcontroller.[1] In addition, while detection methods exist for active keyloggers that may or may not draw power from the host PC [24], none do for the passive, stealthy variety.

PS/2 keyloggers are used to illustrate the approach as they are simpler and easier to understand. Because of the electrical and signaling similarities of USB and PS/2 line drivers, comparable loading effects will be observed when a USB HKL is connected, so the approach would still be effective for USB keyboards. In fact, given the relatively higher speed, it should be easier to detect a USB keylogger, as the HKL load would produce greater distortions at higher frequencies (i.e. because of the slow clock speed of the PS/2 protocol, it is actually more difficult to detect the presence of a HKL). Host-to-keyboard communication is also disregarded (both PS/2 and USB keyboard protocols are bi-directional).

Finally, we attached our keyloggers to a tap point in the middle of the PS/2 cable (details given in Sect. 4.2). Because of the low frequencies of the signaling and short distances involved, the lumped element model [26] still holds,

---

[1] In Sect. 5.2 we do examine the case of an evasive HKL designed to defeat our detection method by reproducing the keyboard's signal exactly.

which implies that the actual point of attachment (i.e. inside or outside the keyboard/PC) is immaterial. Thus, our setup mimics an attacker connecting a HKL to an arbitrary point between the analog interfaces of the keyboard/PC.

In summary, we consider an attacker who has connected a passive PS/2 HKL, designed to conceal its presence, that recovers keystrokes by measuring the line state at any point between the keyboard and the PC.

2.2   Overview of PS/2 Protocol

The PS/2 bus consists of power (+5 V DC at 275 mA), ground, data, and clock lines [4]. During the idle state (i.e. when neither the keyboard or host is transmitting) the clock and data lines are kept at +5 V DC. The keyboard brings the data line low and then the clock line low to signal its intention to transmit. The low state corresponds to ground. The data line is sampled on the falling edge of the clock, which runs between 10–16.7 KHz (Fig. 1a). A passive, stealthy microcontroller-based keylogger, e.g. a self-powered variant of [17], would be connected to the ground, clock, and data lines and configured such that a downward voltage transition on the clock line triggers an interrupt routine in which the data line is sampled to determine whether a one or zero is being transmitted. Data concerning a keystroke is communicated to the host when a key is pressed and again when it is released.

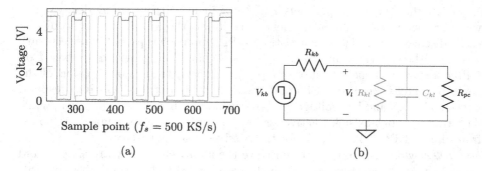

(a)   (b)

Fig. 1. (a) Electrical signal from the keyboard when the SPACE key is pressed (green: clock line; blue: data line; the clock is offset by 250 mV to aid visualization). Data is sampled by the host at the falling edge of the clock. (b) A passive HKL modelled in terms of its input capacitance C_{kl} and resistance R_{kl}. The HKL is connected in parallel with the PC (represented by the load R_{pc}) and keyboard (represented by the square-wave voltage source V_{kb}, with output resistance R_{kb}) (Color figure online).

2.3   First-Order HKL Model

To understand the effects of connecting a HKL, and hence aid in our selection of features for detecting the presence of a keylogger, we modelled the HKL as a first-order RC circuit (Fig. 1b). The model is meant to capture the non-zero capacitance, C_{kl}, and finite input resistance, R_{kl}, of a uC's I/O ports and suggests two ways in which a HKL may affect keyboard signaling.

The first is to notice that when data is transmitted the clock line goes from $+5$ V DC to 0 V DC for each bit; in the presence of a HKL this is roughly equivalent to what is known as the natural response of an RC circuit [26]. The act of bringing the clock line from the high to low state would ideally result in a fast downward drop of the line voltage, $V_l(t)$, however, with a keylogger present, and ignoring the keyboard output resistance for the moment, the line voltage will approach zero according to $V_l(t) = 5 \exp(-t/\tau)$, where $\tau = (R_{kl} \parallel R_{pc})C_{kl}$. A similar analysis holds for when the clock is driven high (the step response). The presence of a HKL thus causes changes in the fall and rise time of the circuit.

The differences in fall/rise times in the absence and presence of a HKL, however, are likely to be small, as the parallel combination of R_{kl} and R_{pc} is likely large (on the order of kΩ) but the capacitance C_{kl} very small (on the order of pF), which leads to a time constant $\tau \sim$ ns. To confirm this we sampled the line voltage of a keyboard with and without a HKL at 40 GS/s using a Tektronix DPO7254C oscilloscope (see Sect. 4.2 for setup details). Figure 2a shows the rising portion of the first clock period without (blue) and with (red) a HKL (the figure is composed of an average of 100 time-aligned signals). Using the procedures set forth in [15] and these signals, fall/rise times were calculated without the HKL as $2.0333 \times 10^{-7}/1.3731 \times 10^{-6}$ s and $2.0350 \times 10^{-7}/1.3782 \times 10^{-6}$ s with. While the fall/rise times are indeed greater in the presence of the HKL, the difference is small; the record-to-record variation is also substantial, with 99 % confidence intervals of $1.9801 \times 10^{-7} \pm 7.5279 \times 10^{-9}$ s/1.2760×10^{-6} $\pm 4.3898 \times 10^{-8}$ s without the HKL and $1.9804 \times 10^{-7} \pm 7.5868 \times 10^{-9}$ s/$1.2815 \times 10^{-6} \pm 5.1446 \times 10^{-8}$ s with. For these reasons, we ignore C_{kl} and examine the effects of R_{kl}, alone.[2]

We note that unless $R_{kl} \gg R_{pc}$, the voltage drop across the load (the PC) as seen by keyboard will be decreased by the parallel combination of R_{kl} and R_{pc} (Fig. 2b). This leads to a second way in which a HKL will perturb the system, namely a decrease of the voltage across the line, V_l. The proof is as follows.

In the absence of a HKL the line voltage is given as

$$V_l = \frac{R_{pc}}{R_{kb} + R_{pc}} V_{kb} \tag{1}$$

Allowing $R_{kl} = \beta R_{pc}$, the parallel combination $R_{eq} = R_{kl} \parallel R_{pc} = \frac{\beta}{1+\beta} R_{pc}$ results in a new line voltage

$$V_l' = \frac{R_{eq}}{R_{kb} + R_{eq}} V_{kb} = \frac{R_{pc}}{\frac{1+\beta}{\beta} R_{kb} + R_{pc}} V_{kb} \leq V_l \tag{2}$$

Eq. 2 is strictly less than Eq. 1 when $\beta \neq \infty$.

---

[2] In Sect. 5.3 we show that HKLs that do not affect line voltage—i.e. those with high input impedance—can still be detected because of their affect on the transient response of the system.

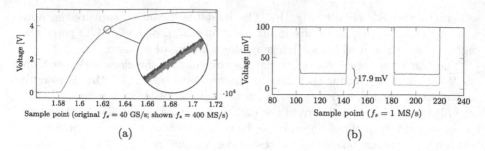

Fig. 2. (a) The rising portion of the first clock period of a keyboard's clock line. It takes the signal longer to transition to the low level when a HKL is present (red) than when it is not (blue); the same holds for the falling portion. (b) The voltage of the clock line with (red) and without a HKL (blue) for the lower portion of the first two clock periods. The level is less due to the loading effects of the HKL (Color figure online).

Given that both the PC and a uC-based HKL likely use the same transistor-level technology to measure the state of line, we take $\beta \approx 1$. Furthermore, to measure a voltage we would expect both the PC and HKL to present a very high resistance, while the keyboard, acting as a voltage source, would present a comparatively low resistance [26]. Assuming that R_{kl} and R_{pc} are approximately 1 MΩ and R_{kb} approximately 500 Ω the difference in the line voltage when a HKL is present at $V_{kb} = 5$ V would be $V_l - V_l' = 2.5$ mV.

Figure 2b shows the lower portion of the first two clock periods of the clock line in the absence (blue) and presence (red) of a HKL (1000 records were time-aligned and averaged). As the figure indicates, the line voltage when a HKL is connected is indeed lower than when it is not and the difference is commensurate with the above calculation (the difference is also apparent and slightly greater for the upper portion of the signal). We also observed differences in the change of voltage for the HKL and no HKL case (i.e. $V_l - V_l'$) between keyboards, which can be explained by assuming that keyboard resistance, R_{kb}, differs between keyboards, where a lower R_{kb} leads to a smaller change in voltage. Similarly, the low voltage level of clocks for keyboards probably differs due to the fact that keyboards have different ground path resistances.

Finally, we note that our model assumes that the resistance and capacitance for a HKL are constant for all frequencies and line voltages, which, in general, is not the case. Given the low frequency of the PS/2 clock, frequency-dependent effects are apt to be slight. Changes in the resistance of the HKL, R_{kl}, for different line voltages could, however, be noticeable because of the constancy of the HKL's input port leakage current over a range of input voltages. For example, the maximum leakage current of a popular microcontroller is 1 µA over the input voltage range of [0,3.3] V [33]. A HKL built using this uC would present a resistance of 25 kΩ at 25 mV and 3.3 MΩ at 3.3 V. This suggests that in searching for the decreases in line voltage that signal the presence of a HKL, we should focus on the upper level of a signal, as by Eqs. 1 and 2, a larger relative drop would be produced for larger values of V_{kb}. The input-voltage dependency of resistances also opens another avenue for possible detection: a HKL may be present if the observed deviation of the line voltage for the high and low levels of the clock is not equal.

3 Physical-Layer Detection of Keyloggers

Having proposed a mechanism by which a HKL may be detected, we introduce an anomaly detection architecture meant to leverage the mechanism to determine if a HKL has been attached. We describe its main components, including feature extraction and feature comparison. The extraction routine will focus on those areas of the signal most likely to display differences in the presence of a HKL, while the comparison routine will be sensitive to the slight changes our theory predicts will result from a HKL but still be robust to noise.

3.1 Proposed Architecture

To detect HKLs using the loading effects outlined above, we propose to incorporate a physical layer detection engine within the PC to perform anomaly detection based on the state of the clock line (Fig. 3a). The engine would be situated between the external keyboard interface of the PC and the internal keyboard interface so as to detect a HKL connected at any point between, or even inside, the PC and keyboard. The clock line is monitored because, while the data signal depends on the keypress, the clock signal is invariant with respect to the key being pressed; i.e. it is ubiquitous and repetitive. The detection engine consists of (1) a high-resolution analog-to-digital converter (ADC) or sampler to measure the clock line, (2) a routine $f(\cdot)$ that extracts features from the sampled data, (3) a metric $d(\cdot)$ by which to compare features of a newly sampled keypress to a baseline feature set, and (4) a database to store training and test data. Feature extraction and comparison are described in the following sections.

As the effect of a HKL on the line state amounts to a few millivolts or tens of millivolts decrease, it is necessary to employ a high-resolution sampler in the detector. By excluding transient effects—i.e. changes in fall and rise times—from the feature set, in addition to the fact that the PS/2 clock is less than 20 KHz, a comparatively low-speed ADC should prove sufficient. Given an ADC with an allowable input range of 0–5 V, a 12-bit ADC would achieve a resolution of ≈1.25 mV. Such an ADC can be had for as cheaply as $3.00 [2].

3.2 Feature Extraction

Our detection theory suggests, and is borne out by data, that a HKL will produce macroscopic effects on the line voltage. As such, it is sufficient to use the raw voltage measurements for features. We note that principal component analysis, factor analysis, or linear discriminant analysis could be used to reduce the

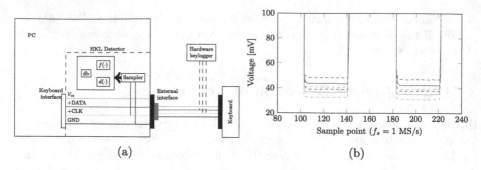

(a)   (b)

Fig. 3. The proposed architecture for detecting hardware keyloggers at the physical layer. A sampler measures the voltage of the clock line. When a key is pressed the corresponding samples are processed to check if they match a baseline acquired in the absence of a HKL. (b) The mean of two periods of the lower portion of the clock signal, using 1000 records, without (blue) and with (red) a HKL. The dashed lines give the 99 % confidence intervals for the means, which indicates that the line voltage for the two cases can be seemingly equivalent at times (Color figure online).

number of features or find the most powerful features in the future, though we did not find these techniques necessary to detect our HKL. As indicated in part by Fig. 2, we have found that a HKL affects the higher and lower levels of the clock to a different degree. Because of this, we have opted to extract samples from the lower and upper portions, and consider each set separately. The latter effect implies that it is only necessary to use a subset of the samples from each level for detection purposes. We use the same reasoning to justify the use of only the keydown portion of the keystroke for detection purposes.

The first step of our feature extraction procedure ($f(\cdot)$ in Fig. 3a) is to obtain the samples corresponding to the keydown portion of the keystroke from a record. To accomplish this an alignment routine takes the maximum of the correlation between a record and a reference signal for the keyboard to indicate the point in the record at which the reference is best aligned with the keydown signal, and then returns a contiguous subset of the record containing just the sample points encompassing the keydown clock signal. The reference signal consists of the keydown portion of a single record obtained in the absence of a HKL.

From the keydown portion of the record, roughly the first 1.5 periods of the clock (the entire first period and the upper half of second) are then used with Algorithms 1 and 2 to obtain the sample points of the lower and upper portions, respectively, of the truncated the clock signal. These sample points form two separate distributions to be used in our comparison function ($d(\cdot)$ in Fig. 3a), discussed next. The extraction procedure allows for the inclusion of some points belonging to the transient; this allows us to include transient effects not captured by our model but that could nonetheless serve as distinguishing features.

Algorithm 1. Extract lower level sample points from clock signal	**Algorithm 2.** Extract upper level sample points from clock signal

Input   : **R** (a sample point-by-record matrix of line measurements for the clock signal)
 Output   : S (sample points of **R** in the clock's lower level)
 $S = \varnothing$;
 foreach $R_i \triangleq R_{*,i} \in \mathbf{R}$ **do**
     $\{X \subset R_i : \forall x \in X < mean(R_i)\}$;
     $\{Y \subset R_i : \forall y \in Y \leq mean(X)\}$;
     $\{Z \subset R_i : \forall z \in Z \leq \mu(Y) + \sigma(Y)\}$;
     $//\mu(\cdot)$ and $\sigma(\cdot)$ compute the mean and standard deviation of the elements
     $S \leftarrow S \cup Z$;
	Input : **R** (a sample point-by-record matrix of line measurements for the clock signal)
	 Output : S (sample points of **R** in the clock's upper level)
	 $S = \varnothing$;
	 foreach $R_i \triangleq R_{*,i} \in \mathbf{R}$ **do**
	     $\{X \subset R_i : \forall x \in X > mean(R_i)\}$;
	     $\{Y \subset R_i : \forall y \in Y \geq mean(X)\}$;
	     $\{Z \subset R_i : \forall z \in Z \geq \mu(Y) - \sigma(Y)\}$;
	     $//\mu(\cdot)$ and $\sigma(\cdot)$ compute the mean and standard deviation of the elements
	     $S \leftarrow S \cup Z$;

3.3 Feature Comparison

Figure 3b shows the mean (solid) and 99 % confidence intervals (dashed) of 1000 records acquired for a keyboard with a keylogger present (red) and in its absence (blue). The signals vary with respect to time and that individual signals with and without the HKL overlap, but that the means, and possibly the variances, are different when the HKL is connected compared to when it is not. Because of the overlap and variation observed, a simple distance metric, such as the Euclidean one, would require a large threshold to keep false positives low, but would also produce an unacceptable number of false negatives. To accommodate both variation and overlap we propose to use a distance metric designed for comparing distributions known as the *earth mover's distance* (EMD).[3]

Put simply, the EMD is a measure of the cost of transforming one histogram to another [27]. In our case, the sample points extracted from the lower, or upper, portion of the first 1.5 clock periods serve as the distribution, and we are interested in the cost of transforming the distribution of a record(s) when the line is in an unknown state to a baseline built for the keyboard in a known state (keylogger absent). If the cost is too high—i.e. if the distribution is too far from the baseline—we assert a HKL has been attached.

Specifically, considering samples from only one of the levels, we build a training distribution D_{trn} from the extracted features of a number of records procured in the absence of a HKL. A test distribution D_{tst} is then constructed from records collected from one or more keystrokes. To test for the presence of a HKL we employ the EMD: if $d(D_{tst}, D_{trn}) \leq T$, where T is a threshold, established to during a training phase, that results in an acceptable number of false positives, the records are said to have been acquired in the absence of a HKL. This procedure is followed for every keystroke or series of keystrokes.

The reference signal necessary to extract features from records and the training distribution for comparing those features to a threshold are stored in the database of our proposed detection engine.

---

[3] Properly speaking, we use a variant of the EMD for non-normalized histograms, where we have selected the l_1 norm for the ground distance metric [27].

4   Experimental Setup and Results

Results validating the first-order model given in Sect. 2 are presented. The HKL designed to conduct experiments on is explained and an overview of our experimental setup and procedures given.

4.1   Keylogger Design

Our HKL was built using a Texas Instruments (TI) Tiva C Series TM4C123G LaunchPad, which is based on the TI TM4C123GH6PM microcontroller [32]. It is modeled on [17] (the only commercially available passive HKL we are aware of) and has similar specifications (e.g. the input leakage currents are the same order of magnitude). A passive HKL is *ipso facto* maximally evasive with respect to current active HKL detection methods. As our methodology relies only on observing deviations present on the clock line, we did not configure the uC to sample the data line or even connect it to the data line. One pin on the uC was set as an input and the uC was configured to issue an interrupt on the falling edge of the pin; an LED was blinked for each keystroke to verify proper operation.

In keeping with the premise of the work—to detect passive and stealthy keyloggers—the uC was powered using the USB bus, not the PS/2 bus; the input pin was also kept floating to maximize its impedance (i.e. R_{kl}) and make the HKL nominally evasive with regards to our detection approach. A floating input pin is generally discouraged as the input can be easily shifted by environmental factors such as noise, leading to spurious readings. It was felt, however, that activating the internal pull-up or pull-down resistors would affect the line voltage noticeably and therefore bias the experiments in favor of our approach.

4.2   Data Collection

Our experimental setup (Fig. 4a) consisted of a single PC for test and measurement purposes; i.e. the PC measured its own clock line voltage (mimicking our proposed architecture [Fig. 3a]). As the PC (a Dell Optiplex GX620) lacked a PS/2 port, a USB-to-PS/2 converter was used to connect the test keyboards. This had the side benefit of allowing us to attach a USB keyboard to control the system without interfering with the keyboard under test. To automate the data collection process a linear motor was setup to press the space bar every 1.2 s for 0.3 s (a 20 % duty cycle square wave with a period of 1.5 s was used with a switch to turn the motor on and off).

The line voltage was measured by connecting a sampler to a tap point midway between the two ends of the PS/2 cable (Fig. 4b). Our choice of sampler was a Measurement Computing USB-2500 Series DAQ board. The DAQ was configured to use a full-scale voltage of 10 V and sample at 1 MS/s. Given the board's 16 bit ADC, we were able to measure signals with a resolution of $\approx 153 \, \mu V$. Upon detecting the first falling edge of the clock, the sampler would acquire data for the next 35 ms. This sampling period allowed us to capture the clock for both

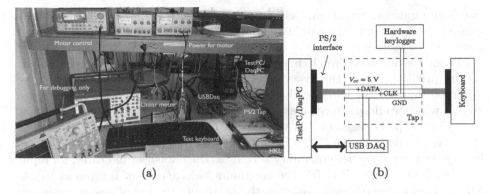

Fig. 4. (a) Experimental setup: the keyboards were secured in place so that the linear motor struck approximately the same place on the spacebar for each keyboard. (b) A schematic diagram of the setup. The dashed box represents an electrical tap in the PS/2 cable that was created by cutting the cable, striping the wires, and then soldering the exposed wires to binding posts.

the keydown and keyup signals sent by the keyboard, though only the clock corresponding to the keydown press was used in our analysis.

We collected data from a total of 25 keyboards, consisting of eight different models, from two manufacturers (Dell and Logitech) and two different places of manufacture (China and Thailand). For each keyboard 1000 keystrokes were recorded without the keylogger, followed by another 1000 keystrokes with the keylogger attached. It took approximately 50 min per keyboard to acquire both sets of data.

The reference signal, used for aligning signals in the feature extraction procedure (Sect. 3.2), for each keyboard was obtained from the first record captured for the keyboard without the HKL. Because the clock signal does not vary substantially from keyboard-to-keyboard, the negative (falling) threshold-based trigger that was set on the sampler to detect the beginning of the clock would consistently initiate the sampling sequence at nearly the same point of the clock signal. This enabled us to use the same set of sample points for the reference signal and extraction of the first 1.5 periods of the clock, again, described in Sect. 3.2, for each keyboard.

4.3 Discussion

The average difference of the line voltage in the absence and presence of the HKL (i.e. $V_l - V_l'$) was found to be 23.7 mV for the upper level of the clock and 4.11 mV for the lower level. We attribute the difference in the voltage drop between the two levels to a change in the input resistance. Indeed, according to [33] the nominal and maximum leakage currents of the uC at 5 V are 30 μA and 60 μA, respectively, while at 50 mV they are 1 nA and 1 μA. This suggests that $R_{kl} = [83.3 \text{ k}\Omega, 166.6 \text{ k}\Omega]$ at 5 V while at 25 mV, $R_{kl} = [25 \text{ k}\Omega, 25 \text{ k}\Omega]$. Using the maximum leakage currents and assuming a $\beta = 1$ with $V_{kb} = 500\Omega$ the predicted differences, by (1) and (2), would amount to $30\,\mathrm{mV}$ and $471\,\mu\mathrm{V}$ for the high and low level, respectively.

While the observed drop in line voltage for the high level roughly corresponds to the predicted drop, the lower level differs by an order of magnitude. The observed drop for the lower level could be explained if the leakage current were $10\,\mu\mathrm{A}$, which would produce an expected drop of $3.4\,\mathrm{mV}$. The documentation for the uC ([33], p. 4) suggests that the leakage current for *most* GPIO pins is less than $1\,\mu\mathrm{A}$ so perhaps the GPIO pin used in our HKL has a higher than average leakage current. Another possibility is that, as the datasheet indicates, for input voltages between $-0.3\,\mathrm{V}$ to $0\,\mathrm{V}$ the maximum leakage current is given as $10\,\mu\mathrm{A}$. Mismatches in the internal biasing of the uC due to the use of a separate power supply for the uC, intended to maintain the HKL's stealth, could conceivably make the input appear in this range to the uC.

To detect the differences in the line state, distances between a training distribution, built for each keyboard from fixed a number of records, and test distributions based on varying numbers of records were computed using the EMD metric. Individual training distributions for the keyboards were built from 25 randomly selected records captured without the keylogger attached. The EMD implementation we used requires that the number of sample points in the training and test distributions be equal. To satisfy this requirement we removed randomly selected samples from the larger distribution to make it equal in size to the smaller distribution. For all the test cases—i.e. whatever the number of records used to build the test distribution—the maximum number of sample points used was limited to 256 in order to keep the EMD calculation tractable.

Table 1. The equal error rate, and corresponding thresholds, achieved using N records to build the test distribution (training distribution fixed at 25 records). The left part of the table gives results for distributions built using the lower clock level while the right gives results for the upper clock level. We are able to reliably detect the presence of the HKL, for all 25 keyboards, after 25 keystrokes by observing the lower level and only 10 keystrokes by observing the upper. Sample points is the nominal number of sample points used in the EMD calculation.

N	EER (%)			T			Sample	EER (%)			T			Sample
	mean	max	median	mean	max	min	points	mean	max	median	mean	max	min	points
1	7.56	31.6	2.8	0.001	0.004	0.001	34	2.42	8.40	2.2	0.016	0.125	0.006	32
2	2.92	13.6	0.6	0.002	0.008	0.001	68	0.67	3.20	0.4	0.039	0.250	0.019	65
3	1.86	16.5	0	0.004	0.016	0.002	104	0.22	1.20	0	0.064	0.500	0.031	97
4	0.98	6.4	0	0.004	0.016	0.003	135	0.12	0.08	0	0.084	0.500	0.031	129
5	0.72	7.0	0	0.006	0.031	0.004	167	0.06	1.50	0	0.104	0.500	0.057	161
10	0.32	5.0	0	0.011	0.063	0.004	256	0	0	0	0.173	0.500	0.063	256
15	0.24	4.6	0	0.012	0.063	0.004	256	0	0	0	0.178	0.500	0.125	256
20	0.16	4.0	0	0.012	0.063	0.004	256	0	0	0	0.193	0.500	0.063	256
25	0	0	0	0.012	0.063	0.004	256	0	0	0	0.175	0.500	0.125	256

To evaluate the efficacy of our approach, we calculated the equal error rate (EER) on a per keyboard basis. Table 1 reports the average, maximum, and median (the minimum was always zero) EER for test distributions built from $N = \{1, 2, 3, 4, 5, 10, 15, 20, 25\}$ consecutive records (training/test distributions built from the lower level on the left and the upper level on the right). As we observed a larger voltage drop for the upper level of the clock, we anticipated that it would be easier to detect the HKL at the higher voltage, and indeed this was so. However, even with the small differences observed at the lower level, our approach is able to reliably detect (i.e. achieve an EER = 0) the presence of the HKL after 25 keystrokes, while for the upper level this same feat is achieved with only 10 keystrokes. Figure 5a and b show the distances between training and test distributions, using $N = 10$ for the high level and $N = 25$ for the low level comparisons, along with their respective EER thresholds.

We were able to further lower the number of keystrokes needed to detect the keylogger to five by fusing the outputs of the upper and lower distance calculations using unanimous voting. That is, for a set of records to be declared free of the HKL, the distances for both the upper and lower level distributions would need to fall within their respective thresholds. To evaluate the fusion of the distance tests, we established the thresholds needed to guarantee zero false-positives for each test distribution. Thus, the keylogger could be detected if the distance for either test distribution built from records captured with the HKL attached was greater than the specified thresholds. Zero false negatives were achieved when $N = 5$ for both high and low level distributions.

5 Feature Stability and Countermeasures

It is shown that while the features used for HKL detection are dependent on the environment, this dependency can be modelled and thus accounted for. Attacker countermeasures, both active and passive, are also considered and neutralized.

5.1 Stability of Features

The variability apparent in Figs. 3b, 5a, and b suggests that the line voltage is a stochastic process. This begs the question: can we track the state of the line using training data acquired at an earlier time? In an attempt to offer a partial answer to this question we acquired a second round of data without the keylogger attached and used the training distributions for the first dataset to calculate the distance between the two. We found that the distances calculated using the upper clock level were within the thresholds established for the earlier dataset; i.e. were able to successfully re-identify that the line was not encumbered with the HKL. In the case of the lower level, however, the distance between the training and test distribution were greater than the previously established thresholds; i.e. we falsely identified the line as having the HKL attached.

We hypothesize that our inability to track the lower line voltage is due to temperature-induced variations, as such small voltages ($\approx 25\,\mathrm{mV}$ for the lower

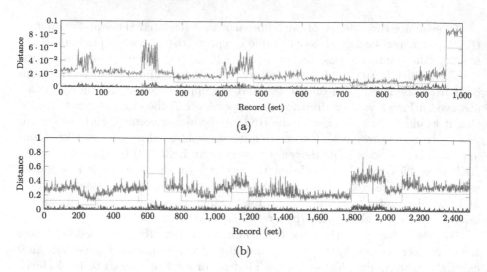

Fig. 5. The earth mover's distance between a training distribution and a test distribution built from records without a keylogger attached (blue) and with a keylogger attached (red) for all 25 keyboards (x-axis; records are grouped). EER thresholds shown in green. Since there is no overlap we are able to detect the HKL. (a) Features extracted from lower level of clock with $N = 25$ and (b) features extracted from upper level of clock with $N = 10$. The spike in the distance for records 601–700 results from a faulty keyboard (Color figure online).

clock level) could be shifted by thermal noise over time. However, temperature-induced changes to the line voltage could be compensated for by employing noise models to equalize line measurements taken at different temperatures. This implies that temperature readings need to be recorded when data is taken in order to take into account the discrepancy between the temperature of new data and the temperature at which the training data was acquired.

To test the above hypothesis, we performed an experiment wherein temperature sensors (the TI LM35DT [31]) were placed next to four suspected points of influence; viz. the keyboard under test, the Measurement Computing DAQ board, the site of PS/2 cable tap, and the uC-based HKL. A National Instrument USB-6008 series DAQ was used to record the output of the sensors. Every 30 s for 24 h[4] a key was pressed and the output of the sensors were measured 100 times, in addition to the voltage of the PS/2 clock line. Using 20 % of the captured data, selected at random, for each of the 23 keyboards as training data we performed a linear regression on the remaining 80 % using the model $F \sim 1 + T$,

---

[4] A slight change was made to our experimental setup to accommodate the duration of the data runs. Instead of the space bar being manually pressed, a program was written that toggled the NUMLOCK state. Since the OS state of this key and the NUMLOCK LED must be consistent, the PC would signal the keyboard that it had a scancode to send by bringing the clock line low, which would then cause the keyboard to generate a clock signal that we were able to subsequently capture.

where T denotes the average measured temperature during which the record was captured and F the mean of the lower portion of the clock signal of the record (our feature of interest). An average $R^2 = 0.99$ indicates that the line voltage is a strong function of temperature; the sensor that provided the best fit was nearest the PS/2 tap point.

5.2 Active and Evasive Keyloggers

In our threat model (Sect. 2.1) we pointed out that active keyloggers that rely on GPIO ports to capture keystrokes from the keyboard and then replay them to the PC should be easily detectable as the input/output ports do not capture the nuances of the keyboards signaling. In this section we argue that even a specially built keylogger that took pains to accurately measure and reproduce the keyboard's signals would be unlikely to remain undetected.

It has been demonstrated [6,9] that, under some circumstances, physical layer identification systems are vulnerable to an attacker replaying a signal from a device using an arbitrary waveform generator (AWG) or digital-to-analog converter (DAC). In the experiments carried out in these works, an attacker acquires a digital copy of a device's signal using an analog-to-digital converter (ADC) and then reproduces it using a DAC. As most uCs are equipped with an ADC and DAC (or can be easily outfitted with them), we could imagine an attacker attempting to mount a similar attack on our proposed PLD system by creating an active HKL that samples the keyboard's signal using the ADC and then replays it to the PC using the DAC. Leaving aside the exact characteristics of each converter necessary to carry out the attack (sampling rates and resolution, chiefly), we point out that the ADC/DAC would still cause loading effects that would make it detectable.

Firstly, the finite resistance associated with the ADC input would cause a drop in the line voltage, which would mean that an attacker cannot know the true value of the keyboard's output. Secondly, the non-zero output impedance of the DAC would cause a decrease in the voltage measured by the PC (this can be seen by the replacement of V_{kb} and R_{kb} with V_{dac} and R_{dac} in Eq. 1). Now, the attacker could attempt to compensate for these loading effects by calibrating the HKL to the system they wish to attach it to. However, this procedure is quite invasive, and noticeable, as it requires that the attacker obtain the resistances of the PC and keyboard. The measurements required to deduce these values require that both the PC and keyboard be powered, as their port impedance would change in the absence of power. To accomplish this would require that the attacker sever at least the clock line between the two, which our PLD could be programmed to notice.

Additionally, we note that measuring and replaying the line state continuously using an ADC/DAC would be more energy intensive than simply measuring and replaying the binary state of the line via GPIOs, leading to a shorter period of keylogging. Also, a simple active HKL would cut off bi-directional communication between the PC and keyboard as the replay is one-way. It may be possible to design an HKL that senses the keyboard taking control of the line, but this seems nontrivial and could introduce delays in signal propagation that are detectable.

Finally, it may also be possible to detect/counter a self-powered active HKL employing a DAC by shorting the keyboard line. The short works as a counter because a stealthy HKL will have a limited power supply, as it is self-powered, so drawing the maximum amount of current possible via a short would increase its power consumption and decrease its operational lifetime. In addition, the DAC could probably not sustain a significant current draw without damage. Detection is also possible using a short: as the keyboard draws its power from the PC a short should result in a spike of current on the V_{CC} line, of a known amount. The presence of a HKL could be deduced by the absence of such a spike, or a spike of equivalent magnitude.

5.3 Passive and Evasive Keyloggers

As noted in Sect. 2.3, a HKL can be detected due to differences in fall/rise time (transient response) or voltage drops. In this work we focused on voltage drops because transient effects are small for the HKL we considered (time constant on the order of a nanosecond). An attacker attempting to evade our level-based detection approach could equip their HKL with a high input impedance comparator, based on the LT1793 op-amp [22], for example, at the input stage to ensure an undetectable voltage drop. With an input impedance of 10 TΩ, such an op-amp would effectively make $R_{eq} = R_{pc}$ (order of MOhm), which would result in $V_l = V_l'$. A high input impedance comparator would, however, produce a time constant ($\tau = R_{eq}C_{kl}$, $C_{kl} \sim$ pF) on the order of microseconds, which would distort the clock voltage to a noticeable degree (due to changes in the rise/fall time of the circuit). This does beg the question: can an attacker select a R_{kl} such that the transient response is unchanged and the drop immeasurable? We would argue no, as follows.

Assume that an attacker can arbitrarily set the resistance of the HKL. It is the attacker's prerogative to select an R_{kl} that produces an equivalent resistance as small as possible (to minimize the time constant), yet large enough so that the resulting voltage drop across R_{eq} is less than can be resolved by the ADC. The minimum equivalent resistance to accomplish this is

$$R_{eq} = \frac{V_l - r}{V_{kb} - V_l + r} R_{kb} \qquad (3)$$

where r is the minimum resolvable voltage drop (see Appendix for derivation). For the ADC used in the paper $r = 150\,\mu\text{V}$, which yields $R_{eq} = 943$ kΩ. Ignoring the capacitance of the additional resistors needed to effect the target resistance, the capacitance of a LT1793 op-amp is 1.5 pF, which produces a time constant on the order of microseconds. Even an $r = 1$ mV requires $R_{eq} = 714$ kΩ, which still produces a time constant on the order of a microsecond. Additionally, attaching the op-amp to the clock line is likely to produce more than 1.5 pF of capacitance.

To validate the above claim we replaced our HKL with a resistor (representing R_{eq}) and 3 pF capacitor and acquired 1000 clock line measurements for each keyboard; fresh comparison data without the resistor and capacitor was also collected. The resistor value was selected experimentally for each keyboard such that the resulting voltage drop could not be detected by our Measurement Computing DAQ. On average, the minimum equivalent resistance for our collection of keyboards was 6 MΩ; i.e. an attacker able to tune the input resistance of their HKL to 6 MΩ would ensure that it is undetectable to our level-based approach, while at the same time minimizing the time constant (and hence rise/fall times) of the circuit. The 3 pF capacitance was used to represent the capacitance of the HKL input pin and the connection to the PS/2 line. An estimate of 3 pF was made as a lower bound based on the assumption that the HKL would be mounted on a printed circuit board (PCB) to accomodate lower capacitance surface mount components, which introduces parasitic capacitances due to the groundplane (0.5 pF cm^{-2} [30]), traces (0.8 pF cm^{-1} [30]), and bondwires (0.1 pF to 0.15 pF for 2 mm wire lengths [16]). Our detection approach consisted of extracting the rise and fall times (calculated according to [15]) of the first five edges of the portion of the clock relating to the down keypress. Instead of the EMD, which was found to be unable to distinguish between the HKL and no HKL cases, the Kullback-Leibler (KL) divergence [21] was employed for comparing training and test distributions.

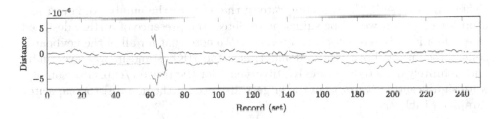

Fig. 6. The Kullback-Leibler divergence between a training distribution and a test distribution built from records without a keylogger attached (blue) and with a keylogger attached (red) for 23 keyboards (x-axis; records are grouped). EER thresholds shown in green. Since there is no overlap, aside from keyboard seven, we are able to detect the HKL. Features consist of the rise times for the first five rising edges of the clock with $N = 100$. The spike in the distance for records 61–70 results from a faulty keyboard (Color figure online).

Given expected rise/fall times on the order of a microsecond, we did not expect to be able to discern a difference in rise/fall times using a 1 MS/s ADC. As such, a Tektronix DPO2024 oscilloscope equipped with a Tektronix P6139B probe (10 MΩ and 8 pF input resistance and capacitance, respectively) was used. Using a sampling rate of 125 MS/s[5] with 25 keystrokes for training/detection using the rise time resulted in an average ERR of 0.02 %, while 100 keystrokes for

---

[5] We note that while 125 MS/s ADCs are more expensive than the 1 MS/s variety, they can still be had for less than $15, e.g. the LTI LTC2251 [23].

Table 2. The equal error rate, and corresponding thresholds, achieved using N records to build the test distribution (training distribution fixed at 25 records). The left part of the table gives results for distributions built using the fall times of the first five falling edges, while the right gives results for distributions built from the rise times of the first five rising edges. We are able to reliably detect the presence of the HKL, for most keyboards, after 50 keystrokes by observing the fall times and only 25 keystrokes by observing the rise times.

N	EER (%)			T			EER (%)			T		
	mean	max	median	mean	max	min	mean	max	median	mean	max	min
1	4.59	9.98	4.31	−0.74	−0.66	−0.86	3.75	9.69	3.51	−6.04	−2	−12
2	2.73	5	3.16	−0.08	−0.07	−0.19	2.11	4.94	1.93	−2.4	−1.5	−4.5
4	1.12	2.5	1.28	−0.26	−0.05	−0.45	0.7	2.24	0.61	−3.62	−0.5	−7.5
5	1	1.93	1.15	−0.39	−0.03	−0.93	0.54	1.68	0.37	−5.82	−3.5	−9.5
10	0.39	0.99	0.41	−0.275	−0.1	−0.45	0.15	0.81	0.53	−8	−7	−9
20	0.10	0.5	0.04	−1.5	−1	−2.5	0.05	0.42	0.01	−17	−11	−26
25	0.09	0.4	0.06	−1.6	−0.6	−2.6	0.02	0.18	0	−21.5	−14	−29
50	0.02	0.1	0	−2.8	−1.8	−3.8	0.03	0.08	0	−32.5	−30	−35
100	0.01	0.1	0	−6.1	−5.7	−6.5	0.001	0.03	0	−64.5	−62	−67

training/testing yielded an average EER of 0.001 % (Fig. 6). This suggests that either an increase in the sampling rate of the ADC or the number of keystrokes used for detection would be sufficient to detect the presence of a HKL designed to evade a level-based detection approach. We note that for all of the keyboards considered, using both rise and fall times, the HKL stand-in was eventually and definitely detected; i.e. the KL divergence for the resistor/capacitor samples were significantly greater than the largest distance for the non-resistor/capacitor samples (Table 2).

6 Conclusion and Future Work

Inspired by the observer effect, we hypothesized that a HKL would have a measurable effect on its host system. Specifically, we built a detection methodology based on the theory that the HKL would cause the voltage of the clock line to drop. This prediction was substantiated through experiments wherein it was shown that 25 keystrokes were necessary to identify the presence of a HKL when the lower level of the clock was used for detection, while the upper level required only 10 keystrokes and was shown to be more consistent across time. A combined approach based on unanimous voting reduced the detection time to five keystrokes. It was found that the features used to identify the presence of a HKL are sensitive to temperature. Furthermore, it was shown experimentally that an attacker cannot escape detection by modifying the input resistance of the HKL, if the transient characteristics of the clock line are monitored.

Future work includes the long-term observation of keyboard signals to understand and incorporate the effects of ageing. Adaptive thresholding schemes may prove useful in this regard. Secondly, to complement detection, investigations of active countermeasures against HKL should be undertaken, including the permanent disabling of HKLs through electrical means. Finally, research should be undertaken to identify features that are not based on the clock signal level. The ultimate aim of this work should be to discover features in the keyboard signaling that are sensitive to the presence of a HKL but invariant with respect to the keyboard resistance/voltage and the PC resistance.

Acknowledgements. The authors would like to thank Li Yin and Heidi Harper of Utah State University for their assistance in collecting data.

Appendix: Optimal Selection of HKL Input Resistance

The attacker seeks to minimize the difference between the line voltage with and without the HKL in order to evade the level-based detection approach, while simultaneously minimizing the time constant associated with the HKL to lessen the increase of the rise/fall times of the clock signal. The former goal can be realized by choosing $R_{kl} \gg R_{pc}$ to ensure that $R_{eq} = R_{kl} \parallel R_{pc} = R_{pc}$. This, however, is achieved at the expense of the latter goal, as the time constant $R_{eq}C_{kl}$ can only be decreased by selecting R_{kl} such that $R_{eq} < R_{pc}$, due to the fact that the HKL capacitance is fixed. The minimum value of R_{eq}, and by extension the optimal input impedance of the HKL, necessary to evade the level-based approach while minimizing the time constant of the HKL is calculated as follows.

Allow r to represent the minimum resolvable voltage drop of the ADC employed in the detector. Evading the level-based detection approach requires $V_l - V_l' = r$, where r may be expressed in terms of the quantities controllable and/or known by the attacker as

$$r = V_l - \frac{R_{eq}}{R_{kb} + R_{eq}} V_{kb} \tag{4}$$

Defining

$$V_m = \frac{R_{eq}}{R_{kb} + R_{eq}} V_{kb} \tag{5}$$

and rearranging terms yields

$$V_l - r = V_m \tag{6}$$

Furthermore, manipulation of (5) gives

$$R_{eq} = \frac{V_m}{V_{kb} - V_m} R_{kb} \tag{7}$$

By substituting (6) into (7) we arrive at

$$R_{eq} = \frac{V_l - r}{V_{kb} - V_l + r} R_{kb} \tag{8}$$

□

References

1. ABC News: Former Cal State student gets year in prison for rigging campus election (2013). http://abcnews.go.com/US/cal-state-student-year-prison-rigging-campus-election/story?id=19682401
2. Analog Devices: AD7265 Differential/Single-Ended Input, Dual 1 MSPS, 12-Bit, 3-Channel SAR ADC (2006), datasheet
3. Chahrvin, S.: Keyloggers–your security nightmare? Comput. Fraud Secur. **2007**(7), 10–11 (2007)
4. Chapweske, A.: The ps/2 mouse/keyboard protocol (2003). http://www.computer-engineering.org/ps2protocol
5. Danev, B.: Physical-layer Identification of Wireless Devices. Ph.D. thesis, ETH Zurich, Zurich, Switzerland (2011)
6. Danev, B., Luecken, H., Capkun, S., Defrawy, K.E.: Attacks on physical-layer identification. In: Proceedings of the Third ACM Conference on Wireless Network Security (WiSec 2010), pp. 89–98. ACM, New York (2010)
7. Danev, B., Zanetti, D., Capkun, S.: On physical-layer identification of wireless devices. ACM Comput. Surv. (CSUR) **45**(1), 6 (2012)
8. Daniels, T.E., Mina, M., Russell, S.F.: A signal fingerprinting paradigm for physical layer security in conventional and sensor networks. In: Proceedings of the International Conference on Security and Privacy for Emerging Areas in Communnication Networks (SecureComm), pp. 219–221. IEEE Computer Society (2005)
9. Edman, M., Yener, B.: Active attacks against modulation-based radiometric identification. Technical report, Rensselaer Polytechnic Institute, Department of Computer Science (2009), technical Report
10. Erbskorn, J.W.: Detection of Intrusions at Layer ONe: The IEEE 802.3 normal link pulse as a means of host-to-network authentication A preliminary performance analysis and survey of environmental effects. Master's thesis, Iowa State University, Ames, IA (2009)
11. Gerdes, R., Mina, M., Russell, S., Daniels, T.: Physical-layer identification of wired ethernet devices. IEEE Trans. Inf. Forensics Secur. **7**(4), 1339–1353 (2012)
12. Gerdes, R.M.: Physical layer identification: methodology, security, and origin of variation. Ph.D. thesis, Iowa State University, Ames, IA (2011)
13. Gerdes, R.M., Daniels, T.E., Mina, M., Russell, S.F.: Device identification via analog signal fingerprinting: a matched filter approach. In: Proceedings of the Network and Distributed System Security Symposium (NDSS). The Internet Society (2006)
14. Greene, M., Parker, M.: Method and system for detecting a keylogger that encrypts data captured on a computer, 25 July 2006, US Patent App. 11/492,581
15. IEEE: Standard for transitions, pulses, and related waveforms (2011), IEEE Std 181–2011
16. Karim, N., Agrawal, A.: Plastic packages electrical performance: reduced bond wire diameter. In: NEPCON WEST, pp. 975–980 (1998)
17. KeeLog: Open source DIY hardware keylogger (2012). http://www.keelog.com/diy.html
18. KeeLog: Keygrabber Module (2013). http://www.keelog.com/
19. KeyCarbon: Keycarbon Raptor (2012). http://www.keycarbon.com/
20. KeyCarbon: Keycarbon PCI (2013). http://www.keycarbon.com/
21. Kullback, S., Leibler, R.A.: On information and sufficiency. Ann. Math. Stat. **52**, 79–86 (1951)
22. Linear Technology: LT1793 JFET Input Op Amp (1999), datasheet

23. Linear Technology: LTC2251/LTC2250 ADCs (2005), datasheet
24. Mihailowitsch, F.: Detecting hardware keyloggers, November 2010. https://deepsec.net/docs/Slides/2010/DeepSec_2010_Detecting_Hardware_Keylogger.pdf. [DeepSec 2010 Presentation]
25. Nakra, B.C., Chaudhry, K.K.: Instrumentation Measurement and Analysis. McGraw-Hill Education (India) Pvt Limited (2009)
26. Nilsson, J.W., Riedel, S.: Electric Circuits. Prentice Hall, Upper Saddle River (2010)
27. Pele, O., Werman, M.: A linear time histogram metric for improved SIFT matching. In: Forsyth, D., Torr, P., Zisserman, A. (eds.) ECCV 2008, Part III. LNCS, vol. 5304, pp. 495–508. Springer, Heidelberg (2008)
28. Salkind, N.: Encyclopedia of Research Design. SAGE Publications, Thousand Oaks (2010)
29. Sapra, K., Husain, B., Brooks, R., Smith, M.: Circumventing keyloggers and screendumps. In: 2013 8th International Conference on Malicious and Unwanted Software: "The Americas" (MALWARE), pp. 103–108, October 2013
30. Texas Instruments: High Speed Analog Design and Application Seminar: High Speed PCB Layout Techniques (2004), presentation
31. Texas Instruments: LM35 Temperature Sensors (2013), datasheet
32. Texas Instruments: Tiva TM4C123GH6PM microcontroller (2013), datasheet
33. Texas Instruments: Use conditions for 5-v tolerant gpios on Tiva C series TM4C123x microcontrollers (2013), application Report
34. The New York Times: Credit card data breach at Barnes & Noble stores (2012). http://www.nytimes.com/2012/10/24/business/hackers-get-credit-data-at-barnes-noble.html?_r=3&
35. Zaitsev, O.: Skeleton keys: the purpose and applications of keyloggers. Netw. Secur. **2010**(10), 12–17 (2010)

Reverse Engineering Intel Last-Level Cache Complex Addressing Using Performance Counters

Clémentine Maurice[1,2]([✉]), Nicolas Le Scouarnec[1], Christoph Neumann[1], Olivier Heen[1], and Aurélien Francillon[2]

[1] Technicolor, Rennes, France
[2] Eurecom, Sophia Antipolis, France
clementine@cmaurice.fr

Abstract. Cache attacks, which exploit differences in timing to perform covert or side channels, are now well understood. Recent works leverage the last level cache to perform cache attacks across cores. This cache is split in *slices*, with one slice per core. While predicting the slices used by an address is simple in older processors, recent processors are using an undocumented technique called *complex addressing*. This renders some attacks more difficult and makes other attacks impossible, because of the loss of precision in the prediction of cache collisions.

In this paper, we build an automatic and generic method for reverse engineering Intel's last-level cache complex addressing, consequently rendering the class of cache attacks highly practical. Our method relies on CPU hardware performance counters to determine the cache slice an address is mapped to. We show that our method gives a more precise description of the complex addressing function than previous work. We validated our method by reversing the complex addressing functions on a diverse set of Intel processors. This set encompasses Sandy Bridge, Ivy Bridge and Haswell micro-architectures, with different number of cores, for mobile and server ranges of processors. We show the correctness of our function by building a covert channel. Finally, we discuss how other attacks benefit from knowing the complex addressing of a cache, such as sandboxed *rowhammer*.

Keywords: Complex addressing · Covert channel · Cross-Core · Last level cache · Reverse engineering · Side channel

1 Introduction

In modern x86 micro-architectures, the cache is an element that is shared by cores of the same processor. It is thus a piece of hardware of choice for performing attacks. Cache attacks like covert and side channels can be performed in virtualized environments [16,22,27,33,35–37], breaching the hypervisor isolation at the hardware level. Caches are also exploited in other types of attacks,

© Springer International Publishing Switzerland 2015
H. Bos et al. (Eds.): RAID 2015, LNCS 9404, pp. 48–65, 2015.
DOI: 10.1007/978-3-319-26362-5_3

such as bypassing kernel ASLR [8], or detecting cryptographic libraries in virtualized environments [17].

Cache attacks are based on difference of timings: the access to a cached memory line is fast, while the access to a previously evicted cache line is slow. Cache attacks can operate at all cache levels: level 1 (L1), level 2 (L2) and Last Level Cache (LLC). Attacks on the L1 or L2 cache restrict the attacker to be on the same core as the victim. This is a too strong assumption on a multi-core processor when the attacker and the victim migrate across cores [27,35]. We thus focus on cache attacks on the last level cache, which is shared among cores in modern processors. Attacks on the last level cache are more powerful as the attacker and the victim can run on different cores, but they are also more challenging. To perform these attacks, the attacker has to target specific sets in the last level cache. He faces two issues: the last level cache is physically addressed, and modern processors map an address to a slice using the so-called *complex addressing* scheme which is undocumented.

A first set of attacks requires shared memory and evicts a specific line using the clflush instruction [7,16,36,38]. However, a simple countermeasure to thwart such side channels is to disable memory sharing across VMs, which is already done by most cloud providers.

Without using any shared memory, an attacker has to find addresses that map to the same set, and exploit the cache replacement policy to evict lines. On processors that do not use complex addressing, huge pages are sufficient to enable side channels by targeting a precise set [14]. On recent processors that use complex addressing, this difficulty can be bypassed by evicting the whole LLC [22], but the temporal resolution makes it impossible to perform side channels. Liu et al. [20] and Oren et al. [24] construct eviction sets by seeking conflicting addresses, enabling fine-grained covert and side channels. This works without reverse engineering the complex addressing function, but has to be performed for each attack.

Hund et al. [8] manually and, as we show, only partially reverse engineered the complex addressing function to defeat kernel ASLR on a Sandy Bridge processor. The challenge in reversing the complex addressing function is to retrieve all the bits. Indeed, previous approaches rely on timing attacks with conflicting cache sets. As the set bits are fixed, they cannot be retrieved this way. Previous work was also incomplete because the function differs for processors with different numbers of cores, as we will show.

Reversing this addressing function also gains momentum [29] in discussions about the exploitation of the so-called *rowhammer* vulnerability. Indeed, *rowhammer* can cause random bit flips in DRAM chips by accessing specific memory locations repeatedly [19]. The exploitation of this vulnerability uses the clflush instruction [28]. This instruction has been disabled [3] in the Native Client sandbox [2] due to this security issue. Reversing the addressing function could lead to new ways to exploit *rowhammer* without relying on the clflush instruction.

In this paper, we automate reverse engineering of the complex cache addressing in order to make these attacks more practical. In contrast to previous work that reverse engineered the function manually, we develop a fully automatic app-roach to resolve the complex addressing of last level cache slices. Our technique relies on performance counters to measure the number of accesses to a slice and to determine on which slice a memory access is cached. As a result, we obtain a translation table that allows determining the slice used by a given physical address (Sect. 3). In the general case, finding a compact function from the map-ping is NP-hard. Nevertheless, we show an efficient algorithm to find a compact solution for a majority of processors (which have 2^n cores). As a result, we pro-vide new insights on the behavior of the last level cache, and refine many previous works (e.g., Hund et al. [8]). In particular, we obtain a more complete and more precise description than previous work, *i.e.*, taking into account more bits of the memory address and fixing the partially incorrect functions of prior work. We evaluate our method on processors of different micro-architectures with various numbers of cores (Sect. 4). We demonstrate the correctness of our function by building a *prime+probe* covert channel (Sect. 5). Finally, we discuss the differ-ence between our findings and the previous attempts of reverse engineering this function, as well as other applications (Sect. 6).

Contributions

In summary, this paper presents the following main contributions:

1. We introduce a generic method for mapping physical addresses to last level cache slices, using hardware performance counters.
2. We provide a compact function for most processor models (with 2^n cores).
3. We validate our approach on a wide range of modern processors.
4. We show, and discuss, practical examples of the benefits to cache attacks.

2   Background

In this section, we give details on cache internals for Intel processors post Sandy Bridge micro-architecture (2011). We then review attacks that exploit cache interferences to perform covert and side channels. Finally, we provide background on hardware performance counters.

2.1   Cache Fundamentals

The processor stores recently-used data in a hierarchy of caches to reduce the memory access time by the processor (see Fig. 1). The first two levels L1 and L2 are usually small and private to each core. The L3 is also called Last Level Cache (LLC). It is shared among cores and can store several megabytes. The LLC is *inclusive*, which means it is a superset of the lower levels.

Caches are organized in 64-byte long blocks called *lines*. The caches are *n-way associative*, which means that a line is loaded in a specific set depending on its address, and occupies any of the n lines. When all lines are used in a set, the

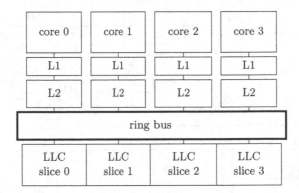

Fig. 1. Cache architecture of a quad-core Intel processor (since Sandy Bridge micro-architecture). The LLC is divided into slices, and interconnected with each core by a ring bus.

replacement policy decides the line to be evicted to make room for storing a new cache line. Efficient replacement policies favor lines that are the least likely to be reused. Such policies are usually variations of Least Recently Used (LRU).

The first level of cache is indexed by virtual addresses, and the two other levels are indexed by physical addresses. With caches that implement a *direct addressing* scheme, memory addresses can be decomposed in three parts: the tag, the set and the offset in the line. The lowest $\log_2(\text{line size})$ bits determine the offset in the line. The next $\log_2(\text{number of sets})$ bits determine the set. The remaining bits form the tag.

The LLC is divided into as many slices as cores, interconnected by a ring bus. The slices contain sets like the other levels. An undocumented hashing algorithm determines the slice associated to an address in order to distribute traffic evenly among the slices and reduce congestion. In contrast to direct addressing, it is a *complex addressing* scheme. Potentially all address bits are used to determine the slice, excluding the lowest $\log_2(\text{line size})$ bits that determine the offset in a line. Contrary to the slices, the sets are directly addressed. Figure 2 gives a schematic description of the addressing of slices and sets.

2.2 Cache Attacks

System memory protection prevents a process from directly reading or writing in the cache memory of another process. However, cache hits are faster than cache misses. Thus by monitoring its own activity, *i.e.*, the variation of its own cache access delays, a process can determine the cache sets accessed by other processes, and subsequently leak information. This class of cache attacks is called *access-driven attacks*.

In a *prime+probe* attack [23,25,26,30], the attacker fills the cache, then waits for the victim to evict some cache sets. The attacker reads data again and determines which sets were evicted. The access to these sets will be slower for the attacker because they need to be reloaded in the cache.

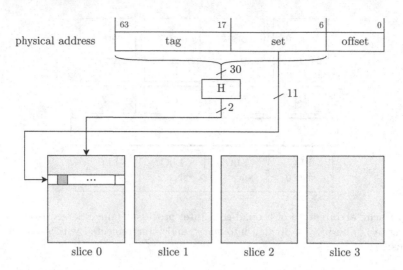

Fig. 2. Complex addressing scheme in the LLC with 64B cache lines, 4 slices and 2048 sets per slice. The slice is given by a hash function that takes as an input all the bits of the set and the tag. The set is then directly addressed. The dark gray cell corresponds to one cache line.

The challenge for this type of fine-grained attack is the ability to target a specific set. This is especially difficult when the targeted cache levels are physically indexed and use complex addressing.

2.3   Hardware Performance Counters

Hardware performance counters are special-purpose registers that are used to monitor special hardware-related events. Such events include cache misses or branch mispredictions, making the counters useful for performance analysis or fine tuning. Because performance counters require high level of privileges, they cannot be directly used for an attack.

The registers are organized by performance monitoring units (called PMON). Each PMON unit has a set of *counter registers*, paired with *control registers*. Performance counters can only be used to measure the global events that happen at the hardware level, and not for a process in particular. This adds noise and has to be considered when performing a measurement.

There is one PMON unit, called CBo (or C-Box), per LLC slice. Each CBo has a separate set of counters, paired to control registers. Among the available events, LLC_LOOKUP counts all accesses to the LLC. A mask on the event filters the type of the request (data read, write, external snoop, or any) [9,11,12].

Performance counters depend on the processor, but the CBo counters and the LLC_LOOKUP event are present in a wide range of processors, and documented by Intel.[1] Some adaptations are needed between different types of processors. Indeed, for Xeon Sandy Bridge, Xeon Ivy Bridge, Xeon Haswell and Core processors, the MSR addresses and the bit fields (thus the values assigned to each MSR) vary, but the method remains similar. Reading and writing MSR registers needs to be done by the kernel (ring 0) via the privileged instructions rdmsr and wrmsr.

3 Mapping Physical Addresses to Slices Using Performance Counters

In this section, we present our technique for reverse engineering the complex addressing function, using the performance counters. Our objective is to build a table that maps a physical address (for each cache line) to a slice (e.g., Table 1).

Table 1. Mapping table obtained after running Algorithm 1. Each address has been polled 10000 times.

Physical address	CBo 0	CBo 1	CBo 2	CBo 3	Slice
0x3a0071010	**11620**	1468	1458	143	0
0x3a0071050	626	**10702**	696	678	1
0x3a0071090	498	567	**10559**	571	2
0x3a00710d0	517	565	573	**10590**	3
...	...	...	...	...	...

This is performed using Algorithm 1. First, monitoring of the LLC_LOOKUP event is set up by writing to control registers (MSR). Then, one memory address is repeatedly accessed (Listing 1.1) to generate activity on the corresponding slice. The counter performance registers are then read for each slice (each CBo). Next, the virtual address is translated to a physical address by reading the file /proc/pid/pagemap. Finally, the physical address is associated to the slice that has the most lookups. Such monitoring sessions are iterated with different addresses to obtain a set of pairs (physical address, slice) that, eventually, forms a table.

The number of times the address needs to be polled is determined experimentally to differentiate the lookup of this particular address in a slice from the noise of other LLC accesses. We empirically found that polling an address 10 000 times is enough to distinguish the correct slice from noise without ambiguity, and to reproduce the experiment on different configurations. The polling itself is carefully designed to avoid access to memory locations other than the tested address (see Listing 1.1). To this end, most of the variables are put in registers,

---

[1] For the Xeon range (servers): processors of the micro-architecture Sandy Bridge in [9], Ivy Bridge in [11], and Haswell in [12]. For the Core range (mobiles and workstations), in [10] for the three aforementioned micro-architectures.

Algorithm 1. Constructing the address to slice mapping table.

1: *mapping* ← new table
2: **for each** addr **do**
3:     **for each** slice **do**
4:         write MSRs to set up monitoring LLC_LOOKUP event
5:     **end for**
6:     polling(addr)   // see Listing 1.1
7:     **for each** slice **do**
8:         read MSRs to access LLC_LOOKUP event counter
9:     **end for**
10:    *paddr* ← translate_address(addr)
11:    find slice *i* that has the most lookups
12:    insert (*paddr*, *i*) in *mapping*
13: **end for**

---

and the only access to main memory is performed by the `clflush` instruction that flushes the line (in all cache hierarchies). The `clflush` instruction causes a lookup in the LLC even when the line is not present.

Listing 1.1 Memory polling function.

```
1: void polling(uintptr_t addr){
2:    register int i asm ("eax");
3:    register uintptr_t ptr asm ("ebx") = addr;
4:    for(i=0; i<NB_LOOP; i++){
5:       clflush((void*)ptr);
6:    }
7: }
```

Table 2 shows the characteristics of the CPUs we tested. Scanning an address per cache line, *i.e.*, an address every 64 B, takes time, but it is linear with the memory size. Scanning 1 GB of memory takes a bit less than 45 min. We now estimate the storage cost of the mapping table. The lowest 6 bits of the address are used to compute the offset in a line, hence we do not need to store them. In practice, it is also not possible to address all the higher bits because we are limited by the memory available in the machine. For a processor with c slices, the slice is represented with $\lceil log_2(c) \rceil$ bits. A configuration of e.g., 256 GB ($= 2^{38}$) of memory and 8 cores can be represented as a table with an index of 32 ($= 38 - 6$) bits; each entry of the table contains 3 bits identifying the slice and an additional bit indicating whether the address has been probed or not. The size of the table is thus $2^{32} \times 4$ bits $= 2$ GB.

Note that the attacker does not necessarily need the entire table to perform an attack. Only the subset of addresses used in an attack is relevant. This subset can be predefined by the attacker, e.g., by fixing the bits determining the set. Alternatively, the subset can be determined dynamically during the attack, and the attacker can query an external server to get the corresponding slice numbers.

Table 2. Characteristics of the Intel CPUs used in our experimentations (mobile and server range).

Name	Model	μ-arch	Cores	Mem
config_1	Xeon E5-2609 v2	Ivy Bridge	4	16 GB
config_2	Xeon E5-2660	Sandy Bridge	8	64 GB
config_3	Xeon E5-2650	Sandy Bridge	8	256 GB
config_4	Xeon E5-2630 v3	Haswell	8	128 GB
config_5	Core i3-2350M	Sandy Bridge	2	4 GB
config_6	Core i5-2520M	Sandy Bridge	2	4 GB
config_7	Core i5-3340M	Ivy Bridge	2	8 GB
config_8	Core i7-4810MQ	Haswell	4	8 GB
config_9	Xeon E5-2640	Sandy Bridge	6	64 GB

4 Building a Compact Addressing Function

4.1 Problem Statement

We aim at finding a function, as a compact form of the table. The function takes n bits of a physical address as input parameters. In the remainder, we note b_i the bit i of the address. The function has an output of $\lceil log_2(c) \rceil$ bits for c slices. To simplify the expression and the reasoning, we express the function as several Boolean functions, one per bit of output. We note $o_i(b_{63}, \ldots, b_0)$ the function that determines the bit i of the output.

Our problem is an instance of Boolean function minimization: our mapping can be seen as a truth table, that can consequently be converted to a formula in Disjunctive Normal Form (DNF). However, the minimization problem is known as NP-hard, and is thus computationally difficult [4].

Existing work on Boolean function minimization does not seem suitable to reconstruct the function from this table. Exact minimization algorithms like Karnaugh mapping or Quine-McCluskey have an exponential complexity in number of input bits. In practice those are limited to 8 bits of input, which is not enough to compute a complete function. The standard tool for dealing with a larger number of inputs is Espresso, which relies on non-optimal heuristics. However, it does not seem suited to handle truth tables of hundreds of millions of lines in a reasonable time.[2] It also gives results in DNF, which won't express the function compactly if it contains logical gates other than AND or OR. Indeed, we provided lines for a subset of the address space to Espresso, but the functions obtained were complex and we did not succeed to generalize them manually. They were generated from a subset, thus they are only true for that subset and do not apply to the whole address space.

---

[2] At the time of camera ready, Espresso has been running without providing any results for more than 2000 h on a table of more than 100.000.000 lines, which only represents the sixth of the 64 GB of memory of the machine.

We thus need hints on the expression of the function to build a compact addressing function. We did this by a first manual reconstruction, then followed by a generalization. We have done this work for processors with 2^n cores, which we consider in the remainder of the section.

4.2   Manually Reconstructing the Function for Xeon E5-2609 v2

We now explain how one can manually reverse engineer a complex addressing function: this is indeed how we started for a Xeon E5-2609 v2 (*config_1* in Table 2). In Sect. 4.3, we will explain how this can be automated and generalized to any processor model with 2^n cores. The following generalization removes the need to perform the manual reconstruction for each setup.

We manually examined the table to search patterns and see if we can deduce relations between the bits and the slices. We performed regular accesses to addresses which were calculated to fix every bit but the ones we want to observe, e.g., regular accesses every 2^6 bytes to observe address bits $b_{11} \ldots b_6$. For bits $b_{11} \ldots b_6$, we can observe addresses in 4kB pages. For the higher bits (b_{12} and above) we need contiguous physical addresses in a bigger range to fix more bits. This can be done using a custom driver [8], but for implementation convenience we used 1 GB pages. Across the table, we observed patterns in the slice number, such as the sequences (0,1,2,3), (1,0,3,2), (2,3,0,1), and (3,2,1,0). These patterns are associated with the XOR operation of the input bits, this made the manual reconstruction of the function easier.

We obtained these two binary functions:

$$o_0(b_{63}, \ldots, b_0) = b_6 \oplus b_{10} \oplus b_{12} \oplus b_{14} \oplus b_{16} \oplus b_{17} \oplus b_{18} \oplus b_{20} \oplus b_{22} \oplus b_{24} \oplus b_{25}$$
$$\oplus b_{26} \oplus b_{27} \oplus b_{28} \oplus b_{30} \oplus b_{32} \oplus b_{33}.$$

$$o_1(b_{63}, \ldots, b_0) = b_7 \oplus b_{11} \oplus b_{13} \oplus b_{15} \oplus b_{17} \oplus b_{19} \oplus b_{20} \oplus b_{21} \oplus b_{22} \oplus b_{23} \oplus b_{24}$$
$$\oplus b_{26} \oplus b_{28} \oplus b_{29} \oplus b_{31} \oplus b_{33} \oplus b_{34}.$$

We confirmed the correctness of the obtained functions by comparing the output of the slice calculated with the function against the entire mapping table obtained with the MSRs.

4.3   Reconstructing the Function Automatically

Our manual reconstruction shows that each output bit $o_i(b_{63}, \ldots, b_0)$ can be expressed as a series of XORs of the bits of the physical address. Hund et al. [8] manually reconstructed a mapping function of the same form, albeit a different one. In the remainder, we thus hypothesize, and subsequently validate the hypothesis, that the function has the same form for all processors that have 2^n cores.

The fact that the function only relies on XORs makes its reconstruction a very constrained problem. For each Boolean function $o_i(b_{63}, \ldots, b_0)$, we can analyze the implication of the address bits independently from each other, in order to access only a handful of physical addresses. Our algorithm finds two addresses that only differ by one bit, finds their respective slices using performance counters, and compares the output. If the output is the same, it means that the bit is not part of the function. Conversely, if the output differs, it means that the bit is part of the function. Note that this only works for a XOR function. This algorithm is linear in number of bits.

To implement the algorithm, we use huge pages of 1 GB on Xeon processors (resp. 2 MB on Core processors), which is contiguous physical memory naturally aligned on the huge page size. The offset in a huge page is 30-bit (resp. 21-bit) long, therefore the lowest 30 bits (resp. 21 bits) in virtual memory will be the same as in physical memory. We thus calculate offsets in the page that will result in physical addresses differing by a bit, without converting virtual addresses to physical addresses. To discover the remaining bits, we allocate several huge pages, and convert their base virtual address to physical address to find those that differ by one bit. In order to do this, we allocate as many huge pages as possible.

Table 3. Functions obtained for the Xeon and Core processors with 2, 4 and 8 cores. Gray cells indicate that a machine with more memory would be needed to determine the remaining bits.

		37	36	35	34	33	32	31	30	29	28	27	26	25	24	23	22	21	20	19	18	17	16	15	14	13	12	11	10	09	08	07	06
2 cores	o_0				⊕		⊕		⊕	⊕	⊕	⊕	⊕		⊕		⊕		⊕	⊕	⊕		⊕		⊕		⊕						⊕
4 cores	o_0				⊕	⊕		⊕		⊕	⊕	⊕	⊕	⊕		⊕		⊕		⊕	⊕	⊕		⊕		⊕		⊕					⊕
	o_1			⊕	⊕		⊕		⊕	⊕		⊕		⊕	⊕	⊕	⊕	⊕	⊕	⊕		⊕		⊕		⊕		⊕			⊕		
8 cores	o_0		⊕	⊕		⊕	⊕		⊕	⊕	⊕	⊕	⊕	⊕		⊕		⊕		⊕	⊕	⊕		⊕		⊕		⊕					⊕
	o_1	⊕		⊕	⊕	⊕		⊕		⊕	⊕		⊕		⊕	⊕	⊕	⊕	⊕	⊕		⊕		⊕		⊕		⊕			⊕		
	o_2	⊕	⊕	⊕	⊕			⊕	⊕		⊕	⊕			⊕	⊕		⊕			⊕			⊕	⊕					⊕			

To evaluate the algorithm, we retrieved the function for all models from *config_1* to *config_8* of Table 2, results are summarized in Table 3. The functions are given for the machine that has the most memory, to cover as many bits as possible. We remark that the functions, for a given number of cores, are identical among all processors, for all ranges of products and micro-architectures. Using the above mentioned algorithm, we obtained those functions quickly (from a few seconds to five minutes in the worst cases). We also remark that we have in total 3 functions o_0, o_1 and o_2 for all processors, and that the functions used only depends on the number of cores, regardless of the micro-architecture or the product range. While in retrospective this seems to be the most straightforward solution to be adopted by Intel, this was far from evident at the beginning of our investigations. Now that the functions are known, an attacker can use them to perform his attacks without any reverse engineering.

5   Using the Function to Build a Covert Channel

To verify empirically the correctness of the function, we build a covert channel. This covert channel uses similar principles to the one of Maurice et al. [22]. It is based on the fact that the LLC is inclusive, *i.e.*, when a line is evicted from the LLC, it is also evicted from the L1 and L2. With this property, a program on any core can evict a line from the private cache of another core. This property can then be used by two programs to communicate. The work in [22] bypasses the complex addressing issue by evicting the whole LLC. However, the LLC typically stores a few megabytes, and thus the sender needs to access a buffer that is the size of (or bigger than) the LLC to evict it entirely. Having the complex addressing function, the sender targets a set in a slice, and thus evicts a cache line with much fewer accesses. For example, in the case of a 12-way associative LLC, assuming a pseudo-LRU replacement policy, the sender needs approximately 12 accesses to evict the whole set.

In this covert channel, the sender creates a set of physical addresses that map to the same set, using the function and the translation from virtual to physical addresses. It repeatedly accesses these addresses to send a '1', and does nothing to send a '0'. The receiver has a set of physical addresses that map to the same LLC set as the sender's. When the sender sends a '1', it evicts the data of the receiver from the LLC, and thus from its private L1 cache. The receiver consequently observes a slow access to its set.

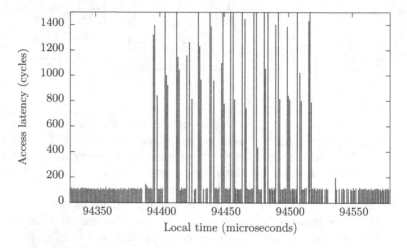

Fig. 3. Receiving interleaved '0's and '1's to test the raw bitrate of the covert channel.

We conduct an experiment on *config_1* to estimate the bitrate of this covert channel, in which the sender transmits interleaved '0's and '1's. Figure 3 illustrates the measurements performed by the receiver. According to the measurements, 29 bits can be transmitted over a period of 130 microseconds, leading to a bitrate of approximately 223 kbps.

6   Discussion

6.1   Dealing with Unknown Physical Addresses

The translation from virtual to physical addresses is unknown to the attacker in most practical setups, like in virtualized or sandboxed environments. We now describe a possible extension to the covert channel described in Sect. 5 to avoid using this address translation.

Similarly to the work of Liu et al. [20] and Irazoqui et al. [14], the sender and the receiver both use huge pages. The cache index bits are thus the same for virtual and physical addresses. Using the function only on the bits in the offset of the huge page, the sender is able to create a set of addresses that map to the same set, in the same slice. As some bits of the physical address are unknown, he does not know the precise slice. However, he does know that these addresses are part of a single set, in a single slice.

The receiver now performs the same operation. The receiver has only the knowledge of the index set to target, but he does not know in which of the n slices. He thus creates n sets of addresses, each one being in a different slice. He then continuously accesses each of these sets. The receiver will only receive transmitted bits in a single set: from now on, he can target a single set. The sender and the receiver are effectively accessing the same LLC set in the same slice.

6.2   Other Applications

Reverse engineering the complex addressing function is orthogonal to performing cache attacks. Indeed, knowing the correct addressing function can help any fine-grained attack on the LLC. Cache attacks rely on the attacker evicting data from a cache level. This can be done by the clflush instruction. However, it requires shared memory in a covert or side channel scenario, and it is not available in all environments. We thus focus on building attacks without this instruction. To perform an attack on the LLC, the attacker needs to create an eviction set, and to subsequently access the data to evict the lines that are currently cached. There are two methods to find an eviction set: a *dynamic* approach based on a timing attack that does not require the function, and a *static* approach that uses the function to compute addresses that belong to an eviction set. Building a static eviction set has the advantage of being faster than building a dynamic one. Indeed, the function is already known, whereas the dynamic set has to be computed for each execution. Moreover, Gruss et al. [6] showed that dynamically computing a set to achieve an optimal eviction is a slow operation.

Hund et al. [8] defeated KASLR using the static approach. Similarly, Irazoqui et al. [14] used a static approach on a Nehalem CPU that does not use complex addressing. Yet, their attack requires understanding the slice selection, and thus having the complex addressing function for more recent CPUs. Concurrently to this work, Gruss et al. [6] used the complex addressing function to build a proof-of-concept of the *rowhammer* attack without the clflush instruction.

Rowhammer is not a typical cache attack, since it exploits a bug on the DRAM to flip bits. However, the bug is triggered by frequent accesses to the DRAM, *i.e.*, non-cached accesses. The original exploits used the `clflush` instruction, that is not available in e.g., Javascript. An attack that seeks to avoid using the `clflush` instruction thus also needs to compute an eviction set.

6.3   Comparison to Previously Retrieved Functions

We observe that the functions we obtained differ from the ones obtained by Hund et al. [8], and Seaborn [29]. In particular, Hund et al. found that the functions only use the tag bits (bits b_{17} to b_{31}). We argue that their method does not infer the presence of the bits used to compute the set (bits b_6 to b_{16}). Indeed, as they searched for colliding addresses, they obtained addresses that belong to the same slice and the same set. As in this case the set is directly mapped to the bits b_6 to b_{16}, addresses that collide have the same values for these bits. Therefore, if the function that computes the slice uses the bits b_6 to b_{16}, the method of [8] is not able to retrieve them. On the contrary, our method retrieves the slices regardless of the sets, leading to a complete function.

We also observe that the function we retrieved for 2 cores is the same as the one retrieved in [29], albeit a more complete one. However, the function we retrieve for 4 cores does not use the same bits as the one retrieved in [8]. We argue that we do have access to the ground truth (*i.e.*, the slices accessed), whereas they rely on *indirect measurements*. Several correct functions can however be retrieved, as the slices can be labeled differently from one work to another.

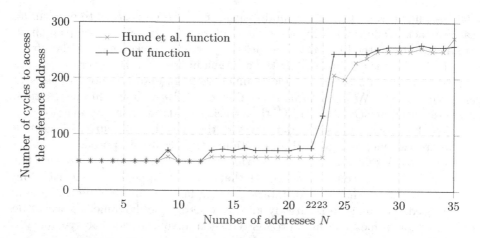

Fig. 4. Median number of cycles to access a reference address, after accessing N addresses in the same set, which is calculated using [8] and our function. Results on 100 runs, on $config\_1$ (Ivy Bridge with a 20-way associative LLC).

To compare our function against [8], we performed the following experiment. Using the retrieved addressing function, we constructed a set of physical addresses that are supposed to map the same set (thus the same slice). We accessed N different addresses from this set. We then measured the access time to the first reference address accessed, to see if it was evicted from the cache. Figure 4 shows the median number of CPU cycles to access the reference address for different values of N, for 100 runs. The function that is the most precise should have a memory access time spike the closest $N = 20$ (which is the cache associativity). We observe that both functions have a spike slightly after $N = 20$. We note that the spike occurs for a value $N > 20$ and not exactly $N = 20$: it is most likely due to the fact that the replacement policy on Ivy Bridge is not strictly LRU, but a variant called Quad-Age LRU [18]. In practice, both functions are able to evict a cache line with few accesses. However, our function seems more precise than the one of [8], leading to fewer accesses to evict a cache line ($N = 23$ accesses for our function, $N = 24$ for [8]), and a sharper transition. This also confirms the correctness of our function.

7   Related Work

Hardware performance counters are traditionally used for performance monitoring. They have also been used in a few security scenarios. In defensive cases, they are used to detect an anomalous behavior such as malware detection [5], integrity checking of programs [21], control flow integrity [34], and binary analysis [32]. Uhsadel et al. [31] used performance counters in offensive cases to profile the cache and derive a side-channel attack against AES. However, the performance counters can only be read with high privileges, *i.e.*, in kernel-mode, or being root in user-mode if a driver is already loaded. Contrary to this attack, we use performance counters to infer hardware properties offline, and our subsequent cache attack does not need high privileges.

The Flush+Reload attack [36] relies on shared memory, and more precisely on shared libraries, to evict lines of cache, using the `clflush` instruction. In this attack, the attacker leverages the shared and inclusive LLC to run concurrently to the victim on separate cores, including on separate virtual machines. Flush+Reload has been used to attack implementations of RSA [36], AES [16] and ECDSA [1]. It has also been used to find a new side channel that revives a supposedly fixed attack on CBC encryption mode [13], and to detect cryptographic libraries [17]. Gruss et al. [7] presented a generic technique to profile and exploit cache-based vulnerabilities, using Flush+Reload. Memory sharing can be easily disabled in virtualized environments (which is already the case in the cloud environment), effectively rendering impossible the Flush+Reload attack. On sandboxed environments, like Javascript or Native Client [2], the ability to perform the Flush+Reload attack is also compromised by the absence of `clflush` instruction [3]. Understanding how complex addressing works allows performing cache attacks in these environments, without the need of shared memory or `clflush`.

Simultaneously to our work, Irazoqui et al. [14], Liu et al. [20], and Oren et al. [24] have extended the Prime+Probe attack to the LLC. They are thus able to perform side channels on the LLC without any shared memory. They construct a set of addresses that map to the same set as the line to evict. Irazoqui et al. [14] have used a Nehalem processor that does not use complex addressing. Therefore huge pages are sufficient to construct this set of addresses. Liu et al. [20], and Oren et al. [24] targeted more recent processors that use complex addressing. They, however, performed their attacks without reverse engineering the complex addressing function. Thus, even if we share the same motivation, *i.e.*, performing cache attacks on recent processors without any shared memory, our works are very different in their approaches. We also note that our work has a broader application, as it contributes to a better understanding of the undocumented complex addressing function, possibly leading to other types of attacks.

Other work is directly interested in retrieving the function, and several attempts have been made to reverse engineer it. Hund et al. [8] performed a manual reverse engineering for a 4-core Sandy Bridge CPU. Their method uses colliding addresses, *i.e.*, *indirect measurements*, to derive the function. They used this function to bypass kernel ASLR. Very recently, and also simultaneous to our work, Seaborn [29] continued the work of [8], with a 2-core Sandy Bridge CPU. The intended goal is to exploit the *rowhammer* bug with cached accesses, without the `clflush` instruction. Gruss et al. [6] subsequently demonstrated a *rowhammer* attack on Javascript, using the complex addressing function. In contrast, we do not use the same method to retrieve the addressing function as [8,29]. Our method, using performance counters, performs *direct measurements*, *i.e.*, retrieves the exact slice for each access. We thus show that the functions in [8,29] are partially incorrect, even though they are sufficient to be used in practice. We also derive a function for all processors with 2^n cores, automating the reverse engineering. Different from these two works, we also have tested our method on a large variety of processors. Concurrently to our work, Irazoqui et al. [15] worked on automating this reverse engineering, and evaluated their work on several processors. However, their method is similar to Hund et al. [8], and thus suffers from the same limitations.

8   Conclusions

In this paper, we introduced a novel method to reverse engineer Intel's undocumented complex addressing, using hardware performance counters. The reversed functions can be exploited by an attacker to target specific sets in the last level cache when performing cache attacks. Contrary to previous work, our method is automatic, and we have evaluated it on a wide range of processors, for different micro-architectures, numbers of cores, and product ranges. We also obtained a more complete and more correct description of the complex addressing function than previous work, *i.e.*, taking into account more bits of the memory address. In the general case with any number of cores, we automatically built a table that maps physical addresses to cache slices. This table already enables to perform targeted cache attacks but may require an important amount of storage. In the case of CPUs with 2^n cores we provided a compact function that maps addresses to slices, rendering the attacks even more effective. We demonstrated a covert channel to prove the correctness of our function, and discussed other applications such as exploiting the *rowhammer* bug in Javascript.

Our work expands the understanding of these complex and only partially documented pieces of hardware that are modern processors. We foresee several directions for future work. First, a compact representation for CPUs with a number of cores different from 2^n would generalize our findings. Second, we believe that new attacks could be made possible by knowing the complex addressing of a cache. Finally, we believe that understanding the complex addressing function enables the development of countermeasures to cache attacks.

Acknowledgments. We would like to thank Mark Seaborn, Mate Soos, Gorka Irazoqui, Thomas Eisenbarth and our anonymous reviewers for their valuable comments and suggestions. We also greatly thank Stefan Mangard and Daniel Gruss for the collaboration on the exploitation of the *rowhammer* bug in Javascript, for which we applied the findings of this article after its submission.

References

1. Benger, N., van de Pol, J., Smart, N.P., Yarom, Y.: "Ooh Aah.. Just a Little Bit": a small amount of side channel can go a long way. In: Batina, L., Robshaw, M. (eds.) CHES 2014. LNCS, vol. 8731, pp. 75–92. Springer, Heidelberg (2014)
2. Chrome Developers. Native Client. https://developer.chrome.com/native-client. Accessed 2 June 2015
3. Chrome Developers. Native Client Revision 13809, September 2014. http://src.chromium.org/viewvc/native_client?revision=13809&view=revision. Accessed 2 June 2015
4. Crama, Y., Hammer, P.L.: Boolean Functions: Theory, Algorithms, and Applications. Cambridge University Press, New York (2011)
5. Demme, J., Maycock, M., Schmitz, J., Tang, A., Waksman, A., Sethumadhavan, S., Stolfo, S.: On the feasibility of online malware detection with performance counters. ACM SIGARCH Comput. Architect. News 41(3), 559–570 (2013)
6. Gruss, D., Maurice, C., Mangard, S.: Rowhammer.js: a remote software-induced fault attack in JavaScript. arXiv:1507.06955v1 (2015)
7. Gruss, D., Spreitzer, R., Mangard, S.: Cache template attacks: automating attacks on inclusive last-level caches. In: Proceedings of the 24th USENIX Security Symposium (2015)
8. Hund, R., Willems, C., Holz, T.: Practical timing side channel attacks against kernel space ASLR. In: Proceedings of the 2013 IEEE Symposium on Security and Privacy (S&P 2013), pp. 191–205. IEEE, May 2013
9. Intel. Intel® Xeon® Processor E5-2600 Product Family Uncore Performance Monitoring Guide. 327043–001:1–136 (2012)
10. Intel. Intel® 64 and IA-32 Architectures Software Developer's Manual, vol. 3 (3A, 3B & 3C): System Programming Guide. 3(253665) (2014)
11. Intel. Intel® Xeon® Processor E5 v2 and E7 v2 Product Families Uncore Performance Monitoring Reference Manual. 329468–002:1–200 (2014)
12. Intel. Intel® Xeon® Processor E5 v3 Family Uncore Performance Monitoring Reference Manual. 331051–001:1–232 (2014)

13. Irazoqui, G., Eisenbarth, T., Sunar, B.: Lucky 13 strikes back. In: Proceedings of the 10th ACM Symposium on Information, Computer and Communications Security (AsiaCCS 2015), pp. 85–96 (2015)

14. Irazoqui, G., Eisenbarth, T., Sunar, B.: S$A: a shared cache attack that works across cores and defies VM sandboxing–and its application to AES. In: Proceedings of the 36th IEEE Symposium on Security and Privacy (S&P 2015) (2015)

15. Irazoqui, G., Eisenbarth, T., Sunar, B.: Systematic reverse engineering of cache slice selection in Intel processors. In: Proceedings of the 18th EUROMICRO Conference on Digital System Design (2015)

16. Irazoqui, G., Inci, M.S., Eisenbarth, T., Sunar, B.: Wait a minute! A fast, Cross-VM attack on AES. In: Stavrou, A., Bos, H., Portokalidis, G. (eds.) RAID 2014. LNCS, vol. 8688, pp. 299–319. Springer, Heidelberg (2014)

17. Irazoqui, G., IncI, M.S., Eisenbarth, T., Sunar, B.: Know thy neighbor: crypto library detection in cloud. Proc. Priv. Enhancing Technol. 1(1), 25–40 (2015)

18. Jahagirdar, S., George, V., Sodhi, I., Wells, R.: Power management of the third generation Intel Core micro architecture formerly codenamed Ivy Bridge. In: Hot Chips 2012 (2012). http://hotchips.org/wp-content/uploads/hc_archives/hc24/HC24-1-Microprocessor/HC24.28.117-HotChips_IvyBridge_Power_04.pdf. Accessed 16 July 2015

19. Kim, D.-H., Nair, P.J., Qureshi, M.K.: Architectural support for mitigating row hammering in DRAM memories. IEEE Comput. Archit. Lett. 14(1), 9–12 (2014)

20. Liu, F., Yarom, Y., Ge, Q., Heiser, G., Lee, R.B.: Last-level cache side-channel attacks are practical. In: Proceedings of the 36th IEEE Symposium on Security and Privacy (S&P 2015) (2015)

21. Malone, C., Zahran, M., Karri, R.: Are hardware performance counters a cost effective way for integrity checking of programs. In: Proceedings of the Sixth ACM Workshop on Scalable Trusted Computing (2011)

22. Maurice, C., Neumann, C., Heen, O., Francillon, A.: C5: cross-cores cache covert channel. In: Almgren, M., Gulisano, V., Maggi, F. (eds.) DIMVA 2015. LNCS, vol. 9148, pp. 46–64. Springer, Heidelberg (2015)

23. Neve, M., Seifert, J.-P.: Advances on access-driven cache attacks on AES. In: Biham, E., Youssef, A.M. (eds.) SAC 2006. LNCS, vol. 4356, pp. 147–162. Springer, Heidelberg (2007)

24. Oren, Y., Kemerlis, V.P., Sethumadhavan, S., Keromytis, A.D.: The spy in the sandbox: practical cache attacks in JavaScript and their implications. In: Proceedings of the 22nd ACM Conference on Computer and Communications Security (CCS 2015) (2015)

25. Osvik, Dag Arne, Shamir, Adi, Tromer, Eran: Cache attacks and countermeasures: the case of AES. In: Pointcheval, David (ed.) CT-RSA 2006. LNCS, vol. 3860, pp. 1–20. Springer, Heidelberg (2006)

26. Percival, C.: Cache missing for fun and profit. In: Proceedings of BSDCan, pp. 1–13 (2005)

27. Ristenpart, T., Tromer, E., Shacham, H., Savage, S.: Hey, you, get off of my cloud: exploring information leakage in third-party compute clouds. In: Proceedings of the 16th ACM Conference on Computer and Communications Security (CCS 2009), pp. 199–212 (2009)

28. Seaborn, M.: Exploiting the DRAM rowhammer bug to gain kernel privileges, March 2015. http://googleprojectzero.blogspot.fr/2015/03/exploiting-dram-rowhammer-bug-to-gain.html. Accessed 2 June 2015

29. Seaborn, M.: L3 cache mapping on Sandy Bridge CPUs, April 2015. http://lackingrhoticity.blogspot.fr/2015/04/l3-cache-mapping-on-sandy-bridge-cpus.html. Accessed 2 June 2015
30. Tromer, E., Osvik, D.A., Shamir, A.: Efficient cache attacks on AES, and counter-measures. J. Cryptology **23**(1), 37–71 (2010)
31. Uhsadel, L., Georges, A., Verbauwhede, I.: Exploiting hardware performance counters. In: Proceedings of the 5th International Workshop on Fault Diagnosis and Tolerance in Cryptography (FDTC 2008), pp. 59–67 (2008)
32. Willems, C., Hund, R., Fobian, A., Felsch, D., Holz, T.: Down to the bare metal: using processor features for binary analysis. In: Proceedings of the 28th Annual Computer Security Applications Conference (ACSAC 2012), pp. 189–198 (2012)
33. Wu, Z., Xu, Z., Wang, H.: Whispers in the hyper-space: high-speed covert channel attacks in the cloud. In: Proceedings of the 21st USENIX Security Symposium (2012)
34. Xia, Y., Liu, Y., Chen, H., Zang, B.: CFIMon: detecting violation of control flow integrity using performance counters. In: Proceedings of the 42th International Conference on Dependable Systems and Networks (DSN 2012), pp. 1–12 (2012)
35. Xu, Y., Bailey, M., Jahanian, F., Joshi, K., Hiltunen, M., Schlichting, R.: An exploration of L2 cache covert channels in virtualized environments. In: Proceedings of the 3rd ACM Cloud Computing Security Workshop (CCSW 2011), pp. 29–40 (2011)
36. Yarom, Y., Falkner, K.: Flush+Reload: a high resolution, low noise, L3 cache side-channel attack. In: Proceedings of the 23th USENIX Security Symposium (2014)
37. Zhang, Y., Juels, A., Reiter, M.K., Ristenpart, T.: Cross-VM side channels and their use to extract private keys. In: Proceedings of the 19th ACM Conference on Computer and Communications Security (CCS 2012) (2012)
38. Zhang, Y., Juels, A., Reiter, M.K., Ristenpart, T.: Cross-tenant side-channel attacks in PaaS clouds. In: Proceedings of the 2014 ACM SIGSAC Conference on Computer and Communications Security (CCS 2014), pp. 990–1003. ACM Press, New York (2014)

Hardware-Assisted Fine-Grained Code-Reuse Attack Detection

Pinghai Yuan[1,2]([✉]), Qingkai Zeng[1,2], and Xuhua Ding[3]

[1] State Key Laboratory for Novel Software Technology,
Nanjing University, Nanjing, China
pinghaiyuan@gmail.com
[2] Department of Computer Science and Technology,
Nanjing University, Nanjing, China
zqk@nju.edu.cn
[3] School of Information Systems, Singapore Management University,
Singapore, Singapore
xhding@smu.edu.sg

Abstract. Code-reuse attacks have become the primary exploitation technique for system compromise despite of the recently introduced Data Execution Prevention technique in modern platforms. Different from code injection attacks, they result in unintended control-flow transfer to victim programs without adding malicious code. This paper proposes a practical scheme named as *CFIGuard* to detect code-reuse attacks on user space applications. CFIGuard traces every branch execution by leveraging hardware features of commodity processors, and then validates the traces based on fine-grained control flow graphs. We have implemented a prototype of CFIGuard on Linux and the experiments show that it only incurs around 2.9 % runtime overhead for a set of typical server applications.

Keywords: Code-reuse attack · Control flow integrity · Indirect branch tracing

1 Introduction

There are abundant schemes focusing on software vulnerability mitigation. Data Execution Prevention (DEP) [4,34], Stack Smashing Protector (SSP) [12] and coarse-grained Address Space Layout Randomization (ASLR) [33] have been widely adopted in commodity platforms. For instance, DEP marks a memory page either non-executable or non-writable such that it can effectively defend against code injection attacks. However, DEP and the other two mechanisms fall short of defending against advanced code-reuse attacks, such as Return-oriented Programming (ROP) [30] and just-in-time ROP [32], which have been used by hackers in real-life cyberspace attacks.

This situation has prompted active research on fine-grained ASLR [15,18, 25,31,38] and Control Flow Integrity (CFI) [3] mechanisms to counter code-reuse attacks. ASLR aims to hide the address space layout from the attacker in

H. Bos et al. (Eds.): RAID 2015, LNCS 9404, pp. 66–85, 2015.
DOI: 10.1007/978-3-319-26362-5_4

a bid to hinder effective construction of malicious code. However, its security-by-obscurity approach cannot withstand sophisticated attacks that infers the address space layout via various channels. CFI works by checking a program's execution flow against predetermined Control-Flow Graphs (CFGs), thus provides strong protection by detecting control-flow violation. Unfortunately, CFI has not been widely adopted to protect applications in practice, mainly due to its large overhead for code preprocessing and runtime checking. Moreover, CFI lacks of code transparency in the sense that it demands modification either on the source code [2] or the binary code of the protected application [41, 43]. This hassle also hinders a wide adoption of CFI.

However, existing CFI works still face the security challenge in practice. For instance, the inter-module transfers that span over two modules can hardly be restricted without information extracted by a whole program analysis, which in turn needs a tough engineer work. Furthermore, since many works enforce context-free CFI with static CFGs, so they cannot prevent a backward-transfer issued by a *ret* instruction back to a caller which is valid according to the CFGs but does not issue current function invocation. Their security guarantees become worse as many recent works enforce coarse-grained CFI [9,13,16,29]. The deadly point of most CFI works is that they are crippled and made ineffective once control-flow has already been diverted due to their imperfect protection.

This paper presents CFIGuard, a fully transparent code-reuse attack detection engine for user applications. Our approach is to monitor every executed indirect branch during the lifetime of a process, and to identify abnormal control transfers diverting from the control flow graph. The core of CFIGuard is a novel combination of two hardware features widely available on modern x86 processors: Last Branch Recording (LBR) and Performance Monitor Unit (PMU). We name the technique as *LBR + PMU* whereby LBR records the jump-from and jump-to addresses of every branch instruction execution and PMU sets off a non-maskable interrupt triggered by a programmable counter. The interrupt handler then validates the records by consulting the corresponding fine-grained CFGs. Relying mainly on hardware for instruction-level monitoring allows for completely transparent operation, without the hassle of modifying the protected applications. Applying fine-grained CFGs for attack detection guarantees a strong security protection. The runtime overhead of LBR + PMU is lowered by filtering out direct transfer whose executions dominate the total of all branch executions.

We have built a prototype of CFIGuard on Linux. It can selectively protect any Linux application as long as its CFG is in place. Besides detecting traditional ROP attacks, CFIGuard can counter stop JOP [7], the recent just-in-time ROP [32] and blind-ROP [6] attacks. To measure the effectiveness of CFIGuard, we have conducted a variety of security tests using the RIPE benchmark [39], including stack/heap overflow vulnerabilities coupled with shell code injection or ROP attacks. Our evaluation results indicate that CFIGuard can precisely catch the attacks on the spot. Performance evaluation results show that CFIGuard introduces negligible runtime overhead for most applications.

The main contributions of our work are:

- The key observation that control flow hijacking on security breaches can be *precisely* captured by using the LBR mechanism coupling with PMU.
- The design of CFIGuard which is the first system to detect code-reuse attacks and enforce fine-grained CFI protection with hardware support.
- A prototype implementation of CFIGuard on Linux with security and performance evaluations to demonstrate its effectiveness and efficiency.

2   Background: Hardware Features

Recent years have seen several proposed schemes utilizing hardware features on modern x86 processors to mitigate control-flow hijacking attacks. Among them, CFIMon [40] uses Branch Trace Store (BTS) [19] while kBouncer [26] and ROPecker [11] rely on LBR [19]. Besides using debug facilities, CFIGuard also makes use of PMU [19]. Note that on multicore systems, each core has its own BTS, LBR and PMU facilities. We now briefly explain these three hardware features.

Branch Trace Store. BTS records all branches execution in the user/kernel space into a memory buffer. It can be configured to halt the monitored program when the recording buffer is full and to resume as well. However, since BTS does not support branch type filtering, all types of jumps, calls and returns are recorded without distinction. Since validating direct branches on a platform with DEP protection is an action of gilding the lily, using BTS alone may introduce unnecessary false positive to security systems such as CFIMon [40].

Last Branch Recording. Like BTS, LBR also records both source and destination addresses of each branch execution. However, LBR stores the traces in a set of Model-Specific Registers (MSRs) in a round-robin fashion. The current design of LBR feature does not generate interrupt when the LBR buffer is full. As a result, the oldest records are flushed away with upcoming ones.

To monitor a user space code execution, kBouncer [26] and ROPecker [11] have deliberately to hook into system calls or use a sliding window in order to trigger page faults. Even so, LBR automatically flushes away most of the records and these approaches can only check a small portion of branch executions. The advantages of LBR over BTS are that (i) incurs negligible overhead for recording the branch traces, and (ii) supports a filtering mechanism based on combination of Code Privilege Level (CPL) and branch instruction types.

Performance Monitoring Unit. PMU is a performance measuring and counting unit provided by most modern x86 processors. PMU can work in interrupt-based mode, in which a counter called PMC increases for each occurrence of the monitored event and a non-maskable interrupt is thrown out whenever PMC overflows. PMU can monitor a wide range of events including cache-missing, branch mis-predictions, and even the execution of certain types of branches.

3 Practical Indirect Branch Tracing for Code-Reuse Attack Detection

The proposed approach uses runtime process monitoring to identify the execution of code that exhibits code-reuse behavior. A code-reuse attack, such as an ROP attack, consists of several instruction sequences called gadgets scattering among code segments of the victim program. A gadget always ends with an indirect branch instruction that transfers control to the subsequent gadget whose address is specified in the injected malicious "payload" prepared by the attacker.

In code-reuse attacks, the branch instruction at the end of a gadget is either an unintended instruction (a.k.a. truncated instruction) or jumps to an unintended target. The former refers to an instruction code beginning at the middle of a valid instruction generated by the compiler, which is possible because instructions on x86 platforms are of variable lengths and not aligned. An unintended target is an instruction address where the current branch is not expected to jump to according to the CFG. By recording both jump-from and jump-to addresses of every indirect branch execution and then validating each record with a fine-grained CFG, CFIGuard can detect a code-reuse attack before its code completes a malicious operation.

In this section, we discuss in detail how CFIGuard combines Last Branch Recording and Performance Monitoring Unit to record every indirect branch execution. Then we describe how CFIGuard uses this information to detect code-reuse attacks.

3.1 Branch Tracing vs Other Approaches

The targets of direct branches are hard-coded in the code segments. With DEP [4,34] protection, they are free from being tempered with. On the contrary, indirect branches are vulnerable to control-flow hijacking as the memory regions storing their target addresses, such as the stack and the heap, are always writable. Therefore, as in previous schemes, our work exclusively focuses on protecting the execution of *indirect call*, *indirect jump* and *ret* instructions. There are several approaches that can be applied to protect their executions with different protection granularity, transparency level and deployment effort.

Software Hardening Approach. This approach extends the compiler to insert runtime checks in the executable at compile time [20,35]. They always provide fine-grained protection on the selected branch types because they can strictly restrict the dynamically computed target of each branch with the information extracted from the source code. However, this approach requires recompilation of the target applications and the dependent libraries. An alternative is to have binary instrumentation or rewriting. It is advantageous over the compiler based method as it does not require the source code, but only debug symbols [2] or relocation information [43]. Nonetheless, this benefit is at the cost of weaker security assurance as it is challenging to obtain a fine-grained CFG [16] from the binary.

Runtime Monitoring Approach. kBouncer [26], ROPecker [11] and CFIMon [40] utilize hardware features provided by mainstream processors to protect user space code. They record and check the jump-from and jump-to addresses of each branch execution without instrumenting the binary. Nonetheless, they apply heuristic rules to identify attacks, an approach which is unreliable as compared with CFG [17]. In addition, due to the limitation of the LBR capability, kBouncer [26] and ROPecker [11] can only check a small portion of branch executions, thus their security protection is inadequate and vulnerable [9,16].

CFIGuard's Approach. Similar to kBouncer and ROPecker, our system only monitors the execution of indirect branches at runtime. The difference is that we can trace every branch execution by coupling LBR with PMU. To compare with the BTS-based CFIMon [40], CFIGuard achieves a better performance by filtering out direct branches at the hardware level. Moreover, CFIGuard provides more reliable protection as it identifies attacks by consulting fine-grained CFGs.

3.2 Using LBR + PMU for Security Enhancement

In our system, PMU counts branch executions while LBR records of them. LBR + PMU traces all indirect branch executions by turning on LBR's filtering mechanism and by configuring PMU to monitor indirect branch executions with a properly initialized PMC to ensure that an interrupt is triggered before the LBR buffer is full.

LBR + PMU can be configured to generate an interrupt once every N branch executions by initializing PMC with different values. By setting N to 1, LBR + PMU would interrupt the monitored program at every indirect branch execution and thus we can detect the attack at the first place. However, this setting has a high performance toll. We observe that setting N to the LBR buffer size (16 for the CPU model we used) can achieve the best performance while recording all executions of user-level indirect branches.

Filtering Out Direct Branches. Both LBR and PMU support filtering according to CPL and branch types. LBR provides a dedicated control register MSR_LBR_SELECT for filtering; PMU can set a sub-event mask for this purpose. Table 1 lists the available filtering flags provided by LBR + PMU. An indirect branch instruction is filtered out if its corresponding type flag is unset; otherwise, it is recorded into the LBR buffer. Note that, branch types in this table are independent with each other and therefore we can set the combination "CPL_USER + NEAR_IND_CALL + NEAR_IND_JMP + NEAR_RET" to record all user space indirect branch executions.

Managing LBR + PMU. With a slight modification to the system kernel, we develop a driver to manage LBR + PMU and export a system call interface to applications. A user can execute a spawner application to launch a protected program under the monitoring of LBR + PMU. Once monitored, we tag the protected program with a new flag field of its Process Control Block (PCB). When the protected program is switched in/out, we turn on/off LBR + PMU and

Table 1. Branch filtering flags provided by LBR + PMU.

Flag	Meaning	Instruction example
CPU_USER	Branches occurring in ring 3	-
CPU_KERNEL	Branches occurring in ring 0	-
JCC	Conditional branches	jz loc_8048418
NEAR_REL_CALL	Near relative calls	call sub_80482F0
NEAR_IND_CALL	Near indirect calls	call eax
NEAR_REL_JMP	Near relative jumps	jmp sub_8048390
NEAR_IND_JMP	Near indirect jumps	jmp eax
NEAR_RET	Near returns	ret

restore/save related registers. In other words, the state of LBR + PMU becomes a part of process context. When enforcing CFI, an effective method to maintain the context is to erase the LBR buffer and to reset PMC to 0, after security checking but before switching out. Note that PMC needs to be reinitialized before exiting the interrupt handler such that PMU can generate an interrupt again. Consequently, CFIGuard can protect multiple programs in parallel.

4   Identify Control-Flow Violation

The execution of reused-code is identified by examining two types of control-flow violations: (a) running a programmer unintended indirect branch instruction; (b) an intended branch jumps to an unintended target. Therefore, we perform attack detection by consulting the corresponding CFGs.

4.1   Security Checking Scheme

In this work, a branch instruction execution is also referred to as a *transfer* defined by an address pair (jump-from, jump-to) which are the source and destination addresses of a branch execution, respectively. At runtime, an indirect branch could result in different transfers from the same source address but to different destination addresses. The execution of a transfer is deemed legal if and only if its source and destination addresses match a specific CFG edge. There is a special treatment for inter-module transfers, whose destination addresses are out of current module and thus cannot be depicted by the CFG of current module. For those transfers, we separately check their jump-from and jump-to addresses with the exit-point of the source module and the entry-point of the landing module, respectively. As a result, this strategy gives us the flexibility to generate constraint data of the current module without any information about other modules.

Figure 1 illustrates our runtime security enforcement wherein Fig. 1(a) shows our CFGs along with a few code snippets taken from the application and its dynamically linked libraries. Besides holding the data about in-module indirect transfers, those CFGs also list the entry-points and exit-points of the current module. *Entry-points* are the addresses where external branches that jump into the current module, while *exit-points* are addresses of indirect branches that jump out of the current module. In those CFGs, we use labels instead of addresses. In particular, for each instruction location A in the disassembler output of IDA [1], we associate it with a symbolic label "lab_A".

Figure 1(b) shows the idea of validating a record in the security check by consulting the CFGs. In this figure, a smile sign means to accept a record if the record is identified as a legal transfer, while a stop sign means to reject a record if it is identified as an illegal one. For instances, a record (lab_147c, lab_132e) is rejected because the CFG of the library shows that there is no branch instruction starting at lab_147c. This record must be due to an unintended instruction. A record (lab_83f5, lab_8052) is also rejected because the CFG of application shows that target address lab_8052 is unintended for the ret instruction at lab_83f5. The other are accepted because they are compliant to the CFGs.

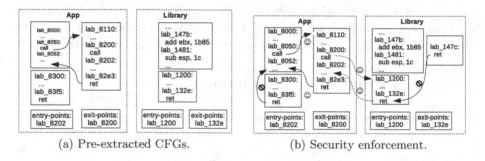

(a) Pre-extracted CFGs.   (b) Security enforcement.

Fig. 1. Our runtime security enforcement.

4.2 Control-Flow Constraint: Call-Site CFG

CFIGuard uses the CFG data structure directly for detecting control-flow violation without reducing its complexity as in coarse-grained CFI [23,24,43]. As a benefit, the attack detection logic of CFIGuard is unified and strict. In practice, we prefer fine-grained CFGs for the purpose to achieve strong security protection.

We construct a dedicated target table for each indirect branch. In addition, a table is built to store the addresses of intended branch instructions, exit-points and entry-points. Therefore, the constraint data consists of four components.

1. The first component is a bitmap for jump-from addresses where valid indirect branch instructions are located. Each byte (uniquely identified by an address) of the code segment corresponds to a bit in this bitmap. If a byte is the beginning of an indirect branch instruction, the corresponding bit is set to 1; otherwise it is set to 0. This bitmap can verify the legitimacy of source addresses of each LBR record.

2. The second is a hash table stores the connectivity between a jump-from and its target table. A hash table entry has three fields: the key (i.e., jump-from addresses), the location of the target table, and an entry index of the collided element.
3. The third is a series of target tables each of which stores a set of jump-to addresses of a particular branch. The size of those tables varies across branches as each branch has a different number of targets. For management, each target table is prepended with a header that provides rich information. A header has three fields: the size of current target table, the branch instruction type, and a permission bit indicating whether an inter-module transfer is allowed or not. The second and third fields provide information to validate the legitimacy of the destination address of each LBR record. Note that the header's last field also defines whether current branch is an exit-point.
4. The fourth component is the entry-points where control flows into current module. This part is also implemented using a bitmap. Similar to the bitmap for jump-from addresses, each bit of this bitmap indicates where valid entry-points are located.

Therefore, the first three components are involved when CFIGuard validates intra-module transfer records while all of them are needed when checking exit-points and entry-points in case of inter-module transfers. On a side note, our constraint data only uses the offsets to the code segment base rather than absolute addresses. Consequently, it is not affected by the base address where the executable's code segment is loaded into the memory. Hence, such a CFG can be accessed concurrently by multiple threads, and even shared by many programs at runtime.

4.3   Code-Reuse Attack Detection Triggers

Before describing the runtime detection phase, we first introduce two types of events that trigger the detection logic: an interrupt issued by LBR + PMU and invocation of a system call.

Hardware Interrupt. When LBR + PMU generates an interrupt, the CPU control is passed to the interrupt handler in the kernel and LBR stops recording branches because it is configured to monitor user space code only. For simplicity, in our current implementation, the interrupt handler directly invokes the security check function. Other alternatives include to invoke it in a kernel thread or in a user-mode process. Each scheme has its own advantages and disadvantages, and we remark that all of them can benefit from the isolation capability provided by hardware.

System Calls. By default, we check LBR records in batch mode. This scheme can allow an attacker to execute an average of $N/2$ invalid indirect branches before LBR + PMU issues an interrupt. In other words, the attacker may launch a malicious system call before the interrupt performs a security validation. To deal with such attacks, we ensure the security by postponing any system call execution after LBR buffer inspection. To this end, we hook into the system call handlers (e.g., `sysenter_entry` and `system_call` routines of the Linux kernel) to invoke our security check.

Runtime Detection. For each LBR record, we process it in the following steps

- Step 1. Identify whether it is an execution trace of an intra-module transfer by using the kernel API (e.g., `find_vma` in Linux) to retrieve the Virtual Memory Area (VMA) manager that covers the current source (or destination) address. In Linux, each code or data segment of a program has its own VMA whose meta-data is maintained by a manager. A record is considered as an intra-module transfer if its source and destination addresses are covered by the same VMA. Otherwise, it is an inter-module transfer.
- Step 2. Convert the address pair to offsets in order to be compliant to the format of the aforementioned constraint data. To this end, the source (or destination) address is subtracted with the base address where the current code segment is loaded in the memory and maintained by the VMA manger.
- Step 3. Retrieve the CFG of the recorded branch instruction's source address. The VMA manager has a new field named `cfg_info` that points to the buffer storing the CFG. Note that all CFGs are priorly loaded into the kernel space before running the protected program, and are bound to the `cfg_info` fields when running kernel routines `fork()` or `exec()`.
- Step 4. Finally, we perform code-reuse attack detection by checking this record with CFGs.

5   Implementation of CFIGuard

We have implemented a prototype of CFIGuard on the Linux kernel version 3.13.11. Currently, CFIGuard supports Intel Ivy Bridge architecture and focuses on preventing user-level attacks only. The prototype runs in two phases: the offline CFG recovering phase and the online CFI enforcing phase. During the offline phase, CFIGuard builds a table of target addresses for each branch and then generates the constraint data for the binaries. During the second phase, CFIGuard employs LBR + PMU to record every indirect branch execution and performs attack detection by consulting CFGs.

5.1   Control-Flow Constraint

Extracting Control-Flow Graph. We develop a Python script based on IDA [1] to collect call-sites from binaries. If the call-site is a direct call, we can easily get its target. Otherwise, we analyse the source code to collect targets of an indirect call. We use the method applied in forward-CFI [35] to construct target tables for indirect calls based on the source code. Specifically, we classify all functions into different categories based on the types of their return values and parameters. An indirect function invocation (using a function pointer) can only target the category that has the same type of the pointer. The target tables of indirect calls are fed to our Python script.

With the information about call-sites, we can construct the target tables for `ret` instructions. Then we analyze the Procedure Linkage Table (PLT) entries and switch-case tables to construct the target tables for `indirect jump` instructions. Note that, if function pointers in a switch-case jump table are hard-coded in a read-only segment, they cannot be tampered with because of DEP protection. Therefore, jump instructions (e.g., `jmp jtable[edx*4]`) with such a target set can hardly be exploited by attackers if the compiler implements the jump table lookups correctly, i.e., jumping out of this table is impossible. We state this fact of those jump instructions by not listing their jump-to addresses in their target tables. Instead, we set the *size* field of the headers of their target tables with a specific value as an indication. This scheme could accelerate the security checking and also save memory overhead.

The exit-points include: (a) PLT entries that invoke library functions; (b) `ret` instructions at the end of exported functions of the current module; (c) indirect calls of exported function that invoke external call-back functions. Meanwhile, the entry-points are composed of instructions next to call-sites that invoke PLT entries or external library functions.

In case that the source code of the protected program is not available, we can recover CFG from its binary as in coarse-grained CFI schemes [43,44]. In fact, the CFGs recovered by those works are accurate enough for CFIGuard because the CFGs are utilized without reduction.

Storing Control-Flow Graph. The CFGs are stored in the form of bitmaps and tables described below.

Jump-from address bitmap. This bitmap is implemented as an array of words. Each word has 32-bits, thus it can track 32 code bytes or 32 addresses with the lowest bit corresponding to the lowest address.

Connectivity hash table. This hash table stores the connectivity between a jump-from address and its target table. It is a sparse table with a density around 50 %. Moreover, it is open addressed and represented using arrays, thus have near-linear search time.

Target tables. The addresses of each table are sorted in an ascending order such that we can quickly locate a target when validating the jump-to address of a LBR record.

Bitmap of entry-points. In order to save the memory overhead, the entry-point bitmap is merged with the jump-from address bitmap. An entry-point must be an address of an intended instruction, so the merged bitmap does not add extra bit for validating jump-from addresses.

Moreover, we add a header to manage the constraint data, which contains metadata including the location of bitmap and hash table, as well as the size of hash table. Figure 2 illustrates a part of the constraint data of an exemplary application.

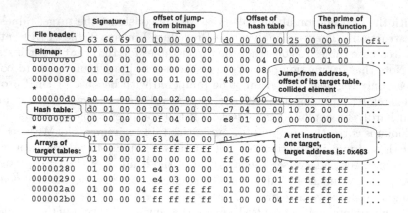

Fig. 2. The constraint data of a demo application

5.2   Hardware Monitor: LBR + PMU

Figure 3 is the diagram of the LBR + PMU monitor. LBR is configured by IA32_DEBUG_MSR and MSR_LBR_SELECT registers which are used for enabling/disabling LBR and branch type filtering, respectively. PMU is configured by three registers. In fact, modern CPUs generally offer several PMU units and we select the first one denoted as PMU0 in our processor. Register IA32_PERF_GLOBAL_CTRL is used to enable PMU0. Meanwhile, Register IA32_PERFEVSEL0 sets the BR_INST_EXEC bits for monitoring and sets a sub-event mask for branch type filtering.

The driver of LBR + PMU exports several interfaces for management: (a) an interface to enable/disable the monitor; (b) an interface to support branch type filtering; and (c) an interface to (re-)initialize PMC0.

5.3   Security Check

We implement the security check functionality as two Loadable Kernel Modules (LKMs) with one for loading the constraint data and the other for policy enforcement.

LKM for Loading Constraint Data. This module uses kernel buffers to store constraint data of the application and its dynamically linked libraries. All pages of these buffers are set with VM_RESERVED attribute to ensure that they are not swapped out at runtime. This configuration makes the constraint data to be available for the interrupt handler. Moreover, each buffer is exported to the user as a memory-mapping file under the "/proc" file system, and the files are protected by the access policies of the Linux system. As a result, a privileged user can upload constraint data files into the kernel buffers before running a protected program.

This module also hooks into the *exec()* kernel routine to bind the constraint data file to the VMA instance of the corresponding code segment after the

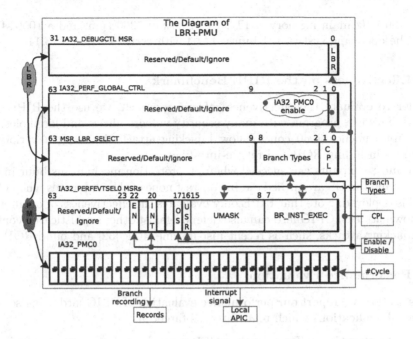

Fig. 3. The diagram of LBR + PMU

protected program is loaded into the memory. Consequently, the right constraint data is retrieved from the VMA instance during the security check.

LKM for Security Enforcement. The module inserts hooks in the interrupt handler "intel_pmu_handle_irq()" and the system call table to intercept LBR + PMU's interrupts and system calls, respectively. The security check is bound to a function pointer exported by the Linux kernel, which is initialized when this module is installed.

5.4 Launching CFIGuard System

Current implementation needs a few manual operations to protect a program at runtime, but we leave it as our future work to automate the entire process. We first install the LKM for loading the constraint data and then upload constraint data to the exported "/proc" files. Next, we install the LKM for security enforcement. After that, a user application can be launched with CFIGuard protection.

6 Evaluation

All evaluation experiments are performed on a PC with an Intel Core i5-3470 processor with 4 cores. Each core has 32 k L1 instruction and L1 data cache and a 256 K L2 data cache. The four cores share a 6 MB L3 cache. The platform has

4 GB 1066 MHz main memory, a 1TB SCSI disk of 7200 rpm, and a 1000 Mbps NIC. The operating system is Ubuntu 14.04 with kernel version 3.13.11.

6.1 Effectiveness on the RIPE Benchmark

In order to evaluate the effectiveness of our approach, we use the RIPE [39] testbed. This is a program with many security vulnerabilities and loopholes. Its test script launches 3940 control flow hijacking attacks by using a variety of techniques including ROP and return-into-libc.

Around 80 exploits can succeed when all protection mechanisms built in the platform and the OS are turned on. In contrast none of them succeeds when CFIGuard is deployed. Note that RIPE only evaluates the effectiveness of countering the known attacks. CFIGuard can also defend against other sophisticated control flow hijacking attacks, such as recent just-in-time ROP [32] and blind-ROP [6].

6.2 Performance Evaluation

In this section, we report our performance evaluation of CFIGuard using several real-world applications which many attacks target at.

Target Applications. To show that CFIGuard can be efficiently applied to a variety of applications in practice, we choose different types of server applications listed in Table 2, including Apache Web Server, Mysql Database and the vsftpd FTP server.

Table 2. Different types of real-world applications for benchmarking

Application	Performance matrix	Parameters
Apache	Throughput of *get*	20 clients send 50000 requests
Mysql	Runtime overhead	16 clients issue 10000 transactions
vsftpd	Throughput	10 clients download/upload a 10Mb file

Contribution of Branch Type Filtering. The filtering of direct branches dramatically releases the hardware burden on recording and results in low frequency of interrupts and low performance overhead. We utilize Linux's Perf tool to count the execution rounds of indirect branches and that of all branches. The results are shown in Table 2 below. On average, the execution rounds of indirect branches take only 16.7 % of the total amount. Therefore, the branch filtering mechanism of LBR + PMU effectively trims the runtime overhead as compared to monitoring all branches.

Performance Results. We evaluate those server applications with a performance matrix shown in Table 2. Figure 4 depicts the performance overhead for protecting these applications with CFIGuard. From this figure, we can see that CFIGuard incurs low performance overhead, with only 2.9 % on average, and a maximum 5.6 % on Apache. Most of the cost (around 83 %) is attributed to

Table 3. The execution records of indirect branches and their ratio in total.

Server	# of branch exec. (in million)	# of ind. branch exec. (in million)	Percentage (%)	Remarks
Apache	99.8	19.3	19.3	Get a 8 Kb file
Mysql	7619.5	1416.1	18.6	Size of queried table is 32000
vsftpd-download	307.2	293.3	13.6	Download a 10 Mb file
vsftpd-upload	1926.0	2730	15.2	Upload a 10 Mb file

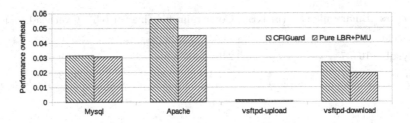

Fig. 4. Performance overhead of CFIGuard

LBR + PMU monitoring. Our overhead is lower than that of CFIMon [40] which reports a 6.1 % overhead. The result means that CFIGuard can be applied to certain real-world server applications in daily use (Table 2).

Figure 5(a) shows the overhead of CFIGuard when web clients get files of different sizes from an Apache server. The performance overhead is less than 1 % when the file size is larger than 4 KB, but increases as the file getting smaller (note that Fig. 4 shows the average cost across different file sizes). This is because when the file is large, the task is more I/O intensive. For small-size files, the server consumes more CPU cycles relatively. The throughput of *apache-get* running with CFIGurad is 88 % of its native throughput when the file size is 1 KB. Figure 5(b) shows the runtime of CFIGuard when database clients queries tables of different sizes hosted by a Mysql server. The time overhead of CFIGuard is around 3.7 % on average.

6.3 Memory Overhead

Table 4 shows the memory space used by CFIGuard to store the constraint data for a target application as compared to the application's own memory cost. The overhead mainly is attributed to the jump-from address bitmap and the target tables. Because the instruction set of x86 architecture consists of instructions with variable length, we have to track every code byte with a bit. As a result,

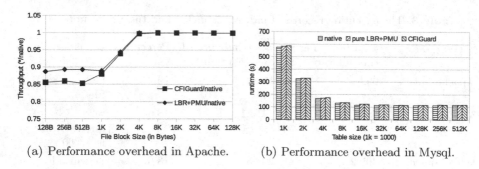

(a) Performance overhead in Apache.   (b) Performance overhead in Mysql.

Fig. 5. Performance overhead of CFIGurad in Apache and Mysql.

Table 4. The memory overhead of CFIGurad

Servers	Binary file size (in KB)	Constraint file size (in Kb)	Overhead (%)
Apache	568	136	24.0
Mysql	10437	2492	23.9
vsftpd	167	54	32.3

the overhead is at least 1/8. The memory overhead introduced by target tables is mainly for two reasons. Firstly, a small portion of `ret` instructions have too many targets (e.g., more than 256). Secondly, although all `ret` instructions of the same function have a common target set, each of them has its own target table according to our design. Note that the constraint data for shared libraries can be shared by different processes, which significantly saves the system wide memory cost.

7   Discussion

7.1   Return-into-app Attack

A dynamically linked library such as `libc.so` may export many functions. The backward inter-module transfers issued by `ret` instructions in those functions can hardly be depicted by a static CFG. Most existing mechanisms provide no protection or imprecise protection for those transfers to bypass the hassle. Hence, backward inter-module transfers are generally vulnerable at present. In the same vein as the `return-to-libc` attack, we name it the `return-into-app` attack as it is prone to redirect those transfers to invalid targets located at the application. CFIGuard mitigates such attacks by dictating that those transfers can only target the legitimate entry-points of the landing module. Because a typical program has far less entry-points than the number of indirect branch targets, the attack can hardly be launched under the protection of CFIGuard comparing with other CFI solutions such as MIP [23] and CCFIR [43].

7.2 Implications on Hardware Enhancement

The LBR buffer size of modern processors are much larger than their predecessors. Using a large LBR buffer can dramatically reduce the amount of interrupts triggered by LBR + PMU. Moreover, we call for integrating LBR and PMU together as a single facility in the upcoming generation of processors.

8 Related Work

8.1 Code-Reuse Attacks

The idea of code-reuse attack was proposed by Solar Designer [14] in 1997. Return-into-libc attacks are applied to applications on x86 processors in [22]. In 2007, Shacham et al. [30] proposed ROP (Return-Oriented-Programming). Unlike return-into-libc, ROP reuses short code snippets (called gadgets) which is more flexible to construct the malicious payload. Moreover, ROP is shown to be Turing complete in the sense that the attacker can accomplish any task. Bletsch et al. [7] proposed Jump-Oriented Programming (JOP) which reuses gadgets ended with indirect jump instructions to implement malicious functionality. In 2013, Snow et al. [32] proposed just-in-time ROP to undermine varies fine-grained ASLR solutions. There are other variants of ROP attacks. For example, String-Oriented Programming (SOP) [27]) uses a format string bug to exploit applications that are protected by a combination of weak ASLR, DEP, and SSP. Bosman et al. [8] proposed Signal-Oriented Programming (SROP) which employs Linux's SIGRETURN signal to load data from the stack into a register. If an attacker controls the data on the stack, he can initialize one or more registers with his data, then launches ROP or JOP attacks. Bittau et al. [6] proposed blind-ROP. Although such an attack is launched under a special circumstance, it demonstrates that a remote server is still vulnerable even when an attacker does not have any information about the server application.

8.2 Mitigation

Recent years have seen a surge of new techniques to mitigate code-reuse attacks. The two mainstream approaches are Address Space Layout Randomization (ASLR [33]) and Control Flow Integrity (CFI [3]). Runtime monitoring is also proposed as an alternative to ASLR and CFI.

Address Space Layout Randomization. The fundamental rationale of ASLR is that it is difficult for the adversary to collect available gadgets to construct an ROP chain when he lacks the knowledge of the address layout of the target code, which is achieved via randomizing the address space. Many fine-grained ASLR solutions have been proposed to increase the entropy of randomization [15, 18, 25, 31, 38]. The limitations of ASLR are summarized below. First, many fine-grained ASLR solutions make the libraries no long sharable [5]. Because of the changing of code positions, operands of control flow instructions, such as those of conditional jumps, vary from different randomized instances. As a result, security is achieved at the cost of the share-ability of libraries. Secondly, ASLR can hardly stop just-in-time ROP [32]. If a program has memory exposure vulnerabilities, an attacker may dynamically discover the randomized code layout and construct the ROP payload accordingly on the fly. Ironically, code inflation caused by fine-grained ASLR provides more available gadgets at the attacker's disposal. Lastly, ASLR does not withstand return-into-libc attack. As return-into-libc is proved to be Turing complete [36], ASLR offers limited security assurance.

Control Flow Integrity Enforcement. CFI schemes insert security checks before indirect branch instruction at the compilation phase [20,23,24,35,37] or through binary rewriting [2,43,44]. We describe several CFI schemes below.

The classic CFI implementation [2] uses function-level unique IDs as the control-flow constraint and allocates the same ID for an indirect branch instruction and its allowed targets. It rewrites the protected binary by inserting an ID before each target and a security check before each indirect branch instruction. The security check holds an ID and ID-comparing instructions. A control-flow transfer is allowed only if its jump-to target holds the same ID as that of security check.

HyperSafe [37] enforces the finest-grained CFI because it statically constructs a specific target table for each indirect branch instruction. It rewrites the protected program by replacing an indirect branch instruction with a direct jump to an external check routine, which at run-time consults the target tables to validate transfers before launching the original transfers.

CCFIR [43] is a 3-ID implementation according to the classic CFI work. It classifies the valid targets of all indirect branch instructions into three sets and stores them in a dedicated code region called *springboard*. Generally speaking, CCFIR performs security checks as other aligned-chunk CFI works such as PittSFIeld [21] and NaCli [41], because it detects attacks by checking whether the target is an aligned entries in the springboard. However, CCFIR allows an indirect branch to jump to an invalid target address belonging to the assigned set. Therefore, CCFIR only enforces coarse-grained CFI and can be circumvented by advanced attacks [16]. Other coarse-grained solutions, including MIP [23] and bin-CFI [44], also suffer from the same security issue [9,13,16,29].

Forward-CFI [35] focuses on protecting forward indirect transfers, i.e. `indirect call` and `indirect jump`. It is implemented by the compiler's CFI enforcement on the intermediate code. Thus it can easily produce security enhanced binaries after compilation. However, it needs a huge effort to be adopted in real-world systems as the users have to recompile all involved code. Moreover, to protect only certain types of indirect transfers is problematic in security. Some recently proposed schemes also suffer from the same limitation [20,28,42].

Runtime Monitoring. Hardware features provided by modern processors are used to monitor the code execution in several schemes such as kBouncer [26], ROPecker [11] and CFIMon [40]. The first two use LBR whereas the last uses BTS. Due to the limitation of hardware facilities, kBouncer and ROPecker can only capture a small portion of indirect branch executions, while CFIMon has to capture and examine executions of all types of branches. Moreover, all of them are limited by the accuracy because they require heuristic rules to identify attacks [9,10,13,16,29].

9 Conclusion

We have described the design and implementation of CFIGuard, a transparent security system that identifies control-flow integrity violation caused by code-reuse attacks. By creatively combining Last Branch Recording and Performance Monitoring Unit, CFIGuard records every execution of indirect branches during the lifetime of a process and validates the records in a separated security check by consulting fine-grained CFGs. CFIGuard introduces negligible runtime overhead on real-world applications. We demonstrate that our prototype implementation on Linux can effectively detect various advanced attacks, including return-into-libc and ROP.

In our future work, we plan to extend CFIGuard to protect just-in-time compiled code and the operating system kernel, and also to port our implementation to Windows systems.

Acknowledgments. This work has been partly supported by National NSF of China under Grant No. 61170070, 61572248, 61431008, 61321491; National Key Technology R&D Program of China under Grant No. 2012BAK26B01.

References

1. IDA: http://www.hex-rays.com/ida/index.shtml
2. Abadi, M., Budiu, M., Erlingsson, Ú., Ligatti, J.: Control-flow integrity. In: CCS 2005 (2005)
3. Abadi, M., Budiu, M., Erlingsson, Ú., Ligatti, J.: A theory of secure control flow. In: Lau, K.-K., Banach, R. (eds.) ICFEM 2005. LNCS, vol. 3785, pp. 111–124. Springer, Heidelberg (2005)
4. Andersen, S., Abella, V.: Data Execution Prevention: Changes to Functionality in Microsoft Windows XP Service Pack 2, Part 3: Memory Protection Technologies (2004)
5. Backes, M., Nürnberger, S.: Oxymoron: making fine-grained memory randomization practical by allowing code sharing. In: USENIX 2014 (2014)
6. Bittau, A., Belay, A., Mashtizadeh, A., Mazieres, D., Boneh, D.: Hacking blind. In: SP 2014 (2014)
7. Bletsch, T., Jiang, X., Freeh, V.W., Liang, Z.: Jump-oriented programming: a new class of code-reuse attack. In: ASIACCS 2011 (2011)
8. Bosman, E., Bos, H.: Framing signals - a return to portable shellcode. In: SP 2014 (2014)
9. Carlini, N., Wagner, D.: ROP is still dangerous: breaking modern defenses. In: USENIX 2014 (2014)
10. Casteel, K.: A Systematic Analysis of Defenses Against Code Reuse Attacks. Ph. D. thesis, Massachusetts Institute of Technology (2013)

11. Cheng, Y., Zhou, Z., Yu, M., Ding, X., Deng, R.H.: ROPecker: a generic and practical approach for defending against ROP attacks. In: NDSS 2014 (2014)
12. Cowan, C., Pu, C., Maier, D., Hinton, H., Walpole, J., Bakke, P., Beattie, S., Grier, A., Wagle, P., Zhang, Q.: StackGuard: automatic adaptive detection and prevention of buffer-overflow attacks. In: USENIX 1998 (1998)
13. Davi, L., Lehmann, D., Sadeghi, A.-R., Monrose, F.: Stitching the gadgets: on the ineffectiveness of coarse-grained control-flow integrity protection. In: USENIX 2014 (2014)
14. Designer, S.: Getting around non-executable stack (and fix). Bugtraq (1997)
15. Gupta, A., Kerr, S., Kirkpatrick, M.S., Bertino, E.: Marlin: making it harder to fish for gadgets. In: CCS 2012 (2012)
16. Göktaş, E., Athanasopoulos, E., Bos, H., Portokalidis, G.: Out of control: overcoming control-flow integrity. In: SP 2014 (2014)
17. Göktaş, E., Athanasopoulos, E., Polychronakis, M., Bos, H., Portokalidis, G.: Size does matter: why using gadget-chain length to prevent code-reuse attacks is hard. In: USENIX 2014 (2014)
18. Hiser, J., Nguyen-Tuong, A., Co, M., Hall, M., Davidson, J.: ILR: where'd my gadgets go? In: SP 2012 (2012)
19. Intel: Intel 64 and IA-32 Intel Architecture software developer's manual (2001)
20. Jang, D., Tatlock, Z., Lerner, S.: SAFEDISPATCH: securing C++ virtual calls from memory corruption attacks. In: NDSS 2014 (2014)
21. Mccamant, S., Morrisett, G.: Evaluating SFI for a CISC architecture. In: USENIX 2006 (2006)
22. Nergal: The advanced return-into-lib (c) exploits: PaX case study. Phrack Magazine, Volume 0x0b, Issue 0x3a, Phile# 0x04 of 0x0e (2001)
23. Niu, B., Tan, G.: Monitor integrity protection with space efficiency and separate compilation. In: CCS 2013 (2013)
24. Niu, B., Tan, G.: Modular control-flow integrity. In: PLDI 2014 (2014)
25. Pappas, V., Polychronakis, M., Keromytis, A.: Smashing the gadgets: hindering return-oriented programming using in-place code randomization. In: SP 2012 (2012)
26. Pappas, V., Polychronakis, M., Keromytis, A.D.: Transparent ROP exploit mitigation using indirect branch tracing. In: USENIX 2013 (2013)
27. Payer, M., Gross, T.R.: String oriented programming: when ASLR is not enough. In: PPREW 2013 (2013)
28. Prakash, A., Hu, X., Yin, H.: vfGuard: strict protection for virtual function calls in COTS C++ binaries. In: NDSS 2015 (2015)
29. Schuster, F., Tendyck, T., Pewny, J., Maaß, A., Steegmanns, M., Contag, M., Holz, T.: Evaluating the effectiveness of current anti-ROP defenses. In: Stavrou, A., Bos, H., Portokalidis, G. (eds.) RAID 2014. LNCS, vol. 8688, pp. 88–108. Springer, Heidelberg (2014)
30. Shacham, H.: The geometry of innocent flesh on the bone: return-into-libc without function calls (on the x86). In: CCS 2007 (2007)
31. Shioji, E., Kawakoya, Y., Iwamura, M., Hariu, T.: Code shredding: byte-granular randomization of program layout for detecting code-reuse attacks. In: ACSAC 2012 (2012)
32. Snow, K.Z., Monrose, F., Davi, L., Dmitrienko, A., Liebchen, C., Sadeghi, A.-R.: Just-in-time code reuse: on the effectiveness of fine-grained address space layout randomization. In: SP 2013 (2013)
33. PaX Team: PaX address space layout randomization (ASLR) (2003)

34. PaX Team: PaX non-executable pages design & implementation (2003)
35. Tice, C., Roeder, T., Collingbourne, P., Checkoway, S., Erlingsson, Ú., Lozano, L., Pike, G.: Enforcing forward-edge control-flow integrity in GCC & LLVM. In: USENIX 2014 (2014)
36. Tran, M., Etheridge, M., Bletsch, T., Jiang, X., Freeh, V., Ning, P.: On the expressiveness of return-into-libc attacks. In: Sommer, R., Balzarotti, D., Maier, G. (eds.) RAID 2011. LNCS, vol. 6961, pp. 121–141. Springer, Heidelberg (2011)
37. Wang, Z., Jiang, X.: HyperSafe: a lightweight approach to provide lifetime hypervisor control-flow integrity. In: SP 2010 (2010)
38. Wartell, R., Mohan, V., Hamlen, K.W., Lin, Z.: Binary stirring: self-randomizing instruction addresses of legacy x86 binary code. In: CCS 2012 (2012)
39. Wilander, J., Nikiforakis, N., Younan, Y., Kamkar, M., Joosen, W.: RIPE: runtime intrusion prevention evaluator. In: ACSAC 2011 (2011)
40. Xia, Y., Liu, Y., Chen, H., Zang, B.: CFIMon: detecting violation of control flow integrity using performance counters. In: DSN 2012 (2012)
41. Yee, B., Sehr, D., Dardyk, G., Chen, J.B., Muth, R., Ormandy, T., Okasaka, S., Narula, N., Fullagar, N.: Native client: a sandbox for portable, untrusted x86 native code. In: SP 2009 (2009)
42. Zhang, C., Song, C., Chen, K.Z., Chen, Z., Song, D.: VTint: defending virtual function tables integrity. In: NDSS 2015 (2015)
43. Zhang, C., Wei, T., Chen, Z., Duan, L., Szekeres, L., McCamant, S., Song, D., Zou, W.: Practical control flow integrity and randomization for binary executables. In: SP 2013 (2013)
44. Zhang, M., Sekar, R.: Control flow integrity for COTS binaries. In: USENIX 2013 (2013)

Networks

Haetae: Scaling the Performance of Network Intrusion Detection with Many-Core Processors

Jaehyun Nam[1]([✉]), Muhammad Jamshed[2], Byungkwon Choi[2], Dongsu Han[2], and KyoungSoo Park[2]

[1] School of Computing, KAIST, Daejeon, South Korea
[2] Department of Electrical Engineering, KAIST, Daejeon, South Korea
{namjh,ajamshed,cbkbrad,dongsu_han,kyoungsoo}@kaist.ac.kr

Abstract. In this paper, we present the design and implementation of Haetae, a high-performance Suricata-based NIDS on many-core processors (MCPs). Haetae achieves high performance with three design choices. First, Haetae extensively exploits high parallelism by launching NIDS engines that independently analyze the incoming flows at high speed as much as possible. Second, Haetae fully leverages programmable network interface cards to offload common packet processing tasks from regular cores. Also, Haetae minimizes redundant memory access by maintaining the packet metadata structure as small as possible. Third, Haetae dynamically offloads flows to the host-side CPU when the system experiences a high load. This dynamic flow offloading utilizes all processing power on a given system regardless of processor types. Our evaluation shows that Haetae achieves up to 79.3 Gbps for synthetic traffic or 48.5 Gbps for real packet traces. Our system outperforms the best-known GPU-based NIDS by 2.4 times and the best-performing MCP-based system by 1.7 times. In addition, Haetae is 5.8 times more power efficient than the state-of-the-art GPU-based NIDS.

Keywords: Many-core processor · Network intrusion detection system · Parallelism · Offloading

1 Introduction

High-performance network intrusion detection systems (NIDSes) are gaining more popularity as network bandwidth is rapidly increasing. As traditional perimeter defense, NIDSes oversee all the network activity on a given network, and alarm the network administrators if suspicious intrusion attempts are detected. As the edge network bandwidth of large enterprises and campuses expands to 10+ Gbps over time, the demand for high-throughput intrusion detection keeps on increasing. In fact, NIDSes are often deployed at traffic aggregation points, such as cellular core network gateways or near large ISP's access networks, whose aggregate bandwidth easily exceeds a multiple of 10 Gbps.

Many existing NIDSes adopt customized FPGA/ASIC hardware to meet the high performance requirements [4,13]. While these systems offer monitoring

© Springer International Publishing Switzerland 2015
H. Bos et al. (Eds.): RAID 2015, LNCS 9404, pp. 89–110, 2015.
DOI: 10.1007/978-3-319-26362-5_5

throughputs of 10+ Gbps, it is often very challenging to configure and adapt such systems to varying network conditions. For example, moving an FPGA application to a new device requires non-trivial modification of the hardware logic even if we retain the same application semantics [25]. In addition, specialized hardware often entails high costs and a long development cycle.

On the other hand, commodity computing hardware, such as multi-core processors [3,15] and many-core GPU devices [2,9], offers high flexibility and low cost because of its mass production advantage. In addition, recent GPU-based NIDSes [23,34] enable high performance, comparable to that of hardware-based approaches. However, adopting GPUs leads to a few undesirable constraints. First, it is difficult to program GPU to extract the peak performance. Since GPU operates in a single-instruction-multiple-data (SIMD) fashion, the peak performance is obtained only when all computing elements follow the same instruction stream. Satisfying this constraint is very challenging and often limits the GPU applicability to relatively simple tasks. Second, large number of GPU cores consume a significant amount of power. Even with recent power optimization, GPUs still use a significant portion of the overall system power. Finally, discrete GPUs incur high latency since packets (and their metadata) need to be copied to GPU memory across the PCIe interface for analysis. These extra PCIe transactions often exacerbate the lack of CPU-side memory bandwidth, which degrades the performance of other NIDS tasks.

Recent development of system-on-chip many-core processors [8,16] has bridged the technology gap between hardware- and software-based systems. The processors typically employ tens to hundreds of processing cores, allowing highly-flexible general-purpose computation at a low power budget without the SIMD constraint. For example, EZchip TILE-Gx72 [16], the platform that we employ in this paper, has 72 processing cores where each core runs at 1 GHz but consumes only 1.3 Watts even at full speed (95 watts in total). With massively parallel computation capacity, a TILE platform could significantly upgrade the performance of NIDS.

In this paper, we explore the high-performance NIDS design space on a TILE platform. Our guiding design principle is to balance the load across many cores for high parallelism while taking advantage of the underlying hardware to minimize the per-packet overhead. Under this principle, we design and implement Haetae, our high-performance NIDS on TILE-Gx72, with the following design choices. First, we run a full NIDS engine independently on each core for high performance scalability. Unlike the existing approach that adopts the pipelining architecture [24], our system removes all the inter-core dependency and minimizes CPU cycle wastes on inter-core communication. Second, we leverage the programmable network interface cards (NICs) to offload per-packet metadata operations from regular processing cores. We also minimize the size of packet metadata to eliminate redundant memory access. This results in significant savings in processing cycles. Finally, Haetae dynamically offloads the network flows to host-side CPU for analysis when the system experiences a high load. We find that the host offloading greatly improves the performance by exploiting available computing cycles of different processor types.

We implement Haetae by extending open-source Suricata [14] optimized for TILE-Gx72 processors. Our evaluation shows that Haetae achieves 79.3 Gbps for large synthetic packets, a factor of 1.7 improvement over the MCP-based Suricata. Our system outperforms Kargus [23], the best-known GPU-based NIDS, by a factor of 2.4 with 2,435 HTTP rules given by Snort 2.9.2.1 [29] that Kargus used. With real traffic traces, the performance of Haetae reaches 48.5 Gbps, which is 1.9 times higher throughput than that of the state-of-the-art GPU-based NIDS. In terms of power efficiency, Haetae consumes 5.8 times less power than the GPU-based NIDS.

While we focus on the development of Haetae on TILE-Gx72 in this paper, we believe that our design principles can be easily ported to other programmable NICs and many-core processors as well.

2   Background

In this section, we provide a brief overview of many-core processors using EZchip TILE-Gx72 as a reference processor. We then describe the operation of a typical signature-based NIDS.

2.1   Overview of EZchip TILE-Gx

Figure 1 shows the architecture of the EZchip TILE-Gx72 processor with 72 processing cores (called tiles in the TILE architecture). Each tile consists of a 64-bit, 5-stage very-long-instruction-word (VLIW) pipeline with 64 registers, 32 KB L1 instruction and data caches, and a 256 KB L2 set-associative cache. TILE-Gx72 does not provide a local L3 cache, but the collection of all L2 caches serves as a distributed L3 cache, resulting in a shared L3 cache of 18 MB. Fast L3 cache access is realized by a high-speed mesh network (called iMesh),

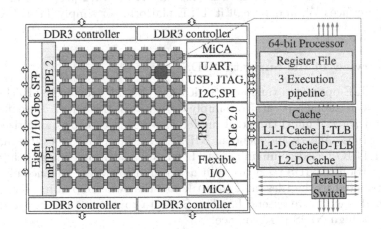

Fig. 1. Overall architecture of TILE-Gx72 processor

which provides lossless routing of data and ensures cache coherency among different tiles. The power efficiency comes from relatively low clock speed (1 to 1.2 GHz), while a large number of tiles provide ample computation cycles.

The TILE-Gx72 processor contains special hardware modules for network and PCIe interfaces as well. mPIPE is a programmable packet I/O engine that consists of ten 16-bit general-purpose processors dedicated for packet processing. mPIPE acts as a programmable NIC by directly interacting with the Ethernet hardware with a small set of API written in C. mPIPE is capable of performing packet I/O at line speed (up to 80 Gbps), and its API allows to perform direct memory access (DMA) transactions of packets into the tile memory, inspect packet contents, and perform load-balancing. The primary goal of the mPIPE module is to evenly distribute incoming packets to tiles. Its packet processors help parse packet headers and balance the traffic load across all tiles: a feature that closely resembles the receive-side scaling (RSS) algorithm available in modern NICs. The mPIPE processors can be programmed to check the 5-tuples of each packet header (*i.e.*, source and destination IP addresses, source and destination ports, and protocol ID) and to consistently redirect the packets of the same TCP connection to the same tile.

Besides the mPIPE module, the TILE-Gx72 processor also has the TRIO hardware module, which performs bidirectional PCIe transactions with the host system over an 8-lane PCIev2 interface. The TRIO module maps its memory region to the host side after which it handles DMA data transfers and buffer management tasks between the tile and host memory. TRIO is typically used by the host system to manage applications running in a TILE platform. Since the TILE platform does not have direct access to block storage devices, some TILE applications also use TRIO to access host-side storage using FUSE. In this work, we extend the stock TRIO module to offload flow analyzing tasks to the host machine for Haetae.

The TILE processors are commonly employed as PCIe-based co-processors. TILEncore-Gx72 is a PCIe device that has the TILE-Gx72 processor and eight 10 GbE interfaces [5], and we call it TILE platform (or simply TILE-Gx72) in this paper.

2.2   Overview of the Suricata NIDS

We use a TILE-optimized version of Suricata v1.4.0 [14] provided by EZchip. We refer to it as baseline Suricata (or simply Suricata) in this paper. Baseline Suricata uses a *stacked* multi-threaded model where each thread is affinitized to a tile, and it runs a mostly independent NIDS engine except for flow table management and TRIO-based communication. It follows a semi-pipelining architecture where a portion of NIDS tasks are split across multiple tiles. The incoming traffic is distributed to the tiles, and each tile has the ownership of its share of the traffic. In this work, we extend baseline Suricata to support the design choices we make for high NIDS performance.

Incoming packets to Suricata go through the following five NIDS modules.

1. The **receive** module reads packets through packet I/O engines. In commodity desktop and server machines, such packet I/O engines may include PF_RING [11], PSIO [20], and DPDK [7]. Haetae, on the other hand, uses EZchip's mPIPE module for network I/O communication. After receiving a batch of packets from the mPIPE module, the NIDS allocates memory for each ingress packet and initializes the corresponding packet data structure.
2. The **decode** module parses packet headers and fills the relevant packet substructures with protocol-specific metadata. As a last step, it registers the incoming packets with the corresponding flows.
3. The **stream** module handles IP defragmentation and TCP segment reassembly. It also monitors IP-fragmented and TCP-segmented evasion attacks as mentioned in [21].
4. The **detect** module inspects the packet contents against attack signatures (also known as rules). This phase performs deep packet inspection by scanning each byte in the packet payloads. It first checks if a packet contains possible attack strings (*e.g.*, multi-string matching) and if so, more rigorous regular expression matching is performed to confirm an intrusion attempt. This two-stage pattern matching allows efficient content scanning by avoiding regular expression matching on the innocent traffic.
5. Finally, the **output** module logs the detection of possible intrusions based on the information from the matched signatures.

3 Approach to High Performance

In this section, we identify the performance bottlenecks of baseline Suricata on the TILE platform and describe our basic approach to addressing them.

3.1 Performance Bottlenecks of Suricata

A typical performance bottleneck of a signature-based NIDS is its pattern matching. However, for TILE-Gx72, we find that parallel execution of pattern matching may provide enough performance while per-packet overhead related to metadata processing takes up a large fraction of processing cycles.

To demonstrate this, we measure the performance of a multi-pattern matching (MPM) algorithm (Aho-Corasick algorithm [17], which is the de-facto multi-string matching scheme adopted by many software-based NIDSes [14,23,29,34]). Figure 2(a) shows the performance of the MPM algorithm on the TILE platform without packet I/O and its related NIDS tasks. For the experiment, we feed in newly-created 1514B TCP packets with random payloads from the memory to the pattern matching module with 2,435 HTTP rules from the Snort 2.9.2.1 ruleset. We observe that the performance scales up linearly as the number of cores grows, peaking at 86.1 Gbps with 70 cores. The pattern matching performance is reasonable for TILE-Gx72 that has eight 10G network interfaces.

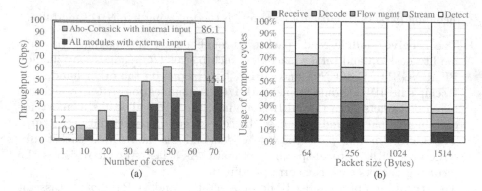

Fig. 2. Performance bottleneck analysis of Baseline Suricata: (a) Throughputs of the Aho-Corasick algorithm over varying numbers of TILE-Gx72 cores, (b) CPU usage breakdown of Suricata modules over various packet size

However, if we generate packets over the network, the overall performance drops by more than 40 Gbps. This means that modules other than pattern matching must be optimized for overall performance improvement. To reveal a detailed use of processing cycles, we measure the fraction of compute cycles spent on each NIDS module. The results in Fig. 2(b) show that tasks other than pattern matching (i.e., the detect module) take up 28 to 72 % of total processing cycles, depending on the packet size. The tile usage for the non-pattern matching portion is a fixed overhead per packet as the fraction gets higher for smaller packets.

Our detailed code-level analysis reveals that these cycles are mostly used to process packet metadata. They include the operations, such as decoding the protocol of each packet, managing concurrent flows, and reassembling TCP streams for each incoming packet. In this work, we focus on improving the performance of these operations, since the overall NIDS performance often depends on the performance of these operations while leveraging the unique hardware-level features of TILE-Gx72.

3.2   Our Approach

Our strategy for a high-performance NIDS is two folds. First, we need to parallelize pattern matching as much as possible to give the most compute cycles to the performance-critical operation. This affects the basic architecture of the NIDS, which will be discussed in more detail in the next section. Second, we need to reduce the overhead of the per-packet operation as much as possible. For the latter, we exploit the special hardware provided by the TILE-Gx72 platform. More specifically, our system leverages mPIPE and TRIO for offloading some of the heavy operations from regular tiles. mPIPE is originally designed to evenly distribute the incoming packets to tiles by their flows, but we extend it to perform per-packet metadata operations to reduce the overhead on regular tiles. The key challenge here is that the offloaded features need to be carefully chosen because the mPIPE processors provide limited compute power and memory access privilege. TRIO is mostly used to communicate with the host-side CPU for monitoring the application behavior. We extend the TRIO module to pass the analyzing workload to the host side when the TILE platform experiences a high load. That is, we run a host-side NIDS for extra flow analysis. The challenge here is to make efficient PCIe transfers to pass the flows and to dynamically determine when to deliver the flows to the host side. We explain the design in more detail in the next section.

4   Design

In this section, we provide the base design of Haetae, and describe three optimizations: mPIPE computation offloading, lightweight metadata structure, and dynamic host-side flow analysis.

4.1   Parallel NIDS Engine Architecture

Haetae adopts the multi-threaded parallel architecture where each thread is running a separate NIDS engine, similar to [23]. Each NIDS engine is pinned to a tile, and repeats running all NIDS tasks in sequence from receive to output modules. This is in contrast to the pipelining architecture used by earlier TILE-based Suricata [24] where each core is dedicated to perform one or a few modules and the input packets go through multiple cores for analysis. Pipelining is adopted by earlier versions of open-source Suricata, but it suffers from a few fundamental limitations. First, it is difficult to determine the number of cores that should be assigned for each module. Since the computation need of each module varies for different traffic patterns, it is hard to balance the load across cores. Even when one module becomes a bottleneck, processing cores allocated for other modules cannot help alleviate the load of the busy module. This leads to load imbalance and inefficient usage of computation cycles. Second, pipelining tends to increase inter-core communication and lock contention, which is costly in a high-speed NIDS. Since an NIDS is heavily memory-bound, effective cache usage is critical for good performance. In pipelining, however, packet metadata and payload have to be accessed by multiple cores, which would increase CPU cache bouncing and reduce the cache hits. Also, concurrent access to the shared packet metadata would require expensive locks, which could waste processing cycles.

To support our design, we modify baseline Suricata to eliminate any shared data structures, such as the flow table. Each thread maintains its own flow table while it removes all locks needed to access the shared table entry. Incoming packets are distributed to one of the tiles by their flows, and a thread on each tile analyzes the forwarded flows without any intervention by other threads. Since each thread only needs to maintain a small amount of flow ranges, dividing the huge flow table into multiple pieces for each thread is not a big trade-off. Thus, this *shared-nothing architecture* ensures high scalability while it simplifies the implementation, debugging, and configuration of an NIDS.

One potential concern with this design is that each core may not receive the equal amount of packets or flows from the NICs. However, recent measurements in a real ISP show that a simple flow-based load balancing scheme like RSS more or less evenly distributes the flows among the processing cores [35]. According to the study, the maximum difference in the number of processed flows per each core on a 16-core server is within 0.2 % of all flows at any given time with real traffic. This implies that the randomness of IP addresses and port numbers used in real traffic is sufficient to distribute the packet load evenly among the tiles.

4.2   MPIPE Computation Offloading

With the highly-scalable system architecture in place, we now focus on optimizing per-tile NIDS operations. Specifically, we reduce the packet processing overhead on a tile by offloading some common computations to the mPIPE programmable hardware module. When a packet arrives at a network interface, mPIPE allocates a packet descriptor and a buffer for the packet content. The packet descriptor has packet metadata such as timestamps, size, pointer to the packet content as well as some reserved space for custom processing. After packet reception, the software packet classifier in mPIPE distributes the packet descriptors to one of the tile queues, and the tile accesses the packet content with the packet descriptor. mPIPE allows the developers to replace the packet classifier with their custom code to change the default module behavior.

Programming in mPIPE, however, is not straightforward due to a number of hardware restrictions. First, in the case of mPIPE, it allows only 100 compute cycles per packet to execute the custom code at line rate. Second, the reserved space in the packet descriptor is limited to 28 bytes, which could be too small to perform intensive computations. Third, mPIPE embedded processors are designed mainly for packet classification with a limited instruction set and programming libraries. They consist of 10 low-powered 16-bit processors, which do not allow flexible operations such as subroutines, non-scalar data types (*e.g.*, structs and pointers), and division (remainder) operations.

Given these constraints, Haetae offloads two common packet processing tasks of an NIDS: packet protocol decoding and hash computation for flow table lookup. We choose these two functions for mPIPE offloading since they should run for every packet but do not maintain any state. Also, they are relatively simple to implement in mPIPE while they save a large number of compute cycles on each tile.

Figure 3 shows how the customized mPIPE module executes protocol decoding and flow hash computation. A newly-arriving packet goes through packet decoding and flow hash functions, saving results to the reserved area of an mPIPE packet descriptor. Out of 28 bytes of total output space, 12 bytes are used for holding the packet address information (*e.g.*, source and destination addresses and port numbers) and 4 bytes are used to save a 32-bit flow hash result. The remaining 12 bytes are employed as a bit array to encode various information: whether it is an IPv4 or IPv6 packet, whether it is a TCP or UDP packet, the length of a TCP header in the case of the TCP packet, etc.

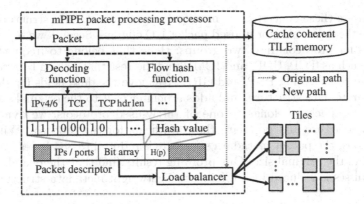

Fig. 3. Design of the mPIPE engine with decoding and hash computations

Each bit can indicate multiple meanings depending on protocols. After these functions, a load balancer determines which tile should handle the packet, and the packet descriptor along with the packet is directly passed onto the L2 cache of the tile that handles the packet, a feature similar to Intel data direct I/O [6]. As a result, each NIDS thread can proceed with the pre-processed packets and avoids memory access latencies.

Our micro-benchmarks show that mPIPE offloading improves the performance of the decode and flow management modules by 15 to 128 % (in Sect. 6). Since these are per-packet operations, the cycle savings are more significant with smaller packets.

4.3 Lightweight Metadata Structure

mPIPE computation offloading confirms that reducing the overhead of per-packet operation greatly improves the performance of the overall NIDS. The root cause for performance improvement is reduced memory access and enhanced cache access efficiency. More efficient cache utilization leads to a smaller number of memory accesses, which minimizes the wasted cycles due to memory stalls. If the reduced memory access is a part of per-packet operation, the overall savings could be significant since a high-speed NIDS has to handle a large number of packets in a unit time.

To further reduce the overhead of per-packet memory operation, we simplify the packet metadata structure of baseline Suricata. Suricata's packet metadata structure is bloated since it has added support for many network and transport-layer protocols over time. For example, the current data structure includes packet I/O information (*e.g.*, PCAP [10], PF_RING [11], mPIPE), network-layer metadata (*e.g.*, IPv4, IPv6, ICMP, IGMP) and transport-layer metadata (*e.g.*, TCP, UDP, SCTP). The resulting packet metadata structure is huge (1,920 bytes), which is not only overkill for small packets but also severely degrades the cache utilization due to redundant memory access. Also, the initialization cost for metadata structure (*e.g.*, memset() function calls) would be expensive.

To address these concerns, we modify the packet metadata structure. First, we remove the data fields for unused packet I/O engines. Second, we separate the data fields for protocols into two groups: those that belong to frequently-used protocols such as TCP, UDP, and ICMP and the rest that belong to rarely-used protocols such as SCTP, PPP, and GRE. We move the data fields for the latter into a separate data structure, and adds a pointer to it to the original structure. If an arriving packet belongs to one of rarely-used protocols, we dynamically allocate a structure and populate the data fields for the protocol. With these optimizations, the packet metadata structure is reduced to 384 bytes, five times smaller than the original size. Our profiling results find that the overall number of cache misses is reduced by 54 % due to lightweight metadata structures.

4.4   Flow Offloading to Host-Side CPU

Since TILE-Gx72 is typically attached to a commodity server machine, we could improve the NIDS performance further if we harness the host-side CPU for intrusion detection. The TILE-Gx72 platform provides a TRIO module that allows communication with the host machine. We exploit this hardware feature to offload extra flows beyond the capacity of the TILE processors to the host-side CPU.

The net performance increase by host-side flow offloading largely depends on two factors: (i) how fast the TILE platform transfers the packets to the host machine over its PCIe interface, and (ii) the pattern matching performance of the host-side NIDS. In our case, we use a machine containing two Intel E5-2690 CPUs (2.90 GHz, 16 cores in total) that run Kargus with only CPUs [23]. Since the performance of the Aho-Corasick algorithm in Kargus is about 2 Gbps per CPU core [23], the host-side NIDS performance would not be an issue given the 8-lane PCIev2 interface (with 32 Gbps maximum bandwidth in theory) employed by the TILE platform.

We first describe how we optimize the TRIO module to efficiently transfer packets to the host side, and explain which packets should be selected for offloading. Also, we determine when the packets should be offloaded to the host machine to maximize the performance of both sides.

Efficient PCIe Communication. Baseline Suricata provides only rudimentary host offloading support mainly used for remote message logging; since the TILE platform does not have built-in secondary storage, it periodically dispatches the batched log messages from its output module to the host-side storage via its TRIO module. Since log transmission does not require a high bandwidth, the stock TRIO module in the baseline Suricata code is not optimized for high-speed data transfer. First, the module does not exploit zero-copy DMA support. Second, it does not exercise parallel I/O in PCIe transactions, incurring a heavy contention in the shared ring buffer. Our measurement shows that the stock TRIO module achieves only 5.7 Gbps of PCIe data transfer throughput at best out of the theoretical maximum of 32 Gbps.

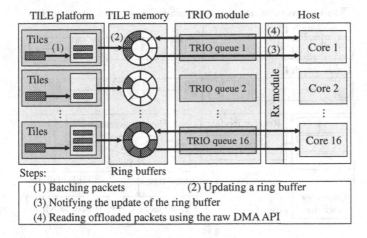

Fig. 4. Design of the offloading module with the TRIO engine

We exploit three features in the TRIO module to maximize the PCIe transfer performance for high host-side NIDS throughput. First, we develop a zero-copying offloading module with the raw-DMA API provided by the TRIO engine. The raw-DMA API ensures low-latency data transfer between the TILE platform and the host. It requires physically-contiguous buffers to map the TILE memory to the host-side address space. For zero-copy data transfer, we pre-allocate shared packet buffers at initialization of Suricata, which are later used by mPIPE for packet reception. Packets that need to be offloaded are then transferred via the TRIO module without additional memory copying, which greatly saves compute cycles. Second, we reduce the contention to the shared ring buffer by increasing the number of TRIO queues. The baseline version uses a single ring buffer, which produces severe contention among the tiles. We increase the number to 16, which is the maximum supported by our TILE platform. This allows parallel queue access both from tiles and CPU cores. Finally, we offload multiple packets in a batch to amortize the cost incurred due to per-packet PCIe transfer. Our packet offloading scheme is shown in Fig. 4. We find that these optimizations are very effective, improving the performance of PCIe transfer by 5 to 28 times over the stock version.

Dynamic Flow Offloading. We design the TRIO offloading module to fully benefit from the hardware advantage of the TILE platform. We make the TILE platform handle as much traffic as possible to minimize the power consumption and the analyzing latency. To determine when to offload the packets to the host side, each tile monitors whether it is being under pressure by checking the queue size in mPIPE. A large build-up in the queue indicates that the incoming load may be too large for the tile to catch up.

Figure 5 shows the design of the dynamic offloading algorithm in Haetae. The basic idea is similar to opportunistic packet offloading to GPU in [23], but

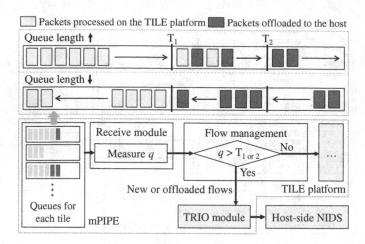

Fig. 5. Dynamic flow offloading

the unit of offloading is a flow in our case, and the task for offloading is the entire flow analysis instead of only pattern matching. In our algorithm, we use two thresholds to determine whether a new flow should be offloaded or not. If the queue length (q) exceeds the first threshold (T_1), a small portion (L_1) of new flows are chosen to be offloaded to the host machine. If it successfully curbs the queue size blowup, Haetae reverts to TILE-only flow analysis and stops offloading to the host side. However, if the queue size increases beyond the second threshold (T_2), a larger portion (L_2, typically, $L_2 = 1$) of new flows is offloaded to the host machine, which helps drain the queue more quickly. When the queue length exceeds the second threshold, the system keeps the offloading rate to L_2 until the queue length goes below the first threshold (T_1). This two-level offloading scheme prevents rapid fluctuation of the queue length, which would stabilize flow processing in either mode.

The unit of offloading should be a flow since the host-side NIDS is independent of the TILE-side NIDS. The host-side NIDS should receive all packets in a flow to analyze the protocol as well as reassembled payload in the same flow. To support flow-level offloading, we add a bit flag to each flow table entry to mark if a new packet belongs to a flow being offloaded or not. This extra bookkeeping, however, slightly reduces the per-tile analyzing performance since it is rather heavy per-packet operation.

5   Implementation

We implement Haetae by extending a TILE-optimized Suricata version from EZchip. This version optimizes the Aho-Corasick algorithm with special TILE memory instructions, and uses a default mPIPE packet classifier to distribute incoming packets to tiles. To support the design features in Sect. 4, we implement per-tile NIDS engine, mPIPE computation offloading, lightweight packet metadata structure, and dynamic host-side flow offloading. This requires a total of 3,920 lines of code modification of the baseline Suricata code.

For shared-nothing, parallel NIDS engine, we implement a lock-free flow table per each tile. By assigning a dedicated flow table to each NIDS engine, we eliminate access locks per flow entry and improve the core scalability. The flow table is implemented as a hash table with separate chaining, and the table entries are pre-allocated at initialization. While the baseline version removes idle flow entries periodically, we adopt lazy deletion of such entries to reduce the overhead of per-flow timeouts. Idle flow entries are rare, so it suffices to delete them in chain traversal for other activities only when there is memory pressure. To maximize the parallelism, we run an NIDS engine on 71 tiles out of 72 tiles. The remaining tile handles shell commands from the host machine.

Supporting lightweight packet metadata structure is the most invasive update since the structure is used by all modules. To minimize code modification and to hide the implementation detail, we provide access functions for each metadata field. This requires only 360 lines of code modification, but it touches 32 source code files.

Implementing mPIPE computation offloading is mostly straightforward except for flow hash calculation. Baseline Suricata uses Jenkin's hash function [1] that produces a 32-bit result, but implementing it with a 16-bit mPIPE processor requires us to emulate 32-bit integer operations with 16-bit and 8-bit native instructions. Also, we needed to test whether protocol decoding and hash calculation is within the 100-cycle budget so as not to degrade the packet reception performance. mPIPE offloading modifies both the existing mPIPE module and Suricata's decode and flow management modules, which requires 130 and 100 lines of new code, respectively.

For dynamic host-side flow offloading, we implement 1,700 lines of code on the tile side and 1,040 lines of code on the host side. First, we modify the receive module to measure the load of each tile and to keep track of the flows that are being offloaded to the host. Second, we implement the tile-to-host packet transfer interface with a raw DMA API provided by TRIO. Finally, we modify the CPU-only version of Kargus to accept and handle the traffic passed by the TILE platform.

6   Evaluation

Our evaluation answers three aspects of Haetae:

1. We quantify the performance improvement and overhead of mPIPE and host-side CPU offloading. Our evaluation shows that the mPIPE offloading improves the performance of the decode and flow management modules by up to 128 % and the host-side CPU offloading improves the overall performance by up to 34 %.

2. Using synthetic HTTP workloads, we show the breakdown of performance improvement for each of our three techniques and compare its overall performance with Kargus with GPU and baseline Suricata on the TILE platform. The result shows that Haetae achieves up to 2.4x improvements, over Kargus and baseline Suricata.
3. Finally, we evaluate the NIDS performance using real traffic traces obtained from the core network of one of the nation-wide cellular ISPs in South Korea. Haetae achieves a throughput of 48.5 Gbps, which is a 92 % and 327 % improvement respectively over Kargus and baseline Suricata.

6.1   Experimental Setup

We install a TILE-Gx72 board on a machine with dual Intel E5-2690 CPUs (octacore, 2.90 GHz, 20 MB L3 cache) with 32 GB of RAM. We run Haetae on the TILE platform and CPU-based Kargus on the host side. Each NIDS is configured with 2,435 HTTP rules from the Snort 2.9.2.1 ruleset. For packet generator, we employ two machines that individually have dual Intel X5680 CPUs (hexacore, 3.33 GHz, 12 MB L3 cache) and dual-port 10 Gbps Intel NICs with the 82599 chipset. Our packet generator is based on PSIO [20] that can transmit packets at line rate (40 Gbps each) regardless of packet size. For real traffic evaluation, we replay 65 GB of packet traces obtained from one of the largest cellular ISPs in South Korea [35]. We take the Ethernet overhead (such as preamble (8B), interframe gap (12B), and checksum (4B)) into consideration when we calculate a throughput.

6.2   Computation Offloading Overhead

This section quantifies the performance benefit and overhead of mPIPE and TRIO offloading.

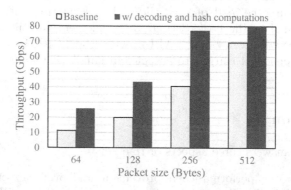

Fig. 6. Throughputs of the decoding and flow management modules with mPIPE offloading. The throughputs are line rate (80 Gbps) for 1024 and 1514B packets.

MPIPE Offloading Overhead. We first verify whether offloaded computations adversely affect mPIPE's packet I/O throughput. For this, we disable all NIDS modules other than the receive module, and compare the packet acquisition throughputs with and without mPIPE computation offloading. We generate TCP packets of varying size from 64 to 1514 bytes and measure the throughput for each packet size. Our result shows that even with mPIPE computation offloading packet I/O achieves line rates (80 Gbps) regardless of packet size. This confirms that the offloaded computations are within the cycle budget of the mPIPE processors, and offloading does not adversely affect the packet I/O performance.

We then evaluate the performance improvement achieved by mPIPE offloading. Figure 6 compares the performances with and without offloading. To focus on the performance improvement by packet reception and flow management, we enable the receive, decode, and flow management modules and disable other modules (e.g., stream and detect modules) for the experiments.

The mPIPE offloading shows 15 to 128 % improvement over baseline Suricata depending on the packet size. Because mPIPE offloading alleviates per-packet overhead, improvement with small packets is more noticeable than with large packets. In sum, the results show that computation offloading to mPIPE brings significant performance benefits in the NIDS subtasks.

TRIO Offloading Overhead. We now measure TRIO's throughput in sending and receiving packets over the PCIe interface. Note this corresponds to the maximum performance improvement gain achievable using host-side flow offloading. We compare the throughputs of our optimized TRIO module and the existing one. Figure 7(a) shows the throughputs by varying packet sizes. The original TRIO module cannot achieve more than 5.7 Gbps of throughput because it first copies data into its buffer to send data across the PCIe bus. Such additional memory operations (i.e., memcpy()) significantly decrease the throughputs. Our optimized TRIO is up to 28 times faster. The relative improvement increases as the packet size increases because the overhead of DMA operation is amortized. The throughput saturates at 29 Gbps over for packets larger than 512B, which is comparable to the theoretical peak throughput of 32 Gbps for an 8-lane PCIe-v2 interface. Note that the raw channel rate of a PCIe-v2 lane is 5 Gbps, and the use of the 8B/10B encoding scheme limits the peak effective bandwidth to 4 Gbps per lane. Figure 7 (b) shows end-to-end throughputs of Haetae with the CPU-side flow offloading by varying packet size. By exploiting both the TILE processors and host-side CPUs, we improve the overall NIDS performance by 18 Gbps, from 61 to 79.3 Gbps, for 1514B packets. While the overall performance is improved, we notice that the TILE-side performance degrades by 9 Gbps (to 52 Gbps in Fig. 7(b)) when TRIO offloading is used. This is because extra processing cycles are spent on PCIe transactions for packet transfers. We also note that the improvement with larger packets is more significant. This is because the PCIe overhead is relatively high for small-sized packets and the CPU-side IDS throughput with small packets is much lower compared to its peak throughput obtained for large packets. Despite the fact, the flow offloading improves the performance by 79 % for 64B packets. Given that the average packet size in real traffic is much larger than 100B [35], we believe that the actual performance improvement would be more significant in practice.

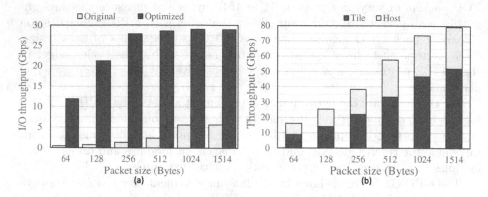

Fig. 7. TRIO performance benchmarks: (a) TRIO throughputs with and without our optimizations, (b) Throughputs with flow offloading

6.3   Overall NIDS Performance

Figure 8 shows the performance breakdown of the three key techniques under synthetic HTTP traffic. The overall performance ranges from 16 to 79 Gbps depending on the packet size. mPIPE offloading and metadata reduction achieve 33 % (1514B packets) to 88 % (64B packets) improvements and CPU-side flow offloading achieves 32 % additional improvement on average. Through the results, we find that reducing the per-packet operations significantly improves the overall NIDS performance, and we gain noticeable performance benefits by utilizing the host resources.

Figure 9(a) shows the performances of Haetae compared to other systems under the synthetic HTTP traffic. We compare with the baseline Suricata, customized for Tilera TILE-Gx processors, and Kargus with two NVIDIA GTX580 GPUs. In comparison with baseline Suricata, Haetae shows 1.7x to 2.4x performance improvement. We also see 1.8x to 2.4x improvement over Kargus in throughput (except for 64B packets). The relatively high performance of Kargus for 64B packets mainly comes from its batched packet I/O and batched function calls, which significantly reduces the overhead for small packets. In case of Haetae, we find that batch processing in mPIPE is ineffective in packet reception due to different hardware structure.

Here, we compare Haetae with a pipelined NIDS design in [24]. Because the source code is not available, we resort to indirect comparison by taking the performance number measured using a TILE-Gx36 processor from [24]. Since the clock speeds of the TILE-Gx36 (1.2 GHz) and TILE-Gx72 (1.0 GHz) processors

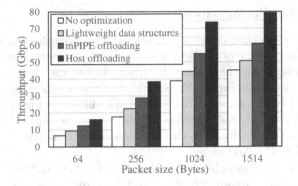

Fig. 8. Breakdown of performance improvement by each technique

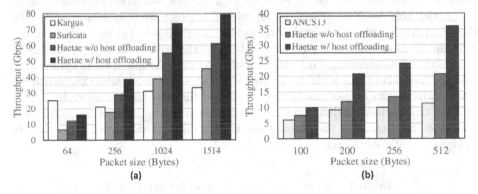

Fig. 9. Performance comparison with (a) synthetic HTTP workloads, (b) the NIDS proposed in ANCS '13 [24] (36 tiles)

are different, we scale down the performance numbers in the paper. For fair comparison, we use only 36 tiles for Haetae but increase the number of rules (7,867 rules), similar to [24]. Figure 9(b) shows the final results. While previous work achieves 6 to 11.3 Gbps for 100 to 512B packets, Haetae without host offloading achieves 7.4 to 20.6 Gbps for the same size, which is 1.2 to 1.8x more efficient. Moreover, Haetae with host offloading achieves 1.7 to 3.2x improvements over the previous work. The improvements come from two main reasons. First, unlike pipelining, Haetae's parallel architecture reduces load imbalance and inefficient usage of the tiles. We observe that the performance of [24] flattens at 512B packets, presumably due to the overheads of pipelining. Second, Haetae saves the computation cycles by applying the mPIPE offloading and the lightweight metadata structures.

In terms of power consumption, Haetae is much more efficient: Haetae with host offloading (TILE-Gx72 and two Intel E5-2690 CPUs) shows 0.23 Gbps per watt while Kargus (two Intel X5680 CPUs and two NVIDIA GTX580 GPUs) achieves only 0.04 Gbps per watt, spending 5.8x more power than Haetae.

6.4   Real Traffic Performance

We evaluate the performance with real traffic traces obtained from a 10 Gbps LTE backbone link at one of the largest mobile ISPs in South Korea. We remove unterminated flows from the real traffic traces and shape them to increase the overall transmission rate (up to 53 Gbps). The real traffic trace files are first loaded into RAM before packets are replayed. The files take up 65 GB of physical memory (2M TCP flows, 89M packets). To increase the replay time, we replay the files 10 times repeatedly. Like the previous measurements, we use the same ruleset (2,435 HTTP rules) as well.

Table 1 shows the throughputs of Haetae and other NIDSes. With the real traces, Haetae is able to analyze 4.2x and 1.9x more packets than Baseline Suricata and Karugs respectively. While Haetae achieves up to 79.3 Gbps with the synthetic workload, the throughput with the real workload decreases due to two major reasons. First, the modules related to flows are fully activated. Unlike the synthetic workload, the real workload has actual flows. The flow management module needs to keep updating flow states and the stream module also needs to reassemble flow streams. Thus, these modules consume much more cycles with the real workload than with the synthetic workload. Second, while the synthetic workload consists of packets of the same size, the real traffic has various data and control packets of different sizes. The average packet size of the real traffic traces is 780 bytes, and the throughput is 16 % lower than that of 512B packets in the synthetic workload.

Table 1. Performance comparison with the real traffic

IDS	Baseline Suricata	Kargus	Haetae
Throughput	11.6 Gbps	25.2 Gbps	48.5 Gbps

7   Related Work

We briefly discuss related works. We categorize the previous NIDS works into three groups by their hardware platforms: dedicated-hardware, general-purpose multi-core CPU, and many-core processors.

NIDS on Dedicated-hardware: Many works have attempted to scale the performance of pattern matching with dedicated computing hardware, such as FPGA, ASIC, TCAM, and network processors. Barker et al. implement the Knuth-Morris-Pratt string matching algorithm on an FPGA [18]. Mitra et al. develops a compiler that converts Perl-compatible regular expression (PCRE) rules into VHDL code to accelerate the Snort NIDS [27]. Their VHDL code running on an FPGA achieves 12.9 Gbps of PCRE matching performance. Tan et al. implement the Aho-Corasick algorithm on an ASIC [32]. Yu et al.

employ TCAMs for string matching [36] while Meiners et al. optimize regular expression matching with TCAMs [26]. While these approaches ensure high performance, a long development cycle and a lack of flexibility limit its applicability.

NIDS on Multi-core CPU: Snort [29] is one of the most popular software NIDSes that run on commodity servers. It is initially single-threaded, but more recent versions like SnortSP [12] and Para-Snort [19] support multi-threading to exploit the parallelism of multi-core CPU. Suricata [14] has the similar architecture as Snort and it allows multiple worker threads to perform parallel pattern matching on multi-core CPU.

Most of multi-threaded NIDSes adopt pipelining as their parallel execution model: they separate the packet receiving and pattern matching modules to a different set of threads affinitized to run on different CPU cores so that the incoming packets have to traverse these threads for analysis. As discussed earlier, however, pipelining often suffers from load imbalance among the cores as well as inefficient CPU cache usage.

One reason for the prevalence of pipelining in early versions of multi-threaded software NIDSes is that popular packet capture libraries like pcap [10] and network cards at that time did not support multiple RX queues. For high performance packet acquisition, a CPU core had to be dedicated to packet capture while other CPU cores were employed for parallel pattern matching. However, recent development of multi-queue NICs and multi-core packet I/O libraries such as PF_RING [11], PSIO [20], netmap [28] allows even distribution of incoming packets to multiple CPU cores, which makes it much easier to run an independent NIDS engine on each core. Haetae takes the latter approach, benefiting from the mPIPE packet distribution module while it avoids the inefficiencies from pipelining.

NIDS on Many-core Processors: Many-core GPUs have recently been employed for parallel pattern matching. Gnort [33] is the seminal work that accelerates multi-string and regular expression pattern matching using GPUs. Smith et al. confirm the benefit of the SIMD architecture for pattern matching, and compare the performance of deterministic finite automata (DFA) and extended finite automata (XFA) [30] on G80 [31]. Huang et al. develop the Wu-Manber algorithm for GPU, which outperforms the CPU version by two times [22]. More recently, Snort-based NIDSes like MIDeA [34] and Kargus [23] demonstrate that the performance of software engines can be significantly improved by hybrid usage of multi-core CPU and many-core GPU. For example, Kargus accepts incoming packets at 40 Gbps with PSIO [20], a high-performance packet capture library that exploits multiple CPU cores. It also offloads the Aho-Corasick and PCRE pattern matching to two NVIDIA GPUs while it performs function call batching and NUMA-aware packet processing. With these optimizations, Kargus achieves an NIDS throughput over 30 Gbps on a single commodity server.

Jiang et al. have proposed a Suricata-based NIDS on a TILE-Gx36 platform with 36 tiles [24]. While their hardware platform is very similar to ours, their NIDS architecture is completely different from Haetae. Their system adopts pipelining from Suricata and mostly focuses on optimal partitioning of tiles for tasks. In contrast, Haetae adopts per-tile NIDS engine and focuses on reducing per-packet operations and offloading flows to host machine. We find that our design choices provide performance benefits over their system: 20 to 80 % performance improvement in a similar setting.

8   Conclusion

In this paper, we have presented Haetae, a highly scalable network intrusion detection system on the Tilera TILE-Gx72 many-core processor. To exploit high core scalability, Haetae adopts the shared-nothing, parallel execution architecture which simplifies overall NIDS task processing. Also, Haetae offloads heavy per-packet computations to programmable network cards and reduces the packet metadata access overhead by carefully re-designing the structure. Finally, Haetae benefits from dynamic CPU-side flow offloading to exploit all processing power in a given system. We find that our design choices provide a significant performance improvement over existing state-of-the-art NIDSes with great power efficiency. We believe that many-core processors serve as a promising platform for high-performance NIDS and our design principles can be easily adopted to other programmable NICs and many-core processors as well.

Acknowledgments. We thank anonymous reviewers of RAID 2015 for their insightful comments on our paper. This research was supported in part by SK Telecom [G01130271, Research on IDS/IPS with many core NICs], and by the ICT R&D programs of MSIP/IITP, Republic of Korea [14-911-05-001, Development of an NFV-inspired networked switch and an operating system for multi-middlebox services], [R0190-15-2012, High Performance Big Data Analytics Platform Performance Acceleration Technologies Development].

References

1. A hash function for hash table lookup. http://www.burtleburtle.net/bob/hash/doobs.html
2. AMD: OpenCL Zone. http://developer.amd.com/tools-and-sdks/
3. AMD Opteron Processor Solutions. http://products.amd.com/en-gb/opteroncpu result.aspx
4. Check Point IP Appliances. http://www.checkfirewalls.com/IP-Overview.asp
5. EZchip TILEncore-Gx72 Intelligent Application Adapter. http://tilera.com/products/?ezchip=588&spage=606
6. Intel Data Direct I/O Technology. http://www.intel.com/content/www/us/en/io/direct-data-i-o.html
7. Intel DPDK. http://dpdk.org/
8. Kalray MPPA 256 Many-core processors. http://www.kalrayinc.com/kalray/products/#processors
9. NVIDIA: What is GPU Computing? http://www.nvidia.com/object/what-is-gpu-computing.html
10. PCAP. http://www.tcpdump.org/pcap.html

11. PF_RING. http://www.ntop.org/products/pf_ring
12. SnortSP (Security Platform). http://blog.snort.org/2014/12/introducing-snort-30.html
13. Sourcefire 3D Sensors Series. http://www.ipsworks.com/3D-Sensors-Series.asp
14. Suricata Open Source IDS/IPS/NSM engine. http://suricata-ids.org/
15. The Intel Xeon Processor E7 v2 Family. http://www.intel.com/content/www/us/en/processors/xeon/xeon-processor-e7-family.html
16. TILE-Gx Processor Family. http://tilera.com/products/?ezchip=585&spage=614
17. Aho, A.V., Corasick, M.J.: Efficient string matching: an aid to bibliographic search. Commun. ACM **18**(6), 333–340 (1975)
18. Baker, Z.K., Prasanna, V.K.: Time and area efficient pattern matching on FPGAs. In: Proceedings of the ACM/SIGDA International Symposium on Field-Programmable Gate Arrays (FPGA), pp. 223–232. ACM (2004)
19. Chen, X., Wu, Y., Xu, L., Xue, Y., Li, J.: Para-snort: A multi-thread snort on multi-core ia platform. In: Proceedings of the Parallel and Distributed Computing and Systems (PDCS) (2009)
20. Han, S., Jang, K., Park, K., Moon, S.: Packetshader: a gpu-accelerated software router, vol. 41, pp. 195–206 (2011)
21. Handley, M., Paxson, V., Kreibich, C.: Network intrusion detection: Evasion, traffic normalization, and end-to-end protocol semantics. In: USENIX Security Symposium, pp. 115–131 (2001)
22. Huang, N.F., Hung, H.W., Lai, S.H., Chu, Y.M., Tsai, W.Y.: A GPU-based multiple-pattern matching algorithm for network intrusion detection systems. In: Proceedings of the International Conference on Advanced Information Networking and Applications - Workshops (AINAW), pp. 62–67. IEEE (2008)
23. Jamshed, M.A., Lee, J., Moon, S., Yun, I., Kim, D., Lee, S., Yi, Y., Park, K.: Kargus: a highly-scalable software-based intrusion detection system. In: Proceedings of the ACM Conference on Computer and Communications Security (CCS), pp. 317–328 (2012)
24. Jiang, H., Zhang, G., Xie, G., Salamatian, K., Mathy, L.: Scalable high-performance parallel design for network intrusion detection systems on many-core processors. In: Proceedings of the ACM/IEEE Symposium on Architectures for Networking and Communications Systems (ANCS). IEEE Press (2013)
25. Kuon, I., Tessier, R., Rose, J.: FPGA architecture: Survey and challenges. In: Foundations and Trends in Electronic Design Automation, vol. 2, pp. 135–253. Now Publishers Inc. (2008)
26. Meiners, C.R., Patel, J., Norige, E., Torng, E., Liu, A.X.: Fast regular expression matching using small TCAMs for network intrusion detection and prevention systems. In: Proceedings of the 19th USENIX conference on Security, pp. 8–8. USENIX Association (2010)
27. Mitra, A., Najjar, W., Bhuyan, L.: Compiling PCRE to FPGA for accelerating Snort IDS. In: Proceedings of the ACM/IEEE Symposium on Architecture for Networking and Communications Systems (ANCS), pp. 127–136. ACM (2007)
28. Rizzo, L.: netmap: a novel framework for fast packet i/o. In: USENIX Annual Technical Conference. pp. 101–112 (2012)
29. Roesch, M., et al.: Snort - lightweight intrusion detection for networks. In: Proceedings of the USENIX Systems Administration Conference (LISA) (1999)
30. Smith, R., Estan, C., Jha, S., Kong, S.: Deflating the big bang: fast and scalable deep packet inspection with extended finite automata. ACM SIGCOMM Comput. Commun. Rev. **38**, 207–218 (2008)

31. Smith, R., Goyal, N., Ormont, J., Sankaralingam, K., Estan, C.: Evaluating gpus for network packet signature matching. In: Proceedings of the IEEE International Symposium on Performance Analysis of Systems and Software (ISPASS) (2009)
32. Tan, L., Sherwood, T.: A high throughput string matching architecture for intrusion detection and prevention. In: ACM SIGARCH Computer Architecture News, vol. 33, pp. 112–122. IEEE Computer Society (2005)
33. Vasiliadis, G., Antonatos, S., Polychronakis, M., Markatos, E.P., Ioannidis, S.: Gnort: high performance network intrusion detection using graphics processors. In: Lippmann, R., Kirda, E., Trachtenberg, A. (eds.) RAID 2008. LNCS, vol. 5230, pp. 116–134. Springer, Heidelberg (2008)
34. Vasiliadis, G., Polychronakis, M., Ioannidis, S.: Midea: a multi-parallel intrusion detection architecture. In: Proceedings of the ACM Conference on Computer and Communications Security (CCS), pp. 297–308 (2011)
35. Woo, S., Jeong, E., Park, S., Lee, J., Ihm, S., Park, K.: Comparison of caching strategies in modern cellular backhaul networks. In:Proceeding of the Annual International Conference on Mobile Systems, Applications, and Services (MobiSys), pp. 319–332. ACM (2013)
36. Yu, F., Katz, R.H., Lakshman, T.V.: Gigabit rate packet pattern-matching using tcam. In: Proceedings of the IEEE International Conference on Network Protocols(ICNP), pp. 174–183. IEEE (2004)

Demystifying the IP Blackspace

Quentin Jacquemart[1]([✉]), Pierre-Antoine Vervier[2], Guillaume Urvoy-Keller[3],
and Ernst Biersack[1]

[1] Eurecom, Sophia Antipolis, France
quentin.jacquemart@eurecom.fr, erbi@e-biersack.eu
[2] Symantec Research Labs, Sophia Antipolis, France
Pierre-Antoine_Vervier@symantec.com
[3] University of Nice Sophia Antipolis, CNRS, I3S, UMR 7271,
06900 Sophia Antipolis, France
urvoy@unice.fr

Abstract. A small part of the IPv4 address space has still not been
assigned for use to any organization. However, some of this IP space
is announced through BGP, and is, therefore, globally reachable. These
prefixes which are a subset of the *bogon* prefixes, constitute what we call
the *blackspace*.It is generally admitted that the blackspace stands to be
abused by anybody who wishes to carry out borderline and/or illegal
activities without being traced.

The contribution of this paper is twofold. First, we propose a novel
methodology to accurately identify the IP blackspace. Based on data
collected over a period of seven months, we study the routing-level characteristics of these networks and identify some benign reasons why these
networks are announced on the Internet. Second, we focus on the security
threat associated with these networks by looking at their application-
level footprint. We identify live IP addresses and leverage them to fingerprint services running in these networks. Using this data we uncover
a large amount of spam and scam activities. Finally, we present a case
study of confirmed fraudulent routing of IP blackspace.

1 Introduction

The global BGP (Boder Gateway Protocol) routing table now contains over 600 k
distinct IPv4 prefixes. A few of these prefixes should not be globally announced
(such as the private IP space) and are collectively referred to as *bogon* prefixes.
A subset of bogon prefixes, which we call the *blackspace*, is composed only of
prefixes that have not been assigned for use to any organization.

These unallocated, yet globally announced and reachable blackspace prefixes traditionally hold a bad reputation. On top of uselessly cluttering up the
global routing table, there have been reports of DDoS (Distributed Denial of
Service) attacks originated from blackspace address blocks [19]. Spammers are
also believed to abuse the blackspace in order to stealthily announce and abuse
routes [8]. By extension, it is admitted that the blackspace stands to be abused
by anybody who wishes to carry out borderline and/or illegal activities without
being traced.

© Springer International Publishing Switzerland 2015
H. Bos et al. (Eds.): RAID 2015, LNCS 9404, pp. 111–132, 2015.
DOI: 10.1007/978-3-319-26362-5_6

Because it is unallocated, hijacking a blackspace prefix is more likely to go unnoticed. Traditional hijacking detection tools, such as Argus [16], focus on "regular" prefix hijackings, i.e. situations in which the hijacked prefix is announced by the attacker alongside the owner's legitimate announcement. In the case of blackspace prefixes, there is no rightful owner, and thus no legitimate announcement that can be used to find an anomaly. Consequently, hijacking blackspace prefixes is out of the detection scope of state-of-the-art monitoring tools. Hijacking a blackspace prefix is also different from hijacking a *dormant* prefix, as analyzed in [22]. Dormant prefixes have been handed out for active use to organizations, but are globally unannounced; whereas blackspace prefixes are unallocated, and *should not* be globally announced.

Therefore, it is recommended to filter out bogons (including the blackspace), so as to minimize the window of opportunity of potential abusers. Unfortunately, the blackspace constantly varies in size and shape, according to new prefix assignments and prefix returns that are carried out daily by different Internet actors. Filtering out bogons is therefore inconvenient and tricky. In order to automate the process as much as possible, Team Cymru provides multiple lists with different levels of granularity that can be included directly in a BGP router's configuration [18].

This paper focuses on the study of blackspace prefixes and aims to clarify what the blackspace contains. A partly similar study, which encompassed all bogon prefixes [8], was carried out over 10 years ago. The formal reporting of malicious events carried out from the blackspace, [19], is even older. Back then, the IPv4 landscape was much different from today's, and the results provided by these works are not applicable anymore in today's Internet.

We start by detailing the method that we use to isolate the blackspace prefixes from the BGP routing table. We then provide a thorough study of the blackspace networks on two different levels. First, we look at the information we extract from the BGP control plane and study the size of the blackspace. We then study the persistence and change in the blackspace through time. We characterize the origin ASes (Autonomous Systems) that actively announce blackspace by using semantic information (e.g. WHOIS records). Second, we look at the data plane and focus exclusively on the security threat associated with the blackspace prefixes. In order to do so, we actively seek live IP addresses and extract the domain name for these machines. We check the websites running in the blackspace, analyze their content, and check if their URLs are known to be malicious. We use an IP blacklist to locate hosts that are associated with adware, scam, phishing, and other malicious activities. Finally, we check for spamming activities and show how some spammers skillfully abuse the unallocated IP space in order to remain anonymous.

This paper is organized in the following way. Section 2 details the method and the datasets we use in order to locate the blackspace inside the BGP routing table. Section 3 details our analysis results: Sect. 3.1 studies the size and variation of the blackspace; Sect. 3.2 details the BGP topology characteristics of the blackspace prefixes; Sect. 3.3 details the active measurements we do on blackspace networks, as well as a detailed threat analysis. Section 4 discusses the shortcomings of our approach. Section 5 provides a summary of the existing work and this domain, and how our efforts differ, and improve the current state-of-the-art. Finally, Sect. 6 summarizes our findings and provides a few ways to improve our system.

2 Isolating the Blackspace

In this Section, we detail how we isolate the blackspace prefixes within the global BGP routing table by using a combination of distinct datasets that provide information about IP assignments. This step is necessary because there is no information on how the current bogon list [18] is populated. We show later, in Sect. 5, that our methodology for identifying the IP blackspace is more accurate and finer grained than previous efforts.

2.1 IP Space Assignation Hierarchy

To better understand our methodology, it is perhaps best to first briefly mention how the IP address space is divided into multiple blocks by distinct institutions before being assigned to end users, such as ISPs, corporations, or academic institutions. First, the IANA (Internet Assigned Numbers Authority) is in charge of distributing /8 prefixes to RIRs (Regional Internet Registries). There are five RIRs, each responsible for a different geographical area. In turn, RIRs allocate IP address space to LIRs (Local Internet Registries), such as ISPs, large corporations, academic institutions, etc. LIRs enforce their RIR's policies and distribute IP address blocks at the local level, i.e. to end users [1,14].

2.2 Definitions

Bogon prefixes have traditionally been loosely defined as any IP prefix in the BGP routing table that should not be globally reachable. More precisely, following the definitions of [18], a prefix is a **bogon** if any of the three following conditions is true: (i) it is a **martian** prefix, i.e. if it is a prefix that was reserved for special use by an RFC, such as the private IP address space; (ii) the prefix belongs to a block that was not assigned to any RIR by the IANA; (iii) the prefix belongs to a block that was not assigned by a RIR to a LIR, or to an end user.

We define the **blackspace** prefixes as the set of bogon prefixes that are not martians and that are announced in BGP. In other words, it is the set of BGP-announced prefixes that have not been assigned for use – either because it still belongs to the IANA pool, or because a RIR has not assigned it to an ISP or an end user. We explicitly remove martian prefixes because they are most likely the result of a local route leak caused by a misconfiguration [8]. Moreover, since these prefixes are internally routed in a lot of networks, we are unlikely to reach martian-originating networks from our own, rendering any standard network diagnostics utility such as ping or traceroute pointless.

2.3   Internet Routing Registries

The IRRs (Internet Routing Registries) are a set of distributed databases maintained by the five RIRs where network operators can provide information regarding their network on a voluntary basis. In particular, the `inetnum` objects contain
information regarding IP address space assignment [2]. Consequently, the IRR
databases sound like the ideal starting point to isolate the IP blackspace. We
need to access the database of each RIR, and extract the IP ranges mentioned in
`inetnum` objects. We then have to check the prefixes announced in BGP against
the ones we found in the IRRs, and keep those that do not match.

Unfortunately, things are not quite that simple. Like previously stated, providing information in the IRR databases is in no way mandatory, and even
though it is considered as a good practice for LIRs to maintain their allocation
information up to date, they are in no way required to do so. Additionally (and
somehow consequently), the IRR databases are manually updated, and thus are
plagued with typical human errors, such as typos. For example, some `inetnum`
objects end their network on a .225 IP address, where the right value would be
255; some objects explicitly discard their net address, and/or their broadcast
address, etc. Due to these reasons, we cannot expect to have an exact mapping
between the BGP prefixes and the IRR prefixes. As a result, if we cannot match a
BGP prefix to an IRR prefix, we take into consideration `inetnum` objects that are
within the BGP prefix (i.e. `inetnum` objects that are more specific than the BGP
prefix). If over 95 % of the address space of the BGP prefix is covered by more
specific IRR prefixes, we consider the BGP prefix has having been assigned, and
that providing a matching IRR entry was overlooked. Our reasoning is that each
customer of LIRs (which may be other ISPs) potentially wishes to update the
IRR database, if only to update the management information of their network,
such as technical and administrative contact details.

2.4   RIR Statistics Files

Every day, each RIR publishes a report – sometimes known as the delegation
report – on the current status of the use they make of resources they have been
allocated, including IP address space [3]. This report breaks down each RIR's
IP address pool into four distinct states: ALLOCATED, ASSIGNED, AVAILABLE,
and RESERVED. The first two states, ALLOCATED and ASSIGNED, are similar in
the fact that they both have been marked as usable by someone by the RIR,
i.e. these addresses can be announced. The difference is that ALLOCATED space
ought to be used by LIRs for suballocation, whereas ASSIGNED space should not
– i.e. it should be used directly by the LIR or end user. As the name suggests, the
AVAILABLE state contains addresses that have not been ALLOCATED or ASSIGNED
to any entity. Finally, the RESERVED state is somehow an intermediate between
the other states: it has not been ALLOCATED (or ASSIGNED) to anybody, but is
also not AVAILABLE for such purposes. For example, these addresses might be
reserved for the growth of a LIR, returns that have not been cleared yet, or
experimental space [3]. In this classification, the blackspace is shared between

RESERVED and AVAILABLE states: in both cases there should not be any public BGP announcement for these addresses.

2.5   Blackspace Computation Process

Our BGP dataset is built on the data provided by the RIPE RIS collectors [15]. We daily fetch the routing table of each of the 13 active, geographically diverse routers, and create a list of all globally reachable routes. In the same time, we daily extract all `inetnum` objects from each IRR database, and we compare these two datasets as described in Sect. 2.3. We then remove from the remaining BGP prefixes the parts for which there exists an IRR entry. For illustrative purposes, let's consider (a real-world case) where a /21 prefix is announced in BGP, and where only one of the /22 more specific prefixes has an `inetnum` entry. We remove the /22 that is in the IRR from the blackspace, leaving only the other /22 in it. At this point, there is a one-to-n relationship between the prefixes in the blackspace and the prefixes as announced in BGP: a single BGP-announced prefix can result in multiple entries in the blackspace once the registered parts have been removed.

We further filter the results by discarding prefixes that are marked as ASSIGNED or ALLOCATED by RIRs in their statistics files. Once more, there are cases in which the remaining prefixes are in multiple states wrt. the statistics files states, e.g. the IP space is ALLOCATED and RESERVED. In this situation, we only keep the part of address space that is either RESERVED or AVAILABLE.

It is noteworthy that, although using both the IRRs and the statistics files might appear redundant, there are documented inconsistencies between the two distinct datasets [10]. Because we aim at investigating the blackspace, it is essential to use these multiple sources in order to circumvent the limitations inherent to each dataset and to focus exclusively on real blackspace prefixes so as to avoid introducing bias in our results.

3   Blackspace Analysis

In this Section, we study the blackspace networks over a period of seven months, between September 2014 and March 2015. In Sects. 3.1 and 3.2, we consider the routing-level characteristics of the blackspace networks, and identify some patterns for legitimate blackspace announcements. Then, in Sect. 3.3, we seek to determine the security threat posed by the blackspace networks by looking at the application-level services running in these networks, and by checking whether they were involved in some malicious activities like spamming or scam website hosting. Finally we provide a case study of a confirmed case of cybercriminals who carried out nefarious activities such as spamming by abusing AVAILABLE IP space.

3.1   Prevalence and Persistence

In this Section, we focus on a few essential aspects of the blackspace by looking at the size, temporal characteristics, and variation of the blackspace. In order to observe those, we computed the blackspace once per day between September 1st, 2014 and March 31, 2015 with the method detailed in Sect. 2. We compute the blackspace once a day because the IRR databases we use and the RIR statistic files are updated with this same frequency.

During our observation, the number of globally distinct prefixes from our collector routers varied between 550k and 600k prefixes. These prefixes route around 180 equivalent /8 IP addresses, i.e. the equivalent of 180 class A networks, or 180×2^{24} IP addresses. The reason we focus on the number of IP addresses instead of the number of prefixes is that, because of the methodology explained in Sect. 2, the relationship between a BGP prefix and a blackspace prefix is a one-to-many. By taking an aggregated BGP prefix and removing parts of it, we virtually inflate the number of prefixes in the blackspace, even though this larger number of prefixes actually represents a smaller IP space, rendering the prefix count meaningless. Figure 1 plots the daily number of IP addresses in the blackspace, as seen from a global BGP point of view. It shows that the blackspace size normally varies between 10^{-2} and 10^{-1} eqv. /8. It also shows that this number is relatively stable, apart from two peaks in October 2014 and January 2015. We investigated the reasons behind these peaks and attributed them to the announcement of 192.0.0.0/2 between October 15, 2014 and October 20, 2014; and a series of smaller prefixes between January 24, 2015 and January 29, 2015. We classify these events as routing leaks because they meet the criterias behind BGP misconfigurations detailed in [11]: a relative short-duration, and low visibility. Only three collector routers received the a route for 192.0.0.0/2 in October, and only one received the multiple prefixes in January 2015. Moreover, in both cases, only a single Autonomous System path (AS path) was seen, and the origin AS was a private AS number. All in all, Fig. 1 shows that the entirety of the blackspace could generally be contained in a single prefix, whose CIDR length would be between a /10 and a /15.

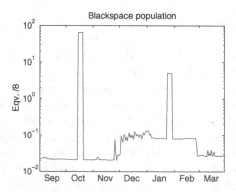

Fig. 1. Number of IP addresses in the blackspace, between September 1st, 2014 and March 31, 2015.

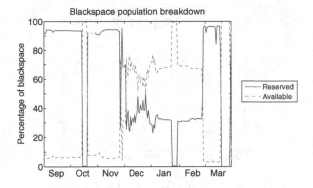

Fig. 2. Daily proportion of RESERVED and AVAILABLE address space in the blackspace, between September 1st, 2014 and March 31, 2015.

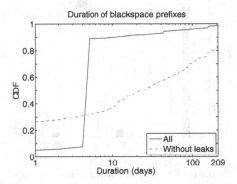

Fig. 3. Persistence of blackspace prefixes.

As mentioned in Sect. 2, a prefix in the blackspace has no `inetnum` entry in the IRR, and has not been allocated for use by a RIR. Figure 2 breaks down the statuses attributed to these IP addresses. Route leaks excluded, most of the blackspace is actually due to RESERVED resources, which are set aside by RIRs because they cannot be allocated right away.

Figure 3 plots the Cumulative Distribution Function (CDF) of the number of consecutive days a single prefix was included in the blackspace. The plain line plots this duration for all blackspace prefixes, including the many transient ones that were the results of the two route leaks already observed in Fig. 1. The dashed line plots the same duration, but excludes the prefixes resulting from these leaks. The difference between these two curves implies that a lot of distinct prefixes were added to the blackspace due to the leak of routes. Indeed, the plain CDF shows that most blackspace prefixes are detected during four or five consecutive days, which is precisely the duration of the two leaks observed in Fig. 1. On the other hand, the dotted CDF shows that 50 % of blackspace prefixes that are not the result of these leaks are seen for at least 12 days, and that around 28 % of them are seen during one day or less. In order to know how

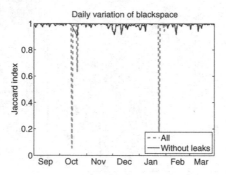

Fig. 4. Day-to-day variation of the blackspace prefixes.

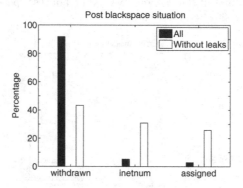

Fig. 5. Situation of the prefix after if left the blackspace.

much the blackspace varies daily, Fig. 4 plots the Jaccard index in-between two successive days. We compute the Jaccard index between days d and $d + 1$ as the ratio of the number of blackspace prefixes that are detected on both days, divided by the total number of distinct blackspace prefixes detected on day d and $d + 1$. A Jaccard index value of 1 indicates that the computed blackspaces for days d and $d + 1$ are identical. Conversely, a Jaccard index value of 0 indicates that the computed blackspaces for days d and $d + 1$ are 100 % different. The closer to 1 the value is, the more similar the two blackspaces are. Once again, the variation is quite high when the route leaks start and finish, as shown by the full line; but there is not a lot of daily variation otherwise (as shown by the dashed curve).

The duration of a prefix in the blackspace (Fig. 3) as well as the variation of the blackspace (Fig. 4) imply that some prefixes leave the blackspace. This is possible if any of the three following conditions are met: (i) the prefix is withdrawn from BGP; (ii) an `inetnum` entry is added in the IRR; (iii) the prefix is marked as ALLOCATED or ASSIGNED by a RIR. Figure 5 plots the distribution of each event for prefixes that exited the blackspace during our observation period. Again, the values are plotted for all entries, and also only for entries that were not the result of route leaks. In both situations, the most likely cause is that the prefix has been withdrawn. The second cause is the creation of an `inetnum` entry in an IRR database. If the IRR entry is more specific than the blackspace prefix, another (more) specific prefix will be included in the blackspace instead. Consequently, a bit less than 45 % of prefixes leave the blackspace because the BGP announcement was withdrawn. On the other hand, the other 55 % become allocated (in one way or another) afterwards; which implies that half of the prefixes included in the blackspace are, potentially, used in good faith by the announcers. However, the other half, which globally amounts to a /11 network, does not end up as a registered network.

3.2 BGP Characterization

In the previous Section, we saw that there are many blackspace prefixes, many of which are long-lasting. In this Section, we focus on the BGP characteristics of blackspace prefixes. We first focus on the origin AS of the blackspace prefixes to shed light on their uses. Where we cannot, we look at the temporal evolution of the blackspace prefix along with its origin AS in order to better understand the root cause.

AS numbers are assigned a status by RIRs, just like IP blocks (see Sect. 2): either ALLOCATED, ASSIGNED, AVAILABLE or RESERVED. Figure 6 plots the daily proportion of each AS status for ASes that originate a blackspace prefix. The plot has been further broken down by explicitly classifying the private AS numbers (between 64,512 and 65,535 [12]) separately from the RESERVED set. As can be seen by the black/squared line private ASNs are responsible for a large number of prefixes, but only during the two route leaks. In fact, all leaked prefixes are originated from a private ASN. ALLOCATED, ASSIGNED and RESERVED ASNs all roughly account for a third of blackspace prefixes, and AVAILABLE ASNs account for less than 10 % of those. Just like with IP blocks, RESERVED and AVAILABLE ASNs are not ALLOCATED, and thus should not be in use. Yet, two thirds of the blackspace prefixes are originated by these ASes.

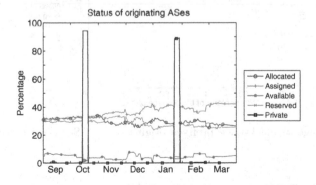

Fig. 6. Daily status of the ASNs originating a blackspace prefix.

Figure 7 plots the percentage of blackspace prefixes for ASes that announce (at least) one blackspace prefix. The plot is further subdivided by AS status, but we excluded the private AS numbers, as they were the result of route leaks (see Fig. 6). Here, both of the ALLOCATED and ASSIGNED statuses behave similarly, with more than 90 % of them announcing less than 1 % of blackspace prefixes. Less than 10 % of ALLOCATED (and around 20 % of ASSIGNED) ASes originate more than a quarter of blackspace prefixes. On the other hand, close to 70 % of RESERVED and AVAILABLE ASes *only* announce blackspace prefixes. To put this into perspective, the (global) average number of announced prefixes by ALLO-CATED ASes is 229; by ASSIGNED ASes is 340; by RESERVED ASes is four, and by AVAILABLE ASes is two. In order to find out who operates these networks, we look at the names of the corporations behind these ASes (using [9]). We get 185 network names for ALLOCATED or ASSIGNED ASes that originate blackspace prefixes, for which we located the corporation website using mostly popular web search engines. We were able to resolve 178 names to mostly telephone or cable companies and ISPs (of all sizes and shape: tier-1 to tier-3, from dial-up to business-grade fiber providers, all around the world), hosting and cloud providers, data centers, IT service companies, and world-wide tech companies. Other companies operated as advertising, airlines, bank and insurances, con-structions, courier and parcel delivery services, e-commerce, Internet exchange points, law firms, medical companies, military contractors, and online news. We could not resolve seven names. One was established as a company, but the web-site did not work, one used a name too generic to be found, and for three we could not locate any further information. The two remaining ASes appear to have been registered by individuals in Eastern Europe who also own other ASNs which are known to send spam – but do not originate blackspace prefixes at the same time.

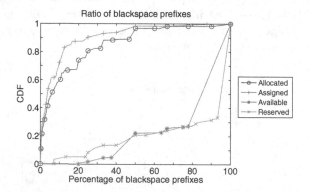

Fig. 7. Percentage of blackspace prefixes originated by ASes according to that AS's status.

Because the RESERVED and AVAILABLE ASes are not registered, we were not able to find registration information for them. Instead, we looked at the BGP topology of these prefixes, and investigated on the evolution of the blackspace prefix through time. For 33 % of the cases where a blackspace prefix is originated from a RESERVED AS, the origin AS remains RESERVED throughout the whole observation period. The prefixes were marked as RESERVED. These networks are usually single-homed and peer either directly with a tier-1 provider, or with a tier-3. The other 66 % prefixes show a state transition from, or to, RESERVED. In all the cases we observed, this was due to a network owner either bringing up a new network, or decommissioning an old one. For example, half a dozen blackspace prefixes were originated from a RESERVED AS for six months through a tier-1 AS. On one day, the AS status changed to ASSIGNED and the name matched a well-known airline. The next day, the prefixes were all given inetnum entries in the IRR. Our interpretation is that the prefixes and ASN were RESERVED for the growth of said airline, and that they started using these resources before the paperwork had been fully processed. In another case, the prefixes and ASN were ALLOCATED, but one day turned to RESERVED. By looking up the company's name, we were able to find a letter from ICANN, informing the company that they had breached their registrar accreditation agreement by failing to meet technical requirements, and also by failing to pay the accreditation fees. The day following the date of the letter, all of that company's resource where changed to RESERVED. In some cases, there are transitions from ALLOCATED, to RESERVED, and then back to ALLOCATED. In this situation, we believe the situation was similar to the one of the last example, except that they corrected their behaviour to meet the requirements during the grace period. In the case of AVAILABLE ASes, there were only a handful of situations in which the AS (and the announced blackspace prefix) ended up as ALLOCATED or ASSIGNED. In these situations, it was the result of a new network being connected to the global Internet.

In conclusion, by looking at the routing-level characteristics, we were able to identify a set of blackspace prefixes that appear to be benign. Some prefixes appear to be in the blackspace because they have just been allocated, or because they are being phased out. Moreover, some blackspace networks are originated by tier-1 ISPs. Consequently, these networks are unlikely to be maliciously announced. All other networks need to be further analyzed in order to assess their threat level. To carry out this analysis, the next Section will be focusing on uncovering the application-level services running in the blackspace and seeking for hosts associated with malicious network activities.

3.3   Data Plane and Application-Level Analysis

A. Introduction. In the previous Sections, we have explored the routing-level characteristics of blackspace networks. We have identified a small number of network practices leading to benign blackspace announcements. In order to be able to assess the security risk that is posed by the remaining set of blackspace prefixes, we need to know more about their network activities, e.g. which application-level services are running and whether they are known to be the source of some malicious network traffic. For this, we first need to find out live

Table 1. Breakdown of application-level activities in the blackspace.

Domain-based reputation (Sect. 3.3.B)	Total	Domain names	556
		Hostnames	1,428
	Malicious	Domain names	35
		Hostnames	222
		IP addresses	142
		IP prefixes	81
	Benign	Domain names	5
IP-based reputation (Sect. 3.3.C)	Malicious	IP addresses	46
		IP prefixes	28
Spam (Sect. 3.3.D)	Malicious	IP addresses	206,404
		IP prefixes	58
SPAMTRACER [22] (Sect. 3.3.E)	Malicious	IP prefixes	82

IP addresses and domain names, and we will then look at the services that these machines are running and check them against logs of malicious network activities. Table 1 summarizes our findings.

In order to discover live IP addresses, we lightly probed each of the blackspace networks once per day in February and March 2015, except for ten days between Feb 16 and Feb 26 when our modem broke down. Using zmap [7], we sent a TCP SYN packet to each IP address included in a blackspace prefix on ports 21 (FTP), 22 (SSH), 25 (SMTP), 80 (HTTP), 137 (NetBios), 179 (BGP), and 443 (HTTPS). We run the scan from a machine located in AS3215 (Orange), and wait for SYN/ACK replies. Please note that the number of ports that we can scan is limited by the bandwidth we have been allowed to use for our experiments. The particular choice of the port number reflects what we believe to be the most popular services running on the Internet.

Figure 8 plots the number of SYN/ACK received per day and per port from the blackspace. There is quite a large number of web servers running in the blackspace. We customarily get replies from between 6 k and 8 k machines on port 80, and 2.5 k machines on port 443. Next is port 22, with around 1 k daily SYN/ACKs. There are around 100 FTP servers, and around 50 hits on port 179, suggesting that these IP addresses are border routers. Finally, we only get a handful of TCP replies on the NetBios port, and no reply at all on port 25.

Figure 9 plots the variation of the live IP addresses in the blackspace, which indicates the persistence of these IP addresses. As we can see, the variation is quite high. These results need to be put into perspective of Fig. 4 which showed that there was a very small variation in the blackspace networks. This suggests that the hosts inside blackspace networks are not static, but dynamically come and go. In other words, these networks appear to be actively configured, and not left in a 'legacy' state.

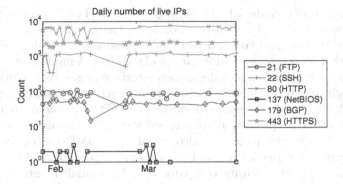

Fig. 8. Daily number of SYN/ACK packets received from the blackspace.

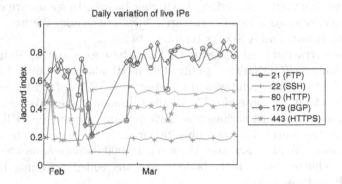

Fig. 9. Day-to-day variation of live IP addresses in the blackspace.

B. Websites, URLs, and Domain Names. In the previous Section, we located a set of highly volatile live IP addresses in the blackspace, and we saw that we found thousands of web servers daily. In this Section, we look at the contents of these websites and their associated URLs and domain names which we match with a domain whitelist and blacklist. A simple way to know what's going on with these servers is to check the web page they serve. As a result, we supplement our scan with a simple HTTP client that just fetches the default page returned by the server, using the simple request `GET / HTTP/1.0`.

Using the returned HTTP headers, we find that over 90 % of pages inside the blackspace are served by an Apache server; then come IIS, and Cisco IOS. Other pages are returned by nginx and lighthttpd, various application platforms, even including a print server. Because we get thousands of pages per day, we cannot manually go through all of them. In order to help our analysis, we used an unsupervised machine learning tool that clustered our pages based on the similarity of their raw content. We get between 60 and 80 clusters. The most important one contains over 4000 Apache error pages. This implies that, for the most part, the default page of web servers located in the blackspace is an Apache error page. Other clusters include default web pages of each HTTP daemon (e.g. your installation was successful). Websites hosted in the blackspace are usually in small clusters containing two or three IP addresses, which we checked in order to conclude that they represent wide variety of websites. A number of login pages are available, either to enter a configuration interface (e.g. a router/printer configuration login page), but also web applications such as Microsoft applications (e.g. Outlook Web Access), remote desktops (e.g. Citrix), content management systems, and other proprietary corporate software. A large airline consistently served their default web page. We also found some SME businesses, such as technology firms (e.g. tier-3 ISPs and local shops), a second-hand car dealer, a law firm, and a private security company. Finally, a small number of clusters contained online forums. From the content of the topics available on the default page, their content varied from standard community interest (e.g. online gaming), to obvious copyright infringing file sharing boards. In some rare cases, the retrieved page contained a lot of obfuscated JavaScript code. We used wepawet [5,25] to check it out, and it always remained benign.

We further extracted from a passive DNS database we maintain all fully qualified domain names (FQDNs) that resolved to an IP address within a blackspace IP prefix at the time the prefix was announced in BGP. We found a total 1,428 distinct FQDNs that accounted for 556 distinct domain names. We then checked these domain names against various blacklists including Spamhaus DBL [17] and VirusTotal [23][1] to search for scam, phishing or malware hosting activities associated with them. We also used the Alexa top 10,000 domain names as a means to determine whether some truly benign domains ended up being hosted on blackspace IP address space.

The correlation yielded 35 domains deemed malicious by the queried blacklists. These malicious domains were observed in no less than 222 different FQDNs, which appear to have resolved to 142 distinct IP addresses in 81 distinct blackspace IP address blocks. However, five domain names were also found in the Alexa top 10,000 ranked websites suggesting they were most probably benign. All of these were whitelisted, and belonged to well-known web applications, airlines, and technology companies. The remaining 516 domains could not be classified as either benign or malicious. From these observations we can see that while some blackspace announcements seem to be related to legitimate activities, cybercriminals also appear to leverage such IP address space when performing nefarious activities.

C. Malicious IP Addresses. In order to locate host-level malicious activities inside blackspace prefixes, we were able to secure a list of malicious IP addresses from a IP-based reputation system that we maintain for operational purposes. These IP addresses were classified as either adware, phishing, scam, and other kinds of miscellaneous activity.

We looked for IP addresses that were included in blackspace prefixes exclusively on the days during which we detected the prefix in the blackspace. In

---

[1] VirusTotal includes more than 60 different website and domain scanning engines.

other words, we explicitly discarded any matching IP address and its covering blackspace prefix where a match occurred outside of the blackspace period, even if there were matches during the blackspace period. The reasoning behind this (overly) strict matching is that we are looking for malicious activity that is the result of an individual abusing the blackspace in order to remain hidden. Thus, any matching malicious activity outside of the blackspace period could be argued to be the result of a previous owner of the prefix, and not from the blackspace itself. With these strict matches, we matched 46 malicious IP addresses in 28 distinct blackspace prefixes. Four of these IPs addresses were involved in scam activities, and the remaining 42 others in phishing activities.

We then looked into these eight BGP prefixes to see if we could obtain more information from the announcements. One of the BGP prefixes was RESERVED and originated by an AS that was marked as AVAILABLE, through what appears to be a tier-3 ISP in Thailand. Six of the other BGP prefixes were also all RESERVED, and originated by registered ASes. Two of these were country-wide ISPs, one was a television by satellite broadcaster, and one belonged to a hosting provider. A European prefix was being announced by the AS of a Japanese corporation, on which we were unable to find any information.

The remaining BGP prefix is 192.0.0.0/2, which we had previously classified as a route leak becaused it mached the descriptions in [11]. This prefix was announced between October 15, 2014 and October 20, 2014. This announcement resulted in an additional 2,970 prefixes in the blackspace (see Fig. 1). Among these, 22 contain IP addresses marked as malicious, exactly during the announcement period. More precisely, a single /24, as well as a /19, both contain 11 individual malicious IP addresses, a /22 contains five, a /20 contains two. The remaining four IP addresses are spread across different blackspace prefixes. It is important to stress that the matches were done exclusively on the blackspace period. Actually, none of these prefixes were routable before or after this leak. The route also had a low visibility: it was only seen by 3 (out of 13) RIPE RIS collector routers; and there is only one single AS path leading to the origin. The origin AS was 65000, a private AS number (Fig. 6), and the route was propagated through one cloud services and hosting provider, and then through a tier-3 ISP in the USA. Section 4 further discusses this peculiar situation.

D. Spam Campaigns. In an effort to further characterize the footprints of blackspace prefixes while they were announced and determine whether they pose a security threat to the Internet, we extracted spam source IP addresses in these prefixes that were blacklisted in Spamhaus SBL and DROP (Don't Route Or Peer) [17], Uceprotect [21], PSBL [13] and WPBL [24]. Furthermore, we retained only those IP prefixes where spam activities were exclusively reported while the prefixes were announced as blackspace to ensure that the observed activities were not related to the previous or next status of the prefixes. We identified a total of 206,404 distinct spam sources in 58 IP prefixes. Figure 10 shows the BGP announcements and blacklisted spam sources related to a sample of 15 out of 58 blackspace prefixes while they were announced as blackspace.

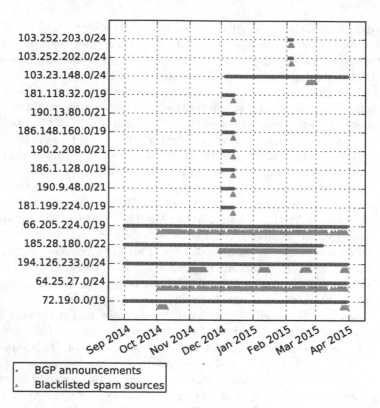

Fig. 10. BGP announcements and blacklisted spam sources related to IP prefixes while they were announced as blackspace. For the sake of conciseness, only 15 out of 58 prefixes that were blacklisted are depicted.

Finally, we correlated the list of blackspace IP prefixes with the output of SPAMTRACER [22], a system specifically designed to identify network IP address ranges that are hijacked by spammers to enable them to send spam while remaining hidden. Relying on a combination of BGP and traceroute data collected for networks seen originating spam and a set of specifically tailored heuristics, the system identifies those spam networks that exhibit a routing behavior likely indicating they were hijacked. We found that 82 IP prefixes were reported by SPAMTRACER as hijacked spam networks at the same time we identified them as being part of the blackspace.

E. Case Study. Starting from the 82 particularly suspicious blackspace prefixes we uncovered a very interesting phenomenon that we describe in-depth here below. Looking closely at how these 82 network prefixes were announced in BGP revealed that they were all advertised via one AS: AS59790 "H3S Helge Sczepanek trading as H3S medien services". Based on this intriguing observation, we decided to extract from all identified blackspace IP prefixes every of those

that were advertised via AS59790. Surprisingly we discovered that no less than
476 IP prefixes in total (82 of them seen originating spam by SPAMTRACER)
were advertised via AS59790 between October 17, 2014 and January 8, 2015
and that **all of them were part of the blackspace** at the time of the BGP
announcements. Furthermore, all blackspace prefixes actually correspond to IP
address space allocated by the IANA to AfriNIC (the African RIR) but not yet
ALLOCATED or ASSIGNED by AfriNIC to any organization. Looking at the AS
paths in the BGP announcements of the 476 networks

$$\{AS_{collector}, \dots, AS174, \textbf{AS59790}\} \tag{1}$$

$$\{AS_{collector}, \dots, AS174, \textbf{AS59790}, AS201509\} \tag{2}$$

reveals that AS59790 was always connected to a single upstream provider AS174
"Cogent Communications (US)", a cross-continent tier-1 ISP. From the AS paths
we can also see that when AS59790 did not appear as the BGP origin AS (case
1) it was apparently used to provide transit to AS201509 (case 2). AS59790
"H3S Helge Sczepanek trading as H3S medien services (DE)" was ASSIGNED
on September 30, 2014 and AS201509 "Sky Capital Investments Ltd. (DE)"
was ASSIGNED on October 17, 2014, shortly before they started to be used to
announce the blackspace prefixes. Both ASes were registered in the RIPE region
to what appear to be organizations active in the finance industry in Germany.
However, we were unable to find any information regarding these organizations
through extensive web searches. The description of AS59790 and AS201509 in
the IRR reveals that they are in fact under the control of the same person. We
were unable to establish contact or to get any further information by contacting
RIPE.

In summary,

- AS59790 and AS201509 were used to announce a total of 476 blackspace
  prefixes over a period of approximately three weeks;
- these ASes were never used to announced any non-blackspace prefix;
- some of the blackspace prefixes announced were used to send spam, according
  to [22].

The evidence presented here above suggests that these ASes were involved in
malicious BGP announcements of IP blackspace. Moreover, a recent article from
Dyn [6] reported on similar evidence about AS59790 being involved in fraudulent
routing announcements of unallocated African IP address space. This case study
thus tends to confirm the assumption that blackspace IP prefixes are purposefully
used to source different types of malicious network traffic, such as spam, likely
in an effort to hinder traceability.

4   Discussion

In this Section, we address the shortcomings and weaknesses of our methodology.

The results presented in Sect. 3 offer a granularity of one day. This can be explained by the following reasons. First, the data sources that we use to compute the blackspace – i.e. the IRR databases and the RIR delegated files – are only updated once per day. Second, because we are actively probing the blackspace networks, we are effectively limited by the capacity of our Internet connection. In order to comfortably run this scan in its entirety (i.e. the equivalent /10 blackspace on 7 ports, with the additional web crawling), we need, on average, 17 h. As a result, we cannot do more than a single scan per day. Third, and consequently, we use routing table dumps from RIPE RIS instead of BGP messages. Routing table dumps are generated every 8 h and contain the entirety of the routes known by the router. The dumps of BGP messages are generated every 5 min and contain all the BGP messages exchanged between the collector routers and one of its peers. With those, we would obtain a much better granularity of data, maybe even include more prefixes in the blackspace. However, since we were mainly focusing on the accurate detection of blackspace prefixes, and on the discovery of the network footprints that they have, as well as the malicious activities they carry out, we think our results are still representative. Short-lived hijacks occurring in the blackspace would not enable an attacker to host a scam website, for example.

Our probing is done from a single machine located in AS3215 (Orange). While this gives us plenty of control over the environment in which our experiment is deployed, it comes at the price of a few drawbacks. First, we don't know anything regarding the BGP-view of the network we are connected in. In other words, we are using BGP data from RIPE RIS as the source of our control-plane data, and the Orange network in order to explore the connectivity. Even though Orange is a tier-1 network, we could not find any direct peering between 'our' AS and a RIPE collector. Actually, AS3215 is routed through AS5511 – better known as OpenTransit – which contains Orange's tier-1 infrastructure. This potentially leads to false negative in our measurements, especially in the case low-visibility prefixes, such as the route leak of 192.0.0.0/2 in which we detected malicious IP addresses (Sect. 3.3.C). Would probes sent from our vantage point have reached the originating network, or would they have been dropped because there would be no "route to host"? The optimal way to carry out these measurements is from a machine that runs BGP so as to assess the reachability of the destination.

At the beginning of Sect. 3, we saw two BGP events leading to a sudden and massive increase of the blackspace size. We classified these events as route leaks because they were only seen by a handful of RIPE collectors – three collectors for the leak in October; one collector for the one in January – and because there was only a single AS path between the collector(s) and the origin. However, because we also detected malicious activities inside of them, the question of whether these events were deliberate attacks disguised as route leaks needs to be raised. Unfortunately, we cannot provide a definite answer. But a recent report underlined highly localised BGP hijacks, engineered to have a very low footprint, and to remain invisible from the point of views of route collectors [20].

5   Related Work

The oldest report of malicious activities carried out from the bogon address space dates back to 2001 with [19], where the author provided an analysis of the attacks carried out against an active web site. A large proportion of attacks originated from bogon addresses: 13 % from within the bogons of classes A, B, and C; 53 % from classes D (multicast) and E (future use). All in all, by properly filtering incoming traffic at a border router, 66 % of attacks could easily be mitigated.

As a result, Team Cymru set up the bogon reference project [18], which precisely defines the different categories of bogon prefixes. We used this as the basis of our definitions in Sect. 2. Additionally, multiple lists of bogon prefixes are offered to network owners who wish to filter bogons out of their networks, which can be retrieved in many convenient ways and formats. These lists vary according to the desired level of precision. The bogon lists contain the prefixes still reserved in the IANA pool, as well as prefixes reserved by RFCs for specific use cases. The *full* bogon list supplements these prefixes with prefixes that have been allocated to RIRs by the IANA, but not by RIRs to ISPs or end users. These lists are dynamic, and network operators that use them should update their filters accordingly. Unfortunately, the methodology used to populate these lists is not disclosed. By comparing the full bogon list with our blackspace list, we were able to identify key differences. First, the full bogon list does not make use of the IRRs, as evidenced by many prefixes for which an inetnum object could be found. Second, the full bogon list appears to implement some heuristics based on the status of the prefixes. For example, we noticed that prefixes whose status transitioned from either ALLOCATED or ASSIGNED to RESERVED were not listed in the full bogon list. We also noticed that some prefixes that were RESERVED for a long time were not listed, although it might be that the transition happened before our data was gathered. We ignore the motivations behind these heuristics. However, the comparison of our blackspace list with the full bogon list on the same day shows that using the IRR databases in addition to the RIR delegation files improves the accuracy of the list.

In 2004, Feamster et al. [8] provided the first formal study of bogon prefixes by looking into the prevalence and persistence of bogon announcements, as well as the origin ASes leaking these prefixes. However, the authors did not explicitly focus on the blackspace, but rather on the equivalent of the (simple) bogon list. Consequently, 70 % of the analyzed events actually involve the prefixes reserved for the private IP space. Only 40 % of the events lasted longer than a day. In our analysis, this value is of 75 % (Fig. 3). The rest of the study cannot be directly mapped onto our results, even though the beginning of Sect. 3 provides results to similar questions. However, with the authors' methodology, there is a one-to-one mapping between the BGP routing table and the bogon analysis. With this, they can focus on the number of bogon prefixes announced by an AS. In our case, we have a one-to-n relationship between the BGP prefix and the blackspace prefixes because we divide the BGP announcement in separate parts that may have been assigned independently. The authors also focus on the effect of bogon filtering and show that network operators who filter out bogon prefixes usually do not update their filters in timely fashion, resulting in reachability issues and potential denial of service. It is also worth noting that the bogon prefixes used for the study were composed of the 78 /8 prefixes that still belonged to the IANA pool back then (excluding class E). Today, the IANA pool only consists of one single /8 prefix, 0.0.0.0/8 (also excluding 240.0.0.0/4). As a result, the IP address space inside which our studies have been conducted is much different.

6   Conclusion

In this paper, we focused on the IP blackspace, which is composed of the set of prefixes that are globally announced through BGP but have not been assigned for use to any entity. We presented a thorough methodology to compute the blackspace by using a combination of data sources reflecting the current allocations of the IP space. We saw that the daily blackspace address space is equivalent to a /10 prefix, and that the prefixes that compose it change over time. We actively studied those networks from the BGP control plane point of view, and also from the data plane point of view. While we showed that some of the blackspace is composed of prefixes that are either being phased out of the Internet or being installed, a significant part of it does not result from normal network operations, such as assignments and decommissions. By cross-checking with various reliable security data sources, we were able to isolate malicious activities that only occurred during a period in which the monitored prefixes were inside the blackspace. Even by using our strict matching rules, and our limited, targeted view of these networks, the amount of malicious activities is significant. In particular, we showed through a validated case study that cybercriminals **do** abuse blackspace prefixes to carry out nefarious activities while also hindering their traceability.

Consequently, this paper confirms how important it is to precisely filter blackspace prefixes out of BGP. Because state-of-the-art hijacking detection tools (such as Argus [16]) do not focus on detecting this particular form of hijack, filtering out routes to the blackspace is the only active counter-measure that can be used today against blackspace hijacks. However, the shape of the blackspace is dynamic, and previous studies [4,8] have illustrated that, when a bogon filter has been setup, it is obsolete because it is not updated, thereby affecting the connectivity towards networks that are being added to the Internet. Moreover, the current source of bogon filtering [18] does not take into account `inetnum` entries from IRR databases, thus including – and preventing access to – networks that have been assigned to a customer.

This paper also underlines the difficulty of using a ground truth in BGP. Even though the prefixes that we focused on all have in common the fact that they should not even be used on the public Internet, we were able to show cases where their use was the result of legitimate practices. As a result it is still quite difficult to automate the estimation of the danger resulting from a particular prefix in the blackspace.

We plan to improve on our system in the following ways. First, we plan to define a set of reliable heuristics that would discard benign blackspace announcements and only retain those that are potentially harmful, thus increasing the quality of filters installed on routers. Second, we would like to supplement our probing system with a traceroute infrastructure that would enable us to geographically locate the origin of these networks, and the diversity of their connectivity. This would enable us to see if there are specific parts of the networks that hijackers prefer to abuse. Third, we need to view the BGP control plane, as well as the data plane from the same vantage point in order to make sure we reach low visibility routes. For this, we need a set of geographically diversified machines that run BGP – each connected to a different set of peers – and from which we can run our measurement experiments. If this can be achieved, a bonus point would be to make the system run in real time, by detecting and probing networks as they come and go in the BGP routing table. Our results currently focus on the IPv4 address space, inside of which the unallocated space is getting smaller every day. It would be interesting to do the same measurements with IPv6, and see how the results compare. As a final remark, note that we are able to provide interested parties with more detailed results and to discuss future work that can be undertaken with this dataset and infrastructure.

References

1. APNIC: Understanding address management hierarchy. http://www.apnic.net/services/manage-resources/address-management-objectives/management-hierarchy
2. APNIC: Using Whois: Quick Beginners Guide. http://www.apnic.net/apnic-info/whois_search/using-whois/guide
3. ARIN: Extended Allocation and Assignment Report for RIRs. https://www.arin.net/knowledge/statistics/nro_extended_stats_format.pdf
4. Bush, R., Hiebert, J., Maennel, O., Roughan, M., Uhlig, S.: Testing the reachability of (new) address space. In: Proceedings of the 2007 SIGCOMM Workshop on Internet Network Management, INM 2007, pp. 236–241 (2007)
5. Cova, M., Kruegel, C., Vigna, G.: Detection and analysis of drive-by-download attacks and malicious JavaScript code. In: Proceedings of the World Wide Web Conference (WWW) (2010)
6. Madory, D.: The Vast World of Fraudulent Routing, January 2015. http://research.dyn.com/2015/01/vast-world-of-fraudulent-routing/. Accessed 5 June 2015
7. Durumeric, Z., Wustrow, E., Halderman, J.A.: ZMap: fast internet-wide scanning and its security applications. In: Proceedings of the 22nd USENIX Security Symposium, August 2013
8. Feamster, N., Jung, J., Balakrishnan, H.: An empirical study of "bogon" route advertisements. Comput. Commun. Rev. 35(1), 63–70 (2004)
9. Huston, G.: AS names. http://bgp.potaroo.net/cidr/autnums.html
10. Huston, G.: RIR Resource Allocation Data Inconsistencies. http://www.cidr-report.org/bogons/rir-data.html
11. Mahajan, R., Wetherall, D., Anderson, T.: Understanding BGP misconfiguration. SIGCOMM Comput. Commun. Rev. 32(4), 3–16 (2002)
12. Mitchell, J.: Autonomous System (AS) Reservation for Private Use. RFC 6996, July 2013

13. Passive Spam Block List. http://psbl.org/
14. RIPE NCC: FAQ: Becoming a member. https://www.ripe.net/lir-services/member-support/info/faqs/faq-joining
15. RIPE NCC: Routing Information Service. http://www.ripe.net/ris/
16. Shi, X., Xiang, Y., Wang, Z., Yin, X., Wu, J.: Detecting prefix hijackings in the internet with argus. In: Proceedings of the 12th ACM SIGCOMM Internet Measurement Conference, IMC 2012, pp. 15–28 (2012)
17. Spamhaus. http://www.spamhaus.org/
18. Team Cymru: The Bogon Reference. http://www.team-cymru.org/bogon-reference.html
19. Thomas, R.: 60 Days of Basic Naughtiness: Probes and Attacks Endured by an Active Web Site. http://www.team-cymru.org/documents/60Days.ppt, March 2001
20. Toonk, A.: Recent BGP routing incidents - malicious or not. Presentation at NANOG 63, February 2015
21. Uceprotect. http://www.uceprotect.net/
22. Vervier, P.A., Thonnard, O., Dacier, M.: Mind your blocks: on the stealthiness of malicious BGP hijacks. In: NDSS 2015, Network and Distributed System Security Symposium, February 2015
23. VirusTotal. https://www.virustotal.com/
24. Weighted Private Block List. http://www.wpbl.info/
25. Wepawet. http://wepawet.cs.ucsb.edu

Providing Dynamic Control to Passive Network Security Monitoring

Johanna Amann[1]([✉]) and Robin Sommer[1,2]

[1] International Computer Science Institute, Berkeley, USA
[2] Lawrence Berkeley National Laboratory, Berkeley, USA
{johanna,robin}@icir.org

Abstract. Passive network intrusion detection systems detect a wide range of attacks, yet by themselves lack the capability to actively respond to what they find. Some sites thus provide their IDS with a separate control channel back to the network, typically by enabling it to dynamically insert ACLs into a gateway router for blocking IP addresses. Such setups, however, tend to remain narrowly tailored to the site's specifics, with little opportunity for reuse elsewhere, as different networks deploy a wide array of hard- and software and differ in their network topologies. To overcome the shortcomings of such ad-hoc approaches, we present a novel *network control framework* that provides passive network monitoring systems with a flexible, unified interface for active response, hiding the complexity of heterogeneous network equipment behind a simple task-oriented API. Targeting operational deployment in large-scale network environments, we implement the design of our framework on top of an existing open-source IDS. We provide exemplary backends, including an interface to OpenFlow hardware, and evaluate our approach in terms of functionality and performance.

1 Introduction

Network intrusion detection and prevention systems (IDS and IPS, respectively) detect a wide range of attacks, including port- and address scans for reconnaissance, SSH brute-forcing, attempts to exploit specific vulnerabilities (e.g., Heartbleed), and also complex multi-step APT-style attacks. An *IPS* operates *inline* within the network's forwarding path, enabling the system to actively react to an intrusion by, e.g., blocking the specific connection or more generally any traffic originating from the same IP address. Operationally, however, inline operation often remains impractical, as it adds a complex device into the forwarding path that increases latencies and jitter, and risks causing disruption if malfunctioning. Furthermore, for the largest of environments—such as the quickly growing set of 100 G *Science DMZs* [20]—arguable no IPS (or firewall) can today operate at their line rates at all [9]. More commonly, network environments thus deploy a passive *IDS* instead, operating out-of-band on an independent copy of the network traffic coming from a tap or SPAN port. To still support active response in that setting, some sites then provide their IDS with a separate control channel

© Springer International Publishing Switzerland 2015
H. Bos et al. (Eds.): RAID 2015, LNCS 9404, pp. 133–152, 2015.
DOI: 10.1007/978-3-319-26362-5_7

back to the network, most typically by having it dynamically insert ACLs or null routes into a gateway router for blocking IP addresses. Such setups, however, tend to remain narrowly tailored to the site's network topology and the specific equipment it deploys, offering little opportunity for reuse elsewhere and posing challenges for testing, maintenance, and extension.

To overcome the shortcomings of such ad-hoc approaches, we present a novel *network control framework* that provides passive network monitoring systems with a flexible, unified interface for active response, hiding the complexity of heterogeneous network equipment behind a simple task-oriented API. We structure our network control framework around four low-level traffic control primitives: dropping, whitelisting, redirection, and modification. From these, we then compose a set of higher-level tasks that an IDS can chose to deploy, such as blocking IP addresses, shunting traffic for load shedding, quarantining infected hosts, and enforcing quality-of-service guarantees. Internally, we map the primitives to rules that the network control framework forwards to a set of pre-configured backends representing the network's devices able to carry out the corresponding actions (e.g., routers, switches, firewalls). When multiple components can execute a rule, the network control framework automatically selects the most appropriate. It also transparently unifies inconsistencies between device semantics.

Our framework targets operational deployment in large-scale network environments with link capacities of 10 G and beyond. We implement the design of our framework on top of an existing open-source IDS that such environments commonly deploy. We provide exemplary backends for OpenFlow and *acld* [1], as well as a generic backend driving command-line tools (which we demonstrate with Linux iptables). Using the OpenFlow backend, we evaluate our approach through case studies involving real-world tasks and traffic. We release our implementation as open-source software under BSD license [14].

Overall, our work offers a new capability combining the advantages of unobtrusive passive monitoring with the ability to actively react swiftly and comprehensively through a unified architecture that can replace today's ad-hoc setups. While our discussion focuses primarily on the security domain, the network control framework's potential extends more broadly to traffic engineering applications well, as our quality-of-service use case demonstrates.

We structure the remainder of this paper as follows: Sect. 2 discusses use cases for our system. Section 3 presents the design of the network control framework, and Sect. 4 describes our implementation. Section 5 introduces the backends that the network control framework currently supports, and Sect. 6 evaluates the framework. Section 7 discusses the related work before our paper concludes in Sect. 8.

2   Use Cases

We begin by discussing four high-level IDS use-cases that our network control framework facilitates. Traditionally, a site would implement each of these separately, typically with homegrown scripts that cater to their network environment. The network control framework instead offers a high-level API that supports these use cases directly, internally breaking them down into lower-level rules that it then carries out through an appropriate backend.

Dynamic Firewall. The network control framework enables an IDS to dynamically block traffic that it deems hostile. Typical examples include stopping a connection exhibiting illegitimate activity, and dropping connectivity for hosts probing the network. In contrast to a traditional firewall, an IDS can derive such decisions dynamically by analyzing session content and tracking over time the state of any entities it observes. For example, the Lawrence Berkeley National Laboratory (LBNL), a research lab with a staff size of about 4,000 and 100 G connectivity, blocks an average of about 6,000 to 7,000 IPs each day using a custom setup that interfaces the Bro IDS [17] with their border router through a separate daemon process, *acld* [1]. Indiana University, which has more than 100,000 students and multiple 10GE uplinks, blocks an average of 500 to 600 IPs per day, also using a custom setup processing data from Bro and Snort.

Shunting. Flow shunting [7,11] reduces the load on an IDS by asking the network to no longer send it further traffic for high-volume connections that it has identified as benign. In scientific environments, shunting typically targets large file transfers: once identified as such, there remains little value in inspecting their content in depth. Shedding the corresponding load leaves more resources for inspecting the remaining traffic, which in turn then allows a site to provision less IDS capacity than the full volume would require. Two sites using this approach effectively are LBNL and UIUC's *National Center for Supercomputing Applications* (NCSA). Both places currently implement shunting for GridFTP traffic with custom scripts that exploit the specifics of their network environments. On a typical day in these environments, shunting reduces the total traffic volume by about 37 % and 32 %, respectively.

Quarantine. When an IDS identifies a local system as compromised, it can—as a protective measure—redirect any new connections from that host to an internal web server that informs the user of the problem. Traditionally, implementing such a quarantine mechanism constitutes a complex task operationally, as it needs to interact closely with the local network infrastructure. For example, the Munich Scientific Network (MSN) deploys a custom NAT system [21] for quarantining that implements the corresponding logic for local end-user systems by combining a number of existing software components.

Quality-of-Service. Going beyond the security domain, the network control framework also facilitates more general traffic engineering applications. By steering traffic to different switch ports or VLANs, one can route entities over paths with different properties. For example, a Science DMZ might want to send a high-volume data transfer onto a different *virtual circuit* that provides bandwidth guarantees [15]. Another use case is bandwidth throttling. For DDOS mitigation, one can move a local target server to a different ingress path enforcing a rate-limit, thereby relieving pressure for the remaining traffic. Likewise, a network monitor might decide to throttle individual P2P clients that it finds exceeding their bandwidth quota.

3   Design

In this work, we introduce a network control framework that enables passive monitoring applications to transparently exercise control over heterogeneous network components like switches, routers, and firewalls. In this section, we discuss the design of the network control framework, starting with its overarching objectives in Sect. 3.1.

3.1   Objectives

Our design of the network control framework aims for the following objectives:

Simple, Yet Flexible API. The network control framework's API needs to provide sufficient abstraction to make it straight-forward to use, yet remain flexible to support a variety of use cases. The API should support common high-level tasks directly (like blocking and shunting), while leaving lower-level functionality accessible that enables users to compose their own.

Unification of Heterogeneous Network Components. Sites deploy a variety of network equipment with different capabilities and semantics. The network control framework needs to unify their differences through an API that abstracts from device specifics.

Support for Complex Topologies. As networks can have complex structures, the network control framework needs to support instantiating multiple backends simultaneously, to then chose the most appropriate for each rule. For example, actions that block traffic might need to address a different device than reducing the load on the IDS through shunting. Likewise, one device may support a specific operation better, or more efficiently, than another (e.g., MAC address filtering vs. IPv6 filtering; or when dropping traffic, being closer to the source).

Unification of Forwarding and Monitoring Path. The network control framework provides control over both traffic that the network forwards and traffic that the IDS receives for processing from its tap or SPAN port. Even though the effect of manipulating them is quite different—rules on the forwarding path affect end-users, while the monitoring path only changes what the IDS' analyzes— the corresponding operations remain conceptually similar. The network control framework should thus unify the two behind a single interface.

Low Latency. The network control framework has to apply new rules rapidly. The main difference between a passive IDS and an inline IPS is the latency with which active response takes place. While network control framework can fundamentally not match an IPS' instantaneous action, the network control framework must add as little delay as possible to any latency that the devices impose that it controls.

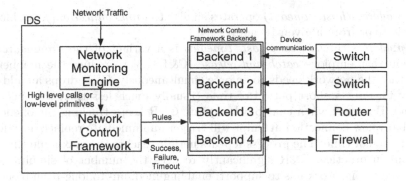

Fig. 1. Basic architecture.

3.2 Architecture

Figure 1 shows the overall architecture of the network control framework, located inside an IDS as a subcomponent. The IDS deploys its standard detection mechanisms (signatures, analysis scripts, etc.) to asses the traffic it sees. Once it decides to take action (e.g., block a scanner), it directs the network control framework to carry that out, using either its *high-level API* if that supports the use case directly through one of its operations, or *lower-level primitives* to compose non-standard functionality. In the former case, the network control framework internally maps the high-level API call to a sequence of corresponding low-level primitives. In either case, it then forwards the primitives to a set of *backends* in the form of *rules* for them to install. Each backend corresponds to a device on the network able to carry out actions. When operators register their devices with the network control framework, they provide the corresponding backend instance with the information how to communicate with the physical device (e.g., the IP address of an OpenFlow switch), as well as potentially further context information about the device's capabilities and location (e.g., the IP space behind a switch). They also assign each backend a priority. For each new rule, the network control framework then iterates through all available backends, from highest priority to lowest priority, until one confirms that it successfully executed the desired action. If no backend accepts the rule, the operation fails. In the following subsections, we elaborate further on the main parts of this overall scheme.

3.3 High-Level Operations

The network control framework supports eight predefined high-level operations, which provide for the most common IDS use cases:

drop_connection(connection, timeout) facilitates dynamic firewalling by terminating a connection through blocking its packets on the forwarding path. It receives the connection's 5-tuple as a parameter, as well as a timeout indicating the duration for the block to stay in place.

drop_address(host, timeout) operates similar to *drop_connection()*, yet blocks all traffic to or from a given IP address.

drop_address_catch_release(host, timeout) is a variant of the *drop_address()* operation that employs *catch-and-release* (C&R) [8] to reduce the number of blocks that the network needs to enforce simultaneously. C&R drops an address initially for only a short period of time (usually much less than the specified timeout). However, when that block expires, C&R keeps tracking the offending IP, and any new connection attempt will trigger an immediate reblock, now for a longer period of time. The process repeats until it reaches the maximum timeout duration. In practice, C&R significantly reduces the number of simultaneous blocks that the network has to support, enabling medium- to long-term blocking while remaining parsimonious with switch &router memory resources.

shunt_flow(flow, timeout) drops a unidirectional flow (specified in the form of its 5-tuple) from the *monitoring* path for a specified duration. This allows, e.g., to remove a large file transfer from the IDS' input stream. As on high-volume connections the bulk of the data tends to flow in one direction only, this operation leaves the other side of the session unaffected.

quarantine(Infected, DNS server, Quarantine server, timeout) isolates an internal host (infected) by blocking all of its traffic except for DNS, which it reroutes to a Quarantine server running an instrumented DNS server that always returns the IP address of itself for any hostname lookup. The quarantine server also runs a web server that can then serve a web page to the host informing end users of the reason for quarantining them.

redirect(flow, destination port, timeout) redirects a unidirectional flow to a different output port on a switch. This allows, e.g., to control quality-of-service properties by steering the traffic to a dedicated port/link.

whitelist(prefix, timeout) whitelists a network prefix so that no other network control framework operation will affect it. This serves as a safety measure, e.g., to avoid blocking critical servers or, more generally, IP space from upstream service providers like Amazon or Google.

All of these operations returns an opaque handle associated with the changes they put in place. An additional *remove(handle)* function uninstalls the operation even before it timeout expires.

3.4 Low-Level Primitives

After introducing the high-level operations of the network control framework in Sect. 3.3, this section shows how users can manually create lower-level rules through a more verbose, but powerful API that directly exposes the primitives underlying the network control framework.

Generally, a *rule* describes an action to perform on a traffic subset through a set of attributes; see Table 1. Each rule consists of three primary components: *(i)* the *type* of action to perform (e.g., *drop*); *(ii)* the *entity* to apply the action to (e.g., a specific IP address); and *(iii)* the *target* network path to operate on (forwarding or monitoring). The rule type specifies the action to perform on all of the entity's traffic, with four choices currently supported: *drop* (drop all traffic matching entity), *whitelist* (leave entity unaffected of any other

Table 1. Summary of network control framework rules.

Rule Specification:

Type	Type of Rule (*Drop*, *Modify*, *Redirect*, or *Whitelist*).
Target	Rule targets either the *Forward* or *Monitor* path.
Entity	*Entity* (IP Address, Mac, Flow or Connection) to match.
Timeout	Interval after which the rule is expired (default: No timeout).
Priority	Rule priority; higher priority rules take precedence (default: 0).
Mod	Modification Specification (mandatory for *Modify* rules).
RedirectTo	Port Specification (mandatory for *Redirect* rules).
Location	String description of Rule. (optional)

Entities:

Address Entity: *IP Address*	Specifies an IP address; traffic from and to address is matched.
MAC Entity: *Mac Address*	Specifies a MAC address; traffic from and to address is matched.
Connection Entity: *Source IP, Source Port, Destination IP, Destination Port*	Specifies a bi-directional connection by its 5-tuple.
Flow Entity: *Src. & Dest. Network, Src. & Dest. Port, Src. & Dest. MAC*	Specifies an uni-directional flow; wildcards allowed for all fields.

Modification Specification:

4-tuple	Modify any or all of source, destination IP and port. (optional)
Source & Dest. MAC	Modify source and/or destination MAC. (optional)
Output port	Specify output port (optional).

rule), *redirect* (steer entity to a different output port), and *modify* (change content of entity's packets). The network control framework supports five types of entities: unidirectional *flows*, bi-directional *connections*, *IP addresses*, *network prefixes*, and layer-2 *MAC addresses*. Rules specify flows/connections through their 5-tuples, with support for wildcards as tuple elements. For IPs, prefixes, and MACs, a rule always matches any traffic involving that entity, regardless of direction. In addition to the three mandatory *type*, *entity*, and *target* attributes, Table 1 shows further options that rules support, including: *Priority* resolves conflicts if multiple rules match the same traffic; *Modify* augments modify actions by defining the change to perform; and *RedirectTo* specifies the target port. Internally, the network control framework converts all the high-level operations from Sect. 3.3 into such rules. For example, consider *shunt_flow*. In this case, the network control framework creates a rule as follows, dropping all traffic for the specified 5-tuple on the monitoring path:

```
Rule(Type=Drop, Entity=Flow([5-tuple]), Target=Monitor)
```

Implementing *quarantine* is more complex, with four separate rules:

```
Rule(Type=Drop, Entity=Flow(SrcIp=[Infected]), Target=Forward)

Rule(Type=Redirect, Priority=1,
    Entity=Flow(SrcIP=[Infected], DstIp=[DNS server], DstPort=53/udp),
    Modify(DestIp=[Quarantine Srv]), Target=Forward)

Rule(Type=Redirect, Priority=1,
    Entity=Flow(SrcIp=[Quarantine Srv], SrcPort=53/udp, DstIp=[Infected]),
    Modify(SrcIp=[DNS Server]), Target=Forward)
```

```
Rule(Type=Whitelist, Priority=1,
    Entity=Flow(SrcIp=[Host], DstIp=[QuarantineHost], DstPort=80/tcp),
    Target=Forward)
```

The first rule blocks all traffic from the infected host using the default priority of 0. The second and third higher priority rules modify *(i)* DNS requests from the quarantined host to go to the dedicated quarantine server, and *(ii)* DNS server responses to appear as coming from the original server. The fourth rule permits port 80 requests from the infected host to the quarantine server.

3.5 Adaptability to Networks

The network control framework's support for multiple backends enables pushing out a rule to the device most appropriate for putting it into effect. Consider, for example, an environment with several switches, each responsible for a specific IP subnet. One can add each of them to the network control framework by instantiating a corresponding backend, configuring each to only accept rules for the switch's IP range. When installing a rule, the network control framework will iterate through the backends until reaching the appropriate switch, which will signal that it can handle it. As another example, an environment could block traffic by deploying a combination of a firewall and a router. The router could drop individual IP addresses efficiently using its hardware lookup tables, but might not be able to match on other fields like TCP/UDP ports and would hence reject corresponding requests. The less efficient firewall would then provide a fall-back accepting all other rules.

Backend priorities allow to fine-tune the selection of backends further. When instantiating multiple backends with the same priority, the network control framework will install a rule through *all* of them. This supports, e.g., the case of multiple border routers connecting to different upstream providers: blocking IPs should take effect on all of their links. Shunting on the monitoring path provides an example for using different priorities. Generally, shunting should happen as close to the tap as possible. As a fallback, however, in case the closest switch does not support the necessary drop rule, one can always have the local IDS host itself filter out the traffic at the NIC level; that way the packets at least do not reach the IDS' processing. To support this scenario, one would instantiate a high priority backend for the switch, and a low priority backend for kernel-level filtering on the IDS system.

3.6 Unifying State Management

The network control framework installs control rules dynamically as the IDS identifies corresponding patterns. Typically, such rules remain valid only for moderate periods of time, from a few minutes to hours. Afterwards, they need to expire so that network behavior reverts back to normal and resources on the devices free up. The network control framework thus supports timeouts as an intrinsic part of its architecture; all operations and rules include them. Internally, however, handling timeouts requires managing the corresponding state, which poses a challenge. While some backends can support rule expiration directly through device mechanisms (e.g., OpenFlow can time out rules), not all have that capability (e.g., acld). For backends without corresponding support, the network control framework includes a software implementation as an optional service that a backend can leverage. If activated, the network control framework tracks the backend's active rules with their expiration times, sending it explicit removal requests at the appropriate time. Even if a device supports rule expiration in hardware, a backend might still chose to rely on the network control framework's implementation instead if the device's expiration semantics do not align with the network control framework's API requirements. In either case, from the user's perspective the network control framework reports a notification when a rule expires, including—if the backend supports it—more detailed information about traffic it has matched during its lifetime. Generally, hardware switches track such metrics and the network control framework passes it along.

State management introduces a challenge when either the IDS or a device restarts, as generally that means the system will loose any rules it has installed. On the IDS side, one can conceptually solve that rather easily by having the system retain state persistently across restarts, either through serialization at termination time or by directly maintaining the information in a on-disk database. Once the system is back up again, it can then timeout any rules that have expired during the downtime, sending removal commands to their backends. On the device side, handling restarts proves more challenging. One approach would be replaying all the rules from IDS memory. That however could impose significant load on the device (e.g., imagine reinstalling thousands of IP address blocks). It would also require actually *recognizing* that a device has restarted, a task that turns out difficult to perform for some backends (e.g., OpenFlow switches do generally not signal restarts explicitly). Therefore, the network control framework accepts that rebooting a switch means that it will loose all its rules; the framework will continue operation as if nothing had happened. In practice the impact of this approach remains low, as due to the dynamic nature of rules in our use cases, their lifetime tends to remain short anyways. For rules that target individual flows, chances are the session will have terminated already when the device is back up. Even for long-lived flows, reverting back to normal operation occasionally usually proves fine (e.g., when shunting, load will increase back to the full level briefly). For more general rules, the higher-level analysis can often compensate for the rare case of a device restart by retriggering the original action. For example, when dropping with catch-and-release (see Sect. 2), the IDS will immediately reblock the offender on its next connection attempt. Internally, if the network control framework manages rule expiration it will eventually still send removals for rules that no longer exist after a device restart, which however the backend can ignore.

4   Implementation

We implement the design of the network control framework on top of the open-source Bro Network Security Monitor [5,17]. Bro provides an apt platform for active response as its event-based, Turing-complete scripting language facilitates complex custom policies taking decisions. Furthermore, Bro allows us to implement the network control framework fully inside this language as well, whereas other IDS would typically require integration at a lower level.

4.1   User Interface

The network control framework's user interface consists of a new script-level Bro framework that provides script writers with an interface closely following the design we present in Sect. 3, exposing both the high-level operations as well as the low-level primitives to their custom logic. In the following, we examine two real-world examples of how a Bro user can leverage the network control framework to react to network activity the system observes.

First, consider the case of a high-volume supercomputing environment aiming to shunt all GridFTP [2] data flows, thereby lessening the load on their Bro setup. In this case, as Bro already includes the capability to identify GridFTP transfers, one can hook the network control framework's high-level *shunt_flow* function, contained in the *NetControl* namespace to Bro's corresponding event by writing a handler like this:

```
event GridFTP::data_channel_detected(c: connection) {
    NetControl::shunt_flow([$src_h=c$id$orig_h, $src_p=c$id$orig_p,
                           $dst_h=c$id$resp_h, $resp_p=c$id$resp_p], 1hr);
}
```

Second, assume we want to block the IP addresses of hosts performing a port or address scan. For that, we hook into Bro's alarm reporting ("notices"):

```
event log_notice(n: Notice::Info) {
  if ( n$note == Address_Scan || n$note == Port_Scan )
    NetControl::drop_address(n$src, 10min);
}
```

Inserting low-level rules likewise closely follows the design from Sect. 3, mapping the rule attributes from Table 1 to corresponding Bro data types. For example, the following shows the actual implementation of the shunt_flow operation in the Bro scripting language. For the most part, the function just converts Bro's data structures into the format that the network control framework expects:

```
function shunt_flow(f: flow_id, t: interval) : string {
  local flow = Flow(
      $src_h=addr_to_subnet(f$src_h), $src_p=f$src_p,
      $dst_h=addr_to_subnet(f$dst_h), $dst_p=f$dst_p
      );
  local e: Entity = [$ty=FLOW, $flow=flow];
  local r: Rule = [$ty=DROP, $target=MONITOR, $entity=e, $expire=t];
  return add_rule(r);
}
```

Since the actual rule operations will execute asynchronously, the network control framework uses Bro events to signal success or failure, as well for reporting a rule's removal along with the corresponding statistics (see Sect. 3.6).

4.2 Adding Backends

As discussed in Sects. 3.2 and 3.5, the network control framework supports multiple backends simultaneously with different priorities. In our Bro implementation, one adds backends at initialization time through corresponding script code:

```
local backend = NetControl::create_backend_Foo([...]);
NetControl::activate(backend, 10);
```

The `create_plugin_Foo` function is part of the backend's implementation and receives any arguments that it requires, for example the IP address and port of a switch to connect to. `activate` then adds the newly minted instance to the network control framework, specifying its priority as well (10 in this example).

The network control framework deploys a plugin model for implementing new backends, making it easy to augment it with support for further devices. Each backend plugin has to implement three functions for *(i)* instantiating a backend of that type, *(ii)* adding rules, and *(iii)* removing rules. Instantation returns an instance of a Bro data type describing the backend with its functions and features (e.g., if the plugin can handle rule expiration itself). Both the add and removal functions receive the backend instance along with the rule as their parameters. The add function returns a boolean indicating if the backend could execute the rule.

5 Backends

In this section we present the different types of backends that our implementation of the network control framework currently supports through plugins that we have implemented: OpenFlow in Sect. 5.1, *acld* in Sect. 5.2, Bro's built-in packet filter in Sect. 5.3, and finally a generic command-line interface in Sect. 5.4.

5.1 OpenFlow

OpenFlow [13] is an SDN protocol that allows applications to control the forwarding plane of a switch (or router) by inserting or removing rules. As switches with OpenFlow support have become both common and affordable, the protocol provides an ideal target for the network control framework to support a range of devices across vendor boundaries. We added OpenFlow support to our implementation in two steps: *(i)* we created a separate abstraction inside Bro, an *OpenFlow module*, that exposes OpenFlow's primitives to Bro scripts through a corresponding API; and *(ii)* we wrote an OpenFlow backend plugin for the network control framework that uses the OpenFlow module for interfacing to

OpenFlow devices. We chose to separate the two, as OpenFlow support may prove useful for applications beyond the network control framework as well.

In a OpenFlow deployment, applications typically do not talk to devices directly, but instead interface to an *OpenFlow controller* that serves as the middle-man. The controller is the component that speaks the actual OpenFlow protocol with the switch ("southbound"), while exposing an external API (e.g., a REST interface) to clients ("northbound"). Unfortunately, there is no standardized northbound interface; depending on the choice of a controller, the mechanisms differ. For our case study, we leveraged the Ryu SDN Framework [19].

Ryu enables creating custom controllers in Python, fully supporting versions OpenFlow 1.0 to 1.3. We leveraged the Ryu API to write an OpenFlow controller interfacing Ryu to Bro's communication protocol, using the *Broker* messaging library [6]. On the Bro side, the OpenFlow module maps OpenFlow messages into corresponding Broker messages, essentially creating our own communication mechanism between the two systems.[1] Figure 2 summarizes the full architecture when using the network control framework with OpenFlow: Messages pass from the network control framework's OpenFlow backend into the OpenFlow module, which in turn sends them over to the controller via Broker. Results travel the same way in reverse.

As an additional feature, the OpenFlow backend supports callback functions that can inspect and modify any OpenFlow messages it generates before passing them on. This allows to, e.g., use fields that OpenFlow supports yet have no equivalent inside the framework (e.g., input ports, or VLAN priorities).

OpenFlow's lack of success messages posed a particular implementation challenge for the backend. Generally, OpenFlow does not acknowledge rules that were successfully installed; it only reports error cases. With the network control framework that proves problematic, as its approach to iterate through all backends make it important to confirm an action's execution. One solution would be to just assume that a rule was successfully applied after a certain amount of

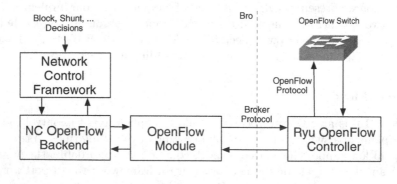

Fig. 2. OpenFlow architecture.

---

[1] Indeed, our Bro OpenFlow module remains independent of Ryu and could support other controllers as well if one extended them with a similar receiver component.

time has passed with no error message. However, this would require choosing a conservative timeout and hence significantly delay the success signal back to the network control framework, contrary to our objective of keeping latencies low. We instead solved this challenge by using OpenFlow's *barrier messages*. When a switch receives a *barrier request*, it will answer with a *barrier reply*, yet only after it has fully processed all preceeding OpenFlow messages. Hence, once the plugin receives a barrier reply, it knows that any operations that have not prompted an explicit error message so far, must have succeeded.

The OpenFlow backend assumes that it can insert rules without conflicting with other applications talking to the same controller and/or switch. In practice, one can typically resolve potential conflicts between applications by associating priorities with the OpenFlow rules, which the backend supports. More generally, Porras et al. [18] present an enhanced controller that mediates conflicts.

5.2 Acld

Acld [1] is a Unix daemon that acts as a middle-man for blocking IP addresses, address pairs, ports, and more; interfacing to a range of hard- and software switches and firewalls, including from Cisco, Juniper, and Force10, as well as BSD ipfw. Acld is, e.g., used by LBNL.

We created an Acld backend for the network control framework that compiles rules into acld's command syntax and then sends them over to the daemon for execution, using again Bro's communication library Broker to implement that communication.[2] Since the actions that acld supports are more limited than the rules that the network control framework can express, the backend checks first if a rule has an acld equivalent, declining it otherwise. Acld does not support rule expiry itself. Instead, the network control framework keeps track of all its rules and removes them automatically after their timeout period.

5.3 IDS Packet Filter

We also provide a backend that targets Bro itself. Bro provides an internal packet filter that allows excluding traffic from further processing early in its processing pipeline. Doing so removes the CPU overhead associated with that traffic, including in particular stream reassembly and protocol analysis. As Papadogiannakis et al. [16] demonstrate, such early filtering can significantly improve IDS performance. We implemented a network control framework backend plugin that emits rules for this Bro-internal packet filter, enabling the network control framework to execute rules for the monitoring path on the IDS system itself. Usually, this backend will represent a fall-back option: if another backend can filter the traffic earlier, that would be the better choice; but if that capability is not available, filtering late remains better than not all.

---

[2] Currently, Bro talks to an intermediary Python script, which in turn relays commands to acld through TCP. We plan to integrate Broker into acld directly in the future.

5.4   Generic Command-Line Interface

As a generic backend, we implemented a command-line interface that allows users
to specify shell commands to execute for installing and removing rules, making
it easy to support network components that come with command-line clients.
As an example, we used this to implement network control framework support
for Linux iptables. Our iptables implementation uses Broker again, similar to
the Ryu OpenFlow interface. In this case, we implemented a Broker backend
for the network control framework itself, which passes the low-level network
control framework data structures to a Broker endpoint outside of Bro. We then
implemented a Python script that receives these Broker messages and executes
custom shell commands that the user specifies through a YAML configuration
file. To pass parameters to these commands (e.g., IP addresses), the Python
script replaces a set of predefined macros with the corresponding values from
the network control framework rules. Each shell command executes inside a
separate thread so that even rapid sequences of rules do not lead to delays.[3] For
Linux iptables, we use the following command-line for blocking an IP address:

```
iptables -A INPUT [?address:-s . ][?proto:-p . ][?conn.orig_h:-s . ]
  [?conn.orig_p: --sport . ][?flow.src_h: -s . ][?flow.src_p: --sport .]
  [?conn.resp_h:-d . ][?conn.resp_p: --dport . ][?flow.dst_h: -d . ]
  [?flow.dst_p: --dport . ] -j DROP
```

Here, the macro syntax tells the Python script to replace each pair of brackets
with either an appropriate command line option if the corresponding network
control framework attribute is defined, or just an empty string if not. The entry
to remove a rule works accordingly.

6   Evaluation

In this section we evaluate functionality and performance of the network control
framework on the basis of the use cases we discuss in Sect. 2. We use the network
control framework's OpenFlow backend for all experiments and measurements.

6.1   Functionality

We implemented all the use cases we discuss in Sect. 2—dynamic firewalling,
shunting, quarantining, and QoS—in a variety of lab setups in different environments. For these experiments, we connected the network control framework to
three different OpenFlow-capable hardware switches: an IBM G8052 (firmware
version 7.11.2.0), an HP A5500-24 G-4SFP (Comware version 5.20.99), and an
Pica8 Open vSwitch P-3930 (PicOs 2.5.2). In each case, we validated correct
operation through manually generating corresponding traffic and confirming that
the switches indeed had installed the anticipated OpenFlow rules. We conclude
that our network control framework generally indeed operates as expected.

---

[3] As this could potentially reorder rules, users can optionally disable threading.

During our testing, we however noticed a number of differences between the OpenFlow implementations of the three switches. Most importantly, while all the switches offer OpenFlow 1.3, they differ in the feature set they support. For example, the HP A5500 only supports one output target per rule, making it impossible to duplicate traffic from one input port to two target ports—generally a desirable capability for network monitoring setups.[4] Both the IBM G8052 and the Pica8 P-3930 support this operation. Neither the IBM nor the HP switch can modify IP-level information (e.g., IP addresses or ports), preventing the network control framework's corresponding modifications from working with them. The Pica8 switch provides this functionality. Finally, the size of the switches' flow tables differ across the three devices—yet with all of them remaining rather small: the HP switch offers the largest table, yet still only supports two times 3,072 distinct entries.

6.2   Performance

In terms of performance, we examine two scenarios: the latency of blocking attacks and malicious content as well as the effectiveness of shunting traffic.

Filtering. As our first scenario, we examine the latency of blocking attacks and malicious content. When adding block rules, the main operational concern is the speed with which it takes effect; the delay between the decision and implementation should be as small as possible.

To test this scenario, we examined one hour of connection logs representing all external port 80 traffic on the Internet uplinks of the University of California at Berkeley (UCB). The upstream connectivity consists of two 10GE links with a daytime average rate of about 9 Gb/s total. During that hour, there were 9,392,623 established HTTP connections. To generate a test-load for automatic blocking, we pretended that every thousandth HTTP connection was carrying malicious content and thus had to be blocked, turning into an average of 2.6 network control framework operations per second. This level is quite a bit higher than what even large environments encounter in practice. Consulting with the operations team at LBNL, their system blocked, e.g., an average of 269 and 308 IPs per hour on May 28th and June 1st respectively. In their most active hour during those days, they blocked 616 IPs, i.e., 0.17 per second. At Indiana University, 23,875 blocks executed in total during May 2015, corresponding to 0.009 per second. Our testing workload exceeds these rates significantly, hence putting more strain on the setup than currently found in operational settings.

By extracting from the connection logs the timestamps and originator IP addresses of all "malicious" connections, we generated execution traces of network control framework operations matching what a live Bro would have executed during that hour of traffic. Replaying these traces through Bro triggers the actual OpenFlow messages with correct timing in a repeatable way. We

---

[4] While the lack of this feature does not affect the network control framework directly, it could prevent using it in combination with further static monitoring rules.

performed two measurements with this replay approach: *(i)* blocking all future traffic *from* the offending IP addresses, and *(ii)* blocking all future traffic *from or to* those addresses; the latter requires two OpenFlow rule insertions, doubling their frequency to an average of 5.2 per second.

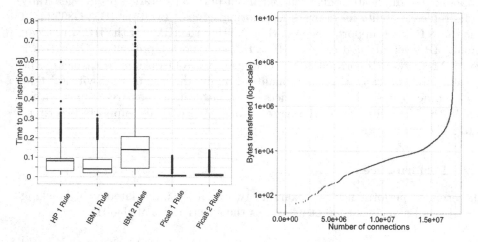

Fig. 3. Box plot of rule insertion latency with uni- and bi-directional rules for different OpenFlow hardware switches.

Fig. 4. TCP connection sizes at UCB (2015-05-07, 15:00-16:00) (Bytes axis log-scaled).

Figure 3 shows the delays from the moment Bro decided to insert a rule to the time when the success notification arrived back for most combinations of the three switches and the two measurements.[5] For all combinations shown, the rules took less than a second to insert, with the mean values being much lower. For example, for the IBM G8052, the median latency for bi-directional blocks was 141 ms; 42 ms for uni-directional. The Pica8 P-3039 showed the most impressive results with median times of 11 ms and 8.5 ms, respectively. For comparison, LBNL's operations team currently reports latencies around 300 ms on average when performing blocks with their home-built solution, i.e., more than an order of magnitude more than the combination of the network control framework with a (good) OpenFlow switch.

These results demonstrate that the network control framework supports high-speed rule execution even at levels substantially exceeding what operational environments currently require. Our measurements however also show the impact of hardware choices on blocking efficiency.

As a second evaluation, we determine how much data can typically still go through during the "gap time", meaning the period between when an IDS determines that a connection should be blocked, and the time when the network

---

[5] We excluded the HP A5500 with bi-directional rules due to problematic behavior when inserting rules that way: The average latency was >10 s, with many rules timing out and never getting an acknowledgment from the switch.

implements that decision. This is the additional latency that passive monitoring incurs in comparison to an inline IPS, with which blocks take effect instantaneously.

For this scenario, we assume a detector that inspects the header of HTTP requests to determine whether to deem them malicious, issuing blocks at the end of the header at the latest. We capture a 1 h packet trace of port 80 connections at the uplink of UCB, taken on 2015-05-01 at 16:00-17:00. Due to the fact that the traffic volume at UCB is more than a single machine can handle, we record a representative subset. Specifically, we use $\frac{1}{28}$ of all flows, corresponding to a slice of traffic that the organization's load-balancer setup sends to one of their in total 28 backend Bro machines. The resulting trace contains 159,474 HTTP connections.

We replay the trace file using a custom version of Bro, which we instrumented to output for each HTTP session (i) the packet timestamp of when the header was completed; (ii) the remaining duration of that connection from that point onwards; (iii) and the number of bytes transferred during intervals of I ms after completion of the header, with values for I chosen to correspond to the latencies we measured above for installing rules into the OpenFlow switches.

First, we measure how many connections terminate before they can be blocked using an uni-directional block with the different switches, assuming their block-time is either within the median or the 75 % percentile.

Table 2 shows the results of this evaluation. The table shows the median and 75 % block-speeds for the different switches. Assuming these values, we evaluate (i) how many connections terminate before a block can be installed, and (ii) what the median, mean and maximum amount of bytes are that could be transferred over the connection before the block was engaged.

These results show that, with the right hardware, the network control framework incurs latencies small enough that it would indeed have been able to stop most connections before their completion.

Shunting. As a second scenario, we examined the effectiveness of shunting traffic with the network control framework, using again network traffic from UCB's Internet uplink. This time, we examined flow logs of one hour of all TCP connections during the same peak traffic time as in Sect. 6.2. During that hour, the link saw 17,238,227 TCP connections, with a maximum volume of 7.5 GB and a total volume of 2.1 TB.

Table 2. Block times, connections that were not blocked in time, median, mean and maximum bytes transferred before block was engaged for OpenFlow switches.

Switch	Block time	Not blocked	Med. transferred	Mean transferred	Max transferred
Pica8 (Med)	8.5 ms	4,229 (2.7 %)	0	1.6 k	68 k
Pica8 (75P)	11 ms	8,273 (5.1 %)	12	2.3 k	101 k
IBM (Med)	41 ms	27,848 (17.4 %)	194	9.5 k	1.1 MB
IBM (75P)	89 ms	41,965 (26.3 %)	526	27 k	4.0 MB
HP (Med)	82 ms	38,381 (24 %)	454	23 k	4.5 MB
HP (75P)	93 ms	43,128 (27 %)	537	28 k	5.0 MB

Figure 4 plots the distribution of connection sizes, with the x-axis showing the number of connections and the y-axis their volume in log-scale.[6] We find the connection sizes highly heavy-tailed, with a small number of connections making up the bulk of the data. The mean connection size is 123 KB, the median is 2 KB.

Looking at the connections in more detail, there are 106 connections transferring more than 1 GB of data, making up 12 % of the total traffic; 1999 with more than 100 MB (36 %); and 24,106 with more than 10 MB (65 %). Assuming that we instructed the network switch to shunt each connection after reaching 1000, 100 or 10 MB respectively, we would shunt 53 %, 26 % or 6.5 % of the total TCP data transferred over the network link.

As this evaluation shows, traffic shunting can be effective even outside of scientific lab environments with their strong emphasis on bulk transfers. The university network we examine here exhibits a highly diverse traffic mix, with typical end-user traffic contributing most of the activity. Still, shunting would provide significant load reduction. Our implementation of the network control framework makes this easy to setup and control through just a few lines of Bro script code.

7 Related Work

There is a substantial body of academic work evaluating the interplay of network monitoring and software defined networking in different ways. The original OpenFlow paper [13] already suggests that applications might want to process individual packets instead of operating at the flow-level, as the OpenFlow API exposes it. Xing et al. [25] implement a prototype system using Snort to analyze packets via an OpenFlow controller. A this incurs significant computational cost, the authors use their system only up to a few thousand packets per second.

Shirali-Shareza et al. [22] examine the problem of controllers not being suitable to access packet-level information from the network. They propose an OpenFlow sampling extension, which allows the switch to only send a subset of a flow's packets to the controller. However, this approach is not suitable for use with network monitoring systems that rely on seeing the full packet stream for, e.g., TCP reassembly. Braga et al. [4] implement a lightweight DDOS flooding attack detector by regularly querying a network of OpenFlow controllers for flow information. They do not inspect raw packet contents. Van Adrichem et al. [24] present a system using OpenFlow to calculate the throughput of each data flow through the network over time by querying OpenFlow switches in variable intervals. Their results are within a few percent of direct traffic observation.

Slightly related to our work, Ballard et al. [3] present a language and system for traffic redirection for security monitoring at line rate. They implement a language to define how traffic should flow through the network as well as the system that applies the rules in an OpenFlow-capable network. Snortsam [23] is a plugin for the Snort IDS, allowing automated blocking of IP addresses on

---

[6] The connections reporting a size of 0 were not fully established.

a number of different hard- and software firewalls and routers. In comparison to our approach, Snortsam remains more limited, only allowing the blocking of source/destination IP addresses or single connections. SciPass [10] is an Open-Flow controller application designed to help scaling network security to 100 G networks. It supports using OpenFlow switches for load-balancing to IDS systems as well as traffic shunting. For the purpose of our paper, an application like SciPass could become another backend, just like our OpenFlow interface, and thus complement our design.

Porras et al. [18] present an enhanced OpenFlow controller mediating conflicting rules that independent applications might insert; an approach that one could use in conjunction with the network control framework's OpenFlow backend. Gonzalez et al. [11] introduce shunting as a hardware primitive in the context of an inline FPGA device with a direct interface to an IDS. Campbell et al. [7] evaluate its effectiveness inside 100 G scientific environments, using a simulation driven by Bro connection logs. The network control framework facilitates transparent operational deployment of this powerful capability. Related to shunting, Maier et al's Time Machine [12] leverages the heavy-tailed nature of traffic for optimizing bulk storage.

8 Conclusion

In this paper we present the design and implementation of a *network control framework*, a novel architecture enabling passive network monitoring systems to actively control network components, such as switches and firewalls. Our design provides a set of high-level operations for common functionality directly, while also offering access to lower-level primitives to perform custom tasks. As one of its key features, the framework supports controlling multiple network devices simultaneously, installing each rule at the component most appropriate to carry it out.

We assess the feasibility of our design by implementing the framework on top of the open-source Bro Network Security Monitor, and assess its functionality and performance through an OpenFlow backend connecting to three hardware switches in realistic settings. We find that the network control framework supports workloads beyond what even large-scale environments currently require. Going forward, we consider this framework a key abstraction for providing more dynamic security response capabilities than operators have available today. We anticipate that, in particular, the largest of today's network environments—with links of 100 G, and soon beyond—will benefit from the framework's capabilities in settings that no inline IPS can support.

Acknowledgments. We would like to thank Aashish Sharma, Keith Lehigh, and Paul Wefel for their feedback and help.

This work was supported by the National Science Foundation under grant numbers ACI-1348077 and CNS-1228792. Any opinions, findings, and conclusions or recommendations expressed in this material are those of the author(s) and do not necessarily reflect the views of the NSF.

References

1. ACL blocker notes. http://www-nrg.ee.lbl.gov/leres/acl2.html
2. Allcock, W., Bester, J., Bresnahan, J., Chervenak, A., Liming, L., Tuecke, S.: GridFTP: Protocol Extensions for the Grid. Grid ForumGFD-R-P.020 (2003)
3. Ballard, J.R., Rae, I., Akella, A.: Extensible and scalable network monitoring using OpenSAFE. In: INM/WREN (2010)
4. Braga, R., Mota, E., Passito, A.: Lightweight DDoS flooding attack detection using NOX/OpenFlow. In: LCN (2010)
5. Bro Network Monitoring System. https://www.bro.org
6. Broker: Bro's Messaging Library. https://github.com/bro/broker
7. Campbell, S., Lee, J.: Prototyping a 100g monitoring system. In: PDP (2012)
8. Presentation slides–Anonymized for submission (2014)
9. ESnet: Science DMZ Security - Firewalls vs. Router ACLs. https://fasterdata.es.net/science-dmz/science-dmz-security/
10. GlobalNOC: SciPass: IDS Load Balancer & Science DMZ. http://globalnoc.iu.edu/sdn/scipass.html
11. Gonzalez, J., Paxson, V., Weaver, N.: Shunting: a hardware/software architecture for flexible, high-performance network intrusion prevention. In: ACM Communications and Computer Security (CCS) Conference, Washington, D.C (2007)
12. Maier, G., Sommer, R., Dreger, H., Feldmann, A., Paxson, V., Schneider, F.: Enriching network security analysis with time travel. In: Proceedings of the ACM SIGCOMM (2008). http://www.icir.org/robin/papers/sigcomm08-tm.pdf
13. McKeown, N., Anderson, T., Balakrishnan, H., Parulkar, G., Peterson, L., Rexford, J., Shenker, S., Turner, J.: OpenFlow: enabling innovation in campus networks. CCR 38(2), 69–74 (2008)
14. Network Control framework and utility code. http://icir.org/johanna/netcontrol
15. OSCARS: On-Demand Secure Circuits and Advance Reservation System. http://www.es.net/engineering-services/oscars/
16. Papadogiannakis, A., Polychronakis, M., Markatos, E.P.: Improving the accuracy of network intrusion detection systems under load using selective packet discarding. In: EUROSEC (2010)
17. Paxson, V.: Bro: a system for detecting network intruders in real-time. Comput. Netw. 31(23–24), 2435–2463 (1999)
18. Porras, P., Cheung, S., Fong, M., Skinner, K., Yegneswaran, V.: Securing the software-defined network control layer. In: Proceedings of the 2015 Network and Distributed System Security Symposium (NDSS), February 2015
19. Ryu SDN Framework. http://osrg.github.io/ryu/
20. Science DMZ - A Scalable Network Design Model for Optimizing Science Data Transfers. https://fasterdata.es.net/science-dmz
21. Security and NAT Gateway for the Munich Scientific Network (MWN). https://www.lrz.de/services/netzdienste/secomat_en/
22. Shirali-Shahreza, S., Ganjali, Y.: FleXam: flexible sampling extension for monitoring and security applications in openflow. In: HotSDN (2013)
23. Snortsam - A Firewall Blocking Agent for Snort. https://www.snortsam.net
24. Van Adrichem, N., Doerr, C., Kuipers, F.: OpenNetMon: network monitoring in OpenFlow software-defined networks. In: NOMS (2014)
25. Xing, T., Huang, D., Xu, L., Chung, C.J., Khatkar, P.: SnortFlow: a OpenFlow-based intrusion prevention system in cloud environment. In: GREE (2013)

Hardening

Probabilistic Inference on Integrity for Access Behavior Based Malware Detection

Weixuan Mao[1], Zhongmin Cai[1(✉)], Don Towsley[2], and Xiaohong Guan[1]

[1] MOE KLINNS Lab, Xi'an Jiaotong University, Xi'an, Shaanxi, China
{wxmao,zmcai,xhguan}@sei.xjtu.edu.cn
[2] School of Computer Science, University of Massachusetts, Amherst, MA, USA
towsley@cs.umass.edu

Abstract. Integrity protection has proven an effective way of malware detection and defense. Determining the integrity of subjects (programs) and objects (files and registries) plays a fundamental role in integrity protection. However, the large numbers of subjects and objects, and intricate behaviors place burdens on revealing their integrities either manually or by a set of rules. In this paper, we propose a probabilistic model of integrity in modern operating system. Our model builds on two primary security policies, "no read down" and "no write up", which make connections between observed access behaviors and the inherent integrity ordering between pairs of subjects and objects. We employ a message passing based inference to determine the integrity of subjects and objects under a probabilistic graphical model. Furthermore, by leveraging a statistical classifier, we build an integrity based access behavior model for malware detection. Extensive experimental results on a real-world dataset demonstrate that our model is capable of detecting 7,257 malware samples from 27,840 benign processes at 99.88% true positive rate under 0.1% false positive rate. These results indicate the feasibility of our probabilistic integrity model.

Keywords: Probabilistic graphical model · Integrity protection · Malware

1 Introduction

In spite of considerate effort by security researchers and engineers, attackers continue to craft malicious code (malware). A recent security threat report by Symantec states that there were more than 317 million new pieces of malware created in 2014, which is 26% more than in 2013 [27]. Being faced with ever-growing and increasingly sophisticated malware, it is important to develop more effective defenses from essential perspectives of security [28].

Integrity protection has proven an effective way of malware detection and defense [4,7,23,28]. Determining the integrity of subjects and objects is fundamental to integrity protection [26]. The integrity of a subject or an object refers to the trustworthiness of its contents. Integrity is typically divided into levels,

© Springer International Publishing Switzerland 2015
H. Bos et al. (Eds.): RAID 2015, LNCS 9404, pp. 155–176, 2015.
DOI: 10.1007/978-3-319-26362-5_8

e.g., *trusted* and *untrusted*, *high* and *low*, etc. Integrity protection aims at preventing trusted objects from being accessed inappropriately, e.g., it forbids an untrusted program from writing a trusted file. Prior work manually defines the number of integrity levels, and assigns integrity levels to subjects and objects either manually or by rules. For example, previous work usually defines two integrity levels [4,7,26]. Learning from previous attacks, Sun et al. treat Media players and games as having low integrity [26], LOMAC treats system files as having high integrity, and builds on a rule that assigns a subject a low integrity, if it read an object with low integrity [7]. Windows Vista treats Internet Explorer as having low integrity, and Vista files as having high integrity [11]. It is feasible to define integrity levels either manually or by rules, when the number of subjects and objects is small, and the behaviors of subjects are simple. However, given hundreds of thousands subjects and objects in a modern operating system, it is challenging and error-prone to assign integrity levels to all of them manually. And, given the intricate behaviors of subjects, it is neither flexible nor adaptive to assign integrity levels to them by rules.

This paper aims to determine integrity levels for all system subjects, i.e., programs, and system objects, i.e., files and registries, based on access behaviors of benign programs. Our method builds on two primary security policies, "*no read down*" and "*no write up*". These two policies, first proposed by Biba [4], have become the basis of integrity protections in modern operating systems [7,12,26]. These policies make connections between integrity levels and access behaviors. Our method determines the integrity levels of subjects and objects based on these connections. Unlike earlier work, it makes no assumption of the total number of integrity levels and needs no knowledge obtained from previous attacks.

The integrity level of system subjects and objects may change in different executions and contexts. We model integrity levels as random variables to capture their uncertainties. Meanwhile, each observation of access behavior, involving a pair of system subject and object, implies an ordering of their integrity levels between them, according to "no read down" and "no write up" security policies. This ordering of integrity level defines a joint integrity level (joint distribution) of the subject-object pair. Thus, we build a probabilistic generative model to capture these connections, and derive the joint distribution of the integrity levels of each pair, based on observations of access behaviors of benign programs. To obtain the integrity levels of each subject and object, we aggregate the joint integrity level of each pair to build a pairwise Markov network. We then employ message passing based inference on this pairwise Markov network, i.e., loopy belief propagation, to obtain integrity levels of all subjects and objects.

Furthermore, we employ a statistical classifier to build an integrity based access behavior model for malware detection. We conduct a set of experiments to evaluate our model by comparing with baseline models, on a data set consisting of 27,840 executions of 534 benign programs and 7,257 executions of malicious programs. Our encouraging results demonstrate the usefulness of our access behavior model for malware detection based on determined integrity levels, and the feasibility of our model on determining integrity levels for system subjects and objects.

The contributions of this paper are summarized as follows:

- Modeling integrity level of system subjects and objects under two primary security policies. We propose a probabilistic generative model to capture the connection between the joint integrity level of each pair of system subjects and objects, and observations of access behaviors of benign programs, corresponding to "no read down" and "no write up" security policies.
- Probabilistic graphical model on joint integrity levels of all subject-object pairs. We build a probabilistic graphical model, pairwise Markov network, to characterize joint integrity levels of all pairs, and leverage a message passing based inference to further characterize integrity levels of all subjects and objects.
- An integrity based access behavior model for malware detection. We employ a statistical classifier, random forest, to build an access behavior model for malware detection, based on integrity levels of accessed objects of programs.
- Extensive experimental results on a real data set demonstrate the feasibility and capability of our model. On a data set consisting of 27,840 executions of 534 benign programs and 7,257 executions of malicious programs, our experimental results of malware detection exhibit a 99.88 % true positive rate at 0.1 % false positive rate.

The paper is organized as follows. We first introduce the background and related work in Sect. 2. We then explain our probabilistic integrity model and inference, and our model of malware detection in Sect. 3. After demonstrating our experimental results in Sect. 4, Sect. 5 concludes our work and states future work.

2   Background and Related Work

2.1   Integrity Protection

Integrity protection has been demonstrated to be an effective way of protecting modern operating systems [7,12,23,26]. It determines when information flows are allowed based on the integrity levels of subjects and objects. One of the most fundamental and well-known integrity protection models is the Biba model [4], which defines policies as follows.

- A subject is allowed to read an object only if its integrity is lower than or equal to that of the object (no read down).
- A subject is allowed to write an object only if its integrity is higher than or equal to that of the object (no write up).

The Biba model provides security policies for integrity protection, and was initially proposed as a mandatory access control (MAC) model in military, government systems. We refer to "no read down" as *NRD*, and "no write up" as

NWU in the following paper. However, Biba is too restrictive for modern operating systems [21]. Follow-up research aimed to build a more applicable model from two perspectives: (1) Determine the integrity level of subjects and objects. (2) Devise policies for these integrity levels.

Prior work assigns integrity levels to subjects and objects, and devises policies under integrity levels either manually or by rules [7,23,26]. LOMAC is a Linux extension of Biba model. It defines two integrity levels, high and low. System files are assigned high integrity levels and the network is assigned a low integrity level. LOMAC changes the integrity level of subjects and objects according to the *low water mark* principle, i.e., if a subject with high integrity reads an object with low integrity, the integrity of the subject is assigned to low [7]. This provides a mechanism of capturing changes of integrity levels of subjects and objects dynamically. However, its way of determining static integrity levels of subjects and objects relies on limited rules. Sun et al. devise elaborate rules to assign integrity levels, either high or low, to subjects and objects, and define policies based on their experiences on benign and malicious information flow [26]. In their later work, they apply integrity protection with similar policies into software installation, and propose a Secure Software Installer to prevent untrusted software from modifying files used by trusted software [25]. Their rules require a large number of examples of both attacks and defenses. Although these rules may provide an effective protection, it is expensive to devise such rules, and difficult to make them flexible enough to deal with newly emerging attacks and benign programs. Hsu et al. provide a framework for recovering from malicious programs and their effects based on integrity. They focus on the NRD policy, because they do not aim to prevent malware but only to recover from intrusions [12]. Mao et al. leverage graph centrality to measure the importance of systems subjects and objects, which is treated as a proxy for integrity [20]. However, there is still a gap between the importance of graph structure and integrity in operating systems. Beside these efforts by security researchers, one commercial example is the Mandatory Integrity Control (MIC) in Windows Vista. It labels the integrity levels of file objects as either Low, Medium, High, or System. As a default, critical Vista files are labeled System, other objects are labeled Medium, and Internet Explorer is labeled Low. MIC designs policies to enforce security with the help of user account control (UAC) [1,11,19]. However, it highly relies on judgment of users, which makes it unusable for ordinary users [3].

Previous integrity protection model suffer from two shortcomings. Firstly, it is difficult to determine the integrity levels of all subjects and objects, as there are hundreds of thousands and intricate behaviors between them. Prior work usually manually assigns integrity levels to a small subset of subjects and objects based on their experiences in attacks, and then uses a rule-based approach to determine others [7,11,25,26]. Unlike prior work, which predefines the number of possible integrity levels, we make no assumption about the number of integrity levels in operating systems, but determine it from access behaviors of benign programs. We aim to determine the integrity level for each subject and object, relying on knowledge of benign programs, but not malicious programs. Secondly, mandatory control policies and manually devised rules cannot accommodate real-world operation very well without the introduction of numerous exceptions in the face of crafty attackers and diverse benign programs. We employ a statistical classifier to extract policies for benign and malicious programs with respect to their access behaviors under our integrity levels.

2.2 Behavior Based Malware Detection

Prior work on behavior based malware detection usually employs heuristic, rule-based or statistical learning algorithms to construct behavior models or specifications for programs [2,6,8,16,17]. It successfully trades false positives off against false negatives. However, it relies on statistical discriminations between benign and malicious programs only, and neglects the essence of malware from a security perspective, i.e., violations of security policies. Our method leverages the integrity level of objects involved in access behaviors, which pays more attention to violations of security policies of programs. Under the integrity level derived from our model, we observe discriminations not only in statistics, but also from a security perspective in our experimental results.

3   Methodology

3.1   Overview

In this section, we present our method for deriving integrity levels of system subjects and objects, and malware detection. It consists of two components: (1) Probabilistic integrity model and inference. (2) Malware detection utilizing the integrity levels. Figure 1 illustrates the framework of our method in this paper.

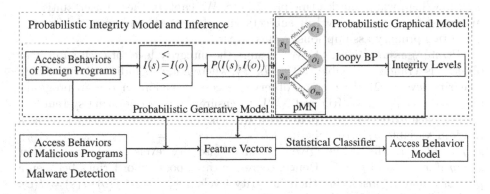

Fig. 1. Framework of our method for deriving integrity levels and malware detection

Since the integrity levels of system subjects (programs) and objects (files or registries) may change in different executions and contexts, we represent the integrity levels as random variables to capture their uncertainties in real operating systems. The first component of our method, probabilistic integrity model and inference, consists of two steps: (i) Given all observed access behaviors, we infer the joint integrity level (joint distribution) of each subject-object pair, under proposed a probabilistic generative model for access behaviors. Depending on which of the two primary security policies NRD and NWU applies, each observed access behavior implies an ordering of the integrity levels of a subject-object pair. The possible orderings include $<, =, >$. Moreover, the orderings within a subject-object pair implies its joint integrity level (joint distribution). (ii) We aggregate the joint distributions of integrity levels for all pairs of subjects and objects to construct a pairwise Markov network (pMN) that provides a joint distribution of integrity levels for all subjects and objects. Our goal is to characterize the distribution of the integrity levels of each subject and object from the pMN. Furthermore, we employ loopy belief propagation (loopy BP), a message passing approximate inference algorithm, to infer the marginal distributions of the integrity levels for subjects and objects.

Once we characterize the integrity levels, we extract feature vectors to describe access behaviors of programs. Resorting to a statistical classifier, we build a model of malware detection, that accounts for the security meanings of access behaviors. In this paper, we focus on system subjects and objects, i.e., programs, files and registries.

3.2 Probabilistic Integrity Model

Probabilistic Integrity and Pairwise Relationship. It is not easy to determine the exact integrity level of subjects and objects. For example, due to the varying behaviors and intents, a program may exhibit different integrity levels in different executions and contexts. Meanwhile, accessed by these programs, the integrity level of a file or registry may be changed according to security policies, e.g., low/high water mark principle [7], etc. We capture these uncertainties by modeling the integrity level of subjects and objects as random variables, and make two primary assumptions in this paper.

Primary assumptions: (1) We assume the integrity level of each subject or object i is a random variable $I(i) \in \{L, H\}$, where L and H indicate low and high integrity levels. (2) We assume observed access behaviors of benign programs obey security policies NRD and NWU to ensure a secure operating system.

For each subject-object pair (s, o), we denote their joint integrity level as a random variable $J_I(s, o)$, where $P(J_I(s, o) = (x, y)) = P(I(s) = x, I(o) = y)$, $x, y \in \{L, H\}$. Meanwhile, given a pair of integrity levels (x, y), we say that $x < y$ if $x = L$ and $y = H$. Hence, there are three possible orderings between a pair of s and o considering their integrity levels, i.e., $I(s) < I(o)$, $I(s) = I(o)$, $I(s) > I(o)$. Note that, the integrity level of s may be higher than that of o in one execution, but lower than that of o in another execution. Therefore, we represent the order between s and o as a random variable $E_I(s, o)$ with three possible values, i.e., $E_I(s, o) \in \{I(s) < I(o), I(s) = I(o), I(s) > I(o)\}$. Thus, we obtain $P(J_I | E_I)$ by $P(J_I | E_I) = \frac{P(E_I | J_I) P(J_I)}{P(E_I)} \propto P(E_I | J_I) P(J_I)$ as follows.

(1) If E_I is $I(s) < I(o)$, then,

$$P(J_I = (L, H)|E_I) = 1; \text{ otherwise, } 0. \tag{1}$$

(2) If E_I is $I(s) = I(o)$, then,

$$P(J_I = (L, L)|E_I) = P(LL), P(J_I = (H, H)|E_I) = P(HH); \text{ otherwise, } 0, \tag{2}$$

where $P(LL) = \frac{P(J_I=(L,L))}{P(J_I=(L,L))+P(J_I=(H,H))}$, $P(HH) = \frac{P(J_I=(H,H))}{P(J_I=(L,L))+P(J_I=(H,H))}$

(3) If E_I is $I(s) > I(o)$, then,

$$P(J_I = (H, L)|E_I) = 1; \text{ otherwise, } 0. \tag{3}$$

Probabilistic Generative Model for Access Behavior. An access event is an observed access behavior. We refer to system call events related to files or registries as *access events*. Each access event involves a subject and an object, and we divide all access events into two types, *read* and *write*, according to their information flows [13].

One execution of a program s consists of a set of access events. In each execution, there are three possible access behaviors between a subject s and an object o, i.e., *Read-only* (r), *Write-only* (w), *Read & Write* (r & w) [13]. Thus, once s accesses o, we represent the access behavior of s on o as a random variable with three possible values, and s takes one of three possible access behaviors on o in each execution. We denote the probabilities that s reads-only, writes-only, and reads & writes o as $P_r(s, o)$, $P_w(s, o)$, and $P_{r\&w}(s, o)$.

Furthermore, for a program s with different executions, we assume the access behavior of s in one execution is independent of its behavior in other executions. We define $Acc(s, o)$ to be the access behavior of s on o among all executions, consisting of $N_{r,(s,o)}$, $N_{w,(s,o)}$ and $N_{r\&w,(s,o)}$, which are the number of executions that s reads-only, writes-only and reads & writes, and they obey a multinomial distribution, i.e., $Acc(s, o) = (N_{r,(s,o)}, N_{w,(s,o)}, N_{r\&w,(s,o)}) \sim$ Multi$(N_{(s,o)}, P_r(s, o), P_w(s, o), P_{r\&w}(s, o))$, where $N_{(s,o)}$ is the total number of executions of program s that accesses object o.

With our second primary assumption, the relationship between the access behavior of s on o and their integrity levels can be interpreted as follows: If $I(s) < I(o)$, then s reads-only o, i.e., $P_r(s, o) = 1$ and $P_w(s, o), P_{r\&w}(s, o) = 0$; if $I(s) > I(o)$, then s writes-only o, i.e., $P_w(s, o) = 1$ and $P_r(s, o), P_{r\&w}(s, o) = 0$; if $I(s) = I(o)$, then s can perform any of behaviors, i.e., $0 < P_r(s, o), P_w(s, o), P_{r\&w}(s, o) < 1$. However, as mandatory security policies, there may exist violations of them in commercial operating systems [21]. Our model allows violations of security policies by assuming the distribution of access behavior of s on o not only depends on the order of integrity levels between them, but also on the distribution of access behavior under violations. We assume the distribution of access behavior under violations is identical to that under equal integrity, i.e., $I(s) = I(o)$. Thus, the distribution of all access behaviors is derived by combining that under order of integrity levels and that under violations, which results in a random variable T representing the prior distribution of the distribution of access behavior. Based on the above analysis and assumptions, we build a probabilistic generative model, which is a hierarchical Bayesian model, for the access behavior of programs and accessed objects with their integrity levels as shown in Fig. 2. Assumptions of conditional probabilities in the model are presented in Eqs. (4)–(7).

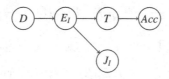

Fig. 2. A generative model for the access behavior with integrity levels

Equation (4) presents a Dirichlet prior D of the integrity ordering to deal with the lack of a sufficient number of observations in the data set. Equation (5) indicates the categorical distribution of the integrity ordering, where the probability of $I(s) < I(o)$, $I(s) = I(o)$, and $I(s) > I(o)$ are d_1, d_2, and d_3 respectively. Before presenting the multinomial distribution of access behaviors with parameters t_1, t_2, and t_3 in Eq. (7), Eq. (6) presents the prior T of this multinomial distribution conditioning on the integrity ordering, which aims to model access behaviors by combining both the security policies, i.e., NRD and NWU, and potential violations in commercial operating systems. Combining with the relationship between E_I and J_I as shown in Eqs. (1)–(3), this generative model provides a way to model the access behavior with joint integrity level of subjects and objects. Moreover, it offers a way to infer the joint integrity level $J_I(s, o)$ given observations of access behaviors, which is presented in the following subsection.

$$D = (d_1, d_2, d_3) \sim \mathrm{Dir}(\alpha_1, \alpha_2, \alpha_3), \tag{4}$$

$$E_I | D \sim \mathrm{Cat}(3, d_1, d_2, d_3), \tag{5}$$

$$T = (t_1, t_2, t_3) | E_I \sim \begin{cases} \mathrm{Dir}(1 + \beta_1, \beta_2, \beta_3), & \text{if } I(s) < I(o), \\ \mathrm{Dir}(\beta_1, \beta_2, \beta_3), & \text{if } I(s) = I(o), \\ \mathrm{Dir}(\beta_1, 1 + \beta_2, \beta_3), & \text{if } I(s) > I(o), \end{cases} \tag{6}$$

$$Acc | T \sim \mathrm{Multi}(N, t_1, t_2, t_3). \tag{7}$$

Probabilistic Graphical Model on Integrity. Our goal is to characterize the integrity level of each subject and object by marginal distributions, i.e., $P(I(s))$ and $P(I(o))$. To achieve this goal, we need to aggregate the joint integrity levels of all pairs of subjects and objects, and calculate the marginal integrity distribution for subjects and objects. We achieve this goal using a probabilistic graphical model, or more accurately, *pairwise Markov network* (pMN). Pairwise Markov networks are the simplest subclass of Markov networks. A pMN is an undirected probabilistic graphical model $G(V, E, \Psi)$, where V is a set of nodes representing random variables, E is a set of edges representing relationships between nodes with factors defined in Ψ, each edge is associated with a factor over a pair of nodes [14]. In our problem, the pMN is a bipartite graph, where each node represents the integrity level of a subject or object, a subject is connected with an object if there exists an observed access event associated with them. There is no edge between two subjects or two objects. Meanwhile, we encode the joint integrity level J_I for each pair of subject and object into each edge, the factor on each edge is joint integrity level J_I. Figure 3 illustrates an example of a pMN consisting of four pairs of subjects and objects. Since the bipartite graph constructed from a real data set contains loops, we compute an approximate inference on the integrity level of each subject and object as shown in the following subsection.

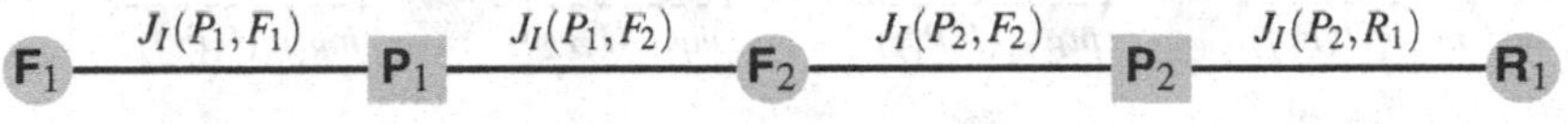

Fig. 3. An example of pairwise Markov network

3.3 Probabilistic Inference

Inference on Joint Integrity Level of Each Pair. Under the generative model shown in Fig. 2, the Bayes estimator $\hat{P}_E$ for the integrity ordering given access events is

$$\hat{P}_E = P(E_I|Acc) = \sum_{D,T} P(E_I, D, T|Acc), \propto \sum_{D,T} P(Acc|T)P(T|E_I)P(E_I|D)P(D),$$

$$= \sum_T P(Acc|T)P(T|E_I) \sum_D P(E_I|D)P(D). \tag{8}$$

More specifically, the probabilities of all possible orderings are

$$\hat{P}_{E_I}(<) = P(< |Acc) = \frac{\alpha_1}{\alpha_1 + \alpha_2 + \alpha_3} \frac{(\beta_1 + \beta_2 + \beta_3)(N_r + \beta_1)}{\beta_1(N + \beta_1 + \beta_2 + \beta_3)}/\Sigma, \tag{9}$$

$$\hat{P}_{E_I}(=) = P(= |Acc) = \frac{\alpha_2}{\alpha_1 + \alpha_2 + \alpha_3}/\Sigma, \tag{10}$$

$$\hat{P}_{E_I}(>) = P(> |Acc) = \frac{\alpha_3}{\alpha_1 + \alpha_2 + \alpha_3} \frac{(\beta_1 + \beta_2 + \beta_3)(N_w + \beta_2)}{\beta_2(N + \beta_1 + \beta_2 + \beta_3)}/\Sigma, \tag{11}$$

where $\Sigma = \frac{\alpha_1}{\alpha_1+\alpha_2+\alpha_3} \frac{(\beta_1+\beta_2+\beta_3)(N_r+\beta_1)}{\beta_1(N+\beta_1+\beta_2+\beta_3)} + \frac{\alpha_2}{\alpha_1+\alpha_2+\alpha_3} + \frac{\alpha_3}{\alpha_1+\alpha_2+\alpha_3} \frac{(\beta_1+\beta_2+\beta_3)(N_w+\beta_2)}{\beta_2(N+\beta_1+\beta_2+\beta_3)}$.
More details of the derivation are presented in Appendix.
Our estimator $\hat{P}(J_I(s,o))$ for the joint distribution of integrity levels is,

$$\hat{P}(J_I(s,o)) = P(J_I(s,o)|Acc) = \sum_{E_I(s,o)} P(J_I(s,o)|E_I(s,o))P(E_I(s,o)|Acc). \tag{12}$$

Inference on Integrity Level of Subject and Object. There exist loops in our pairwise Markov network. Hence, the estimation of marginal distributions for such graphs is known to be NP-complete. Loopy belief propagation provides an approximate and efficient way of inference based on *message passing*. It has proven to be a successful at inferring on marginal distributions over loopy graph in various domains, such as object tracking in computer vision, error-correcting code, etc [14]. In particular, researchers have applied loopy belief propagation to solve problems in security area by modeling them as classification problems [18, 29]. We apply this method to our problem to infer the probabilistic integrity level of each subject and object.

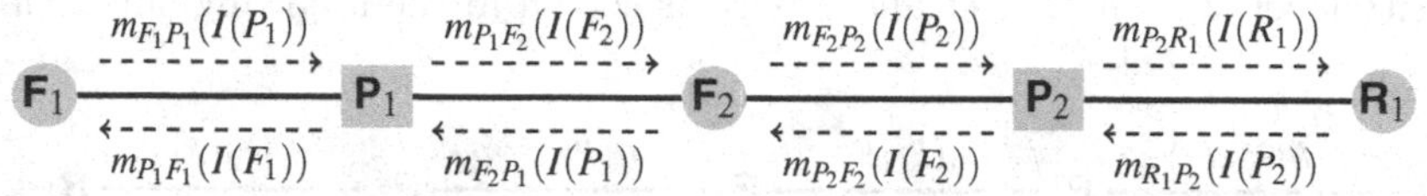

Fig. 4. Message passing of loop belief propagation on the pMN shown in Fig. 3

The loopy belief propagation works as follows. Each node sends messages to its adjacent nodes, as shown in Fig. 4, according to

$$m_{ij}(x_j) = \sum_{x_i \in \{low, high\}} \pi_i(x_i)\Psi_{ij}(x_j|x_i) \prod_{k \in N(i)\backslash j} m_{ki}(x_i), \qquad (13)$$

where $m_{ij}(x_j)$, $i \in N(j)$ indicates the message from adjacent nodes of node j, $\pi_i(x_i)$ is the prior of node i. $\Psi_{ij}(x_i|x_j)$ is the conditional probability of integrity level of x_i given that of x_j, which is derived as follows.

$$\Psi_{ij}(x_i|x_j) \propto P(x_i, x_j) = \hat{P}(J_I(x_i, x_j)) = \sum_{E_I(x_i,x_j)} P(J_I(x_i,x_j)|E_I(x_i,x_j))P(E_I(x_i,x_j)|Acc).$$

$$(14)$$

Substituting Eqs. (1)–(3), (9)–(11) into Eq. (14), we can easily derive the conditional probability $\Psi_{ij}(x_i|x_j)$. The message $m_{ij}(x_j)$ reveals that how the node i thinks about the level of node j. In each iteration, the message of all nodes will be updated. The order of message updating is not important. The iteration stops when the message of nodes converge, i.e., there is no significant changes of messages between iterations, or when a sufficient number of iterations is reached. Then, we compute the marginal distribution of integrity for each node, a.k.a. the belief of node, as follows.

$$b_i(x_i) = C\pi_i(x_i) \prod_{k \in N(i)} m_{ki}(x_i), \qquad (15)$$

where C is a normalization constant to ensure that the integrity probabilities add up to 1, i.e., $\sum_{x_i \in \{L,H\}} b_i(x_i) = 1$. Here, $b_i(L)$ and $b_i(H)$ indicate probabilities that i has *low* and *high* integrity level respectively.

3.4 Malware Detection

There exist violations in commercial modern operating systems under NRD and NWU security policies [21]. In order to accommodate violations, we employ a statistical learning technique to extract more adaptive security policies for malware detection. Before we describe this technique, we first show how to recover the integrity level of subjects and objects under the probabilistic notation.

Integrity Level. The integrity levels of subjects and objects are recovered by taking into account the probability that the subject/object has *high* integrity, i.e., $P(I(i) = H)$, which is the belief of a subject/object $b_i(H)$. We sort subjects and objects by their beliefs of $b_i(H)$ in decreasing order, and assign the integrity level to all subjects and objects from the highest to the lowest. We treat the subjects and objects with same beliefs as having the same integrity level. The ranking positions under the sort are treated as the integrity levels of subjects and objects.

Malware Detection. For program i, we create a feature vector $\mathbf{X}_i$ for it. The feature vector is similar to [20], but with column normalization. More specifically, $\mathbf{X}_i$ is

$$\mathbf{X}_i = \left[\mathbf{x}_i^{(\text{file,read})}, \mathbf{x}_i^{(\text{file,write})}, \mathbf{x}_i^{(\text{reg,read})}, \mathbf{x}_i^{(\text{reg,write})} \right], \tag{16}$$

$$\mathbf{x}_i^{(k,l)} = \left[x_{i1}^{(k,l)}, ..., x_{ir}^{(k,l)}, ..., x_{iL^{(k)}}^{(k,l)} \right]. \tag{17}$$

Here $x_{ir}^{(k,l)}$ is the fraction of objects of type $k \in \{\text{file, registry}\}$ accessed under operation $l \in \{\text{read, write}\}$ at integrity level r. $\mathbf{x}_i^{(k,l)}$ is the vector of these fractions at all integrity levels. $L^{(k)}$ is the total number of integrity levels of objects of type k.

Once we create feature vectors for both benign and malicious processes, we train a statistical classifier to build an access behavior model for malware detection.

3.5 Time Complexity

The main time complexity of malware detection model consists of two parts: (1) Integrity determination. (2) Malware classification.

To analyze the time complexity of the first part, we assume the number of edges is E in our pairwise Markov network, which corresponds to the number of subject-object pairs. Our model employ loopy belief propagation, which is a iterative algorithm running in $O(4E(s+1))$, where s is the number of iterations. In each iteration, we need to calculate messages on both directions of each edge, and each direction contains two types of messages, i.e., L and H. That is the reason of the constant before the number of edges. We observe $s \ll E$[1]. Hence,

---

[1] In fact, we find s is about 7 in our experiments.

we can say, our probabilistic integrity model run in the linear time to the number of edges in our pairwise Markov network, i.e., $O(E)$.

The time complexity of malware classification depends on the statistical classifier we employ, we analyze it in our experimental results.

4 Experimental Evaluation

4.1 Evaluation Methodology

To evaluate our model, we design a set of experiments to empirically answer three questions: (1) Do the determined integrity levels support malware detection from a perspective of security policies? (2) What is the performance of our malware detection model? (3) What is the running time of our probabilistic integrity model in experiments?

Experimental Settings. *Benign programs*: We employ Process Monitor [22] to collect the access behaviors of programs under eight different users' normal usages without interfering with their daily usages, which run on systems running Microsoft Windows XP SP3. Among eight users, two of them are male undergraduates who were working on their final year projects, and six others are graduates consisting of one female student and five male students, whose behaviors include writing, programing, web surfing, etc. The data collection takes place over periods of 7 to 16 days, and we finally obtain access behaviors of 27,840 executions from 534 benign programs.

Malicious programs: We download a collection of 270 K malware samples from VxHeaven, which is a website providing information about viruses [30]. We randomly select 9 K samples, run them in our sandbox which is with Windows XP SP3 on VMWare without network connection, and monitor their behaviors with Process Monitor. After running each sample for five minutes, we revert the virtual machine to a clean snapshot so that different samples do not interfere with each other. Since not all samples exhibit file or registry access activities, we finally obtain access behaviors of 7,257 malware samples. The families of final malware samples are listed in Table 1.

Table 1. Number of malware samples in each family

Family	Samples	Family	Samples	Family	Samples	Family	Samples
Backdoor	25	Trojan-Banker	75	Trojan-Clicker	37	Trojan-PSW	216
Trojan-Spy	768	Trojan-Dropper	128	Trojan-GameThief	278	Trojan-IM	3
Trojan-Mailfinder	5	Trojan-Ransom	2	Trojan.Win32	575	Virus.BAT	1
Virus.JS	3	Virus.MSIL	18	Virus.MSWord	3	Virus.Multi	24
Virus.NSIS	1	Virus.Win32	2527	Virus.WinHLP	5	Worm.BAT	12
Worm.MSIL	4	Worm.Win32	2547				

Training and testing sets: Because the executions of benign programs are collected from eight users, we set up eight experiments. In each experiment, we select the executions of benign programs from one user as a benign testing set, and those from seven other users as benign training set. We infer the probabilistic integrity level of objects from the benign training set. Meanwhile, we randomly select 80 % malware samples as a malicious training set and the remaining ones as a malicious testing set. We repeat the experiment 20 times. The results of 20 repetitions are averaged and illustrated in the following subsections.

Hyperparameters: To avoid priors dominating the data in our generative model as shown in Eqs. (4) and (6), we choose Jeffreys priors, i.e., α_1, α_2, α_3, β_1, β_2, and β_3 are equal to 0.5, which are non-informative priors and invariant under transformation [9].

New objects: It is very common to come across new objects which do not appear in the training set. For example, objects are newly created by processes in the testing set. We employ a heuristic method to assign probabilistic integrity level to new objects, which is similar to the approach in [20], but from a probabilistic perspective. More specifically, we assign probabilistic integrity level to new objects according to the directory it is stored in. The probability that the new object has high integrity level equals to the probability that its parent directory has high integrity level, which equals to the highest probability that the child objects of the parent directory have high integrity level.

Statistical classifier: We employ random forests, implemented in Scikit-learn [24], as our classifier. Random forests is an ensemble learning method for classification (and regression) that operate by constructing a multitude of deci-sion trees at training time. It not only exhibits the same advantage of decision trees, but also overcomes the main disadvantage of decision trees, namely over-fitting [5]. Moreover, we observe that the results are comparable in performance to other classifiers, e.g., k-nearest neighbors, logistic regression, and support vec-tor machine. We do not demonstrate them in this paper considering page limits.

Baseline. We compare our method to two baseline models for determining integrity levels. The first baseline model ($B1$) strictly obeys NRD and NWU, which forms a lattice constructed from access behaviors of benign programs. The lattice consists of partial orders of integrity levels between subjects and objects determined by observed access events under NRD and NWU. The layers in the hierarchical structure of the lattice indicate integrity levels. Figure 5 illustrates the lattice constructed from our data set of benign programs. We observe four layers in this hierarchical structure, which indicates four possible integrity levels of subjects and objects. The lattice is shown as integrity levels increasing from bottom to top. We employ $B1$ because it is a mandatory integrity protection, which relies solely on NRD and NWU security policies.

The second baseline model ($B2$) is the importance based malware detec-tion model introduced in [20]. It assigned importance values to all subjects and objects by examining their structures in a dependency network, and employed statistical classifiers to detect malware based on the assigned importance values

- Program
- File
- Registry

GIN
GSCC
GOUT

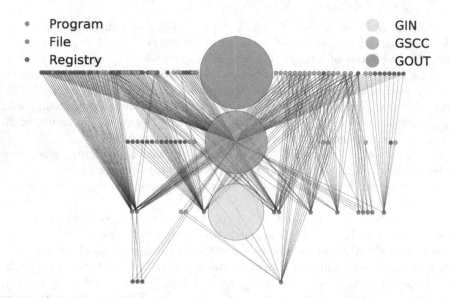

Fig. 5. The lattice constructed from access events of benign programs in our data set. GSCC stands for giant strongly connected component, GIN represents in-neighbors of the GSCC but without any edge from the GSCC, and GOUT represents out-neighbors of the GSCC but without any edge to the GSCC. Each small node indicates either a subject (program) or an object (file or registry).

of objects. The reason for choosing B2 is that this paper has similar goal with that, although there is a gap between importance values and integrity levels.

4.2   Integrity Levels and Security Policies

To explore the appropriateness of the derived integrity levels, we examine the differences exhibited between benign and malicious programs from the perspective of their compliance to security policies NRD and NWU. That is, we investigate the violations of security policies for benign and malicious processes based on the derived integrity levels. We define a violation of NRD or NWU when a process reads an object with low integrity level, and writes an object with high integrity level.

Let p be a process, O_r be the set of reading objects of p, O_w be the set of writing objects of p, $o_r \in O_r$, $o_w \in O_w$. Strictly, according to the NRD and NWU policies, the integrity levels of p, o_r and o_w should satisfy $I(p) \leq I(o_r)$ and $I(p) \geq I(o_w)$, i.e., $I(p) - I(o_r) \leq 0$ and $I(o_w) - I(p) \leq 0$. Because of difficulty in determining $I(p)$, we employ a proxy $I(o_w) - I(o_r) \leq 0$, by summing up the two criteria, to examine violations. A violation happens to the process p when $I(o_w) - I(o_r) > 0$. We refer to a *violation* as a pair of reading and writing objects where the integrity level of the reading object is lower than that of the writing object. If the determined integrity levels of objects are correct, few violations would appear in benign processes, while many violations would appear in malicious processes.

We examine violations in processes by two simple indicators based on our proxy for violation: (1) *Fraction of violation.* In each execution, we count the fraction of violations among all pairs of reading objects and writing objects, e.g., $\frac{\sum_{o_r,o_w} \mathbb{1}(I(o_w)-I(o_r)>0)}{|O_r||O_w|}$, where $\mathbb{1}()$ is an indicator function, $|O_r|$ and $|O_w|$ are the sizes of set O_r and O_w. (2) *Largest violation.* This refers to the difference between the lowest integrity level of all reading objects and the highest integrity level of all writing objects in one execution, e.g., $\max_{o_r,o_w} I(o_w) - I(o_r)$. These two simple indicators demonstrate why the integrity levels of objects are useful to detect malware from a perspective of security policies. Figure 6 exhibits fraction of violations, while Fig. 7 illustrates largest violations, for benign and malicious processes w.r.t. integrity levels of access objects determined by baselines and our model, in terms of box plots. These results are obtained from all testing sets of eight experiments which are presented in the above subsection. A box plot splits these results into quartiles. The interquartile range box represents the middle 50 % of the results. The whiskers, extending from either side of the box, represent the ranges for the bottom 5 % and the top 5 % of the results.

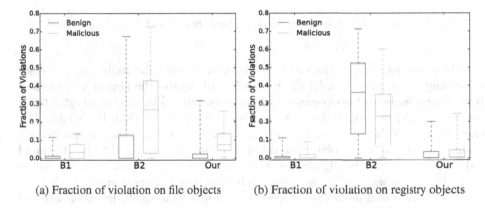

(a) Fraction of violation on file objects   (b) Fraction of violation on registry objects

Fig. 6. Fraction of violation under integrity levels from baseline and our models

In Fig. 6(a), as we expected, there are fewer violations in benign processes than in malicious processes, w.r.t. integrity levels of accessed file objects, under all three models. Using the Kolmogorov–Smirnov (KS) test, we find significant differences ($p \ll 10^{-4}$) between benign and malicious processes under all three models in Fig. 6(a). The KS test is a nonparametric test to evaluate whether two samples come from the same population. These results indicate each model can be used to determine integrity levels. We also find that our model is more able to discriminate between benign and malicious processes than the two baseline models, with respect to integrity levels of accessed file objects. This indicates that our model does a better job at determining integrity levels for file objects.

With respect to the integrity levels of accessed registry objects, we do not observe obvious difference between benign and malicious processes in Fig. 6(b), although significant differences ($p \ll 10^{-4}$) are found under KS test. There are two possible reasons: (1) All models fail to determine the integrity levels of registry objects. (2) Benign processes do not obey NRD and NWU policies when they access registry objects.

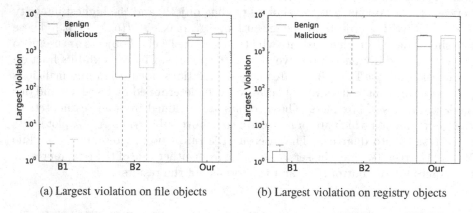

(a) Largest violation on file objects   (b) Largest violation on registry objects

Fig. 7. Largest violation under integrity levels from baseline and our models

Moreover, we explore the difference between benign and malicious processes according to the largest violation. Figure 7(a) illustrates the largest violations of benign and malicious processes on file objects, while Fig. 7(b) illustrates those on registry objects. Since the total number of integrity levels in B1 is much less than those in other two models, we show the largest violation in logarithmic scale. Similar results are observed in Fig. 7(a) and (b) compared to Fig. 6(a) and (b). Meanwhile, we find significant differences ($p \ll 10^{-4}$) under the KS test in all cases. As shown in Fig. 7(a), our model achieves the greatest discrimination between benign and malicious processes according to integrity levels of accessed file objects. It implies the ability of our model for malware detection even with camouflages. However, we find similar failures of all three models in distinguishing malicious programs from benign programs, which due to similar possible reasons as we aforementioned.

We observe obvious differences between benign and malicious processes by examining either of these two indicators. However, the fraction of violation may suffer from *mimicry* or *camouflaged attacks*, where malicious processes run under the cover of some benign processes [10,15]. For example, if malware deliberately read many file objects with the highest integrity levels, then the numerator in the fraction of violations will be overwhelmed by the denominator in the fraction, which leads to as small fraction of violations as benign processes. Compared with the fraction of violation, the indicator of largest violation is much more robust. However, one potential failure of the largest violation indicator is false positive. There are benign processes which modify objects with high integrity level while read objects with low integrity level. Usually, these processes are some special processes, such as system services. We can include them in a whitelist, and reduce the false positives of the largest violation indicator.

4.3   Detection Results

Although simple indicators, e.g., fraction of violations, largest violation, etc., provide us ways of understanding why a model works, they usually fail to achieve promising performance on malware detection. As presented in Sect. 3.4, we employ random forests to extract adaptive security policies under determined integrity levels and build a model for malware detection. With three models for determining integrity levels, we evaluate their performance on malware detection with the ROC curve and the area under ROC curve (AUC). We train models with the benign and malicious training sets, and evaluate them on the benign and malicious testing sets, as stated in Sect. 4.1.

Table 2 exhibits average true positive rates (TPRs) of three models at specific false positive rates (FPRs) among all experiments. We choose these four FPRs, because they are four representative FPRs to evaluate a method of malware detection in practice. Meanwhile, we emphasis the most outperformed results of our models compared with baseline models, i.e., 99.88 % TPF at 0.1 % FPR, on average. In most cases, our model achieves better performance than two baseline models.

Table 2. Performance under different models of determining integrity level

Model	FPR	True Positive Rate (TPR)								Average TPR
		U1	U2	U3	U4	U5	U6	U7	U8	
B1	0%	0%	0%	0%	0%	0%	0%	0%	0%	0%
	0.1%	92.09%	83.59%	70.30%	76.08%	53.35%	79.79%	64.10%	43.10%	70.30%
	0.5%	96.75%	91.75%	92.55%	88.50%	86.18%	90.31%	90.98%	76.89%	89.24%
	1.0%	98.09%	96.64%	95.18%	92.52%	91.85%	91.54%	94.19%	90.08%	93.76%
B2	0%	99.52%	82.34%	97.58%	98.22%	88.16%	99.40%	0%	99.73%	83.11%
	0.1%	100%	90.02%	99.27%	99.85%	92.92%	99.53%	70.21%	99.73%	93.94%
	0.5%	100%	99.60%	99.86%	100%	99.57%	99.66%	95.32%	99.73%	99.21%
	1.0%	100%	99.93%	100%	100%	99.86%	99.66%	99.16%	99.86%	99.80%
Our	0%	99.45%	99.49%	99.51%	97.15%	98.30%	99.71%	4.48%	98.31%	87.05%
	0.1%	99.98%	99.98%	99.95%	99.89%	99.87%	99.94%	99.61%	99.85%	99.88%
	0.5%	99.99%	100%	99.98%	99.98%	99.97%	99.98%	99.89%	99.93%	99.97%
	1.0%	100%	100%	99.98%	99.99%	99.99%	99.99%	99.94%	99.97%	99.98%

To further compare the performance of the three models, we conduct a Wilcoxon rank-sum test to evaluate whether one model significantly outperforms the other in terms of AUC. The Wilcoxon signed-rank test is a non-parametric statistical hypothesis test used when comparing two related samples to assess whether their population mean ranks differ. Table 3 illustrates the test statistic and its significance between each pair of models. A negative value of the test statistic indicates that the first model performs worse than the second model shown at the beginning of the row.

Table 3. Results of Wilcoxon rank-sum tests on AUCs of different models

Models	U1	U2	U3	U4	U5	U6	U7	U8	All
B1 v.s. B2	-5.41**	-5.41**	-5.41**	-5.41**	-5.41**	-5.41**	-5.41**	-5.41**	-15.47**
B1 v.s. Our	-5.41**	-5.41**	-5.41**	-5.41**	-5.41**	-5.41**	-5.41**	-5.41**	-15.47**
B2 v.s. Our	-2.89*	-5.41**	-0.14 (0.89)	-0.81 (0.41)	-2.84*	-0.77 (0.44)	-3.68**	-4.25**	-5.44**

* Indicates significance under 0.01.
** Indicates significance under 0.0001.
p-value is shown in parenthesis if it is not significant under these two levels.

In Table 3, from column U1 to U8, we perform hypothesis testing on results of 20 runnings within each experiment. The last column presents the result of hypothesis testing on results of runnings of all experiments. We observe significant improvements of our model compared with baseline models.

Furthermore, Fig. 8 illustrates average ROCs of eight experiments under our probabilistic integrity level, which provides better understandings of the performance.

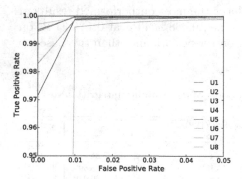
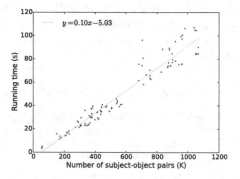

Fig. 8. Average ROC of eight experiments under our model

Fig. 9. Scatter plot of running time in seconds against problem size in thousands

4.4 Running Time

The time complexity of the employed classifier, random forests, has been well studied, which is, $mn \log n$, where m is the number of trees in random forests, we find $m = 10$ is optimal in our experiments, n is the number of processes, a.k.a. data points [5]. Hence, we do not present its running time.

We explore the running time of our probabilistic integrity model, since the running time of loopy belief propagation in practices varies in different problems. We vary the problem size, which is the number of subject-object pairs, by randomly selecting different portions of subjects and their involving subject-object pairs. Figure 9 illustrates a scatter plot of running time in seconds against problem size in thousands, and its fitting with linear regression. We observe strongly linear relationship, supported by significant coefficients and $R^2 = 0.93$ in the linear regression, between the running time and the problem size. This result verifies the linear time complexity of our probabilistic integrity model, and demonstrates the feasibility of a runtime malware detection.

5   Conclusion and Future Work

In spite of considerate effort by security researchers and engineers, it has been demonstrated that attackers move faster than defenders. This paper presents a probabilistic model on access behaviors of programs, and integrity levels of programs, files and registries. We employ probabilistic inferences to determine integrity levels of these system subjects and objects. Combining with a statistical classifier, we build a integrity based access behavior model for malware detection. The encouraging experimental results indicate the feasibility and usefulness of our model. The linear time complexity of our probabilistic integrity model is both proofed by our theoretical analysis, and verified by our experimental results.

Our model can be extended to subject and objects in other granularities, which are constrained by similar security policies. Meanwhile, our model can be adapted to determine levels of other security attributes, e.g., confidentiality, according to corresponding security policies, e.g., Bell-LaPadula model.

We believe our probabilistic integrity model will be enhanced, when acquiring knowledge from both benign and malicious programs. Thus, building a model to combine access behaviors of both benign and malicious programs will be our future work.

Acknowledgments. We would like to thank our shepherd, Manos Antonakakis, and the anonymous reviewers for their insightful comments that greatly helped improve the presentation of this paper. This work is supported by NFSC (61175039, 61221063, 61403301), 863 High Tech Development Plan (2012AA011003), Research Fund for Doctoral Program of Higher Education of China (20090201120032), International Research Collaboration Project of Shaanxi Province (2013KW11) and Fundamental Research Funds for Central Universities (2012jdhz08). Any opinions, findings, and conclusions or recommendations expressed in this material are the authors' and do not necessarily reflect those of the sponsor.

Appendix- Derivation of Eq. (8)

$P(E_I|Acc) \propto \sum_T P(Acc|T)P(T|E_I) \sum_D P(E_I|D)P(D)$, where

$$\sum_D P(E_I|D)P(D) = \begin{cases} \sum_D d_1 P(D) = \mathbb{E}_D(d_1) = \frac{\alpha_1}{\alpha_1+\alpha_2+\alpha_3}, & \text{if } I(s) < I(o), \\ \sum_D d_2 P(D) = \mathbb{E}_D(d_2) = \frac{\alpha_2}{\alpha_1+\alpha_2+\alpha_3}, & \text{if } I(s) = I(o), \\ \sum_D d_3 P(D) = \mathbb{E}_D(d_3) = \frac{\alpha_3}{\alpha_1+\alpha_2+\alpha_3}, & \text{if } I(s) > I(o). \end{cases} \tag{18}$$

And then,

(1.) If $I(s) < I(o)$:

$$P(< |Acc) \propto \frac{\alpha_1}{\alpha_1 + \alpha_2 + \alpha_3} \Delta \int_T t_1^{N_r} t_2^{N_w} t_3^{N_{r\&w}} \frac{t_1^{\beta_1} t_2^{\beta_2-1} t_3^{\beta_3-1}}{B(1+\beta_1,\beta_2,\beta_3)} \, dT,$$

$$= \frac{\alpha_1}{\alpha_1 + \alpha_2 + \alpha_3} \Delta \frac{B(N_r + \beta_1 + 1, N_w + \beta_2, N_{r\&w}\beta_3)}{B(1+\beta_1,\beta_2,\beta_3)},$$

$$= \frac{\alpha_1}{\alpha_1 + \alpha_2 + \alpha_3} \Delta \frac{\beta_1 + \beta_2 + \beta_3}{\beta_1} \frac{N_r + \beta_1}{N + \beta_1 + \beta_2 + \beta_3} \Omega, \quad (19)$$

where $\Delta = \frac{\Gamma(N+1)}{\Gamma(N_r+1)\Gamma(N_w+1)\Gamma(N_{r\&w}+1)}$, $\Omega = \frac{B(N_r+\beta_1, N_w+\beta_2, N_{r\&w}+\beta_3)}{B(\beta_1,\beta_2,\beta_3)}$, and $B(\beta_1,\beta_2,\beta_3) = \frac{\Gamma(\beta_1)\Gamma(\beta_2)\Gamma(\beta_3)}{\Gamma(\beta_1+\beta_2+\beta_3)}$.

(2.) If $I(s) = I(o)$:

$$P(= |Acc) \propto \frac{\alpha_2}{\alpha_1 + \alpha_2 + \alpha_3} \Delta \int_T t_1^{N_r} t_2^{N_w} t_3^{N_{r\&w}} \frac{t_1^{\beta_1-1} t_2^{\beta_2-1} t_3^{\beta_3-1}}{B(\beta_1,\beta_2,\beta_3)} \, dT = \frac{\alpha_2}{\alpha_1 + \alpha_2 + \alpha_3} \Delta\Omega.$$

$$(20)$$

(3.) If $I(s) > I(o)$:

$$P(> |Acc) \propto \frac{\alpha_3}{\alpha_1 + \alpha_2 + \alpha_3} \Delta \int_T t_1^{N_r} t_2^{N_w} t_3^{N_{r\&w}} \frac{t_1^{\beta_1-1} t_2^{\beta_2} t_3^{\beta_3-1}}{B(\beta_1,\beta_2+1,\beta_3)} \, dT,$$

$$= \frac{\alpha_3}{\alpha_1 + \alpha_2 + \alpha_3} \Delta \frac{\beta_1 + \beta_2 + \beta_3}{\beta_2} \frac{N_w + \beta_2}{N + \beta_1 + \beta_2 + \beta_3} \Omega.$$

$$(21)$$

Summing up Eqs. (19)–(21), we derive the posterior distribution of E_I given Acc, i.e., $P(E_I|Acc)$, as shown in Eqs. (9)–(11).

References

1. Anderson, R.: Security Engineering: A Guide to Building Dependable Distributed Systems. John Wiley & Sons (2008)
2. Apap, F., Honig, A., Hershkop, S., Eskin, E., Stolfo, S.J.: Detecting malicious software by monitoring anomalous windows registry accesses. In: Wespi, A., Vigna, G., Deri, L. (eds.) RAID 2002. LNCS, vol. 2516, p. 36. Springer, Heidelberg (2002)
3. Bellovin, S.M.: Security and usability: windows vista, July 2007. https://www.cs.columbia.edu/smb/blog/2007-07/2007-07-13.html
4. Biba, K.J.: Integrity considerations for secure computer systems. ESD-TR 76–372, MITRE Corp. (1977)
5. Breiman, L.: Random forests. Mach. Learn. 45, 5–32 (2001)
6. Canali, D., Lanzi, A., Balzarotti, D., Kruegel, C., Christodorescu, M., Kirda, E.: A quantitative study of accuracy in system call-based malware detection. In: Proceedings of the 2012 International Symposium on Software Testing and Analysis, pp. 122–132. ACM (2012)
7. Fraser, T.: Lomac: low water-mark integrity protection for cots environments. In: IEEE Symposium on Security and Privacy (S&P), pp. 230–245 (2000)

8. Fredrikson, M., Jha, S., Christodorescu, M., Sailer, R., Yan, X.: Synthesizing near-optimal malware specifications from suspicious behaviors. In: IEEE Symposium on Security and Privacy (S&P), pp. 45–60 (2010)
9. Gelman, A., Carlin, J.B., Stern, H.S., Rubin, D.B.: Bayesian data analysis, vol. 2. Taylor & Francis (2014)
10. Gu, Z., Pei, K., Wang, Q., Si, L., Zhang, X., Xu, D.: LEAPS: detecting camouflaged attacks with statistical learning guided by program analysis. In: 45th Annual IEEE/IFIP International Conference on Dependable Systems and Networks (DSN). IEEE (2015)
11. How the integrity mechanism is implemented in Windows Vista (2014). http://msdn.microsoft.com/en-us/library/bb625962.aspx,
12. Hsu, F., Chen, H., Ristenpart, T., Li, J., Su, Z.: Back to the future: a framework for automatic malware removal and system repair. In: 22nd Annual Computer Security Applications Conference, ACSAC 2006, pp. 257–268. IEEE (2006)
13. King, S.T., Chen, P.M.: Backtracking intrusions. ACM Trans. Comput. Syst. **23**, 51–76 (2005)
14. Koller, D., Friedman, N.: Probabilistic graphical models: principles and techniques. MIT press (2009)
15. Kruegel, C., Kirda, E., Mutz, D., Robertson, W., Vigna, G.: Automating mimicry attacks using static binary analysis. In: Proceedings of the 14th conference on USENIX Security Symposium, vol. 14, pp. 11–11. USENIX Association (2005)
16. Kruegel, C., Mutz, D., Valeur, F., Vigna, G.: On the detection of anomalous system call arguments. In: Snekkenes, E., Gollmann, D. (eds.) ESORICS 2003. LNCS, vol. 2808, pp. 326–343. Springer, Heidelberg (2003)
17. Lanzi, A., Balzarotti, D., Kruegel, C., Christodorescu, M., Kirda, E.: Accessminer: using system-centric models for malware protection. In: Proceedings of the 17th ACM conference on Computer and Communications Security (CCS), pp. 399–412. ACM (2010)
18. Manadhata, P.K., Yadav, S., Rao, P., Horne, W.: Detecting malicious domains via graph inference. In: Kutyłowski, M., Vaidya, J. (eds.) ICAIS 2014, Part I. LNCS, vol. 8712, pp. 1–18. Springer, Heidelberg (2014)
19. Mandatory Integrity Control (2014). http://msdn.microsoft.com/en-us/library/windows/desktop/bb648648
20. Mao, W., Cai, Z., Guan, X., Towsley, D.: Centrality metrics of importance in access behaviors and malware detections. In: Proceedings of the 30th Annual Computer Security Applications Conference (ACSAC 2014). ACM (2014)
21. Mao, Z., Li, N., Chen, H., Jiang, X.: Combining discretionary policy with mandatory information flow in operating systems. ACM Trans. Inf. Syst. Secur. (TISSEC) **14**(3), 24 (2011)
22. Mark Russinovich, B.C.: Process monitor (2014). http://technet.microsoft.com/en-us/sysinternals/bb896645
23. Muthukumaran, D., Rueda, S., Talele, N., Vijayakumar, H., Teutsch, J., Jaeger, T., Edwards, N.: Transforming commodity security policies to enforce Clark-Wilson integrity. In: Proceedings of the 28th Annual Computer Security Applications Conference (ACSAC 2012). ACM (2012)
24. Pedregosa, F., Varoquaux, G., Gramfort, A., Michel, V., Thirion, B., Grisel, O., Blondel, M., Prettenhofer, P., Weiss, R., Dubourg, V., et al.: Scikit-learn: machine learning in python. J. Mach. Learn. Res. **12**, 2825–2830 (2011)
25. Sun, W., Sekar, R., Liang, Z., Venkatakrishnan, V.N.: Expanding malware defense by securing software installations. In: Zamboni, D. (ed.) DIMVA 2008. LNCS, vol. 5137, pp. 164–185. Springer, Heidelberg (2008)

26. Sun, W., Sekar, R., Poothia, G., Karandikar, T.: Practical proactive integrity preservation: a basis for malware defense. In: IEEE Symposium on Security and Privacy (S&P), pp. 248–262 (2008)
27. Symantec. Internet Security Threat Report, April 2015. https://www4.symantec.com/mktginfo/whitepaper/ISTR/21347932_GA-internet-security-threat-report-volume-20-2015-social_v2.pdf
28. Sze, W.-K., Sekar, R.: A portable user-level approach for system-wide integrity protection. In: Proceedings of the 29th Annual Computer Security Applications Conference (ACSAC 2013), pp. 219–228. ACM (2013)
29. Tamersoy, A., Roundy, K., Chau, D.H.: Guilt by association: large scale malware detection by mining file-relation graphs. In: Proceedings of the 20th ACM SIGKDD international conference on Knowledge Discovery and Data Mining, pp. 1524–1533. ACM (2014)
30. VXHeaven (2010). http://vx.netlux.org/

Counteracting Data-Only Malware
with Code Pointer Examination

Thomas Kittel[(✉)], Sebastian Vogl, Julian Kirsch, and Claudia Eckert

Technische Universität München, München, Germany
{kittel,vogls,kirschju,eckert}@sec.in.tum.de

Abstract. As new code-based defense technologies emerge, attackers
move to data-only malware, which is capable of infecting a system without introducing any new code. To manipulate the control flow without
code, data-only malware inserts a control data structure into the system,
for example in the form of a ROP chain, which enables it to combine
existing instructions into a new malicious program. Current systems try
to hinder data-only malware by detecting the point in time when the malware starts executing. However, it has been shown that these approaches
are not only performance consuming, but can also be subverted.

In this work, we introduce a new approach, Code Pointer Examination (CPE), which aims to detect data-only malware by identifying
and classifying code pointers. Instead of targeting control flow changes,
our approach targets the control structure of data-only malware, which
mainly consists of pointers to the instruction sequences that the malware
reuses. Since the control structure is comparable to the code region of
traditional malware, this results in an effective detection approach that
is difficult to evade. We implemented a prototype for recent Linux kernels that is capable of identifying and classifying all code pointers within
the kernel. As our experiments show, our prototype is able to detect
data-only malware in an efficient manner (less than 1 % overhead).

Keywords: VMI · Introspection · CFI · CPI · CPE · Pointer examination · OS Integrity · Linux · kernel · Data-only malware

1 Introduction

Malware is without doubt one of the biggest IT security threats of our time. This
is especially true for kernel-level malware, which runs at the highest privilege
level and is thus able to attack and modify any part of the system, including the
operating system (OS) itself. However, even kernel-level malware has a weakness that is well-suited for its detection: in order to execute, the malware has
to load its malicious instructions onto the victim's system and thereby effectively change its codebase. This makes current kernel-level malware vulnerable
to code integrity-based defense mechanisms, which prevent or detect malicious
changes to the code regions of the system. It is not surprising that validating

© Springer International Publishing Switzerland 2015
H. Bos et al. (Eds.): RAID 2015, LNCS 9404, pp. 177–197, 2015.
DOI: 10.1007/978-3-319-26362-5_9

the integrity of the system's code regions became a key approach to counter-act malware. In the meantime, commodity OSs employ a multitude of mechanisms that protect the system's codebase (e.g. W⊕X, secure boot, etc.) and researchers presented sophisticated Code Integrity Validation (CIV) frameworks that are capable of reliably and efficiently detecting malicious changes to the code regions of userspace programs [20] as well as modern OS kernels [17].

As code integrity mechanisms become more and more widespread, attackers are forced to find new ways to infect and control a system. A likely next step in malware evolution is thereby *data-only malware*, which solely uses instructions that already existed before its presence to perform its malicious computations [14]. To accomplish this, data-only malware employs code reuse techniques such as return-oriented programming (ROP) or jump-oriented programming (JOP) to combine existing instructions into new malicious programs. This approach enables the malware form to evade all existing code-based defense approaches and to persistently infect a system without changing its codebase [30]. Despite this capability and the substantial risk associated with it, there only exist a handful of countermeasures against data-only malware so far, and those can often be easily circumvented [6, 9, 13, 24].

In this paper, we explore a new approach to the detection of data-only malware. The key idea behind this approach is to detect data-only malware based on "malicious" pointers to code regions. For simplicity we refer to them as code pointers. Similar to traditional malware, data-only malware has to control which reused instruction sequence should be executed when. To achieve this, data-only malware makes use of a control structure that contains pointers to the instructions that should be (re)used. This control structure can essentially be seen as the "code region" of the data-only program that the malware introduces. By identifying malicious code pointers in memory, we in essence aim to apply the idea of code integrity checking to the field of data-only malware by detecting malicious control data within the system. For this purpose, we introduce the concept of Code Pointer Examination (CPE).

The idea behind CPE is to identify and examine each possible code pointer in memory in order to classify it as benign or malicious. This is essentially a two-step process: In the first step, we iterate through the entire memory of the monitored machine with a byte by byte granularity in order to identify all code pointers. In the second step, we classify the identified code pointers based on heuristics. As our experiments showed, this approach results in an effective and high-performance (less than 1 % overhead) detection mechanism that can detect data-only malware and is well-suited for live monitoring as well as forensic investigations.

Since the OS is the integral part of the security model that is nowadays used on most systems, we focus our work primarily on the Linux *kernel*. We chose this OS, since it is open and well documented, which makes it easier to understand and reproduce our work. However, the concepts and ideas that we present are equally applicable to userspace applications and other OSs such as Windows.

In summary we make the following contributions:

- We present CPE, a novel approach to identify and classify code pointers in 64-bit systems.
- We highlight data structures that are used for control flow decisions in modern Linux kernels and thus must be considered for control flow validation.
- We provide a prototype implementation and show that it is both effective and efficient in detecting control structures of data-only malware.

2 Background

In this section we discuss foundations required for the rest of the paper.

Protection Mechanisms. Intel provides two new protection mechanisms to make it significantly harder for an attacker to introduce malicious code or data into the kernel. The first protection mechanism is Supervisor Mode Execution Protection (SMEP). SMEP ensures that only code that is marked as *executable* and *supervisor* is executed in kernel mode. In particular, if the CPU is trying to fetch an instruction from a page that is marked as a *user* page while operating with a Current Privilege Level (CPL) that is equal to zero, SMEP will generate a protection fault. SMEP is usually used together with the No-eXecute (NX) bit, which marks a page as not executable.

The second protection mechanism is Supervisor Mode Access Prevention (SMAP). This feature can basically be seen as SMEP for data; it raises a fault if data that is marked as *user* in the page tables is accessed within the kernel. With both of these features enabled, the kernel is thus unable to access any userspace memory. In combination, this significantly reduces the amount of memory that is usable as gadget space for an attacker.

Runtime Code Validation. A key idea that our work builds upon is runtime code validation. While code-based defense mechanisms such as W⊕X and secure boot ensure the integrity of code at load time, runtime code validation guarantees that all code regions of a system are coherent and valid at any point in time during its execution [17]. For this purpose, the code of the protected system is constantly monitored and the legitimacy of all observed changes is verified. As a result, any modification or extension of the existing codebase can be detected and prevented. To illustrate this, we briefly describe the runtime code validation framework presented by Kittel et al. [17], which serves as a foundation for this work.

Kittel et al. created a runtime code validation framework that is capable of reliably validating the integrity of all kernel code pages at runtime. To isolate the monitoring component from the protected system, the proposed system makes use of virtualization. Once monitoring begins, the validation framework first iterates through the page tables of the system to obtain a list of all executable supervisor pages. Since the page tables are the basis for the address translation conducted by the underlying hardware, this approach effectively enables the framework to reliably determine which memory regions are marked as executable and could thus contain instructions.

In the next step, the monitor obtains the list of loaded kernel modules from the monitored system using virtual machine introspection (VMI). Based on this information the framework simulates the loading process of each of the modules as well as the kernel image to obtain a trusted and known-to-be-good state of the code regions that can later on be compared to the current state of the code regions. To accomplish this, the framework requires access to a trusted store that contains all modules as well as the kernel binary that are executing in the monitored system. This trusted store is implemented by storing all trusted binary files within the hypervisor.

Once the loading process has been simulated, the trusted code pages contain all load time changes that the kernel applies. However, modern kernels may also patch code regions at runtime in order to increase compatibility and performance. As a result, the trusted code pages may at this point still differ from the code pages that are currently used by the monitored system. To identify whether runtime changes have been applied, each of the trusted code pages is compared byte by byte with its counterpart in the protected system. If a difference is observed, the framework attempts to validate the changes by determining whether the change was conducted by one of runtime patching mechanisms that the kernel uses. The individual validation steps thereby heavily depend on the hardware configuration of the monitored system as well as the runtime patching mechanisms that it uses. The interested reader can find an overview of the individual runtime patching mechanisms employed by the Linux kernel in [17].

Data-only Malware. Runtime code validation frameworks effectively hinder an attacker from introducing malicious instructions into a system as this new code will be detected and prevented from execution. To be able to control a system under such circumstances, attackers must thus resort to malware forms that leave the codebase of the attacked system untouched. The only malware form that is currently known to be capable of such a feat is data-only malware, which alters the control flow of the infected system based on specially crafted data structures [14,30].

In particular, data-only malware reuses the instructions that already existed on the target system before the malware arrived to perform its malicious operations. This is achieved by applying code reuse techniques, commonly used in the field of binary exploitation, to the problem of malware creation. Well-known examples of such techniques are ROP [27], JOP [3] and ret2libc [4].

To control the execution of the system, code reuse techniques leverage a control data structure that consists of pointers to existing instruction sequences. In general one cannot reuse arbitrary instruction sequences; instead, each of the reused sequences must fulfill a particular property. For example, in the case of ROP, each reused instruction sequence must end with a `return` instruction. The property of the `return` instruction is thereby that it will load the address which currently resides on top of the stack into the instruction pointer. This enables us to control the execution of the system as follows: our first reused instruction sequence will point the stack pointer to our control data structure in memory. Since the control structure now resides on the stack, the execution of the **return** instruction at the end of each reused sequence will obtain the address of the next sequence from the control structure and initiate its execution. Consequently, the **return** instruction provides the "transition" between the individual sequences whose addresses are contained within the control structure.

While code reuse *exploits* usually only make use of a very small control data structure that simply allocates a writable and executable memory region which is then used to execute traditional shellcode, control data structures of data-only malware are in general quite large. The reason for this is that data-only *malware* solely relies on code reuse to function. Each functionality that the malware provides must be implemented by code reuse. The result are huge chains that contain hundreds of reused instruction sequences [30]. However, due to the increasing proliferation of code integrity mechanisms, attackers will likely transition to this type of malware to attack modern OS kernels.

3 Attacker Model and Assumptions

In this work we assume that the monitored system is protected by a virtualization-based runtime code integrity validation framework. In addition, we assume that an attacker has gained full access to the monitored system, which she wants to leverage to install kernel malware. While the attacker can, in principle, modify any part of the system, the code validation framework will detect some of the changes that the attacker may conduct. Most importantly, it will detect any changes to executable kernel code and will in addition enforce SMEP and SMAP from the hypervisor-level. As a result, the attacker is forced to use data-only malware to infect the kernel. In this process, the control structure that is used by the attacker must reside within kernel's memory space since SMAP is in place. We also assume that the kernel's *identity mapping* which maps the entire physical memory into kernel space is marked as usermode in the page tables. A similar approach was previously proposed by Kemerlis et al. [15], in which pages that are used by userspace applications are temporarily unmapped from the identity mapping. Finally, we assume that the data-only malware introduced into the system by the attacker is persistent, i. e. will permanently reside within the memory of the target system, as otherwise it could not be triggered by an external event. Notice that this is usually the case for malware as Petroni and Hicks [22] showed.

4 Related Work

There is a plethora of work that is concerned with verifying the integrity of software. The existing research can thereby be roughly divided into two parts. The first branch of research focuses on the integrity of the system's code regions. This led to the development of various frameworks that are capable of validating the integrity of the codebase of applications as well as the kernel code sections [12,17,20]. This work builds upon said research by assuming that the code of the monitored system cannot be modified by an attacker due to fact that it is protected by such a framework.

The second branch of research, which our work belongs to, focuses on the integrity of the kernel's data and especially the kernel's *control* data. A popular approach in this regard is Control Flow Integrity CFI validation, which aims to dynamically validate the target of each branch instruction [1,16]. This is accomplished by tracing and monitoring every indirect branch and the current stack pointer of the inspected machine, implementing a shadow stack, or using the performance counters of the monitored system to trace unpredicted branches [7,21,33,34]. Unfortunately, however, current approaches not only suffer from a significant performance overhead, but also rely on invalid assumptions, which makes them vulnerable to evasion attacks [6,9,13,26].

Instead of ensuring control flow integrity for the entire kernel, there also have been approaches that solely focus on the discovery of hooks, which are often used by rootkits and other malware forms to intercept events within the system [31,32]. During this process, existing approaches rely on the assumption that only persistent control data can be abused for hooking. As in the case of CFI, this assumption is invalid and can be used to circumvent existing mechanisms by targeting transient control data instead [30]. Thus, neither hook-based detection nor CFI mechanisms are currently capable of countering data-only malware.

In addition, there has been work aiming to reconstruct the kernel data structures and their interconnection on the hypervisor level in order to provide data integrity checking [5,11,19,25]. The basic idea hereby is to parse the entire kernel code to be able to reconstruct the dependencies of different data structures (points-to analysis) and to construct a map of kernel data structures. However, current approaches are so far unable to reconstruct the entire graph of kernel data structures, which allows data-only malware to evade detection by leveraging techniques such as DKSM [2].

An alternative approach, similar to the one proposed in this work, aims to scan for pointers to executable code in 32-bit userspace memory [23,28]. Unfortunately, this approach has a high number of false positives on 32-bit systems. Therefore, each detected code pointer is further analyzed using *speculative code execution*.

Finally, Szekeres et al. [29] introduced the concept of Code-Pointer Integrity (CPI), the requirement to enforce the integrity of code pointers in memory. An implementation of CPI that is based on memory splitting was then proposed by Kuznetsov et al. [18]. In their work they introduce a compile time instrumentation approach that protects control flow relevant pointers. The basic idea thereby is to separate control flow relevant pointers into a separated space in memory and to limit access to that area. Thus they split process memory into a safe region and a regular region, where the safe region is secured by the kernel and can only be accessed via memory operations that are *autogenerated and proven at compile time* [18]. However, Evans et al. [10] showed that restricting access to pointers in memory is not enough, since this separation can still be broken with the help of side channel attacks.

5   Approach

In this work we aim to detect the control data structure of persistent data-only malware. In the process, we want to achieve three main goals:

Isolation. Since the main goal of our framework is to *detect* rather than to *prevent* kernel data-only malware infections, it is crucial that the detection framework is strongly isolated from the monitored target system. This is why we will leverage virtualization as a building block for our framework.

Performance. The overhead incurred by our detection framework on the monitored system should be as small as possible. Since we use virtualization as a foundation for our framework, it is thereby of particular importance that we keep the number of Virtual Machine (VM) exists as small as possible as they will heavily impact the performance of the overall approach.

Forensic. Due to the ever increasing number of malware attacks, the investigation of incidents becomes more and more important in order to understand the approach of an successful attacker and to avoid future breaches. This is why another crucial goal of our framework is to support forensic investigations in addition to live monitoring. In this regard, its particular important that an human investigator can easily assess and analyze the situation once an anomaly is detected by our framework.

The key idea behind our approach is to detect persistent data-only malware based on its control structure. As described in Sect. 2, the control structure is the most important component of data-only malware that essentially defines which reused instruction sequence should be executed when. Due to this property it is comparable to the code section of traditional malware, which makes it highly suitable as a basis for a detection mechanism.

To detect the control structure in memory, we use a three-step process. In the first step, we start by checking the integrity of important control flow related kernel objects. This is done for multiple reasons. First, we can use additional contextual information about these kernel objects, and second, these objects contain a lot of code pointers by design. By validating these objects at the beginning, we can increase the performance of our approach, as the code pointer within these known objects do not need to be validated in the following steps. We refer to this step as *Kernel Object Validation*.

In the second step, we *identify* all code pointers within the kernel's memory space. Based on this information, in the third step we *classify* the identified code pointers into benign and malicious code pointers applying multiple heuristics. The combination of these latter two steps is the *Pointer Examination* phase. Figure 1 provides an overview of this process. In the following, we describe these steps in more detail. For the sake of simplicity, we thereby focus on the Intel x64_64 bit architecture and the Linux OS. However, most of what we present is equally applicable to other OSs such as Windows. While this section provides an overview of our approach, we defer a discussion of the implementation details to Sect. 6.

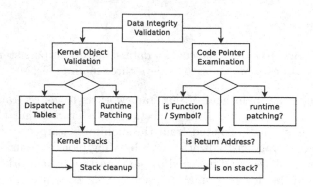

Fig. 1. Pointer classification within the proposed framework.

5.1   Control Flow Related Data Structures

We first describe control flow relevant kernel objects that we check using special semantic knowledge in the first step of our process.

Kernel Dispatcher Tables and Control Flow Registers. The most traditional control flow related data structures are the system call table and the interrupt descriptor tables. As control flow related data structures have already seen a lot of attention, we only mention this type of data structures here for sake of completeness. Our system checks every entry within these tables and ensures that it points to the correct function. This can be done by comparing the entire object to the corresponding version inside a trusted reference binary. In this step, we also validate the values of all control flow relevant registers such the model-specific registers MSRs and the *Debug* registers.

Tracepoints. Tracepoints are another type of data structure that is control flow relevant. An administrator can use the tracepoints feature to insert arbitrary hooks into the kernel's control flow that are executed whenever a certain point in the kernel's control flow is hit and the corresponding tracepoint is enabled. The addresses of the callback functions are stored in a list and are sequentially called by the kernel once the tracepoint is triggered. Tracepoints impose a big problem for control flow integrity validation as arbitrary function addresses can be inserted into all tracepoint locations at runtime. To counter this threat, we ensure that every hook that is installed with this mechanism calls a valid function within the Linux kernel.

Control Structures For Kernel Runtime Patching. To manage different runtime-patching mechanisms, the kernel maintains a variety of data structures. These data structures in turn contain pointers to kernel code, as they need to store the locations where kernel code should be patched at runtime. In our approach we check the integrity of the related data structures.

Kernel Stacks. Another examined type of data structure is the kernel stack of each thread in the system. We separate each kernel stack into three parts: At the very beginning of the stack, the active part of the stack is located. This part is empty if the corresponding process is currently executing in userspace. Next to the active part of the stack, old obsolete stack content is residing. On the very top of the stack, after all usable space, resides a structure called `thread_info`. It contains the thread's management information, for instance a `task_struct` pointer and the address limit of the stack.

While it is possible to validate the active part of the stack and its management structure, an attacker could use the old, currently unused stack space to hide persistent data-only malware. Therefore, this space is filled with zeros by our framework when used in live monitoring mode. Otherwise the unused stack regions are displayed to the forensic analyst for diagnosis and verification.

5.2   Pointer Identification

After we have validated control flow relevant data structures, we identify all other code pointers in memory in the second step. To identify code pointers, first of all we need to obtain a list of all executable memory regions within kernel space. For this purpose, we make use of the page tables used by the hardware. We also generate a list of all readable pages that do not contain code, as these pages contain the kernel's data. Note that using this approach we are also able to support Address Space Layout Randomization (ASLR).

Equipped with a list of all kernel code and data pages, we identify all kernel code pointers by iterating through each data page byte by byte and interpreting each 64-bit value as a potential pointer. If the potential pointer points to a code region (i.e., the 64-bit value represents an address lying within one of the code pages), we consider it to be a code pointer. While it seems that this very simple approach might produce many false positives, we like to stress that we did not observe any false positives during our experiments with various 64-bit Linux kernels. In our opinion the primary reason for this is that the 64-bit address space is much larger than the former 32-bit address space and makes it thus much more unlikely that non pointer values looking like pointers appear within memory.

5.3   Pointer Classification

After we have found a pointer, we classify it based on its destination address in order to decide whether it is malicious or benign. In a legitimate kernel there are multiple targets which a pointer is *allowed* to point to. In the following, we list those valid targets and describe how we are able to determine to which category the pointer belongs to.

Function Pointers. One important type of kernel code pointers are *function pointers*, which are frequently used within the kernel. To determine whether a code pointer is a function pointer, we make use of symbol information that is extracted from a trusted reference binary of the monitored kernel. Amongst these symbols are all functions that the kernel provides. We leverage the symbol list to verify whether a code pointer points to a function or not. In the former case, we consider the pointer to be benign. Otherwise, we continue with the classification process in order to determine whether the code pointer belongs to one of the other categories discussed below. Note that this implies that our approach might still be vulnerable to data-only malware that solely makes use of return-to-function (ret2libc).

Return Addresses. Another important type of code pointers are *return addresses*. In contrast to a function pointer, which must point to the beginning of a function, a return address can point to any instruction within a function that is preceded by a call instruction. To identify whether a code pointer is a return address, we leverage multiple heuristics. Note that most of the return addresses are located on a stack which is already checked during the Kernel Object Validation phase.

Pointers Related to Runtime Patching. A third type of pointer destinations are addresses that are stored by the kernel and point to a location where dynamic code patching is performed. While most of these pointers are contained within special objects that are checked in the Kernel Object Validation step as previously described, there are still some exceptions that must be considered separately.

Unknown Pointer Destinations. Any code pointer pointing into executable code which can not be classified into one of the above categories is considered to be malicious.

As we intend to identify kernel level data-only malware with our approach and we assume that the malware is persistently stored in memory, we propose to execute CPE in regular intervals.

6   Implementation

After describing the general idea of our approach, we cover the details of our implementation in this section. The code pointer examination framework presented in this work is based on our kernel code integrity framework [17]. This framework provides multiple advantages for our implementation:

First, it keeps track of all kernel and module code sections and ensures their integrity during runtime. In addition, it keeps track of all functions and symbols that are available inside the monitored kernel, as it already resembles the Linux loading process. This ensures that the information about the monitored kernel is binding by its nature, that is, it reflects the actual state of the monitored system. In our implementation we can use this database as a ground truth to classify kernel code pointers.

Secondly, the underlying framework keeps track of all dynamic runtime code patching that is conducted by the Linux kernel. We use this information to identify and validate data structures that are related to kernel runtime patching.

Third, our approach is usable for multiple hypervisors, while most of the features can also be used to analyze memory dumps in a forensic scenario. Currently tests have been conducted with both KVM as well as XEN.

6.1   Kernel Object Validation

Before we scan the kernel's memory for pointers, we check the integrity of important kernel data structures. This allows to minimize the parts of kernel data that may contain arbitrary function pointers or other pointers into executable kernel code. The validation of those structures leverages semantic information about the kernel that was generated by the underlying code validation framework or manually collected while analyzing the kernel. In the following, we only list a couple of examples to illustrate the requirement of this step.

First, we validate various dispatcher tables and the kernel's read-only data segments. These locations usually contain a lot of kernel code pointers, whereas the target of each pointer is well defined. The validation is performed by comparing these objects to the trusted reference versions of the binaries that are loaded by the underlying validation framework.

Next, we validate kernel data structures used for runtime patching. These are for example: Jump Labels (__start___jump_table), SMP Locks (__smp_locks), Mcount Locations (__start_mcount_loc), and Ftrace Events (__start_ftrace_events). To validate these structures we semantically compare them to the data extracted from trusted reference binaries by the underlying framework. In addition to these runtime patching control data structures, there also exist data structures in the kernel that are used to actually conduct the runtime patch. For clarification, we discuss one example for legitimate kernel code pointers related to self-patching: the kernel variables bp_int3_handler and bp_int3_addr.

To understand why these pointers are required, we explain how runtime patching takes place in the Linux kernel. If the kernel patches a multibyte instruction in the kernel, it can not simply change the code in question. The kernel's code would be in an inconsistent state for a short period of time, which might lead to a kernel crash. Thus, the kernel implements a special synchronization method. It first replaces the first byte of the change with an *int3* instruction. As a result, every CPU trying to execute this instruction will be trapped. Then the rest of the space is filled with the new content. As a last step, the kernel replaces the first byte and notifies all waiting CPUs. During this process the address containing the *int3* instruction is saved in the variable bp_int3_addr.

This enables the *int3* interrupt handler upon invocation to determine whether the interrupt originates from the patched memory location or not. While the interrupt handler will simply process the interrupt normally in the latter case, it will in the former case invoke a specific handler whose address is stored within the variable bp_int3_handler. In the case of a patched jump label, for example, the *handler variable* will point to the instruction directly after the patched byte sequence, which effectively turns the sequence into a *NOP* sequence during the patching process. Since both of the bp_int3 variables are not reset after patching is complete, they always point to the last patched location and the last handler respectively. To solve this issue, our framework checks whether the current value of the bp_int3_addr points to a self patching location and if the handler address matches the type of patching conducted.

Finally, we iterate through all pages that contain a stack. Each process running in a system owns its own kernel stack that is used once the application issues a system call. To gather the addresses of all stacks from the monitored host, we iterate through the list of running threads (`init_task.tasks`) and extract their corresponding stacks. In case the process is not currently executing within the kernel, the current stack pointer is also saved within that structure. Ideally the process is currently not executing in kernel space in which case its stack must be *empty*. Otherwise we must validate the contents of the stack.

In order to validate a stack we use the following approach: For each *return address* found on the stack, we save the addresses of two functions. First, we save the address of the function that the return address is pointing to (`retFunc`). In addition, we also extract the address of the target, of the call instruction preceding the *return address* (`callAddr`). This is possible, since in most cases, the destination of the call is directly encoded in the instruction, or a memory address is referenced in the instruction that can in turn be read from the introspected guest system's memory.

This information is then used to validate the next return address that is found on the stack. In particular, the `callAddr` of the next frame needs to match the `retFunc` of the previous stack frame, as the previous function must have called the function, that the return address is pointing to.

Since it is not possible to extract all call targets using the method described above, we use an additional mechanism to extract all possible targets of indirect calls: we monitor the execution of the test systems in a secure environment and activate the processor's Last Branch Register (LBR) mechanism in order to extract the call and the target address of every indirect branch instruction executed by the system's CPU. Using this mechanism we generated a whitelist of targets for each call for which the target address is generated during runtime. This list is then also used by our stack validation component. With this we were, in our experiments, able to validate most of the kernel stacks within our test system. While this mechanism is not perfect yet, it certainly reduces the attack surface further.

The entire problem arises because the stack is currently not designed to be verifiable even under normal circumstances. However, the kernel developers currently discuss an enhancement to the code that would make stack validation more reliable, which could, once implemented, be used to improve our current approach and would allow removal of the whitelist.[1]

6.2   Code Pointer Examination

After we have checked important data structures, we scan through the rest of kernel data memory to find pointers to executable kernel code. This is achieved using the following steps: We first extract the memory regions of executable kernel code sections in the monitored virtual machine using the page tables structure. As a second step, we extract the data pages of the monitored guest

---

[1] https://lkml.org/lkml/2015/5/18/545.

system. For this purpose, we obtain all pages that are marked as supervisor and not executable in the page tables. These pages contain the data memory of the kernel and therefore all pointers that are accessible from within the Linux kernel. Note that the information we use for our analysis is binding, since it is derived from either the hardware or the trusted kernel reference binaries.

Having obtained the code and data pages, we iterate through the extracted pages in a byte by byte manner. We interpret each eight byte value (independently of its alignment) as a pointer and check whether it points into one of the memory locations that was identified as containing kernel code. If we found a pointer that points to executable kernel memory we first check if its destination is contained in the list of valid functions.

In case the pointer does not point to a valid function, we check if the pointer is a return address. There are currently multiple approaches used in our framework to identify a return address. First and foremost, a return address must point to an instruction within a function that is preceded by `call` instruction. Consequently, our initial check consists of validating whether the instruction it points to is actually contained within the function.

For this purpose, we disassemble the function the pointer allegedly points to from the beginning and verify that the value of the pointer points to a disassembled instruction and not somewhere in between instructions. In such a case, we additionally ensure a `call` instruction resides before the instruction the pointer points to. If any of these conditions fail, we consider the code pointer not to be a valid return address and continue to the next category.

Most of the return addresses used within the kernel are stored within one of the kernel stacks. However, there exist a few functions within the kernel that save the return address of the current function to be able to identify the current caller of that function. This was first introduced as a debug feature to print the address of the calling function to the user in case of an error. However, in the meantime this feature is also used for other purposes such as timers. For example, the struct `hrtimer` contains a pointer `start_site` that points to the instruction after the call instruction that started the timer.

With such a feature in place and used by the kernel it is hard to differentiate between legitimate return addresses and specially crafted control structures for code reuse techniques. To limit this problem we created a whitelist of all calls to functions that contain the problematic instruction and only allow return addresses in the kernel's data segment if they point to one of the functions in question.

If the pointer does not point to a valid function or a return address, the pointer is considered as malicious and a human investigator is notified. At this point the system also enriches the error message with the name of the function or symbol the pointer is pointing into.

7 Evaluation

In this section, we evaluate our approach using the prototype implementation described in Sect. 6. In order to determine whether our framework is able to

achieve the goals set in Sect. 5, we first determine its performance characteristics, before we evaluate its effectiveness against data-only malware in both
live monitoring as well as forensic applications. We follow this with an in-depth
discussion of the security aspects of our system.

7.1 Experiments

Our host system consisted of an AMD Phenom II X4 945 CPU with 13 GB of
RAM running Linux kernel version 3.16 (Debian Jessie). As guest systems we
used two different VMs running Linux 3.8 as well as Linux 3.16. Each VM had
access to two virtual CPUs and 1 GB of RAM. In these experiments, we used
XEN as the underlying hypervisor.

Performance and False Positives. First of all, we evaluated the performance
of our system as well as its susceptibility to false positives. For this purpose, we
used the *Phoronix-Test-Suite* to run a set of Benchmarks on our system. In detail,
we ran the *pts/kernel* test suite. We conducted these benchmark three times on
each test kernel. During the first set of tests, we disabled all external monitoring
to obtain a baseline of the normal system performance. In the second test set, we
enabled the code validation component to be able to differentiate between the
overhead of our framework and the code validation system. Finally, we enabled
both the code validation component as well as our new pointer validation module
in order to identify the additional overhead that our system incurs. During the
tests, the integrity validation component was executed in a loop, if enabled, to
stress the guest system as much as possible. The results of the benchmarks of
each set of experiments as well as the overall performance degradation are shown
in Table 1 for Linux 3.8 and in Table 2 for Linux 3.16.

   While evaluating the Linux 3.8 kernel, the kernel contained 80 code pages
and 426 data pages. One complete *Code Integrity Validation* was completed in
255.8 ms, while in the experiment with Code Integrity Validation *and* Pointer
Examination enabled, one iteration took 567.58 ms (that is 341.78 ms for CPE).
The Linux 3.16 kernel that was used during our evaluation contained 408 code
pages and 986 data pages. The Code Integrity Validation alone took 639.8 ms
per iteration, while the combined CIV and Pointer Examination took 962.0 ms
per iteration (that is 322.2 ms for CPE). Note that these values are mean values.
This shows that it takes less than 1 ms on average to check the integrity of one
page.

   As one can see the performance overhead that our framework incurs is very
small. In fact, the use of the underlying Code Validation Component incurs
a larger overhead than our CPE framework. The performance impact of our
system is for the most benchmarks well under one percent. The main reason for
this is that our framework, in contrast to many other VMI-based approaches,
uses passive monitoring of the guest system whenever applicable. As a result,
the guest system can execute through most of the validation process without
being interrupted by the hypervisor, which drastically reduces the performance
overhead of the monitoring. Only for the FSMark benchmark a performance

Table 1. Results of the Phoronix Test Suite for Linux 3.8.

Test (Unit)	w/o	CIV (%)	CIV &CPE (%)
FS-Mark (Files/s)	32.57	30.10 (8.21%)	31.73 (2.65%)
Dbench (MB/s)	69.84	66.53 (4.98%)	71.54 (−2.38%)
Timed MAFFT Alignment (s)	20.63	20.70 (0.34%)	20.63 (0.00%)
Gcrypt Library (ms)	2857	2853 (−0.14%)	2837 (−0.70%)
John The Ripper (Real C/S)	1689	1689 (0.00%)	1688 (0.06%)
H.264 Video Encoding (FPS)	35.38	35.23 (0.43%)	35.31 (0.20%)
GraphicsMagick 1 (Iter/min)	95	95 (0.00%)	95 (0.00%)
GraphicsMagick 2 (Iter/min)	58	58 (0.00%)	58 (0.00%)
Himeno Benchmark (MFLOPS)	593.59	585.73 (1.34%)	586.24 (1.25%)
7-Zip Compression (MIPS)	4715	4702 (0.28%)	4706 (0.19%)
C-Ray - Total Time (s)	130.96	131.00 (0.03%)	130.99 (0.02%)
Parallel BZIP2 Compression (s)	36.35	36.58 (0.63%)	36.47 (0.33%)
Smallpt (s)	445	445 (0.00%)	446 (0.22%)
LZMA Compression (s)	234.50	236.39 (0.81%)	236.12 (0.69%)
dcraw (s)	124.24	124.38 (0.11%)	124.35 (0.09%)
LAME MP3 Encoding (s)	25.20	25.19 (−0.04%)	25.19 (−0.04%)
Ffmpeg (s)	27.00	27.02 (0.07%)	26.82 (−0.67%)
GnuPG (s)	15.34	14.98 (−2.35%)	14.94 (−2.61%)
Open FMM Nero2D (s)	1137.17	1148.95 (1.04%)	1144.94 (0.68%)
OpenSSL (Signs/s)	173.70	173.73 (−0.02%)	173.80 (−0.06%)
PostgreSQL pgbench (Trans/s)	115.11	114.69 (0.37%)	115.21 (−0.09%)
Apache Benchmark (Requests/s)	10585.45	10481.21 (0.99%)	10506.23 (0.75%)

degradation of about 2.65 % is noticed on Linux 3.8. This degradation can not be seen in the results of the benchmark on Linux 3.16. While using the guest system with monitoring enabled, we did not observe any noticeable overhead from within the guest system. This clearly shows that our framework can achieve the performance goal set in Sect. 5 and is, from a performance point of view, well suited for real world applications. Sometimes the results even showed that the tests were better with our pointer examination framework enabled than without our framework. We argue that this may be due to the fact that the performance impact of our system is much smaller than the impact of other standard software within the tested Debian system that also influenced the result.

At the same time we did not observe any false positives during our experiments. That is, when enabled, our system could classify all of the pointers it encountered during the validation process using the heuristics we described in Sect. 5. However, note that we can, due to the design of our system, not rule

Table 2. Results of the Phoronix Test Suite for Linux 3.16.

Test (Unit)	w/o	CIV (%)	CIV & CPE (%)
FS-Mark (Files/s)	30.90	31.37 (−1.50%)	31.67 (−2.43%)
Dbench (MB/s)	61.42	60.76 (1.09%)	61.04 (0.62%)
Timed MAFFT Alignment (s)	20.74	20.79 (0.24%)	20.75 (0.05%)
Gcrypt Library (ms)	3747.00	3740 (−0.19%)	3733 (−0.37%)
John The Ripper (Real C/S)	1693.00	1693 (0.00%)	1692 (0.06%)
H.264 Video Encoding (FPS)	34.60	34.32 (0.82%)	34.35 (0.73%)
Himeno Benchmark (MFLOPS)	598.71	582.78 (2.73%)	585.78 (2.21%)
7-Zip Compression (MIPS)	4850.00	4805 (0.94%)	4730 (2.54%)
C-Ray - Total Time (s)	89.80	89.81 (0.01%)	89.80 (0.00%)
Parallel BZIP2 Compression (s)	31.25	31.41 (0.51%)	31.37 (0.38%)
Smallpt (s)	407.00	407 (0.00%)	407 (0.00%)
LZMA Compression (s)	236.62	241.49 (2.06%)	242.17 (2.35%)
dcraw (s)	117.54	117.47 (−0.06%)	117.29 (−0.21%)
LAME MP3 Encoding (s)	23.39	23.41 (0.09%)	23.40 (0.04%)
GnuPG (s)	13.72	13.65 (−0.51%)	13.98 (1.90%)
OpenSSL (Signs/s)	173.63	173.37 (0.15%)	173.57 (0.03%)
Apache Benchmark (Requests/s)	9504.78	9156.01 (3.81%)	9383.66 (1.29%)

out false positives entirely. We perform a more detailed discussion about the possibility of encountering false positives in Sect. 7.2.

Malware Detection. Having evaluated the performance of our system and touched upon its susceptibility to false positives, we continued to evaluate the effectiveness of our framework against data-only malware. For this purpose, we infected our test VMs with the persistent data-only rootkit presented by Vogl et al. [30]. We chose this rootkit, since it is, to the best of our knowledge, the only persistent data-only malware available to date.

While our framework did not detect any malicious code pointers during the performance experiments, our system immediately identified the various malicious control structures used by the rootkit. In particular, our system identified the modified `sysenter` MSR and the modified system call table entries for the `read` and the `getdents` system call during the prevalidation step and thus classified the system as malicious. As these hooks are also found by other systems, we then removed these obvious manipulations manually and once more validated the system state. While the prevalidation step yielded no results in this case, the pointer validation found all of the malicious code pointers in memory. This proves that our framework can be very effective against data-only malware even if the malware avoids the manipulation of key data structures such as the system call table.

Finally, to evaluate the usefulness of our framework in forensic applications, we conducted an experiment where we randomly installed the rootkit on the test VMs while we periodically took snapshots of the guest systems. Our system detected all of the infected snapshots reliably.

7.2   Discussion

In this section, we provide a detailed discussion of the security of our system.

False Positives. Although we did not encounter false positives throughout our experiments, we cannot rule out false positives entirely, since our system relies on heuristics to identify code pointers. However, we like to stress that we consider the likelihood of encountering false positives in our system to be quite small on a 64-bit architecture. To encounter a false positive with our system, we essentially would need to find a value in kernel space that contains the address of a kernel code section even though it is not a pointer. Since the virtual address space on a 64-bit system has a size of $1.8 * 10^{19}$ bytes and the kernel code section typically only has a size of 15 megabytes at maximum, the chance of encountering such a rare case, if all values in memory were uniformly distributed would be merely $8.5 * 10^{-11}\%$. And that is only the case if the kernel is not optimized as the kernel code section even becomes smaller in this case. However, we admit that this is only the case if the kernel is mapped to a random location within the address space and not directly to the beginning or the end of the address space. In other words, we consider a 64-bit address space to be sufficiently large that the chance of arbitrary data looking like a pointer by chance are small at best. Consequently, we assume that false positives are not a big issue in most scenarios. In case of false positives, one could further analyze the detected pointers using speculative code execution as proposed by Polychronakis [23]. Note that an attacker could also introduce benign data into the system that will be identified as code pointers by our system. We argue that this kind of tampering with our system should still be identified as malicious.

ret2libc. When searching for malicious pointers in memory, we currently do not penalize pointers that point to function entry points. As a consequence, our system is at the moment unable to detect data-only malware that solely makes use of entire kernel functions to perform its malicious computations. While this is certainly a weakness of our approach, it is important to note that this is a very common limitation that almost all existing defense mechanisms against code reuse attacks face [8, 26]. In fact, to the best of our knowledge, the detection of ret2libc attacks still remains an open research problem.

In addition, while ret2libc is a powerful technique that is very difficult to detect, we argue that it is actually quite difficult to design pure data-only malware that solely relies on entire functions to run on a 64-bit architecture. The main reason for this is that in contrast to 32-bit systems, function arguments in Linux and Windows are no longer passed on the stack on a 64-bit architecture, but are provided in registers instead. As a consequence, to create 64-bit ret2libc data-only malware, an attacker must actually have access to "loader" functions that allow her to load arbitrary function arguments into the registers that the calling conventions dictate. Otherwise, without access to loader functions, the attacker is unable to pass arguments to any of the functions she wants to invoke, which significantly restricts her capability to perform attacks.

It goes without saying that such loader functions are probably rare if they exist at all. A possible approach to further reduce the attack surface could thus be to analyze the kernel code for such loader functions. If they should exist, one can then monitor the identified functions during execution to detect their use in ret2libc attacks. We plan to investigate this idea in more depth in future work.

Return Addresses. If an attacker requires gadgets in addition to entire functions to execute her persistent data-only malware (e.g. to load function arguments into registers), she can only use a gadget that is directly following a call instruction. The only location that she can place the required control structure to without being detected is the kernel stack of a process. Should a code pointer that points inside a function appear anywhere else within the kernel memory, it will be classified and identified as malicious by our system. In addition, due to the fact that our system enforces SMAP from the hypervisor, the control structure cannot be placed in userspace if it should be executable from kernelspace. This only leaves a kernel stack for kernel data-only malware. But even here the attacker faces various constraints. First of all, she can only make use of gadgets that appear legitimately in the code and that are preceded by a call instruction, since all other pointers into a function would be classified as malicious. Secondly, as the kernel stack where the control structure resides may also be used by the process it belongs to, the attacker must ensure that her persistent control structure is not overwritten by accident. While this is not necessarily an issue for data-only exploits, this is crucial in the case of persistent data-only malware as the persistent control structure of the malware must never be changed uncontrollably. Otherwise, if the control structure would be modified in an unforeseen way, it is very likely that the malware will fail to execute the next time it is invoked. This is comparable to changing the code region of traditional malware. This is also why our system zeroes all data that belongs to a memory page that is part of the kernel stack, but currently resides at a lower address than the stack pointer points to as a final defense layer. Since this data should be unused in a legitimate scenario, zeroing it will not affect the normal system behavior. However, in the case of persistent data-only malware, this approach may destroy the persistent control structure of the malware, which will thwart any future execution. This will be case if the malware is currently executing while our system performs the validation. Since an attacker cannot predict when validations occur as our system resides on the hypervisor-level, this makes it difficult for her to stay unnoticed in the long run.

As a further enhancement one could set the kernel stacks of processes that are currently not executing to not readable within the page tables. This could for example be done during the process switch. As a result, the attacker would only be able to use her control structure when the process on whose kernel stack the structure resides is currently executing. This raises the bar if the attacker wants to hook the execution of all processes instead of just one, which is generally the case.

Taking all this into account we argue that while our system cannot eliminate persistent data-only malware entirely, it significantly reduces the attack surface. In future work, we plan to further enhance our detection by developing novel techniques to validate the legitimacy of a kernel stack that are also applicable in forensic scenarios. In addition we plan to investigate the applicability of our approach to userspace applications or an Android environment.

8   Conclusion

In this paper, we have proposed *Code Pointer Examination*, an approach that aims to detect data-only malware by identifying and classifying pointers to executable memory. To prove the validity and practicability of our approach, we employed it to examine all pointers to executable kernel memory in recent Linux kernels. In the process, we discussed important control flow relevant data structures and mechanisms within the Linux kernel and highlighted the problems that must be solved to be able to validate kernel control data reliably. Our experiments show that the prototype, which we implemented based on the discussed ideas, is effective in detecting data-only malware, while only incurring a very small performance overhead (less than 1 % in most of the benchmarks). In combination, with code integrity validation, we thus provide the first comprehensive approach to kernel integrity validation. While our framework still exhibits a small attack surface, we argue that it considerably raises the bar for attackers and thus provides a new pillar in the defense against data-only malware.

Acknowledgments. We thank the anonymous reviewers for their insightful comments. This work was supported by the Bavarian State Ministry of Education, Science and the Arts as part of the FORSEC research association.

References

1. Abadi, M., Budiu, M., Erlingsson, U., Ligatti, J.: Control-flow integrity. In: Proceedings of the 12th ACM conference on Computer and Communications Security, CCS 2005, pp. 340–353. ACM, New York (2005)
2. Bahram, S., Jiang, X., Wang, Z., Grace, M., Li, J., Srinivasan, D., Rhee, J., Xu, D.: DKSM: subverting virtual machine introspection for fun and profit. In: Proceedings of the 29th IEEE International Symposium on Reliable Distributed Systems (SRDS 2010), New Delhi, October 2010
3. Bletsch, T., Jiang, X., Freeh, V.W., Liang, Z.: Jump-oriented programming: a new class of code-reuse attack. In: Proceedings of the 6th ACM Symposium on Information, Computer and Communications Security, ASIACCS 2011, pp. 30–40. ACM, New York (2011)
4. C0ntex. Bypassing non-executable-stack during exploitation using return-to-libc
5. Carbone, M., Cui, W., Lu, L., Lee, W., Peinado, M., Jiang, X.: Mapping kernel objects to enable systematic integrity checking. In: Proceedings of the 16th ACM conference on Computer and Communications Security (CCS 2009), pp. 555–565. ACM (2009)

6. Carlini, N., Wagner, D.: ROP is still dangerous: breaking modern defenses. In: 23rd USENIX Security Symposium (USENIX Security 2014), pp. 385–399. USENIX Association, San Diego, August 2014

7. Cheng, Y., Zhou, Z., Yu, M., Ding, X., Deng, R.H.: ROPecker: a generic and practical approach for defending against ROP attacks. In: 21st Annual Network and Distributed System Security Symposium, NDSS 2014, February 23–26, 2014, San Diego (2014)

8. Davi, L., Liebchen, C., Sadeghi, A.-R., Snow, K. Z., Monrose, F.: Isomeron: Code randomization resilient to (just-in-time) return-oriented programming. In: Proceeding 22nd Network and Distributed Systems Security symposium (NDSS) (2015)

9. Davi, L., Sadeghi, A.-R., Lehmann, D., Monrose, F.: Stitching the gadgets: on the ineffectiveness of coarse-grained control-flow integrity protection. In: 23rd USENIX Security Symposium (USENIX Security 2014), pp. 401–416. USENIX Association, San Diego, August 2014

10. Evans, I., Fingeret, S., González, J., Otgonbaatar, U., Tang, T., Shrobe, H., Sidiroglou-Douskos, S., Rinard, M., Okhravi, H.: Missing the point (er): on the effectiveness of code pointer integrity (2015)

11. Feng, Q., Prakash, A., Yin, H., Lin, Z.: MACE: high-coverage and robust memory analysis for commodity operating systems. In: Proceedings of the 30th Annual Computer Security Applications Conference, ACSAC 2014, pp. 196–205. ACM, New York (2014)

12. Gilbert, B., Kemmerer, R., Kruegel, C., Vigna, G.: DYMO: tracking dynamic code identity. In: Sommer, R., Balzarotti, D., Maier, G. (eds.) RAID 2011. LNCS, vol. 6961, pp. 21–40. Springer, Heidelberg (2011)

13. Göktaş, E., Athanasopoulos, E., Polychronakis, M., Bos, H., Portokalidis, G.: Size does matter: why using gadget-chain length to prevent code-reuse attacks is hard. In: 23rd USENIX Security Symposium (USENIX Security 2014), pp. 417–432. USENIX Association, San Diego, August 2014

14. Hund, R., Holz, T., Freiling, F.C.: Return-oriented rootkits: bypassing kernel code integrity protection mechanisms. In: Proceedings of 18th USENIX Security Symposium (2009)

15. Kemerlis, V.P., Polychronakis, M., Keromytis, A.D.: Ret2dir: rethinking kernel isolation. In: 23rd USENIX Security Symposium. USENIX Association, August 2014

16. Kemerlis, V.P., Portokalidis, G., Keromytis, A.D.: kGuard: lightweight kernel protection against return-to-user attacks. In: Proceedings of the 21st USENIX Conference on Security Symposium, Security 2012. USENIX Association, Berkeley (2012)

17. Kittel, T., Vogl, S., Lengyel, T.K., Pfoh, J., Eckert, C.: Code validation for modern OS kernels. In: Workshop on Malware Memory Forensics (MMF), December 2014

18. Kuznetsov, V., Szekeres, L., Payer, M., Candea, G., Sekar, R., Song, D.: Code-pointer integrity. In: 11th USENIX Symposium on Operating Systems Design and Implementation (OSDI 2014), pp. 147–163. USENIX Association, Broomfield, October 2014

19. Lin, Z., Rhee, J., Zhang, X., Xu, D., Jiang, X.: SigGraph: Brute force scanning of kernel data structure instances using graph-based signatures. In: Proceedings of the Network and Distributed System Security Symposium (NDSS). IEEE (2011)

20. Litty, L., Lagar-Cavilla, H.A., Lie, D.: Hypervisor support for identifying covertly executing binaries. In: Proceedings of the 17th Usenix Security Symposium, pp. 243–258. USENIX Association, Berkeley (2008)

21. Pappas, V., Polychronakis, M., Keromytis, A.D.: Transparent rop exploit miti-gation using indirect branch tracing. In: Presented as part of the 22nd USENIX Security Symposium (USENIX Security 2013), pp. 447–462. USENIX, Washington, D.C. (2013)
22. Petroni, Jr., N.L., Hicks, M.: Automated detection of persistent kernel control-flow attacks. In: Proceedings of the 14th ACM conference on Computer and communi-cations security, CCS 2007. ACM, New York (2007)
23. Polychronakis, M., Keromytis, A.D.: ROP payload detection using speculative code execution. In: 6th International Conference on Malicious and Unwanted Software (MALWARE), pp. 58–65. IEEE (2011)
24. Sadeghi, A.-R., Davi, L., Larsen, P.: Securing legacy software against real-world code-reuse exploits: utopia, alchemy, or possible future? - keynote -. In: 10th ACM Symposium on Information, Computer and Communications Security (ASIACCS 2015), April 2015
25. Schneider, C., Pfoh, J., Eckert, C.: Bridging the semantic gap through static code analysis. In: Proceedings of EuroSec 2012, 5th European Workshop on System Security. ACM Press, April 2012
26. Schuster, F., Tendyck, T., Liebchen, C., Davi, L., Sadeghi, A.-R., Holz, T.: Coun-terfeit object-oriented programming: On the difficulty of preventing code reuse attacks in C++ applications. In: 36th IEEE Symposium on Security and Privacy, Oakland, May 2015
27. Shacham, H.: The geometry of innocent flesh on the bone: return-into-libc with-out function calls (on the x86). In: Proceedings of the 14th ACM conference on Computer and Communications Security, CCS 2007, pp. 552–561. ACM, New York (2007)
28. Stancill, B., Snow, K.Z., Otterness, N., Monrose, F., Davi, L., Sadeghi, A. R.: Check my profile: leveraging static analysis for fast and accurate detection of ROP gadgets. In: 16th Research in Attacks, Intrusions and Defenses (RAID) Symposium, October 2013
29. Szekeres, L., Payer, M., Wei, T., Song, D.: SoK: eternal war in memory. In: Pro-ceedings of the 2013 IEEE Symposium on Security and Privacy, SP 2013, pp. 48–62. IEEE Computer Society, Washington, DC (2013)
30. Vogl, S., Pfoh, J., Kittel, T., Eckert, C.: Persistent data-only malware: function hooks without code. In: Proceedings of the 21th Annual Network & Distributed System Security Symposium (NDSS), February 2014
31. Wang, Z., Jiang, X., Cui, W., Ning, P.: Countering kernel rootkits with lightweight hook protection. In: Proceedings of the 16th ACM conference on Computer and Communications Security, CCS 2009, pp. 545–554. ACM, New York (2009)
32. Wang, Z., Jiang, X., Cui, W., Wang, X.: Countering persistent kernel Rootkits through systematic hook discovery. In: Lippmann, R., Kirda, E., Trachtenberg, A. (eds.) RAID 2008. LNCS, vol. 5230, pp. 21–38. Springer, Heidelberg (2008)
33. Xia, Y., Liu, Y., Chen, H., Zang, B.: CFIMon: detecting violation of control flow integrity using performance counters. In: Proceedings of the 2012 42nd Annual IEEE/IFIP International Conference on Dependable Systems and Net-works (DSN), DSN 2012, pp. 1–12. IEEE Computer Society, Washington, DC (2012)
34. Zhang, C., Wei, T., Chen, Z., Duan, L., Szekeres, L., McCamant, S., Song, D., Zou, W.: Practical control flow integrity and randomization for binary executables. In: IEEE Symposium on Security and Privacy (SP), pp. 559–573. IEEE (2013)

Xede: Practical Exploit Early Detection

Meining Nie[1], Purui Su[1,2]([envelope]), Qi Li[3], Zhi Wang[4], Lingyun Ying[1],
Jinlong Hu[5], and Dengguo Feng[1]

[1] Trusted Computing and Information Assurance Laboratory,
Institute of Software, CAS, Beijing, People's Republic of China
purui@iscas.ac.cn
[2] State Key Laboratory of Computer Science,
Institute of Software, CAS, Beijing, China
[3] Tsinghua University, Beijing, China
[4] Florida State University, Tallahassee, USA
[5] South China University of Technology, Guangzhou, China

Abstract. Code reuse and code injection attacks have become the
popular techniques for advanced persistent threat (APT) to bypass
exploit-mitigation mechanisms deployed in modern operating systems.
Meanwhile, complex, benign programs such as Microsoft Office employ
many advanced techniques to improve the performance. Code execution patterns generated by these techniques are surprisingly similar to
exploits. This makes the practical exploit detection very challenging,
especially on the Windows platform. In this paper, we propose a practical exploit early detection system called Xede to comprehensively detect
code reuse and code injection attacks. Xede can effectively reduce false
positives and false negatives in the exploit detection. We demonstrate
the effectiveness of Xede by experimenting with exploit samples and
deploying Xede on the Internet. Xede can accurately detect all types of
exploits. In particular, it can capture many exploits that cannot be captured by mainstream anti-virus software and detect exploits that fail to
compromise the systems due to variations in the system configurations.

Keywords: Exploits · Code injection · Code reuse · ROP · Detection

1 Introduction

Advanced persistent threat (APT) is a stealthy, continuous, and targeted attack
against high-value targets, such as enterprises and government agencies. It is
often motivated by major financial or political reasons. There are a stream of
recent infamous attacks that cause vast consumer data breach and other dis-
astrous consequences [4–6]. APT has since become a major security concern to
these organizations. APT often employs zero-day (or recently-disclosed) vulnerabilities in popular programs, such as Microsoft Office, Internet Explorer, Adobe
Flash, and Adobe Acrobat [37,40], to penetrate the defenses of its target. Traditional signature-based (black-listing) malware and intrusion detection systems

© Springer International Publishing Switzerland 2015
H. Bos et al. (Eds.): RAID 2015, LNCS 9404, pp. 198–221, 2015.
DOI: 10.1007/978-3-319-26362-5_10

have increasingly become ineffective against APT. Meanwhile, white-listing is not only inconvenient for end users due to compatibility issues, but also incapable of catching malicious inputs (unless there is a formal definition of all valid and secure inputs). Instead, an effective defense against APT should focus on the early detection of exploits. Exploits often violate some code or control-flow integrity. For example, code injection attacks introduce new (malicious) code into the system, while return-oriented programming (ROP [39], a typical code reuse attack) manipulates the control flow to execute its gadgets, short code snippets that each ends with a return instruction. An exploit detection system checking these integrities could detect a wide spectrum of exploits.

However, the practical exploit detection is still a challenging problem, especially for the Windows systems. Remote network exploits against common Windows applications are the most prevailing attack surface [37]. Popular Windows applications, such as Microsoft Office, often employ the following advanced techniques that are surprisingly similar to exploits. If not carefully vetted, these programs could be mistakenly classified as malicious files, leading to high false positives. *First*, many large Windows functions generate dynamic code to improve performance or extend the functionality. We analyze 7 common targets in Windows and find that all these applications generate a large quantity of dynamic codes. An exploit detection system should separate the generated code from the injected malicious code. *Second*, some applications may replace or adjust the return addresses on the stack for obscure reasons. We also saw the example code that pushes return addresses directly to the stack, instead of through the call instructions. These irregular behaviors disrupt security mechanisms like the shadow stack expect the call and return instructions to be matched. Exploit detection systems need to accommodate these special but common program tricks to reduce false positives. *Third*, benign windows applications may have many short code sequences that resemble gadgets and are wrongfully detected as such by existing schemes. For instance, we analyzed a large amount of samples collected from the Internet, and found that most of them contain many small gadget sequences. In particular, we observed around 5,000 false positives when simple ROP detection schemes are employed to analyze one PDF file. Furthermore, commodity operating systems have incorporated exploit mitigation techniques such as data-execution prevention (DEP [17]) and address space layout randomization (ASLR [26]). These techniques significantly raise the bar for reliable exploits. Many exploits are tied to a specific run-time environment. If the detector has a different setting other than the target system, the exploits often trigger exceptions. This can and should be leveraged for the exploit detection.

In this paper, we propose Xede, a practical exploit early detection system to protect against APT. Xede can be deployed at the gateway to scan the incoming traffic, such as emails, or deployed as a web service to scan files for exploit detection. Xede has three major detection engines: exploit exception detector, code injection detector, and code reuse detector. The first component detects failed attack attempts by monitoring exceptions. Many exploits rely on the specific system configurations. Xede uses a variant of software configurations (e.g., OS with different patching levels) to induce the instability of exploits. Our experiments reveal that around 70 % of the malware samples are unstable, causing run-time exceptions. The second component detects (malicious) injected code by comparing the executed instructions against a list of benign instructions. This list is timely updated with the legitimate dynamically generated code to reduce false positives. Code injection attacks are often combined with code reuse attacks to bypass the DEP protection. Xede's third component focuses on the code reuse detection. It can detect both the more popular return-oriented programming (ROP) attacks and jump-oriented programming (JOP) attacks. Surprisingly, our experiments show that around 20 % of exploits contain a mix of return-based and jmp-based gadgets. Xede's code reuse detector can accommodate all the previously-mentioned eccentric program behaviors. With these three components, Xede can detect many different types of exploits, including zero-day exploits. We have built a prototype of Xede for the Windows operating systems. Our evaluation demonstrates that Xede is highly effective in detecting exploits. For example, we can detect all the malware samples we collected from the Internet. We have also deployed Xede on the Internet as a public service [42] to scan user-provided suspicious files.

2   Background

In order to exploit a vulnerability of a program, the following three steps need to be performed. Firstly, attackers need to construct memory layout of the program to host shellcode and data. Secondly, the attackers hijack the control flow of the program to injected shellcode directly or by constructing ROP gadgets. Lastly, the shellcode is executed to exploit the vulnerability. Note that shellcode could be injected into memory of target processes by either direct code injection, i.e., by code injection attacks, or constructing instruction chains through a serious of ROP gadgets, i.e., ROP attacks. Nowadays it is not easy to directly construct code injection attacks since the DEP defense mechanism employed in Windows does not allow direct code injection on writable and executable memory space. To address this issue, ROP gadgets are used to construct shellcode by leveraging indirect branch instructions, i.e., ROP gadgets, in target processes. Besides ROP gadgets that usually end with ret instructions, JOP gadgets ending with indirect jmp instructions can be used to construct shellcode as well [8]. In this paper, for simplicity, we collectively call them ROP gadgets.

To launch pure code injection attacks, the attackers can arrange memory layout to host shellcode by using heap spray or stack overflow. As shown in Fig. 1, the attackers can use the HeapAlloc function to allocate the shellcode at the addresses of 0x06060606, 0x0A0A0A0A, and 0x0C0C0C0C, respectively. The control flow of the program can be hijacked to the shellcode by altering the function pointer or return address, and the pointer or the address will point to the location of the injected shellcode. For instance, the function pointer in Fig. 1 is changed to 0x0C0C0C0C that is the location of the injected shellcode. Once the altered function pointer is invoked, the shellcode will be executed. Unlike code injection attacks, ROP attacks identify ROP gadgets and construct the stack including the addresses of the ROP gadgets. As shown in Fig. 1, gadgets are located at different locations, e.g., at **0x5e861192** and **0x5e81372a**. When the ESP register points to the address of the first gadget, i.e., **0x0x5e861192**, the control flow of program will be redirected to the gadgets by leveraging a ret instruction. The gadgets are executed one by one according to the addresses stored on the stack. Eventually, the **WriteProcessMemory** function is called to finish exploit execution.

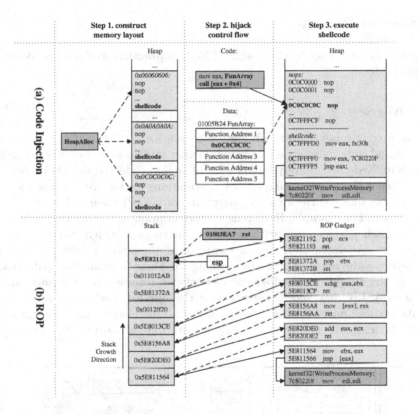

Fig. 1. Exploits examples with different exploitation techniques.

Normally, code injection attacks are easier to construct. However, the data execution prevention (DEP) mechanism raises the bar for code injection attacks. Therefore, it is not easy to directly inject executable code into memory with DEP-enabled systems. ROP attacks are immune to DEP but can be throttled by the address space layout randomization (ASLR) mechanism. To evade these prevention mechanisms, attackers adopt hybrid approaches to launch attacks, i.e., they can construct ROP gadgets to bypass the prevention mechanisms and leverage code injection attack to execute shellcode.

Key Observation. Benign programs contain some attack patterns, e.g., dynamic code, mismatching of call and return instructions, and small gadget sequence, which make exploit detection harder. However, exploits generated by different attack techniques share a common pattern that they redirect the control flow to some abnormal places other than the original ones. Specifically, the control flow is redirected to the pre-constructed shellcode or the first ROP gadget. Hence, we could detect different exploits by detecting unexpected jumps according to different attack features.

3   System Design

In this section, we describe the design of Xede, a practical exploit early detection system, in detail.

3.1   Overview

Xede is a comprehensive exploit detection platform. It can detect both code injection and code reuse attacks. Code injection attacks introduce alien code into the system. Xede accordingly builds a list of benign code and detects branches to the injected code by comparing branch destinations to that list. Meanwhile, code reuse attacks like return-oriented programming (ROP) have distinctive control flow patterns. For example, ROP reuses short snippets of the existing code called gadgets. Each gadget ends with a return instruction which "returns" to the next gadget. As such, ROP has a sequence of unbalanced returns. Xede can thus detect code reuse attacks by looking for these control flow patterns. In addition, the ubiquitous deployment of exploit mitigation mechanisms, such as DEP and ASLR, has significantly raised the bar for working exploits. Many exploits become unreliable as a result of that. This observation is leveraged by Xede to heuristically detect exploits by monitoring "abnormal" exceptions.

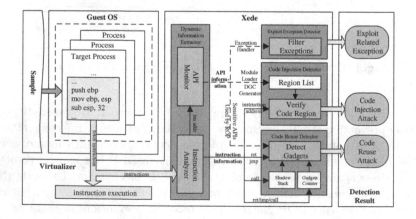

Fig. 2. The architecture of Xede

Figure 2 shows the architecture of Xede. Xede can be based on a whole-system emulator like QEMU or a dynamic binary translation based virtualization platform, such as VirtualBox and VMware workstation. At run-time, the virtualizer feeds the details of executed instruction to Xede. Xede has four major components. A dynamic information extractor extracts the run-time information of the running system, such as the executed instructions, exceptions, and the loaded modules. That information is passed to the three exploit detection engines: exploit exception detector, code injection detector, and code reuse detector. They try to detect exploits with abnormal exceptions, injected instructions, and characteristic code-reuse control flow patterns, respectively. In the rest of this section, we will describe each module.

3.2   Dynamic Information Extractor

Xede is based on a system emulator. This allows Xede to monitor every aspect of the target system. Xede is particularly interested in the details of certain executed instructions and critical API calls. The emulator passes the executed instructions and their operands to Xede. If it is a branch instruction, Xede checks whether the branch target points to a benign code block to detect injected code. Moreover, Xede uses the virtual machine introspection technology [24] to reconstruct the high-level API calls. Xede is interested in three types of API functions: the functions that load a kernel module or a shared library, the functions that handle exceptions, and the functions that are often misused by code reuse attacks (e.g., those that change the memory protection). The parameters and return values of those API calls allow Xede to identify valid code regions, catch abnormal exceptions, and detect code reuse attacks.

3.3   Exploit Exception Detector

Most commodity operating systems support two exploit mitigation mechanisms: DEP and ASLR. The former prevents code from being overwritten and data from being executed. Accordingly, no injected code can be immediately executed. It must be made executable first. The latter randomizes the layout of a process to prevent the attacker from locating useful gadgets. Many exploits have severe compatibility issues. They often trigger exceptions when the target software configurations change. Because of these issues, exploits are significantly harder to be perfect. On the other hand, popular attack targets, such as Microsoft Office, Adobe Acrobat and Flash, and Oracle Java virtual machine, all run fairly stable under normal operations. An exception in these programs may signify an ongoing attack. Therefore, Xede tries to detect *failed* exploits by monitoring the exceptions caused by these programs. Most existing exploit detection systems focus solely on detecting *successful* exploits. Xede instead can detect both successful and failed exploits.

There are two challenges to this approach: *first*, a process may cause various benign exceptions during its execution. For example, the kernel may swap out a part of the process to relieve the memory pressure. If that part is accessed by the process, an exception will be raised by the hardware. Hence, we must be able to distinguish these benign exceptions from the ones caused by the attacks. *Second*, complex commercial programs like Microsoft Office often try to handle exceptions if they can to provide a smooth user experience. There are many different ways to handle an exception. This could confuse the exploit detection systems. Therefore, we need to have a single unified method to catch exceptions. There are 23 different exceptions in the Windows operating system roughly in the following five categories: memory-related, exception-related, debugging-related, integer-related, and floating-point-related. Exceptions caused by exploits most likely fall into the first category. For example, they may read or write invalid data areas or execute illegal instructions. Memory-related exceptions are handled by the page fault handler in the kernel (i.e. the `MmAccessFault` function in Windows), which may further deliver them to the faulting user process.

To address the first challenge, we need to separate benign exceptions from ones caused by attacks. Programs can cause benign exceptions in the following two scenarios: *first*, the kernel uses demand paging to reduce memory consumption. For example, it may load a part of the process address space lazily from the disk, or swaps some memory pages out to the disk if they have not been used for a long time. *Second*, the user process itself might use memory-related exceptions to implement lazy memory allocation. For example, some programs use large data containers with an unknown length. The memory is only allocated when the data is accessed and an exception is raised. Microsoft Power Point 2007 uses this approach to manage Object Linking and Embedding (OLE) data. Xede has to exclude both cases from the exploit detection otherwise there will be lots of false positives. The first case is rather straightforward to exclude. The page fault handler (`MmAccessFault`) recognizes that this page fault is caused by a valid-but-not-present page. It reads the accessed data from the backing store and returns `STATUS_SUCCESS` to restart the instruction. Exceptions caused by attacks instead cause `MmAccessFault` to return `STATUS_ACCESS_VIOLATION`. However, `MmAccessFault` also returns `STATUS_ACCESS_VIOLATION` for the second case. To solve this problem, we first compare the faulting instruction address against the list of legitimate code. An alert will be raised by Xede if the instruction is illegitimate. Otherwise, we record the faulting data address expecting the program to allocate new memory for it. The next time a new data region is allocated, we check whether it covers the previous faulting data address. If so, the exception is considered to be benign.

3.4 Code Injection Detector

Even though modern operating systems like Windows enforce data execution prevention, code injection is still possible. For example, some (old) programs or libraries have mixed code and data pages. These pages must be made executable and writable, violating the DEP principle. If a program can dynamically generate code, its address space could contain writable and executable pages. Moreover, the memory protection can also be changed by system calls. Xede accordingly has a code inject detector, which builds at run-time a list of legitimate code regions and checks whether an executed instruction is in the list or not.

Legitimate Code Regions: A process consists of many different executable modules. For example, the kernel inserts the standard dynamic loader into the process to start a new one. The loader then loads the main program together with its linked shared libraries. The program itself can load additional dynamic libraries at run-time. Moreover, other processes, such as the input method editor (IME), can inject code into the process. Xede needs to identify all these executable modules. To this end, Xede hooks the API functions that may load code into a process. Their run-time parameters and return values provide the necessary information for Xede to locate the loaded executable (the program or a shared library) and know the base address of the executable. Xede then parses the executable to find the offset and size of its code section. The run-time code location is the base plus the offset. Correspondingly, we also monitor the API calls that unload an executable and remove the associated code section from the list of legitimate code regions. This list is also kept up-to-date with dynamically generated code.

Dynamically Generated Code: Dynamic code generation is a popular method to improve program performance. For example, modern browsers rely on just-in-time compiling to speedup JavaScript programs. This makes it possible to run large complex applications such as Google Maps in the browser. Xede requires a simple and generic way to recognize dynamically generated code. To that end, Xede hooks the related API calls to monitor memory allocations and memory protection changes.

To generate dynamic code, a process can allocate a block of writable-and-executable memory and then write the code into it, or it can save the code in the already-allocated writable memory and calls a system API to make the memory executable. In either case, Xede hooks the memory allocation and modification APIs. If a block of memory is made executable, we add it to the list of legitimate code region list. Likewise, if a block of memory loses its execution permission or is freed, we remove it from the code region list. Note that these two methods can only allocate execute memory in the page granularity (4KB for x86-32). Nevertheless, there are some unsafe programs that generate code using the executable heap. That is, the whole heap is made writable and executable. It is thus unnecessary for these programs to explicitly allocate executable memory pages. They could just use the ordinary `malloc` and `free` functions to manage executable memory. A simple solution would add the whole heap section to the executable code region. This leads to a high false negative rate for Xede because code injected in the heap is mistaken as benign code. To identify the exact regions of the generated code, we observe that well-designed programs use `NtFlushInstructionCache` to flush the instruction cache if new code is generated or the existing code is modified (self-modifying code). Xede thus hooks this function and adds the memory block specified in its parameters to the benign code region list (we merge continuous regions to reduce the list size.) On architectures with relaxed cache consistency mode, the instruction cache must be flushed for the generated/modified code to take effect. This is not strictly necessary for the x86 architecture which provides transparent instruction cache flushing. However, we expect most commercial programs (i.e., the poplar targets of attacks) to follow the correct practice to flush the cache because Windows does support several different architectures (e.g., ARM).

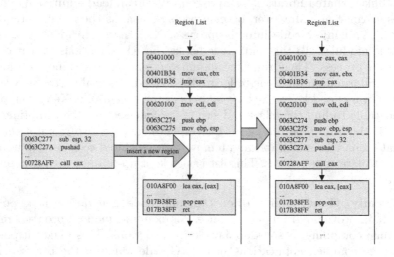

Fig. 3. Merge adjacent code regions

Code Injection Detection: Xede detects the injected code by checking whether an executed instruction lies in the list of benign code regions. However, it is prohibitively time-consuming to check this for every single instruction. Xede instead validates this property when the control flow is changed. In other words, it only checks that the destination of each branch instruction is within the code region list. This coincides with the concept of basic blocks. Each basic block is a linear sequence of instructions with only one entry point and one exit point. To guarantee correctness, we must ensure that each basic block lies within a single region. The code region list we built should not have problems in this regard if the program is correct. Figure 3 shows how this requirement is fulfilled by merging adjacent blocks of dynamically generated code. In addition, many basic blocks target another basic block in the same region. Xede thus verifies whether a branch target is within the current list, and only falls back to the whole list if that quick check fails.

3.5 Code Reuse Detector

With the wide-spread deployment of DEP and ASLR, code reuse attacks have become one of the most popular attack vectors. Fine-grained code reuse attacks include return-oriented programming (ROP) and jump-oriented programming

(JOP). ROP uses return instructions to chain gadgets, while JOP uses jump instructions instead. ROP is often used by attackers to bypass DEP. Xede can detect both ROP and JOP. Xede detects JOP by identifying sequences of gadget-like instructions. In this paper, we omit the details of the JOP detection, and focus on the more practical and more popular ROP attacks instead.

In ROP, each gadget ends with a return instruction. When a gadget returns, it pops the address of the next gadget off the stack and "returns" to it. A typical ROP attack consists of 17 to 30 gadgets [9]. This introduces a sequence of erratic return-based control flow transfers. For example, unlike legitimate return instructions that jump to a valid return site (i.e., an instruction preceded by a call instruction), gadgets often do not mimic a return site. As such, one way to detect ROP is to check whether the return target is preceded by a call instruction. Unfortunately, this method can be easily bypassed by call-preceded gadgets [7]. On the other hand, normal program execution has (mostly) balanced call and return pairs, but ROP causes mismatch between them (more returns than calls). This provides a more precise and reliable method to detect ROP. Specifically, Xede maintains a shadow stack for return addresses. It pushes the return address to the stack when a call instruction is executed, and pops the return address at the top of the stack and compares it to the actual return address when a return instruction is executed. This approach can detect ROP attacks because, when an ROP attack overwrites the stack with its gadget addresses, these addresses are not added to the shadow stack. However, it cannot be applied to the Windows platform due to various erratic behaviors of benign programs. We observe all of the following cases:

1. The program may replace the return address on stack with a completely different return address, causing the call-return mismatch.
2. The exception handling, setjmp/longjmp, and call/pop sequences introduces extra call instructions without the matching return instructions. For example, a program must be compiled as position-independent executable (PIE) to benefit from ASLR. PIE uses the PC-relative addressing mode to access its code and data. However, the x86-32 architecture does not natively support this addressing mode. Compilers instead emulate it by calling the next instruction and immediately popping the return address off the stack.
3. The program may adjust the return address on the stack (for unknown reasons), but usually within a few bytes.

As such, return addresses on the stack might be added, removed, and changed during the normal program execution. Xede needs to handle all these cases to reduce false positives.

First, to handle added return addresses, we search the shadow stack top-down for possible matches. If a match is found, we consider this return benign and pop the excessive returns above it. Note that this will not conflict with recursive functions whose return addresses might appear on the stack many times because normal recursive functions have matched call and return pairs. *Second*, to handle removed return addresses, we observe that normal program often removes only a single extra return address from the stack at a time. Therefore, Xede only considers it an ROP attack if there are N consecutive mismatched return addresses. According to our observation, an exploit can be accurately captured if the enhanced shadow stack captures three consecutive mismatched return addresses. Therefore, in our prototype, we use three for N. A normal real-world ROP attack usually uses 17 to 30 gadgets [9], say, to arrange gadgets and store parameters. Under some rare conditions, the attacker might be able to launch an ROP attack with two gadgets, one to make the injected shellcode executable (e.g., with the `VirtualProtect` function, assuming the parameters to this function happen to be placed.) and the other to execute the shellcode. To defeat ROP attacks with a very short gadget sequence, Xede hooks 52 most common APIs used by ROP attacks and checks whether these functions are "called" by a return instruction. If so, Xede considers it an ROP attack and raises an alert. *Third*, to handle changed return addresses, we analyze a number of common executables and find that return addresses mostly change by less than or equal to 16 bytes. Therefore, if a return address does not match the return address on the top of the stack, we check whether they are within 16 bytes of each other. If so, we consider the return address has been changed by the program itself and do not raise an alert. In addition, to avoid repeating the above time-consuming heuristics, we add any detected special cases to a white list and quickly check if a potential mismatch is discovered.

Xede can also detect ROP attacks that use stack pivoting. Stack pivoting points `esp`, the top of the stack, to a buffer under the attacker's control, such as a maliciously constructed heap area. The fake stack facilitates the attacker to carry out complex ROP attacks. To detect stack pivoting, we verify whether the `esp` register points to a valid stack area when we detect a potential mismatch of return addresses. We can retrieve the base and length of the stack from the thread control blocks in the guest operating system, such as the following fields in the Windows TEB (thread environment block) structure: `teb->NtTib->StackBase` and `teb->NtTib->StackLimit`.

4   Implementation

We have implemented a prototype of Xede based on QEMU, a generic open-source emulator. QEMU allows us to flexibly instrument instructions/basic blocks and introspect the guest memory. However, the design of Xede is not tied to QEMU. It is equally applicable to other hardware emulators (e.g., Bochs) and binary-translation based virtualization systems (e.g., VMware workstation and Oracle VirtualBox).

Figure 4 shows the overall architecture of our QEMU-based prototype. QEMU parses the guest instructions and further translates them into basic blocks. Basic blocks may further be linked into super blocks (i.e., translation blocks of QEMU). As previously mentioned, Xede has four major components. The dynamic information extractor retrieves the instruction details and hooks important API calls. As such, each time a new instruction is parsed, and its information is passed to this module for bookkeeping. The module also

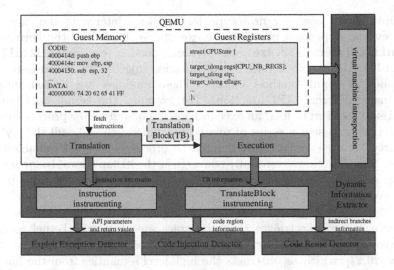

Fig. 4. Xede prototype based on QEMU

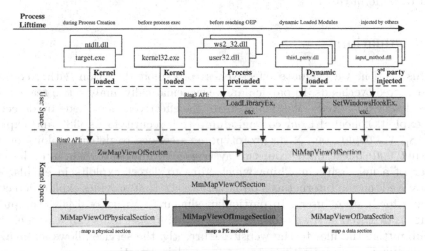

Fig. 5. Xede introspects Windows libraries

inserts a call back to the entry point of each interested API function (e.g., `NtFlushInstructionCache`) to catch its parameters and return values. The API call data is used by the second module, exploit exception detector, to detect failed exploits. To reduce the overhead of address validation, code injection detector only validates the branch targets to ensure that they jump to legitimate code regions. As such, it inserts a callback at the end of each basic block (this is where branch instructions are located.) The last module, code reuse detector, instruments indirect branch instructions (i.e., indirect calls, indirect jumps, and returns).

Figure 5 shows how our prototype for Windows intercepts the executable loading events. A process may include executables loaded by the kernel (e.g., ntdll.dll and kernel32.exe), the dynamic loader (e.g., user_32.dll and ws2_32.dll), the process itself, and libraries injected by third-party programs such as input method editors. These modules are loaded into the process using different API functions. For example, the kernel uses function ZwMapViewOfSection to load an executable section, and a user process can load dynamic libraries using a series of related functions such as LoadLibraryEx. A third-party library can be injected into the process with SetWindowsHookEx. However, these functions eventually converge at the MiMapViewofImageSection function. As such, Xede hooks this function to intercept the executable module loading events.

Xede leverages the guest kernel states to improve the preciseness of the detection. For example, it retrieves the valid stack area from the kernel to detect stack pivoting. This technology is commonly known as virtual machine introspection [20,24], which reconstructs the high-level semantics from the low-level raw data such as the memory and disk images. Our semantic analyzer is developed to perform this task.

5   Evaluation

In this section, we evaluate effectiveness of exploit detection with Xede and the incurred overheads. In particular, we systematically analyze two real exploit cases detected by Xede. We demonstrate the effectiveness of Xede by detecting real exploits collected from contagiodump [10], securityfocus [38], and exploit-db [18]. We deploy our Xede prototype as a service to detect exploits on the Internet and collect data from two systems. We integrate Xede into the mail server of a university in China which aims to detect exploits in emails, and deploy Xede on the Internet as a pubic service [42] that provides exploit detection services for Internet users. In particular, similar to VirusTotal [43], the public service is deployed as a web service so that any Internet users can scan their files by submitting the files to the website. Currently, the service allows anonymous sample submissions from the Internet for exploit detection.

5.1   Effectiveness Evaluation

Detection with Exploit Samples. We use exploits downloaded from some websites, e.g., contagiodump [10], securityfocus [38], and exploit-db [18], to evaluate the effectiveness of exploit detection. Overall we collect 12501 exploits that are included in doc/docx/rtf files, xls/xlsx files, ppt/pptx files, and pdf files. Table 1 shows the results of exploit detection. Xede accurately detects all of these exploits. Xede detects that more than 75 % exploits are generated by using the code injection techniques. In particular, among these exploits, 51.47 % exploits adopt the ROP techniques, which validates that most of exploits combine ROP and code injection techniques, and around 19.85 % exploits leverage JMP-based

Table 1. Exploit sample proportion with different exploitation techniques.

Exploit techniques	Sample proportion
code injection	75 %
ret-based gadgets	51.47 %
jmp-based gadgets	19.85 %
exploit exception	25 %

gadgets. 25 % exploits are captured because they raise abnormal execution exceptions. Furthermore, we do not observe any pure ROP attacks.

Real Deployment Detection. We collected 1,241 samples submitted by the anonymous Internet users during three months, and collected 10,144 attachments from our university email system for one month. Specifically, we selected 5,000 active users and randomly sampled their incoming emails with a rate of 3 %, and analyzed 20 popular types of the samples attached in the emails. This results in 62,500 emails and 10,144 attachments. Note that, we collected the emails before the email filters. Table 2 shows the breakdown of file types collected in real world deployment. Xede detects 136 exploits, among which 4 and 132 exploits are from the emails and the public service, respectively. Most of the exploits are pdf files and the files generated by MS office suites. They account for 30.9 % and 58.1 %, respectively. The rest are some swf files, html/htm files, and wps files. We confirm these exploits by manual analysis. Although we observe the attacks constructed by these exploits, only 44.12 % of exploits successfully succeed, which means that these exploits heavily rely on special system environments. Therefore, it is necessary to capture and detect the exploits that do not succeed to compromise the systems. Table 3 shows the success rate of different exploits. Xede can detect all these exploits no matter if they are successfully executed, which shows that the exploit detection in Xede is independent of the target system configurations. Note that, in the experiments, we do not differentiate legitimate and malicious application "crashes" because we do not observe any legitimate "crashes".

Many exploits detected by Xede cannot be captured by the existing anti-virus software. We confirm it by using some commercial virus software, i.e., Kaspersky 2015, Mcfee AntiVirus Plus, Avira Free Antivirus 2015, and Norton 2015. Overall, all these software cannot correctly detect the exploits. As shown in Table 4, Kaspersky achieves the lowest false negative that is around 15.44 %. It only detects 115 exploits out of 136 exploits, and the rest 21 exploits cannot be detected by any anti-virus software. The results reveal that many exploits can evade detection with signature matching. It demonstrates that a generic detection system is essential to detect exploits by identifying malicious operations of software.

For the 11,249 samples that Xede did not raise an alert, we used the previously-mentioned anti-virus products to cross-validate whether Xede introduced any false negatives. None of those samples were identified by them as

Table 2. Breakdown of sample file types collected in real world deployment.

Sample type	The number of email samples	The number of submitted samples	Total number
doc/docx/dot	5840	154	5994
pdf	153	241	394
swf	2	49	51
xls/xlsx	778	112	890
html/htm	80	102	182
rtf	110	120	230
ppt/pptx/pps	82	144	226
wps	58	20	78
txt/ini	2611	115	2726
jpg/png/gif	411	180	591
chm	19	4	23
Total Number	10144	1241	11385

Table 3. Success rate of different exploits.

Sample type	The number of detected exploits	Succeed exploit	Failed exploit	Success rate
doc/docx	58	43	15	74.14 %
pdf	42	4	38	9.52 %
swf	8	0	8	0 %
xls/xlsx	11	8	3	72.73 %
htm/html	6	3	3	50 %
rtf	6	1	5	16.67 %
ppt/pptx/pps	4	1	3	25 %
wps	1	0	1	0 %

Table 4. False negatives of commercial anti-virus software.

AV software	Version	Date of DB update	False negative
Kaspersky	15.0.2.361	24/05/2015	21
McAfee	18.0.204	24/05/2015	49
Avira	15.0.10.434	24/05/2015	22
Norton	22.2.0.31	24/05/2015	32

malicious. Note that false negatives are still possible if both Xede and those anti-virus products miss the attacks. Moreover, to roughly estimate how many of these 11,249 samples may be detected by existing approaches [16,30,34] as malicious (possible false positives), we recorded the suspicious patterns detected (but eventually dismissed) by Xede in these samples. Particularly, we found that 879 xls samples cause Excel to generate more than 90KB dynamic code each, and most doc samples each lead to over 4,500 mismatched call and ret instructions in Microsoft Word. All these cases may be mis-identified as malicious by existing approaches. Xede did not raise alerts for these cases.

5.2 Case Study

We analyze two different exploit samples that detected by our Xede. One sample can successfully compromise a system by leveraging the vulnerability reported by CVE-2012-0158, and the other sample leveraging the vulnerability reported by CVE-2014-1761 fails to launch the attack due to wrong system configurations.

Case 1: CVE-2012-0158. We analyze an exploit that leverages the vulnerability named with CVE-2012-0158 [14] that is a buffer overflow vulnerability in the ListView and TreeView ActiveX controls in the MSCOMCTL.OCX library. The vulnerability is leveraged against a Doc file that combines ROP and code injection technique. In order to evade Data Execution Prevention (DEP), the Doc file invokes the system call `VirtualAlloc` to allocate a block of executable memory by constructing a ROP chain, and injects the shellcode into the space. We run the exploit in Windows 7 as guest OS with Office 2003 SP1. In order to systematically analyze the exploit techniques leveraged by the exploit, we do not terminate the exploit after it is detected. Instead, we allow Xede to detect all attacks in the exploit.

ROP Detection. Xede detects 12 anomalous `return` operations. We find that the returned address by executing the first `return` instruction is `0X7c809a81` that is exactly the address of the system call `VirtualAlloc`. By analyzing the stack information, we obtain the parameters of the system call as follows. `VirtualAlloc(0x001210b0, 0x0001000, 0x00001000, 0x0000040)`. After the system call is executed, a block of executable memory is allocated. We confirm that the memory later will be injected with the shellcode. Moreover, we detect 45,039 gadget-like sequences of instructions. But, we do not find any jmp-based gadgets.

Code Injection Detection. During execution of the exploit, Xede records 53 legal code regions and 47 regions that are executable sections generated by the modules (e.g., DLL and EXE modules). As we discussed in Sect. 3, once instructions are not executed in a legal region, Xede will treat it as an attack. Overall, Xede detect 133,643 attacks. In particular, by analyzing the first five attacks, we find that the instructions are within the memory block allocated by the `VirtualAlloc` function. It means that these instructions are the code injected by the attackers. We confirm that the code is shellcode by manual analysis. We identify several instructions that should not be invoked by Doc files, e.g., to release PE files or invoke CMD scripts.

Case 2: CVE-2014-1761. Now we analyze another Doc sample that leverages the vulnerability of CVE-2014-1761 [15] that is executed in Windows XP OS with Office 2003 SP3. When we open the sample file, the Word application crashes. We do not find anomalies by monitoring invoked APIs.

Exploit Exception Detection. Xede identifies anomaly address access at 0x909092e4. We confirm the sample is an exploit by running in Windows 7 OS with Office 2010 SP1. The possible reason why the exploit fails is that the part of shellcode, i.e., 0x9090, is treated as the address and the shellcode cannot be correctly located. Therefore, the exploit was not correctly executed due to the mismatched software versions.

Summary. As we observed, most exploits combine different exploitation techniques, i.e., ROP and code injection, which similar to the exploit sample above. ROP is used to evade the DEP mechanism, and the attacks finally are mounted by executing injected shellcode. According to the two exploit sample above, we show that how Xede detects exploits no matter if they can be successfully executed.

5.3   Performance Evaluation

In this experiment we evaluate the overheads incurred by Xede and the overheads during Xede bootstrapping. The experiment is performed in an Ubuntu 12.04 server with 3.07 GHz Intel Xeon X5675 CPU and 32 GB memory. We measure the overheads incurred by Xede compared with pure QEMU. As shown in Fig. 6, Xede consumes around 60 % of CPU cycles that consumed by QEMU during the bootstrapping within the 60 seconds. The possible reason is that exploit execution incurs many virtual machine introspections during Xede bootstrapping. Note that, Xede can effectively detect most exploits during this period. After the bootstrapping, Xede does not introduce extra significant CPU consumption.

We compare the CPU utilization rate and memory overhead by measuring the resource assumption in a Guest OS with 256 MB assigned memory (see Figs. 7 and 8). We can observe that Xede does not incur many CPU cycles after bootstrapping. The CPU utilization rate in QEMU with Xede and QEMU without Xede are around 0.12 % and 0.08 %, respectively. Similarly, Xede does not introduce significant memory overheads. Therefore, Xede is very lightweight. Furthermore, we measure the overheads with parallel exploit detection. Figure 9 illustrates the resource consumption with 80 Xede instances. Memory consumption is stable and the consumption rate is within 90 %. CPU utilization rate is around 6 % except some utilization rate bursts. Thus, Xede is scalable to parallel exploit detection.

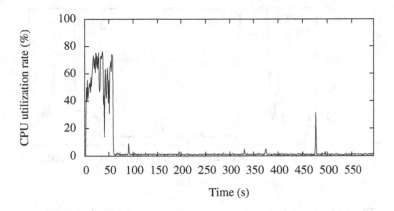

Fig. 6. Increased CPU consumption by Xede compared with QEMU.

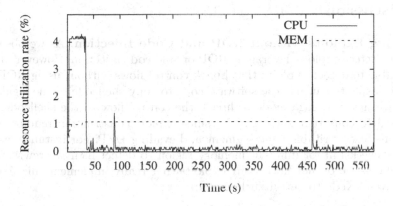

Fig. 7. CPU cycles and memory consumed by Xede.

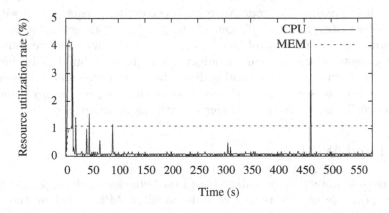

Fig. 8. Increased CPU and memory consumption by Xede compared with QEMU.

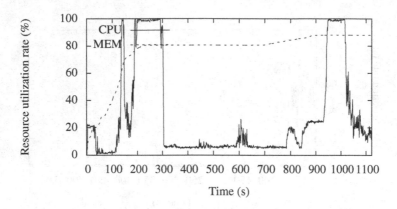

Fig. 9. CPU and memory consumption with 80 Xede instances.

6 Discussion

Detecting Exploits without ROP and Code Injection. As we observed, Xede can detect exploits leveraging ROP or/and code injection. However, it may not be able to detect exploits that hijack control flows without using ROP. For example, exploits can use the software code to copy shellcode to the legal code region and leverage legal code to hijack the control flow to the shellcode. It is very hard to construct such exploits since exploit construction requires strict conditions, e.g., writable code segment and evading DEP. For instance, we can compute checksum for different memory region to detect memory rewriting. In real practice, we do not notice any exploits that really implement this. We can easily extend Xede to detect such exploits.

Accuracy of ROP Detection. Xede does not count the number of gadgets where source and destination addresses of jmp are same. It significantly reduces the miscounted gadgets, and thereby reduces false positives of detecting JOP. However, it is possible to evade Xede by constructing gadget chains with the same intermediate gadgets, i.e., gadget *1*->gadget *x*->gadget *2*->gadget *x*-> ⋯. In order to perform control flow hijacking from the intermediate gadgets to different gadgets, a large amount of gadgets are required to build chains between gadgets, e.g., between gadget *1* and gadget *x* in the example above. However, it is really difficult to such gadget chains, and we did not observe any attacks in real practice. Thus, we do not consider the attacks in this paper.

7 Related Work

Malicious code detection is mainly based on behavior analysis [2,3,19,27,45, 46]. The principle of this technique is to monitor APIs called by the target process and then check if the process behaves properly via analyzing the API sequence. The behavior analysis techniques are also widely adopted in current anti-virus software, such as FireEye [19] and WildFire [45]. The shortcomings of the approaches are also obvious. They need to configure corresponding behavior policies for different types of samples. By analyzing API sequence, it is very difficult either to describe the comprehensive behaviors of a benign software or to accurately define the possible behaviors of malicious code [25]. Moreover, exploits are very sensitive to the system environment. If a victim software version does not match the expected environment, the exploit will abort and the malicious behaviors cannot be identified.

Recently more researches are conducted to detect exploits by identifying shellcode [31,35,44]. Shellcode detection approaches intend to scan the content of the sample file before the file execution and then to detect whether the file includes shellcode characteristics. Polychronakis et al. [31] use a set of runtime heuristics to identify the presence of shellcode in arbitrary data streams. The heuristics identify machine-level operations that are inescapably performed by different shellcode types, such as reading from FS:[0x30], writing to FS:[0]. Wang et al. [44] blindly disassembles each network request to generate a control flow graph, and then uses novel static taint and initialization analysis algorithms to determine if self-modifying (including polymorphism) and/or indirect jump code obfuscation behavior is collected. Such line of approaches shares an important shortcoming. Content in data files is the same to the actual layout in process memory. For example, shellcode hiding in a Doc file will be parsed and reorganized by its host process, i.e., winword.exe. Therefore, it is not easy to accurately identify the presence of shellcode in different data files. Moreover, since shellcode representation may not be fundamentally different in structure from benign payloads [28], these approaches inevitably suffers from significant false positive rates.

Exploit detection by enforcing Control Flow Integrity (CFI) generates a complete control flow graph (CFG) of samples (or, the host process of the sample file if the sample is a data file) by performing static pre-analysis [1,21,47]. It monitors the execution of the target process, analyzes each instruction executed, and verifies the legitimacy of each control flow transfer by checking whether the flow transfer exists in the CFG. Zhang et al. [47] classify the destination addresses of indirect control flow transfer into several categories, such as code pointer constants, computed code addresses, exception handling addresses, and verify these destination addresses according to the results of static analysis. Unfortunately, the CFI approaches cannot be adopted in real systems because of the following reasons. Firstly, aiming to construct complete CFGs, CFI usually requires source code of program or debug information of whole program. The information of proprietary software is not always available. We could build CFG without those information with some tools, such as IDA [22], but the accuracy and coverage of CFG cannot be guaranteed. Secondly, the CFI approaches usually cannot verify the legitimacy of control flow transfer in dynamic code, which widely exists in modern software. Lastly, they suffers from the problems of inefficiency and high complexity [21].

Taint analysis employs a dynamic tracing technique to detect exploits [11–13, 29,33,41]. It marks input data from tainted sample, and then monitors program execution to track how the tainted attribute propagates and to check if the tainted data is used in dangerous ways. However, as far as we know, all existing taint analysis engines are unable to fully support analysis of the entire Intel instruction set. Hence, the accuracy of the analysis results cannot be guaranteed. Moreover, taint analysis needs to parse each instruction executed by the target processes, and record all addresses of tainted data, The computation complexity and complexity is not acceptable in real practice [36].

The prevention mechanisms, such as ASLR [26] and DEP [17], are adopted to protect against malicious code exploits. More exploits leverage the ROP technique to evade the mechanisms. ROP is hard to detect because it uses the existing legal instruction sequences to construct shellcode, instead of injecting shellcode. Last Branch Recording (LBR) [23], a recent technique released with Intel processors, is used to analyze the executed indirect branch instructions to see if there exists an excessively long chain of gadget-like instruction sequences. LBR-based approaches [9,30] rely on hardware for instruction-level monitoring, which introduces small runtime overhead and transparent operations. Unfortunately, these approaches have some inherent drawbacks. The LBR stack can include only 16 records, and is shared by all running processes and threads. Hence, the stack may not have enough space to record sufficient data. Moreover, these approaches cannot observe the actual path of instruction execution between two indirect jumps, thereby they cannot accurately count the number of instructions. Therefore, the LBR-based approaches may not be accurate to analyze and detect exploits. Similar to Xede, shadow stack and speculative code execution are adopted to detect ROP. For example, Davi et al. [16] utilized shadow stack to detect ROP. However, the system is built upon the PIN subsystem and cannot instrument the kernel code. Polychronakis et al. [32] used speculative code execution to analyze non-randomized modules and is unable to detect exploits leveraging randomized modules.

8   Summary

In this paper, we present the design and implementation of Xede, an exploit detection system. Xede comprehensively detect different types of exploits, e.g., generated by pure code injections, pure ROP, and hybrid exploitation techniques. We have implemented a prototype of Xede with QEMU. The evaluation demonstrates that Xede can effectively detect different exploits according experiments with samples and real world deployment on the Internet. In particular, with real world deployment, Xede detects a large number of exploits that cannot be captured by mainstream anti-virus software and exploits that raise abnormal execution exceptions due to mismatched execution environments.

Acknowledgement. We would like to thank our shepherd Christopher Kruegel, and the anonymous reviewers for their insightful comments. This work is partially supported by the National Basic Research Program of China (973 Program) (Grant

No.2012CB315804), and the National Natural Science Foundation of China (Grant No.91418206).

References

1. Abadi, M., Budiu, M., Erlingsson, U., Ligatti, J.: Control-flow integrity. In: Proceedings of the 12th ACM Conference on Computer and Communications Security, pp. 340–353. ACM (2005)
2. Amnpardaz. http://jevereg.amnpardaz.com/
3. Anubis. https://anubis.iseclab.org/
4. Flame Malware. http://en.wikipedia.org/wiki/Flame_malware
5. Sony Pictures Entertainment hack. http://en.wikipedia.org/wiki/Sony_Pictures_Entertainment_hack
6. Stuxnet. http://en.wikipedia.org/wiki/Stuxnet
7. Carlini, N., Wagner, D.: Rop is still dangerous: breaking modern defenses. In: USENIX Security Symposium (2014)
8. Checkoway, S., Davi, L., Dmitrienko, A., Sadeghi, A.R., Shacham, H., Winandy, M.: Return-oriented programming without returns. In: Proceedings of the 17th ACM Conference on Computer and Communications Security, pp. 559–572. ACM (2010)
9. Cheng, Y., Zhou, Z., Yu, M., Ding, X., Deng, R.H.: Ropecker: a generic and practical approach for defending against rop attacks. In: Symposium on Network and Distributed System Security (NDSS) (2014)
10. contagiodump. http://contagiodump.blogspot.com/
11. Costa, M., Crowcroft, J., Castro, M., Rowstron, A., Zhou, L., Zhang, L., Barham, P.: Vigilante: end-to-end containment of internet worms. ACM SIGOPS Oper. Syst. Rev. **39**, 133–147 (2005). ACM
12. Crandall, J.R., Chong, F.: Minos: architectural support for software security through control data integrity. In: International Symposium on Microarchitecture (2004)
13. Crandall, J.R., Su, Z., Wu, S.F., Chong, F.T.: On deriving unknown vulnerabilities from zero-day polymorphic and metamorphic worm exploits. In: Proceedings of the 12th ACM Conference on Computer and Communications Security, pp. 235–248. ACM (2005)
14. CVE-2012-0158. http://cve.mitre.org/cgi-bin/cvename.cgi?name=CVE-2012-0158
15. CVE-2014-1761. http://cve.mitre.org/cgi-bin/cvename.cgi?name=CVE-2014-1761
16. Davi, L., Sadeghi, A.R., Winandy, M.: Ropdefender: a detection tool to defend against return-oriented programming attacks. In: Proceedings of the 6th ACM Symposium on Information, Computer and Communications Security, pp. 40–51. ACM (2011)
17. Data Execution Prevention. http://en.wikipedia.org/wiki/Data_Execution_Prevention
18. exploit-db. http://www.exploit-db.com/
19. FireEye. http://www.fireeye.com/
20. Garfinkel, T., Rosenblum, M.: A virtual machine introspection based architecture for intrusion detection. In: Proceedings of the 10th Network and Distributed System Security Symposium, Febuary 2003
21. Goktas, E., Athanasopoulos, E., Bos, H., Portokalidis, G.: Out of control: overcoming control-flow integrity. In: 2014 IEEE Symposium on Security and Privacy (SP), pp. 575–589. IEEE (2014)

22. IDA Pro. https://www.hex-rays.com/products/ida/
23. Intel: Intel 64 and IA-32 Architectures Software Developerś Manual, Febuary 2014
24. Jiang, X., Wang, X., Xu, D.: Stealthy malware detection through VMM-based "Out-Of-the-Box" semantic view reconstruction. In: Proceedings of the 14th ACM Conference on Computer and Communications Security, October 2007
25. Lanzi, A., Balzarotti, D., Kruegel, C., Christodorescu, M., Kirda, E.: Accessminer: using system-centric models for malware protection. In: Proceedings of the 17th ACM Conference on Computer and Communications Security, pp. 399–412. ACM (2010)
26. Larsen, P., Homescu, A., Brunthaler, S., Franz, M.: SoK: automated software diversity. In: Proceedings of the 2014 IEEE Symposium on Security and Privacy, SP 2014 (2014)
27. LastLine. https://www.lastline.com/
28. Mason, J., Small, S., Monrose, F., MacManus, G.: English shellcode. In: Proceedings of the 16th ACM Conference on Computer and Communications Security, pp. 524–533. ACM (2009)
29. Newsome, J., Song, D.: Dynamic taint analysis for automatic detection, analysis, and signature generation of exploits on commodity software (2005)
30. Pappas, V., Polychronakis, M., Keromytis, A.D.: Transparent rop exploit mitigation using indirect branch tracing. In: USENIX Security, pp. 447–462 (2013)
31. Polychronakis, M., Anagnostakis, K.G., Markatos, E.P.: Comprehensive shellcode detection using runtime heuristics. In: Proceedings of the 26th Annual Computer Security Applications Conference, pp. 287–296. ACM (2010)
32. Polychronakis, M., Keromytis, A.D.: Rop payload detection using speculative code execution. In: 2011 6th International Conference on Malicious and Unwanted Software (MALWARE), pp. 58–65. IEEE (2011)
33. Portokalidis, G., Slowinska, A., Bos, H.: Argos: an emulator for fingerprinting zero-day attacks for advertised honeypots with automatic signature generation. ACM SIGOPS Oper. Syst. Rev. **40**, 15–27 (2006). ACM
34. Rabek, J.C., Khazan, R.I., Lewandowski, S.M., Cunningham, R.K.: Detection of injected, dynamically generated, and obfuscated malicious code. In: Proceedings of the 2003 ACM Workshop on Rapid malcode, pp. 76–82. ACM (2003)
35. Ratanaworabhan, P., Livshits, V.B., Zorn, B.G.: Nozzle: A defense against heap-spraying code injection attacks. In: USENIX Security Symposium, pp. 169–186 (2009)
36. Schwartz, E.J., Avgerinos, T., Brumley, D.: All you ever wanted to know about dynamic taint analysis and forward symbolic execution (but might have been afraid to ask). In: 2010 IEEE Symposium on Security and Privacy (SP), pp. 317–331. IEEE (2010)
37. Secunia: Secunia vulnerability review 2015. Technical report, Secunia (2014). http://secunia.com/vulnerability-review/
38. securityfocus. http://www.securityfocus.com/
39. Shacham, H.: The geometry of innocent flesh on the bone: return-into-libc without function calls (on the x86). In: Proceedings of the 14th ACM Conference on Computer and Communications Security, October 2007
40. Snow, K.Z., Monrose, F.: Automatic hooking for forensic analysis of document-based code injection attacks (2012)
41. Suh, G.E., Lee, J.W., Zhang, D., Devadas, S.: Secure program execution via dynamic information flow tracking. ACM Sigplan Not. **39**, 85–96 (2004). ACM
42. TCA Malware Analysis platform. http://www.tcasoft.com/

43. VirusTotal. https://www.virustotal.com/
44. Wang, X., Jhi, Y.C., Zhu, S., Liu, P.: Still: exploit code detection via static taint and initialization analyses. In: 2008 Annual Computer Security Applications Conference, ACSAC 2008, pp. 289–298. IEEE (2008)
45. WildFire.   https://www.paloaltonetworks.com/products/technologies/wildfire. html
46. XecScan. http://scan.xecure-lab.com/
47. Zhang, M., Sekar, R.: Control flow integrity for cots binaries. In: Usenix Security, pp. 337–352 (2013)

Attack Detection I

Preventing Exploits in Microsoft Office Documents Through Content Randomization

Charles Smutz$^{(\boxtimes)}$ and Angelos Stavrou

George Mason University, Fairfax, USA
{csmutz,astavrou}@gmu.edu

Abstract. Malware laden documents are a common exploit vector, often used as attachments to phishing emails. Current approaches seek to detect the malicious attributes of documents through signature matching, dynamic analysis, or machine learning. We take a different approach: we perform transformations on documents that render exploits inoperable while maintaining the visual interpretation of the document intact. Our exploit mitigation techniques are similar in effect to address space layout randomization and data randomization, but we implement them through permutations to the document file layout.

We randomize the data block order of Microsoft OLE files in a manner similar to the inverse of a filesystem defragmention tool. This relocates malicious payloads in both the original document file and in the memory of the reader program. Through dynamic analysis, we demonstrate that our approach indeed subdues in the wild exploits in both Office 2003 and Office 2007 documents while the transformed documents continue to render benign content properly. We also show that randomizing the compression used in zip based OOXML files mitigates some attacks. The strength of these mechanisms lie in the number of content representation permutations, and the method applies where raw document content is used in attacks. Content randomization methods can be performed offline and require only a single document scan while the user-perceived delay when opening the transformed document is negligible.

1 Introduction

Leveraging documents as a vehicle for exploitation remains a very popular form of malware propagation that is sometimes more effective than mere drive-by downloads [2]. Malicious documents are documents that have been modified to contain malware, but are engineered to pose as benign documents with useful content. For this reason, they are often called Trojan documents. Malware-bearing documents typically exploit a vulnerability in the document reader program, but they can also be crafted to carry exploits in the form of an embedded object such as a media file. Another class of malicious documents are used as a stepping stone and while they do not take advantage of a software flaw, they rely on the user to execute a macro or even a portable executable. Often social engineering is used as part of the delivery vector to enhance the likelihood that victims will execute the malware contained within the document.

© Springer International Publishing Switzerland 2015
H. Bos et al. (Eds.): RAID 2015, LNCS 9404, pp. 225–246, 2015.
DOI: 10.1007/978-3-319-26362-5_11

For years, client side exploits, including attacks against document readers, have become more prevalent [6]. Despite efforts at improving software security, new vulnerabilities in document readers are still present today. For instance, there were 17 CVEs issued for Microsoft Office in 2013 and 10 in 2014, many of which were severe vulnerabilities facilitating arbitrary code execution. Document file types, such as PDF and Microsoft Office documents, are consistently among the top file types submitted to VirusTotal, implying current widespread concern over the role of documents as malware carriers. The impetus to stop Trojan documents is elevated due to their pervasive use in targeted espionage campaigns, such as those waged against non-governmental organizations (NGOs) [4,8,11].

Numerous approaches have been proposed to detect malicious documents. Signature matching, dynamic analysis, and machine learning based approaches are used widely in practice. Despite these many approaches, malware authors continue to evade detection and exploit computers successfully. Mitigations which seek to defeat many classes of memory misuse based exploits, such as address space layout randomization (ASLR) and data execution prevention (DEP), are implemented in modern operating systems. However, these protections are commonly circumvented and exploitation is still possible [23]. Despite extensive research and significant investments in protective technology, document exploits continue to remain a viable and popular vector for attack.

Our primary contribution is to demonstrate that modifications to documents between creation and viewing can hinder misuse of document content, adding additional exploit protection, while leaving them semantically equivalent with very little end-user impact. The proposed approach is inspired by operating system based exploit protections. Instead of seeking to detect the exploits in documents, we seek to defeat exploits by scrambling the malicious payloads used in attacks. While address space layout randomization is performed by the operating system, we induce exploit protections in the reader program through modifications to the input data. We modify a document at the file format level, resulting in a transformed document which will render the same as the original, but in which malicious content is disarranged and made inoperative. The transformed document is used in place of the original document. The document transformation should occur between the document creation and document open. Network gateways, such as web proxies or mail servers, or network clients such as web browsers or mail clients are ideal places to utilize our mechanisms. Hence, deployment of our technique requires no modification to the vulnerable document reader or client operating system.

We explore various methods of document content randomization (DCR). Microsoft Office formats are particularly amenable to document content fragment randomization (DCFR) where we rearrange the layout of blocks in a document file, without modifying the extracted data streams. We show that it is possible to relocate malicious content in both the document file and document reader memory. We also show that document content encoding randomization (DCER) breaks exploits in practice by changing the raw representation of the data in the file without changing the decoded stream. The strength of DCR rests in the number of unique content representations that can be created. For DCFR, this is driven by the number of block order permutations. For DCER, the number of possible encodings is the limiting factor.

We evaluate these content randomization techniques by testing them against hundreds of real world maldocs taken from VirusTotal. We test DCR on the three most prevalent exploits in both .doc and .docx files in our malicious document corpus. We find that most attacks are mitigated. Furthermore, we measured the performance of document transformation and found it to be comparable to an anti-virus scan. Opening a transformed document is at most 3 % slower than normal. We also validated that the transformed document rendered the same as the original document. Lastly, we examine the limits of DCR in the face of possible bypass techniques such as omelette shellcode.

The applicability of DCR is limited to foiling exploits that attempt to access exploit material in a manner inconsistent with the way the document reader accesses document data. Potential issues with DCR include breaking intrusion detection system signatures and cryptographic signatures applied to the raw document file.

2 Related Work

Detection of malicious documents using byte level analysis has long been studied and deployed widely despite recognized weaknesses in detecting new or polymorphic samples [13,22,24].

Dynamic analysis of documents can provide additional detection power, but it comes with computational cost, difficulty of implementation, and ambiguity in discerning malware [27]. Applying machine learning to various features extracted from documents, such as structural properties, has been shown to be effective but has also been challenged by mimicry attacks and adversarial learning [14,20,21]. We differ from most document centric defenses. Instead of seeking to detect the malicious content, we modify documents to foil exploit progression.

Our work builds upon years of research in probabilistic exploit mitigations typically implemented in the operating system. Address space layout randomization (ASLR) [26] is adopted widely. It is effective in defeating many classes of exploits, but is circumvented through limitations in implementation [19], use of heap sprays [28], or data leakage. As return oriented programming and similar techniques [18] have become popular, mechanisms to relocate or otherwise mitigate code (gadget) reuse have been proposed [16,29].

ASLR incurs little run time overhead because it relies on virtual memory techniques where address translation and relocation are already performed. Code level approaches such as instruction set randomization have also been proposed but are computationally prohibitive [9]. Data space randomization enciphers program data with random keys, but this method is not feasible in practice due to deployment difficulty and computational expense [3]. Instead of implementing these protection mechanisms in the execution environment, we seek to induce barriers to malware by modification to the document.

3   Microsoft Office File Formats and Exploit Protections

We here describe the commonly used Microsoft Office file formats. The OLE Compound Document Format was used as the default by Office 97-2003 and is used in the files whose extension is typically .doc, .ppt, and .xls. Beginning in Office 2007, the default file format is Office Open XML which use the .docx, .pptx, and .xslx extensions. We also explain the most important exploit protection mechanisms provided by Office and Windows, such as ASLR and DEP.

3.1   OLE Compound Document Format

The file format used by Office 97-2003 is called by many names including Compound File Binary Format and OLE Compound Document Format. We refer to this format as the "OLE" file format throughout this paper, as many of the libraries and utilities for parsing this format use variations of this name.

The OLE Compound Document format supports the storage of many independent data streams and borrows many structures from filesystems, especially the FAT filesystem. OLE files are used as a container for many file types including Office 97-2003 (.doc/.ppt/.xls), Outlook Message (.msg), Windows Installer (.msi), Windows Thumbnails (Thumbs.db), and ActiveX or OCX controls (.ocx). All of these file formats use the OLE format as a base container, implementing their own data structures inside of streams stored by the OLE format. In this way, the OLE file format can be compared to the zip archive which serves at the base container for diverse file formats including Java Archives (.jar), Office Open XML Documents (.docx/.pptx./.xlsx), and Mozilla Extensions (.xpi).

Like a filesystem, the OLE format is comprised of many data blocks or sectors. The vast majority of OLE files use a 512 byte sector size, but other sizes are possible. Blocks in the OLE file are allocated and linked using allocation tables. The individual data streams are logically organized in a hierarchical structure similar to the file/folder organization of a filesystem. There is a directory entry for each OLE stream containing the name of the file, the location of the first sector, and other metadata such as modification times. The OLE format also supports mini-streams which divide normal size sectors into 64 byte sectors, using a second, embedded allocation table.

Except for the header, which must be located in the first sector, all of the contents in an OLE file can be located arbitrarily within the OLE file. Furthermore, there is no requirement for the various data streams to be arranged in order or in contiguous blocks, although it is the norm.

The OLE format serves as a container for arbitrary data streams. Individual file formats use this basic container but implement their own format for the data in the various streams. We do not describe the particular OLE-based file formats as they vary widely, are often proprietary and poorly documented, and our study relies on the common container capability of OLE files.

3.2 Office Open XML File Format

The Office Open XML (OOXML) File Format became the default file format for Office documents starting in Office 2007. These files use the extensions of .docx, .pptx, and .xlsx. This format has been codified in international standards ECMA-376 and ISO/IEC 29500.

The OOXML file format uses a zip file as a container, with individual objects stored as files in the zip. The majority of the content in an OOXML file is XML data. The document content is represented as XML with markup that is unique to the OOXML format, but which is generally similar to other markup such as HTML. The contents of an OOXML document can be modified by unzipping the archive, modifying it with a text editor, and zipping the archive. However, the relatively complex markup requires extensive knowledge to make major changes.

While text and formating can be represented using XML, other content, such as images, are embedded in the document as separate files in the zip archive. Some of the binary objects embedded in OOXML files utilize the OLE format. Example of these files include Office 2003 files, some multimedia files, equations, ActiveX controls, and executables.

3.3 Microsoft Office Exploit Protections

Macro based viruses have long been an issue in Office documents. All recent Office versions disable the automatic execution of macros. The OOXML file format assigns macro based files a separate extension, such as .docm instead of .docx, making inadvertent execution of macros extremely difficult. The OOXML format is designed to minimize the amount of binary content and improve the readability in the text content of documents, making the file format easier to validate and simplifying the parser.

Data Execution Prevention (DEP) was enabled in Office 2010, which prevents execution of arbitrary shellcode in the heap and has generally forced the adoption of ROP code re-use techniques. ASLR was enabled by default in Windows Vista. Office running on versions of Windows since Vista will have the benefit of ASLR for operating system libraries, but ASLR was not enabled for all Office provided libraries until Office 2013. Hence, up until Office 2013, we observe use of ROP gadgets from Office libraries without the need for an ASLR bypass.

Throughout this paper, we refer to the container format common to Office 2003 and many other files as OLE. We refer specifically to Office 2003 or Office 2007 files by their extension: .doc or .docx respectively. While we refer to these file formats by the file extension of the document files (.doc/.docx) for brevity, we also included the presentation (.ppt/.pptx) and spreadsheet (.xls/.xlsx) files in our study. Our study relies on file format characteristics which are common across the document, presentation, and spreadsheet file variations.

4 Approach

Inspired by the simplicity and generality of ASLR-like techniques, we seek to obtain similar exploit mitigation outcomes through transformations to input data. The properties of a document can often directly and predictably influence various run time attributes of the opening application. The memory of a reader program is necessarily influenced by the file which it opens. We seek to find practical ways to make exploitation more difficult by content induced variations to the document file and reader memory. We call this general approach document content randomization (DCR).

We study two specific forms of document entropy infusion: document content fragment randomization (DCFR) and document content encoding randomization (DCER). DCFR is analogous to ASLR in that the order of data blocks in the document file is randomized. DCER can be compared to data space randomization because we randomize file level encoding. Both of these approaches apply to data stored in document files, but they can affect memory as files and subfiles are loaded into memory.

These transformations are envisioned to operate on documents during transfer between the potentially malicious source and the intended victim. They could be employed in network gateways such as email relays or web proxies where modification is already supported. In practice, filtering based on blacklists and anti-virus scanning is already common at these points. The modifications to the document could also be implemented on the client. For example, the web browser could employ the mechanisms presented here at download time, similar to other defenses such as blacklists and anti-virus.

We focus on Office documents, but most of the high level principles discussed here apply to other file formats. Specifically, we seek to mitigate exploits in two common document formats: Office 2003 (.doc) and Office 2007 (.docx).

4.1   Content Randomization in .doc Files

The most promising opportunity to apply DCR to .doc files is at the raw document file level. Malicious content is often stored in the raw document file and accessed through the filesystem during exploitation. Typically, file level access of malicious content occurs later in the exploitation phase and this content is usually malicious code, whether it be shellcode or a portable executable. Sourcing malicious content from the file is surprisingly common in document based exploits.

The authors observed obfuscated portable executables embedded in the raw document file of 96 % of the malicious Office 2003 documents in the Contagio document corpus [17]. This set of malicious documents, observed in targeted attacks, includes files that were 0 day attacks when collected. Retrieving additional malicious content from the raw document file is also common in PDF files used in targeted email attacks, while web based PDF exploits usually load their final payload through web download.

File level access most frequently is achieved through standard file access mechanisms, such as reading the file handle. Because most client object exploits, including document exploits, are triggered by opening a malicious file, a handle to the exploit file is usually already available in the reader application. While the malicious content may be embedded raw into the document file, exploits

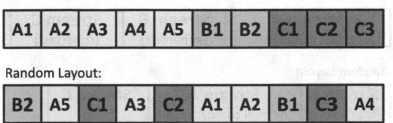

Fig. 1. OLE Fragmentation: The order of blocks in data streams is randomized, fragmenting the payloads

typically employ signature matching evasion techniques, such as trivial XOR encryption. The malicious content accessed through the raw document is sometimes accessed by offset, but typically an egg hunt is employed, where the file is searched for a specific marker. In most .doc files, we observed the shellcode and portable executables embedded within the bounds of the structure of the document, but simply appending malicious content to the end of an existing document is possible and is used sometimes.

We defeat raw file reflection by malware by performing file level content fragmentation (DCFR). OLE based file formats such as .doc files are especially accommodating of this technique. Typically, the streams in an OLE file are sequentially stored. However, re-ordering can occur and is expressly allowed. To implement this approach we built an OLE file block randomizer. It simply creates a new OLE file functionally equivalent to the original except that the layout of the data blocks is randomized. This is accomplished by randomizing the location of the data blocks, and then adjusting the sector allocation tables and directory data structures accordingly. This is essentially the inverse of running a filesystem defragmentation utility. An example of fragmentation of three OLE data streams is given in Fig. 1. Note that the blocks in the data streams are typically sequentially arranged. We randomize the order of the data blocks across all the streams. In the event that any data exists in the raw document file stream but is not contained in valid OLE sectors, the data is not transfered to the new randomized document.

Re-ordering data blocks, or DCFR, in an OLE provides a consistently effective and quantifiable way to prevent access to malicious content in raw document files without impacting normal use. Since OLE files do not implement any form of encoding at the container level, DCER is not a practical option.

4.2   Content Randomization in .docx Files

We also studied the use of document content in .docx exploits. We found a small number of OOXML files where the raw zip container was accessed for a malicious payload. These attacks simply included the malicious payload, usually

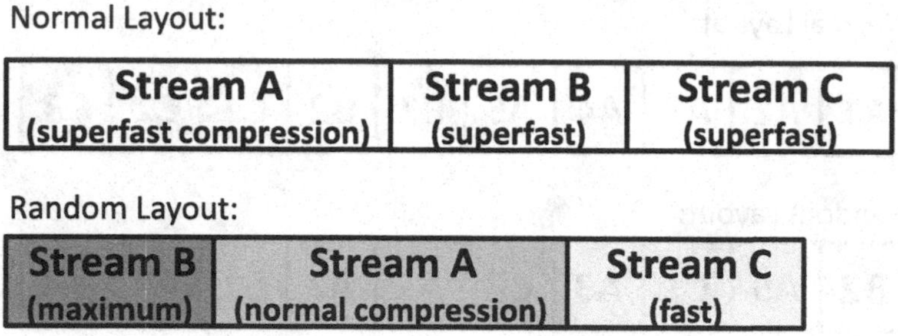

Normal Layout:

Stream A (superfast compression)	Stream B (superfast)	Stream C (superfast)

Random Layout:

Stream B (maximum)	Stream A (normal compression)	Stream C (fast)

Fig. 2. ZIP Encoding Randomization: The order and compression level of data streams is randomized

an encrypted portable executable, in the zip file without compression. It is then trivially located in the file through an egg hunt, similar to that done in OLE files.

We devised two simple ways to introduce entropy in the OOXML file. First, we randomized the order of the files in the zip archive. This defeats access based on offset. We also re-compressed the zip data streams, randomly selecting one of four deflate compression levels (superfast, fast, normal, maximum). Figure 2 demonstrates transformation of a simple zip file with three subfiles. Note that the order of the files in archive and the compression used on each file is randomized. Office uses superfast compression, the lowest compression level, so our archive randomization usually results in smaller files. Compression level randomization is enough to foil simple access to file content, even if an egg hunt is used. Therefore, content encoding randomization (DCER) applied at the file level is applicable to some .docx exploits.

However, most .docx exploits gain access to the final malware payload through a web download or through an egg hunt in memory. We found a common method of performing scriptless heap sprays in contemporaneous exploits that can be mitigated by DCFR [1,12]. In this heap spray technique, first observed in CVE-2013-3906, many ActiveX objects containing primarily heap spray data are read when the document is opened and loaded into the heap. These objects are loaded into memory raw, without interpretation or parsing. It is not clear why these objects are loaded into memory in this manner, while other embedded files do not receive the same treatment. Dynamic analysis by the authors confirmed that these embedded ActiveX objects are loaded directly in memory, while most other data from the document is not loaded into memory wholesale. Even if these ActiveX controls are not activated, they represent a simple and effective way to introduce content directly into the memory of the reader program.

Heap sprays are used to defeat ASLR. They ensure that the malicious payload can be located with high certainty through duplication of the malicious payload across a large memory address range, even if the address of a single copy can not be predicted. Only one copy of the malicious payload is needed for successful exploitation. Traditionally, heap sprays contain shellcode. However, DEP prevents execution from the heap. In the case of exploits targeting systems with DEP, the heap is commonly sprayed with ROP gadgets and a stack pivot is used to move the stack into the sprayed region. These attacks successfully evade ASLR and DEP. We observed this technique for scriptless heap sprays used for both traditional shellcode and to implement fake stacks implementing malicious ROP chains. While these two techniques have been observed, this ability to easily and predictably influence the reader process's memory could be used for other attacks such as object corruption exploits. This general technique is also used to load single copies of arbitrary content, including portable executables, into memory which is later egg-hunted and used in exploits.

Since these ActiveX objects use the same OLE container format that Office 2003 documents use, we use the same OLE fragmentation techniques to defeat these scriptless heap sprays. We randomized the layout of all OLE files embedded in .docx files, regardless of their role. When these objects are loaded into RAM, the content is scrambled, but can still be retrieved by a document reader which implements the OLE decoding routines. These scriptless heap sprays in .docx files represent an example of how document content directly influences reader memory.

For .docx files, we perform both file level encoding randomization and fragmentation of objects to be loaded into memory.

4.3   Strength of Content Randomization Mechanisms

Like other probabilistic exploit protections, one can calculate the likelihood of exploit success in the face of brute force attacks against DCR. Methods such as ASLR obfuscate the location of malicious payloads. Document content randomization does this as well. However, content based malicious payloads are very frequently located via egg hunts or are duplicated in heap sprays, obviating randomized relocation. In practice, the primary protection power lies in randomization of the content representation, whether through fragmentation or through encoding.

In the simple case, the probability of a payload that has been randomly fragmented being in proper order is the inverse of the number of possible permutations or $1/n!$ where n is the number of fragments. In practice, this should be adjusted to account for other data mixed in with the malicious payload, repetition of the malicious payloads, and other limitations or constraints. For example, when OLE DCFR is employed, the number of fragments that influence the possible permutations is not just the number of fragments in the malicious payload, but includes all of the sectors that are randomized.

When we perform DCER on .docx files, we randomly select between four deflate compression levels. This is adequate for all the samples we observed where DCER has effect because they all involve data streams that are originally uncompressed. This is, however, a very small number of permutations. Part of the strength of DCER is also rooted in how difficult the encoding of the content is to reverse or circumvent. Compression makes generating a specific post compression malicious payload more difficult through transformations and restrictions in the encoded output. For example, repeated byte sequences, such as the high order bytes in addresses used in ROP gadgets, are not found in compressed output. Unlike straightforward fragmentation, the constraining power of encoding is more difficult to quantify. Individual implementations of deflate are deterministic, but they are also allowed great latitude in how the encoding occurs. The same data stream can have many byte level representations using the same encoding method. If an entropy inducing compressor/encoder is used, the number of encoding induced permutations could be quantified.

The strength of DCR lies in the ability to fragment or encode malicious payloads in an unpredictable and constraining manner. This strength can be quantified as proportional to the number of randomized content permutations. We address possible DCR evasion approaches in Sect. 7.

5   Exploit Protection Evaluation

We evaluated the effectiveness of our content based exploit protections on hundreds of malicious Office documents sourced from VirusTotal. These documents were downloaded daily from the recent uploads to VirusTotal over the course of months. Our downloads were limited primarily by our monthly download limit on VirusTotal. We obtained 64,617 unique .doc files between May 2013 and March 2015 and 32,383 unique .docx files between November 2013 and March 2015, averaging 98 .doc and 66 .docx files per day. Of these collected documents, 40720 .doc and 2901 .docx files were labeled by at least one AV engine as malicious in a scan conducted two weeks following initial submission. Of these malicious documents, 1085 .doc and 578 .docx files were labeled by the anti-virus engines as utilizing a known exploit. The majority of the non-exploit malicious documents were identified by the anti-virus engines as utilizing macros.

As our study advances methods to break exploits using mechanisms not applicable to pure social engineering attacks, we focused our evaluation solely on maldocs leveraging a software vulnerability. Furthermore, to be able to better explain how our mechanisms applied to specific exploits, we utilized only those maldocs which were labeled by anti-virus engines to use a single exploit. We were left with 962 .doc and 363 .docx files after inconsistent exploit labels were removed. Of these documents, we found all exploits for which we were able to replicate successful exploitation and for which there were at least 20 samples. This resulted in 3 exploits in .doc files and 3 exploits in .docx files. Surprisingly, the malicious documents were distributed heavily across a small number of particularly popular exploits. For example, the three top exploits in the .docx file types comprised 306 of the 363 files, with 225 of these samples in the most popular exploit. In the event that we had many samples for a given exploit, we randomly selected a subset achieving a maximum of 100 documents to test and a maximum of 50 viable maldocs per exploit. In total, there were 343 documents tested and 217 documents demonstrating successful malware execution across these 6 sets.

To test for exploitation, we attempted dynamic execution of the Trojan documents by opening them in a virtual machine. To achieve successful exploitation, we utilized various configurations of software including both Windows XP and Windows 7 and Office 2007 and Office 2010. The ROP based exploits required specific versions of the libraries from which they reuse code. Since one of the exploits selected for our testing is in Adobe Flash, we also installed the appropriate version of Flash player. We considered the malware execution successful when malicious code was executed or requested from the network that would have been executed. Successful exploitation occurred in 217 or 63 % of the malicious documents we tested. We attribute this relatively low malware success rate to VirusTotal being used by malware authors for testing, sometimes testing unreliable or incomplete exploits. For example, in a few of the successful exploits we observed calc.exe, the malware "hello world", as the final payload. There were a small number of apparent false positives by AV as well.

Taking these successful malicious document based exploits, we applied our document content based mitigations and re-ran the documents. We considered the exploit blocked by DCR when the final malware payload was blocked. We observed the differences in malware execution through both host based and network based instrumentation. In a very small number of cases, DCR was not possible due to the malicious document having defective structure. These failures were considered blocked as well, but are due to the rudimentary file validation provided by performing content randomization.

Generally, the malicious documents we observed employ a portable executable as the final malicious payload. Most of these executables are extracted from the raw document file, many are downloaded from an external server, and a few are extracted from document reader memory. In many of the Trojan documents, the original document file is overwritten by a benign document, which is opened and presented to the user. Most of the malware immediately beacons to a controller node, but a small minority of the malware performed other actions such as infecting other files on the local system. We observed dropped benign documents and malware that correlate to recent reports of targeted attacks against NGOs [4,8] as well as more opportunistic crimeware.

When the document based exploit is blocked by DCR, the document reader typically crashes. However, sometimes instead of crashing, the reader enters an infinite loop, presumably performing an egg hunt that is never successful. When a decoy benign document is provided by the malware, it is either never opened due to a failure in malware execution or the benign document is scrambled due to DCR and the attempt to open the document fails because the file is invalid. When DCR interrupts file-level access, shellcode that is attempting to extract a portable executable or additional shellcode from the document file is interrupted. When memory fragmentation is effective, it scrambles either shellcode or ROP chains, preventing exploitation earlier. Table 1 contains the high level results of our evaluation.

CVE-2009-3129 is triggered by a malformed spreadsheet that causes a memory corruption error. All of the successful exploits were .xls spreadsheet files. In all of these exploits, the pattern of extracting an encrypted portable executable

Table 1. DCR Exploit Protection Evaluation

CVE	File Type	Blocked	Total	Block Rate	Effective Mechanism
2009-3129	.xls	36	36	100 %	File Fragmentation
2011-0611	.doc, .xls	29	29	100 %	File Fragmentation
2012-0158	.doc, .xls	50	50	100 %	File Fragmentation
2012-0158	.pptx, .xlsx	4	10	40 %	File Encoding
2013-3906	.docx	42	42	100 %	Memory Fragmentation
2014-4114	.ppsx, .docx	2	50	4 %	File Validation
All-		163	217	75.1 %	-

and benign decoy document is employed. Due to raw access to the document file, all of these exploits were defeated by file level DCFR.

CVE-2011-0611 is actually a vulnerability in Adobe software products, including Flash player, but it is most often observed inside of Office documents. This exploit triggers a type confusion error through a malformed Flash file embedded in the Office document. We were able to observe successful exploitation in both .doc and .xls files. Like the other exploits embedded in OLE based file formats, all of the exploits are defeated by file level DCFR because the malicious executable and decoy document are extracted from the raw document file.

It is interesting to observe that this exploit in Adobe products was utilized so heavily in Office files. It is likely that part of the reason this exploit was embedded in Office documents was to leverage the social engineering of email based attacks.

CVE-2012-0158 is caused by malformed ActiveX controls that corrupt system state. While originally reported in RTF documents, our VirusTotal sourced malware contained a large number of 2012-0158 exploits in the OLE container as well. We observed successful exploitation in both .doc and .xls files, which was defeated by file level document fragmentation.

We also observed 2012-0158 in OOXML based files. These .docx based 2012-0158 were much less common than the .doc version, making this set the smallest in our evaluation. We observed both .pptx slideshows and .xlsx spreadsheet files containing viable exploits.

This vulnerability exists in the MSCOMCTL library which handles ActiveX controls. Until May 2014 (CVE-2014-1809), ASLR was not enabled on this library on all versions of Office (including Office 2013) and on all version of Windows (including Windows 7 and Windows 8). Since this library is easily locatable, it is trivial to re-use code from the same library as is used for the initial vulnerability. Due to this lack of OS level exploit mitigations and the simplicity of exploitation, DCR, including memory fragmentation, does not block this exploit. It is noteworthy that since the ActiveX controls used in this exploit are OLE files, our DCR mechanisms fragmented these objects. However, since the access to these objects comes through legitimate means, the layout randomization provides no mitigation power.

However, some exploits are foiled because they use anomalous access to the raw document file. In the case where the raw document is accessed, the encrypted malicious payload is stored in the zip container without compression. Our re-compression of the zip streams with a randomly selected compression level defeats this file level access.

CVE-2013-3906 is a vulnerability in the TIF image format parser that permits memory corruption resulting in possible code execution. This exploit was manifest in .docx documents. Some of these exploits use ROP chains, while some use traditional shellcode. The ROP based exploits can evade DEP using a stack pivot and code re-use. Since ASLR is not enabled on the MSCOMCTL library, this library is used for gadgets in the ROP based exploits. Hence, the ROP formulation of the exploit was able to evade both ASLR and DEP as implemented at the time. However, in either the case of traditional shellcode or ROP chains, the 2013-3906 exploits are defeated through fragmentation of ActiveX objects used to implement a scriptless heap spray. The majority of the 2013-3906 samples we observed attempt to load final malware via HTTP requests. The other exploits load the final malware in memory using the same ActiveX control loading mechanism, such that these payloads are also fragmented.

The CVE-2014-4114 vulnerability is not caused by a software coding flaw, but rather policy that allows remote code to be executed. In this vulnerability, an ActiveX control allows execution of a remote .inf file which then allows execution of a portable executable. The malware is most typically downloaded via Windows file sharing (SMB/CIFS). The vast majority of these maldocs were .ppsx files which are presentations that open automatically as slide shows. There were a small number of .docx files as well. Since this vulnerability is a policy flaw, mitigations such as ASLR and DEP do not apply. Similarly, DCR does not apply even though we fragment the OLE ActiveX controls implementing the exploit. We only block a small number of these exploits because our file fragmenter identifies them as improperly formatted.

Overall, we are able to block over 75 % of the exploits in our evaluation set. If 2014-4114, which is not a traditional memory safety vulnerability, is excluded, then DCR blocks over 96 % of the exploits in our evaluation set.

6   Performance Evaluation

The core performance characteristics of DCR are the time required to perform the document transformation and the overhead incurred when opening the document. The document content randomization time was evaluated by performing DCR on a number of documents. The file open overhead was measured by timing the document reader opening and rendering the document, comparing the times from the original and randomized documents. We also validated that the view of the document presented to the user remained invariant by scripting Office to open the document and print it as a PDF. We compared the resulting PDFs

Table 2. DCR Performance

File type	Transform speed	Render overhead
.doc	68.9 Mbps	0 %
.docx	43.1 Mbps	2.9 %

created from the original and modified documents to ensure equivalence in rendering. The results of the performance evaluation of DCR are summarized in Table 2.

6.1 .doc DCR Performance

To evaluate the computational expense of performing the document content randomization, we measured the time to perform this operation on a 1000 document, 249 MB, set randomly selected from the Govdocs corpus [7]. The average time to perform the document fragmentation was 28.9 s using a single thread on a commodity server. This equates to 68.9 Mbps of throughput in a single thread. To put this execution time in perspective, we scanned the same corpus with ClamAV which required an average 28.7 s to complete. Performing this content fragmentation on a single 248 K sample (close to average document size) yielded an average 0.028 second execution time. The DCR operations are similar in cost to that incurred by a common anti-virus engine and result in a delay that should be acceptable for most situations.

To test the performance impact of DCR on document opening and rendering, this set of benign documents was converted to PDF using Microsoft Office and powershell scripting. There were 39 documents that were removed from this set because they required user input to open or printing was prohibited by Office. The most common cause of failing to print was invocation of protected view, which limits printing, apparently because they were created by old versions of Office (the Govdocs corpus contains some very old documents). Other obstacles to automation included prompting for a password or prompting the user as a result of automated file repair actions. In addition, following OLE file format fragmentation, an additional 125 documents opened in protected view which prevented automated printing. These files apparently triggered some file validation heuristics in Office. The same mechanisms used to break exploits can also be used for malicious intent, such as evading virus scanners. All content was present, and it was later discovered that the validation heuristic did not trigger reliably on independent formulations of the same original document–some transformations would trigger this protected view and some would not. This protection built into Office triggers on some particular block layouts but the exact criteria was not discovered by the authors. If DCR is to be use widely, it would be necessary to understand and prevent triggering of this heuristic, although documents from untrusted sources (email or web) are already opened in protected view anyway.

The test data set therefore contained 836 documents totaling 197 MB. It took about 15 min for the documents to be converted to PDFs which equals just over 1 second per document. Performing multiple trials, there was no consistent difference in speed between the original and the fragmented documents. The differences in mean open times between the original and fragmented documents was 1/50th of the 95 % confidence interval. Therefore, the randomized documents take no longer to open and render. This is expected as there is no additional work required to reassemble the randomized streams. Any effects resulting from less efficient read patterns seem to be masked by file caching.

Having converted both the original and fragmented documents to PDF documents, the resulting PDFs were compared for similarity. Since the PDFs had unique attributes such as creation times, none of the PDFs generated from rendering the original documents were identical to those generated from the fragmented documents. However, they were very similar in all respects. The average difference in size of the resulting PDFs was 40 bytes, with 513 of the PDF pairs having the exact same size. The average binary content similarity score of these derivative document pairs was 87 (out of 100) using the ssdeep utility [10]. Manual review of a small number of samples also confirmed the same content in the fragmented documents as in the original documents.

6.2 .docx DCR Performance

The performance impact of .docx DCR was similarly evaluated. To measure the cost of performing our embedded object layout randomization, we compiled a corpus of benign .docx files from the Internet, using a web search with the sole criteria of seeking .docx files. The search yielded a wide diversity of sites with no known relevant bias on the part of the researchers.

This corpus consisted of 341 files weighing in at 76 MB. Executing our utility required an average 14.3 s from which we derive a single threaded bandwidth of 43.1 Mbps. Scanning the same corpus with ClamAV required 28.0 s, nearly double the time required for our mechanism. The time to execute on a single 225 KB document, which was an average size document in this corpus, was 0.034 s.

As with .doc files, we tested the impact on rendering by converting both the original and randomized documents to PDF using Office. The outcome was a mean open time of 268.5 s for the original documents and 276.3 s for the DCR documents. This 2.9 % increase in document render time following document fragmentation is greater than the 95 % confidence interval for these trials. This slow down is very likely due to the use of higher levels of compression in the zip container. By default, Microsoft Office uses deflate compression with the fastest compression level while our randomized compression levels are spread between four compression levels. Indeed, the corpus of randomized documents was 8 % smaller than the original document set.

This performance evaluation excluded one of the 341 documents that crashed Office post randomization. This document did not appear to be malicious in any way, but simply contained a large number of ActiveX controls that triggered a bug in Office following fragmentation. We did not determine the exact cause of this crash, but did isolate it to the fragmented OLE based ActiveX objects. Since it caused a crash instead of causing a file validation/parsing error, we do not consider it evidence of a fundamental issue with our approach, but rather a bug in Office or a special case our randomizer needs to handle.

Beyond the zip container, the vast majority of the documents in this benign corpus were not modified. Of the 341 documents, only 10 documents had OLE sub-objects on which fragmentation was performed, including the crash inducing document. Since this number was so small, the user visible representation of these samples were validated manually. Both the original and the modified document were opened and compared. Barring the aforementioned single document, randomizing the OLE objects embedded in .docx files maintained the integrity of the original document as presented to the user.

For both .doc and .docx files, the CPU time required to perform document randomization is reasonable–comparable with that of signature matching based detectors. The overhead on document open is negligible. We observed an issue with heuristic detections triggering protected view in about 12 % of .doc files. We also seemed to trigger of a bug for a single .docx file. Barring these exceptions, the transformed documents provided the same display to the user as is produced by the original.

7   Content Randomization Evasion

Document content randomization is effective against many exploits created without knowledge that it would be used. If it is to remain effective following wide-scale deployment, it must be resilient to evasion. The strength of malicious payload fragmentation lies in the number of fragments required for the payload. For fragmentation to be effective, the size of the malicious payload must be larger than the fragmentation block size.

The OLE containers used in .docx heap sprays employ a default block size of 64 bytes which is much smaller than the shellcode required for a meaningful exploit. In most of the examples we observed, the shellcode was approximately 500 bytes in length. As a comparison, we studied a collection of 32-bit windows shellcode snippets packaged with the Metasploit Framework. The functionality of these code blocks ranged from stubs that act as building blocks to complete malicious payloads. The average size of all of these components is 289 bytes. In most situations, these shellcode blocks will be extended a small amount with exploit specific register setup and shellcode encoding. The size of the larger shellcode components is comparable with the approximately 500 byte shellcode observed in the .docx scriptless heap sprays. Shellcode that provides functionality for a full malicious payload is invariably larger than can fit within the 64 byte default size restriction imposed by content fragmentation.

Current exploits are not resilient to malicious payload fragmentation because it is not currently widely deployed. However, the documented countermeasure to limits on payload size is to perform an egg hunt per payload block, which has been styled omelette shellcode [5]. Omelette shellcode locates and combines multiple smaller eggs into a larger buffer, reconstructing a malicious payload from many small pieces. The omelette approach adds at least one more stage to the exploit, in exchange for accommodating fragmentation of the malicious content.

A typical heap spray involves filling a portion of the heap with the same malicious content repeated many times, with each repetition being a valid entry point. This approach would be altered for an optimal omelette based exploit. One would spray the heap with the omelette code solely, then load a single copy of the additional shellcode eggs into memory outside the target region for the spray.

When multiple egg hunts are used to defeat malicious payload fragmentation, then the primary mitigation power is shifted to the size of a block in which the reassembly code must reside. Each egg containing the partitioned payload could have an arbitrarily small size with a few bytes overhead for a marker used to locate the egg and an identifier to facilitate proper re-ordering. The size of the omelette code is invariably the bottleneck of the technique. If the omelette code can fit fully within a fragmentation block, then malicious payload fragmentation will not be effective.

Therefore, for omelette shellcode to operate, it must be loaded in a single 64 byte block or it will be fragmented and re-ordered. Most openly available examples of omelette shellcode, which are designed specifically to be as compact as possible, are about 80–90 bytes [25]. Of course, it may be possible to shrink the size of the omelette functionality in a given exploit and probabilistic attacks are possible.

However, if the 64 byte block size provides insufficient fragmentation, this block size could be dropped to a level rendering any sort of egg hunt infeasible. The size of these blocks in OLE files is tunable. It is also noteworthy that the cutoff between normal and small block streams can be changed and that the block size for the normal streams is also tunable. Ergo, this flexibility in size applies generally to both normal and small OLE streams. Due to the arbitrary tuning of OLE block sizes, it is not feasible to prevent malicious payload fragmentation by shrinking the payload size using techniques such as omelette shellcode.

In exploring malicious payload size limitations, we use shellcode because methods such as omelette shellcode are relatively well documented. The same general principles apply to other situations such as ROP based exploits. Typical ROP chains are similar in size to the shellcode, so the fragmentation of DCFR is equally effective. The ROP chains we saw in the CVE-2013-3906 heap sprays were about 1000 bytes in length. Therefore small block OLE fragmentation should be able to disrupt ROP chains as well, even if omelette style techniques are employed. The same arguments should apply to .doc file level content randomization. To the degree that exploits cannot implement malicious payload reconstruction mechanisms, then file level content randomization will remain effective.

Because document content randomization is not used widely, no examples of malicious documents could be found in the wild that used countermeasures such as omelette code. However, observations made during the manual validation performed for current exploits indicate that DCR would still be successful.

In our study of Office documents, we saw a relatively small number of exploits that were defeated by encoding based content randomization. We observed no attempts to counter this exploit protection, and there is a dearth of studies that apply to DCER evasion. As such, counterevasion strategies are necessarily speculative.

One likely DCER evasion approach would be to anticipate the encoding and adjust the payload accordingly. Some encodings are so simplistic that they could be defeated by preparing the malicious payload so that it appears as desired post encoding. For example, if base64 were a possible encoding, it would likely be possible to prepare a malicious payload that was operable following encoding despite some restrictions in content [15]. This approach would be more difficult with encoding mechanisms such as compression which have greater complexity. Even if attackers were able to circumvent the tighter constraints caused by compression, an arbitrarily large number of compression representations are possible because of the latitude afforded in compression algorithms such as deflate. Adding a custom, entropy infusing, compressor to the existing DCR mechanisms would be operationally feasible.

Assuming there are enough possible encodings to make brute forcing infeasible, the indirect approach, analogous to omelette shellcode, would be to implement a decoder. If a very small decoder can be created, then it might be used to decode a larger payload. Trivial encodings such as hexascii or base64 may well be possible to implement in a very small decoder. Assuming an encoding method such as deflate compression is used, it is not likely that a sufficiently small decoder can be created to make this method worthwhile. We studied the compiled object size of a few common decompress only deflate implementations designed specifically for small size, including miniz and zlib's puff, and found the smallest to be 5 KB. When compared with other decoders used in exploits, this is relatively large. It seems that scenarios where using an over 5 KB decoder is useful for defeating content encoding based would be rare.

When attacked directly, DCFR's strength is driven by minimum fragment size which drives the number of fragments and the resulting number of possible permutations. It is not feasible to drop the size of a malicious payload small enough to evade the granularity provided by DCFR in OLE files. DCER's evasion resistance lies in both the constraints imposed by the encoding techniques employed and the number of possible encodings. It seems that the flexibility provided by encoding, especially compression, should allow sufficient entropy to make defeating DCER infeasible.

8 Discussion

Not all exploits are directly impacted by DCR and some vulnerabilities may be formulated to circumvent DCR. For example, the malicious documents foiled through OLE file randomization could be modified to load the final malicious executable through a web download instead of extracting it from inside the document file. Similarly, the OOXML documents defeated through memory content location randomization could use a scripted heap spray instead of relying on document content loaded into memory. However, these changes might cause the exploit to run afoul of additional mitigations such as restrictions on ability to download executables or restrictions on the execution of macros. Hence, DCR is enabled by environmental controls such as restrictions on web downloads, Office based protections such as disabling of scripting, and operating system controls such as DEP. If these complementary protection mechanisms are not used, DCR will not be as effective. To the degree that security controls that drive attackers to use raw file content become more prevalent, DCR should increase in applicability, including in other file formats.

Some forms of DCR are more difficult to circumvent than others because they operate much earlier in the exploitation process where the attacker has lower control over the system. For example, DCR that defeats heap sprays is more resilient than that which disrupts egg hunts that extract the final malicious payload. In our evaluation, the older exploits were interrupted later in the exploitation process while the newer exploits occur much earlier. It appears that complimentary mitigations in the operating system (ALSR and DEP) constrain exploit authors to use document content earlier in the exploits.

DCR is an attractive mitigation technique because it incurs a very low performance impact. Transforming the document requires roughly the same computational resources that are already commonly employed to perform signature matching on both network servers and client programs. DCR incurs a very small performance penalty when the transformed document is opened because this mechanism leverages the file stream reassembly routines already executed by the document reader.

Just as virtual memory mechanisms enable ASLR with little overhead, the parsing and reassembly that enables multiple file level representations of the same logical document allows for efficient DCR. Any situation where data is referenced indirectly, providing for multiple possible low level representations, could potentially be used to implement exploit protections similar to DCR. We focus on content fragmentation because the file formats studied here support a large degree of layout changes. Content encoding randomization is only effective in a small number of Office exploits. However, other document and media formats might not support the same level of data fragmentation but may support arbitrary encoding or compression. The PDF format is a good candidate for file level DCER to prevent raw file reflection based malware retrieval. There is an opportunity for studying the limits of DCER, especially in document formats such as PDF where there are multiple options for encoding, the encodings can be combined for the same stream, and encoding mechanisms themselves can be tweaked. For example, instead of using standard compression levels for the deflate method, one could use probabilistic Huffman coding trees and randomized use of LZ77 data deduplication. Operating system based encoding or data randomization techniques generally have been unsuccessful due to computational overhead and the difficulty of deploying the technique which requires modifying system libraries as well as applications. However, DCER has the potential to be computationally feasible because the content encoding already occurs.

DCR is likely to be employed in situations where many multiple repeated exploitations attempts are not easy, lowering concern of probabilistic attacks. For example, document based attacks usually require the user to take an action to view the document. Because of how client applications are used, probabilistic attacks requiring numerous attempts, similar to those employed against network daemons to defeat ASLR, are not likely to be possible.

While DCR does not impact the content of the document as interpreted by the document reader and viewed by the user, it does change the raw document file. This could potentially impact some signature matching systems which operate on raw files instead of interpreting as the document reader does. Also, cryptographic signatures such as those used in signed emails would not validate correctly on the transformed document. Solutions to these issues have yet to be elaborated, but potential solutions are promising. For example, signature matching systems can implement file parsing. Signature validation systems could operate on an invariant logical representation of the parsed document, instead of a potentially arbitrary file level representation.

9   Conclusions

We designed and evaluated exploit protections using transformations performed on documents between production and consumption. Document content fragment and encoding randomization are effective in scrambling exploit critical content in document files and in document reader process memory. We evaluated the ability to mitigate current exploits in Office 2003 (.doc) and Office 2007 (.docx) file formats using hundreds of malicious documents, demonstrating a memory misuse exploit block rate of over 96 %. The overhead of transforming documents is comparable in run time to a common anti-virus engine and the added latency of opening a content layout randomized document is negligible for .doc and about 3 % for .docx files. The transformed documents are functionally equivalent to the original documents, barring the exploit protections that are induced. The evasion resistance of content randomization is rooted in the number of raw content permutations possible. File content randomization should be applicable to other file formats as complementary controls force attackers to use direct access to file content to advance their attacks.

Acknowledgments. The authors would like to thank all of the reviewers for their valuable comments and suggestions. This work is supported by Lockheed Martin Corporation and the National Science Foundation Grant No. CNS 1421747 and II-NEW 1205453. Opinions, findings, conclusions and recommendations expressed in this material are those of the authors and do not necessarily reflect the views of Lockheed Martin, the NSF, or US Government.

References

1. 5 attackers & counting: Dissecting the "docx.image" exploit kit, December 2013. http://www.proofpoint.com/threatinsight/posts/dissecting-docx-image-exploit-kit-cve-exploitation.php
2. Security threat report 2014: Smarter, shadier, stealthier malware. Technical report, Sophos Labs (2014)
3. Bhatkar, S., Sekar, R.: Data space randomization. In: Zamboni, D. (ed.) DIMVA 2008. LNCS, vol. 5137, pp. 1–22. Springer, Heidelberg (2008)
4. Blond, S.L., Uritesc, A., Gilbert, C., Chua, Z.L., Saxena, P., Kirda, E.: A look at targeted attacks through the lense of an NGO. In: 23rd USENIX Security Symposium (USENIX Security 2014), pp. 543–558, USENIX Association, San Diego (2014)
5. Bradshaw, S.: The grey corner: omlette egghunter shellcode, October 2013. http://www.thegreycorner.com/2013/10/omlette-egghunter-shellcode.html
6. Dhamankar, R., Paller, A., Sachs, M., Skoudis, E., Eschelbeck, G., Sarwate, A.: Top 20 internet security risks for 2007. http://www.sans.org/press/top20_2007.php
7. Garfinkel, S., Farrell, P., Roussev, V., Dinolt, G.: Bringing science to digital forensics with standardized forensic corpora. Digit. Investig. **6**, S2–S11 (2009)
8. Hardy, S., Crete-Nishihata, M., Kleemola, K., Senft, A., Sonne, B., Wiseman, G., Gill, P., Deibert, R.J.: Targeted threat index: characterizing and quantifying politically-motivated targeted malware. In: Proceedings of the 23rd USENIX Security Symposium (2014)
9. Kc, G.S., Keromytis, A.D., Prevelakis, V.: Countering code-injection attacks with instruction-set randomization. In: Proceedings of the 10th ACM Conference on Computer and Communications Security, CCS 2003, pp. 272–280. ACM, New York (2003)
10. Kornblum, J.: Identifying almost identical files using context triggered piecewise hashing. Digit. Investig. **3**(suppl.), 91–97 (2006)
11. Li, F., Lai, A., Ddl, D.: Evidence of advanced persistent threat: a case study of malware for political espionage. In: 2011 6th International Conference on Malicious and Unwanted Software (MALWARE), pp. 102–109, October 2011
12. Li, H., Zhu, S., Xie, J.: RTF attack takes advantage of multiple exploits, April 2014. http://blogs.mcafee.com/mcafee-labs/rtf-attack-takes-advantage-of-multiple-exploits
13. Li, W.-J., Stolfo, S.J., Stavrou, A., Androulaki, E., Keromytis, A.D.: A study of malcode-bearing documents. In: Hämmerli, B.M., Sommer, R. (eds.) DIMVA 2007. LNCS, vol. 4579, pp. 231–250. Springer, Heidelberg (2007)
14. Maiorca, D., Corona, I., Giacinto, G.: Looking at the bag is not enough to find the bomb: an evasion of structural methods for malicious PDF files detection. In: Proceedings of the 8th ACM SIGSAC Symposium on Information, Computer and Communications Security, ASIA CCS 2013, pp. 119–130. ACM, New York (2013)
15. Mason, J., Small, S., Monrose, F., MacManus, G.: English shellcode. In: Proceedings of the 16th ACM Conference on Computer and Communications Security, CCS 2009, pp. 524–533. ACM, New York (2009)
16. Pappas, V., Polychronakis, M., Keromytis, A.: Smashing the gadgets: hindering return-oriented programming using in-place code randomization. In: 2012 IEEE Symposium on Security and Privacy (SP), pp. 601–615, May 2012
17. Parkour, M.: 11,355+ malicious documents - archive for signature testing and research, April 2011. http://contagiodump.blogspot.com/2010/08/malicious-documents-archive-for.html

18. Shacham, H.: The geometry of innocent flesh on the bone: return-into-libc without function calls (on the x86). In: Proceedings of the 14th ACM Conference on Computer and Communications Security, CCS 2007, pp. 552–561. ACM, New York (2007)

19. Shacham, H., Page, M., Pfaff, B., Goh, E.-J., Modadugu, N., Boneh, D.: On the effectiveness of address-space randomization. In: Proceedings of the 11th ACM Conference on Computer and Communications Security, CCS 2004, pp. 298–307. ACM, New York (2004)

20. Smutz, C., Stavrou, A.: Malicious PDF detection using metadata and structural features. In: Proceedings of the 28th Annual Computer Security Applications Conference, ACSAC 2012, pp. 239–248. ACM, New York (2012)

21. Srndic, N., Laskov, P.: Detection of malicious PDF files based on hierarchical document structure. In: Proceedings of the 20th Annual Network & Distributed System Security Symposium 2013 (2013)

22. Stolfo, S.J., Wang, K., Li, W.-J.: Fileprint analysis for malware detection. In: ACM CCS WORM (2005)

23. Szekeres, L., Payer, M., Wei, T., Song, D.: SoK: eternal war in memory. In: 2013 IEEE Symposium on Security and Privacy (SP), pp. 48–62, May 2013

24. Tabish, S.M., Shafiq, M.Z., Farooq, M.: Malware detection using statistical analysis of byte-level file content. In: Proceedings of the ACM SIGKDD Workshop on CyberSecurity and Intelligence Informatics, CSI-KDD 2009, pp. 23–31. ACM, New York (2009)

25. Team, C.: Exploit notes-win32 eggs-to-omelet, August 2010. https://www.corelan.be/index.php/2010/08/22/exploit-notes-win32-eggs-to-omelet/

26. Team, P.: PaX address space layout randomization (2003). http://pax.grsecurity.net/docs/aslr.txt

27. Tzermias, Z., Sykiotakis, G., Polychronakis, M., Markatos, E.P.: Combining static and dynamic analysis for the detection of malicious documents. In: Proceedings of the Fourth European Workshop on System Security, EUROSEC 2011, pp. 4:1–4:6. ACM, New York (2011)

28. Wei, T., Wang, T., Duan, L., Luo, J.: Secure dynamic code generation against spraying. In: Proceedings of the 17th ACM Conference on Computer and Communications Security, CCS 2010, pp. 738–740. ACM, New York (2010)

29. Zhang, C., Wei, T., Chen, Z., Duan, L., Szekeres, L., McCamant, S., Song, D., Zou, W.: Practical control flow integrity and randomization for binary executables. In: 2013 IEEE Symposium on Security and Privacy (SP), pp. 559–573, May 2013

Improving Accuracy of Static Integer Overflow Detection in Binary

Yang Zhang, Xiaoshan Sun, Yi Deng, Liang Cheng$^{(\boxtimes)}$, Shuke Zeng, Yu Fu, and Dengguo Feng

Trusted Computing and Information Assurance Laboratory, Institute of Software, Chinese Academy of Sciences, Beijing, China
{zhangyang,sunxs,dengyi,chengliang,skzeng,fuyu,feng}@tca.iscas.ac.cn

Abstract. Integer overflow presents a major source of security threats to information systems. However, current solutions are less effective in detecting integer overflow vulnerabilities: they either produce unacceptably high false positive rates or cannot generate concrete inputs towards vulnerability exploration. This limits the usability of these solutions in analyzing real-world applications, especially those in the format of binary executables.

In this paper, we present a platform, called INDIO, for accurately detecting integer overflow vulnerabilities in Windows binaries. INDIO integrates the techniques of pattern-matching (for quick identification of potential vulnerabilities), vulnerability ranking (for economic elimination of false positives), and selective symbolic execution (for rigorous elimination of false positives). As a result, INDIO can detect integer overflow with low false positive and false negative rates.

We have applied INDIO to several real-world, large-size Windows binaries, and the experimental results confirmed the effectiveness of INDIO (all known and two previously unknown integer overflows vulnerabilities were detected). The experiments also demonstrate that the vulnerability ranking technique and other optimization techniques employed in INDIO can significantly reduce false positives with economic costs.

Keywords: Integer overflow detection · Static program analysis · Binary analysis · Vulnerability ranking · Weakest precondition · Symbolic execution

1 Introduction

Integer overflow presents a major class of security vulnerabilities in information systems, or more generally, software-regulated systems (e.g. embedded systems). As reported by the Common Vulnerability and Exploit (CVE), integer overflow has become the second most critical type of coding errors, after buffer overflow, that causes severe security consequences[1].

---

[1] Vulnerability type distributions in cve. CVE (2007), http://cve.mitre.org/docs/vuln-trends/vuln-trends.pdf.

© Springer International Publishing Switzerland 2015
H. Bos et al. (Eds.): RAID 2015, LNCS 9404, pp. 247–269, 2015.
DOI: 10.1007/978-3-319-26362-5_12

Integer overflow emerges when an arithmetic operation attempts to create a numeric value that is too large to be correctly represented in the available storage space. We refer to such arithmetic operations as overflow points. Even though overflow points do not directly compromise security, they can trigger other types of vulnerabilities, such as buffer and heap overflow, and in turn cause significant security consequences.

Both the industry and academia have proposed a variety of solutions in recent years to detecting and mitigating integer overflow vulnerabilities. These solutions can be generally categorized as based on either static analysis (e.g. [15,25–27, 29]) or dynamic analysis (e.g. [7,10,16,24,28,31]). Unfortunately, both these two categories of solutions have their limitations when applied in realistic analyses. In addition to the high computational cost, static analysis solutions typically suffer from high false positive rates. That is, in order to ensure zero omission of integer overflow vulnerabilities, these solutions typically over-estimate the behavior of the program under analysis, which leads to excessive spurious vulnerabilities being reported. The analyst might have to spend significant effort in ruling out false positives before being able to address a genuine vulnerability.

Dynamic analysis based solutions do not have the problem of excessive false positives. In contrast, whenever they report an integer overflow, it is trusted to be real and exploitable. However, the effectiveness of these solutions heavily depends on the set of inputs used to execute the program. It is often challenging to find inputs within reasonable effort that trigger all vulnerabilities in the program. Moreover, most of these solutions need to generate new input or modify the original input at runtime to re-execute the program and explore its state space. This restricts their applicability in checking GUI-based applications, because the behavior of GUI-based applications is triggered by events (e.g., mouse-clicking), whose input scope is hard to fully cover [30]. In fact, most existing dynamic analysis solutions can only examine programs with specific input formats (such as media players, network protocol parsers and file processors).

The limitations of existing solutions exacerbate when the program under analysis is in binary code. The unique characteristics of binary code, including the blur distinction between data and instructions, the prevailing use of indirect addressing and jumps, and the lack of type information, make it a challenging task to reconstruct the syntactic structure and semantics from binary code that, unfortunately, constitutes the premise for existing solutions to proceed their analysis with acceptable accuracy.

However, it is inevitable to detect and fix integer overflow at the binary level, since it is often impractical to do so at the source code level (e.g., due to the unavailability of source code, incomplete code or missing library files). To tackle the difficulties of analyzing binary code, and especially to address the limitations of existing solutions, we propose a static analysis based framework called INDIO (INtegrated Detection of Integer Overflow) to detect and validate integer overflow vulnerabilities in Windows binaries.

INDIO decomposes the task of finding integer overflow in binaries into two steps. Firstly, all suspicious program paths likely to contain integer overflow are identified using pattern matching. We refer to these suspicious paths as *vulnerable paths*. Priority ranking and weakest precondition (WP) calculation are then employed to all vulnerable paths to filter out a significant portion of false positives with economic costs. The second step of detection is based on selective symbolic execution [9], which checks if the vulnerabilities identified in the first step are genuine in a simulated runtime environment. Taint analysis and path pruning are employed prior to symbolic execution to force computationally expensive analysis be only spent on validating suspicious vulnerabilities that are likely to be real. A byproduct of selective symbolic execution is that it generates example program inputs exposing the genuine vulnerabilities. Given that a vulnerability sometimes is embedded in program paths with hundreds of instructions, this feature is particularly helpful to analysts to understand and fix integer overflow vulnerabilities.

We applied INDIO to several real-world windows binaries that have been widely analyzed by existing solutions. INDIO found one previously unknown bug and one fixed but unpublished bug in the GUI library comctl32.dll, and another previously unknown bug in libpng.dll. The two unknown bugs have both been confirmed by their vendors. Our experimental results also show that INDIO is capable of detecting integer overflow with low false positive and false negative rates.

In summary, this paper makes the following contributions:

- We developed an integrated framework, INDIO, to effectively detect integer overflow in Windows binaries. The framework incorporates pattern matching, inter-procedural data- and control-flow analysis, and symbolic execution to quickly detect and validate integer overflow vulnerabilities in Windows binaries. For the genuine vulnerabilities detected, the framework is able to generate example inputs triggering them, in order to assist the understanding and fixing of these vulnerabilities.
- We implemented a collection of optimization techniques, including vulnerability priority ranking, WP calculation, taint analysis and path pruning, to improve the efficiency of integer overflow detection. These techniques enable INDIO to significantly reduce the number of false positives it reports while keeps its false negative rate at a very low level.
- We applied INDIO to a set of widely used Windows binaries, in which INDIO detected two previously unknown integer overflow vulnerabilities.

2   System Overview

INDIO takes x86 binaries (executables and DLLs) as input, and performs a two-stage analysis to detect integer overflow in these binaries. At the end of analysis, INDIO outputs the detected integer overflow vulnerabilities, as well as example inputs to the binaries that expose these vulnerabilities. The detection in INDIO is semi-automatic, and the only human intervention needed is to decide the criteria on which suspicious vulnerabilities should pass to the second stage of analysis.

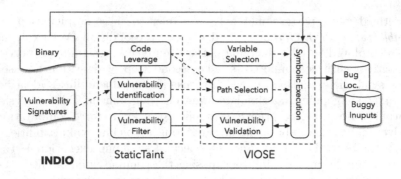

Fig. 1. Architecture of INDIO

The architecture of INDIO, as illustrated in Fig. 1, is consisted of two parts: StaticTaint (Static Identification of Integer Overflow and Taint Analysis), and VIOSE (Validation of Integer Overflow using Symbolic Execution). StaticTaint first performs a quick search in the input binary to identify potentially vulnerable paths by comparing them to known patterns of insecure integer operation and usage; VIOSE conducts symbolic execution along the vulnerable paths identified by StaticTaint and monitors their execution to validate whether they present genuine security threats. If a potential vulnerability is genuine, VIOSE produces example inputs to the binary that expose this vulnerability.

Next we use comct132.dll as a running example to explain how INDIO operates to detect integer overflow. StaticTaint first translates comct132.dll into the Intermediate Representation (IR) using its Code Leverage module (Sect. 3.1), and then searches the IR for code fragments that match vulnerability patterns defined in the Vulnerability Pattern Library (Sect. 3.2). These code fragments are identified as candidate vulnerabilities. For example, the arithmetic operation at 0x5d180c82 in the following code snippet is identified during the search, because the result of multiplication is passed to the memory allocation function _ReAlloc at 0x5d180c8a as a parameter without any overflow check. For each candidate vulnerability, StaticTaint records the address of its overflow points and how the potentially overflowed integer value is used.

```
.text:5d180c2c     ; int __stdcall DSA_InsertItem(HDSA hdsa,
.text:5d180c2c     ; int i, const void *pitem)
.text:5d180c2c     hdsa              = dword ptr  8
.text:5d180c2c     i                 = dword ptr  0Ch
.text:5d180c2c     Src               = dword ptr  10h
    . . .
.text:5d180c82     imul   eax, [esi+0Ch]      ;
.text:5d180c86     push   eax                 ; uBytes
.text:5d180c87     push   dword ptr [esi+4]   ; hMem
.text:5d180c8a     call   \_ReAlloc@8         ; ReAlloc(x,x)
```

The pattern matching process in StaticTaint obviously can cause many false positives, as the trade-off for fast vulnerability identification. To address this, its Vulnerability Filter utilizes two light-weight static analyses, namely priority ranking (Sect. 3.3) and WP calculation (Sect. 3.4) to eliminate as many false positives as possible:

1. The priority ranking algorithm calculates the possibility of a vulnerability being exploited, referenced to as priority, based on how overflowed integers are used by security-sensitive operations (also known as *sinks*). The higher priority a candidate vulnerability has, the more likely it presents a genuine vulnerability. For example, the vulnerability described above has a priority higher than most of other candidate vulnerabilities in comct132.dll, because it uses the overflowed integer to decide the size of memory to be allocated right after the overflowed integer is computed. One can specify a priority threshold to filter out all candidate vulnerabilities with priorities lower than the threshold.

2. The Vulnerability Filter further eliminates the candidate vulnerabilities that are apparently unexploitable. It accomplishes this by using WP calculation and value-range analysis to determine whether the program paths from the program entry point to the sinks corresponding to these vulnerabilities are feasible. Only vulnerabilities with feasible program paths are passed to VIOSE for further validation. For the vulnerability in the above example, the path segments from 0x5d180c2c to 0xbd180c82 and from 0x5d180c82 to 5d180c8a are confirmed as feasible by the WP calculation and value-range analysis, respectively. Thus, it is passed to VIOSE.

Unfortunately, the WP calculation is sometimes incapable of dealing with long or complex program paths: it either cannot terminate within the time limit or generates intricate preconditions that the SMT solver cannot handle. Thus, many false positives might still sneak through StaticTaint. To tackle this, VIOSE validates the candidate vulnerabilities passing through StaticTaint using symbolic execution, which is more accurate than the WP calculation in validating suspicious program paths [25]. VIOSE also employs two heuristics to improve the efficiency and scalability of symbolic execution:

1. It incorporates a taint analysis to reduce the number of symbolic variables to be introduced during symbolic execution. For example, the taint analysis reports that the first parameter of _ReAlloc in the above example has no impact on the sink at 0x5d180c8a, and hence introduces no symbolic variable for this parameter.

2. It also integrates a path pruning process that directs symbolic execution to only considers program paths connecting the program entry point to the overflow points and then to the corresponding sinks (see Sect. 4.2). In the above example, all branches that do not lead to 0x5d180c82 and then to 0x5d180c8a are eliminated from symbolic execution after path pruning.

With the assistance of these two heuristics, the symbolic execution engine in VIOSE validates if the sinks for each candidate vulnerability are reachable from the entry point of the binary. If so, the engine deems the vulnerability as genuine and output example inputs to the binary that trigger the vulnerability. For example, for the above example vulnerability, [hdsa + 8]=0x01000000, [hdsa + 0ch]=0x01005451, [hdsa + 10h]=0x00000010 are generated for the three parameters of DSA_InsertItem, in order to exploit the vulnerability at 0x5d180c8a.

The integration of StaticTaint and VIOSE enables them to compensate the limitations of each other, so as to achieve a balance between the accuracy and efficiency of vulnerability detection. On one hand, StaticTaint incorporates capabilities to filter out a significant portion of false positives, so that the time-consuming symbolic execution in VIOSE is applied to validate much fewer vulnerabilities. On the other hand, VIOSE validates and rules out false positives passing through StaticTaint with more rigorous analysis.

3   StaticTaint: Identify Vulnerabilities with Pattern Match

As illustrated in Fig. 1, StaticTaint is consisted of three modules: the **Code Leverage** module first translates the binary under analysis into an IR; the **Vulnerability Identification** module then traverses the IR to identify all potential integer overflow vulnerabilities based on pre-defined vulnerability patterns; the **Vulnerability Filter** lastly examines the identified vulnerabilities and eliminates false positives. Vulnerabilities passing the Vulnerability Filter are then forwarded to VIOSE for further validation.

3.1   Code Leverage

StaticTaint first reverse-engineers an input binary into an equivalent assembly program using IDA Pro[2], and then eliminates the side-effect of the assembly program by transforming it into an IR using the Code Leverage module.

The IR language used in StaticTaint is derived from that proposed in Vine [22], with augmented support for type information and SSA representation. It includes the following five types of grammatical terms:

- assignment Assign(var, exp), assigning the value of exp to variable var;
- jump statement Jmp(label), which shifts the program's execution to the statement labeled as label;
- conditional jump Cjmp(exp, label1, label2), which directs the program's execution to the statement labeled as label1 if exp is evaluated as true, or to statement labeled as label2 otherwise;
- labeled statement (label, st), where st is any SSA statement and label is a string label assigned to st; and
- function invocation statement Call(exp) that invokes the function whose initial address is the value of exp.

---

[2] Hex-Rays Inc., https://www.hex-rays.com/products/ida/index.shtml (May 2015).

Variables in our IR are divided into memory and register variables, where memory (heap or stack) variables are defined as a combination of functions associated with these variables and their offsets to the bottom of the stack/heap. Each variable in our IR has fields to record its storage size and sign. This is in contrast to Vine, which only records the storage size of variables. The extra sign field enables to collect and calculate the sign information of variables more accurately, which is important to the calculation of correct overflow conditions (see Sect. 3.3) and to the accuracy of subsequent vulnerability validation.

We integrate both control- and data-flow analyses to reconstruct the sign information from binary code. This starts with collecting useful information from the reverse-engineered assembly code to initialize the sign of variables. For example, variables used as array index, memory size and unsigned jumps (such as JA* and JB*) are unsigned, while those used in conditional jump instructions (i.e. JG* and JL*) are signed.

3.2   Vulnerability Identification

StaticTaint considers an arithmetic instruction as a (potential) overflow point, if it involves integer variables and matches with one or several patterns in the Vulnerability Pattern Library (VPL). A pattern in the VPL defines a dangerous way of using a possibly overflowed integer that creates security vulnerabilities. Currently, the VPL used by StaticTaint includes the following patterns:

- **Integer usage in security-sensitive operations.** Integer overflows become vulnerabilities only when they are used in security-sensitive operations, including:
  - **Memory allocation.** If an overflowed integer is used as the size parameter of memory allocation functions (e.g. `malloc` series), the actual size of the memory allocated can be smaller than intended. This may lead to buffer overflow vulnerabilities.
  - **Memory Indexing.** If an overflowed integer is used as the index of an array, a pointer or a structure, one can gain access to unintended memory area, leading to information leakage or memory manipulation.
  - **Conditional judgment.** If an overflowed integer is used in the conditions of conditional jump statements, the program control flow can be manipulated to circumvent necessary checks, e.g. permission checks and data integrity checks.
- **Lack of overflow checking.** Any integer arithmetic operation may cause integer overflow vulnerabilities if it is not followed by overflow checks.
- **Incomplete or wrong input checks.** If the the size and signedness of an integer variable are not properly checked before being used in integer operations (e.g. addition and multiplication), an overflow may occur.

The above patterns are derived from our studies on publicly announced integer overflow vulnerabilities (e.g. those in the CVE database) and from the academic literature (e.g., [10,25]). Of course, the VPL can be continuously updated to capture our evolving understanding of integer overflow vulnerabilities.

Technically, the process of identifying all potential overflow points in a binary based on pattern matching is implemented as an inter-procedural data flow analysis, which proceeds as follows:

1. Traverse the program for vulnerability identification. For every integer arithmetic instruction without a subsequent check on its result, the address of this instruction and the variable storing its result are logged as a possible overflow point in the overflow point list. For example, if the instruction `Assign(c, Add(a, b))` at address 0x401000 commits a potential overflow, an entry (c, 0x401000, 0) is added to the list of overflow points, in which "0" indicates that this instruction is where the integer overflow originates.
2. Broadcast the identification results across the entire program to collect variables whose values are affected by the potentially overflowed integer values. Assuming an instruction `Assign(d, Div(c, 2))` with address 0x401001 immediately following the overflow point, then an entry (d, 0x401001, 1) is created and added to the list of overflow points, where "1" indicates one propagation step away from the overflow point.
3. A second round of traversing is performed on the program to collect the information of how potentially overflowed integer variables are used. If the use of such a variable matches with one or more patterns in the VPL, it is deemed as a potential vulnerability, and an entry *(overflow point, usage information)* is added to the overflow point list. Consider the above example again. Suppose variable c is used in two places: a conditional jump instruction `Cjmp(c, label1, label2)` with address 0x4001005 and a memory allocation instruction with address 0x401008. Then an entry (0x401000, (0x401005, BranchCond), (0x401008, MemAlloc)) is added to the overflow point list, where `BranchCond` represents the use of c in a conditional jump and `MemAlloc` indicates its use in memory allocation.

3.3 Vulnerability Priority Ranking

The vulnerability priority ranking algorithm in the Vulnerability Filter module decides which vulnerabilities warrant further analysis, based on the observation that unintentional overflows are more likely to be exploited than intentional ones. When overflowed integer values are used in different types of sinks, different levels of risk might present to the system security. For example, it has been reported that more than a half of integer overflow vulnerabilities are caused because memory allocation operations use overflowed integer values to decide the size of memory to be allocated [31], while vulnerabilities due to overflowed values being used as the index to dereference memory structures are rare. Thus, memory allocation operations are more critical to system security than sinks like memory dereference operations.

We assign different weights to different types of sinks, according the following rules, to capture their impact to security:

– A high weight is assigned to memory allocation operations.
– A medium weight is assigned to conditional statements.

- A low weight is assigned to memory dereference operations.
- For an arithmetic operation that potentially causes integer overflow, if the program has a check over its result immediately after the operation, then a negative weight is assigned to the check. This is consistent with the experience that the threat of integer overflow can be reduced if appropriate checks are instrumented in the program.

It should be noted that, if further knowledge of integer overflow vulnerabilities and their causes becomes available, the weights assigned to different types of sinks could and should be adjusted accordingly.

Having weights representing different security risks assigned, the Vulnerability Filter is able to calculate the priorities of candidate integer overflow vulnerabilities. Formally, suppose a program has n types of sinks, and an integer overflow vulnerability has its overflowed integer value used in n_i sinks of type i, where $i = 1, 2, .., n$. its priority, p, is calculated following Eq. 1, where:

1. ω_i is the weight assigned to sinks of type i.
2. pc_{ij} is the number of propagation steps from the arithmetic operation that introduces the overflowed integer value (also known as *source*) to the jth use of this value in type i sinks. A propagation step is a transformation over the potentially overflowed integer value, such as applying an Add or Sub operation to the value. Moreover, $pc_{ip} \leq pc_{iq}$ for any $0 \leq p \leq q \leq n_i$.
3. q_i is a constant weakening factor that the analyst assigns to type i sinks. This factor specifies how the threat of using an overflowed integer in a type i sink decreases as the distance (i.e., the number of propagation steps) between this sink and source increases.

$$p - \sum_{i=1}^{n} \sum_{j=0}^{n_j-1} ((\omega_i \quad pc_{ij} \times q_i)/2^j) \tag{1}$$

Intuitively speaking, Eq. 1 formalizes two rules of evaluating potential integer overflow vulnerabilities: (1) the deeper a potentially overflowed value is propagated into the program, the less likely its use in sinks commits real vulnerabilities; and (2) it is more risky to use a potentially overflowed integer value in multiple types of sinks than to use it in multiple sinks of the same type. Hence, if more than one type i sinks use the potentially overflowed integer, these extra sinks only contribute partially to the likelihood of the vulnerability being real (see the 2^j divisor in Eq. 1).

Once the priorities of all identified vulnerabilities are calculated, one can specify a threshold, so that only vulnerabilities with priorities higher than the threshold are passed to VIOSE for further validation. This feature is particularly useful when the time and resource available for vulnerability validation is limited. The selection of such a threshold is based on the user's analysis needs: a higher threshold helps on to spend most resources on validating the most likely vulnerabilities, while a lower threshold helps to gain a better false negative rate.

We have applied the vulnerability priority raking algorithm to a number of Windows binaries, and investigated how the selection of the priority threshold

Table 1. Overflow condition for arithmetic operations

Overflow point	Sign of a and b	Overflow condition
Add(a,b)	Unsigned	$a + b < a$
	Signed	$(a > 0\&b > 0\&a+b < a)\|\|(a < 0\&b < 0\&a+b > a)$
Mul (a,b)	Unsigned	$a! = 0\&(a * b)/a! = b$
	Signed	$a! = 0\&(a * b)/a! = b$
Sub (a,b)	Unsigned	$a < a - b$
	Signed	$(a > 0\&b > 0\&a < a - b)\|(a < 0\&b < 0\&a - b < a)$

impact the false negatives that INIDO finally reported. Experimental results confirmed that with a simple "training" process (see Sect. 5.1) for the threshold selection, the algorithm eliminated 78 % false positives generated by pattern matching without omitting any known vulnerability (see Sect. 5.4).

We acknowledge that Eq. 1 is formalized based on our investigation of known integer overflow vulnerabilities. Even though our experiments demonstrate its effectiveness in distinguishing genuine vulnerabilities from false positives, there is still possibility that it does not accurately capture how integer overflow leads to security vulnerabilities in realistic binaries. Large-scale studies on realistic binaries can certainly help us confirm the rules underlying Eq. 1 and optimize the configuration of its parameters. For example, studies on realistic binaries can improve our understanding on how the distance from overflow points to sinks affects the likelihood of an integer overflow leading to a vulnerability. We leave this to future study.

3.4 Vulnerable Path Calculation

To eliminate the false positives reported by the priority ranking algorithm, we examines whether the WPs associated with the paths from the program's entry point to overflow points are satisfiable. Given an identified vulnerability (i.e., an overflow point and the sink(s) using the overflowed integer value), the tactic validates if it is genuine as follows:

1. The overflow condition c is calculated for the overflow point according to Table 1. This condition, if satisfied, ensures that an overflowed value be assigned to the corresponding variable;
2. All possible paths connecting the program entry point to the overflow point are translated into a Guarded Command Language format (denoted as G);
3. The WP $s = wp(G, c)$ is calculated by following the algorithm in [11] for each of the paths identified in the last step. Thus, if s is satisfied when the program starts, then c is also satisfied when the program executes along the corresponding program path.
4. The STP solver is invoked to solve whether or not s can be satisfied. If not, then the vulnerability is a false positive and hence filtered out.

In addition to the WP calculation, the Vulnerability Filter also implements a mechanism to validate the paths from overflow points to the corresponding sinks, also known as *forward vulnerable paths*. The validation of forward vulnerable paths is based on a simplified value-range analysis [21], in which the values of variables of interest are abstracted as a range over the integer domain. In particular, the values of all integer variables involved are initialized as the entire integer domain and continuously updated during forward execution of the forward vulnerable paths. When conditional jumps are encountered, checks are conducted to see if the current value ranges of related variables can satisfy the branch conditions, so that the execution can eventually lead to the target sinks. If not, the forward vulnerable paths are infeasible, suggesting that the corresponding vulnerabilities are false positives.

Both the WP calculation and value-range analysis are conservative and do not introduce false negatives, when applied to reduce false positives (see Sect. 5.4 for details).

4 VIOSE: Vulnerability Validation with Symbolic Execution

False positives survived from StaticTaint are further examined and eliminated by VIOSE with its Symbolic Execution Engine (SEE). As illustrated in Fig. 1, the SEE in VIOSE maintains a virtual machine as the abstract runtime environment for executing binaries, and its operation is guided by the Vulnerability Validation module. In particular, the Vulnerability Validation module instructs the SEE on which program paths to execute, and monitors the execution results of the SEE.

The complexity of symbolic execution, in terms of symbolic states explored and constraints generated, increases exponentially as the number of symbolic variables involved or the size of the program path increases [1]. Thus, we introduce two components in VIOSE, the Variable Selection and Path Selection modules, to improve the scalability and effectiveness of symbolic execution.

4.1 Symbolic Execution in VIOSE

The SEE in VIOSE is constructed on the top of S2E [9], a platform for exploring and analyzing the behavior of binary code. S2E has a variety of notable features, making it suitable to be used for our analysis: 1. S2E can automatically switch between concretely and symbolically executing the code of interest, within an emulated OS runtime environment (i.e., a virtual machine); 2. the virtual machine in S2E offers a real software stack (libraries, OS kernel, drivers, etc.), rather than abstract models, to emulate the targeted OS environment, which makes the analysis built upon it closer to the reality; and 3. S2E can execute binary code in both user and kernel modes, making it applicable to more binary programs.

The SEE in VIOSE extends S2E with two features to improve the efficiency of symbolic execution:

1. A plug-in is added to S2E, which guides S2E to only execute, symbolically or concretely, instructions commanded by the Vulnerability Validation module. In other words, only instructions relevant to integer overflow are executed.
2. A customization is made to the S2E symbolic execution engine, so that:
   (a) S2E can introduce symbolic parameters for variables and memory locations specified by the user. As a result, instructions involving these variables and memory locations are forced to be executed symbolically.
   (b) When an arithmetic instruction with integer variables is encountered, S2E automatically generates the constraint for the involved integer variables to overflow. However, such a constraint has already been generated by the Vulnerability Filter component of StaticTaint in previous analysis. Thus, the VIOSEs SEE simply retrieves this constraint instead of re-generating it.

Given an entry point and a sink, S2E explores all program paths connecting them. For each of such paths, S2E invokes the STP solver to check if the conjunction of the integer overflow constraint and the path constraints collected along the path is satisfiable. If STP reports back a solution (i.e. certain evaluation of input variables enabling the potential overflow), S2E stops analyzing the rest paths for this pair of (entry point, sink), and reports it as a genuine vulnerability to the Vulnerability Validation module. If the conjunction is found to be unsatisfiable or cannot be solved within a pre-defined time limit, S2E continues to analyze the rest program paths for this pair of (entry point, sink). Only when no solution can be found for the constraint conjunctions of all program paths connecting the entry point and the sink, S2E reports the vulnerability as a false positive.

It is worth noting that the S2E platform performs selective symbolic execution directly on the binary code. Thus, we extend StaticTaint with the feature of mapping all its vulnerability identification results (on the IR level) back to the original binary level, so that these results can be re-used to guide the symbolic execution in S2E. Experiments showed that S2E enables INDIO to achieve 76 % reduction of false positives (see Sect. 5.4).

4.2   Path Pruning and Taint Analysis

As compared to the WP calculation, symbolic execution is more accurate in validating the feasibility of program paths [25], and hence can detect false positives that survive from previous analyses. However, symbolic execution is more computationally expensive than the WP calculation [18], making it a formidable task to validate all suspicious vulnerabilities with symbolic execution. Considering this, VIOSE incorporates the Path Selection module to reduce the number of program paths that symbolic execution needs to explore; and the Variable Selection module to help reduce the number of symbolic variables to be introduced. As a result, symbolic execution in VIOSE can scale up to analyze more complex and larger binaries.

The Path Selection module implements a heuristic algorithm that we previously proposed [5] to identify program instructions and paths irrelevant to integer overflow analysis and remove them from subsequent analysis. The algorithm is essentially a customized control-flow analysis of the program of interest: if in the control flow graph an instruction is not on either a path from the program entry point to an overflow point or on any forward vulnerable paths from the overflow point to its sink(s), the instruction is deemed as irrelevant and thus pruned off. In other words, when symbolic execution is facing more than one branch to proceed, the Path Selection component instructs symbolic execution to take the branch leading to the target sinks. Eliminating irrelevant instructions and paths from symbolic execution can focus the analysis only on the portion of code that matters to integer overflow and consequently improve the analysis efficiency.

The Variable Selection module, on the other hand, reduces the number of symbolic variables introduced during symbolic execution. It is an instance of classic taint analysis, except that it only tracks the tainted program inputs that are used as the operands of overflow points or can influence such operands. For these variables tainted by inputs, the Variable Selection module informs the SEE to introduce symbolic variables. For input variables decided as irrelevant to integer overflow, the Variable Selection module assigns them with random concrete values, since their values have no impact to the corresponding vulnerabilities.

Note that typical taint analysis does not consider the information flow caused by control dependency [18]. Thus, it is possible that variables affecting the control flow (e.g., those used in the conditions of if statements) might be identified as "untainted", and the Variable Selection module will not introduce symbolic variables for them. This might result in some branches of if statements being missed by symbolic execution, and thus affect the result of vulnerability validation. We leave it as future work to enhance our taint analysis to take into account control dependency.

5 Evaluation

We have evaluated the effectiveness and efficiency of INDIO against a number of widely-tested Windows applications and libraries. They are listed in Table 2, among which comctl132.dll and gdi32.dll are both GUI-based libraries and libpng.dll was deemed as "completely free of undefined integer overflows" [10]. We conducted all experiments on a Lenovo desktop with a 2.6 GHz Intel i7 CPU and 4G memory, and the threshold of the priority ranking algorithm was set as 30 (see Sect. 5.1 for explanation). Similar to other static analysis tools, all vulnerabilities reported by INDIO were manually inspected to decide if they were false positives or represented real security issues.

5.1 Effectiveness: Detection of Known Vulnerabilities

In the first set of experiments we applied INDIO to 6 different programs, each of which has a known integer overflow vulnerability. INDIO successfully reported

Table 2. Statistics of detecting known integer overflow vulnerabilities.

Program name	Program version	Advisory ID	Vuln. Identif.	Priority ranking	WP Calc.	Symbolic execution	Rank
comctl32	5.82.2900.2180	eEye reported	401	63	16	2	1
gdi32	5.1.2600.2180	CVE-2007-3034	1029	93	10	1	10
libpng	1.5.13	CVE-2011-3026	525	73	14	2	4
png2swf	0.9.1	CVE-2010-1516	2331	201	8	2	5
jpeg2swf	0.9.1	CVE-2010-1516	2459	176	8	2	5
libwav_plugin	0.8.6h	CVE-2008-2430	22	2	1	1	1

all vulnerabilities contained in these programs. Table 2 summarizes the results, in which column 3 shows the advisory reports for the known vulnerabilities; columns 4-7 show the numbers of suspicious vulnerabilities after each of INDIO's analysis and optimization modules was applied; and column 8 shows the priorities computed for the vulnerabilities. It is obvious from Table 2 that our priority ranking algorithm drastically filters out false positives generated, while keeping false negatives at a negligible level in the experiments.

In fact, we used the first set of experiments as the "training set" to approach a reasonable priority threshold for vulnerability ranking. We first applied INDIO to the training set with threshold = 0 and checked if any known vulnerability listed in Table 2 was missed. The process was repeated by increasing the threshold by 5 each time. The results, illustrated in Fig. 2, showed that the false negatives occurred when the threshold was 35. Thus we set the threshold as 30 in the subsequent experiments.

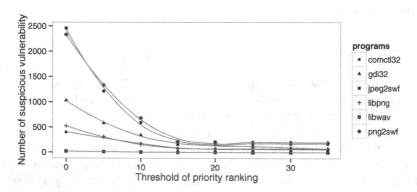

Fig. 2. The number of suspicious vulnerabilities reported by the ranking algorithm fell down as the threshold is rising. When threshold = 35, false negatives occurred.

5.2 False Positive Reduction

The focus of the second set of experiments was to evaluate the effectiveness of INDIO in reducing false positives. In these experiments, we compared the numbers of false positives reported by both INDIO and IntScope [25] for the same set of 9 binaries. The reason why IntScope was chosen for comparison is twofold: (1) IntScope is a renowned static analysis tool for Windows binaries; and (2) to the best of our knowledge, IntScope achieves the lowest false positive rate among existing static integer overflow detection tools, including [8, 25–27].

The comparison results between INDIO and IntScope are summarized in Fig. 3, which demonstrated that INDIO not only reported all the vulnerabilities recorded in [25] but also found a previous unknown vulnerability in comctl32.dll. In terms of false positives, INDIO reported fewer false positives than IntScope for 3 out of the 9 binaries. For the rest 6 binaries, INDIO reported the same number of false positives as IntScope.

The reason why INDIO out-performed IntScope, from the false positive rate perspective, lies in the fact that IntScope only outputs suspicious paths that might contain integer overflow for a single function in the binary, while ignores potential vulnerabilities caused by other functions in the same binary. These suspicious paths need to be further filtered by other auxiliary testing tools to check their validity. INDIO, on the contrary, reports overflow points for each vulnerability in the entire binary, instead of targeting at a certain function in it.

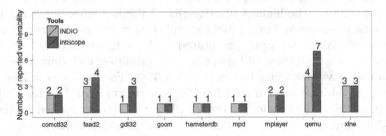

Fig. 3. Numbers of (potential) vulnerabilities reported by INDIO and IntScope. Note that [25] only recorded the number of false positives reported in the functions that contained genuine vulnerabilities, while INDIO reported all false positives reported for the 9 binaries.

5.3 New Bug Detection

In the experiments, INDIO succeeded in finding two vulnerabilities in comctl32.dll and libpng.dll that have not been reported by any tools before. The vendors of these two binaries both confirmed these two vulnerabilities, and released corresponding security patches to fix them[3]. In addition, INDIO also found a vulnerability that has been fixed by the vendor but never been published.

---

[3] Ref. CVE-2013-3195 and CVE-2013-7353.

Analysis of comctl32.dll. comctl32.dll is a Windows system library, providing a set of window control functionalities used by Windows GUI applications. The following code shows the vulnerability we found in its function `DSA_InsertItem`, where it uses the product of `nItemSize` and `nNewItems` as the size of memory to be allocated, without any prior overflow check. Both `nItemSize` and `nNewItems` are 32-bit signed integers, whereas the data type of the second parameter of `ReAlloc` 32-bit unsigned integer. This could cause the product to wrap around to a relatively smaller integer than expected. Malicious attackers can hence exploit this vulnerability by carefully crafting the `nGrow` and `nMaxCount` fields of parameter `hdsa`. For brevity, we refer to this vulnerability as Vulnerability #1. Notably, the security community has not been able to detect Vulnerability #1 for more than a decade.

```
INT DSA_InsertItem (HDSA hdsa, INT nIndex, LPVOID pSrc) {
    INT    nNewItems, nSize;
    ...
    if (nIndex >= hdsa->nItemCount)  nIndex = hdsa->
        nItemCount;
    ...
    nNewItems = hdsa->nMaxCount + hdsa->nGrow;
    nSize = hdsa->nItemSize * nNewItems;
    lpTemp = ReAlloc (hdsa->pData, nSize);
    ...}
```

StaticTaint reported 16 suspicious vulnerabilities, among which Vulnerability #1 was assigned the highest priority (51). VIOSE further determined 14 of them as false positives and generated example inputs for the rest two suspicious vulnerabilities. With the inputs generated by VIOSE, we were able to manually confirm the genuineness of these two vulnerabilities, including Venerability #1 and another vulnerability in function `DPA_GROW`. For the latter vulnerability, Microsoft has released version 5.82.2900.6028 of `comctl32.dll` to fix it without making it aware to the public. In contrast, Wang et al. also applied IntScope to comctl32.dll, but was not able to detect Vulnerability #1. Additionally, we are not aware any dynamic tools having been used to detect vulnerabilities in this GUI library.

Analysis of libpng.dll. The vulnerability we are the first to detect in `libpng.dll-1.5.13` is a typical heap buffer overflow vulnerability caused by integer overflow. To be more specific, its function `png_set_unknown_chunks`(in libpng/pngset.c) used two of its parameters, `info_ptr` and `num_unknowns`, to calculate the size of a memory chunk `np` without any checks, as illustrated in the following code segment. These two unsigned parameters in the multiplication can be very close to the upper limit of unsigned integers. Thus, the size of memory allocated to `np` might be smaller than expected when wraparound occurs during the size calculation. This might result in a segmentation fault when information is copied to `np`. For convenience, we refer to this vulnerability as Vulnerability #2.

```
void PNGAPI png_set_unknown_chunks (png_structp png_ptr,
   png_infop info_ptr, png_unknown_chunkp unknowns, int
      num_unknowns) {
   ...
   np = (png_unknown_chunkp)png_malloc_warn(png_ptr,
      (png_size_t)(info_ptr->unknown_chunks_num +
         num_unknowns)*
      png_sizeof(png_unknown_chunk));
   ...
   png_memcpy(np, info_ptr->unknown_chunks,
      (png_size_t)info_ptr->unknown_chunks_num
      png_sizeof(png_unknown_chunk));
   ...}
```

For this binary StaticTaint first identified 14 suspicious vulnerabilities, out of which Vulnerability #2 was assigned with a priority of 45, lower than 10 other vulnerabilities. VIOSE validated 2 vulnerabilities as genuine, namely Vulnerability #2 and vulnerability CVE-2011-3026 listed in Table 2. As evidence of the genuineness of Vulnerability #2, VIOSE produced an example input, which assigned the fourth argument of png_set_unknown_chunks as 0xffffffff. After manual analysis, we confirmed that this input did trigger Vulnerability #2.

Libpng.dll has been widely analyzed by different approaches [10,14,29], but none of them found Vulnerability #2. For example, IOC, a dynamic integer overflow detection tool using source code instrumentation, asserted that libpng is completely free of undefined integer overflows, after analyzing it against an existing test suite [10]. The reason why IOC failed to detect Vulnerability #2 might lie in that the test suite used to execute the binary did not trigger the size of memory allocated to np to overflow. However, Vulnerability #2 presents a genuine security threat. In fact, according to IOCs integer overflow categorization, Vulnerability #2 falls into the harmful category of "unintentional implementation errors".

5.4 Effectiveness of Optimization

We also evaluated the effectiveness of each optimization technique in INDIO during detecting known vulnerabilities in Sect. 5.1. To do this, we turned on one more optimization technique at one time and recorded the numbers of false positives reported. The experimental results are summarized in Table 2.

Suppose that x and z suspicious vulnerabilities were reported before and after optimization #n was applied to a binary respectively, and y was the number of genuine vulnerabilities in the binary. We calculated the reduction ratio of false positives by optimization #n as $1 - (z - y)/(x - y)$. As demonstrated in Table 2, the priority ranking algorithm eliminated in average 78 % of the suspicious vulnerabilities; the WP calculation eliminated about 85 % of the remaining suspicious vulnerabilities; and lastly the symbolic execution engine was able to filter out about 76 % of the vulnerabilities.

5.5 Efficiency

INDIO spent about 1 hour analyzing an average-size binary, the majority of which was taken by the Vulnerability Filtering module (about 50 % of the cost) and the Vulnerability Validation module (about 35 %). In comparison, IntScope spends about 10 min to analyze an average-size executable [25]. However, their time cost did not take into account the time and effort needed for validating suspicious vulnerabilities, which typically accounts for a significant portion of time cost in vulnerability detection (e.g., 35 % time cost in our experiments).

Nevertheless, we have to admit that INDIO spends more time than IntScope in detecting vulnerabilities. Part of the reason lies in that IntScope only performs taint analysis and symbolic execution during IR traversing. INDIO, on the other hand, not only performs priority ranking and the WP calculation to filter false positives, but also conducts path pruning and taint analysis to improve the effectiveness of VIOSE. This results in about 31 min being spent in these analyses during the IR traversing stage. Considering the benefits of much fewer false positives being reported and more accurate analysis results, we deem the relatively higher time cost by INDIO as an acceptable tradeoff.

It is worth noting that a large part of INDIO's time cost is incurred by solving path constraints generated during the WP calculation and symbolic execution. Our statistics showed that constraint solving took up to 40 % of INDIO's running time. This suggests that the time performance of INDIO could be improved if optimization tactics (e.g., [3,4]) are applied to the constraint solver. We leave this to future work.

5.6 Discussion

Our experiments on a set of binaries that have been widely analyzed by a variety of tools provide encouraging evidence on INDIOs capability of detecting known and unknown integer overflow vulnerabilities. Moreover, as compared to IntScope which is renown for its low false positive rate, INDIO performed more effectively in reducing false positives in our experiments. According to our experience, a static analysis tool with the lower false positive rate is more "user-friendly" to programmers, and hence is easier to be integrated into the software development process.

It is worth noting that the SMT solver employed in INDIO might fail to solve the WP constraints with the constraint's complexity beyond the solver's analytical capability. There are two options to handle such situations: (1) report all paths containing unsolvable WP conditions as vulnerable paths, in order to avoid false negatives; or (2) do not report these paths, in order to reduce the number of false positives. In the current implementation of INDIO, we took the second option, which may lead to false negatives. However, our experiments as described in Sects. 5.1 and 5.2 demonstrate that this choice (with a reasonable timeout for WP calculation) does not result in noticeable increase of false negatives in realistic analysis.

The validity of our experiments are threaten by two factors:

1. The experiment subjects selected might not well represent real (Windows) binaries suffering from integer overflow. In the experiments, we selected a set of Windows binaries that are widely used in common media or image applications. Most of them have been thoroughly studied by an array of integer overflow analysis tools. Thus, they offer us a good basis to compare our tool with existing analysis techniques. In future study, we plan to evaluate INDIO against more comprehensive test benches covering typical integer operation and usage in (Windows) binaries.
2. It is possible that the binaries we studied contain vulnerabilities that have not been uncovered by any tools, which might affect our evaluation of INDIOs false negative rates. In fact, INDIO succeeded in finding two new vulnerabilities from the considered binaries, despite the fact that they have been well checked by a host of tools before [4,10,12 16,20,24,25,29,31]. Nevertheless, an inaccurate estimation of INDIO's false negative rate does not compromise the conclusion we have drawn from the experiments, which is that INDIO is more effective in detecting integer overflow from binaries with a much lower false positive rate.

6   Related Work

Static Binary Analysis. A number of tools have been proposed to use static analysis techniques to detect integer overflow in binaries. For example, Loong Checker [8] retrieves the summary of functions in binaries using value-set analysis and data dependency analysis. Based on the retrieved summaries, Loong Checker applies taint analysis to investigate the use of potentially overflowed integer values in sinks. IntFinder [6] recovers type information from binaries, and then uses it to detect suspicious instructions that might cause integer overflow. Taint analysis is also used in IntFinder to reduce the size of suspicious instructions. Both LoongChecker and IntFinder suffer from the problem of high false positive rates, and have to be used together with dynamic analysis to rule out false positives.

The previous work closest to ours is IntScope [25], which integrates path-sensitive data-flow analysis and taint analysis to identify vulnerable points of integer overflow. Similar to our approach, IntScope also spends expensive symbolic execution-based analysis only on paths on which tainted values are used in sinks.

Unlike these static approaches, INDIO significantly reduces the cost of static analysis using a vulnerability ranking mechanism. Thus, only a small portion of vulnerabilities likely to be genuine are examined with expensive static analysis. INDIO further improves the efficiency and scalability of static analysis using its built-in heuristics, including taint analysis and path pruning. Moreover, the use of S2E gives INDIO better accuracy in symbolic execution than IntScope, which uses abstract memory models to simulate the runtime environment for binaries.

Dynamic Analysis & Symbolic Execution. Fuzz testing (e.g., [12,13]) has been traditionally used to challenge the reliability of systems with excessive malformed test inputs. Recently, fuzz test has evolved to conduct symbolic analysis [12,19,20] or taint analysis [16] on a concrete(seed) input to guide the generation of sensible test inputs that explore program paths of interest (e.g., tainted paths). These evolved fuzz testing techniques have the potential of detecting vulnerabilities in binaries [12,16,24], because the test inputs they generate might explore vulnerable program paths and trigger vulnerabilities.

However, in contrast to static analysis based approaches, fuzz testing and its variants cannot guarantee to generate test inputs that cover all possible paths in binaries or paths that matter. As a result, vulnerabilities might be omitted by these approaches. In addition, the effectiveness of dynamic analysis is limited by the quality of test inputs crafted, which depends on the level of knowledge about the binaries (in particular, the input protocols of the binaries) acquired. Without such knowledge, dynamic analysis becomes less effective in exploring program defects and vulnerabilities. For example, DIODE [20] employs a specific input format parser to reconstruct test input files. It is unknown whether DIODE or tools alike can be applied to GUI-based executables such as comctl32.dll, which are fed by non-file-based inputs.

Dynamic instrumentation tools like DynamoRIO [2] are often used to monitor dynamic execution of binaries. If the binaries are appropriately instrumented, these tools can catch the occurrence of integer overflow. However, they can only be applied to binaries running in user mode, and depend on other techniques to craft inputs that might trigger integer overflow.

Source Code Analysis. Numerous approaches have been proposed to detect integer overflow at the source code level. These approaches either use static analysis to detect integer overflow [26,27], or instrument the source code and check integer overflow at runtime [10,17,31]. IntPatch [31] uses type analysis to locate possible overflow sites and applies backward slicing to find the operations that affect the overflow sites. [27] aims to find multiple vulnerabilities including integer overflow in source code by exploring the code property graph, a novel format of source code representation. However, as stated in [10], one reason why it is challenging to detect integer issues in source code is that different compilers interpret undefined integer operations in different ways, making the pre-compiling analysis approaches unable to detect integer bugs introduced by compilers. To address this issue, the IOC tool [10] instruments the source code with overflow check during compiling and reports overflow sites at runtime. IntFlow [17] follows the same idea of IOC while integrates information flow tracking to reduce the high positive rates troubling IOC.

7   Conclusion

It has been a challenge for static analysis techniques to analyze software programs with acceptable scalability and false positive rates. To address these challenges, we have presented a tool called INDIO that relies on static analysis to detect integer overflow vulnerabilities in Windows binaries, while significantly reduces the analysis cost and the number of false positives being reported. INDIO applies pattern matching to quickly identify potential integer overflow vulnerabilities and establishes a collection of optimization techniques to filter out a significant portion of false positives. INDIO is also capable of generating program inputs that could trigger the genuine vulnerabilities, a feature particularly helpful for the user to understand and fix integer overflow vulnerabilities. Our experiments have confirmed the effectiveness of INDIO in detecting integer overflow vulnerabilities with low false positive rates. The experiments also show that the heuristics employed by INDIO to filter out false positives would not cause false negatives in practices.

As of future work, we plan to conduct more comprehensive experiments to evaluate and optimize the vulnerability priority ranking mechanism, making it to reflect the latest trend of integer overflow vulnerabilities in reality. A guideline can also be established from such experiments to assist the user in adjusting the mechanism (e.g. sink weights, threshold) for their own analysis needs. To mitigate the false negatives caused by the Variable Selection module, we plan to enhance our taint analysis with techniques such as control-flow propagation [23] to trace the dependency among variables more accurately.

Acknowledgments. We are grateful to Yi Zhang, and the anonymous reviewers for their insightful comments and suggestions. This research was supported in part by National Natural Science Foundations of China (Grant No. 61471344).

References

1. Anand, S., Godefroid, P., Tillmann, N.: Demand-driven compositional symbolic execution. In: Ramakrishnan, C.R., Rehof, J. (eds.) TACAS 2008. LNCS, vol. 4963, pp. 367–381. Springer, Heidelberg (2008)
2. Bala, V., Duesterwald, E., Banerjia, S.: Dynamo: a transparent dynamic optimization system. SIGPLAN Not. **35**(5), 1–12 (2000)
3. Cadar, C., Dunbar, D., Engler, D.: KLEE: unassisted and automatic generation of high-coverage tests for complex systems programs. In: Proceedings of the 8th USENIX Conference on Operating Systems Design and Implementation, OSDI 2008, pp. 209–224. USENIX Association, Berkeley (2008)
4. Cha, S.K., Avgerinos, T., Rebert, A., Brumley, D.: Unleashing mayhem on binary code. In: Proceedings of the 2012 IEEE Symposium on Security and Privacy, SP 2012, pp. 380–394. IEEE Computer Society, Washington, DC (2012)
5. Chen, D., Zhang, Y., Cheng, L., Deng, Y., Sun, X.: Heuristic path pruning algorithm based on error handling pattern recognition in detecting vulnerability. In: 2013 IEEE 37th Annual Computer Software and Applications Conference Workshops (COMPSACW), pp. 95–100, July 2013
6. Chen, P., Han, H., Wang, Y., Shen, X., Yin, X., Mao, B., Xie, L.: IntFinder: automatically detecting integer bugs in x86 binary program. In: Qing, S., Mitchell, C.J., Wang, G. (eds.) ICICS 2009. LNCS, vol. 5927, pp. 336–345. Springer, Heidelberg (2009)
7. Chen, P., Wang, Y., Xin, Z., Mao, B., Xie, L.: Brick: a binary tool for run-time detecting and locating integer-based vulnerability. In: International Conference on Availability, Reliability and Security, ARES 2009, pp. 208–215 (2009)

8. Cheng, S., Yang, J., Wang, J., Wang, J., Jiang, F.: Loongchecker: practical summary-based semi-simulation to detect vulnerability in binary code. In: 2011 IEEE 10th International Conference on Trust, Security and Privacy in Computing and Communications (TrustCom), pp. 150–159, November 2011

9. Chipounov, V., Kuznetsov, V., Candea, G.: S2e: a platform for in-vivo multi-path analysis of software systems. In: Proceedings of the Sixteenth International Conference on Architectural Support for Programming Languages and Operating Systems, ASPLOS XVI, pp. 265–278. ACM, New York (2011)

10. Dietz, W., Li, P., Regehr, J., Adve, V.: Understanding integer overflow in C/C++. In: Proceedings of the 34th International Conference on Software Engineering, ICSE 2012, pp. 760–770. IEEE Press, Zurich (2012)

11. Dijkstra, E.: Go to statement considered harmful. In: Classics in Software Engineering (incoll), pp. 27–33. Yourdon Press, Upper Saddle River (1979)

12. Godefroid, P., Levin, M.Y., Molnar, D.: SAGE: whitebox fuzzing for security testing. Commun. ACM **55**(3), 40 (2012)

13. Haller, I., Slowinska, A., Neugschwandtner, M., Bos, H.: Dowsing for overflows: a guided fuzzer to find buffer boundary violations. In: Proceedings of the 22nd USENIX Conference on Security, SEC 2013, pp. 49–64 (2013)

14. Hasabnis, N., Misra, A., Sekar, R.: Light-weight bounds checking. In: Proceedings of the Tenth International Symposium on Code Generation and Optimization, CGO 2012, pp. 135–144. ACM, New York (2012)

15. Long, F., Sidiroglou-Douskos, S., Kim, D., Rinard, M.: Sound input filter generation for integer overflow errors. In: Proceedings of the 41st ACM SIGPLAN-SIGACT Symposium on Principles of Programming Languages, POPL 2014, pp. 439–452. ACM, New York (2014)

16. Molnar, D., Li, X.C., Wagner, D.: Dynamic test generation to find integer bugs in x86 binary linux programs. In: Proceedings of the 18th Conference on USENIX Security Symposium, pp. 67–82. USENIX Association, Berkeley (2009)

17. Pomonis, M., Petsios, T., Jee, K., Polychronakis, M., Keromytis, A.D.: IntFlow: improving the accuracy of arithmetic error detection using information flow tracking. In: Proceedings of the 30th Annual Computer Security Applications Conference, ACSAC 2014, pp. 416–425. ACM, New Orleans (2014)

18. Schwartz, E.J., Avgerinos, T., Brumley, D.: All you ever wanted to know about dynamic taint analysis and forward symbolic execution (but might have been afraid to ask). In: Proceedings of the 2010 IEEE Symposium on Security and Privacy, SP 2010, pp. 317–331 (2010)

19. Sen, K., Marinov, D., Agha, G.: Cute: A concolic unit testing engine for c. SIGSOFT Softw. Eng. Notes **30**(5), 263–272 (2005)

20. Sidiroglou-Douskos, S., Lahtinen, E., Rittenhouse, N., Piselli, P., Long, F., Kim, D., Rinard, M.: Targeted automatic integer overflow discovery using goal-directed conditional branch enforcement. In: Proceedings of the Twentieth International Conference on Architectural Support for Programming Languages and Operating Systems, ASPLOS 2015, pp. 473–486. ACM, New York (2015)

21. Simon, A.: Value-Range Analysis of C Programs: Towards Proving the Absence of Buffer Overflow Vulnerabilities. Springer, Heidelberg (2010)

22. Song, D., Brumley, D., Yin, H., Caballero, J., Jager, I., Kang, M.G., Liang, Z., Newsome, J., Poosankam, P., Saxena, P.: BitBlaze: a new approach to computer security via binary analysis. In: Sekar, R., Pujari, A.K. (eds.) ICISS 2008. LNCS, vol. 5352, pp. 1–25. Springer, Heidelberg (2008)

23. Stephen, M., Dawnsong, M.P.: DTA++: dynamic taint analysiswith targetedcontrol-flow propagation. In: Proceedings of the 18th Annual Network and Distributed System Security Symposium (NDSS), pp. 269–282, February 2011
24. Wang, T., Wei, T., Gu, G., Zou, W.: TaintScope: a checksum-aware directed fuzzing tool for automatic software vulnerability detection. In: 2010 IEEE Symposium on Security and Privacy (SP), pp. 497–512, May 2010
25. Wang, T., Wei, T., Lin, Z., Zou, W.: IntScope: automatically detecting integer overflow vulnerability in x86 binary using symbolic execution. In: Proceedings of the Network and Distributed System Security Symposium (2009)
26. Wang, X., Chen, H., Jia, Z., Zeldovich, N., Kaashoek, M.F.: Improving integer security for systems with KINT. In: Proceedings of the 10th USENIX Conference on Operating Systems Design and Implementation, pp. 163–177 (2012)
27. Yamaguchi, F., Golde, N., Arp, D., Rieck, K.: Modeling and discovering vulnerabilities with code property graphs. In: Proceedings of the 2014 IEEE Symposium on Security and Privacy, SP 2014, pp. 590–604 (2014)
28. Yamaguchi, F., Lindner, F., Rieck, K.: Vulnerability extrapolation: assisted discovery of vulnerabilities using machine learning. In: Proceedings of the 5th USENIX Conference on Offensive Technologies, WOOT 2011, p. 13 (2011)
29. Yamaguchi, F., Wressnegger, C., Gascon, H., Rieck, K.: Chucky: exposing missing checks in source code for vulnerability discovery. In: Proceedings of the 2013 ACM SIGSAC Conference on Computer & Communications Security, pp. 499–510 (2013)
30. Yang, Z., Yang, M., Zhang, Y., Gu, G., Ning, P., Wang, X.S.: AppIntent: analyzing sensitive data transmission in android for privacy leakage detection. In: Proceedings of the 2013 ACM SIGSAC Conference on Computer & Communications Security, CCS 2013, pp. 1043–1054. ACM, New York (2013)
31. Zhang, C., Wang, T., Wei, T., Chen, Y., Zou, W.: IntPatch: automatically fix integer-overflow-to-buffer-overflow vulnerability at compile-time. In: Gritzalis, D., Preneel, B., Theoharidou, M. (eds.) ESORICS 2010. LNCS, vol. 6345, pp. 71–86. Springer, Heidelberg (2010)

A Formal Framework for Program Anomaly Detection

Xiaokui Shu[✉], Danfeng (Daphne) Yao, and Barbara G. Ryder

Department of Computer Science, Virginia Tech, Blacksburg, VA 24060, USA
{subx,danfeng,ryder}@cs.vt.edu

Abstract. Program anomaly detection analyzes normal program behaviors and discovers aberrant executions caused by attacks, misconfigurations, program bugs, and unusual usage patterns. The merit of program anomaly detection is its independence from attack signatures, which enables proactive defense against new and unknown attacks. In this paper, we formalize the general program anomaly detection problem and point out two of its key properties. We present a unified framework to present any program anomaly detection method in terms of its detection capability. We prove the theoretical accuracy limit for program anomaly detection with an abstract detection machine. We show how existing solutions are positioned in our framework and illustrate the gap between state-of-the-art methods and the theoretical accuracy limit. We also point out some potential modeling features for future program anomaly detection evolution.

Keywords: Program anomaly detection · Unified framework · Automata theory · Detection accuracy · Theoretical accuracy limit

1 Introduction

Security problems in program executions – caused by program bugs, inappropriate program logic, or insecure system designs – were first recognized by the Air Force, the Advanced Research Projects Agency (ARPA), and IBM in early 1970s. In 1972, Anderson pointed out the threat of subverting or exploiting a piece of software by a malicious user [2]. This threat was developed to a multitude of real-world attacks in the late 1980s and 1990s including buffer overflow, return-into-libc, denial of service (DoS), etc.

Defenses have been proposed against categories of attacks from the perspectives of hardware (e.g., NX bit), operating system (e.g., address space layout randomization), compiler (e.g., canaries) and software architecture (e.g., sandbox) [56]. Although these defenses create barriers to exploiting a program, they can be circumvented. For example, new program attacks are developed leveraging unattended/uninspected execution elements, such as return-oriented programming [51], jump-oriented programming [5,10], and non-control data attacks [11].

Denning proposed an intrusion detection expert system (IDES) in 1987 [15], which learns how a system should behave (normal profiles) instead of how it

© Springer International Publishing Switzerland 2015
H. Bos et al. (Eds.): RAID 2015, LNCS 9404, pp. 270–292, 2015.
DOI: 10.1007/978-3-319-26362-5_13

should not (e.g., an attack). In this paper, we formalize one area of intrusion detection, namely *program anomaly detection* or *host-based intrusion detection* [52]. The area focuses on intrusion detection in the context of program executions. It was pioneered by Forrest et al., whose work was inspired by the analogy between intrusion detection for programs and the immune mechanism in biology [22].

Two major program anomaly detection approaches have been established and advanced: *n-gram-based dynamic normal program behavior modeling* and *automaton-based normal program behavior analysis*. The former was pioneered by Forrest [23], and the latter was formally introduced by Sekar et al. [50] and Wagner and Dean [59]. Other notable approaches include probabilistic modeling methods pioneered by Lee and Stolfo [40] and dynamically built state machine first proposed by Kosoresow and Hofmeyr [36]. Later work explored more fine-grained models [4,28,30] and combined static and dynamic analysis [24].

Evaluating the detection capability of program anomaly detection methods is always challenging [59]. Individual attacks do not cover all anomalous cases that a program anomaly detection system detects. Control-flow based metrics, such as average branching factor, are developed for evaluating specific groups of program anomaly detection methods [59]. However, none of the existing metrics is general for evaluating an arbitrary program anomaly detection system.

Several surveys summarized program anomaly detection methods from different perspectives and pointed out relations among several methods. Forrest et al. summarized existing methods from the perspective of system call monitoring [21]. Feng et al. formalized automaton based methods in [19]. Chandola et al. described program anomaly detection as a sequence analysis problem [8]. Chandola et al. provided a survey of machine learning approaches in [9]. The connection between an n-gram method and its automaton representation is first stated by Wagner [60]. Sharif et al. proved that any system call sequence based method can be simulated by a control-flow based method [52].

However, several critical questions about program anomaly detection have not been answered by existing studies and summaries.

1. How to formalize the detection capability of any detection method?
2. What is the theoretical accuracy limit of program anomaly detection?
3. How far are existing methods from the limit?
4. How can existing methods be improved towards the limit?

We answer all these questions in this paper. We unify *any existing or future* program anomaly detection method through its detection capability in a formal framework. We prove the theoretical accuracy limit of program anomaly detection methods and illustrate it in our framework. Instead of presenting every proposed method in the literature, we select and explain existing milestone detection methods that indicate the evolution of program anomaly detection. Our analysis helps understand the most critical steps in the evolution and points out the unsolved challenges and research problems.

The contributions of this paper are summarized as follows.

1. We formalize the general security model for program anomaly detection. We prove that the detection capability of a method is determined by the expressiveness of its corresponding language (Sect. 2).
2. We point out two independent properties of program anomaly detection: *precision* and *the scope of the norm*. We explain the relation between precision and deterministic/probabilistic detection methods (Sect. 2).
3. We present the theoretical accuracy limit of program anomaly detection with an abstract machine $\tilde{M}$. We prove that $\tilde{M}$ can characterize traces as precise as the executing program (Sect. 3).
4. We develop a hierarchal framework unifying any program anomaly detection method according to its detection capability. We mark the positions of existing methods in our framework and point out the gap between the state-of-the-art methods and the theoretical accuracy limit (Sect. 5).
5. We explain the evolution of program anomaly detection solutions. We envision future program anomaly detection systems with features such as full path sensitivity and higher-order relation description (Sect. 6).
6. We compare program anomaly detection with control-flow enforcement. We point our their similarities in techniques/results and explain their different perspectives approaching program/process security (Sect. 7).

2   Formal Definitions for Program Anomaly Detection

We formally define the problem of program anomaly detection and present the security model for detection systems. Then we discuss the two independent properties of a program anomaly detection method: the detection capability and the scope of the norm. Last, we give an overview of our unified framework.

2.1   Security Model

Considering both transactional (terminating after a transaction/computation) and continuous (constantly running) program executions, we define a **precise program trace** based on an *autonomous portion of a program execution*, which is a consistent and relatively independent execution segment that can be isolated from the remaining execution, e.g., an routine, an event handling procedure (for event-driven programs), a complete execution of a program, etc.

Definition 1. *A precise program trace* **T** *is the sequence of all instructions executed in an autonomous execution portion of a program.*

T is usually recorded as the sequence of all executed *instruction addresses*[1] and *instruction arguments*. In real-world executions, addresses of *basic blocks* can be used to record **T** without loss of generality since instructions within a basic block are executed in a sequence.

We formalize the problem of program anomaly detection in Definition 2.

---

[1] Instruction addresses are unique identifiers of specific instructions.

Definition 2. *Program anomaly detection is a decision problem whether a precise program trace* **T** *is accepted by a language L. L presents the set of all normal precise program traces in either a deterministic means (L = {**T** | **T** is normal})* *or a probabilistic means (L = {**T** | P(**T**) > η}).*

In Definition 2, η is a probabilistic threshold for selecting normal traces from arbitrary traces that consist of instruction addresses. Either parametric and non-parametric probabilistic methods can construct probabilistic detection models.

In reality, no program anomaly detection system uses **T** to describe program executions due to the significant tracing overhead. Instead, a **practical program trace** is commonly used in real-world systems.

Definition 3. *A practical program trace* $\ddot{\mathbf{T}}$ *is a subsequence of a precise program trace* **T**. *The subsequence is formed based on alphabet* Σ, *a selected/traced subset of all instructions, e.g., system calls.*

We list three categories of commonly used practical traces in real-world program anomaly detection systems. The traces result in *black-box*, *gray-box*, and *white-box* detection approaches with an increasing level of modeling granularity.

- *Black-box level traces:* only the communications between the process and the operating system kernel, i.e., system calls, are monitored. This level of practical traces has the smallest size of Σ among the three. It is the coarsest trace level while obtaining the trace incurs the smallest tracing overhead.
- *White-box level traces:* all (or a part of) kernel-space and user-space activities of a process are monitored. An extremely precise white-box level trace $\ddot{\mathbf{T}}$ is exactly a precise trace **T** where all instructions are monitored. However, real-world white-box level traces usually define Σ as the set of function calls to expose the call stack activity.
- *Gray-box level traces:* a limited white-box level without the complete static program analysis information [24], e.g., all control-flow graphs. Σ of a gray-box level trace only contains symbols (function calls, system calls, etc.) that appear in dynamic traces.

We describe the general security model of a real-world program anomaly detection system in Definition 4. The security model derives from Definition 2 but measures program executions using $\ddot{\mathbf{T}}$ instead of **T**.

Definition 4. *A real-world program anomaly detection system* Λ *defines a language* L_Λ *(a deterministic or probabilistic set of normal practical program traces) and establishes an attestation procedure* G_Λ *to test whether a practical program trace* $\ddot{\mathbf{T}}$ *is accepted by* L_Λ.

A program anomaly detection system Λ usually consist of two phases: *training* and *detection*. Training is the procedure forming L_Λ and building G_Λ from known normal traces $\{\ddot{\mathbf{T}} \mid \ddot{\mathbf{T}}$ is normal$\}$. Detection is the runtime procedure testing incoming traces against L_Λ using G_Λ. Traces that cannot be accepted by L_Λ in the detection phase are logged or aggregated for alarm generation.

2.2   Detection Capability

The detection capability of a program anomaly detection method Λ is its ability to detect attacks or anomalous program behaviors. Detection capability of a detection system Λ is characterized by the precision of Λ. We define *precision* of Λ as the ability of Λ to distinguish different precise program traces in Definition 5. This concept is independent of whether the scope of the norm is deterministically or probabilistically established (discussed in Sect. 2.3).

Definition 5. *Given a program anomaly detection method Λ and any practical program trace $\ddot{T}$ that Λ accepts, the precision of Λ is the average number of precise program traces $\mathbf{T}$ that share an identical subsequence $\ddot{T}$.*

Our definition of program anomaly detection system precision is a generalization of *average branching factor* (using regular grammar to approximate the description of precise program traces) [59] and *average reachability measure* (using context-free grammar to approximate the description of precise program traces) [28]. The generation is achieved through the using of $\mathbf{T}$, the most precise description of a program execution. average in Definition 5 can be replaced by other aggregation function for customized evaluation.

We formalize the relation between the expressive power of L_Λ (defined by detection method Λ) and the detection capability of Λ in Theorem 1.

Theorem 1. *The detection capability of a program anomaly detection method Λ is determined by the expressive power of the language L_Λ corresponding to Λ.*

Proof. Consider two detection methods Λ_1 (L_{Λ_1}) and Λ_2 (L_{Λ_2}) where Λ_1 is more precise than Λ_2, one can always find two precise program traces $\mathbf{T}_1/\mathbf{T}_2$, so that $\mathbf{T}_1/\mathbf{T}_2$ are expressed by L_{Λ_1} in two different practical traces $\ddot{T}_{1\Lambda_1}/\ddot{T}_{2\Lambda_1}$, but they can only be expressed by L_{Λ_2} as an identical $\ddot{T}_{\Lambda_2}$. Because the definition of the norm is subjective to the need of a detection system, in theory, one can set $\mathbf{T}_1/\mathbf{T}_2$ to be normal/anomalous, respectively. In summary, Λ_1 with a more expressive L_{Λ_1} can detect the attack $\mathbf{T}_2$ via practical trace $\ddot{T}_{2\Lambda_1}$, but Λ_2 cannot.

Theorem 1 enables the comparison between detection capabilities of different detection systems through their corresponding languages. It lays the foundation of our unified framework. The more expressive L_Λ describes a normal precise trace $\mathbf{T}$ through a practical trace $\ddot{T}$, the less likely an attacker can construct an attack trace $\mathbf{T}'$ mimicking $\mathbf{T}$ without being detected by Λ.

2.3   Scope of the Norm

Not all anomaly detection systems agree on whether a specific program behavior (a precise program trace $\mathbf{T}$) is normal or not. Even given the set of all practical program traces Σ^* with respect to a specific alphabet Σ (e.g., all system calls), two detection systems Λ_1 and Λ_2 may disagree on whether a specific $\ddot{T} \in \Sigma^*$ is normal or not. Σ^* denotes the set of all possible strings/traces over Σ.

Definition 6. *The scope of the norm S_Λ (of a program anomaly detection system Λ) is the selection of practical traces to be accepted by L_Λ.*

While L_Λ is the set of all normal practical traces, S_Λ emphasizes on the selection process to build L_Λ, but not the expressive power (detection capability) of L_Λ. S_Λ does not influence the detection capability of Λ.

For instance, VPStatic [19] (denoted as Λ_s) utilizes a pushdown automaton (PDA) to describe practical program traces. Therefore, its precision is determined by the expressiveness of context-free languages[2]. S_{Λ_s} is all *legal control flows* specified in the binary of the program. VtPath [18] (denoted as Λ_v) is another PDA approach, but S_{Λ_v} is defined based on dynamic traces. Since dynamic traces commonly forms a subset of all feasible execution paths, there exists $\ddot{T}$ not in the training set of Λ_2. Thus, $\ddot{T}$ will be recognized as anomalous by Λ_2 yet normal by Λ_1. Because the precisions of Λ_1 and Λ_2 are the same, Λ_2 can be made to detect $\ddot{T}$ as normal by including $\ddot{T}$ in its training set (changing S_{Λ_v}).

There are two types of scopes of the norm:

- **Deterministic scope of the norm** is achieved through a deterministic language $L_\Lambda = \{\ddot{T} \mid \ddot{T} \text{ is normal}\}$. Program anomaly detection systems based on finite state automata (FSA), PDA, etc. belong to this category.
- **Probabilistic scope of the norm** is achieved through a stochastic language $L_\Lambda = \{\ddot{T} \mid P(\ddot{T}) > \eta\}$. Different probability threshold η results in different S_Λ and different L_Λ/Λ. Program anomaly detection systems based on hidden Markov model, one-class SVM, etc. belong to this category.

2.4 Overview of Our Unified Framework

We develop a unified framework presenting any program anomaly detection method Λ. Our framework unifies Λ by the expressive power of L_Λ.

We illustrate our unified framework in Fig. 1 showing its hierarchical structure[3]. In Fig. 1, L-1 to L-4 indicate four major precision levels with decreasing detection capabilities according to the expressive power of L_Λ. The order of precision levels marks the potential of approaches within these levels, but not necessarily the practical detection capability of a specific method[4]. Our design is based on both the well-defined levels in Chomsky hierarchy and the existing milestones in the evolution of program anomaly detection.

L-1: context-sensitive language level (most powerful level)
L-2: context-free language level
L-3: regular language level
L-4: restricted regular language level (least powerful level).

---

[2] Context-sensitive languages correspond to pushdown automata.

[3] The hierarchy is reasoned via Chomsky hierarchy [12], which presents the hierarchical relation among formal grammars/languages.

[4] For example, one detection approach Λ_a in L-2 without argument analysis could be less capable of detecting attacks than an approach Λ_b in L-3 with argument analysis.

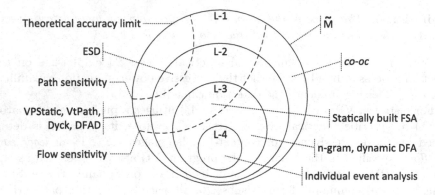

Fig. 1. The hierarchy of our program anomaly detection framework. L-1 to L-4 are four major precision levels with decreasing detection capabilities.

The restricted regular language corresponding to L-4 does not enforce specific adjacent elements for any element in a string (program trace). Two optional properties within L-1, L-2 and L-3 are *path sensitivity* and *flow sensitivity* (Sect. 5.2). We prove the theoretical accuracy limit (the outmost circle in Fig. 1) in Sect. 3 with an abstract detection machine $\tilde{M}$. We abstract existing methods in Sect. 4 and identify their positions in our unified framework in Sect. 5. We present details of our framework and point out the connection between levels in our framework and grammars in Chomsky hierarchy in Sect. 5. We describe the evolution from L-4 methods to L-1 methods in Sect. 6.2.

3 Accuracy Limit of Program Anomaly Detection

We describe an abstract detection machine, $\tilde{M}$, to differentiate between any two precise program traces. Thus, $\tilde{M}$ detects any anomalous program traces given a scope of the norm. A practical program trace $\ddot{\mathbf{T}}$ that $\tilde{M}$ consumes is a precise program trace $\mathbf{T}$. We prove that $\tilde{M}$ has the identical capability of differentiating between traces (execution paths) as the program itself. Therefore, $\tilde{M}$ is the accuracy limit of program anomaly detection models.

3.1 The Ultimate Detection Machine

The abstract machine $\tilde{M}$ is a 9-tuple $\tilde{M} = (Q, \Sigma, \Gamma, A, \Omega, \delta, s_0, Z, F)$ where the symbols are described in Table 1. $\tilde{M}$ operates from s_0. If an input string/trace $\ddot{\mathbf{T}}$ reaches a final state in F, then $\ddot{\mathbf{T}}$ is a normal trace.

$\tilde{M}$ consists of three components: *a finite state machine, a stack Π*, and *a random-access register Υ*. In $\tilde{M}$, both Π and Υ are of finite sizes. Indirect addressing, i.e., the value of a register can be dereferenced as an address of another register, is supported by Υ and $A \subset \Omega$. Because a random-access register can simulate a stack, Π can be omitted in $\tilde{M}$ without any computation

Table 1. Descriptions of symbols in $\tilde{M}$. All sets are of finite sizes.

	Name	Description
Q	States	Set of states
Σ	Input alphabet	Set of input symbols
Γ	Stack alphabet	Set of symbols on the stack
A	Register addresses	Set of addresses of all registers
Ω	Register alphabet	Set of symbols stored in registers
δ	Transition relation	Subset of $Q \times (\Sigma \cup \{\varepsilon\}) \times \Gamma \times \Omega^* \times Q \times \Gamma^* \times \Omega^*$
s_0	Initial state	State to start, $s_0 \in Q$
Z	Initial stack symbol	Initial symbol on the stack, $Z \subseteq Q$
F	Final states	Set of states where $\ddot{\text{T}}$ is accepted, $F \subseteq Q$

ε denotes an empty string.
Ω^* or Γ^* denotes a string over alphabet Ω or Γ, respectively.

power loss. We keep Π in $\tilde{M}$ to mimic the execution of a real-world program. It helps extend $\tilde{M}$ for multi-threading (Sect. 3.3) and unify $\tilde{M}$ in our framework (Sect. 5.1).

A transition in $\tilde{M}$ is defined by δ, which is a mapping from $(\Sigma \cup \{\varepsilon\}) \times Q \times \Gamma \times \Omega^*$ to $Q \times \Gamma^* \times \Omega^*$. Given an input symbol $\sigma \in \Sigma \cup \{\varepsilon\}$, the current state $q \in Q$, the stack symbol $\gamma \in \Gamma$ (stack top), and all symbols in the register $\{\omega_i \mid \omega_i \in \Omega, \ 0 \leq i \leq |A|\}$, the rules in δ chooses a new state $q' \in Q$, pops γ, pushes zero or more stack symbols $\gamma_0 \gamma_1 \gamma_2 \ldots$ onto the stack, and update $\{\omega_i\}$.

3.2   The Equivalent Abstract Machine of an Executing Program

We state the precision of the abstract detection machine $\tilde{M}$ in Theorem 2 and interpreter both *sufficiency* and *necessity* aspects of the theorem.

Theorem 2. $\tilde{M}$ *is as precise as the target program;* $\tilde{M}$ *can detect any anomalous traces if the scope of the norm is specified and* $\tilde{M}$ *is constructed.*

Sufficiency: $\tilde{M}$ has the same computation power as any real-world executing program so that $L_{\tilde{M}}$ can differentiate any two precise program traces.
Necessity: detection machines that are less powerful than $\tilde{M}$ cannot differentiate any two arbitrary precise program traces of the target program.

Although a Turing machine is commonly used to model a real-world program in execution, an executing program actually has limited resources (the tape length, the random access memory size or the address symbol count) different from a Turing machine. This restricted Turing machine is abstracted as linear bounded automaton [34]. We prove Theorem 2 by Lemmas 1 and 2.

Lemma 1. *A program that is executing on a real-world machine is equivalent to a linear bounded automaton (LBA).*

Lemma 2. $\tilde{M}$ *is equivalent to a linear bounded automaton.*

Proof. We prove that $\tilde{M}$ is equivalent to an abstract machine $\ddot{M}$ and $\ddot{M}$ is equivalent to an LBA, so $\tilde{M}$ is equivalent to an LBA.

$\ddot{M}$ is an abstract machine similar to $\tilde{M}$ except that Υ (the register) in $\tilde{M}$ is replaced by two stacks Π_0 and Π_1. $size(\Upsilon) = size(\Pi_0) + size(\Pi_1)$.

We prove that $\tilde{M}$ and $\ddot{M}$ can simulate each other below.

- One random-access register can simulate one stack with simple access rules (i.e., last in, first out) enforced. Thus, Υ can be split into *two non-overlapping register sections* to simulate Π_0 and Π_1.
- Π_0 and Π_1 together can simulate Υ by filling Π_0 with initial stack symbol Z to its maximum height and leaving Π_1 empty. All the elements in Π_0 are counterparts of all the units in Υ. The depth of an element in Π_0 maps to the address of a unit in Υ. To access an arbitrary element e in Π_0, one pops all elements higher than e in Π_0 and pushes them into Π_1 until e is retrieved. After the access to e, elements in Π_1 are popped and pushed back into Π_0.

$\ddot{M}$ **is equivalent to an LBA:** $\ddot{M}$ consists of a finite state machine and three stacks, Π (same as Π in $\tilde{M}$), Π_0, Π_1 (the two-stack replacement of Υ in $\tilde{M}$). $\ddot{M}$ with three stacks is equivalent to an abstract machine with two stacks [48]. Two stacks is equivalent to a finite tape when concatenating them head to head. Thus, $\ddot{M}$ is equivalent to an abstract machine consisting of a finite state machine and a finite tape, which is a linear bounded automaton.

In summary, $\tilde{M}$ is equivalent to an LBA and Lemma 2 holds. $\square$

3.3   Usage and Discussion

Operation of $\tilde{M}$: $\tilde{M}$ consists of a random-access register Υ and a stack Π. The design of $\tilde{M}$ follows the abstraction of an executing program. Π simulates the call stack of a process and Υ simulates the heap. The transition δ in $\tilde{M}$ is determined by the input symbol, symbols in Υ and the top of Π, which is comparable to a real-world process. Given a precise trace **T** of a program, $\tilde{M}$ can be operated by emulating all events (instructions) of **T** through $\tilde{M}$.

Multi-threading Handling: although $\tilde{M}$ does not model multi-threading program executions, it can be easily extended to fulfill the job. The basic idea is to model each thread using an $\tilde{M}$. Threads creating, forking and joining can be handled by copying the *finite state machine* and *stack* of an $\tilde{M}$ to a new one or merging two $\tilde{M}$s. δ needs to be extended according to the shared register access among different $\tilde{M}$s as well as the joining operation between $\tilde{M}$s.

Challenges to Realize $\tilde{M}$ in Practice: $\tilde{M}$ serves as a theoretical accuracy limit. It cannot be efficiently realized in the real world because

1. The number of normal precise traces is infinite.
2. The scope of the norm requires a non-polynomial time algorithm to learn.

The first challenge is due to the fact that a trace $\ddot{T}$ of a program can be of any length, e.g., a continuous (constantly running) program generates traces in arbitrary lengths until it halts. Most existing approaches do not have the problem because they only model short segments of traces (e.g., n-grams with a small n [21], first-order automaton transition verification [19]).

Pure dynamic analysis cannot provide a complete scope of the norm. The second challenge emerges when one performs comprehensive static program analysis to build $\tilde{M}$. For example, one well-known exponential complexity task is to discover induction variables and correlate different control-flow branches.

4   Abstractions of Existing Detection Methods

In this section, we analyze existing program anomaly detection models and abstract them in five categories. We identify their precision (or detection capability) in our framework in Sect. 5.

Finite State Automaton (FSA) Methods represent the category of program anomaly detection methods that explicitly employs an FSA. Kosoresow and Hofmeyr first utilized a deterministic finite state automaton (DFA) to characterize normal program traces [36] via black-box level traces (building a DFA for system call traces). Sekar et al. improved the FSA method by adopting a limited gray-box view [50]. Sekar's method retrieves *program counter* information for every traced system call. If two system calls and program counters are the same, the same automaton state is used in the FSA construction procedure.

Abstraction: all FSA methods explicitly build an FSA for modeling normal program traces. A transition of such an FSA can be described in (1). p_i is an automaton state that is mapped to one or a set of program states. Each program state can be identified by a system call (black-box level traces) or a combination of system call and program counter (gray-box level traces). $s*$ denotes a string of one or more system calls.

$$p_i \xrightarrow{s*} p_{i+1} \tag{1}$$

n-gram Methods represent the category of program anomaly detection methods those utilize sequence fragments to characterize program behaviors. n-grams are n-item-long[5] substrings[6] of a long trace, and they are usually generated by sliding a window (of length n) on the trace. The assumption underlying n-gram methods is that *short trace fragments are good features differentiating normal and anomalous long system call traces* [23]. A basic n-gram method tests whether every n-gram is in the known set of normal n-grams [21].

Abstraction: a set of n-gram (of normal program behaviors) is equivalent to an FSA where each state is an n-gram [60]. A transition of such an FSA can

---

[5] n can be either a fixed value or a variable [45,63].

[6] Lookahead pair methods are subsequent variants of n-gram methods [35].

be described in (2). The transition is recognized when there exist two normal n-grams, $(s_0, s_1, \ldots, s_{n-1})$ and $(s_1, \ldots, s_{n-1}, s_n)$, in any normal program traces.

$$(s_0, s_1, \ldots, s_{n-1}) \xrightarrow{s_n} (s_1, \ldots, s_{n-1}, s_n) \tag{2}$$

Since n-gram methods are built on a membership test, various deterministic [45,62] and probabilistic [17,61] means are developed to define the scope of the norm (the set of normal n-grams) and perform the membership test. And system call arguments were added to describe system calls in more details [7,55,57].

Pushdown Automaton (PDA) Methods represent the category of program anomaly detection methods those utilize a PDA or its equivalents to model program behaviors. DPA methods are more precise than FSA methods because they can simulate user-space call stack activities [18].

An FSA connects control-flow graphs (CFGs) of all procedures into a *monomorphic* graph, which lacks the ability to describe direct or indirect recursive function calls [31,59]. A PDA, in contrast, keeps CFGs isolated and utilizes a stack to record and verify function calls or returns [18,19,29]. Thus, it can describe recursions. However, only exposing the stack when system calls occur is not enough to construct a deterministic DPA [19]. There could be multiple potential paths transiting from one observed stack state Γ_i to the next stack state Γ_{i+1}. Giffin et al. fully exposed all stack activities in Dyck model [30] by embedding loggers for function calls and returns via binary rewriting.

Abstraction: a typical PDA method consumes white-box level traces [19] or gray-box level traces [43]. The internal (user-space) activities of the running program between system calls are simulated by the PDA. Denote a system call as s and a procedure transition as f. We describe the general PDA transition in (3) where Γ_i / Γ_{i+1} is the stack before/after the transition, respectively.

$$p_i, \Gamma_i \xrightarrow{f \text{ or } s} p_{i+1}, \Gamma_{i+1} \tag{3}$$

System call arguments can be added to describe calls in more details like they are used in previous models. In addition, Bhatkar et al. utilized data-flow analysis to provide complex system call arguments verification, e.g., unary and binary relations [4]. Giffin et al. extended system call arguments to environment values, e.g., configurations, and built an environment-sensitive method [28].

Probabilistic Methods differ from deterministic program anomaly detection approaches that they use stochastic languages to define the scope of the norm (Sect. 2.3). Stochastic languages are probabilistic counterparts of deterministic languages (e.g., regular languages). From the automaton perspective, stochastic languages correspond to automata with probabilistic transition edges.

Abstraction: existing probabilistic program anomaly detection methods are probabilistic counterparts of FSA, because they either use n-grams or FSA with probabilistic transitions edges. Typical probabilistic detection methods include hidden Markov model (HMM) [61,64], classification methods [16,37,41,46], artificial neural network [27], data mining approaches [40], etc. Gu et al. presented a supervised statistical learning model, which uses control-flow graphs to help the training of its probabilistic model [32].

Probabilistic FSA does not maintain call stack structures[7], and it constrains existing probabilistic approaches from modeling recursions precisely. In theory, FSA and probabilistic FSA only differ in their scopes of the norm; one is deterministic the other is probabilistic. The precision or detection capability of the two are the same as explained in Sect. 2.3. Different thresholds in parametric probabilistic models define different scopes of the norm, but they do not directly impact the precision of a model.

N-variant Methods define the scope of the norm with respect to the current execution path under detection. They are different from the majority of detection methods that define the scope of the norm as all possible normal execution paths.

In N-variant methods, a program is executed with n replicas [14]. When one of them is compromised, others – that are executed with different settings or in different environments – could remain normal.

The anomaly detection problem in N-variant methods is to tell whether one of the concurrently running replicas is behaving differently from its peers; N-variant methods calculate the behavior distance among process replicas. Gao et al. proposed a deterministic alignment model [25] and probabilistic hidden Markov model [26] to calculate the distances.

Abstraction: existing N-variant models are FSA or probabilistic FSA equivalents. The precision is limited by their program execution description based on n-grams. This description forms a deterministic/probabilistic FSA model underlying the two existing N-variant methods.

5   Unification Framework

We develop a hierarchical framework to uniformly present any program anomaly detection method in terms of its detection capability. We identify the detection capabilities of existing program anomaly detection methods (Sect. 4) and the theoretical accuracy limit (Sect. 3) in our framework.

5.1   Major Precision Levels of Program Anomaly Detection

We abstract any program anomaly detection method Λ through its equivalent abstract machine. Λ is unified according to the language L_Λ corresponding to the abstract machine. We summarize four major precision levels defined in our unified framework in Table 2. We describe them in detail below in the order of an increasing detection capability.

L-4: Restricted Regular Language Level. The most intuitive program anomaly detection model, which reasons events individually, e.g., a system call with or without arguments. No event correlation is recorded or analyzed.

---

[7] Probabilistic PDA has not been explored by the anomaly detection community.

Table 2. Precision levels in our framework (from the most to the least accurate).

Precision levels	Limitation[a]	Chomsky level
L-1 methods	Program execution equivalent	Type-1 grammars
L-2 methods	First-order reasoning	Type-2 grammars
L-3 methods	Cannot pair calls and returns	Type-3 grammars
L-4 methods	Individual event test	Type-3 grammars[b]

[a]The key feature that distinguishes this level from a level of higher precision.
[b]The restricted regular language does not enforce specific adjacent events for any event in a program trace.

An L-4 method corresponds to a restricted FSA, which accepts a simple type of regular languages L_4 that does not enforce specific adjacent elements for any element in a string (practical program trace $\ddot{T}$).

L-4 methods are the weakest detection model among the four. It is effective only when anomalous program executions can be indicated by individual events. For example, sys_open() with argument "/etc/passwd" indicates an anomaly.

A canonical example of L-4 methods is to analyze individual system events in system logs and summarize the result through machine learning mechanisms [16].

L-3: Regular Language Level. The intermediate program anomaly detection model, which records and verifies *first-order event transitions* (i.e., the relation between a pair of adjacent events in a trace, which is an extra feature over L-4 methods) using type-3 languages (regular grammar).

An L-3 method corresponds to an FSA, which naturally describes first-order transitions between states. Each state can be defined as one or multiple events, e.g., a system call, n-grams of system calls. One state can be detailed using its arguments, call-sites, etc. The formal language L_3 used to describe normal traces in an L-3 method is a type-3 language.

L-3 methods consume black-box traces. The monitoring is efficient because internal activities are not exposed. However, L-3 methods cannot take advantage of exposed internal activities of an executing program. For example, procedure returns cannot be verified by L-3 methods because L_3 (regular grammar) cannot pair arbitrary events in traces; L-3 methods cannot model recursions well.

Canonical L-3 methods include DFA program anomaly detection [36], n-grams methods [23], statically built FSA [50], and FSA with call arguments [7].

L-2: Context-free Language Level. The advanced program execution model, which verifies first-order event transitions with full knowledge (aware of any instructions) of program internal activities in the user space.

An L-2 method corresponds to a PDA, which expands the description of an FSA state with a stack (last in, first out). Procedure transitions (nested call-sites) can be stored in the stack so that L-2 methods can verify the return of each function/library/system call. The formal language L_2 used to describe normal traces in an L-2 method is a type-2 (context-free) language.

Gray-box or white-box traces are required to expose program internal activities (e.g., procedure transitions) so that the stack can be maintained in L-2 methods. Walking the stack when a system call occurs is an efficient stack expose technique [18]. However, the stack change between system calls is nondeterministic. A more expensive approach exposes every procedure transition via code instrumentation [30], so that the stack is deterministic.

Canonical L-2 methods include VPStatic [19], VtPath [18], and Dyck [30]. Moreover, Bhatkar et al. applied argument analysis with data-flow analysis (referred to by us as DFAD) [4], and Giffin et al. correlated arguments and environmental variables with system calls (referred to by us as ESD) [28].

L-1: Context-Sensitive Language Level. The most accurate program anomaly detection model in theory, which verifies higher-order event transitions with full knowledge of program internal activities.

L-1 methods correspond to a higher-order PDA, which extends a PDA with non-adjacent event correlations, e.g., induction variables.

We develop Theorem 3 showing that higher-order PDA and $\tilde{M}$ (Sect. 3) are equivalent in their computation power. The proof of Theorem 2 points out $\tilde{M}$ and linear bounded automaton (LBA) are equivalent. Therefore, these three are abstract machines representing the most accurate program anomaly detection.

The formal language L_1 used to describe normal traces in an L-1 method is a type-1 (context-sensitive) language.

We formally describe an L-1 method, i.e., $\tilde{M}$, in Sect. 3. Any other LBA or $\tilde{M}$ equivalents are also L-1 methods.

Theorem 3. *L-1 methods are as precise as the target executing program.*

We provide a proof sketch for Theorem 3. First, $\tilde{M}$ is as precise as the executing program (Theorem 2 in Sect. 3). Next, we give the sketch of the proof that the abstract machine of L-1 methods, i.e., a higher-order PDA, is equivalent to $\tilde{M}$: a higher-order PDA characterizes cross-serial dependencies [6], i.e., correlations between non-adjacent events. Therefore, it accepts context-sensitive languages [53], which is type-1 languages accepted by $\tilde{M}$.

Although the general context-sensitive model (higher-order PDA or $\tilde{M}$) has not been realized in the literature, Shu et al. demonstrated the construction of a constrained context-sensitive language model (*co-oc* in Fig. 1) [54]. The model quantitatively characterizes the co-occurrence relation among non-adjacent function calls in a long trace. Its abstraction is the context-sensitive language Bach [49].

Probabilistic Detection Methods and Our Hierarchy are Orthogonal. The reason is that probabilistic models affect the scope of the norm definition, but not the precision of the detection (explained in Sect. 2.3). For instance, a probabilistic FSA method (e.g., HMM [61,64], classification based on n-grams [16,46]) is an L-3 method. It cannot model recursion well because there is no stack in the model. The precision of a probabilistic FSA method is the same as the precision of a deterministic FSA method, except that the scope of the norm is defined probabilistically. A similar analysis holds for N-variant methods. All existing N-variant methods [25,26] are L-3 methods.

Instruction Arguments are Part of Events in T. However, argument analysis does not increase the precision level of a detection method, e.g., an n-gram approach with argument reasoning is still an L-3 approach.

Table 3. Terminology of sensitivity in program anomaly detection.

	Calling context	Flow	Path	Environment
Sensitive Objects	Call sites	Instruction order	Branch dependency	Arguments configurations
Precision Level[a]	L-4	L-3	L-2	L-2
Description[b]	RL	RL	CFL	CFL

[a]The least precise level required to specify the sensitivity.
[b]The least powerful formal language required for describing the sensitivity.
RL: regular language. CFL: context-free language.

5.2   Sensitivity in a Nutshell

We describe optional properties (sensitivities) within L-1 to L-3 in our hierarchical framework with respect to sensitivity terms introduced from program analysis. We summarize the terminology of sensitivity in Table 3 and explain them and their relation to our framework.

Calling Context Sensitivity concerns the call-site of a call. In other words, it distinguishes a system/function call through different callers or callsites. Calling-context-sensitive methods[8] are more precise than non-calling-context-sensitive ones because mimicked calls from incorrect call-sites are detected.

Flow Sensitivity concerns the order of events according to control-flow graphs (CFG). Only legal control flows according to program binaries can be normal, e.g., [50]. Flow sensitive methods bring static program analysis to anomaly detection and rule out illegal control flows from the scope of the norm.

Path Sensitivity concerns the branch dependencies among the binary (in a single CFG or cross multiple CFGs). Infeasible paths (impossibly co-occurring basic blocks or branches) can be detected by a path-sensitive method. Full path sensitivity requires exponential time to discover. Existing solutions take some path-sensitive measures, e.g., Giffin et al. correlated less than 20 branches for a program in ESD [28].

---

[8] Calling context sensitivity (or context sensitivity in short) in program analysis should be distinguished from the term *context-sensitive* in formal languages. The latter characterizes cross-serial dependencies in a trace, while the former identifies each event (e.g., a system call) in a trace more precisely.

Environment Sensitivity correlates execution paths with executing environments, e.g., arguments, configurations, environmental variables. Several types of infeasible paths such as an executed path not specified by the corresponding command line argument can be detected by an environment-sensitive method [28]. Environment sensitivity is a combination of techniques including data-flow analysis, path-sensitive analysis, etc.

6   Attack/Detection Evolution and Open Problems

In this section, we describe the evolution of program anomaly detection systems using the precision levels in our framework. New solutions aim to achieve better precision and eliminate mimicry attacks. We point out future research directions from both precision and practicality perspectives.

6.1   Inevitable Mimicry Attacks

Mimicry attacks are stealthy program attacks designed to subvert program anomaly detection systems by mimicking normal behaviors. A mimicry attack exploits false negatives of a specific detection system Λ. The attacker constructs a precise trace $\mathbf{T}'$ (achieving the attack goal) that shares the same practical trace $\ddot{\mathbf{T}}_\Lambda$ with a normal $\mathbf{T}$ to escape the detection.

The first mimicry attack was described by Wagner and Soto [60]. They utilized an FSA (regular grammar) to exploit the limited detection capability of n-gram methods (L-3 methods). In contrast, L-2 methods, such as [18,19,30], invalidate this type of mimicry attacks with context-free grammar description of program traces. However, mimicry attacks using context-free grammars, e.g., [20,38], are developed to subvert these L-2 methods.

As program anomaly detection methods evolve from L-4 to L-1, the space for mimicry attacks becomes limited. The functionality of mimicry attacks decreases since the difference between an attack trace and a normal trace attenuates. However, an attacker can always construct a mimicry attack against any real-world program anomaly detection system. The reason is that the theoretical limit of program anomaly detection (L-1 methods) cannot be efficiently reached, i.e., $\tilde{M}$ described in Sect. 3 requires exponential time to build.

6.2   Evolution from L-4 to L-1

A detection system Λ_1 rules out mimicry traces from a less precise Λ_2 to achieve a better detection capability. We describe the upgrade of detection systems from a lower precision level to a higher precision level. Intuitively, L-3 methods improve on L-4 methods as L-3 methods analyze the order of events. We summarize four features to upgrade an L-3 method (abstracted as a general FSA) to L-2 and L-1 methods in Fig. 2.

① expanding a state horizontally (with neighbor states)

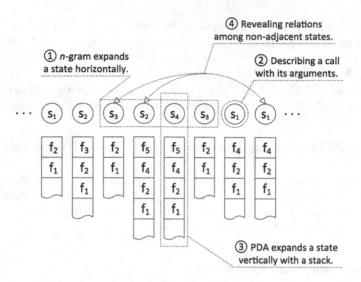

Fig. 2. Four approaches for improving a basic L-3 method (FSA).

② describing details of states (call-sites, arguments, etc.)
③ expanding a state vertically (using a stack)
④ revealing relations among non-adjacent states.

The four features are not equally powerful for improving the precision of an anomaly detection method. ① and ② are complementary features, which do not change the major precision level of a method. ③ introduces a stack and upgrades an L-3 method to an L-2 method. ④ discovers cross-serial dependencies and establishes a context-sensitive language [53], which results in an L-1 method.

Most of the existing program anomaly detection methods can be explained as a basic L-3 method plus one or more of these features. L-3 with ① yields an n-gram method [23]. L-3 with ② was studied in [44]. L-3 with ③ is a basic L-2 method. More than one feature can be added in one program anomaly detection system. L-3 with ① and ② was studied by Sufatrio and Yap [55] and Gaurav et al. [57]. L-3 with ② and ③ was studied by Bhatkar et al. [4] and Giffin et al. [28]. $\tilde{M}$ (described in Sect. 3) provides ③ and ④ as basic features. ② can be added to $\tilde{M}$ to describe each state in more details.

6.3 Open Problems

We point out several open problems in program anomaly detection research.

Precision. As illustrated in our framework (Fig. 1), there is a gap between the theoretical accuracy limit (the best L-1 method) and the state-of-the-art approaches in L-2 (e.g., ESD [28]) and constrained L-1 level (e.g., co-oc [54]).

L-2 models: existing detection methods have not reached the limit of L-2 because none of them analyze the complete path sensitivity. Future solutions can explore a more complete set of path sensitivity to push the detection capability of a method towards the best L-2 method.

L-1 models: higher-order relations among states can then be discovered to upgrade an L-2 method to L-1. However, heuristics algorithms need to be developed to avoid exponential modeling complexity. Another choice is to develop constrained L-1 approaches (e.g., co-oc [54]), which characterize some aspects of higher-order relations (e.g., co-occurrence but not order).

Probabilistic models: existing probabilistic approaches, i.e., probabilistic FSA equivalents, are at precision level L-3. Probabilistic PDA and probabilistic LBA can be explored to establish L-2 and even L-1 level probabilistic models.

Practicality. In contrast to the extensive research in academia, the security industry has not widely adopted program anomaly detection technologies. No products are beyond L-3 level with black-box traces [33]. The main challenges are *eliminating tracing overhead* and *purifying training dataset*.

Tracing Overhead Issue: L-2 and L-1 methods require the exposure of user-space program activities, which could result in over 100 % tracing overhead on general computing platforms [3]. However, Szekeres et al. found that the industry usually tolerates at most 5 % overhead for a security solution [56].

Polluted Training Dataset Issue: most existing program anomaly detection approaches assume the training set contains only normal traces. Unless the scope of the norm is defined as *legal control flows*, which can be extracted from the binary, the assumption is not very practical for a real-world product. A polluted training dataset prevents a precise learning of the scope of the norm for a detection model, which results in false negatives in detection.

7 Control-Flow Enforcement Techniques

Control-flow enforcements, e.g., Control-Flow Integrity (CFI) [1] and Code-Pointer Integrity (CPI) [39], enforce control-flow transfers and prevent illegal function calls/pointers from executing. They evolve from the perspective of attack countermeasures [56]. They are equivalent to one category of program anomaly detection that defines the scope of the norm as legal control flows [52].

7.1 Control-Flow Enforcement

Control-flow enforcement techniques range from the protection of return addresses, the protection of indirect control-flow transfers (CFI), to the protection of all code pointers (CPI). They aim to protect against control-flow hijacks, e.g., stack attacks [42]. We list milestones in the development of control-flow enforcement techniques below (with an increasing protection capability).

Return Address Protection: Stack Guard [13], Stack Shield [58].
Indirect Control-flow Transfer Protection: CFI [1], Modular CFI [47].
All Code Pointer Protection: CPI [39].

7.2 Legal Control Flows as the Scope of the Norm

In program anomaly detection, one widely adopted definition of the scope of the norm S_A is *legal control flows* (Sect. 2.3); only basic block transitions that obey the control flow graphs are recognized as normal. The advantage of such definition is that the boundary of S_A is clear and can be retrieved from the binary. No labeling is needed to train the detection system. This definition of S_A leads to a fruitful study of constructing automata models through static program analysis[9], e.g., FSA method proposed by Sekar et al. [50] and PDA method proposed by Feng et al. [18].

7.3 Comparison of the Two Methods

We discuss the connection and the fundamental difference between control-flow enforcement and program anomaly detection.

Connection. Modern control-flow enforcement prevents a program from executing any illegal control flow. It has the same effect as the category of program anomaly detection that defines the scope of the norm as legal control flows. From the functionality perspective, control-flow enforcement even goes one step further; it halts illegal control flows. Program anomaly detection should be paired with prevention techniques to achieve the same functionality.

Difference. A system can either learn from attacks or normal behaviors of a program to secure the program. Control-flow enforcement evolves from the former perspective while program anomaly detection evolves from the latter. The specific type of attacks that control-flow enforcement techniques tackle is *control-flow hijacking*. In other words, control-flow enforcement techniques do not prevent attacks those obey legal control flows, e.g., brute force attacks. Program anomaly detection, in contrast, detects attacks, program bugs, anomalous usage patterns, user group shifts, etc. Various definitions of the scope of the norm result in a rich family of program anomaly detection models. One family has the same detection capability as control-flow enforcement.

8 Conclusion

Program anomaly detection is a powerful paradigm discovering program attacks without the knowledge of attack signatures. In this paper, we provided a general model for systematically analyzing *(i)* the detection capability of any model, *(ii)* the evolution of existing solutions, *(iii)* the theoretical accuracy limit, and *(iv)* the possible future paths toward the limit.

Our work filled a gap in the literature to unify deterministic and probabilistic models with our formal definition of program anomaly detection. We presented and proved the theoretical accuracy limit for program anomaly detection. We developed a unified framework presenting any existing or future program

---

[9] Dynamically assigned transitions cannot be precisely pinpointed from static analysis.

anomaly detection models and orders them through their detection capabilities. According to our unified framework, most existing detection approaches belong to the regular and the context-free language levels. More accurate context-sensitive language models can be explored with pragmatic constraints in the future. Our framework has the potential to serve as a roadmap and help researchers approach the ultimate program defense without attack signature specification.

Acknowledgments. This work has been supported by ONR grant N00014-13-1-0016. The authors would like to thank Trent Jaeger, Gang Tan, R. Sekar, David Evans and Dongyan Xu for their feedback on this work. The authors would like to thank anonymous reviewers for their comments on stochastic languages.

References

1. Abadi, M., Budiu, M., Erlingsson, U., Ligatti, J.: Control-flow integrity. In: Proceedings of ACM CCS, pp. 340–353 (2005)
2. Anderson, J.P.: Computer security technology planning study. Technicl report, DTIC (October (1972)
3. Bach, M., Charney, M., Cohn, R., Demikhovsky, E., Devor, T., Hazelwood, K., Jaleel, A., Luk, C.K., Lyons, G., Patil, H., Tal, A.: Analyzing parallel programs with pin. Computer **43**(3), 34–41 (2010)
4. Bhatkar, S., Chaturvedi, A., Sekar, R.: Dataflow anomaly detection. In: Proceedings of IEEE S & P, May 2006
5. Bletsch, T., Jiang, X., Freeh, V.W., Liang, Z.: Jump-oriented programming: a new class of code-reuse attack. In: Proceedings of ASIACCS, pp. 30–40 (2011)
6. Bresnan, J., Bresnan, R.M., Peters, S., Zaenen, A.: Cross-serial dependencies in Dutch. In: Savitch, W.J., Bach, E., Marsh, W., Safran-Naveh, G. (eds.) The Formal Complexity of Natural Language, vol. 33, pp. 286–319. Springer, Heidelberg (1987)
7. Canali, D., Lanzi, A., Balzarotti, D., Kruegel, C., Christodorescu, M., Kirda, E.: A quantitative study of accuracy in system call-based malware detection. In: Proceedings of ISSTA, pp. 122–132 (2012)
8. Chandola, V., Banerjee, A., Kumar, V.: Anomaly detection for discrete sequences: a survey. IEEE TKDE **24**(5), 823–839 (2012)
9. Chandola, V., Banerjee, A., Kumar, V.: Anomaly detection: a survey. ACM Comput. Surv. **41**(3), 1–58 (2009)
10. Checkoway, S., Davi, L., Dmitrienko, A., Sadeghi, A.R., Shacham, H., Winandy, M.: Return-oriented programming without returns. In: Proceedings of ACM CCS, pp. 559–572 (2010)
11. Chen, S., Xu, J., Sezer, E.C., Gauriar, P., Iyer, R.K.: Non-control-data attacks are realistic threats. In: Proceedings of USENIX Security, vol. 14, pp. 12–12 (2005)
12. Chomsky, N.: Three models for the description of language. IRE Trans. Inf. Theory **2**(3), 113–124 (1956)
13. Cowan, C., Pu, C., Maier, D., Hintony, H., Walpole, J., Bakke, P., Beattie, S., Grier, A., Wagle, P., Zhang, Q.: StackGuard: automatic adaptive detection and prevention of buffer-overflow attacks. In: Proceedings of USENIX Security, vol. 7, p. 5 (1998)

14. Cox, B., Evans, D., Filipi, A., Rowanhill, J., Hu, W., Davidson, J., Knight, J., Nguyen-Tuong, A., Hiser, J.: N-variant systems: a secretless framework for security through diversity. In: Proceedings of USENIX Security, vol. 15 (2006)
15. Denning, D.E.: An intrusion-detection model. IEEE TSE **13**(2), 222–232 (1987)
16. Endler, D.: Intrusion detection: applying machine learning to solaris audit data. In: Proceedings of ACSAC, pp. 268–279, December 1998
17. Eskin, E., Lee, W., Stolfo, S.: Modeling system calls for intrusion detection with dynamic window sizes. In: Proceedings of DARPA Information Survivability Conference and Exposition II, vol.1, pp. 165–175 (2001)
18. Feng, H.H., Kolesnikov, O.M., Fogla, P., Lee, W., Gong, W.: Anomaly detection using call stack information. In: Proceedings of IEEE Security and Privacy (2003)
19. Feng, H., Giffin, J., Huang, Y., Jha, S., Lee, W., Miller, B.: Formalizing sensitivity in static analysis for intrusion detection. In: Proceedings of IEEE Security and Privacy, pp. 194–208, May 2004
20. Fogla, P., Sharif, M., Perdisci, R., Kolesnikov, O., Lee, W.: Polymorphic blending attacks. In: Proceedings of USENIX Security, pp. 241–256 (2006)
21. Forrest, S., Hofmeyr, S., Somayaji, A.: The evolution of system-call monitoring. In: Proceedings of ACSAC, pp. 418–430, December 2008
22. Forrest, S., Perelson, A., Allen, L., Cherukuri, R.: Self-nonself discrimination in a computer. In: Proceedings of IEEE Security and Privacy, pp. 202–212, May 1994
23. Forrest, S., Hofmeyr, S.A., Somayaji, A., Longstaff, T.A.: A sense of self for unix processes. In: Proceedings of IEEE Security and Privacy, pp. 120–128 (1996)
24. Gao, D., Reiter, M.K., Song, D.: On gray-box program tracking for anomaly detection. In: Proceedings of USENIX Security, vol. 13, p. 8 (2004)
25. Gao, D., Reiter, M.K., Song, D.: Behavioral distance for intrusion detection. In: Proceedings of RAID, pp. 63–81 (2006)
26. Gao, D., Reiter, M.K., Song, D.: Behavioral distance measurement using hidden Markov models. In: Zamboni, D., Kruegel, C. (eds.) RAID 2006. LNCS, vol. 4219, pp. 19–40. Springer, Heidelberg (2006)
27. Ghosh, A.K., Schwartzbard, A.: A study in using neural networks for anomaly and misuse detection. In: Proceedings of USENIX Security, vol. 8, p. 12 (1999)
28. Giffin, J.T., Dagon, D., Jha, S., Lee, W., Miller, B.P.: Environment-sensitive intrusion detection. In: Proceedings of RAID, pp. 185–206 (2006)
29. Giffin, J.T., Jha, S., Miller, B.P.: Detecting manipulated remote call streams. In: Proceedings of USENIX Security, pp. 61–79 (2002)
30. Giffin, J.T., Jha, S., Miller, B.P.: Efficient context-sensitive intrusion detection. In: Proceedings of NDSS (2004)
31. Gopalakrishna, R., Spafford, E.H., Vitek, J.: Efficient intrusion detection using automaton inlining. In: Proceedings of IEEE Security and Privacy, pp. 18–31, May 2005
32. Gu, Z., Pei, K., Wang, Q., Si, L., Zhang, X., Xu, D.: Leaps: detecting camouflaged attacks with statistical learning guided by program analysis. In: Processing of DSN, June 2015
33. Hofmeyr, S.: Primary response technical white paper. http://www.ttivanguard. com/austinreconn/primaryresponse.pdf. Accessed August 2015
34. Hopcroft, J.E.: Introduction to Automata Theory, Languages, and Computation. Pearson Education India, New Delhi (1979)
35. Inoue, H., Somayaji, A.: Lookahead pairs and full sequences: a tale of two anomaly detection methods. In: Proceedings of ASIA, pp. 9–19 (2007)
36. Kosoresow, A., Hofmeyer, S.: Intrusion detection via system call traces. IEEE Softw. **14**(5), 35–42 (1997)

37. Kruegel, C., Mutz, D., Robertson, W., Valeur, F.: Bayesian event classification for intrusion detection. In: Proceedings of ACSAC, pp. 14–23, December 2003
38. Kruegel, C., Kirda, E., Mutz, D., Robertson, W., Vigna, G.: Automating mimicry attacks using static binary analysis. In: Proceedings of USENIX Security, vol. 14, p. 11 (2005)
39. Kuznetsov, V., Szekeres, L., Payer, M., Candea, G., Sekar, R., Song, D.: Code-pointer integrity. In: Proceedings of USENIX OSDI, pp. 147–163 (2014)
40. Lee, W., Stolfo, S.J.: Data mining approaches for intrusion detection. In: Proceedings of USENIX Security, vol. 7, p. 6 (1998)
41. Liao, Y., Vemuri, V.: Use of k-nearest neighbor classifier for intrusion detection. Comput. Secur. 21(5), 439–448 (2002)
42. Liebchen, C., Negro, M., Larsen, P., Davi, L., Sadeghi, A.R., Crane, S., Qunaibit, M., Franz, M., Conti, M.: Losing control: on the effectiveness of control-flow integrity under stack attacks. In: Proceedings of ACM CCS (2015)
43. Liu, Z., Bridges, S.M., Vaughn, R.B.: Combining static analysis and dynamic learning to build accurate intrusion detection models. In: Proceedings of IWIA, pp. 164–177, March 2005
44. Maggi, F., Matteucci, M., Zanero, S.: Detecting intrusions through system call sequence and argument analysis. IEEE TDSC 7(4), 381–395 (2010)
45. Marceau, C.: Characterizing the behavior of a program using multiple-length n-grams. In: Proceedings of NSPW, pp. 101–110 (2000)
46. Mutz, D., Valeur, F., Vigna, G., Kruegel, C.: Anomalous system call detection. ACM TISSEC 9(1), 61–93 (2006)
47. Niu, B., Tan, G.: Modular control-flow integrity. SIGPLAN Not. 49(6), 577–587 (2014)
48. Papadimitriou, C.H.: Computational Complexity. John Wiley and Sons Ltd., New York (2003)
49. Pullum, G.K.: Context-freeness and the computer processing of human languages. In: Proceedings of ACL, Stroudsburg, PA, USA, pp. 1–6 (1983)
50. Sekar, R., Bendre, M., Dhurjati, D., Bollineni, P.: A fast automaton-based method for detecting anomalous program behaviors. In: Proceedings of IEEE Security and Privacy, pp. 144–155 (2001)
51. Shacham, H.: The geometry of innocent flesh on the bone: Return-into-libc without function calls (on the x86). In: Proceedings of ACM CCS, pp. 552–561 (2007)
52. Sharif, M., Singh, K., Giffin, J.T., Lee, W.: Understanding precision in host based intrusion detection. In: Kruegel, C., Lippmann, R., Clark, A. (eds.) RAID 2007. LNCS, vol. 4637, pp. 21–41. Springer, Heidelberg (2007)
53. Shieber, S.M.: Evidence against the context-freeness of natural language. In: Kulas, J., Fetzer, J.H., Rankin, T.L. (eds.) The Formal Complexity of Natural Language, vol. 33, pp. 320–334. Springer, Heidelberg (1987)
54. Shu, X., Yao, D., Ramakrishnan, N.: Unearthing stealthy program attacks buried in extremely long execution paths. In: Proceedings of ACM CCS (2015)
55. Sufatrio, Yap, R.: Improving host-based IDS with argument abstraction to prevent mimicry attacks. In: Proceedings of RAID, pp. 146–164 (2006)
56. Szekeres, L., Payer, M., Wei, T., Song, D.: SoK: eternal war in memory. In: Proceedings of IEEE Security and Privacy, pp. 48–62 (2013)
57. Tandon, G., Chan, P.K.: On the learning of system call attributes for host-based anomaly detection. IJAIT 15(6), 875–892 (2006)
58. Vendicator: StackShield. http://www.angelfire.com/sk/stackshield/. Accessed August 2015

59. Wagner, D., Dean, D.: Intrusion detection via static analysis. In: Proceedings of IEEE Security and Privacy, pp. 156–168 (2001)
60. Wagner, D., Soto, P.: Mimicry attacks on host-based intrusion detection systems. In: Proceedings of ACM CCS, pp. 255–264 (2002)
61. Warrender, C., Forrest, S., Pearlmutter, B.: Detecting intrusions using system calls: alternative data models. In: Proceedings of IEEE S&P, pp. 133–145 (1999)
62. Wee, K., Moon, B.: Automatic generation of finite state automata for detecting intrusions using system call sequences. In: Proceedings of MMM-ACNS (2003)
63. Wespi, A., Dacier, M., Debar, H.: Intrusion detection using variable-length audit trail patterns. In: Debar, H., Mé, L., Wu, S.F. (eds.) RAID 2000. LNCS, vol. 1907, pp. 110–129. Springer, Heidelberg (2000)
64. Xu, K., Yao, D., Ryder, B.G., Tian, K.: Probabilistic program modeling for high-precision anomaly classification. In: Proceedings of IEEE CSF (2015)

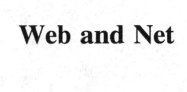

Web and Net

jÄk: Using Dynamic Analysis to Crawl and Test Modern Web Applications

Giancarlo Pellegrino[1]([⊠]), Constantin Tschürtz[2], Eric Bodden[2], and Christian Rossow[1]

[1] Center for IT-Security, Privacy, and Accountability (CISPA), Saarland University, Saarbrücken, Germany
{gpellegrino,crossow}@cispa.saarland
[2] Secure Software Engineering Group, Technische Universität Darmstadt, Darmstadt, Germany
constantin.tschuertz@gmail.com, eric.bodden@sit.fraunhofer.de

Abstract. Web application scanners are popular tools to perform black box testing and are widely used to discover bugs in websites. For them to work effectively, they either rely on a set of URLs that they can test, or use their own implementation of a *crawler* that discovers new parts of a web application. Traditional crawlers would extract new URLs by parsing HTML documents and applying static regular expressions. While this approach can extract URLs in classic web applications, it fails to explore large parts of modern JavaScript-based applications.

In this paper, we present a novel technique to explore web applications based on the dynamic analysis of the client-side JavaScript program. We use dynamic analysis to hook JavaScript APIs, which enables us to detect the registration of events, the use of network communication APIs, and dynamically-generated URLs or user forms. We then propose to use a navigation graph to perform further crawling. Based on this new crawling technique, we present jÄk, a web application scanner. We compare jÄk against four existing web-application scanners on 13 web applications. The experiments show that our approach can explore a surface of the web applications that is 86 % larger than with existing approaches.

1 Introduction

Web application scanners are black box security testing tools that are widely used to detect software vulnerabilities in web applications. As a very essential component, the scanners have to explore all parts of the web application under test. Missing functionality during this exploration step results in parts of the web application remaining untested—leading to potential misses of critical vulnerabilities. To addres this problems, scanners typically expand their initial set of seed URLs. That is, they *crawl* a web application to extract as many different URLs as possible. URLs are then used to send crafted inputs to the web application to detect vulnerabilities. Nowadays, crawlers find new URLs by pattern matching on the HTML content of web sites, e.g., using regular expressions. While this approach can extract URLs in classic web applications, it fails to explore large parts of modern web applications.

© Springer International Publishing Switzerland 2015
H. Bos et al. (Eds.): RAID 2015, LNCS 9404, pp. 295–316, 2015.
DOI: 10.1007/978-3-319-26362-5_14

The advent of JavaScript and client-side communication APIs has increased the complexity of the client-side of web applications. While in the past the client side was merely a collection of static HTML resources, in modern web applications the client side is a full-fledged program written in JavaScript running in a web browser. In these programs, URLs and forms are no longer only static objects, but they may also be the result of client-side computations. For example, JavaScript functions can be used to generate user login forms, to encode user inputs using non-standard HTML form encoding (e.g., JSON), and to include form input values at runtime. Prior work has shown that many URLs in modern web applications are generated dynamically by JavaScript code [1]. As web scanners tend to perform checks on the HTML code, they will fail to cover large parts of web applications. As a result, this leaves a significant fraction of the attack surface of a web application unknown to the underlying vulnerability testing methodology, resulting in incomplete tests.

However, crawling modern web applications is challenging. The difficulties mainly originate from new features introduced by JavaScript. JavaScript programs use an event-driven paradigm, in which program functions are executed upon events. To trigger the execution of these functions, and thus the generation of URLs, a web crawler needs to interact with the JavaScript program. Recently, Mesbah et al. have proposed to combine web-application crawling with dynamic program analysis to infer the state changes of the user interface [2]. However, this approach relies on a number of heuristics which do not cover all the interaction points of the client side. As a result, the largest part of the web application remains unexplored, which ultimately limits the capability to detect vulnerabilities.

In this paper, we address the shortcomings in terms of poor code coverage of existing crawling techniques. We propose a novel approach that combines classic web application crawling and dynamic program analysis. To this end, we dynamically analyze the web applications by hooking JavaScript API function and performing runtime DOM analysis. Using a prototype implementation called jÄk, we show that our methodology outperforms existing web application scanners, especially when it comes to JavaScript-based web applications. Whereas existing tools find only up to 44 % of the URLs, we show that jÄk doubles the coverage of the WIVET web application [3]. We also tested jÄk against 13 popular web applications, showing that in eleven cases it has the highest coverage as compared to existing tools. In summary, we make the following contributions:

- We present a novel dynamic program analysis technique based on JavaScript API function hooking and runtime DOM analysis;
- We propose a model-based web-application crawling technique which can infer a navigation graph by interacting with the JavaScript program;
- We implement these ideas in jÄk, a new open-source web application scanner. We compare jÄk against four existing scanners and show their limitations when crawling JavaScript client-side programs;
- We assess jÄk and existing tools on 13 case studies. Our results show that jÄk improves the coverage of web application by about 86 %.

2 Background

Before turning to our technique, we will briefly describe two JavaScript concepts that are often used in modern web applications. These two, events and modern communication APIs, severely increase the complexity of scans.

2.1 Event Handling Registration

Client-side JavaScript programs use an event-driven programming paradigm in which (i) browsers generate events when something interesting happens and (ii) the JavaScript program registers functions to handle these events. JavaScript supports different event categories: device input events (e.g., mouse move), user interface events (e.g., focus events), state change events (e.g., onPageLoad), API-specific events (e.g., Ajax response received), and timing events (e.g., timeouts). Event handlers can be registered via (i) event handler attributes, (ii) event handler property, (iii) the addEventListener function, or (iv) timing events:

Event Handler Attribute — The registration of an event handler can be done directly in the HTML code of the web application. For example, when the user clicks on the HTML link, the browser executes the code in the attribute onclick:

```
1 | <a href="contact.php" onclick="doSomething"></a>
```

Event Handler Property — Similarly, event handlers can be registered by setting the property of an HTML element. Below is an equivalent example of the previous one. The code first defines a JavaScript function called handler. Then, it searches for the HTML element with the identifier link. Then, it sets the property onclick with the function handler. After that, whenever the user clicks on the link to contact.php, the browser executes the handler function.

```
1 | <a id="link" href="contact.php"></a>
2 |
3 | <script type="text/javascript">
4 |   function handler() { /* do something */ }
5 |   var link = document.getElementsById("link");
6 |   link.onclick = handler;
7 | </script>
```

addEventListener Function — Third, programmers can use addEvent Listener to register events, as shown below. Again, this code searches the HTML element with ID link. Then, it calls addEventListener() with two parameters. The first parameter is the name of the event, in our case the string "click" (for the user click event). The second parameter is the name of the function, i.e., handler.

```
1 | <a id="link" href="contact.php"></a>
2 |
3 | <script type="text/javascript">
4 |   function handler() { /* do something */ }
5 |   var link = document.getElementsById("link");
6 |   link.addEventListener("click", handler);
7 | </script>
```

Timing Events — Finally, timing events are fired only once after a specified amount of time, i.e., timeout event, or at regular time intervals, i.e., interval event. The handler registration for these events is performed via the `setTimeout` and the `setInterval` functions, respectively.

Modern web applications rely heavily on these events to trigger new behavior. Web application scanners thus have to support event-based code.

2.2   Network Communication APIs

The communication between the web browser and the server side has shifted from synchronous and message-based, to asynchronous and stream-oriented. Understanding and supporting modern network communication APIs is thus essential for web application scanners. For example, consider Listing 1.1, which shows the use of the XMLHttpRequest (XHR) API, in which the JavaScript program sends an asynchronous HTTP POST request to the server side.

Listing 1.1. XMLHttpRequest API Example

```
1  var server = "http://foo.com/";
2  var token = "D3EA0F8FA2"
3  var xhr = new XMLHttpRequest();
4  xhr.open("POST", server);
5  xhr.addEventListener("load", function() {
6      // process HTTP response
7  });
8  xhr.send("token=" + token);
```

The JavaScript program first initializes two variables: a URL that identifies the endpoint to which the HTTP request is sent, and a `token` that can be an anti-CSRF token or an API key to allow the client-side JavaScript program to access third-party web service. Then, the JavaScript program instantiates an XMLHttpRequest object for an HTTP POST request and registers a handler to process the server response. Finally, it sets the POST body as `token=D3EA0F8FA2`, and sends the HTTP request to the server.

Classic crawlers statically analyze the HTML and JavaScript code to extract URLs. This makes it hard for them to extract the correct endpoint. Furthermore, classic crawlers cannot extract the structure of the HTTP POST request. We find that four popular crawlers (w3af, skipfish, wget, and crawljax) cannot extract the POST request structure of this example. Two of these crawlers, w3af and skipfish, use regular expressions to extract strings that look like URLs, as a result they may find out URLs when stored in variables such as `server`, however, they will miss the POST parameter `key`. Worse, if the URL would have been generated dynamically, e.g., "`server="http://"+domain+"/";`", then w3af and skipfish could not detect even the first part. Finally, the two other crawlers, wget and crawljax, even fail to detect URLs stored in JavaScript variables. Many parts of modern web applications can only be reached by interpreting such dynamically generated requests, thus limiting the coverage of existing crawlers (cf. Sect. 5).

3   Crawling Modern Web Applications

As explained in the previous section, modern web applications can use JavaScript events to dynamically react to events, and to update the internal and visual state of the web application in response. Figure 1 gives a graphical representation of the page flow of an example toy web application. Initially, the user loads the URL http://foo.com/, which loads the web application's landing page into the browser. This page is then loaded into its initial state and displayed to the user. The user can then interact with the page, for instance submit HTML forms or click HTML links, which will invoke further pages such as http://foo.com/bar/, shown to the right. User events or spontaneous events such as timers can also, however, change the page's internal and visual state, as denoted by the dotted arrows. Those internal states can inflict significant changes to the page's DOM, which is why they should be considered by crawlers as well. Most current crawlers, however, will focus on HTML only, which restricts them virtually to discovering only those HTML page's initial states.

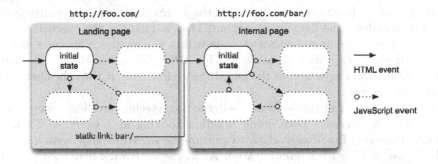

Fig. 1. State changes and page flow induced by clicks and events

We propose a new concept based on dynamic analysis for crawling web applications that overcomes the limitations of existing crawlers. The overall idea is to combine classic web application crawling with program analysis of the client-side of a web application. The crawler starts from a seed URL, e.g., the landing page, and it retrieves the resources of the client-side program, e.g., an HTML page or JavaScript program. Then, it runs the client-side program in a modified JavaScript execution environment to analyze its behavior. From the analysis, the crawler can extract events and URLs which are later used to explore both the client-side program and the server side. Finally, the crawler repeats the analysis until when no more new behaviors can be discovered. Section 3.1 presents our dynamic JavaScript program analyses. Section 3.2 presents the logic to expand the search via crawling.

3.1   Dynamic JavaScript Program Analysis

We deploy dynamic program analysis to monitor the behavior of the JavaScript program and extract events, dynamically-generated URLs and forms, and endpoints for the communication with the server side.

Dynamic analysis of client-side JavaScript programs can be performed in different ways. One approach is to modify the JavaScript interpreter to inspect and monitor the execution of the program. In this setting, whenever an instruction of interest executes, the interpreter executes a hook function instead of or in addition to the original instruction. However, this approach requires one to modify a JavaScript engine, most of which are notoriously complex pieces of software. Furthermore, this approach will bind the technique to a specific engine. Another way to perform dynamic analysis is to insert calls to own JavaScript functions within the source code of the client-side JavaScript program. This approach requires one to process and transform the source code of the program. Unfortunately, the source code of JavaScript programs may not be available as a whole as it may be streamed to the client side at run-time and one piece at a time.

jÄk follows a third option, namely monitoring the execution of the program by hooking functions to APIs inside the JavaScript execution environment. jÄk first initializes the JavaScript engine. Then it modifies the execution environment by running own JavaScript code within the engine. This code installs function hooks to capture calls to JavaScript API functions and object methods, and schedules the inspection of the DOM tree. After that, it runs the client-side JavaScript program.

In the remainder of this section, we detail these techniques. First, we present the basic techniques for performing function hooking in JavaScript. Then we describe the use of function hooking to capture the registration of event handlers and the use of network communication APIs, respectively. Finally we describe how dynamic traces are collected.

Function Hooking. Function hooking is a family of techniques that allows one to intercept function calls to inspect the parameters or alter the behavior of the program. In this section, we present two features of JavaScript that we use to hook functions: *function redefinition* and *set functions*.

Function redefinition is a technique for overwriting JavaScript functions and object methods. Consider the example in Listing 1.2, which shows the use of function redefinition that logs any call to the function `alert`. This is achieved first by associating a new name to the function `alert` (Line 2), and then by redefining the `alert` function (Line 3). The redefinition still behaves as the original `alert`, however, it adds (i.e., hooks) a call to log its use.

While function redefinition can be used to hook arbitrary functions to function calls, it cannot be used when functions are set as an object property, i.e., `obj.prop=function(){[...]}`. To hook functions in these cases, we use so-called *set functions*, which are bound to object properties that are called whenever the property is changed. For example, one can hook the function `myHook` to the property `propr` of the object `obj` as follows:

Listing 1.2. Function hooking via function redefinition

```
1  alert("Hello world!"); // show a popup window
2  var orig_alert = alert;
3  function alert(s) {
4    console.log("call to alert" + s); // hook
5    return orig_alert(s);
6  }
7  alert("Hello world!"); // message is also shown in the console
```

```
Object.defineProperty(obj,"prop",{set:myHook}).
```

Event Handlers Registration. We now show the use of function hooking to capture the registration of event handlers in three of the four registration models: addEventListener function, event handler property, and timing events. For the fourth registration model, i.e., event handler attribute, we do not use function hooking. As in this model handlers are registered as HTML attribute, we captured them by visiting the HTML DOM tree.

Hooking addEventListener — To capture the registration of a new handler, jÄk injects its own function whenever the addEventListener function is called. Listing 1.3 shows an example for the hooking code. The function installHook installs a hook function hook before the execution of a function f of object obj. installHook first preserves a reference to the original function (Line 2). Then, jÄk replaces the original function with its own anonymous function (Line 3 to Line 6). The anonymous function first calls the hook (Line 4) and then the original function (Line 5). Here, the parameters of hook are this and arguments. Both parameters are JavaScript keywords. The first one is a reference to the object instance whereas the latter is a list containing the parameters that will be passed to the function f. Finally, jÄk can use the installHook function to install its hook handler myHook for every call to the function addEventListener of *any* HTML tag element, as shown below:

```
1  installHook(Element.prototype, "addEventListener", myHook)
```

Here Element.prototype is a special object that defines the basic behaviors of all DOM nodes.

Hooking Event Handler Properties — To capture the registration of event handlers via event properties, one can install a hook function as a set function in the

Listing 1.3. Function Hooking for the addEventListener function

```
1  function installHook(obj, f, hook) {
2    var orig = obj[f];
3    obj[f] = function() {
4      hook(this, arguments);
5      return orig.apply(this, arguments);
6    }
7  }
```

DOM elements. However, this approach requires further care. First, the registration of a set function may be overwritten by other set functions installed by the JavaScript program. As opposed to function redefinition, set functions do not guarantee that the hook will remain for the entire duration of the analysis. This can be solved by first redefining the `defineProperty` function and then monitoring its use. Then, if the hook detects a set-function registration, it will create a new set function which chains jÄk's set function with the one provided by the program. Second, we observed that the registration of set functions for event properties may prevent the JavaScript engine from firing events. This can interfere with the operations of a JavaScript program, e.g., it can break the execution of self-submitting forms[1]. While jÄk's set function will still detect event handler registrations, after the discovery, the JavaScript engine needs to be reinitialized.

Finally, as opposed to function redefinitions, this technique may not work in every JavaScript engine. To install set functions, the JavaScript engine needs to mark the property as *configurable*. Unfortunately, this is an engine-dependent feature. For example, the JavaScript engines of Google and Mozilla, i.e., V8 and SpiderMonkey, support this feature whereas the JavaScript engine of Apple does not allow it. When function hooking on event properties is not allowed, one can instead inspect the DOM tree to detect changes in the event properties.

Hooking Timing Event Handlers — To capture the registration of timing event handlers, it is possible to reuse the `installHook` function of Listing 1.3 as follows:

```
1   installHook(window, "setTimeout", myHook)
2   installHook(window, "setInterval", myHook)
```

where `myHook` is the hook function.

Network Communication APIs. Next, we describe the use of function hooking to dynamically inspect the use of networking communication APIs. We will illustrate an example hooking the XMLHttpRequest API, but the general approach can easily be extended to further communication APIs.

As shown in Sect. 2.2, the XHR API is used in three steps. First, an XHR object is instantiated. Then, the HTTP request method and the URL of the server side is passed to the XHR object via the `open` function. Finally, the HTTP request is sent with the function `send`. jÄk can use `installHook` to inject its hook handler `myHook` for both `open` and `send` as follows:

```
1   installHook(XMLHttpRequest, "open", myHook);
2   installHook(XMLHttpRequest, "send", myHook);
```

Other network communication APIs may require the URL of the endpoint as a parameter to the constructor. For example, WebSocket accepts the URL only in the constructor function as follows: `var ws = new WebSocket(server)`. In general, when one would like to hook a function in the constructor, Line 5 of `installHook` in Listing 1.3 needs to be modified to return an instance of the object, i.e., `return new orig(arguments[0], ...)`.

---

[1] A self-submitting form is an HTML form that is submitted by firing submit or mouse click events within the JavaScript program.

Run-Time DOM Analysis. The DOM tree is a collection of objects each representing an element of the HTML document. The DOM tree can be visited to inspect its current state. Each visit can be scheduled via JavaScript events or it can be executed on-demand. In this paper, we consider three uses of run-time DOM analysis. First, it is used to extract the registration of handlers as HTML attributes. Second, it is used to identify changes in the tree while firing events. Third, it can be used to discover the registration of event handlers when the JavaScript engine does not allow to hook code as set functions.

Collection of Dynamic Traces. After describing how to install jÄk's hook functions, we now turn to the actual behavior of the these functions. In general, jÄk uses hook functions to collect information from the run-time environment at the point of their invocation. This information is then sent to the crawler, which collects them in an execution trace.

For the event handler registration, the hook function depends on the type of event (see, e.g., Listing 1.4). For example, for DOM events, the hook function collects the name of the event, the position in the DOM tree of the source and sends it to the crawler. Instead, for timing events, the hook can collect the timeout set by the caller. In either case, hook functions send trace entries to the crawler via a JavaScript object `trace`, which is mapped to a queue object in the crawler's memory. This object acts as a bridge between the JavaScript execution environment and the crawler's execution environment.

Listing 1.4. Hook Function for the addEventListener and setTimeout

```
1  function addEventListenerHook(elem, args) {
2      path = getPath(elem);
3      entry = {
4          "evt_type"    : args[0], //1st par of addEventListener
5          "evt_source"  : path
6      };
7      trace.push(entry);
8  }
```

```
1  function timeoutHook(elem, args) {
2      entry = {
3          "evt_type"    : "timeout",
4          "time"        : args[1] //1st par of setTimeout
5      };
6      trace.push(entry);
7  }
```

When collecting trace entries for network communication APIs, one has to address two issues. First, the APIs typically require multiple steps to set up a communication channel and to deliver messages to the server side. For example, the XHR API requires at least three steps (Lines 3–8 in Listing 1.1). These steps are not necessarily atomic. In fact, a program may open a pool of XHR connections, and finally call the **send** function of each object. In this case, a single hook will result in a trace which contains uncorrelated trace events: at the beginning a sequence of "open" events with the URL endpoints, and then a sequence of only "send" events with the body being sent.

For these reasons, jÄk defines a hook for each of the API functions and then uses the API object to store the current state of the API calls. For example, Listing 1.5 shows the hook function for the API functions **open** and **send**. The hook function **xhrOpenHook** creates two new object properties in the object **xhr** for the HTTP request method and the URL, respectively. Then, the function **xhrSendHook** collects the content of the two object properties and the body of the HTTP requests, and the sends them to the crawler. Such hooks are thread-safe, and thus even work correctly when JavaScript programs access the network communication API concurrently (e.g., within Web Workers [4]).

3.2 Crawling

In the previous section, we presented the dynamic analysis technique in isolation. In this section, we will integrate the dynamic analysis into our web crawler jÄk. The crawler is model-based, i.e., it creates and maintains a model of the web application which is used at each step to decide the next part to explore. First, we describe how we create the model. Then, we discuss the selection criteria for the next action, and finally the termination conditions.

Navigation Graph. jÄk creates and maintains a navigation graph of the web application which models both the transitions within a client-side program and the transitions between web pages. The model is a directed graph similar to the one shown in Fig. 1, in which nodes are clusters of pages and edges can be events and URLs. Each page p is modeled as a tuple of three elements $p = \langle u, E, L, F \rangle$ where u the web page URL, E is the JavaScript events, L a set of URLs (e.g., linked URLs, server-side endpoints), and F a set of HTML forms. jÄk normalizes all URLs by striping out query string values and sorting the query string parameter lexicographically. Two pages p' and p'' are in the same cluster if (i) u' and u'' are identical and (ii) the two pages are *sufficiently similar*. The similarity is calculated as a proportion between the number of common events, URLs and forms over the total number of events, URLs and forms. Precisely, the similarity is defined as follow:

Listing 1.5. Hook Functions for XHR API

```
1   function xhrOpenHook(xhr, args) {
2     xhr.method = args[0]; //1st par of HTMLHttpRequest.open, i.e., HTTP
          method
3     xhr.url = args[1];     //2nd par, i.e., the URL
4   }
5   function xhrSendHook(xhr, args) {
6     entry = {
7       "evt_type"   : "xhr",
8       "url"        : xhr.url,
9       "method"     : xhr.method,
10      "body"       : args[0] //1st par of XMLHttpRequest.send
11    };
12    trace.push(entry);
13  }
```

$$s(p', p'') = \frac{|E' \cap E''| + |L' \cap L''| + |F' \cap F''|}{|E' \cup E''| + |L' \cup L''| + |F' \cup F''|}$$

Through experimental analysis we determined that a similarity threshold of 0.8 generates the best results for our setting.

Navigating. The dynamic analysis of the JavaScript program generates a runtime trace containing event handler registrations and dynamically-generated URLs. It also includes the result of the DOM-tree analysis such as linked URLs and forms. This information is then sorted into two lists, a list of events and a list of URLs. These lists represent the *frontier of actions* that the crawler can take to further explore the web application.

Each type of action may have a different result. On the one hand, the request of a new URL certainly causes to retrieve a new page and, if the page contains a JavaScript program, then it is executed in a new JavaScript environment. This is not necessarily the case of events. Firing an event may allow the crawler to explore more behaviors of the JavaScript program, i.e., to generate new URLs. However, events may also cause to run a new JavaScript program, for instance by setting `window.location` to a new URL. However, we can block this behavior via function hooking. For these reasons, our crawler gives a higher priority to events with respect to the URLs. When no more events are left in the list, then we process the list of URLs. When all the lists are empty, then the crawler exits.

Visiting the Client-side Program — Events such as click, focus, double click, and mouse movements can be fired within the JavaScript execution environment. To fire an event e, jÄk first identifies the DOM element and then fires the event via the DOM Event Interface [5] function `dispatchEvent`. After that, jÄk observes the result of the execution of the handler via the dynamic analysis. The event handler can cause a refresh of the page, a new page to be loaded, a message to be sent to the server side. To avoid any interference with the server side, when firing events, the hook functions, e.g., for network communication API, will block the delivery of the message.

After having fired an event, jÄk can distinguish the following cases. If the event handler results into a network communication API, then jÄk takes the URL from the trace, and enqueues it in the list of URLs. Similarly, if the event handler sets a new URL (i.e., `window.location=`URL), then jÄk enqueues the URL into the linked-URLs list. If the event handler adds new linked URL and forms, then they are inserted into the appropriate list. Finally, if the event handler registers new events, then jÄk prepares the special event which comprises the sequence of events that lead to this point, e.g., $\hat{e} = \langle e, e' \rangle$ where e is the last fired event and e' is the newly discovered event. Then, $\hat{e}$ is added to the list of events. When the crawler schedules this event to be fired, it fires the events in the given order, i.e., first e and then e'.

Requesting New Pages — The crawler should aim to find pages that contain new content rather than pages with known content. To select the next page, jÄk assigns a priority to each of the URLs in the frontier based on two factors: (i) how many times jÄk has seen a similar URL in the past, and (ii) how scattered over the clusters past URLs are. The priority is thus calculated as the number of similar past URLs over the number of clusters in which the past URLs have been inserted in. If a URL in the frontier was never seen in the past, i.e., the priority is 0, then we force its priority to 2. The crawler processes URLs from the highest to the lower priority.

Termination. Without any further control on the behavior of the crawler, the crawler may enter a loop and never terminate its execution. jÄk thus uses two techniques to terminate its execution. First, it has a hard limit for the search depth. Second, the crawler terminates if it cannot find new content anymore. We describe the termination criteria in the following.

Hard Limits — Crawlers can enter loops in two situations. First, loops can happen across the different web pages of a web applications. This can be caused when crawling infinite web applications such as calendars or, for example, when two pages link to each other. The crawler may visit the first page, then schedule a visit to the second, which again points to the first page. These problems can be solved with a limit on the maximum search depth of the crawler. When the crawler reaches a limit on the number of URLs, it terminates the execution. Second, loops may also occur within single web pages. For example, the handler of an event can insert a new HTML element into the DOM tree and register the same handler to the new element. Similarly as seen for URLs, one can limit the maximum depth of events that can be explored within a web page. When the limit is reached, the crawler will no longer fire events on the same page.

Convergence-based Termination — In addition to these limits, the crawler terminates when the discovered pages do not bring any new content. The notion of *new* content is defined in terms of number of similar pages that the crawler visited in the past. To achieve this, the crawler uses the navigation graph and a limit on the number of pages per cluster. If the cluster has reached this limit, the crawler marks the cluster as *full* and any subsequent page is discarded.

4   Implementation of jÄk

This section presents our actual implementation of jÄk, our web-application scanner which implements the crawler and the program analysis presented in Sect. 3. jÄk is written in Python [6] and based on WebKit browser engine [7] via the Qt Application Framework bindings [8]. We released jÄk at https://github.com/ConstantinT/jAEk/.

jÄk comprises four modules: *dynamic analysis* module, *crawler* module, *attacker* module, and *analysis* module. The *dynamic analysis* module implements the techniques presented in Sect. 3.1. jÄk relies on the default JavaScript engine of WebKit, i.e., the JavaScriptCore, to perform the dynamic analysis. Unfortunately, JavaScriptCore sets the event properties as not configurable. As a result, JavaScriptCore does not allow to use function hooking via set functions. To solve this, jÄk handles these cases via DOM inspection. However, we verified that the JavaScript engines of Google and Mozilla, i.e., V8 [9] and SpiderMonkey [10], allow one to hook set functions. In the future, we plan to replace the JavaScriptCore engine with V8.

The *crawler* module implements the crawling logic of Sect. 3.2. Starting from a seed URL, jÄk retrieves the client-side program and passes it to the dynamic analysis module. The dynamic analysis module returns traces which are used to populate the frontiers of URLs and events. Then, jÄk selects the next action and provides it to the dynamic analysis module. Throughout this process, jÄk creates and maintains the navigation graph of the web application which is used to select the next action. The output of the crawler module is a list of forms and URLs.

Finally, the *attacker* and *analysis* modules test the server side against a number of vulnerabilities. For each URL, the attacker module prepares URLs carrying the attack payload. Then, it passes the URL to the dynamic analysis module to request the URL. The response is then executed within the dynamic analysis module, which returns an execution trace. The analysis module then analyzes the trace to decide if the test succeeded.

5   Evaluation

We evaluate the effectiveness of jÄk in a comparative analysis including four existing web crawlers. Our evaluation consists of two parts. Section 5.1 assesses the capability of the crawlers based on the standard WIVET web application, highlighting the need to integrate dynamic analysis to crawlers. Then, in Sect. 5.2, we evaluate jÄk and the other crawlers against 13 popular web applications.

For our experiments, we selected five web crawlers: Skipfish 3.10b [11], W3af 1.6.46 [12], Wget 1.6.13 [13], State-aware crawler [14], and Crawljax 3.5.1 [2]. We selected Skipfish, W3af, and Wget as they were already used in a comparative analysis against State-aware crawler by prior work (see Doupé et al. [14]). Then, we added Crawljax as it is a crawler closest to our approach.

In our experiment, we used the default configuration of these tools. When needed, we configured them to submit user credentials or session cookies. In addition, we configured the tools to crawl a web application to a maximum depth of four. Among our tools, only W3af does not support bounded crawling[2].

---

[2] W3af implements a mechanism to terminate which is based on the following two conditions. First, W3af does not crawl twice the same URL and then it does not crawl "similar" URLs more than five times. Two URLs are similar if they differ only from the content of URL parameters.

5.1   Assessing the Crawlers' Limitations

First, we use the Web Input Vector Extractor Teaser (WIVET) web application [3] to assess the capabilities of existing crawlers and compare these to jÄk. The WIVET web application is a collection of tests to measure the capability of crawlers to extract URLs from client-side programs. In each test, WIVET places unique URLs in a different part of the client-side program including in the HTML and via JavaScript functions. Then, it waits for the crawler to request the URLs. WIVET tests can be distinguished in static and dynamic tests. A test is static if the unique URL is placed in the HTML document without the use of a client-side script. Otherwise, if the client-side program generates, requests, or uses URLs, then the test is dynamic. WIVET features 11 static tests and 45 dynamic tests. We focus on the dynamic behavior of client-side programs and thus limit the evaluation to running the 45 dynamic tests.

Table 1. Number and fraction of dynamic test passed by the different crawlers

Dynamic test categories	Total	Crawljax	W3af	Wget	Skipfish	jÄk
C1 Adobe Flash event	2	0	2	0	0	0
C2 URL in tag	5	5	5	0	5	4
C3 JS in URL, new loc.	2	2	1	0	1	2
C4 URL in tag, tim. evt.	1	0	1	0	1	1
C5 Form subm., UI evt.	2	2	1	0	1	1
C6 New loc., UI evt.	27	0	6	0	6	26
C7 URL in tag, UI evt.	2	0	2	0	1	2
C8 XHR	4	0	2	0	2	4
Total	45	9	20	0	17	40
In %	100	20	44	0	38	89

As URLs can be placed and used by the JavaScript program in different ways, we manually reviewed WIVET's dynamic tests and grouped them into eight classes. We created these classes by enumerating the technique used by each test. For example, we considered whether a test dynamically places an URL in an HTML tag, if the URL is for Ajax requests, or whether the action is in an event handler. Table 1 shows the eight classes and details the results of each crawler for each class.

As Table 1 shows, all tested crawlers but jÄk fail in more than half of the tests. In average, these tools passed only 25 % of the tests. With the exception of Wget, which failed all the dynamic tests, the success rate ranges from 20 % of Crawljax to 44 % of W3af. jÄk instead passed 89 % of the tests. For the event-based tests (i.e., **C4-7**), W3af, Skipfish and Crawljax succeeded in about 16 % of the tests, whereas for the server communication API tests (i.e., **C8**) they succeeded in 25 % of the tests. By comparison, jÄk achieved 96 % and 100 % of success rate for the classes **C4-7** and **C8**, respectively.

We next discuss the details of these experiments per tool. In total, jÄk passed 40 dynamic tests (89 %). With reference to the classes **C4-7**, jÄk discovered the registration of the events via the hook functions. Then, it fired the events which resulted in the submission of the URL. In only one case, jÄk could not extract the URL which is contained in an unattached JavaScript function. As jÄk uses dynamic analysis, it cannot analyze code that is not executed, and thus it will not discover URLs in unattached functions. Nevertheless, jÄk could easily be extended with pattern-matching rules to capture these URLs. In fact, Skipfish and W3af were the only ones able to discover these URLs. For the class **C8**, jÄk discovered the URL of the endpoint via the hook functions and via DOM tree inspection. In this case, the test requested the URL via the XHR API and inserted it in the DOM tree.

jÄk failed in other four dynamic tests. First, one test of **C2** places a JavaScript statement `javascript:` as action form. jÄk correctly extracts the URLs, however it does not submit to the server side because jÄk does not submit forms during the crawling phase. Other two tests are in the class **C1**. This class contains tests which test the support of ShockWave Flash (SWF) objects. This feature is not currently supported by jÄk. Then, the last test is in **C5**. This test submits user data via a click event handler. jÄk correctly detects the event registration and it fires the event on the container of the input elements. However, the handler expects that the event is fired over the submit button element instead of the container. This causes the handler to access a variable with an unexpected value. As a result, the handler raises an exception and the execution is halted. In a web browser, the execution of the handler would have succeeded as a result of the propagation of the click event from the button to the outer element, i.e., the container[3]. The current version of jÄk does not support the propagation of events, instead it fires an event on the element where the handler has been detected, in this case the container.

Crawljax succeeded only in 9 out 45 tests (20 %). Most of the failed tests store URLs either in the location property of the window object (i.e., classes **C4** and **C6**), or as URL of a linked resource (i.e., class **C7**). The URL is created and inserted in the DOM tree upon firing an event. While Crawljax can fire events, it supports only a limited set of target HTML tags to fire events, i.e., buttons and links. Finally, Crawljax failed in all of the dynamic tests involving Ajax requests (See **C8**).

Skipfish and W3af performed better than Crawljax, passing 38 % and 44 % of the dynamic tests, respectively. These tools extract URLs via HTML document parsing and pattern matching via regular expression. When a URL cannot be extracted from the HTML document, the tools use pattern recognition via regular expressions. This technique may work well when URLs maintain distinguishable characteristics such as the URL scheme, e.g., `http://`, or the URL path separator, i.e., the character "/". However, this approach is not sufficiently generic and cannot extract URLs that are composed dynamically via string concatenation. This is the case for the class **C6** Table 1 in which W3af and Skipfish passed only six tests out of 27. In these six tests, the URL is placed

---

[3] This model is the event *bubbling* and is the default model. Another model is the event *capturing* in which the event are propagated from the outermost to the innermost.

in a JavaScript variable and it maintains the URL path separator. With the use of regular expressions, W3af and Skipfish recognized the string as URL and submitted the server side thus passing the tests. However, in the remaining 21, URLs are created as the concatenation string variables and a JavaScript arrays. While regular expressions may be extended to include these specific cases, they will likely never be as complete as dynamic analysis.

5.2   Assessment Using Web Applications

Finally, we compare jÄk to the other crawlers by crawling popular web applications.

Table 2. Number of unique event-handler registrations extracted by jÄk, grouped by event category

Web Apps.	DDI	DII	UI	Chg	API	Errs.	Cust.	Total
WP	34	220	156	14	0	0	0	424
Gallery	930	7	1,257	23	0	0	303	2,520
phpBB	636	8	729	0	0	0	0	1,373
Joomla	46	144	232	26	0	0	0	448
Tidios w/ WP	14,041	26	3,715	192	111	12	641	18,738
Nibbleblog	12	42	0	7	0	0	0	61
Owncloud 8	826	905	274	53	44	0	134	2,236
Owncloud 4	126	651	234	68	10	0	36	1,125
Piwigo	1,609	1,323	281	44	0	0	40	3,297
Mediawiki	13,538	24,837	18,102	2,174	791	0	5,204	64,646
ModX	6,772	14,626	4,483	19	0	0	0	25,900
MyBB 1.8.1	947	6,034	532	1,502	27	2	442	9,486
MyBB 1.8.4	891	5,339	725	150	28	2	607	7,742

We first evaluated how well the crawlers cover a web application. A measure for the coverage is the code coverage, i.e., the number of lines of code that have been exercised by the testing tool. While this measure is adequate for code-based testing tools, it may not be for web application crawlers. As web crawlers operate in a black-box setting, it has a limited visibility of the web application. In addition, web crawlers do not fuzz input fields, but they rather use a user-provided list of inputs. As a result, it may not exercise all the branches, thus, leaving unvisited significant portion of the web application. An alternative measure can be the number of URLs a crawler can extract.

A web crawler is a component which provides a web scanner with the URLs to be tested. As the goal of a web scanner is the detection of web vulnerabilities, the second aspect to evaluate is the detection power. The detection power can be measured in terms of the number of reported vulnerabilities. Unfortunately, such a metric may not be fair. Prior research has shown that this type of evaluation is not an easy task. Web scanners do not support the same classes of vulnerabilities and they may differentiate the target vulnerabilities. In result, the number of discovered vulnerabilities cannot be comparable among the different crawlers. For this reason, in this paper we limited our comparison to a specific class of vulnerabilities, i.e., reflected XSS. Second, the number of reported vulnerabilities may contain false positives. A false positive happens when the scanner reports the existence of a vulnerability but the vulnerability does not acutally exist. The number of false positives also measures the accuracy of the web scanner and indicates whether a scanner adequately verifies if the observed behavior qualifies as a vulnerability.

Case Studies. We performed our assessment using 13 popular web applications. These applications include three content management systems (i.e., Joomla 3.4.1, Modx-CMS 2.02.14, and Nibbleblog 4.0.1), a blogging tool with plugins (i.e., WordPress 3.7 and 4.0.1, and Tidio 1.1), discussion forum software (i.e., MyBB 1.8.01 and 1.8.04, and phpNN 3.0.12), photo gallery applications (i.e., Gallery 2.7.1 and Piwigo 2.7.1), cloud storage applications (i.e., OwnCloud 4.0.1 and 8.0.3), and wiki web application (i.e., MediaWiki 1.24.2). Among these, the following five web application are already known to be vulnerable to reflected XSS: Modx-CMS, MyBB 1.8.01, phpBB, Piwigo, and OwnCloud 4. These web applications vary in size, complexity, and functionality. We set up these web applications on our own servers. Each web application was installed in a virtual machine. We reset the state of the virtual machines upon each test.

Results. We divide the evaluation results into two parts. First, we investigate the diversity of events that jÄk has found and measure the coverage of the crawlers. Second, we assess how well jÄk performs in detecting XSS vulnerabilities as compared to other scanners.

Coverage — Table 2 shows the number of unique event-handler registrations extracted by jÄk. The number of events are shown for each web application, grouped by event category, i.e., device-dependent input events (DDI), device-independent input events (DII), Change events (Chg), API events, Error events, and custom errors. These events are extracted via the dynamic analysis of the client-side JavaScript program of the case studies.

Table 2 shows that web applications can rely on JavaScript events in a moderate way, i.e., Nibbleblog, or more heavily, i.e., Mediawiki. Most of the registered event handlers are of the device input and UI categories. Just these events amount to 68 % of all events, whereas UI events amount to 22 %.

Next we show asses whether jÄk outperforms existing crawlers in terms of coverage. To this end, we measure the number of unique URL structures each crawler found. The URL structure is a URL without the query string values. Table 3 shows the results, excluding all URLs for static and external resources. Numbers in bold mark the tool that extracted the highest number of URL structures. The symbol * indicates that the results of W3af and Skipfish do not take into account invalid URLs that have been found via URL forgery (as explained

Table 3. Coverage of the web applications in terms of unique URL structures, excluding linked and static resources, e.g., CSS documents, external JS files, and images. The symbol * indicates the numbers which do not count URL forgery by W3af and Skipfish.

Web Apps.	jÄk	Crawljax	W3af	Wget	Skipfish
WP	21	15	17*	34	17*
Gallery	180	7	35	33	24
phpBB	50	11	44	27	27
Joomla	4	5	7*	3	5*
Tidios w/ WP	166	21	251*	218	35*
NibbleBlog	7	6	7*	5	7*
OwnCloud 8	98	2	54*	44	14*
OwnCloud 4	80	–	58	10	61
Piwigo	277	15	58	13	24
Mediawiki	1,258	24	480	265	776*
ModX	57	2	21	41	34*
MyBB 1.8.1	152	22	95	131	126
MyBB 1.8.4	152	12	92	135	128
Total	2502	142	1219	959	1278

later). jÄk extracted the highest number of unique URL structures in 10 applications. In one application, i.e., Nibbleblog, jÄk, W3af, and Skipfish extracted the same number of URL structures. In the remaining two web applications, W3af extracted the highest number of web applications. In the case of Joomla, W3af extracted 3 URL structures more than jÄk, whereas in the case of Tidios, W3af extracted 251 URLs against 166 of jÄk.

To interpret these results qualitatively, we sought to assess to what extent the surfaces explored by each tool relate to the one explored by jÄk. A way to measure this is to analyze the URLs extracted by jÄk and each of the other tools, and to calculate the complement sets. These two sets will contain the following URLs. The first set contains URLs that are extracted by jÄk and missed by each of the other crawlers. The second set contains the URLs that are not discovered by jÄk but are extracted by the other tool. The number of URLs in each of these sets is shown in Table 4. When compared with the other tools, on average, jÄk explored a surface of the web applications which is 86 % larger than the one of the other tools. Then, the amount of surface which jÄk did not explore range from 0.5 % of Crawljax to 22 % of Skipfish.

Table 4. Unique URLs discovered only by jÄk (+) and missed by jÄk (-).

Groups	Crawljax	W3af	Wget	Skipfish
Surf. discovered only by jÄk	+98%	+85%	+70%	+90%
Surf. missed by jÄk	-0.5%	-18%	-20%	-22%

To further understand the potential misses by jÄk, we manually inspected a random sample of 1030 (15 %) of the URLs that are not discovered by jÄk. We were able to identify eight classes of URLs, as shown in Table 5. URL forgery refers to URLs which are not present in the web application but are forged by the crawler. The vast majority of the URLs that jÄk "missed", i.e., 75 % of the URLs, are URLs that were forged by W3af and Skipfish. Forging means that these tools implement a crawling strategy which attempts to visit hidden parts of the web application. Starting from a URL, they systematically submit URLs in which they remove parts of the path. For example, W3af derives from URLs like http://foo.com/p1/p2/p3, other URLs, i.e., http://foo.com/p1/p2, http://foo.com/p1/, and http://foo.com/. It is important to notice that these URLs are not valid URLs of the web application. For this reason, we corrected the results in Table 3 by deducting the percentage of forged URLs. Next, the class static resources include style-sheet documents or external JS files with a different document extension, e.g., .php. This is an error introduced by our URL analysis which failed in recognizing these documents as static. The third class of URLs (5.34 %) is the one of unsupported actions such as form submission during crawling. Then, the fourth class contains URLs that were not extracted because they belong to a user session different from the one used by jÄk. This may be solved by using jÄk in parallel with multiple user credentials. The fifth class contains URLs that are due to bugs both in jÄk and in Skipfish. The sixth class contains URLs that are generated while crawling. We have two types of these URLs: URLs with timestamps and URLs generated by, for example, creating new content in the web application. 1,36 % of the URLs, we could not find the origin of the URL nor the root cause. Finally, 1,26 % of the URLs are of W3af that does not implement a depth-bounded crawling and thus might crawl the applications deeper than other crawlers.

Detection — Finally, we measure how the improved crawling convergence translates into the detection of XSS vulnerabilities in the 13 web applications. For these tests, we had to exclude Wget and Crawljax, as they are pure crawlers and as such cannot discover vulnerabilities.

jÄk discovered XSS vulnerabilities in three of the five web applications, i.e., phpBB, Piwigo, and MyBB 1.8.1. However, jÄk could not find known vulnerabilities in OwnCloud 4 and ModX. Manual analysis revealed that the vulnerability as described in the security note of OwnCloud 4 is not exploitable. For ModX, jÄk could not discover the URL. The URL is added in the DOM tree by an event handler. jÄk correctly fires the events, but the code of the handler is not executed because it verifies that the target is an inner tag. This shortcoming is the same that cause to fail the test in the C5 class of Table 1. In a regular browser, due to the implicit rules for the propagation of events, the user will click on the inner tag and the outer one will be executed. As a future work, we plan to reproduce the event propagation as implement by regular browsers.

The other tools detected only known vulnerabilities in MyBB, and had issues with false positives. Both W3af and Skipfish detected the XSS vulnerability in MyBB 1.8.1. Furthemore, in Mediawiki W3af reported 49 XSS vulnerabilities and Skipfish one vulnerability, respectively. However, in both cases, these were false positives. Finally, Skipfish reported 13 false positives in Gallery. In our experiments, jÄk did not report any false positive. This is the result of using dynamic analysis for the detection of XSS attacks: if an attack is successful, the test payload is executed and visible in the dynamic trace.

Table 5. Origin of the URLs that were not discovered by jÄk

URL Origin	URLs	Fraction
URL Forgery	774	75.15%
Static resources	57	5.53%
Unsupp. action	55	5.34%
User session mgmt.	53	5.15%
Bugs	47	4.56%
New content	17	1.65%
Unknown	14	1.36%
Beyond max depth (W3af)	13	1.26%
Total	**1030**	**100,00%**

6 Related Work

In this section we review works closely related to our paper. We focus on two areas: analysis of existing web application scanners, and novel ideas to improve the current state of the art of scanners.

Bau et al. [15] and Doupé et al. [16] presented two independent and complementary studies on the detection power of web application scanners. Both works concluded that while web scanners are effective in the detection of reflected XSS and SQLi, they still poorly perform in the detection of other classes of more sophisticated vulnerabilities. According to these works, one of the reason of these results is the lack of support of client-side technology. Furthermore, Doupé et al. explored in a limited way the problem of web application coverage focusing on the capability of scanners to perform multi-step operations. As opposed to these works, in this paper we mainly focused on the problem of the coverage of web applications and detailed the shortcomings of four web application scanners.

Recently, there have been new ideas to improve the state of the art of web application scanner. These works included the support of client-side features and explored the use of reasoning techniques together with black-box testing. The most notable of these works are the *state-aware-crawler* by Doupé et al. [14], *Crawljax* by Mesbah et al. [2], *AUTHSCAN* by Guangdong et al. [17], and *SSOScan* by Zhou et al. [18]. State-aware-crawler proposed a model inference algorithm based on page clustering to improve the detection of higher-order XSS and SQLi. However, this technique focus mainly on the detection of state-changing operations and it does not take into account the dynamic features of client-side programs. Similarly, Crawljax proposed a model inference technique based on "user-clickable areas" in order to crawl hidden parts of AJAX-based web applications. However, Crawljax uses static heuristics that do not satisfactorily cover the dynamic interaction points between the user and the UI. As opposed to Crawljax, jÄk does not rely on these heuristics and uses a technique which can detect the registration of event handlers via function hooking. Finally, AUTHSCAN and SSOScan are black-box testing tools that focus on the Web-based Single Sign-On functionalities integrated in web applications. AUTH-SCAN extends the classical design verification via model checking with the automatic extraction of formal specifications from HTTP conversations. SSOScan is a vulnerability scanner that targets only Facebook SSO integration in third-party web applications. Neither of the two tools is a web application scanner, and they do not support crawling web applications. As opposed to jÄk, the focus of these tools is on improving the detection power of security testing tools. Nevertheless, the proposed testing technique may be integrated into jÄk to detect other classes of vulnerabilities.

A work closely related to our approach is Artemis [19]. Artemis is a JavaScript web application testing framework which supports the generation and execution of test cases to increase the client-side code coverage. Starting from an initial input (e.g., event), Artemis explores the state space of the web application by probing the program with new inputs. Inputs are generated and selected by using different strategies in order to maximize, e.g., code branches or number of read/write access of object properties. At each step, Artemis resets the state of the client and server side to a known state and continues the exploration. From the angle of input generation, Artemis and our approach shares common points. For example, both approaches explore the client side by firing events and observing state changes. However, Artemis and our approach differ on the assumption of the availability of the server side. While Artemis assumes complete control of the state space of the server side, our approach does not make this assumption and targets the exploration of a live instance of the server side.

7   Conclusion

This paper presented a novel technique to crawl web applications based on the dynamic analysis of the client-side JavaScript program. The dynamic analysis hooks functions of JavaScript APIs to detect the registration of events, the use of network communication APIs, and find dynamically-generated URLs and user forms. This is then used by a crawler to perform the next action. The crawler creates and builds a navigation graph which is used to chose the next action. We presented a tool jÄk, which implements the presented approach. We assessed jÄk and four other web-application scanners using 13 web applications. Our experimental results show that jÄk can explore a surface of the web applications which is about 86 % larger than the other tools.

Acknowledgements. This work was supported by the German Ministry for Education and Research (BMBF) through funding for the project 13N13250, EC SPRIDE and ZertApps, by the Hessian LOEWE excellence initiative within CASED, and by the DFG within the projects RUNSECURE, TESTIFY and INTERFLOW, a project within the DFG Priority Programme 1496 *Reliably Secure Software Systems* $-RS^3$.

References

1. Zhou, J., Ding, Y.: An analysis of URLs generated from javascript code. In: 2012 IEEE/ACIS 11th International Conference on Computer and Information Science (ICIS), vol. 5, pp. 688–693 (2012)
2. Mesbah, A., van Deursen, A., Lenselink, S.: Crawling ajax-based web applications through dynamic analysis of user interface state changes. ACM Trans. Web **6**(1), 3:1–3:30 (2012)
3. Urgun, B.: Web Input Vector Extractor Teaser (2015). https://github.com/bedirhan/wivet
4. Hickson, I.: A vocabulary and associated APIs for HTML and XHTML (2014). http://dev.w3.org/html5/workers/
5. van Kesteren, A., Gregor, A., Ms2ger, Russell, A., Berjon, R.: W3C DOM4 (2015). http://www.w3.org/TR/dom/
6. The Python Software Foundation: Python (2015). https://www.python.org/
7. Apple Inc.: The WebKit Open Source Project (2015). https://www.webkit.org/
8. Riverbank Computing Limited: PyQt - The GPL Licensed Python Bindings for the Qt Application Framework (2015). http://pyqt.sourceforge.net/
9. Google Inc.: V8 JavaScript Engine (2015). https://code.google.com/p/v8/
10. Mozilla Foundation: SpiderMonkey (2015). https://developer.mozilla.org/en-US/docs/Mozilla/Projects/SpiderMonkey
11. Zalewski, M.: Skipfish (2015). https://code.google.com/p/skipfish/
12. Riancho, A.: w3af: Web Application Attack and Audit Framework (2015). http://w3af.org/
13. Nikšić, H., Scrivano, G.: GNU Wget (2015). http://www.gnu.org/software/wget/
14. Doupé, A., Cavedon, L., Kruegel, C., Vigna, G.: Enemy of the state: a state-aware black-box vulnerability scanner. In: Proceedings of the 2012 USENIX Security Symposium (USENIX 2012), Bellevue, WA (2012)
15. Bau, J., Bursztein, E., Gupta, D., Mitchell, J.: State of the art: automated black-box web application vulnerability testing. In: 2010 IEEE Symposium on Security and Privacy (SP) (2010)
16. Doupé, A., Cova, M., Vigna, G.: Why Johnny can't pentest: an analysis of black-box web vulnerability scanners. In: Kreibich, C., Jahnke, M. (eds.) DIMVA 2010. LNCS, vol. 6201, pp. 111–131. Springer, Heidelberg (2010)
17. Guangdong, B., Guozhu, M., Jike, L., Sai, S.V., Prateek, S., Jun, S., Yang, L., Jinsong, D.: Authscan: Automatic extraction of web authentication protocols from implementations. In: 2013 Annual Network and Distributed System Security Symposium (NDSS). The Internet Society (2013)
18. Zhou, Y., Evans, D.: Ssoscan: automated testing of web applications for single sign-on vulnerabilities. In: 23rd USENIX Security Symposium (USENIX Security 2014), pp. 495–510. USENIX Association, San Diego, CA (2014)
19. Artzi, S., Dolby, J., Jensen, S.H., Møller, A., Tip, F.: A framework for automated testing of javascript web applications. In: Proceedings of the 33rd International Conference on Software Engineering, ICSE 2011, pp. 571–580. ACM, New York, NY, USA (2011). http://doi.acm.org/10.1145/1985793.1985871

WYSISNWIV: What You Scan Is Not What I Visit

Qilang Yang[✉], Dimitrios Damopoulos, and Georgios Portokalidis

Stevens Institute of Technology, Hoboken, NJ, USA
{qyang5,ddamopou,gportoka}@stevens.edu

Abstract. A variety of attacks, including remote-code execution exploits, malware, and phishing, are delivered to users over the web. Users are lured to malicious websites in various ways, including through spam delivered over email and instant messages, and by links injected in search engines and popular benign websites. In response to such attacks, many initiatives, such as Google's Safe Browsing, are trying to make the web a safer place by scanning URLs to automatically detect and blacklist malicious pages. Such blacklists are then used to block dangerous content, take down domains hosting malware, and warn users that have clicked on suspicious links. However, they are only useful, when scanners and browsers address the web the same way. This paper presents a study that exposes differences on how browsers and scanners parse URLs. These differences leave users vulnerable to malicious web content, because the same URL leads the browser to one page, while the scanner follows the URL to scan another page. We experimentally test all major browsers and URL scanners, as well as various applications that parse URLs, and discover multiple discrepancies. In particular, we discover that pairing Firefox with the blacklist produced by Google's Safe Browsing, leaves Firefox users exposed to malicious content hosted under URLs including the backslash character. The problem is a general one and affects various applications and URL scanners. Even though, the solution is technically straightforward, it requires that multiple parties follow the same standard when parsing URLs. Currently, the standard followed by an application, seems to be unconsciously dictated by the URL parser implementation it is using, while most browsers have strayed from the URL RFC.

1 Introduction

The popularity of the web has made it the prime vehicle for delivering malicious content to users, including browser exploits, malware, phishing, and web attacks, like cross-site scripting (XSS) [32] and cross-site request forgery (CSRF) [17] attacks. Such attacks are prevalent; Microsoft alone reported that more than 3.5 million computers visited a website containing a web-based exploit in the first quarter of 2012 [35]. The prominence of such attacks has lead to the development of many approaches [20, 22, 27, 30, 37] that automatically detect pages containing malicious content, leading to free and commercial tools [3–6, 8–13, 26, 36] that

© Springer International Publishing Switzerland 2015
H. Bos et al. (Eds.): RAID 2015, LNCS 9404, pp. 317–338, 2015.
DOI: 10.1007/978-3-319-26362-5_15

can scan URLs and routinely crawl the web to identify and filter, quarantine, warn, or take down malicious sites.

Users can reach malicious content by clicking on URLs, which have been injected by attackers into legitimate sites or the results of search engines and spread through spam sent over email and messages. Services which scan pages for malicious content, i.e., URL scanners, follow the same URLs to fetch content from servers and classify it as malicious or benign. Thus, it is essential that when a scanner follows a URL, it visits the same page that the user would visit through his browser or client application.

This paper presents an experimental study on how browsers and URL scanners parse URLs. Our experiments reveal discrepancies on how URLs are parsed, with browsers and URL scanners frequently following different standards and introducing their own rules. As a result, including a character like the backslash in a URL can lead a browser to one web page, while the scanner visits another. Essentially, attackers can hide their malicious content from the scanner, while users can still access it. This constitutes a new evasion strategy for attackers that want to avoid detection from URL scanners. While it may not always be available to them, as certain scanner-browser pairs will treat URLs the same way, this evasion strategy is powerful because it is not based on obfuscating content, but simply requires the inclusion of a character in their URLs.

Looking at Google Safe Browsing, in particular, we show that it transforms backslashes contained in URLs to forward slashes before it accesses a URL, a behavior which has been also noted by web developers in the past [2,28]. On the other hand, Firefox, which uses its malicious-URL database to warn users that are about to accessing malicious sites, does not. Instead, it encodes the backslash character using percent-encoding (aka URL-encoding). As such, an attacker targeting Firefox browsers could essentially hide his exploit from initiatives like Google's Safe Browsing. We have disclosed the issue to both Google and Firefox, who are working on a solution.

The problem is a general one, as every URL scanner tested has exhibited a behavior that creates opportunities for attackers. Technically, the solution to the problem is not a hard one, however, it requires coordination and agreement among the involved parties (i.e., browser and URL scanner developers). Unfortunately, it is also exacerbated by the fact that various applications parse text and automatically create links, when they identify URL patterns. We conducted tests with various applications and libraries, and we discovered that there also discrepancies on what they consider as acceptable URL patterns, leading to another instance of the same problem.

In summary, the contributions of this paper are the following:

- We identify a new evasion strategy made possible because browsers and URL scanners do not parse URLs consistently
- We develop an experimental methodology to reveal discrepancies on how browsers and scanners transform URLs
- We test all major browsers and URL scanners and show that the problem is general

- We test a variety of popular applications that dynamically create links for URL-like text and also discover discrepancies
- We examine popular libraries used for parsing URLs and discover that they follow different RFCs.

2 Background

2.1 URL Encoding and Canonicalization

A uniform resource locator (URL) is a generic way to access a resource over the Internet and is most commonly used to access a service or page over the web. A URL is a uniform resource identifier (URI) and it is an Internet standard with the latest RFC describing it being RFC-3986 [1]. Its syntax is familiar and follows the format shown below.

$$\text{scheme:}// \underbrace{\text{[user:password@]domain:port}}_{\text{authority}} \text{/path?query\#fragment}$$

URLs aim to be generic so that they can be used for a variety of protocols and by a variety of applications. However, as the web has increased in popularity, URLs are used by an increasing number of applications and have been extended with new features (e.g., internationalization), causing some contemporary implementations to stray from the RFC. The web Hypertext Application Technology Working Group (WHATWG), in an attempt to provide a more current standard, has defined the *URL Living Standard* [45]. Below, we discuss some basic aspects of URLs and URL parsing.

Delimiter A generic URI consists of a hierarchical sequence of components referred to as the scheme, authority, path, query, and fragment. Each component corresponds to a piece of information that is necessary to locate a unique resource. Hence, identifying components correctly when parsing a URL is critical for both browsers and servers. Several delimiters are applied in the URL syntax to help separate components. These are the colon (:), the at sign (@), the slash (/), the question mark (?), and the number sign (#).

URL-Encoding or Percent-encoding is a mechanism for encoding information in a URI to represent a data octet in a component, when the corresponding character of the octet is outside the allowed character set or is being used for a special purpose such as the delimiter of, or within, the component. A percent-encoded character is a character triplet, which consists of the percent character (%) and two hexadecimal digits representing the octet's numeric value. For example, %3F is the percent-encoding of the question mark character (?). In percent-encoding format, the uppercase hexadecimal digits and the corresponding lowercase digits are equivalent and exchangeable.

Canonicalization or normalization refers to the process of converting data from one representation to a "standard" or canonical form. Generally, this is done to correctly compare data for equivalence, enumerate distinct data values, improve various algorithms, etc. On URLs, it is mainly done to determine, if two URLs are equivalent and it can include operations such as removing the default HTTP port (i.e., 80), converting the domain to lowercase, and resolving a path that contains a dot or double dot. Occasionally, applications introduce their own canonicalization rules, such as removing duplicate slashes ($//$ → $/$), automatically completing incomplete IP address, deleting extra leading dots in the authority part, etc.

2.2   URL Scanners

Because of the importance of web browsers and the multitude of attacks targeting them or being delivered through them, several approaches [3–13,20,26,36] have developed URL scanners. A URL scanner is a service that analyzes a URL, enabling the identification of viruses, worms, trojans, phishing and other kinds of malicious content detected by antivirus engines or website scanners. URL scanner services are commonly accessed through an online web service, a browser extension, a third party library, or a public web-based API.

Scanners have two main interfaces. The first, allows users to submit or report a URL for immediate or later scanning [3,4,8–11,13,20]. The scanner will then retrieve the content and scan it to determine maliciousness. Some scanners [4, 10] also consult multiple third-party scanners to determine if the content is malicious. The second interface, enables users to query whether a URL has been found to be malicious using the scanner's malicious-URLs database (blacklist). The database is queried looking for an exact or partial match. Regarding the ownership of the blacklist, some scanners maintain their own blacklist [5,6,26, 36], while others use third-party blacklists [12]. Finally, scanners can be divided into two categories: the ones that only check the content of submitted URLs and the ones that follow links within the submitted page [3,8,11,13,26].

Among many URL scanners, there are two that are widely used in daily life, though sometimes users may not be aware of them. The first one is Google Safe Browsing [26], a Google service that helps applications check URLs against Google's constantly updated lists of suspected phishing, malware, and unwanted software pages. It is available through a series of web-based APIs. Google Safe Browsing as a scanner service is integrated into Chrome and Firefox, and even Safari uses its database. The second one is Microsoft's SmartScreen filter [36], a malware and phishing filter that is integrated in several Microsoft products including Internet Explorer and Hotmail. Any time a user gets a warning when visiting a web page in these browsers, it means that the URL is in one of the two scanners' blacklist or both.

3   The Problem

Figure 1 depicts the process, where URLs, which have been submitted by users or obtained by crawling the web, are scanned for malicious content. Links contained

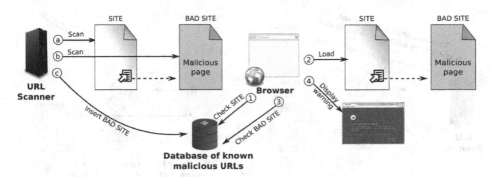

Fig. 1. Modern browsers utilize databases of known malicious URLs, populated by offline URL scanners, to warn and protect users.

within pages are usually also followed and scanned, and when a page is found to contain malicious content, it is inserted into a database. That database can be later used by the browser to prevent users from accessing malicious content. For example, before fetching any page, the browser first checks the URL of that page in the database. If an entry does not exist, it proceeds to load and display the page to the user. If, however, an entry for the URL is found in the database, the browser redirects the user to a page warning him that he is about to visit a page containing malicious content. Even though the user can ignore the warning, research has shown that such warnings are effective in protecting users [14, 23].

This process through which the user is protected from visiting malicious pages can be undermined when scanners and browsers do not parse URLs consistently. There may be many reasons that two programs do not parse a URL the same way. It may be consciously, because their developers chose to support a different standard, or because one of them has adopted additional standards and guidelines. It can also be because of program bugs that cause inconsistent behavior when parsing certain, otherwise legitimate, URLs. Independently of the reason, if the database utilized by a browser was produced by a scanner that treats certain URLs differently than the browser, the user is left exposed to malicious content, which would be otherwise detected and filtered.

The mechanics of such an attack are shown in Fig. 2. An attacker aware of discrepancies in URL parsing can place his malicious content under a URL that brings them about, e.g., *BADURL*. When the scanner processes a page containing this URL, the sought after behavior is triggered causing the scanner to transform the URL to *BADURL'* before accessing it and scanning it. The attacker is essentially able to hide his malicious page from the scanner, so it can never be entered in the database, later used by the browser. It is interesting to note that even if the attacker for some reason placed malicious content under *BADURL'*, causing it to be logged in the database, the browser would actually check *BADURL* instead, which would not match any of the logged entries. The problem is symmetric, in the sense that if the browser is the entity transforming

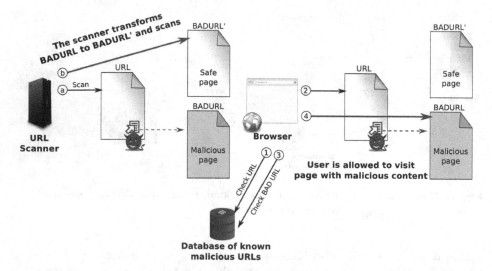

Fig. 2. A scanner parsing URLs differently from a browser allows hiding malicious content from the first, using a carefully crafted URL, while the latter follow it to malicious content.

the URL before accessing it, then the attacker can still hide malicious content by placing it under *BADURL'* while putting innocuous content under *BADURL*.

This problem, which we name *What You Scan Is Not What I Visit* (WYSIS-NWIV), is not limited to browsers, but it can affect any application that creates links for displayed URLs. For example, instant messengers and various web applications, like web mail, do create links for URLs identified in text. Concurrently, there are various products that filter malicious URLs based on databases created by public and proprietary scanners [5,24,38,42]. Each application-scanner pair, where the two do not process URLs the same way, can leave the user exposed to malicious content.

4   Experimental Methodology

To detect discrepancies on how URLs are parsed, we design experiments that will drive browsers and URL scanners with various test inputs. This section describes how we generate the test inputs and the experiments run with browsers and URL scanners.

4.1   Generating Test Inputs

To generate the URL inputs used for testing, we follow a structured approach building on domain knowledge. In particular, we manually examine the following sources to identify high-level patterns of inputs, based on which we generate inputs for testing. The three following resources are used to identify high-level patterns for testing: (i) the RFC 3986 document, (ii) the code base of the Chromium and Mozilla Firefox web browsers, and (iii) the unit tests that come with these browsers. The RFC 3986 specification broadly defines what is allowed, what may be allowed, but also what must be disallowed when a URL is constructed. However, it allows browsers to implement their own policies for "maybe allowed" characters. Thus, based on the study of the URL specification and two open-source web browsers, it would be possible to have discrepancies in some special cases, such as when encountering control characters, special Unicode characters, the backslash character, and encoded delimiters included in the URL path. Furthermore, unit tests provide key examples that web browsers and services should be able to successfully parse for compatibility reasons. Table 1 lists all the test inputs constructed based on the above sources.

Table 1. Inputs used for testing browsers and scanners.

Description of transformation	Generated Tests
Convert the scheme and host to lower case	Equivalence of *HTTP://WWW.EXAMPLE.ORG/PATH* and *http://www.example.org/path*
Decode percent-encoded octets of unreserved characters	URL with sampled character from range %41-%5A ('A'-'Z') and %61-%7A ('a'-'z')
Remove default port	Equivalence of *http://www.example.org:80/path* and *http://www.example.org/path*
Add trailing '/'	Equivalence of *http://www.example.org/path/* and *http://www.example.org/path*
Removing dot-segments ('.')	Equivalence of *http://www.example.org/path/././index.html* and *http://www.example.org/path/index.html* (Number of '.' in the range of 1-5)
Removing the end fragment '#frag'	Equivalence of *http://www.example.org/path/index.html#frag* and *http://www.example.org/path/index.html*
Replacing IP with domain name	Equivalence of *http://www.example.org/path* and *http://10.0.0.1/path*
Limiting protocols	Equivalence of *https://www.example.org/path* and *http://example.org/path*
Removing duplicate slashes	Equivalence of *https://www.example.org/path//index.html* and *http://example.org/path/index.html*
Unicode character handling	Multiple URLs with characters sampled from \x00-\xffffff
Printable characters that need to be percent-encoded	Double quote character *http://www.example.org/path"path*
Backslash character ('\')	*https://www.example.org/path\index.html*
Non–ASCII characters that neeed to be percent-encoded	Multiple URLs with character sampled from range %C0 - %FF
Control characters	URLs including characters \a, \b, \e, \n, \t, \0, \v, \f, \r
Encoded delimiters	URLs including percent-encoded delimiters '#', '?', and '/' in the path
Leading dots	http://...www.example.org (Number of '.' in the range of 1-5)
Whitespace/Tab	*http://www.example.org/pa th* and *http://www.example.org/path%a0path*

4.2   The Experiments

Our first experiment aims to discover differences on how browsers parse and transform URLs, before submitting a request to the server. We developed a browser driver, as a bash script, which launches a browser and requests a URL from the set of test inputs. The browser then performs canonicalization and transformations on the URL and establishes a connection to our server, where it sends the request including the transformed URL. The server was developed using Python on top of the *werkzeug* library and accepts every URL request, logs it, and responds with a default web page. After the page is loaded at the browser, we also extract the URL that was requested from the browser's history database. The URLs requested, received by the server, and stored in the history database are compared to identify discrepancies. To facilitate comparison, we use a unique path prefix on each request that allows us to compare the appropriate URLs.

The second experiment means to evaluate how online URL scanners deal with URLs reported as being malicious, and for scanners that also follow links within the reported pages, discover how they treat the URLs contained within those pages. The latter test serves to establish how a scanner's internal algorithms parse and transform URLs, which reveals how it operates when or if it is used to crawl the web for malicious content. For the first part of this experiment, we manually submit URLs pointing to malicious content to the scanners using the interface provided, most commonly an HTML form. For the latter, we submit URLs pointing to benign pages, which do not directly contain malicious content, but do include URLs pointing to malicious content. All URLs point to our own server that logs information like the remote IP address, other information like the user-agent included in the request, and the timestamp of the request. We also use unique paths in each case to differentiate between scanners.

In the our final experiment, we focus on browsers and URL scanners that work in synergy, such as Chrome and Firefox using Google's Safe Browsing malicious-URLs database. In this test, we submit both benign and malicious websites located in different URL paths, using characters and patterns discovered in the previous experiment to "hide" malicious content from the scanner. The aim is to confirm that we can construct URLs that will point the scanner to safe content, while a browser following the URL will visit malicious content instead.

5   Results

5.1   Browsers

We tested four browser families on three desktop operating systems (OS). We tested Firefox v35.0.1, Chrome v40.0.2214.115, and Opera v27.0.1689.69 on Ubuntu v14.04 LTS, Mac OS X v10.10.2, and Windows 7 SP1. We also tested Safari v8.0.3 on Mac OS X, and Safari v5.1.7 and Internet Explorer (IE) 8.0. 7601.17514 on Windows 7. Our results show that Firefox URL-encodes back-slashes to ($\backslash \rightarrow \%5C$), while every other browser canonicalizes the URL replacing backlashes with forward slashes ($\backslash \rightarrow /$). We also tested three mobile OS:

Android v4.4.2 with Firefox v38.0.5, Chrome v43.0.2357.78, and Opera Mini v29.1, iOS 8 with Chrome v43.0.2357.51, Safari v8.3, and Opera Mini, and Windows Mobile 8.1 with IE and Opera Mini. Once again, Firefox URL-encodes backslashes. Interestingly, Opera Mini on iOS leaves the backslash character unchanged, while every other browser replaces them with slashes. These modifications occur both when a user types a URL in the address bar and when clicking on a link. As a result, browsers doing canonicalization can never access pages hosted on URLs containing a backslash as a legitimate character.

Table 2. The URL scanners considered during testing. All, except Wepawet, scan for both Phishing and malware sites. Some of the scanners, such as VirusTotal, also use third-party databases and scanners.

URL scanners	Available actions			Uses third-party database/scanner
	Scan URL	Query URLs DB	Report URL	
Wepawet	✓			
Google safe browsing		✓	✓	
Virustotal	✓			✓
Sucuri sitecheck	✓			
Gred	✓			
Online link scan	✓			✓
urlQuery	✓			
PhishTank		✓	✓	
Scumware		✓	✓	
WebInspector	✓			
Zscaler Zulu	✓			
SmartScreen filter		✓	✓	
ScanURL		✓		✓
Stopbadware		✓	✓	✓

5.2 URL Scanners

Table 2 lists all the URL scanners we considered in our experiments. We selected several state-of-the-art URL scanners, including products of academic research and freely-accessible production systems. For example, Wepawet [20] is a product of academic research, while VirusTotal [10], Sucuri SiteCheck [8], gred [3], Online Link Scan [4], urlQuery [9], ScanURL [12], PhishTank [5], Scumware [6], WebInspector [11], and Zscaler Zulu URL Risk Analyzer [13] are mature products. We focused our experiments on Google Safe Browsing [26] and Microsoft's SmartScreen Filter [36], as the first is being used by Chrome, Firefox, and Safari, and the latter from IE, for protecting users from malicious URLs. Most scanners permit us to submit URLs (e.g., through a web form) for scanning, returning a report on their state (e.g., whether it is malicious). Others, offer a way to check whether a URL is contained in their database of malicious URL, while, finally, some allow us to report URLs, which will be later checked.

From the scanners listed in Table 2, we tested all that allowed us to submit a URL for scanning or report URLs. We also tested ScanURL, which, after submitting a URL query, provides feedback on the actual URL being searched in the database, granting us this way an indication on the transformations it performs on URLs. There was no way to test stopbadware or SmartScreen Filter. The first did not provide a way to expose how it handles URLs, while the latter is integrated into IE, where the user can use the graphical interface to manually check and report URLs. Because both the URL submission process and filtering is handled by the browser, we cannot test for discrepancies in a meaningful way.

Table 3. The tested URL scanners handle certain characters differently from browsers. Pairs of browsers and scanners that have such discrepancies leave users exposed when the particular scanner is used to filter URLs, as the scanner does not process the same page the browser will visit (e.g., the pairs Chrome/Firefox and Google Safe Browsing).

Scanners	Transformations					
	Manual submission			Injection in submitted page		
	\	%3F (?)	%23 (#)	\	%3F (?)	%23 (#)
Wepawet	%5C‡	%3F	%23	N/A		
VirusTotal	%5C‡	?*	#*	N/A		
gred	deleted*	%3F, %253F	%23, %2523	error*	%3F	%23
Online Link Scan	*	%3F	%23	N/A		
urlQuery	%5C‡	%3F	%23	N/A		
ScanURL	deleted*	%3F	%23	N/A		
PhishTank	*	%3F	%23	N/A		
Scumware	deleted*	%3F	%23	N/A		
WebInspector	/†	%3F	%23	%5C‡	%3F	%23
Zscaler Zulu	/†	%3F	%23	/†	%3F	%23
Google Safe Browsing	varies*•	?*	%23	/†	%3F	%23
Sucuri SiteCheck	deleted*	error*	error*	error*	error*	%23

*Affects pairing with all browsers.
†Affects pairing with browsers that URL encode backslash.
‡Affect pairing with browsers that transform backslash to forward slash.
• Handling of the backslash depends on the character following it.

From all the tested URL patterns, we discovered three transformations that can cause problems when a scanner's database is coupled with a browser to filter malicious URLs (e.g., like Chrome and Firefox using the Google Safe Browsing database). The patterns are: the backslash character (\), and the URL encoded characters ? (%3F) and # (%23). Interestingly, the handling of the backslash character is not well defined in RFC-3986, while ? and # are delimiters in the URL format. The results are summarized in Table 3 and further discussed below.

URL-encoded Delimiters. The characters ? and # are delimiters for URLs and need to be URL-encoded or percent-encoded, if they are present in other parts of the URL, where they are allowed. This way the characters are *escaped*. Our results show that certain scanners unescape these characters, unintentionally transforming the URL, like in the example illustrated below with ? (%3F):

http://www.example.org/path%3Fdistorted → *http://www.example.org/path?distorted*

The underlined part is actually the path requested from the server at www. example.org in each case. As indicated by Table 3, Google Safe Browsing and VirusTotal do such a transformation and, as a result, check a different path, than the one the browser visits. Even worse, Sucuri SiteCheck does not accept %3F at all, treating URLs including it as invalid. Similarly, for %23, the encoded version of #, Sucuri SiteCheck does also not accept it, while VirusTotal unescapes it. Interestingly, when gred encounters either of the two percent-encoded delimiters, it checks two links: the original link, treating the encoded character as an encoded character, and a link where the percent character (%) is itself escaped to %25. gred seems to be very careful in handling form input in this case, accounting for both eventualities, even though no browser seems to treat the % character that way.

Table 4. Examples of URL transformations caused by handling backslash (\) differently.

Original URL	*http://www.example.org/path\distorted*
URL-encoded	*http://www.example.org/path%5Cdistorted*
'\' is canonicalized	*http://www.example.org/path/distorted*
dropped	*http://www.example.org/pathdistorted*
backslash escaped	*http://www.example.org/path\\distorted*

Backslash Handling. Backslash (\) is the character handled in the most inconsistent way among different scanners. We have identified four different transformations that the backslash character is submitted to in our tests: it can be URL-encoded to %5C, canonicalized to (i.e., replaced by) a forward slash (/), simply dropped from the URL, or escaped using another backslash (\\). Examples of these URL transformations are listed in Table 4. Three scanners, Wepawet, Virustotal, and urlQuery escape it by percent-encoding it to %5C. This behavior is akin to the encoding done by Firefox, and as a result pairing any of these scanners with any browser, aside Firefox, would enable an attacker to hide malicious content from the scanner. The reverse happens with Zscaler Zulu that replaces the character with a forward slash, which makes it a bad fit for using with Firefox. ScanURL and Scumware will always completely drop the backslash URL, while Online Link Scan and PhishTank will escape the character using another backslash. In both these cases, using the scanner would expose the user to attacks through such URLs regardless from the browser he is using.

Intra-scanner Backslash Handling Discrepancies. Certain scanners like WebInspector, gred, Google Safe Browsing, and Sucuri SiteCheck, handle the backslash differently depending on how they obtain the URL they are scanning. For example, gred and Sucuri SiteCheck drop it, when we manually submit a URL, while when the URL is in a link within the submitted page, obtained after parsing the submitted page and following the links within, they do not accept it and consider the URL invalid. We establish this by injecting various links within the submitted page and observing that only the ones containing a backslash are not accessed by the scanner. On the other hand, WebInspector canonicalizes backslashes on manual submission, while links injected in pages are URL-encoded. Finally, Google Safe Browsing treats the percent-encoded '?' differently based on how the URL is obtained, while backslashes in manually submitted URLs are processed in a more elaborate way, than when in URLs in pages, where they are transformed to forward slashes. We further discuss Google Safe Browsing below, due to its importance.

Table 5. Examples of how Google Safe Browsing transforms the backslash character when manually reporting URLs.

# Reported URL	Visited URL
1 *http://www.example.org/path\ndistorted*	*http://www.example.org/pathdistorted*
2 *http://www.example.org/path\adistorted*	*http://www.example.org/path%07distorted*
3 *http://www.example.org/path\0distorted*	*http://www.example.org/path*
4 *http://www.example.org/path\x50distorted*	→ *http://www.example.org/pathQdistorted*
5 *http://www.example.org/path\x96distorted*	*http://www.example.org/path%96distorted*
6 *http://www.example.org/path\x0110distorted*	*http://www.example.org/path*
7 *http://www.example.org/path\Qdistorted*	*http://www.example.org/path*

Google Safe Browsing. The backslash character is treated in many different ways by Google Safe Browsing, when a URL is manually reported, which we list below:

1. A backslash specifies a *control character*, when it is followed by one of the following characters: t, n, a, b, 0, and e. Depending on the control character, the URL is transformed in three different ways:
   '\t' '\n' The control character is deleted and the strings before and after it are joined together, as in example 1 in Table 5.
   '\a', '\b' The control character is converted to the corresponding URL-encoded character (%07 and %08 respectively), as in example 2 in Table 5.
   '\0', '\e' The control character and all trailing characters in the URL are deleted, as in example 3 in Table 5.

2. A backslash escapes a *unicode character* when it is followed by the character 'x' ($\backslash x$). In this case, the characters trailing 'x' are retrieved and interpreted as a Unicode character code in hexadecimal. The following sub-cases are possible:

   Character does not require encoding The ASCII representation of the character replaces it, as in example 4 in Table 5.

   Character requires percent-encoding The percent-encoded form of the character replaces it, as in example 5 in Table 5.

   Invalid character If the Unicode character is not allowed in the URL, for example, because it requires two percent-encoded bytes like in the case of $\backslash 0110 \rightarrow \%C4\,\%90$, it is dropped along with all trailing characters, as in example 6 in Table 5.

3. When a backslash is followed by any *other character*, it is treated as an invalid character and it is dropped along with all trailing characters, as in example 7 in Table 5.

5.3   Backslash in Other Applications

Applications, such as instant messengers (IMs), web email, and email clients, dynamically create links when they identify text that resembles a URL. If the information exchanged by such an application is intercepted to scan for potentially malicious URLs [24,38,42], any transformation applied by the application, introduces another point that could be exploited by an attacker (e.g., to bypass URL scanners when performing a spear phishing campaign). We tested various applications with URLs including the backslash character and report our results in Table 6. We focused our efforts on popular operating systems and platforms, such as Mac and Windows on desktops/laptops and iOS and Android on smartphones. Email clients were tested on both Windows and Mac platforms, if available (e.g., eM client and Claws Mail do not have a Mac version). IMs with the exception of Skype and QQ were tested on mobile platforms, since there is a broader variety and are more commonly used on these platforms. Skype and QQ were also tested on Windows and Mac. We do not list Skype's case on iOS, since it does not create links for the tested URLs, essentially failing to recognize URLs with ambiguous characters. Web mail cases and popular sites were tested on both Windows and Mac using Internet Explorer, Chrome, and Firefox.

Most of the tested applications handle backslashes more strictly than browsers and stop processing when a backslash is encountered [45], essentially cropping the URL. However, since no scanner performs such a transformation, *stricter is not safer in this case*. The remainder of the tested applications either canonicalize URLs, transforming backslashes to forward slashes, preserve them, or URL-encode them. An interesting finding is that most of the applications on Android cropped the URL before the first backslash and most of the applications on iOS platform encoded the backslash. Through further investigation, we found that there is a build-in library for finding URLs in plain text, namely `android.util.Patterns.WEB_URL`, which terminates URL pattern matching when it encounters

Table 6. How various other applications transform the backslash character.

	Program	Transformations of backslash (\) in URLs.			
		URL cropped at \	Encoded (%5C)	Canonicalized (\ → /)	Preserved (\)
Instant Messengers	Skype		✓ (Mac)	✓ (Windows)	✓ (Android)
	Hangouts	✓ (Android)	✓ (iOS)		
	QQ	✓ (iOS, Android)	✓ (Mac)		✓ (Windows)
	WeChat	✓ (iOS, Android)			
	Facebook Messenger	✓ (Android)	✓ (iOS)		
	Line	✓ (Android)	✓ (iOS)		
	iMessage		✓ (Mac, iOS)		
	WhatsApp	✓ (Android)	✓ (iOS)		
	Viber	✓ (Android, iOS)			
Web mail	GMail		✓		
	Outlook.com	✓			
	Yahoo! Mail		✓		
	Roundcube Webmail	✓			
Email clients	Opera Mail		✓ (Mac, Windows)		
	Thunderbird		✓ (Mac, Windows)		
	Outlook			✓ (Windows, Mac)	
	Zimbra Desktop			✓ (Mac, Windows)	
	eM client	✓ (Windows)			
	Inky	✓ † (Windows, Mac)			
	Claws Mail				✓ (Windows)
Popular Sites	Facebook	✓			
	Twitter	✓			
	LinkedIn				✓
	Tumblr		✓		

† The entire path part of the URL and part of the domain is cropped.

a backslash. On iOS, the build-in library `dataDetectorWithTypes:NSText CheckingTypeLink` encodes the backslash automatically while searching for URLs. Email clients exhibit more divergence on handling URLs, which indicates that developers create their own URL parser or utilize different libraries to parse URLs. Our results indicate that the standard followed by applications may be unconsciously dictated by the platform and libraries used, some times causing the same application to handle URLs differently based on its platform version.

5.4   Backslash Handling by Different Libraries

Based on the findings presented in the previous section, we further investigate how platforms and libraries handle the backslash character in URLs. We chose some of the most commonly used languages, as reported by IEEE Spectrum [19], and widely used libraries for URL processing used when developing in these languages. The results are presented in Table 7. We observe that different libraries indeed diverge by essentially adhering to different URL RFCs. In *libcurl* 's specifications both RFC 2396 and RFC 3986 are listed, and the library preserves the character. The *cpp-netlib* library obeys RFC 3987, while libraries part of *python 2.6* do not refer to a particular RFC and, interestingly, they handle the character differently. Oracle's Java platform follows the RFC 2396 specification, but when using the *URI* class, the backslash character is not accepted. The *google-http-java-client* library follows RFC 3986. Finally, Ruby's library *net/http* uses RFC 2396. These results indicate that applications may implicitly adopt and RFC for handling URLs based on the libraries used and the platform a developer develops for.

Table 7. How various libraries handle the backslash character. We provide URLs from standard input, parse them using the corresponding libraries, and print the parsed URL to standard output.

Library	Transformations of backslash (\) in URLs.				
	Deleted	Encoded	Canonicalized	Preserved	Error
Libcurl v7.44.0 (C)				✓	
cpp-netlib 0.11.1 (C++)	✓				
Python v2.6.8 – httplib				✓	
Python v2.6.8 – urllib		✓			
Java v1.8.0_31 – java.net (URI class)					✓
Java v1.8.0_31 – java.net (URL class)				✓	
Google-http-java-client v1.20.0 (Java)		✓			
C# v4.6.00079 – System.Net			✓		
Ruby v2.2.2p95 – net/http					✓

6   Discussion

6.1   The Problematic Backslash Character

Web developers have noticed the differences in how different browsers handle the backslash character before us. In a *stackoverflow* post a developer reports that the handling of backslashes from Chrome prevents him from using it legitimately [2]. The response from another user is enlightening: '*The unified solution to deal with backslash in a URL is to use %5C. RFC 2396 did not allow that character in URLs at all (so any behavior regarding that character was just error-recovery behavior). RFC 3986 does allow it, but is not widely implemented, not least because it's not exactly compatible with existing URL processors.*'. More recently, a Google+ user and web developer also identified the discrepancy and pointed that it could lead to another type of vulnerability [28]. In particular, changing the URL can affect the verification of the message origin when using *postMessage()*. They had to update their web application to account for backslash transformations. It is clear that it is unclear which standard each browser and URL scanner adheres to. Moreover, attempts to auto-correct user typos, such as typing a backslash instead of a slash, have been widely adopted by graphical programs, such as browsers. On the other hand, only a few URL scanners seem to be aware of such schemes.

6.2 Impact and Responsible Disclosure

Our results show that there is a clear gap on the use of Google Safe Browsing from Firefox. That is, because an attacker can create URLs including backslashes, which can be followed by Firefox but transformed by Google before checking them for malware. We disclosed the problem to both Google's Safe Browsing team and Mozilla. They have acknowledged it and are working towards a solution. At the moment of writing, the solution is not clear cut due to multi-party involvement. Firefox could adopt canonicalization as the rest of the main stream browsers. Until that happens Google may be looking out for backslashes in encountered URLs. A member of the Google Safe Browsing team has confirmed that such URLs (not the ones submitted by us) are present in their malicious-URLs database, despite our inability to get such URLs scanned. This confirms that even within Google backslash handling is not uniform. Based on our results with various scanners and applications, we suspect that other solutions based on different URL scanners to filter or block malicious URLs are suffering from the same issue.

6.3 Remediation

Adhering Strictly to a Single Standard. The obvious solution to the problem would be that every URL parser implementation adheres to the same standard and be bug-free. Unfortunately, experience has showed that this is probably not a realistic solution. Just recently a bug in how Skype for Windows parses URLs caused it to crash when it parsed the string "http://:" [39]. Browser developers have been devising ways for years to auto-correct common errors made by web developers and display pages that would not be parsed by a strict HTML parser. HTTP, the protocol running the web, is also frequently incorrectly implemented, as a quick search for "incorrect HTTP handling" reveals.

Using Multiple URL Scanners. Our results show that for all tested scanners and browsers, there is no single scanner that could be adopted by any browser and have no discrepancies that leave room for attacks. However, combining multiple scanners could solve the problem, as they would cover different links. As these scanners may already be exchanging data, we designed a test to evaluate whether they already do. More specifically, we checked whether Google Safe Browsing utilizes other scanners' databases. For this test, we created unique URLs that point to a malicious executable file and submit them to each scanner through the appropriate interface. After five days, we check whether the link is stored inside the corresponding scanner's database. We could do this for Virus-Total, Scumware, WebInspector, and Zscaler Zulu that offer a database query interface. Then we access these links through Chrome to check whether they are blocked. Unfortunately, none of them was, indicating that the scanners do not share data.

Broader Scanning and URL Collection. The most viable solution seems to be that when URLs are found to contain characters or patterns, which may be interpreted differently by a client that the scanner checks all possible variations. If such patterns are not broadly used by benign websites, then the additional overhead imposed on the scanner will be relatively small. Our results show that the gred URL scanner already does something like this for %3F (?) and %23 (#). Another option is that scanners take the URLs actually sent by the browser to web servers as-is and use them for scanning. However, this option may violate a user's privacy, as the URL may contain private information and exposes the sites the user visits.

7 Related Work

Identifying malicious web sites before the user visits them to block them, take them down, etc. has been a popular area of research. A score of techniques are used to identify malicious content, using both dynamic and static analysis techniques. While not being exhaustive, we attempt to discuss some of the most prominent works here. Note that the security problem highlighted in this paper does not relate to the techniques and methods used to detect malicious content, such as malware, exploits, and phishing sites. Instead, it has to do with they way users and security systems obtain and parse URLs. That is, security issues arise because an attacker can use a URL to hide his malicious content from a security system, while the client, usually a browser, reaches malicious content through the same URL. Some of the works described below do involve the URL in the classification of web pages used to detect malicious content. It is possible that these approaches could be extended to include heuristics that identify problematic URL patterns as potentially malicious, however, the effectiveness of such measures also depends on how frequently such patterns are encountered on benign sites.

Cova et al. [20] present JSand, a dynamic analysis system that visits web sites using an instrumented browser, collecting run-time events as the browser executes the website. Anomaly detection methods are applied on features extracted from the events to classify websites and identify malicious ones. JSand is part of the Wepawet scanner, which we tested in this work, and utilizes Mozilla's Rhino interpreter. This is probably the reason it processes backslashes in a Firefox-like manner. Prophiler [18] later improves JSand by accelerating the process of scanning web pages by allowing for benign pages to be quickly identified and filtered out. Features extracted from page content, the URL, and information about the host of the page are used to quickly identify benign pages. EvilSeed [29] follows the reverse direction and begins from known malicious websites, which it uses as seeds to search the web more efficiently for malicious content. This is accomplished by extracting terms that characterize the known-to-be malicious sites and using them to query search engines, hence, obtaining results more likely to be malicious or compromised.

In 2007, Google researchers introduced a system for identifying all malicious pages on the web that attempt to exploit the browser and lead to drive-by downloads [41]. Based on the fact that Google already crawls a big part of the web, the researchers begun an effort to extract a subset of suspicious pages that can be more thoroughly scanned. Simple heuristics are used to greatly reduce the number of pages that need to be checked. In a later paper, Provos et al. [40] present results showing the prevalence of drive-by download attacks, using features such as out-of-place inline frames, obfuscated JavaScript, and links to known malware distribution sites to detect them. Their findings estimate that 1.3 % of search queries made to Google returned at least one URL labeled as malicious.

Dynamic analysis techniques that scan the web to identify malicious pages, frequently employ client honeypots. That is, a modified collection of programs that act as a user operating a browser to access a web site. Moshchuk et al. [44] developed Strider HoneyMonkeys, a set of programs that launch browsers with different patch levels, concurrently accessing the same URL, to detect exploits. The approach is based on detecting the effects of a compromise, like the creation of new files, alteration of configuration files, etc.

Some recent works that aim to improve the detection of malicious websites include JStill [47], which performs function invocation-based analysis to extract features from JavaScript code to statically identify malicious, obfuscated code. Kapravelos et al. [30] also focused on detecting JavaScript that incorporates techniques to evade analysis. Another approach, Delta [16], relies on static analysis of the changes between two versions of the same web site to detect malicious content.

Some other works have focused on aspects of the URL itself to detect malicious sites. ARROW [48] looks at the redirection chains formed by malware distribution networks during a drive-by download attack. Garera et al. [25] classify phishing URLs using features that include red-flag keywords in the URL, as well as feature based on Google's page rank algorithm. Statistical features and lexical and host-based features of URLs have been also used in the past to identify malicious URLs with the help of machine learning [33,34,46]. Malicious URLs are frequently hidden by using JavaScript to dynamically generate them on-the-fly. Wang et al. [43] employ dynamic analysis to be extracted such hidden URLs.

Besides the URL scanners mentioned in this paper, there exist another type of scanner called Web Application Scanners. The Web Application Scanner is a kind of scanner that is fed with a URL or a set of URLs, retrieves the pages that URLs pointed to, follows the links inside until identifying all the reachable pages in the application (under a specific domain), analyze the pages with crafted inputs if necessary, and figure out whether this site is vulnerable to some web-specific vulnerabilities (e.g., Cross-Site Scripting, SQL injection, Code Injection, Broken Access Controls). Doupé et al. [21] presents an thorough evaluation of eleven this kind of web application scanners by constructing a vulnerable web site and feeding this website to scanners. Khoury et al. [31] evaluate three scanners against stored SQL injection. Bau et al. [15] analyze eight web application scanners and evaluate their effectiveness against vulnerabilities. For this kind of scanners, they are out of the scope of this paper. In our paper, we assume that the web site is controlled by the attacker and the attacker can planted any malicious content into any link belongs to this site while the web application scanners are targeting the benign sites that may potentially be exploited. The web application scanners usually are not capable of detecting malicious content and phishing pages as well.

8   Conclusions

The procedure of developing a common URL parser framework or enforcing a standardization model can be a hard and challenging task for both application and service vendors, due to expeditious changes in the technology field, and variations and gaps among multiple web services.

In this work, we experimentally test all major browsers and URL scanners, as well as various applications that parse URLs. We expose multiple discrepancies on how they actually parse URLs. These differences leave users vulnerable to malicious web content because the same URL leads the browser to one page, while the scanner follows the same URL to scan another page.

As far as we are aware of, this is the first time browsers and URL scanners have been cross-evaluated in this way. The current work can be used as a reference to anyone interested in better understanding the facets of this fast evolving area. It is also expected to foster research efforts to the development of fully-fledged solutions that put emphasis mostly to the technological, but also to the standardization aspect.

Acknowledgements. We want to express our thanks to the anonymous reviewers for their valuable comments. We would also like to acknowledge Paul Spicer's contribution, who initially investigated the problem.

References

1. Uniform resource identifier (URI): Generic syntax, January 2005. https://www.ietf.org/rfc/rfc3986.txt
2. Different behaviours of treating (backslash) in the url by FireFox and Chrome. stackoverflow, May 2012. http://stackoverflow.com/questions/10438008/different-behaviours-of-treating-backslash-in-the-url-by-firefox-and-chrome
3. gred, March 2015. http://check.gred.jp/
4. Online link scan - scan links for harmful threats! (2015). http://onlinelinkscan.com/
5. PhishTank — join the fight against phishing (2015). http://www.phishtank.com/
6. scumware.org - just another free alternative for security and malware researchers (2015). http://www.scumware.org/

7. Stopbadware — a nonprofit organization that makes the web safer through the prevention, mitigation, and remediation of badware websites, May 2015. https://www.stopbadware.org/
8. Sucuri sitecheck - free website malware scanner, March 2015. https://sitecheck.sucuri.net/
9. urlquery.net - free url scanner, March 2015. http://urlquery.net/
10. VirusTotal - free online virus, malware and URL scanner (2015). https://www.virustotal.com/en/
11. Web inspector - inspect, detect, protect (2015). http://app.webinspector.com/
12. Website/url/link scanner safety check for phishing, malware, viruses - scanurl.net, March 2015. http://scanurl.net/
13. Zscaler zulu url risk analyzer - zulu, March 2015. http://zulu.zscaler.com/
14. Akhawe, D., Felt, A.P.: Alice in warningland: a large-scale field study of browser security warning effectiveness. In: Proceedings of the 22th USENIX Security Symposium, pp. 257–272 (2013)
15. Bau, J., Bursztein, E., Gupta, D., Mitchell, J.: State of the art: automated blackbox web application vulnerability testing. In: 2010 IEEE Symposium on Security and Privacy (SP), pp. 332–345, May 2010
16. Borgolte, K., Kruegel, C., Vigna, G.: Delta: automatic identification of unknown web-based infection campaigns. In: Proceedings of the ACM SIGSAC Conference on Computer and Communications Security (CCS), pp. 109–120 (2013)
17. Burns, J.: Cross site request forgery: an introduction to a common web application weakness. White paper, Information Security Partners, LLC (2007)
18. Canali, D., Cova, M., Vigna, G., Kruegel, C.: Prophiler: a fast filter for the large-scale detection of malicious web pages. In: Proceedings of the International Conference on World Wide Web (WWW), pp. 197–206 (2011)
19. Cass, S.: The 2015 top ten programming languages. http://spectrum.ieee.org/computing/software/the-2015-top-ten-programming-languages
20. Cova, M., Kruegel, C., Vigna, G.: Detection and analysis of drive-by-download attacks and malicious javaScript code. In: Proceedings of the International Conference on World Wide Web (WWW), pp. 281–290 (2010)
21. Doupé, A., Cova, M., Vigna, G.: Why Johnny can't pentest: an analysis of blackbox web vulnerability scanners. In: Kreibich, C., Jahnke, M. (eds.) DIMVA 2010. LNCS, vol. 6201, pp. 111–131. Springer, Heidelberg (2010)
22. Egele, M., Wurzinger, P., Kruegel, C., Kirda, E.: Defending browsers against drive-by downloads: mitigating heap-spraying code injection attacks. In: Flegel, U., Bruschi, D. (eds.) DIMVA 2009. LNCS, vol. 5587, pp. 88–106. Springer, Heidelberg (2009)
23. Egelman, S., Cranor, L.F., Hong, J.: You've been warned: an empirical study of the effectiveness of Web browser phishing warnings. In: Proceedings of the SIGCHI Conference on Human Factors in Computing Systems (CHI), pp. 1065–1074 (2008)
24. FireEye: email security - detect and block spear phishing and other email-based attacks, May 2015. https://www.fireeye.com/products/ex-email-security-products.html
25. Garera, S., Provos, N., Chew, M., Rubin, A.D.: A framework for detection and measurement of phishing attacks. In: Proceedings of the 2007 ACM Workshop on Recurring Malcode (WORM), pp. 1–8 (2007)
26. Google: safe browsing API - google developers (2015). https://developers.google.com/safe-browsing/

27. Ikinci, A., Holz, T., Freiling, F.: Monkey-spider: detecting malicious websites with low-interaction honeyclients. In: Proceedings of Sicherheit, Schutz und Zuverlässigkeit (2008)

28. Imperial-Legrand, A.: Vulnerability writeups. Google+, March 2014. https://plus. google.com/+AlexisImperialLegrandGoogle/posts/EQXTzsBVS7L

29. Invernizzi, L., Benvenuti, S., Cova, M., Comparetti, P.M., Kruegel, C., Vigna, G.: EvilSeed: a guided approach to finding malicious web pages. In: Proceedings of the 2012 IEEE Symposium on Security and Privacy, pp. 428–442 (2012)

30. Kapravelos, A., Shoshitaishvili, Y., Cova, M., Kruegel, C., Vigna, G.: Revolver: an automated approach to the detection of evasive web-based malware. In: Proceedings of the USENIX Security Symposium, pp. 637–652 (2013)

31. Khoury, N., Zavarsky, P., Lindskog, D., Ruhl, R.: An analysis of black-box web application security scanners against stored SQL injection. In: 2011 IEEE Third International Conference on Privacy, Security, Risk and Trust (PASSAT) and 2011 IEEE Third Inernational Conference on Social Computing (SocialCom), pp. 1095–1101, October 2011

32. Kirda, E.: Cross site scripting attacks. In: van Tilborg, H., Jajodia, S. (eds.) Encyclopedia of Cryptography and Security, pp. 275–277. Springer, US (2011)

33. Ma, J., Saul, L.K., Savage, S., Voelker, G.M.: Beyond blacklists: learning to detect malicious web sites from suspicious URLs. In: Proceedings of the International Conference on Knowledge Discovery and Data Mining (KDD), pp. 1245–1254 (2009)

34. Ma, J., Saul, L.K., Savage, S., Voelker, G.M.: Identifying suspicious URLs: an application of large-scale online learning. In: Proceedings of the International Conference on Machine Learning (ICML), pp. 681–688 (2009)

35. Microsoft: Microsoft security intelligence report, volume 13. Technical report, Microsoft Corporation (2012)

36. Microsoft: smartscreen filter (2015). http://windows.microsoft.com/en-us/ internet-explorer/products/ie-9/features/smartscreen-filter

37. Moshchuk, A., Bragin, T., Deville, D., Gribble, S.D., Levy, H.M.: Spyproxy: execution-based detection of malicious web content. In: Proceedings of 16th USENIX Security Symposium on USENIX Security Symposium, SS 2007, pp. 3:1–3:16, USENIX Association, Berkeley, CA, USA (2007). http://dl.acm.org/citation. cfm?id=1362903.1362906

38. proofpoint: targeted attack protection, May 2015. https://www.proofpoint.com/ us/solutions/products/targeted-attack-protection

39. Protalinski, E.: These 8 characters crash Skype, and once they're in your chat history, the app can't start (update: fixed). VentureBeat, May 2012. http://venture beat.com/2015/06/02/these-8-characters-crash-skype-and-once-theyre-in-your-chat-history-the-app-cant-start/

40. Provos, N., Mavrommatis, P., Rajab, M.A., Monrose, F.: All your iFRAMEs point to us. In: Proceedings of the USENIX Security Symposium, pp. 1–15 (2008)

41. Provos, N., McNamee, D., Mavrommatis, P., Wang, K., Modadugu, N.: The ghost in the browser analysis of web-based malware. In: Proceedings of the Workshop on Hot Topics in Understanding Botnets (HOTBOTS) (2007)

42. Symantec: Symantec Web Security.cloud (2015). http://www.symantec.com/ web-security-cloud/

43. Wang, Q., Zhou, J., Chen, Y., Zhang, Y., Zhao, J.: Extracting URLs from JavaScript via program analysis. In: Proceedings of the Joint Meeting on Foundations of Software Engineering (FSE), pp. 627–630 (2013)

44. Wang, Y.M., Beck, D., Jiang, X., Verbowski, C., Chen, S., King, S.: Automated web patrol with strider HoneyMonkeys: finding web sites that exploit browser vulnerabilities. In: Proceedings of NDSS, February 2006
45. WHATWG: URL living standard, May 2015. https://url.spec.whatwg.org/
46. Whittaker, C., Ryner, B., Nazif, M.: Large-scale automatic classification of phishing pages. In: Proceedings of NDSS, February 2010
47. Xu, W., Zhang, F., Zhu, S.: JStill: mostly static detection of obfuscated malicious javascript code. In: Proceedings of the ACM Conference on Data and Application Security and Privacy (CODASPY), pp. 117–128 (2013)
48. Zhang, J., Seifert, C., Stokes, J.W., Lee, W.: ARROW: generating signatures to detect drive-by downloads. In: Proceedings of the International Conference on World Wide Web (WWW), pp. 187–196 (2011)

SDN Rootkits: Subverting Network Operating Systems of Software-Defined Networks

Christian Röpke$^{(\boxtimes)}$ and Thorsten Holz

Horst Görtz Institute for IT-Security (HGI), Ruhr-University Bochum,
Bochum, Germany
{christian.roepke,thorsten.holz}@rub.de

Abstract. The new paradigm of *Software-Defined Networking* (SDN) enables exciting new functionality for building networks. Its core component is the so called *SDN controller* (also termed *network operating system*). An SDN controller is logically centralized and crucially important, thus, exploiting it can significantly harm SDN-based networks. As recent work considers only flaws and rudimentary malicious logic inside SDN applications, we focus on rootkit techniques which enable attackers to subvert network operating systems. We present two prototype implementations: a SDN rootkit for the industry's leading open source controller OpenDaylight as well as a version with basic rootkit functions for the commercial and non-OpenDaylight-based HP controller. Our SDN rootkit is capable of actively hiding itself and malicious network programming as well as providing remote access. Since OpenDaylight intends to establish a reference framework for network operating systems (both open source and commercial), our work demonstrates potential threats for a wide range of network operating systems.

1 Introduction

Over the last few years, the new paradigm of *Software-Defined Networking* (SDN) has attracted a lot of attention from both industry and academia [6,16, 22]. Industry is already adopting SDN technologies and sells SDN-ready products (*e.g.*, OpenFlow-enabled switches and SDN control software), tests feasibility in enterprise networks [11,13], and introduces new ecosystems for SDN-based networks [10]. In academia, a new research area has evolved including security-related topics such as using SDN to enhance network security [1,31] and developing countermeasures against SDN-specific attacks [12,33]. Broadly speaking, SDN physically decouples the *control plane*, on which network control programs decide where traffic is sent to, from the *data plane*, on which packet forwarding hardware forwards traffic to the selected destination. Furthermore, SDN promotes open interfaces to both network devices and physically decoupled network operating systems. Considering the computer market growth after introducing processor chips with open interfaces, SDN enables rapid innovation for the network market [21]. In such a network, the logically centralized network operating system is responsible to program network devices, thus, managing the

© Springer International Publishing Switzerland 2015
H. Bos et al. (Eds.): RAID 2015, LNCS 9404, pp. 339–356, 2015.
DOI: 10.1007/978-3-319-26362-5_16

entire programmable network. The SDN architecture promises hereby to be more dynamic, manageable and cost-effective compared to traditional networks. Concerning security, SDN-based networks benefit from automatism and standard protocols to provide a more adequate and faster reaction on security incidents.

Several security mechanisms for SDN-based networks and especially for network operating systems have been proposed recently. For example, Kreutz *et al.* [15] present security and dependability techniques to secure software-defined networks on a more generic level. FortNOX [29] is based on a security kernel and detects as well as resolves attempts to circumvent existing security flow rules. AvantGuard [33] implements countermeasures to mitigate denial-of-service attacks against SDN controllers launched by network clients. Additionally, Hong *et al.* [12] and Dhawan *et al.* [5] introduce methods to counter SDN-specific attacks which are similar to traditional ARP cache poisoning. With respect to malicious SDN applications, few papers [30,32] study flaws and rudimentary malicious logic and apply sandbox techniques to restrict access to critical operations such as establishing network connections or executing shell commands.

In this paper, we go one step further and investigate rootkit techniques primarily specialized for network operating systems. Compared to previous work, we analyze how attackers can subvert network operating systems via sophisticated malicious SDN applications based on the design principles of rootkits. As a result, we present new challenges and two proof-of-concept implementations for the popular and greatly industry-supported open source OpenDaylight controller as well as for a closed source one. In particular, our SDN rootkit subverts the targeted network operating systems and provides adversely network programming from a remote host, while all carried out manipulations are actively hidden. In addition, we test our SDN rootkit against several available security mechanisms to prove the existence of this threat.

To summarize our work, we provide the following main contributions:

- We investigate sophisticated attacks against modern network operating systems and present new challenges regarding SDN rootkits. Moreover, we develop a new technique for introducing remote access in a SDN-specific fashion.
- We present proof-of-concept implementations of SDN rootkits. In particular, we provide a fully functional version for the industry's leading open source OpenDaylight controller as well as a version with basic functionality for the HP controller. To the best of our knowledge, these are the first prototype implementations of SDN rootkits.
- We test our SDN rootkits against several detection and protection mechanisms and find that current security mechanisms cannot adequately stop SDN rootkits.

2   Background

Before we introduce the concept of SDN rootkits, we first provide background information necessary to understand the SDN-specific aspects of our work.

2.1   Software-Defined Networking

The *Open Networking Foundation* (ONF) [23] is a user-driven organization which is greatly supported by industry. Among others, the ONF publishes SDN standards and defines the SDN architecture [25] by the following layers: (i) *infrastructure layer*, (ii) *control layer*, and (iii) *application layer* (see Fig. 1). The infrastructure layer consists of *programmable network devices* which merely forward network packets. On top, *SDN control software* (also known as SDN controller or network operating system) operates on the control layer and programs the network devices via an open *control data plane interface* (also known as *southbound interface*). Probably the most widely used southbound protocol is *OpenFlow* [19] which facilitates both programming switches via flow tables and requesting their current state. Note that malicious network programming will take place in such flow tables. On the control layer, so called *network services* run inside the control software and provide access to SDN resources while hiding implementation details from the application layer. On the application layer, so called *business applications* operate on a global network view, leveraging network services via an open interface (also known as *northbound interface*). As we will see later, attackers may operate on each of these layers.

To provide an analogy to operating systems like Linux, one can consider that SDN controllers provide interfaces and abstractions for software developers just like an OS. Thus, SDN controllers are also denoted as network operating system [8,32]. Correspondingly, both types of SDN applications (namely, network services and business applications) can be considered as kernel applications and user applications, respectively. In this work, we use the terms NOS and SDN controller interchangeably.

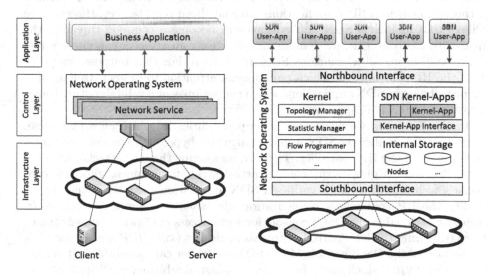

Fig. 1. SDN architecture   **Fig. 2.** NOS components

2.2   Network Operating System Alias SDN Controller

Network operating systems are logically centralized and responsible for controlling the entire SDN, thus, playing a major role. As illustrated in Fig. 2, the
main tasks are providing (i) a global network view, (ii) network statistics, (iii)
a northbound interface as well as a (iv) southbound interface, and (v) programming network devices as required for network operation. A typical SDN scenario
would be reactive network programming: assuming that a switch cannot process
a network packet due to a missing flow table entry, the switch delegates the
forwarding decision to the NOS. The NOS considers the delegated information
as well as the current network state and determines an adequate forwarding
decision which is sent back to the requesting switch, typically, via a flow rule.
Subsequently, such packets are forwarded by the switch according to the previously added flow rule. As we will see in Sects. 3 and 4, the services providing
these functions are the main objectives a SDN rootkit wants to manipulate.

Furthermore, many SDN controllers (*e.g.*, the ones released by HP and Cisco)
support the installation of SDN applications during runtime whereas others, such
as Floodlight [7], are inflexible regarding this. According to Cisco [4], runtime
flexibility is important for implementing business needs. Similarly, HP explicitly
supports runtime flexibility and started the first SDN App Store which hosts
SDN applications (even from third-parties) which are supposed to be installed
during runtime. However, runtime flexibility also makes it easier for attackers to
compromise a NOS, *e.g.*, via malicious SDN applications.

2.3   Motivating Examples

Since there are only a few SDN-based networks nowadays (mostly for research
purposes), malicious SDN applications have not been reported yet. However, we
believe that malicious SDN applications will become a common threat in the
future. To motivate this, we demonstrate how easy an attacker can abuse a real
world NOS to install a malicious SDN application. For that purpose, we penetrate the HP controller [9] which pays special attention to protect itself against
the installation of SDN applications which cannot present a valid signature (often
the case for malicious applications).

In the following, we discuss multiple possibilities by which an attacker can
easily install a malicious SDN application while bypassing existent protection
mechanisms of the HP controller. Thereby, we assume that the attacker has only
unprivileged user rights. In this case, an attacker can, for instance, ignore the controller's web interface which verifies a SDN application's signature and simply
modify the HP controller's configuration file *virgo/configuration/osgi.console.
properties* to enable the OSGi console for local access (`telnet.enabled=true`).
After triggering the HP controller process to restart (*kill -HUP <virgo pid>*), a
connection to the OSGi console of the SDN controller can be established via *tel-
net localhost 2401* which allows an attacker to install arbitrary SDN applications.
Surprisingly, in this case a SDN application must not present a valid signature to
get installed or started. An attacker can also copy a malicious SDN application

into the controller's plugin directory and modify the controller's configuration file *virgo/configuration/config.ini*. Adding an entry here tells the controller to start the previously copied SDN application during startup. After triggering the controller to restart, a configured malicious SDN application can be installed and started, again, without presenting a valid signature.

Since a controller restart may generate unwanted attention, an attacker can also simply copy an arbitrary SDN application to the controller's directory *virgo/pickup*. Since the HP controller uses this directory for hot deployment, any SDN application is automatically installed and started after a few seconds. Surprisingly, malicious SDN applications presenting no valid signature can be also installed this way.

In addition to such flaws, an attacker can also exploit software vulnerabilities which are likely to happen even for NOSs. For example, an attacker could exploit a vulnerability in code verification functions [26,27] or shutdown the entire security system of a NOS, *e.g.*, by exploiting CVE-2012-4681 or CVE-2013-0422. Although we assume that security experts operate a NOS, we want to stress that NOSs may present other vulnerabilities in the future which could be exploited to install malicious SDN applications while bypassing existent protection mechanisms.

2.4   Attacker Model

Similar to attacker models of traditional rootkits, we assume that attackers are able to install a malicious SDN application on a NOS. This may be possible through a compromised SDN App Store or via exploiting design flaws or suitable vulnerabilities of a NOS. While the two former attack scenarios are rather obvious, we want to give a SDN-specific example for the latter case.

Consider that attackers can already write empty files to the controller's file system (CVE-2014-8149) and exploit a vulnerability triggered while parsing network packets which are delegated by a SDN switch (CVE-2015-1166). Assuming additionally that future vulnerabilities might be more critical and that attackers can combine them, a SDN-specific attack scenario would look as follows: A network client (*e.g.*, infected while browsing through the Internet) sends specially crafted packets to a SDN switch which delegates these packets to the NOS due to a missing flow rule. Then, during packet parsing a vulnerability is triggered in the way it allows to write an arbitrary file to the NOS's file system, *e.g.*, to its hot deployment directory. In case of the HP controller, this alone would lead to the installation of our SDN rootkit.

3   SDN Rootkits

Traditional rootkits (*e.g.*, for Windows or Linux) mainly aim at hiding their artifacts in order to remain undetected as long as possible. A mature technique to achieve that is the hooking of selected control data inside an OS (*e.g.*, the system call table) in order to transfer the control flow to the rootkit. While this has remained almost unchanged over the last years, a new technique has been presented recently [34]. It is no longer based on aforementioned control data but uses non-control data for the control transfer. In future networks, however, we face new challenges and require suitable techniques which consider the specifics of SDN-based networks.

3.1   Challenges

In the following, we present SDN rootkit challenges necessary to understand that we can later on provide adequate countermeasures.

Hiding SDN Rootkits from a NOS. Hiding rootkit artifacts from a NOS works similar to hiding them from a commodity OS. Since NOSs are often designed as service-oriented systems, *e.g.*, based on OSGi, the type of artifacts to hide as well as the data structures holding such artifacts differ with respect to traditional rootkits. For example, a SDN rootkit necessarily consumes services in order to perform malicious actions, but it wants to hide itself from the same services to remain undetected. At the same time, however, the service must know its consumers to notify them about new events (which is typically needed by SDN rootkits). Thus, the challenge is to hide rootkit artifacts (*e.g.*, from a service) while it remains capable of performing malicious actions (*e.g.*, based on service notifications).

Hiding a Malicious Network State from the NOS. New and specific to SDN is hiding malicious network programming. This includes adding of malicious flow rules as well as pretending the existence of previously removed (security) flow rules. To make malicious network programming effective, corresponding flow rules must be present (or not) at least in the SDN-enabled switches. Hence, the challenge is to manipulate the NOS's view on the network state despite the fact that it has direct access to the switch's internals as this is part of the SDN paradigm.

Hiding Unwanted Remote Access Communications. Remote access to malicious functions is highly desirable by attackers. Reasonably, such communications should not differ much from normal communication. In SDN-based networks, it is normal to exchange messages between the NOS and the associated switches. However, it is not part of the SDN architecture to provide a connection between network clients (residing in the user network) and the NOS (residing in the management network). Thus, the challenge is to establish a connection which by design should not be possible and which on top does not significantly differ from normal control traffic.

Resolving Non-Existent Rule Conflicts. While hiding malicious flow rules, network operators may want to add similar but legitimate flow rules. For example, assume a legitimate flow rule which matches on the same packet header fields as a malicious one but contains different actions. Adding this legitimate flow rule would cause a rule conflict which must not occur in order to keep malicious behavior hidden. Hence, the challenge is to control the NOS's rule conflict mechanism and to handle possible rule conflicts.

Faking Non-Existent Network Statistics. Assuming that an attacker has already removed a flow rule (*e.g.*, a security rule which blocks traffic from a certain IP address) the flow rule's existence must be pretended. Otherwise, the corresponding security application or a network operator can discover the misconfiguration, thus, revealing the manipulated network state. The challenge is to fake reasonable statistics for the removed flow rules.

3.2 A New Technique for Remote Access

A novel and specific aspect of SDN is establishing a connection between the attacker's host and the SDN rootkit for remote access purposes. Note that such connections are neither part of the SDN architecture nor desirable in any way. However, in the following we present a new technique how this can be achieved for the probably most widely used southbound protocol, *i.e.*, OpenFlow. In OpenFlow, so called *packet-in messages* are sent by OpenFlow-enabled switches in order to delegate forwarding decisions of occurring network packets to the NOS. In response, the NOS determines an adequate decision by taking both packet information and the current network state into account. It then sends this decision back to the requesting switch via a so called *packet-out message*, typically resulting in adding a new flow rule. As illustrated in Fig. 3, attackers can misuse that standard behavior in order to establish a remote access communication.

On the one hand, attackers could send specially crafted packets for which a switch cannot determine a forwarding decision, thus, it delegates such packets

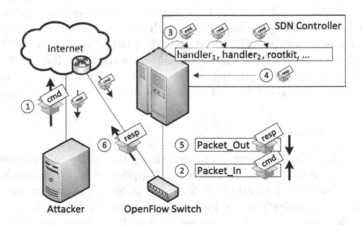

Fig. 3. Remote access via packet-in and packet-out messages

to the NOS. On the other hand, an attacker can install hidden flow rules on each switch which exactly match on the attacker's packets, thus, causing delegation of such packets to the NOS. Inside the NOS, the packet-in message including the attacker's packet (or only the packet's headers) is passed to a registered set of packet-in message handlers. Depending on the NOS, such messages are passed to aforementioned handlers in a sequential fashion allowing each handler to pass the message to the next handler if it cannot provide an adequate forwarding decision. To avoid that other handlers generate responses to the attacker's packets (or even drop the corresponding packet-in message), the SDN rootkit must either ensure that it is the first handler which is called for processing a new packet-in request or that the previous handlers keep passing the packet until the SDN rootkit's packet-in handler is reached.

If the attacker's packets reach the rootkit's handler, it can simply parse the commands (*e.g.*, encoded in the packet's header or the payload) and execute the corresponding malicious actions. Some commands such as *adding a new malicious flow rule* may not necessarily require feedback whereas others like *download the network topology* do. For the latter commands, the SDN rootkit's packet-in handler can create packet-out messages including previously collected information (such as the network topology) which are sent back to the switch. According to the given packet-out settings, the switch forwards the network packet towards the attacker's host. Since such control communications between the NOS and associated switches are normal, attackers can establish a remote access connection which likely remains stealthy.

4   Prototype Implementation

Based on the concept introduced in the last section, we now provide two prototype implementations, one for the industry's leading open source OpenDaylight controller, and another one for the HP controller. OpenDaylight is the foundation for several enterprise NOSs of large companies such as Cisco, IBM, Brocade and Extreme Networks whereas the HP controller is considered as representative for commercial network operating systems. More specifically, we use OpenDaylight's Helium base release (SR1) and the HP controller of version 2.3.5. The current implementation of our SDN rootkit supports the following functions: hiding the rootkit's artifacts, hiding malicious network programming (including rule conflict resolution and faking statistics) as well as providing remote access.

4.1   Rootkit Hiding

For OpenDaylight, there are two main interfaces to display information about NOS internals such as a list of installed SDN applications or running NOS services: a console and a web interface. Since we consider our rootkit to be installed as a normal SDN application, we focus on hiding artifacts which occur inside the NOS during the installation process. It mainly includes the creation of a unique object for each SDN application which is added to the protected list of

installed SDN applications. This object is further on used, for example, to register a new NOS service or to consume an already registered service to implement
its functionality. Accordingly, this unique object is added to a protected list of
registered services and to a protected list of consumers of an already registered
NOS service, respectively. As these lists are protected, they are not supposed to
be modified by SDN applications.

However, we utilize Java reflection and manipulate each of these protected
lists to remove the objects which are added during the installation. This works
fine for the first two lists, $i.e.$, the lists of installed SDN applications and the
one of registered NOS services. But if we remove the rootkit's object from the
consumer list of a NOS service, the SDN rootkit remains unable to react on
service events. Therefore, we additionally replace the OpenDaylight's service
registry which is responsible for notifying the associated consumers of a NOS
service. This is currently implemented by replacing the service's object by an
object of our own registry service. As a result, the SDN rootkit can consume
NOS services while it remains hidden from the NOS.

Since other SDN controllers such as the HP SDN controller are built upon
the same execution environment as OpenDaylight, the presented artifact hiding
works on many other NOS as well. In particular, we implement this basic rootkit
functionality also for the HP controller.

4.2   Malicious Network Programming

To implement malicious network programming, we basically manipulate the
OpenDaylight's view on the network. This view is either cached in protected
flow rule databases or based on information which is directly received from
the network through a so called *read service* and a so called *flow programmer service*. The most interesting databases are: *StaticFlows*, *originalSwView*
and *installedSwView*. *StaticFlows* contains static and pro-actively installed flow
rules which can be managed via OpenDaylight's web interface. For example,
we use this to add security flow rules, *e.g.*, to drop network packets coming
from a certain host. The databases *originalSwView* and *installedSwView* contain the software view of the network. While the former one manages the flow
rules which are requested to be installed, the latter one contains the flow rules
which are actually installed on the switches. The latter two databases are typically used for reactive programming, for example, by the OpenDaylight's load
balancing service.

In addition, OpenDaylight provides direct access to the programmable network through a read service (which allows to read information stored on a network switch) and a flow programmer service (which enables adding and removing
flow rules on such network devices). Figure 4 illustrates how an OpenDaylight
service such as the *statistic manager* can directly access switch information such
as current flow statistics (dashed line). Thereby, it uses the NOS's read service
and sends OpenFlow messages towards the programmable switches in order to
request flow rule statistics such as the byte count or the packet count of a certain flow rule. Figure 5 depicts how OpenDaylight's *Forwarding Rules Manager*

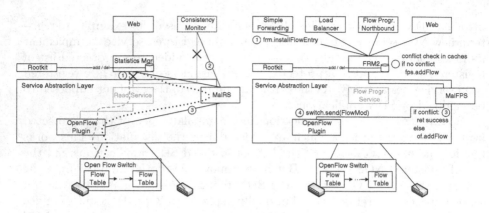

Fig. 4. Read service manipulation   **Fig. 5.** Flow progr. manipulation

(FRM) uses the flow programmer service in order to add and remove a certain flow rule to/from programmable switches (dashed line).

Currently, we implement hiding of malicious flow rules as well as pretending the existence of previously removed security flow rules by invoking the forwarding rules manager's internal functions *addEntryInHw* and *removeEntryInHw*. Inside the FRM, these functions are called after no rule conflicts were detected and after the flow rule caches got updated. However, we facilitate Java reflection and bypass cache updates in order to directly add and remove flow rules to/from the network. Furthermore, we manipulate the view on the network's statistics by replacing the OpenDaylight read service by our own one. As illustrated in Fig. 4, we disconnect the statistics manager (and other read service consumers) and replace it by our own version. Then, we connect our malicious read service to the OpenFlow plugin and thereby control the readable view on the network (dotted line). This is used, for example, to skip statistics of malicious flow rules and to add fake statistics of removed flow rules.

With respect to faking removed flow rules, we also need to consider that a flow rule removal triggers a flow remove event which must be handled to reduce attention. Currently, we wait a few moments after removing a security flow rule and allow the FRM to handle such events. Meaning that the FRM removes the corresponding entries from the affected flow rule caches. Then, we manipulate these flow rule caches and insert fake entries as the corresponding entries would have never been removed.

Concerning flow rule conflicts, we must also control OpenDaylight's rule conflict mechanism. Currently, we replace OpenDaylight's flow programmer service by our own one which enables to check for rule conflicts before OpenDaylight's FRM can do it. In case a network operator adds a new flow rule which is in conflict with a malicious one, our replacement resolves the conflict as follows. First, the malicious flow rule is temporarily stored and removed from the network. Then the new security flow rule is added normally such that the network operator can test its effectiveness, *e.g.*, by sending ping requests. Finally, the malicious flow programmer service waits a certain amount of time, replaces the security flow rule by a fake entry, and restores the previously removed malicious flow rule.

4.3   Remote Access

We realize remote access capabilities to our SDN rootkit functions by implementing the previously introduced technique which is based on OpenFlow's packet-in and packet-out messages. OpenDaylight provides a sequential processing of packet-in events. Meaning that in case of such an event, the corresponding message including the network packet is passed to the packet-in handler which was registered first. This handler can decide to mark that message as being handled or it can pass it to the next handler, *i.e.*, the packet-in handler which was registered second. This continues until either a packet-in handler marks a packet-in message as being handled or all packet-in handlers are called.

In case of OpenDaylight, all default packet-in handlers pass each packet-in message to the next packet-in handler. Therefore, we currently implement remote access capabilities by means of an OpenDaylight packet-in handler which is normally registered but actively hidden by previous rootkit functionality. Commands like `addMalFlow`, `removeSecFlow` and `listTopology` are currently encoded by the TCP source port and parameters like the flow name, matching fields or actions are encoded within the URL of a HTTP GET request. While the former two commands do not require any feedback, the latter command requires to send back the collected information. Beside receiving packet-in messages, each OpenDaylight packet-in handler is also allowed to create and send packet-out messages. We use this to send back confidential information towards the attacker's host.

If installed on a NOS, such a SDN rootkit can be utilized in order to control entire networks. For example, an attacker could remotely send the command `listTopology`. After identifying internal servers which are not supposed to be accessed by external hosts, the attacker could send another command such as `addMalFlow`. Assuming correct network re-programming, at this point the attacker can access internal servers from remote, *e.g.*, to perform further privilege escalation. Network re-programming could also be used to copy internal traffic, thus, forwarding that copy to the attacker. Since SDN is supposed to allow generic network programming, utilizing SDN rootkit functions is a powerful attack.

5   Evaluation

We evaluate our proof-of-concept implementations by performing several tests which aim at revealing rootkit artifacts while performing malicious network programming from a remote host. Therefore, we use standard system tools available for OSGi-based SDN controllers, rule conflict checks included in OpenDaylight, and a state-of-the-art policy checker called NetPlumber [13]. In our evaluation, we use OpenDaylight (Helium release, SR1) and the HP controller (version 2.3.5) as NOSs as well as the popular SDN evaluation tool called *Mininet* [17] which is able to emulate even large networks of OpenFlow-enabled switches.

5.1   Evaluation Setup

Figure 6 illustrates our evaluation environment. Beside a NOS, we run several security mechanisms, *i.e.*, a firewall application, a consistency monitor and (as previously mentioned) a real time policy checker.

We use OpenDaylight's web interface to manually add firewalling flow rules particularly in order to deny the attacker's host h_1 to communicate with host h_2. A consistency monitor frequently tests the consistency between the real network state and the state stored in the internal flow rule caches. As policy checker, we use NetPlumber which sits between the NOS and the switches. It checks at real time if adding a new flow rule or removing an existing flow rule would violate a certain security policy, and blocks programming attempts in case of detected violations.

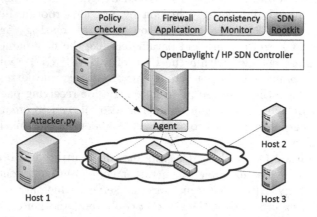

Fig. 6. Evaluation setup

5.2   Testing Artifact Hiding

We test artifact hiding capabilities on both network operating systems. For that purpose, we use several standard system tools provided by the NOS's execution environment which are supposed to reveal the artifacts of unwanted SDN kernel applications such as our SDN rootkit. In particular, we perform the commands `bundles` and `ss` which list installed kernel applications. Additionally, we use the `services` command to display details about all registered services and the `t` command to display information about running threads. Furthermore, we run the `services` and `status` commands to list the kernel applications which consume a registered service. After the installation of our SDN rootkit, however, none of these standard tools show a rootkit artifact on the tested systems.

5.3 Testing Malicious Network Programming

First, we test if the malicious flow rule, which is needed for enabling the remote access to our SDN rootkit, is not only installed on already connected switches, but also on switches which are possibly added during runtime. This malicious flow rule matches on the attacker's remote control packets and, thus, delegates the packets to the SDN controller and forwards them towards the rootkit's packet-in handler. We test this by adding a new switch via the Mininet console followed by performing remote access commands by a host which is only connected to that new switch.

Next, we remotely remove the pre-installed security flow rule which drops network traffic from the attacker's host h_1 to the internal host h_2. This is followed by automatically adding a corresponding fake entry including fake statistics. We verify the manipulated view on the network state by checking OpenDaylight's web console as well as the consistency monitor results which show the same flow rule as it was present before the manipulation. Additionally, we perform a ping test inside of Mininet which is launched by the attacker's host and verify host reachability in spite of a visible security flow rule.

Then, we remotely add a hidden malicious flow rule enabling the attacker to communicate with a server. As result, the attacker's host h_1 becomes able to connect to the server host h_3 whereas the corresponding flow rule does neither appear in OpenDaylight's flow rule caches, in its web console nor is it visible to our consistency monitor.

Finally, we simulate adding a new security flow rule (drop traffic between hosts h_1 and h_3) which would normally trigger a rule conflict because a similar malicious flow rule exists. Since the SDN rootkit is capable of managing this, no rule conflict alert is raised. To the contrary, we can successfully check the effectiveness of this new security flow rule by performing a ping test between host h_1 and host h_3. After some time, however, our SDN rootkit replaces this security flow rule by a fake entry and re-activates the previously disabled malicious flow rule. During this period of time, a network operator could recognize the corresponding rootkit thread which waits a few moments until it performs the aforementioned flow rule replacement and re-activation. Note that at this point another efficiency test would reveal the manipulation.

5.4 Bypassing Policy Checkers

Current policy checkers such as VeriFlow [14] and NetPlumber reasonable sit between the NOS and the associated switch network. Their main task is to block the adding of a new flow rule or the removal of an existing flow rule which would result in a policy violation. Therefore, VeriFlow was implemented inside the SDN controller (due to performance reasons) whereas NetPlumber only simulated network state changes via loading flow rules from local files. Since NetPlumber's implementation is independent from a certain SDN controller (except its agent which is needed to trigger the policy checker), we use this system in our evaluation to perform additional policy checks.

To allow OpenDaylight to run such policy checks before adding or removing flow rules, we implement the NetPlumber agent within OpenDaylight. Reasonably we add policy checks after running OpenDaylight's internal rule conflict tests. Thus, our NetPlumber agent is able to intercept the flow rule programming process of OpenDaylight and consults the NetPlumber policy checker before a new rule is added to the network.

In case of our SDN rootkit, however, these policy checks can be bypassed. In particular, the SDN rootkit directly calls the internal functions *addEntryInHw* and *removeEntryInHw*. Thus, it avoids using the functions *addEntry* and *removeEntry* where OpenDaylight's rule conflict checks as well as the policy checks are implemented. Consequently, malicious flow rules can be added even if a policy violation would be detected normally.

5.5 Bypassing Sandbox Systems

As proposed recently [30,32], sandbox systems help in case SDN applications present flaws or rudimentary malicious logic. In our work, we test if such a system is also able to provide adequate protection against our SDN rootkit. Therefore, we re-implement the latter sandbox system for the OpenDaylight controller as well as for the HP controller. If activated in detection mode, we observe a flood of permission entries including *java.lang.RuntimePermission accessDeclaredMembers* and *java.lang.reflect.ReflectPermission suppressAccessChecks*. Our SDN rookit depends on these permissions and uses corresponding sensitive operations to apply Java reflection. Since legitimate SDN controller components also use Java reflection, correct identification of the calling component is important.

As we implement the SDN rootkit in a separate file, identifying it as potential source for the compromise attack is possible. In protection mode, such permissions can be denied from our SDN rootkit file which results in protecting the SDN controllers from being compromised. However, sandbox configuration can be difficult in practice and misconfiguration is likely to happen (as we will discuss later). Thus, SDN rootkits could use the allowed set of critical operations for a compromise attack. Moreover, if injected into the file of a privileged SDN service (such as a SDN controller core service), a SDN rootkit could utilize these privileges to compromise the NOS. Another option is to simply disable sandboxing as a whole (see CVE-2012-4681 and CVE-2013-0422), thus, performing malicious actions without restrictions.

6   Discussion

Our evaluation shows that the examined SDN controllers do not provide adequate protection against the SDN rootkit. Policy checkers and sandbox systems, however, might be able to tackle the problem if integrated and configured correctly.

With respect to policy checkers (and other external monitoring systems), it is necessary to integrate these entirely independent from the SDN controller. For example, if the agent of the examined policy checker would physically sit between the SDN controller and the associated switches, manipulation of the SDN controller's network view would not be enough to bypass the policy checking. However, the remaining question is whether an attacker, who is able to install a SDN rootkit, is also able to compromise such an external monitoring system.

Concerning sandbox systems, correct configuration is mandatory, otherwise a SDN rootkit may simply use mistakenly granted permissions to run malicious actions. In case of the re-implemented sandbox system, special knowledge of the Java programming language is needed to understand the security implications of occurring sensitive operations. This is similar in case of Rosemary [32] since operators must decide on the system call level if a specific action is allowed, which also requires special knowledge to understand the security implications. Although we assume experts operating SDN controllers, we should consider that network operators might not have such knowledge. In particular, since 50 % to 80 % of network outages occur due to human error [20], misconfiguration is likely to happen in practice. A possible solution could be provided by high-level permissions such as *read topology, add flow rule* or *register for packet-in message handling*. Such a design was proposed by Wen *et al.* [35] and is about to be implemented for the ONOS controller [24]. While such high-level permissions could ease correct sandbox configuration in practice, operators must still guess if such permissions are used in a benign or malicious way.

For future work, we suggest systems similar to current breach detection systems, thus, preventing malicious behavior inside the network operating system. In addition, analysis systems (*e.g.*, NICE [3]) are desirable for current SDN controllers, especially for the Java/OSGi-based ones, since the SDN controllers of many large companies are build upon Java and OSGi. Such an analysis system could be integrated, for instance, in the process of adding SDN applications to a SDN App Store.

7   Related Work

The problem of malicious SDN applications was first addressed by Porras *et al.* [29]. They provide a security kernel for the NOX controller with the focus on detecting and resolving dynamic flow rule tunneling. An enhanced version [28] provides additional security features such as role-based authorization, an OpenFlow-specific permission model and inline flow-rule conflict resolution. While these efforts concentrate on the data plane protection provided on control layer, our SDN rootkit is able to bypass control layer security and, therefore, to compromise the data plane.

Shin *et al.* [32] and Röpke *et al.* [30] provide sandbox techniques to protect the control layer against SDN applications which either present flaws or rudimentary malicious logic. Each of the counteracting sandbox mechanism is based on low-level permissions (*i.e.*, on system call level and on sensitive Java function level) and, therefore, requires special knowledge of the regarding operating systems or the Java programming language. As network operators may have little knowledge regarding these system-level aspects, the possibility of misconfiguration in practice evokes the question of sophisticated attacks through malicious SDN applications.

High-level permission models have been discussed earlier in the literature [35] whereas implementation of similar models in SDN controllers is targeted recently [24, 28]. We believe that these do not entirely solve the problem of sophisticated malicious SDN applications, since operators must still guess whether a critical operation is used in a benign or malicious way, independent of the level's degree.

Finally, we believe that an analysis of SDN applications combined with policy checking at runtime can potentially reveal sophisticated malicious SDN applications. However, current policy checkers [13, 14] focus rather on finding network invariants than on detecting SDN rootkits. Similarly, the analyis system NICE [3] concentrates on finding bugs in OpenFlow applications but not on revealing SDN malware. Approaches for precise analysis of Java reflections [2, 18] could assist for preliminary analysis.

8   Conclusion

Software-defined networking is an emerging technology which crucially depends on secure network operating systems. Commercial network operating systems are often built upon Java and OSGi, for instance, in case of either large enterprises such as Cisco and HP or open source versions such as the industry's leading open source OpenDaylight controller and the carrier-grade ONOS controller. Taking this into consideration, we investigate sophisticated malware attacks against such modern NOS. In particular, we identify new challenges regarding SDN rootkits and develop a new technique for providing remote access by leveraging traditional rootkit techniques and combining these with the SDN specific features. Additionally, we demonstrate via our prototype implementations that modern NOS are vulnerable to sophisticated SDN malware. Even in the presence of available security mechanisms, we are able to subvert and compromise this Achilles' heel of SDN-based networks. Hence, sophisticated SDN malware should be included in the threat model of NOS instead of only considering rudimentary malicious logic.

Acknowledgments. This work has been supported by the German Federal Ministry of Education and Research (BMBF) under support code 01BP12300A; EUREKA-Project SASER.

References

1. Ali, S.T., Sivaraman, V., Radford, A., Jha, S.: A Survey of Securing Networks using Software Defined Networking. To appear in IEEE Transactions on Reliability
2. Bodden, E., Sewe, A., Sinschek, J., Oueslati, H., Mezini, M.: Taming reflection: aiding static analysis in the presence of reflection and custom class loaders. In: International Conference on Software Engineering, ICSE (2011)
3. Canini, M., Venzano, D., Peresini, P., Kostic, D., Rexford, J.: A NICE way to test openflow applications. In: USENIX Symposium on Networked Systems Design and Implementation (2012)
4. Cisco. Extensible Network Controller. www.cisco.com/c/en/us/products/collateral/cloud-systems-management/extensible-network-controller-xnc/data_sheet_c78-729453.html
5. Dhawan, M., Poddar, R., Mahajan, K., Mann, V.: SPHINX: detecting security attacks in software-defined networks. In: Symposium on Network and Distributed System Security (2015)
6. Feamster, N., Rexford, J., Zegura, E.: The Road to SDN. In: ACM Queue: Tomorrow's Computing Today (2013)
7. Floodlight. www.floodlight.openflowhub.org
8. Gude, N., Koponen, T., Pettit, J., Pfaff, B., Casado, M., McKeown, N., Shenker, S.: NOX: towards an operating system for networks. In: ACM SIGCOMM Computer Communication Review (2008)
9. Hewlett-Packard. HP VAN SDN Controller. www.hp.com
10. Hewlett-Packard: HP Open Ecosystem Breaks Down Barriers to Software-Defined Networking (2013). www.hp.com
11. Hölzle, U.: OpenFlow @ Google. Open Networking Summit (2012)
12. Hong, S., Xu, L., Wang, H., Gu, G.: Poisoning network visibility in software-defined networks: new attacks and countermeasures. In: Symposium on Network and Distributed System Security (2015)
13. Kazemian, P., Chang, M., Zeng, H., Varghese, G., McKeown, N., Whyte, S.: Real time network policy checking using header space analysis. In: USENIX Symposium on Networked Systems Design and Implementation (2013)
14. Khurshid, A., Zhou, W., Caesar, M., Godfrey, P.: VeriFlow: verifying network-wide invariants in real time. In: USENIX Symposium on Networked Systems Design and Implementation (2013)
15. Kreutz, D., Ramos, F., Verissimo, P.: Towards secure and dependable software-defined networks. In: ACM SIGCOMM Workshop on Hot Topics in Software Defined Networking (2013)
16. Kreutz, D., Ramos, F.M., Verissimo, P., Rothenberg, C.E., Azodolmolky, S., Uhlig, S.: Software-defined networking: a comprehensive survey. In: Proceedings of the IEEE (2015)
17. Lantz, B., Heller, B., McKeown, N.: A network in a laptop: rapid prototyping for software-defined networks. In: ACM SIGCOMM Workshop on Hot Topics in Software Defined Networking (2010)
18. Livshits, B., Whaley, J., Lam, M.S.: Reflection analysis for java. In: Yi, K. (ed.) APLAS 2005. LNCS, vol. 3780, pp. 139–160. Springer, Heidelberg (2005)
19. McKeown, N., Anderson, T., Balakrishnan, H., Parulkar, G., Peterson, L., Rexford, J., Shenker, S.,Turner, J.: OpenFlow: enabling innovation in campus networks. In: ACM SIGCOMM Computer Communication Review (2008)

20. Networks, J.: Whats behind network downtime? (2008). www-935.ibm.com/services/au/gts/pdf/200249.pdf
21. McKeown, N.: How SDN will shape networking. Open Networking Summit (2011)
22. Nunes, B.A.A., Mendonca, M., Nguyen, X.-N., Obraczka, K., Turletti, T.: A survey of software-defined networking: past, present, and future of programmable networks. In: IEEE Communications Surveys & Tutorials (2014)
23. ONF. Open Networking Foundation. www.opennetworking.org
24. ONOS. Open Network Operating System. http://onosproject.org/
25. Open Networking Foundation: Software-Defined Networking: The New Norm for Networks. White paper, Open Networking Foundation (2012)
26. Oracle. Sun Alert 1000560.1. www.oracle.com (last update in 2008)
27. Oracle. Sun Alert 1000148.1. www.oracle.com, (last update in 2010)
28. Porras, P., Cheung, S., Fong, M., Skinner, K., Yegneswaran, V.: Securing the software-defined network control layer. In: Symposium on Network and Distributed System Security (2015)
29. Porras, P., Shin, S., Yegneswaran, V., Fong, M., Tyson, M., Gu, G.: A security enforcement kernel for openflow networks. In: ACM SIGCOMM Workshop on Hot Topics in Software Defined Networking (2012)
30. Röpke, C., Holz, T.: Retaining control over sdn network services. In: International Conference on Networked Systems (2015)
31. Shin, S., Porras, P., Yegneswaran, V., Fong, M., Gu, G., Tyson, M.: FRESCO: modular composable security services for software-defined networks. In: Symposium on Network and Distributed System Security (2013)
32. Shin, S., Song, Y., Lee, T., Lee, S., Chung, J., Porras, P., Yegneswaran, V., Noh, J., Kang, B.B.: Rosemary: a robust, secure, and high-performance network operating system. In: ACM SIGSAC Conference on Computer and Communications Security (2014)
33. Shin, S., Yegneswaran, V., Porras, P., Gu, G.: AVANT-GUARD: scalable and vigilant switch flow management in software-defined networks. In: ACM Conference on Computer and Communications Security (2013)
34. Vogl, S., Gawlik, R., Garmany, B., Kittel, T., Pfoh, J., Eckert, C., Holz, T.: Dynamic hooks: hiding control flow changes within non-control data. In: USENIX Security Symposium (2014)
35. Wen, X., Chen, Y., Hu, C., Shi, C., Wang, Y.: Towards a secure controller platform for OpenFlow applications. In: ACM SIGCOMM Workshop on Hot Topics in Software Defined Networking (2013)

Android

AppSpear: Bytecode Decrypting and DEX Reassembling for Packed Android Malware

Wenbo Yang[1(✉)], Yuanyuan Zhang[1], Juanru Li[1], Junliang Shu[1], Bodong Li[1],
Wenjun Hu[2,3], and Dawu Gu[1]

[1] Computer Science and Engineering Department,
Shanghai Jiao Tong University, Shanghai, China
wbyang@securitygossip.com
[2] Xi'an Jiaotong University, Xi'an, Shaanxi, China
[3] Palo Alto Networks, Singapore, Singapore

Abstract. As the techniques for Android malware detection are progressing, malware also fights back through deploying advanced code encryption with the help of Android packers. An effective Android malware detection therefore must take the unpacking issue into consideration to prove the accuracy. Unfortunately, this issue is not easily addressed. Android packers often adopt multiple complex anti-analysis defenses and are evolving frequently. Current unpacking approaches are either based on manual efforts, which are slow and tedious, or based on coarse-grained memory dumping, which are susceptible to a variety of anti-monitoring defenses.

This paper conducts a systematic study on existing Android malware which is packed. A thorough investigation on 37,688 Android malware samples is conducted to take statistics of how widespread are those samples protected by Android packers. The anti-analysis techniques of related commercial Android packers are also summarized. Then, we propose AppSpear, a generic and fine-grained system for automatically malware unpacking. Its core technique is a bytecode decrypting and Dalvik executable (DEX) reassembling method, which is able to recover any protected bytecode effectively without the knowledge of the packer. AppSpear directly instruments the Dalvik VM to collect the decrypted bytecode information from the Dalvik Data Struct (DDS), and performs the unpacking by conducting a refined reassembling process to create a new DEX file. The unpacked app is then available for being analyzed by common program analysis tools or malware detection systems. Our experimental evaluation shows that AppSpear could sanitize mainstream Android packers and help detect more malicious behaviors. To the best of our knowledge, AppSpear is the first automatic and generic unpacking system for current commercial Android packers.

Keywords: Code protection · Android malware · DEX reassembling

This work is partially supported by the National Key Technology Research and Development Program of China under Grants No. 2012BAH46B02, the National Science and Technology Major Projects of China under Grant No. 2012ZX03002011, and the Technology Project of Shanghai Science and Technology Commission under Grants No. 13511504000 and No. 15511103002.

H. Bos et al. (Eds.): RAID 2015, LNCS 9404, pp. 359–381, 2015.
DOI: 10.1007/978-3-319-26362-5_17

1   Introduction

As Android malware emerges rapidly, more and more malware detection techniques leverage in-depth program analysis to help understand program and detect malicious behaviors automatically. A range of static and dynamic analysis approaches (e.g., using machine learning techniques to detect malware, using code similarity comparison to classify malware families) have been proposed for detecting malicious Android apps and the progress is significant [7,11,30]. To thwart program analysis based automated malware detection, malware authors gradually adopt code protection techniques [8,26]. Although these techniques are initially designed to counter reverse engineering and effectively resist many program tampering attempts, they are becoming a common measure of malware detection circumvention. Among various code protection techniques, the most popular one is the code packing technique, which transforms the original app to an encrypted or obscured form (a.k.a "packed app"). According to the report [3] released by AVL antivirus team, among over 1 million Android malware samples they detected, the number of code packed malware is about 20,000. Unfortunately, current program analysis techniques and tools do not consider the code packing issue and could not perform effective analysis task on packed code, and thus are not able to detect those kinds of packed malware statically and automatically. In addition, anti-debugging code stubs are frequently injected into a packed app to interfere dynamic analysis based sandbox detection system. In a word, code packing is becoming a main obstacle for the state-of-the-art automated Android malicious code analysis.

To response, this paper conducts a systematic study of packed Android malware, and our work examines the feasibility of universal and automated unpacking for Android applications. The goals and contributions of this paper are twofold: First, we conduct a thorough investigation on large-scale Android malware samples to take statistics of how widespread those malware samples are protected by Android packers. We start the investigation from studying 10 popular commercial Android packers used by malware authors frequently, which cover the majority of existing Android packing techniques, and summarizing the anti-analysis techniques of those commercial Android packers. We then conduct the investigation among 37,688 Android malware samples, which contain 490 code packed malware. The dataset is accumulated from an online Android app analysis system–SandDroid [5] lasting for more than three years in collecting related packed malware samples. To the best of our knowledge, this is the first in-depth investigation on code packed Android malware. Second, to address the challenge of analyzing code packed malware, we propose **AppSpear**, a generic and fine-grained unpacking system for automatically bytecode decrypting and Dalvik executable (DEX) reassembling. As our investigation demonstrates, commercial Android packers are evolving rapidly. Packers' ongoing evolution leads to an endless arms race between packers and unpackers, and it requires a non-trivial amount of efforts for security analysts to tackle this problem. Since the amount of packer and malware increases at a significant speed, manual unpacking is not feasible for large-scale packed malware analysis. To avoid decrypting packed code through manually comprehending different packing algorithms, AppSpear directly instruments the execution to extract all runtime Dalvik Data Structs (DDS) in memory and reassembles them into a normal DEX file. The purpose of AppSpear is to automatically rebuild the code packed app into its normal form so that this rebuilt app is able to be analyzed by program analysis tools. A bytecode decrypting and DEX reassembling process for code packed malware is executed to automatically reverse code protection techniques of Android packers.

Previous unpacking approaches [17,25,28] mainly focus on dumping the loaded DEX data in memory directly to recover the original DEX file. To thwart such memory dump based unpacking, new advanced packers would reload the DEX data into inconsecutive memory regions and modify relevant pointers that point to the data, which leads to a malformed dumped data. Moreover, some information in DEX is crucial to static analysis tools but is irrelevant to dynamic execution (e.g., metadata in DEX file Header). Packers could wipe or modify this kind of information in memory, which makes it difficult to locate a DEX file in memory. Hence, AppSpear adopts a more comprehensive runtime information reassembling approach rather than the simple memory dumping approach. It rebuilds a packed malware through three main steps: First, AppSpear leverages Dalvik VM introspection to circumvent anti-debugging measures of the packer and transparently monitors the execution of the packed app. During the monitoring, it records execution traces and runtime Dalvik Data Structs (DDS) in memory as raw materials for the next step. Second, AppSpear makes use of a proposed DEX reassembling technique to reassemble the collected materials into a normal DEX that is suitable for static analysis. Third, AppSpear makes use of an APK rebuilding technique to re-generate an APK file with inserted anti-analysis code resected.

To validate AppSpear, we first employ all code protection techniques of seven currently available online Android app packing services to pack our test app, and then use AppSpear to unpack the packed samples. AppSpear is able to decrypt every sample and output the reassembled app that corresponds to the original test app well. Further, among the 490 packed malicious apps in all collected 37,688 samples, we select 31 representative samples that are able to execute and use AppSpear to unpack them. All of those samples can be decrypted and reassembled by AppSpear, and the rebuilt apps expose obvious malicious behaviors that could not be detected by static app analysis tools (e.g., AndroGuard) before.

This paper makes the following contributions:

- We perform a thorough investigation on both existing mainstream Android packers and code packed Android malware in the wild. We further summarize typical anti-analysis defenses of Android packers.
- We propose a bytecode decrypting and DEX reassembling technique to rebuild protected apps. Our APK rebuilding process transforms a code packed malware to an unpacked one, which is a feasible form for commodity program analysis.
- We design an automated and generic unpacking system, AppSpear. AppSpear can deal with most mainstream Android packers and the unpacked apps can

be validated by state-of-the-art analysis tools, which are not able to handle the packed form beforehand.

We detail on the investigation of existing Android packers and code packed malware in Sect. 2 and on our proposed unpacking technique in Sect. 3. The experimental evaluation is reported in Sect. 4. Before concluding in Sect. 7 we discuss related work and possible limitations in Sects. 5 and 6.

2   Code Packed Android Malware

The purpose of our investigation includes: (a) to find out the ratio of code packed malware in the wild, and (b) to understand the anti-analysis defenses used by those packers. We conduct a large-scale investigation on 37,668 malware samples collected from the SandDroid online Android app analysis system from 2012 to May 2015. Then we analyze and summarize the anti-analysis techniques used by popular commercial Android packers.

2.1   Investigation

To judge whether a malware sample is packed, and which packer it used to protect itself, we adopt a signature based identification strategy to detect code packed malware. We observe that each commercial Android packer brings its unique native *.so* library, which can be used as the signature of that packer. We first investigate 10 popular commercial Android packers (*Bangcle*, *Ijiami*, *Qihoo360*, etc.) and build a signature database. Then, we collect 37,668 malware samples from 2012 to May 2015 using SandDroid, which detects malware according to the feedback results of 12 main virus scan engines from VirusTotal (F-Secure, Symantec, AntiVir, ESET-NOD32, Kaspersky, BitDefender, McAfee, Fortinet, Ad-Aware, AVG, Baidu-International, Qihoo-360). An app is regarded as malware if more than three virus scan engines detect it.

As Table 1(a) shows, the amount of packed malware increases significantly since 2014. The distribution of packer type used by malicious apps is showed in

Table 1. Summary of packed android malware

(a) Annual statistics

Year	Malware collected	Packed	Ratio
2012	16157	6	0.04%
2013	15443	89	0.58%
2014	5819	376	6.46%
2015	249	19	7.63%

(b) Distribution of packers

Packer	Number of Samples
APKProtect	37
Bangcle	402
NetQin	10
Naga	1
Qihoo360	23
Ijiami	27

Table 1(b). Among those samples, *Bangcle* becomes the most welcome packer, which corresponds to its market share in Android code protection field.

Although most commercial Android packing service providers have stated that every submitted app is first checked by various antivirus products, we still find malware samples protected by those packers. We believe that no packing service provider could prove the accuracy of malware detection. Malicious app may not be detected at the time it was submitted due to the updating latency of the used antivirus products. In this situation, packing services may help produce code packed Android malware in the wild.

2.2 Anti-Analysis Defenses

Android packers often use a variety of defenses to hinder analysis. To comprehend how Android packers obstruct program analysis, we manually analyze 10 commercial Android packers that provide public online packing services. Our analysis indicates that anti-analysis defenses employed by those packers can be classified into three categories. The first category of anti-analysis defenses involve functions that check the static and dynamic integrity of the app (i.e., whether the app is patched or injected with debugging routines). These measures can be easily circumvented if analysts know the tricks beforehand. The second category of anti-analysis measures involve source code level obfuscation, which requires the source code to employ the protection. The third category, which is most complex, involves bytecode hiding.

2.2.1 Integrity Checking

Packers generally check the integrity of their packed apps to decide whether the apps are tampered. They check both the integrity of the static code and the dynamic process. For static code integrity checking, packers often calculate the checksum of the code part to determine whether the code is modified. Specifically, for Android app the certificate of the APK is validated by many packers. For dynamic process integrity checking, packers often calculate the checksum of DEX data loaded in memory at runtime. Moreover, they also detect the existence of debuggers or emulators. Besides the traditional anti-debugging tricks used in desktop Linux system (e.g., to fork subprocesses and *PTRACE* one other, to check */proc/self/status* or */proc/self/wchan*), some packers hook the *write* and *read* syscalls to thwart memory dump based DEX data acquiring. They check whether the code region is accessed or manipulated. If so, such operations will be abandoned.

2.2.2 Source Code Obfuscation

Many developers would obfuscate their source code before their apps are released. Because most Android apps are written in Java, classic Java code obfuscation techniques can be directly employed on Android app. Those techniques mainly include:

- **Identifier mangling**: renaming class names, method names and variable names as meaningless strings or even non-alphabet unicode.
- **String obfuscation**: replacing static-stored strings with dynamic generated ones.
- **Reflection**: hiding method invoking using Java reflection mechanism.
- **Junk code injection**: injecting useless code to change original control flow.
- **Goto injection**: using *goto* to make control flow hard to understand.
- **Instruction replacing**: using a set of instructions to replace one instruction while keeping the semantic of the replaced instruction.
- **JNI control flow transition**: using JNI invoking to hide the real control flow.

Source code obfuscation requires the involving of developers during the development stage. The main problem for source code obfuscation is that it does not provide enough protection strength to counter bytecode level program analysis. Most source code obfuscation techniques only increase the comprehension complexity for manual reverse engineering. Malicious code, which mainly needs to hinder automated program analysis based detection, requires more sophisticated protection.

2.2.3   Bytecode Hiding

When published, the Java source code of an Android app is first compiled with standard Java compiler into Java bytecode files (*.class* files), and these files are then transformed into a DEX file with the *dx* tool provided by Google. Information of bytecode is thus contained in this DEX file. To prevent the analyst from acquiring bytecode information from the app, packers modify the original executables to thwart state-of-the-art analysis tools. Typical measures include *metadata modification* and *DEX encryption*.

In Android app, many metadata could be modified without affecting the normal execution, but the modification significantly affects certain analysis tools. Packers would sabotage program analysis through modifying some crucial metadata of the APK file to create malformed executables, and leverage this as an effective defense to counter analysis. Typical metadata modification measures include:

- **Manifest cheating** [21]: modifying the binary form of the *Manifest.xml* directly and injecting name attribute into <application> with unknown id. Android system will ignore this attribute because the id is unknown. But when typical analysis tools (e.g., *Apktool*) repackage it, this name will be included and is not able to be correctly parsed. Packers can utilize the difference to prevent itself from repackaging.
- **Fake encryption** [1]: setting the encryption flag in ZIP file header though the file is actually not encrypted. Old version of Android($<=4.2$) ignored this flag but decompression modules of APK static analysis tools often check it, which leads to an error.
- **Method hiding** [6]: modifying the *method_idx_diff* and *code_offset* of certain *encoded_method* in DEX file and pointing to another method. It would make the method invisible to most APK static analysis tools.

- **Illegal opcodes** [23]: injecting illegal opcodes or corrupted object in DEX file to break static analysis tools.
- **Anti decompilation** [23]: adding some non-existing classes to break decompiler and prevent them from converting Dalvik bytecode to JAVA.
- **Magic number tampering**: erasing or modifying the magic number of DEX files. It increases the difficulty of locating the DEX file in memory.

Notice that metadata modification measures are actually tricky defenses that do not really hide the bytecode information. Therefore, it is feasible to circumvent these defenses to acquire bytecode with refined static analysis. In addition, with the verification of DEX format becoming stricter, these tricky defenses are not available anymore.

To thoroughly hide bytecode and thwart static analysis, packers employ DEX encryption techniques. Similar to classic code packers on commodity desktop computer platforms, a DEX encryption scheme generally relies on a decrypting stub responsible for decrypting encrypted bytecode at runtime. Packers would place the decrypting stub in native code part of a protected app as an initializer. The encrypted bytecode is first decrypted by the decrypting stub in packer's native code, and then the Dalvik VM will load and execute the decrypted bytecode.

There are generally two types of code releasing strategies for DEX encryption schemes. The first strategy performs a full-code releasing, which decrypts the entire encrypted DEX file before the control flow reaches to it, and does not modify the released DEX file after the transition from unpacking routine to bytecode. The second strategy performs an incremental code releasing, which selectively decrypts only the portion of code that is actually executed, and may encrypt it again after the execution. This strategy is used as a mechanism to prevent memory dump based unpacking. Traditionally, one specific packer generally adopts only one code release strategy (e.g., full-code releasing adopted by *Bangcle* and *APKProtect*). Latest packers, however, start to adopt both kinds of encryption schemes to strength their protections. For instance, the *Baidu* packer will first release a decrypted DEX, which does not contain the original bytecode however. It contains a second decrypting stub responsible for decrypting original bytecode of a method once it is invoked. That is, the packer employs a two-layer encryption based code protection.

The decrypting stub of DEX encryption schemes could be implemented in either Java or native code. DEX file level encryption schemes in Java usually leverage the *DexClassloader* method or the *openDexFile* interface to fulfil a dynamic code loading based DEX releasing. The decrypting stub executes before the DEX file is loaded and releases the decrypted DEX file for the Dalvik VM. However, this kind of code releasing is easily monitored if analysts could hook certain interfaces of Android system services. Thus many schemes prefer the native code, which is more difficult to be analyzed, to fulfil a specific Dalvik bytecode hiding via DEX file encryption. Those schemes tend to encrypt the code at the method level and use native code to directly manipulate memory instead of invoking certain system APIs.

3   AppSpear

3.1   Overview

The target of AppSpear is to fulfil an automated unpacking process against most common Android packers. The involved issues of this process include anti-analysis defense circumvention, DEX decrypting, and executable rebuilding. The most difficult part of this process is how to overcome the deployed DEX hiding techniques. Generally, most Android packers leverage the hybrid code execution style of Android app and implement bytecode decrypting stubs in native code, which are also heavily-packed and obfuscated, thus, difficult to be analyzed and comprehended. Current effective unpacking approaches require a manual reverse engineering to recover the decryption algorithm, and then develop corresponding tools to decrypt the packed bytecode. This process is time-consuming and is easily countered by the packer if it changes its encryption algorithm. To address this challenge, AppSpear adopts a universal Android code unpacking method that does not need to know the detail of the code encryption algorithm. The core intuition of our work is to make use of runtime Dalvik Data Structs (DDS) in memory to reassemble a normal DEX file. When an Android app is installed and executed, its APK file is first decompressed and the belonging DEX file is parsed into different structs of the Dalvik VM instance. The DEX file is a highly structured bytecode data file. Dalvik VM parses the DEX file to initialize the *DexFile* struct and then initializes a series of DDS in memory. These DDS are essential elements of app execution and thus are not allowed to be hidden or arbitrary tampered, otherwise the app will crash. Many packers intentionally modify the mapped DEX data in memory after the DDS initialization to prevent a memory dump based unpacking, but those DDS must be kept accurate to guarantee the stability of the execution. Hence, AppSpear collects those runtime DDS in memory to reassemble the decrypted DEX file.

The feasibility of our work is based on two observations: (1) the packer's functionality is implemented in an independent part of the app (e.g., as a dynamic library), and is responsible for initializing the app by releasing the original DEX bytecode before it is loaded by the Dalvik VM. For most Android packer, there exists a clear boundary between these two parts and a transition process from the packer's code to the original code. This is because the hybrid execution model of Android app restricts the arbitrary control flow transition between DEX execution and native code execution. Generally an app would fulfil the transition only through certain system services. Thus we can detect this boundary by monitoring certain JNI interfaces and determining when to start the DDS collection. (2) No matter how complex the packer encrypts the original data, it seldom modifies the semantic of the original bytecode. After the DEX loading process, it is expected to observe accurate content of the bytecode of the original app from the DDS.

Figure 1 illustrates the overview of AppSpear's unpacking process. In detail, AppSpear employs the unpacking through three main steps: First, to circumvent various anti-analysis measures of Android packers. AppSpear introspects the Dalvik VM to transparently monitor the execution of any packed app. Second,

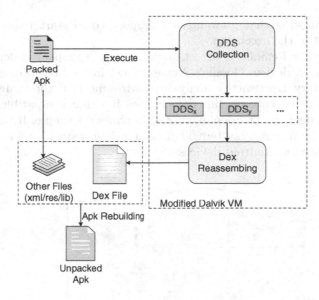

Fig. 1. An overview of AppSpear's unpacking process

AppSpear collects DDS in memory and performs a reassembling process on the collected DDS with some modified methods fixed to re-generate a DEX file, Finally, AppSpear resects anti-analysis code and further synthesizes the DEX file with the manifest file and other resource files from the original packed APK as an unpacked APK. After those three steps, this unpacked app is expected to be analyzed by most regular Android app analyzing tools.

3.2 Transparent Monitoring

Android packers generally adopt complex anti-analysis measures to detect debuggers, emulators and static analysis tools. To effectively circumvent these anti-analysis measures, AppSpear adopts a transparent Dalvik VM instrumentation based bytecode monitoring and retrieving. AppSpear monitors the execution of the app at the Dalvik VM layer, thus is transparent to any bytecode level detection. It is also a very transparent code monitoring to native code level detection because our monitoring is a compilation time instrumentation code injection rather than runtime instrumentation code injection. A runtime instrumentation code injection heavily relies on system provided interfaces (e.g., ptrace) to perform the monitoring, and is easily detected by packers. Compared with them, AppSpear integrates its monitoring code with the Dalvik VM's interpreter and is thus very difficult to be aware of.

AppSpear performs a fine-grained bytecode level instrumentation. We modify the fast interpreter of Dalvik VM to insert an instrumenting stub in each instruction's interpreting handler. Our implementation inserts a function call stub at the very beginning of every opcode's interpretation code. This brings a flexible monitoring that guarantees AppSpear could start unpacking at an arbitrary point of the execution.

To evade typical emulator detecting of packers, AppSpear is deployed on a standard Android device, Google's Nexus phone, instead of an emulator. This guarantees a very trustworthy analyzing environment: if the malware or the packer refuses to execute on this device, then it is not compatible with most other Android devices. The deployment of AppSpear is simple. It only modifies the Dalvik VM's library (/system/lib/libdvm.so) in system, and is compatible to many mainstream Android devices.

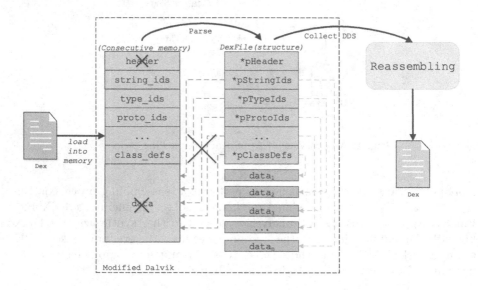

Fig. 2. DEX reassembling

3.3   Dex Reassembling

DEX reassembling of AppSpear is a reverse process of the DEX loading procedure. A Dalvik Data Struct (DDS) is a crucial data structure for the execution of the Dalvik VM. A basic fact for Android app's execution is that the runtime DDS in memory contain the actual execution code and data information of an app. App-Spear leverages this to employ the DEX reassembling process. Dalvik VM maintains 18 DDS parsed from a DEX file during runtime. Those DDS can be classified into two types in our definition: The first type is the index DDS (IDDS) including *Header, StringId, TypeId, ProtoId, FieldId, MethodId, ClassDef* and *MapList*. The main functionality of IDDS is to index the real offset of the second type of DDS: CDDS, which refers to the content DDS (CDDS) including *TypeList, ClassData, Code, StringData, DebugInfo, EncodedArray* and four items related to *Annotation*. This type of DDS mainly store raw data of bytecode content information. Since *Annotation* relevant DDS are seldom related to program's functionality and thus are less important for program analysis, AppSpear currently ignores these parts of items in the process of reassembling. We leave it for future work.

As Fig. 2 shows, in normal DEX loading process, DEX is mapped in consecutive memory. IDDS in initialized *DexFile* struct point to CDDS in the mapped data space. However, packers may modify raw DEX file or data in memory to produce some malformed data structures and lead to an inaccurate analysis. For instance, packers may modify some metadata in DEX file header and set incorrect offset value of certain CDDS. Some packers even re-map different CDDS to new separated memory space and modify the offset value in IDDS to point to the new addresses. Therefore, AppSpear needs to collect DDS in memory and rewrite a new DEX file other than just dumping the mapped DEX in memory to complete the whole unpacking process.

Then we describe the two phases in detail: DDS collection and DEX rewriting.

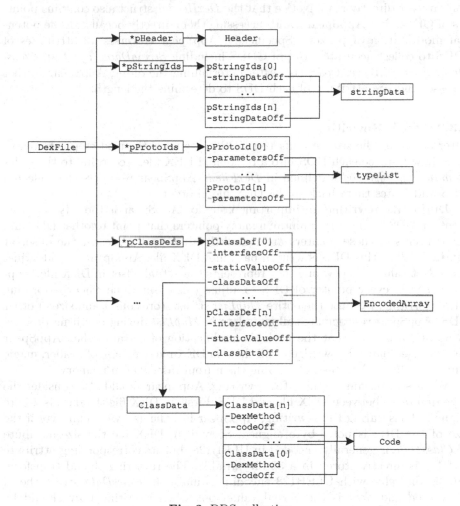

Fig. 3. DDS collection

3.3.1 DDS Collection

AppSpear collects necessary DDS information to help rebuild a normal decrypted DEX file. However, after the DEX loading process a set of information in the original DEX file is either lost or intentionally modified by packer. The main difficulty involves how to precisely acquire the data content of DDS. AppSpear evades these obstructions by reusing the Dalvik VM's parsing methods (e.g., *dexGetXXX* methods in *DexFile.h* [4]), which always provide accurate results.

To collect DDS, AppSpear first introspects the Dalvik VM instance to access the *DexFile* struct through *Method->clazz->pDvmDex->pDexFile* when instructions are being interpreted. Figure 3 depicts the DDS collection process. AppSpear starts the DDS collection from locating the *DexFile* struct and then accessing certain IDDS including *pStringIds, pTypeIds, pProtoIds, pFieldIds, pMethodIds, pClassDefs* in *DexFile* struct. These IDDS are fixed size structs thus their contents are directly read. Notice that the *DexHeader* struct also contains pointers of CDDS, but AppSpear avoids accessing them directly because of the potential modification of packers. Specifically, AppSpear traverses all attributes of IDDS to collect accurate offset of CDDS including *StringData, TypeList, ClassData, EncodedArray, Code*, etc. After determining the offset, AppSpear further accesses the *size* attribute of each DDS to determine the length.

3.3.2 DEX Rewriting

After acquiring the size and offset of DDS in memory, the next step is to determine how to place each DDS into a re-created DEX file. According to the order of *map item type codes* defined in *DexFile.h*, AppSpear re-orders the collected DDS and writes them back to the DEX file in order.

During the rewriting an important issue for AppSpear is the offset adjustment. A DDS in memory maintains many pointers that point to other DDS and the contents of these pointers are reloaded values that represent the offset at runtime. When this DDS is written back into DEX file, AppSpear should adjust this offset value to a new one that represents the actual offset in DEX file. AppSpear checks every pointer of DDS to adjust this offset value when performing DEX rewriting. Because the entire *MapList* struct stores offset and size of other DDS, AppSpear re-calculates all metadata in *MapList* during rewriting process. In addition, in case that the packer's modification of certain value, AppSpear directly uses known knowledge to fill them in DEX file (e.g., size of header, magic number of header) instead of reading them from raw DDS in memory.

What's more, during the DEX rewriting, AppSpear should also consider the type difference between DEX file and DDS. First, in DEX file the data is 4-byte aligned. Thus during the rewriting, AppSpear fills the gap with null byte if the size of the DDS is not 4-byte aligned. Second, in DEX file the size attribute of *ClassData* is generally encoded in ULEB128, but its corresponding attribute in DDS is directly stored in a 32-bit variable. The rewriting should transform this 32-bit value with ULEB128 encoding. Finally, in *ClassData* struct the id of *method* and *field* is the actual value, but when rewriting they should be adjusted into a relative offset to the first id in each *ClassData*. AppSpear would automatically calculate these differences to generate a rewritten DEX file.

3.3.3 Multiple Unpacking

AppSpear needs to collect DDS at certain point of execution (denoted as unpacking point) to guarantee the effectiveness of DEX reassembling. The instruction-level instrumentation of AppSpear proves that it could choose arbitrary point to perform collecting, which is significant for fighting against self-modified packers.

The default unpacking point of AppSpear is determined by an APK's manifest file. We choose the main activity as default unpacking point because packers are not allowed to modify the original four components in Android although they can add new <application> to the manifests file. Once the Dalvik VM's interpretation meets the main activity, AppSpear starts the collection.

A particular difficult point is that an app may load multiple encrypted Dalvik executables at runtime. As a result, our unpacking should also employ DDS collection at each point when a new DEX file is loaded. AppSpear introspects the execution of Dalvik VM and monitors the context. When certain context (e.g., *DexClassloader* is invoked by the app or a new *DexFile* struct is met) is encountered, a DDS collection procedure is triggered. In this way, AppSpear guarantees that any runtime loaded DEX file could also be captured.

One issue for our dynamic analysis based unpacking is that if an encrypted method is not executed during runtime, it would not be able to be decrypted and reassembled into the re-generated app. To handle this, AppSpear traces executed instructions for multiple times, trying to trigger the hidden methods as much as possible. After the tracing phase, AppSpear performs an offline comparison between methods in DEX file and methods in traces. If one method in DEX file does not correspond to that in traces, it will be repaired using the accurate result in traces. Although dynamic analysis will meet the incompleteness issue, AppSpear tries to approach a practically acceptable result. Moreover, if a malicious method is not executed in our device, it is not expected to be triggered in real world devices.

3.4 APK Rebuilding

Many Android app analysis tools require a complete APK file instead of a sole DEX file to perform analysis. Moreover, in our reassembled DEX file there still exists a small amount of anti-analysis code injected by packers to obstruct analysis. AppSpear performs a last step APK rebuilding to solve these issues.

3.4.1 Anti-analysis Code Resecting

Packers usually leverage bugs of some analysis tools to inject code stubs that obstruct the normal analysis. AppSpear resects those code stubs to help analysis. Because those code stubs are very specific and aim at certain analysis tools, they usually have obvious features and are easily detected. AppSpear maintains an empirical database of this kind of code and automatically resects any code stubs in database when encountering.

3.4.2   APK Repackaging

AppSpear combines the reassembled DEX file with materials from the existing packed app including *manifests.xml* and resource files to repackage the app. The manifests file of an app declares the permissions and the entry points of the app. The declared permissions are directly used in our repackaged app while the entry points should be adjusted. Some packers may modify the main entry point to their decrypting stubs so that they could perform DEX decryption before the interpretation of the Dalvik VM. AppSpear would fix this entry point hijacking with the original entry point of the DEX file.

4   Experimental Evaluation

To evaluate the effectiveness of AppSpear, we test malware samples packed by 10 mainstream commercial Android packers, which cover the latest and most complex Android packing techniques. To illustrate and evaluate the effectiveness of our approach on malware detection, 31 packed malware are manually chosen from the collected 490 packed samples of SandDroid to test AppSpear. These 31 samples can run without crashes or exceptions before unpacking and are all of different package names. In other words, we avoid to choose the packed malware from the same original app. The chosen packed malware set covers 6 packers (*Bangcle, Ijiami, Qihoo360, Naga, NetQin,* and *APKProtect*). Notice that latest online Android packing services claim that they do not provide malicious code packing service and there exist no such packed samples detected, we also want to ensure if their countermeasures do take effect and there are no such potential packed malicious apps. So we develop a home brewed malicious app that requires many permissions and collects sensitive data. The test app contains all four main components (*Activity, Service, Broadcast Receiver, Content Provider*) and an *Application* class. We submit this test app to 7 online packing services of *Bangcle* (a.k.a *Secneo*), *Ijiami, Qihoo360, Baidu, Alibaba, LIAPP* and *Dex-Protector,* (*NetQin* and *APKProtect* which appear in malware are not available since the first quarter of 2015) and actually get different packed versions. In a word, we believe that all those 10 packers (7 in existing malware samples and 3 extra online packing services) could help protect malicious apps.

We execute the packed samples on our devices implemented with AppSpear. In our experimental evaluation, AppSpear is deployed on two devices, Galaxy Nexus and Nexus 4 respectively, and the versions of Android operating system are 4.3 and 4.4.2. We build a modified Dalvik VM (in the form of libdvm.so) based on the AOSP source code and replace the default Dalvik VM with our AppSpear integrated one. Notice that our deployment leverages a third-party *Recovery* subsystem (e.g., *CWM* Recovery) to fulfil the system lib replacement and does not require a privilege escalated Android (a.k.a rooted Android), which may fail to pass the integrity checking of some packers.

In our experiment, AppSpear successfully circumvents all anti-debugging and integrity checking measures of these packers, and all of the packed samples on our devices execute stably without occurring exceptions or crashes. Using the default setting, AppSpear conducts the unpacking as soon as the *Main Activity* class invokes the *onCreate* method. Almost all of the samples are unpacked automatically and the corresponding unpacked APK files are generated. As a contrast, existing methodology such as memory dumping either fails and breaks on the halfway due to the various anti-analysis techniques or gets the broken DEX files that cannot be parsed correctly by other analysis tools and need further fix.

4.1   Accuracy of DEX Reassembling

We first evaluate the accuracy and feasibility of the newly generated DEX files. We choose 5 popular static tools to validate the reassemled DEX files. They are DEXTemplate for 010Editor, Baksmali, Enjarify, IDA Pro and AndroGuard. The reason why we choose these five tools is that they are all widely-used and can parse a DEX file to extract information from it. They have their own parsing engines and have no dependency with each other. We consider the failure of DEX parsing as the following conditions:

DEXTemplate for 010Editor is a DEX file parsing template. It will raise errors if the format of a DEX file is invalid. Baksmali is a widely-used disassembler for DEX files. When disassembling invalid DEX files, it will throw exceptions. IDA Pro also supports DEX file disassembling. If it prompts windows indicating parsing error or can not identify the files as DEX when opening the reassembled DEX files, then we regard this condition as DEX parsing failure. Enjarify, which is provided by Google, is a tool for translating Dalvik bytecode to equivalent Java bytecode, aiming to replace dex2jar. When the translation process of a DEX file ends, Enjarify will give the result such as how many classes are translated successfully and how many fail. As long as one class in the whole DEX file fails to be translated, we regard it as an parsing failure. The DEX parsing engine of Androguard is implemented by Python and remains active in open source community. We regard the DEX parsing failure of AndroGuard occurs once it raises errors or exceptions while it is being used to do further static analysis (such as sensitive API extraction in DEX).

The testing set consists of 7 home brewed samples submitted to online packers and 31 malware samples from the collected 490 packed samples, which covers 10 different packers altogether.

The result in Table 2 shows that DEXTemplate for 010Editor, IDA Pro and AndroGuard successfully parse all reassembled DEX files. However, Baksmali

Table 2. Success rate of parsing reassembled DEX

DEXTemplate	Baksmali	Enjarify	IDA Pro	AndroGuard
38/38	37/38	34/38	38/38	38/38

fails to parse only one sample and raises exceptions. The reason is that some illegal instructions, which cause the parsing failure, are intentionally inserted into 9 of 350 classes in that sample. But the exceptions in those 9 classes do not affect the parsing of other 341 classes. Four samples fail when Enjarify tries to translate them to JAR file. Among the 4 samples, 1 % classes on average in each sample appear the parsing errors. After manually checking the reason, we find that these failure result from the limitations presented by Enjarify itself on its homepage. The result proves that the success rate of parsing the reassembled DEX files is high and those few failure cases are mainly caused by the implementation problem of the static tools themselves.

4.2 Unpacking Code Packed Malware

Since AppSpear's target is to rebuild a packed malware into its normal form so that program analysis tools or automated malware detection systems are able to analyze its real behaviors, we implement an in-depth static sensitive behavior analysis tool based on AndroGuard to further evaluate the unpacking results. The tool extracts the sensitive permissions of an APK and counts the number of sensitive behaviors (our tool simply regard the sensitive API calls as sensitive program behaviors) related to those permissions (referring to the map of API and permissions in AndroGuard [2]) before and after unpacking. Since packers do not change the permissions declared in the manifest file, the number of permissions used by samples remains still.

AppSpear conducts the unpacking work on 31 packed malware and the details of our unpacking and analysis results are shown in Table 3. The third column of Table 3 indicates the number of sensitive permissions extracted by our static analysis tool. The fourth column and fifth column indicate the number of sensitive behaviors our static analysis tool counts before and after the AppSpear's unpacking respectively. As Table 3 shows, before the unpacking packers can hide almost all sensitive behaviors of malware which can evade the detection of static analysis tools. After the unpacking of AppSpear, the number of detected sensitive behaviors in unpacked malware increases significantly. This proves that an effective unpacking process is crucial to current malware detection.

Several noticeable observations are also revealed by our experiment: First, the samples packed by *APKProtect* generally possess higher number of sensitive behaviors compared with other samples. After a manual analysis, we find that the packed code of *APKProtect* is not entirely encrypted. Instead, the DEX file is only partially encrypted by *APKProtect*. As a result, some sensitive behaviors are not hidden by the packer before the execution and our static tool can detect them. However, after the unpacking of AppSpear, more hidden sensitive behaviors appear. Second, a malware sample packed by *Bangcle* packer (MD5 sum: 0FA57B3D98C24EABB32C47CA3C47D38A) presents an unusually high number of sensitive behaviors before unpacking. After manually checking the packed sample, we find that it consists of several third-party libraries which contain those sensitive behaviors. Because the packer only packs the main DEX file of the malware, the 102 sensitive behaviors refers to those in third-party libraries.

Table 3. Sensitive behaviors before and after AppSpear's unpacking

Packer Name	Malware Sample	Permissions	Packed	Unpacked
Qihoo360	CE8668B81420CF6843DA4D2EB846C314	6	5	52
	9EC616C1BC4470EE03C4E299C3A616D6	16	5	76
	878CF954DAE814D83BFFC5374E8BF423	12	5	60
Bangcle	6D3D891FC3459CA2A9911D8438966B20	8	0	84
	3FF42BF94C39A9E4B2F0EA50747670B4	6	0	30
	3F6487D723F60B4C80AC7EAB7F22BBCC	13	0	332
	03CA02466849847A26A926D6605927D0	15	0	174
	1D44FA56473B5EC27E75C734062102CA	8	0	13
	020D37EE843411AB749CADF17FC43006	15	0	108
	5F5D6F391148A4E3ACDFF3C57B8EA6EA	10	0	100
	2E06E5A5350EF54342D1328DF216D261	7	0	213
	1AF5B2D290902EE0124239F4315F4B40	9	0	91
	4DA607EDB8D7689B604C775670E5DA6F	6	0	81
	5B5674C8BA87CBC163328B27EFF24392	11	0	230
	07D9EB10587722E26BA93CB47D598641	7	0	65
	3AC41F02613FE1436564AD1C30226416	16	2	6
	9A10E7A615589B0E949F9FF9CBDFE50E	12	0	176
	4E478E2BE20EAC9C0B939FA6ADA60CE5	6	0	30
	0FA57B3D98C24EABB32C47CA3C47D38A	6	102	89
	4B9762D0B4F00E6F1A42D4AA6E984301	21	4	109
NetQin	2C3EB7833C19F35A54C91166BAAE5FCD	11	5	11
	C63AE255C1F3A22DAC47E8BFB400615B	5	5	6
	2A7CADAB7FC61508C70B146B496BDA12	17	5	41
Naga	91815F6F381DB7CA793885873AFFA782	7	0	25
Ijiami	FFB08850111C1D8B061792953588CB88	21	0	109
	A1B22DE648076B8B9515F77326D9DB13	19	0	80
APKProtect	A58DB782081C0A41BE7556FD662F9F09	23	21	30
	67EC17C3B482AC5C1E896A2BB2C64353	5	4	13
	3094CF944D45E48201A8E8EC4C742CD0	2	1	14
	FC272EA7F6A5FE21ED4EADAD8EF34155	9	43	45
	7BB4FB90B8C37311DC6C35AAA15F58C6	2	1	1

After the unpacking of AppSpear, another 89 sensitive behaviors in the unpacked DEX file are detected by our tool, which indicate the real malicious behaviors of this malware sample.

4.3 Home Brewed Samples

Considering the fact that some newly-born packers do not appear in the above malware samples and also even some packers appear, they improve their code packing strength all along, we submit our home brewed sample to 7 latest online packing services to further evaluate the effectiveness of AppSpear. Different from the malware in wild, we have the original DEX file of our home brewed sample before packing, so we can manually verify those unpacked apps by comparing their decrypted and reassembled DEX file with the original one. The content of DEX file in each unpacked app contains the exact components and classes of the original app, which demonstrates the effectiveness of our approach.

To thoroughly understand the detailed advanced packing techniques and prove that AppSpear does defeat the anti-analyses defenses used by those packers, we conduct an in-depth study on verifying the results manually. We find that due to its design principle, AppSpear unpacks the protected app in a unified way without considering certain anti-analyses defenses. For instance, some packers hook system calls (e.g., *write()*) in their own process space to prevent the DEX data from being dumped. If the source address of *write()* is located in the memory scope of the mapped raw DEX data, the content will be modified by the hooking function. AppSpear evades memory dump measures through reassembling and generating a new DEX file instead of reading the raw DEX data, and the unpacking results are accurate. In addition, we manually check each packer's DEX hiding schemes to validate the correctness of our unpacking strategy. We find that the DEX hiding schemes of *Qihoo360*, *LIAPP* and *Bangcle* adopt a full-code unpacking style. Even the encryption algorithms of their DEX hiding schemes are unknown to AppSpear, our DEX reassembling approach easily collects relevant DDS and recovers exactly the same DEX as the original one.

Ijiami. This packer modifies the DEX header to erase the magic number of the DEX file. The measure is used to thwart memory dump based unpacking method, because it is difficult to automatically locate the target DEX data through the memory space of the process without the help of the magic number. Since AppSpear focuses on the *DexFile* struct rather than the raw DEX data in memory, it is not affected by this counter-measure. What's more, *Ijiami* modifies the attribute of *headerSize* in DEX header to a larger value, which crashes some static analysis tools when parsing the unpacked DEX. However, AppSpear has already considered this modification and always uses the correct value to rewrite the reassembled DEX file in the DEX rewriting process.

Alibaba. This packer also applies modifications to the original DEX file. The reassembled DEX file from the sample packed by *Alibaba* packer contains more classes than that in the original DEX file. Some of these injected classes will cause the failure of some static analysis tools such as *dex2jar*. AppSpear considers these classes as anti-analysis code and resects them directly. The DEX hiding scheme also re-maps the *DexCode* of every *DexMethod*, and modifies the *codeOff* attribute in *DexCode* struct to a negative value, AppSpear ignores those modifications and directly acquires data of every DDS to reassemble a new DEX file, thus the reassembled DEX file is accurate.

Baidu. This packer adopts an incremental packing style. It erases the DEX header and inserts native methods as wrapper of some specific 'target' methods (e.g., *onCreate* of *MainActivity*). The code of these methods are patched as NOP until they are executed. When executed, the wrapping native method before the patched method will be first executed to recover the actual bytecode. After the invoking, the bytecode is immediately erased by the wrapping native method after the patched method. AppSpear deals with this situation by adopting instruction level tracing and gets the real bytecode of the target method, and repairs those patched methods using the traced information.

Dexprotector. This packer splits the original DEX file to several DEX files and packs them. AppSpear can monitor dynamic DEX file loading in one process and recover multiple packed DEX files. Besides the packing part of the packer, the recovered DEX files also indicate that *Dexprotector* applies heavy code obfuscation to the original DEX file. AppSpear focuses on hidden code unpacking instead of code de-obfuscation. Source code obfuscation may increase the comprehending complexity for reverse engineering, but it seldom affects the malware detection because the obfuscation is not able to hide privilege API invoking, which directly exposes the malicious intention. Although AppSpear is not able to de-obfuscate this DEX file (de-obfuscation is out of our work's scope), the multiple unpacked DEX files still contain all bytecode information of the original app and are adequate to a later program analysis or malware detection.

5 Discussion

AppSpear is based on dynamic analysis, which means it would suffer from the code coverage issue. If a method is not invoked during runtime, packers would not decrypt the bytecode of this method, then AppSpear can not recover this part of code. Fortunately, AppSpear is deployed on real devices and tries to trigger the hidden methods as much as possible, which can mitigate this shortcoming. From the other side, it is less meaningful for packers to hide a malicious method that is seldom invoked during runtime. From the results of our experiment, we find out that most hidden methods locate on entry point classes or can be easily triggered.

Malware can employ various anti-analysis techniques for emulator or VM evasion [18]. It is feasible that packers can use similar ways to detect AppSpear and then hide the decrypting procedure to defeat our unpacking approach. They can utilize some code features or fingerprint of AppSpear to avoid being analyzed by AppSpear. To thwart such evasion, AppSpear can also use similar anti-detection measures as emulator evading detection proposed in [14].

Besides commercial Android packers, there also exist some home brew packers and some malware may use them to protect the code. Although the methodology of our proposed approach is universal on monitoring and unpacking most kinds of DEX encryption schemes, due to the lack of sample for testing, we can not guarantee that AppSpear could handle those home brew packers perfectly. We leave this as future work. Particularly, some advanced packers transform byte-code into obfuscated native code executables on Android. AppSpear can not de-obfuscate native code obfuscation. Packers may even pack the native code in original APKs even though this kind of code packing technique is still not prevalent on Android. This is one of the limitations of our work and it is possible to be addressed in future with advanced de-obfuscation strategy.

6   Related Work

The topic of code packing have been thoroughly studied in the literature, and several solutions have been proposed for code unpacking [13]. Pedrero et al. [26] present a very comprehensive study on commodity runtime code packers. Their work studied the runtime complexity of packers and evaluated on both off-the-shelf packers and custom packed binaries on desktop computer systems. On the commodity desktop system, a series of automatic unpacking approaches and tools have been proposed. **Polyunpack** [20] performs automatic unpacking by emulating the execution of the program and monitoring all memory writes and instruction fetches, and considers all instructions fetched from previously written memory locations to be successfully unpacked. **Omniunpack** [16] is a real-time unpacker that performs unpacking by looking for written-then-execute pattern. **Renovo** [15] also uses the written-then-execute pattern to perform the unpacking. It instruments the execution of the binary in an emulator and traces the execution at instruction-level. **Pandoras Bochs** [9] is also an emulator based automatic malware unpacking tool, which uses the full system emulator bochs as its engine. **Eureka** [22] uses coarse-grained NTDLL system call monitoring for automated malware unpacking, is only available for Windows packers. These unpacking approaches and tools mainly concern about packers of desktop platforms. Compared with classic Windows and Linux code packers, Android packers are more complex because they involve both native code and Dalvik bytecode, which means a packer should consider both aspects and keep the balance between protection strength and stability. Meanwhile, the analysis tools (e.g., emulators or code instrumentation tools) on Android platform are less powerful. To the best of our knowledge, our work is the first one to study Android packers systematically, and can handle every available commercial packer.

Before our work, there was a range of summarization work that introduces the feature and anti-analysis technique of certain Android packers. Strazzere introduced anti static analysis and anti dynamic analysis code protection techniques in [23,24] separately. Detecting emulator is also an important anti-analysis measure of many packers and is thoroughly discussed in [27]. However, only a few work discuss the bytecode encryption issue in a generic perspective. As far as we know, current bytecode decryption techniques or tools either directly copy DEX data in memory, which is not feasible for unpacking state-of-the-art Android packers, or rely on encryption algorithm reverse engineering, which involves substantial manual efforts. The main shortcoming of many unpacking approaches is that they heavily rely on the specific memory dump based methodology. For instance, Park [17] leverages *wait-for-debug* feature of Android platform to circumvent anti-debugging and then performs a memory dump based unpacking. Yu [28] and Strazzere [25] make some assumptions of the packer's features and leverage these features to locate bytecode, which are already unavailable due to the evolution of the packer. DexHunter [29] mainly focuses on how to locate and dump the DEX in memory. Our proposed DEX reassembling technique settles this deficiency and leads to a more universal unpacking.

The ART runtime has been introduced since Android 4.4.2 to support a more efficient app execution. Although AppSpear is based on the Dalvik VM of Android and focuses on DEX reassembling, which means it is not compatible for those Android versions without Dalvik VM, all apps can also be executed on Dalvik VM even though new ART runtime is supported because of the backward compatibility requirement, So our approach is still effective for a expected long period.

Android malware detection is an active research area and many methods [7, 10,12,19,30] have been proposed to address the large-scale malware analysis issue. However, seldom work considers the code packing issue. Our work is a solution to enhance current malware analysis. The unpacked APK from App-Spear can help program analysis tools, especially those static analysis tools, perform a more accurate malware detection.

7 Conclusion

This paper describes a systematic study of code packed Android malware. Commercial Android packers are analyzed and relevant anti-analysis techniques are summarized. An investigation of 37,688 Android malware samples is then conducted and 490 code packed apps are analyzed with the help of our proposed AppSpear, an automated code unpacking system. AppSpear employs a novel bytecode decrypting and DEX reassembling approach to replace traditional manual analysis and memory dump based unpacking. Experiments demonstrate that our proposed AppSpear system is able to unpack most malware samples protected by popular commercial Android packers, and it is expected to become an essential supplementary process of current Android malware detection.

Acknowledgments. We would like to thank our shepherd, Elias Athanasopoulos, and the anonymous reviewers for their insightful comments that greatly helped improve the manuscript of this paper.

References

1. **An APK Fake Encryption Sample**. https://github.com/blueboxsecurity/DalvikBytecodeTampering
2. **API_permissions.py in AndroGuard**. https://github.com/androguard/androguard/blob/master/androguard/core/bytecodes/api_permissions.py

3. **AVL Malware Report (2014).** http://blog.avlyun.com/2015/02/2137/malware-report/
4. libdex/DexFile.h - platform/dalvik - Git at Google. https://android.googlesource.com/platform/dalvik/+/android-4.4.2_r2/libdex/DexFile.h
5. SandDroid - An automatic Android application analysis system. http://sanddroid.xjtu.edu.cn/
6. Apvrille, A.: Playing Hide and Seek with Dalvik Executables. Hacktivity (2013)
7. Arp, D., Spreitzenbarth, M., Hübner, M., Gascon, H., Rieck, K., CERT Siemens: Drebin: Effective and explainable detection of android malware in your pocket. In: Proceedings of Network and Distributed System Security Symposium (NDSS), 21st (2014)
8. Bilge, L., Lanzi, A., Balzarotti, D.: Thwarting real-time dynamic unpacking. In: Proceedings of European Workshop on System Security, 4th (2011)
9. Böhne, L.: Pandoras bochs: Automatic unpacking of malware. PhD thesis, University of Mannheim (2008)
10. Burguera, I., Zurutuza, U., Nadjm-Tehrani, S.: Crowdroid: behavior-based malware detection system for android. In: Proceedings of the 1st ACM workshop on Security and privacy in smartphones and mobile devices (2011)
11. Crussell, J., Gibler, C., Chen, H.: AnDarwin: scalable detection of semantically similar android applications. In: Crampton, J., Jajodia, S., Mayes, K. (eds.) ESORICS 2013. LNCS, vol. 8134, pp. 182–199. Springer, Heidelberg (2013)
12. Grace, M., Zhou, Y., Zhang, Q., Zou, S., Jiang, X.: Riskranker: scalable and accurate zero-day android malware detection. In: Proceedings of the 10th International Conference on Mobile Systems, Applications, and Services (2012)
13. Guo, F., Ferrie, P., Chiueh, T.: A study of the packer problem and its solutions. In: Lippmann, R., Kirda, E., Trachtenberg, A. (eds.) RAID 2008. LNCS, vol. 5230, pp. 98–115. Springer, Heidelberg (2008)
14. Hu, W.: Guess Where I am: Detection and Prevention of Emulator Evading on Android. HITCON (2014)
15. Kang, M.G., Poosankam, P., Yin, H.: Renovo: a hidden code extractor for packed executables. In: Proceedings of the 5th ACM Workshop on Recurring Malcode (2007)
16. Martignoni, L., Christodorescu, M., Jha, S.: Omniunpack: fast, generic, and safe unpacking of malware. In: Proceedings of the 23rd Computer Security Applications Conference (2007)
17. Park, Y.: We can still crack you! general unpacking method for android packer (not root). In: Black Hat Asia (2015)
18. Petsas, T., Voyatzis, G., Athanasopoulos, E., Polychronakis, M., Ioannidis, S.: Rage against the virtual machine: hindering dynamic analysis of android malware. In: Proceedings of the 7th European Workshop on System Security (EuroSec) (2014)
19. Rasthofer, S., Arzt, S., Miltenberger, M., Bodden, E.: Harvesting runtime data in android applications for identifying malware and enhancing code analysis. Technical report (2015)
20. Royal, P., Halpin, M., Dagon, D., Edmonds, R., Lee, W.: Polyunpack: automating the hidden-code extraction of unpack-executing malware. In: Proceedings of the 22nd Computer Security Applications Conference (2006)
21. Schulz, P., Matenaar, F.: Android reverse engineering and defenses. http://bluebox.com/wp-content/uploads/2013/05/AndroidREnDefenses201305.pdf
22. Sharif, M., Yegneswaran, V., Saidi, H., Porras, P.A., Lee, W.: Eureka: a framework for enabling static malware analysis. In: Jajodia, S., Lopez, J. (eds.) ESORICS 2008. LNCS, vol. 5283, pp. 481–500. Springer, Heidelberg (2008)

23. Strazzere, T.: Dex Education: Practicing Safe Dex. Black Hat, USA (2012)
24. Strazzere, T.: Dex education 201: anti-emulation. HITCON (2013)
25. Strazzere, T., Sawyer, J.: ANDROID HACKER PROTECTION LEVEL 0. DEF CON 22 (2014)
26. Ugarte-Pedrero, X., Balzarotti, D., Santos, I., Bringas, P.G.: SoK: deep packer inspection: a longitudinal study of the complexity of run-time packers. In: Proceedings of IEEE Symposium on Security and Privacy 36th (2015)
27. Vidas, T., Christin, N.: Evading android runtime analysis via sandbox detection. In Proceedings of ACM symposium on Information, computer and communications security, 9th (2014)
28. Yu, R.: Android packers: facing the challenges, building solutions. In: Proceedings of the 24th Virus Bulletin International Conference (2014)
29. Zhang, Y., Luo, X., Yin, H.: Dexhunter: toward extracting hidden code from packed android applications. In: Proceedings ESORICS (2015)
30. Zhou, Y., Wang, Z., Zhou, W., Jiang, X.: Hey, You, get off of my market: detecting malicious apps in official and alternative android markets. In: Proceedings of the 19th Network and Distributed System Security Symposium (NDSS) (2012)

HELDROID: Dissecting and Detecting Mobile Ransomware

Nicoló Andronio, Stefano Zanero, and Federico Maggi[✉]

DEIB, Politecnico di Milano, Milano, Italy
nicolo.andronio@mail.polimi.it,
{stefano.zanero,federico.maggi}@polimi.it

Abstract. In ransomware attacks, the actual target is the human, as opposed to the classic attacks that abuse the infected devices (e.g., botnet renting, information stealing). Mobile devices are by no means immune to ransomware attacks. However, there is little research work on this matter and only traditional protections are available. Even state-of-the-art mobile malware detection approaches are ineffective against ransomware apps because of the subtle attack scheme. As a consequence, the ample attack surface formed by the billion mobile devices is left unprotected.

First, in this work we summarize the results of our analysis of the existing mobile ransomware families, describing their common characteristics. Second, we present HELDROID, a fast, efficient and fully automated approach that recognizes known and unknown scareware and ransomware samples from goodware. Our approach is based on detecting the "building blocks" that are typically needed to implement a mobile ransomware application. Specifically, HELDROID detects, in a generic way, if an app is attempting to lock or encrypt the device without the user's consent, and if ransom requests are displayed on the screen. Our technique works without requiring that a sample of a certain family is available beforehand.

We implemented HELDROID and tested it on real-world Android ransomware samples. On a large dataset comprising hundreds of thousands of APKs including goodware, malware, scareware, and ransomware, HELDROID exhibited nearly zero false positives and the capability of recognizing unknown ransomware samples.

1 Introduction

Theorized back in 1996 [1], ransomware attacks have now become a reality. A typical ransomware encrypts the files on the victim's device and asks for a ransom to release them. The miscreants implement various extortion tactics (as explained in Sect. 2), which are both simple and extremely effective. In the "best" case, the device is locked but data is actually left in place in untouched; in the worst case, personal data is effectively encrypted. Therefore, even if the malware is somehow removed, in absence of a fresh backup, the victims have no other choice than paying the requested ransom to (hope to) regain access to their data. McAfee Labs [2] and the FBI [3] recently concluded that the ransomware trend

© Springer International Publishing Switzerland 2015
H. Bos et al. (Eds.): RAID 2015, LNCS 9404, pp. 382–404, 2015.
DOI: 10.1007/978-3-319-26362-5_18

is on the rise and will be among the top 5 most dangerous threats in the near future.

In parallel, mobile malware is expanding quickly and steadily: McAfee Labs recently reported a 100 % growth in Q42014 since Q42013 [2, p.28], VirusTotal receives hundred of thousands of Android samples every week[1], making them the fourth most submitted file type. Unfortunately, mobile devices are not immune by ransomware. A remarkable wave infected over 900,000 mobile devices in a single month *alone* [4]. Moreover, Kaspersky Labs [5] tracked a another notable mobile campaign, revealing a well-structured distribution network with more than 90 hosts serving the malicious APKs, more than 400 URLs serving the exploits, one controller host, and two traffic-driving networks. Alarmingly, the cyber criminals are one step ahead of the defenders, already targeting mobile users. Given the wide attack surface offered by mobile devices along with the massive amount of sensitive data that users store on them (e.g., pictures, digital wallets, contacts), we call for the need of mobile-specific ransomware counter-measures. Our goal in this paper is to make a first step in this direction.

Current Solutions. To the best of our knowledge, current mitigations are commercial cleanup utilities implementing a classic signature-based approach. For example, SurfRight's HitmanPro.Kickstart [6] is a bootable USB image that uses a live-forensics approach to look for artifacts of known ransomware. Other tools such as Avast's Ransomware Removal [7] (for Android) release the ransomed files by exploiting the naïve design of certain families (i.e., SimpLocker) to recover the encryption key, which fortunately is not generated on a per-infection basis. The research community knows very well that such approaches lack of generality. Also, they are evidently limited to known samples, easy to evade, and ineffective against new variants. From the users' perspective, signature based approaches must be constantly updated with new definitions, and are rarely effective early.

Research Gap. To our knowledge, no research so far have tackled this emerging threat. Even state-of-the-art research approaches (e.g., [8]), which demonstrated nearly-perfect detection and precision on non-ransomware Android malware, recognized only 48.47 % of our ransomware dataset (see Sect. 8). The reason is because ransomware schemes are essentially mimicry attacks, where the overall maliciousness is visible only as a *combination* of legitimate actions. For instance, file encryption or screen locking alone are benign, while the combination of *unsolicited* encryption and screen locking is certainly malicious. Thus, it is not surprising that generic malware-detection approaches exhibit a low recall.

Proposed Approach. After manually analyzing a number of samples of Android ransomware variants from all the existing families, our key insight is to recognize specific, distinctive features of the ransomware tactics with respect to all other malware families — and, obviously, to goodware. Specifically, our

---

[1] https://www.virustotal.com/en/statistics/.

approach is to determine whether a mobile application attempts to *threaten* the user, to *lock* the device, to *encrypt* data — or a combination of these actions.

We implemented HELDROID to analyze Android applications both statically and dynamically. In particular, HELDROID uses static taint analysis and lightweight emulation to find flows of function calls that indicate device-locking or file-encryption behaviors. Our approach to detecting threatening behavior — a core aspect of ransomware — is a learning-based, natural language processing (NLP) technique that recognizes menacing phrases. Although most of our analysis is static, the threatening-text detector does execute the sample in case no threatening text is found in the static files. This allows to support off-band text (e.g., fetched from a remote server).

Overall, HELDROID is specific to the ransomware schemes, but it does not rely on any family in particular. Moreover, the detection features are parametric and thus adaptable to future families. For instance, the taint-analysis module relies on a single configuration file that lists interesting sources and sinks. Similarly, the threatening-text detector supports several languages and new ones can be added with little, automatic training.

Evaluation Results. We tested HELDROID on hundreds of thousands of samples including goodware, generic malware, and ransomware. HELDROID correctly detected all the ransomware samples, and did not confused corner-case, *benign* apps that *resembled* some of the typical ransomware features (e.g., screen locking, adult apps repackaged with *disarmed* ransomware payload). Overall, HELDROID outperformed the state-of-the-art approach for Android malware detection (see Sect. 8). HELDROID performed well also against unknown ransomware samples, missing only minority of cases where the language was not supported out of the box. This was easily fixed with 30 min of work (i.e., find a textbook in Spanish and re-train the NLP classifier). The detection heuristics of HELDROID exhibited only a dozen of false positives over hundreds of thousands non-ransomware apps.

Prototype Release. We provide access to HELDROID through an API (on top of which we implemented a simple Android client), and release our dataset for research purposes: http://ransom.mobi.

Original Contributions. In summary:
- We are the first at looking at the ransomware phenomenon against mobile devices. We provide a retrospective view of the past two years and distill the characteristics that distinguish mobile ransomware from goodware (and from other malware).
- We propose three generic indicators of compromise for detecting Android ransomware activity by recognizing its distinguishing features. The novel aspects of our approach include a text classifier based on NLP features, a lightweight Smali emulation technique to detect locking strategies, and the application of taint tracking for detecting file-encrypting flows.

- We implement (and evaluate) our approaches for the Android platform and open them to the community as a JSON-based API service over HTTP. This is the first public research prototype of its kind.

2 Background and Motivation

Fascinatingly, the idea of abusing cryptography to create extortion-based attacks was first theorized and demonstrated back in 1996 [1]. The authors defined the concept of *cryptovirus* as a *"[malware] that uses public key [...] to encrypt data [...] that resides on the host system, in such a way that [...] can only be recovered by the author of virus"*.

Based on this definition, *ransomware* can be seen as an advanced, coercive cryptovirus. Coercion techniques, also seen in various *scareware* families, include threatening the victim of indictments (e.g., for the detention of pornographic content, child pornography), violation of copyright laws, or similar illegal behavior. In pure scareware, the cyber crooks exploit the fear and do not necessarily lock the device or encrypt any data. In pure ransomware, before or after the threatening phase the malware actually locks the device and/or encrypts sensitive content until the ransom is paid, usually through money transfer (e.g., MoneyPak, MoneyGram) or crypto currencies. Although digital currency was not used in practice back in 1996, curiously, Young and Yung [1] foresaw that *"information extortion attacks could translate in the loss of U.S. dollars if electronic money is implemented."* Notably, CryptoLocker's main payment mechanism is, in fact, Bitcoin [9,10].

2.1 Motivation

Noticing the rapid succession of new families of mobile ransomware, as summarized in Table 1, we downloaded and manually reverse engineered a few samples for each family, noticing three, common characteristics. From this manual analysis we hypothesize that these independent characteristics are representative of the typical mobile ransomware scheme and can be combined in various ways to categorize a sample as scareware, ransomware, or none of the previous.

Device Locking. All families doing device locking use one among these three techniques. The main one consists in asking for device-administration rights and then locking the device. Another technique is to superimpose a full-screen alert dialog or activity. The third technique consists in trapping key-pressure events (e.g., home or back button), such that the victim cannot switch away from the "lock" screen.

Data Encryption. Some samples do not actually have any encryption capability, even if they claim so; alternatively, they may include encryption routines that are however never called. To our knowledge, only the SimpLocker family

Table 1. Timeline of known Android ransomware or scareware families (we exclude minor variants an aliases). E = Encrypt, L = Lock, T = Threaten.

First Seen	Name	Extort	E	L	T	Target and notes
May 2014	Koler (Reveton) [5]	$300	✗	✓	✓	Police-themed screen lock; localized in 30 countries; spreads via SMS
Jun 2014	Simplocker [12]	$12.5[a]	✓	✓	✓	All files on SD card; uses hardcoded, non-unique key
Jun 2014	Svpeng [13]	$200	✗	✓	✓	Police-themed screen lock
Aug 2014	ScarePackage [14]	$100	✗	✓	✓	Can take pictures and scan the device for banking apps or financial details
Early 2015	New Simplocker [11]	$200	✓	✓	✓	Per-device keys; advanced C&C

[a]Corresponding to, approximately, 260 UAH.

currently implements file encryption. In the first version, the encryption key was hardcoded, whereas the second version [11] generates a per-device key. Nevertheless, samples of this family never call any decryption routine, arguably leaving data permanently unavailable even after payment (unless unlocking is performed through a separate app).

Threatening Text. All current families display threatening messages of some sort. We noticed that families localized in English rely on MoneyPak for payments, whereas families localized in Russian accept credit cards as well.

2.2   Goals and Challenges

Having considered the threat posed by ransomware, the potential attack surface comprising billions of Internet-connected devices and the limitations of current countermeasures, our high-level goal is to overcome the downsides of signature-based approaches, and recognize both known and novel ransomware variants robustly by generalizing the insights described in Sect. 2.1.

Achieving our goal is challenging. Recognizing variants requires a robust model of their characterizing features that has both generalization and detection capabilities, in order to catch both new and known ransomware implementations, possibly in an adaptive way. For example, the task of modeling and recognizing threatening text must account for localization, creating a model that can be quickly re-adapted to new languages *before* new ransomware campaigns start spreading. Similar observations apply to other characterizing features.

2.3   Scope and Assumptions

Although ransomware detection is by no means tied exclusively to the mobile world, in this work we focus on Android ransomware. Mobile ransomware is

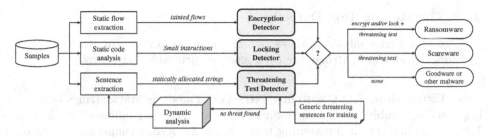

Fig. 1. Android samples are statically analyzed for extracting "artifacts" that typical of ransomware tactics (encryption, locking, threatening). If no threatening text is found, off-band text is analyzed by collecting strings allocated by the sample while running in an instrumented sandbox.

indeed evolving quickly, with 5 families in less than one year (May 2014–Jan 2015), and self-replicating capabilities since the first release.

We focus on challenges that are unique to the ransomware-detection problem (i.e., detecting locking strategies, encryption operations and threatening messages). In this work, we set aside: related problems already tackled by current or past research such as (anti-)evasion techniques, or other aspects that are typical of malicious software *in general*). In Sect. 7 we discuss the impact of our choices.

3   HeLDroid's Approach

In this section we describe how, at a *conceptual* level, HeLDroid analyzes each Android APK file to decide whether it is a ransomware sample.

As summarized in Fig. 1, we employ three, independent detectors, which can be executed in parallel. Each detector looks for a specific indicator of compromise typical of a ransomware malware. The **Threatening Text Detector** uses text classification to detect coercion attempts (Sect. 3.1). If the result of this classifier is positive, but the others are not, we label the sample as "scareware". This means that the application limits itself to displaying some threatening text to convince the victim in doing some action. If also the **Encryption Detector** (Sect. 3.2) and/or the **Locking Detector** (Sect. 3.3) are triggered, this means that the application is actively performing either action on the infected device. In this case, we label the sample as "ransomware". We designed deterministic decision criteria based on static analysis to detect encryption or locking operations. Note that if the **Threatening Text Detector** is not triggered, the sample is discarded and cannot be considered as ransomware or scareware. Although these three detectors could be combined in other ways (e.g., by including weighting), in this work we consider the presence of threatening text as mandatory for a ransomware author to reach her goal. This aspect is discussed thoroughly in Sect. 7.

3.1   Threatening Text Detector

The goal of this analysis is to recognize menacing phrases in statically and dynamically allocated strings (i.e., sequences of printable characters).

Text Extraction. HELDROID first extracts and analyzes static strings by parsing the disassembled code and resource files (e.g., assets, configuration files). If HELDROID detects no threatening text, then it analyzes dynamically allocated strings: It runs the sample in a sandbox, captures a network traffic dump (i.e., PCAP), decodes application-layer protocols (e.g., HTTP) and extracts strings from the resulting data. The sandbox that we employ also extracts strings allocated dynamically (e.g., as a result of a decryption), but none of the current samples used these measures.

Text Classification. To estimate whether a string contains threatening sentences, we use a natural language processing (NLP) supervised classifier. We train it on generic threatening phrases, similar to (and including) those that typically appear in ransomware or scareware samples. More precisely, we train the classifier using phrases labeled by us as *threat*, *law*, *copyright*, *porn*, and *money*, which typically appear in scareware or ransomware campaigns. Note that no ransomware samples are actually needed to train our classifier: All we need are the sentences. As opposed to being able to isolate a sample, knowing the sentences early is easy (e.g., by taking a screenshot or by leveraging reports given by the first victims).

This phase is further detailed in Sect. 4.1. Its **output** is a ternary decision: "ransomware" threatening text (i.e., accusing the user and asking for payment), "scareware" text (i.e., accusing the user), or "none".

Localization. Our NLP classifier supports localization transparently: It tells whether a given sentence is "threatening" in any of the languages on which it has been trained on. In the unlucky case where localized training phrases are unavailable for training, in Sect. 6.2 we show, as a proof of concept, that these can be easily obtained by running automatic translators on existing sentences found in known ransomware or scareware.

Other Sources of Text. From a technical point of view, the text can be displayed via other means than strings (e.g., images). However, we focus on the core problem, which is that of deciding whether a *text* contains threatening phrases. As discussed in Sect. 7, extracting text from images and videos is easily performed with off-the-shelf OCR software. Recall that, among the goals of the attacker, the ransom-requesting message must be readable and understandable by the victim: It is thus against his or her goals to try to evade OCRs, making the text difficult to read as a side effect.

3.2   Encryption Detector

We check whether the (disassembled) code of the sample under analysis contains traces of unsolicited file-encryption operations.

Unsolicited file-encryption operations are usually implemented by reading the storage (e.g., external storage), looping over the files, invoking encryption routines on each of them, and deleting the original files. Therefore, we are interested in finding execution flows that originate from file-reading operations and terminate into encryption routines. To this end, we rely on a fast, static taint-analysis technique to track flows originating from functions that access the storage (e.g., `getExternalStorageDirectory()`), ending into functions that write encrypted content and delete the original files (e.g., `CipherOutputStream`, `delete()`). We are well aware that a malware author can embed cryptographic primitives rather than using the Android API. Fortunately, recent research [15,16] has already tackled this problem.

Details aside, the **output of this phase** is a binary decision on whether there are significant traces of unsolicited file-encryption operations or not.

3.3   Locking Detector

We check if the application under analysis is able to lock the device (i.e., to prevent navigation among activities). This can be achieved in many ways in Android, including the use of the native screen locking functionality, dimming, immortal dialogs, and so forth. Focusing on the most common techniques that we encountered in real-world Android ransomware we designed a series of heuristics based on lightweight emulation, which can be extended to include other locking techniques in the future.

The most common technique to enact device locking consists in inhibiting navigation among activities through the *Home* and *Back* buttons. This is achieved by handling the events that originate when the user clicks on such buttons on the phone and preventing their propagation. The net result is that the ransomware application effectively forces the device to display an arbitrary activity. Another technique consists in asking the user to let the application become a device administrator, thus allowing it to lock the device. This functionality is part of Android and is normally used for benign purposes (e.g., remote device administration in enterprise scenarios).

To detect if any of these locking technique is executed, we implemented a static code-analysis technique, described in Sect. 4.3. Essentially, we track each Dalvik instruction, including method calls, and check whether there exists an execution path that matches a given heuristic. We created one heuristic per locking strategy. For example, we verify whether the event handler associated to the *Home* button returns always `true`, which means that the event handling cannot propagate further, resulting in a locked screen.

Details aside, the **output of this phase** is a binary decision on whether there are significant traces of device-locking implementations or not.

The overall **final output** of HELDROID, obtained by aggregating the outputs of the three detectors, is a ternary decision: ransomware, scareware, or none.

4 System Details

This section describes the details of HELDROID. The technical implementation details are glanced in Sect. 5.

4.1 Threatening Text Detector Details

We use a supervised-classification approach that works on the text features extracted as follows:

1. **Language Detection:** a simple frequency analysis determines the language of the text (see Sect. 5.1 for the implementation details).
2. **Sentences Splitting:** we use a language-specific segmenter that splits the text into *sentences*.
3. **Stop-word Removal:** we remove all stop words (e.g., "to", "the", "an", "and").
4. **Stemming:** we reduce words to their *stems* (e.g., "fishing," "fished," and "fisher" become "fish").
5. **Stem Vectors:** We map each sentence to a set of *stem vectors*, which are binary vectors that encode which stems are in the sentence.

In *training* mode, each stem vector t is stored in a training set T. At *runtime*, the stem vectors obtained from the app under analysis are used to query the classifier, which answers "ransomware," "scareware," or "other," based on the following scoring algorithm.

Scoring. As suggested in the text-classification literature [17], scoring is based on the cosine similarity $s(x,t) \in [0,1]$ between the query stem vector x and every $t \in T$. Since we operate in a boolean space, it can be reduced to $s(\hat{x}, \hat{t}) = \frac{|\hat{x} \cap \hat{t}|}{\sqrt{|\hat{x}|} \cdot \sqrt{|\hat{t}|}}$, where $\hat{x}$ and $\hat{t}$ are the stem sets (i.e., the set data structures that contain strings denoting each stem), which is computed in $O(\min(|\hat{x}|, |\hat{t}|))$.

To score the entire text x, the classifier categorizes its sentences $\forall c \in x$ by maximizing the cosine similarity $s(c,t)\ \forall t \in T$. We denote the score of the best-scoring sentence $c^\star$ as $m(c^\star)$. The best score is calculated within each category. We actually computes two scores, $m(c^\star)_{\text{money}}$ for the best-scoring sentences about "money," and $m(c^\star)_{\text{accusation}}$ for other "accusation" sentences (i.e., threat, law, copyright, porn).

Decision. We label the text as "scareware" if $m_{\text{accusation}}$ exceeds a threshold, and "ransomware" if also m_{money} exceeds. The threshold is set adaptively based on the minimum required score for a sentence to be considered relevant for our analysis. The idea is that short sentences should have a higher threshold, since it is easier to match a greater percentile of a short sentence; instead, longer sentences should have a lower threshold, for the same reason.

Setting thresholds is typically a problematic, yet difficult-to-avoid part of any heuristic-based detection approach. Setting one single threshold is easier, but makes the decision more sensitive to changes (i.e., one single unit above the threshold could signify a false detection). Therefore, we set *bounds* rather than single threshold values, which we believe leave more room for customization. By no means we claim that such bounds are good for future ransomware samples. As any heuristic-based system, they must be adjusted to keep up with the evolution of the threat under consideration. However, by setting them on the known ransomware samples of our dataset, our experiments show that HELDROID can detect also never-seen-before samples. More details are in Sect. 5.2.

4.2 Encryption Detector Details

Using a static taint-tracking technique, we detect file encryption operations as flows from `Environment.getExternalStorageDirectory()` (1 source) to the `CipherOutputStream` constructor, `Cipher.doFinal` methods, or its overloads (8 sinks). Clearly, tracked flows can involve other, intermediate function calls (e.g., copy data from filesystem to memory, then pass the reference to the buffer to an encryption function, and finally write on the filesystem).

An explanatory example taken from a real-world ransomware sample[2] follows: The underlined lines mark the tracked flow. More sources and sinks can be flexibly added by simple configuration changes, although our results show that the aforementioned ones are enough for current families.

Listing 1.1. Flow source of an encryption operation

```
.class public final Lcom/free/xxx/player/d;

# ...

.method public constructor <init>(Landroid/content/Context;)V ...

# getExternalStorageDirectory is invoked to get the SD card root

invoke-static {}, Landroid/os/Environment;->getExternalStorageDirectory()Ljava/io/File;
move-result-object v0
invoke-virtual {v0}, Ljava/io/File;->toString()Ljava/lang/String;
move-result-object v0
new-instance v1, Ljava/io/File;
invoke-direct {v1, v0}, Ljava/io/File;-><init>(Ljava/lang/String;)V

# This invocation saves all files with given extensions in a list
# and then calls the next method

invoke-direct {p0, v1}, Lcom/free/xxx/player/d;->a(Ljava/io/File;)V
return-void
.end method

.method public final a()V
#

# A new object for encryption is instantiated with key
# 12345678901234567890

new-instance v2, Lcom/free/xxx/player/a;
const-string v0, "12345678901234567890"
invoke-direct {v2, v0}, Lcom/free/xxx/player/a;-><init>(Ljava/lang/String;)V ...

# If files were not encrypted, encrypt them now

const-string v3, "FILES_WERE_ENCRYPTED"
invoke-interface {v2, v3, v0}, Landroid/content/SharedPreferences;->getBoolean(Ljava/lang/String;Z)Z
move-result v2
if-nez v2, :cond_1
invoke-static {}, Landroid/os/Environment;->getExternalStorageState()Ljava/lang/String;
move-result-object v2
const-string v3, "mounted"

# ...

# Inside a loop, invoke the encryption routine a on file v0, and
# delete it afterward

invoke-virtual {v2, v0, v4}, Lcom/free/xxx/player/a;->a(Ljava/lang/String;Ljava/lang/String;)V

new-instance v4, Ljava/io/File;
invoke-direct {v4, v0}, Ljava/io/File;-><init>(Ljava/lang/String;)V
invoke-virtual {v4}, Ljava/io/File;->delete()Z

# ...
.end method
.end class
```

[2] MD5: c83242bfd0e098d9d03c381aee1b4788.

Listing 1.2. Flow sink of an encryption operation.

```
.class public final Lcom/free/xxx/player/a;

# ...

.method public final a(Ljava/lang/String;Ljava/lang/String;)V
    .locals 6

    # A CipherOutputStream is initialized and used to encrypt the file
    # passed as argument, which derives from an invocation to

    new-instance v0, Ljava/io/FileInputStream;
    invoke-direct {v0, p1}, Ljava/io/FileInputStream;-><init>(Ljava/lang/String;)V
    new-instance v1, Ljava/io/FileOutputStream;

    invoke-direct {v1, p2}, Ljava/io/FileOutputStream;-><init>(Ljava/lang/String;)V
    iget-object v2, p0, Lcom/free/xxx/player/a;->a:Ljavax/crypto/Cipher;

    const/4 v3, 0x1
    iget-object v4, p0, Lcom/free/xxx/player/a;->b:Ljavax/crypto/spec/SecretKeySpec;

    iget-object v5, p0, Lcom/free/xxx/player/a;->c:Ljava/security/spec/AlgorithmParameterSpec;

    invoke-virtual {v2, v3, v4, v5}, Ljavax/crypto/Cipher;>init(ILjava/security/Key;Ljava/security/spec/AlgorithmParameterSpec;)V

    new-instance v2, Ljavax/crypto/CipherOutputStream;
    iget-object v3, p0, Lcom/free/xxx/player/a;->a:Ljavax/crypto/Cipher;
    invoke-direct {v2, v1, v3}, Ljavax/crypto/CipherOutputStream;-><init>(Ljava/io/OutputStream;Ljavax/crypto/Cipher;)V

    # ...
.end method
.end class
```

If any of these flows are found, HELDROID marks the sample accordingly.

4.3 Locking Detector Details

As a proof of concept, we implement a detection heuristic for each of the three most common screen-locking techniques found in Android ransomware.

- Require **administration privileges** and call `DevicePolicyManager.lockNow()`, which forces the device to act as if the lock screen timeout expired.
- **Immortal Activity.** Fill the screen with an activity and inhibit navigation through back and home buttons by overriding the calls to `onKeyUp` and `onKeyDown`. Optionally, the activity cover the software-implemented navigation buttons if the application declares the `SYSTEM_ALERT_WINDOW` permission.
- **Immortal Dialog.** Show an alert dialog that is impossible to close and set a flag in the window parameters.

Detecting whether an app calls the `lockNow` method is easy. We start from searching for the specific permission bit (`BIND_DEVICE_ADMIN`) in the manifest. If found, we parse the Smali assembler code of the application until we find a call to the `lockNow` method.

For the immortal activity technique we are interested in the handling of the `onKeyDown` and `onKeyUp` methods, which are called when a key is pressed or released. They accept as first argument a parameter `p1` containing the numeric code of target key; their return value determines whether the event is considered handled or not (i.e., whether to pass the same event to other underlying View components). An example[3] follows.

---

[3] MD5 `b31ce7e8e63fb9eb78b8ac934ad5a2ec`.

Listing 1.3. Locking operation example.

```
.method public onKeyDown(ILandroid/view/KeyEvent;)Z
  .locals 1

  # p1 = integer with the key code associated to the pressed key.

  const/4 v0, 0x4 # 4 = back button
  if-ne p1, v0, :cond_0
  iget-object v0, p0, Lcom/android/x5a807058/ZActivity;->q:Lcom/android/zics/ZModuleInterface;

  if-nez v0, :cond_0
  iget-object v0, p0, Lcom/android/x5a807058/ZActivity;->a:Lcom/android/x5a807058/ae;

  # we track function calls as well invoke-virtual {v0},

  Lcom/android/x5a807058/ae;->c()Z :cond_0

  const/4 v0, 0x1 # True = event handled -> do not forward
  return v0
.end method
```

We first locate the **onKeyDown** and **onKeyUp** methods and parse their Smali code. Then we proceed by performing a lightweight Smali emulation. Essentially, we parse each statement and "execute" it according to its semantic. The goal is to verify the existence of an execution path in which the return value is *true*. We examine those **if** statements that compare **p1** with constant integer values. Our emulation technique tracks function calls as well.

Similarly, we detect immortal dialogs by checking if **FLAG_SHOW_WHEN_LOCKED** is set when calling **Landroid/view/Window;->setFlags** in an any **AlertDialog** method, usually in the constructor, and that the same dialog is marked as uncancelable via **setCancelable(false)**.

The immortal activity and dialog techniques can be implemented with a Window instead of an Activity or Dialog object, but we consider this extension exercise for the reader.

5 Implementation and Technical Details

This section describes the relevant technical details of HELDROID.

5.1 Natural Language Processing

We implement the **Threatening Text Detector** on top of *OpenNLP*, a generic, extensible, multi-language NLP library. The sentence splitter and the stemmer [18] are language specific: Adding new languages simply requires training on an arbitrary set of texts provided by the user. For example, we added Russian by training it on a transcript of the *XXVI Congress of the CPSU and Challenges of Social Psychology*[4] and a Wikipedia article about law[5]. In addition, Sect. 6.2 we show how to add new languages to the threatening text classifier.

Our stop-words lists come from the *Stop-words Project*[6]. The language identification is performed with the Cybozu open-source library [19], released and maintained since 2010.

---

[4] http://www.voppsy.ru/issues/1981/816/816005.htm.
[5] https://ru.wikipedia.org/wiki/.
[6] https://code.google.com/p/stop-words/.

5.2   Text Classification Thresholding

To determine whether the score m of a sentence with respect to the accusation or money categories we proceed as follows. More formally, we want to determine whether $m_{accusation}$ or m_{money} exceed a threshold. In doing this, we account for the contribution of all sentences (and not only the best scoring ones).

For example, consider the sentences: *"To unlock the device you need"* ($m = 0.775$), $m =$ *"to pay 1,000 rubles"* ($m = 0.632$), and *"Within 24 h we'll unlock your phone"* ($m = 0.612$). The maximum score is 0.775, but since there are other relevant sentences this value should be increased to take them into account. To this end, we increase the score m as follows:

$$\hat{m} = m + (1 - m) \cdot \left(1 - e^{- \sum\limits_{i=1}^{n} (s(c_i) - t(c_i))} \right)$$

where $s(c) - t(c)$ is capped to zero, n is the number of sentences in that category set, c_i the i-th sentence in the stem vector c, and $t : c \mapsto [0, 1]$ is an adaptive threshold function.

Let us pretend for a moment that $t(c)$ is not adaptive, but set to 0.6. Then the sum of $s(c) - t(c)$ is $0.032 + 0.012 = 0.044$. As you can see, $\hat{m}$ is not very different from m because the scores of second and third sentence are just slightly above their detection threshold.

Instead, the idea behind $t(c)$ is that short sentences should have a higher threshold, since it is easier to match a greater percentile of a short sentence; instead, longer sentences should have a lower threshold, for the dual reason:

$$t(c) = \tau_{max} - \gamma(c) \cdot (\tau_{max} - \tau_{min}), \quad \gamma(c) = \frac{\sum\limits_{c_i \in c} c_i - \sigma_{min}}{\sigma_{max} - \sigma_{min}}$$

with $\gamma(c)$ capped in $[0, 1]$. The summation yields the number of 1 s in the stem vector of sentence c. σ_{min} and σ_{max} are constants that represent the minimum and maximum number of stems that we want to consider: sentences containing less stems than σ_{min} will have the highest threshold, while sentences containing more stems than σ_{max} will have the lowest threshold. Highest and lowest threshold values are represented by τ_{min} and τ_{max}, which form a threshold bound.

These parameters can be set by first calculating the score of all the sentences in the training set. Then, the values are set such that the classifier distinguishes the ransomware in the training set from generic malware or goodware in the training set. Following this simple, empirical procedure, we obtained: $\tau_{min} = 0.35$, $\tau_{max} = 0.63$, $\sigma_{min} = 3$, and $\sigma_{max} = 6$.

5.3   Dynamic Analysis

If no threatening text is found in statically allocated strings, we attempt a last-resort analysis. In an emulator, we install, run and let the sample run for 5'. After launching the app, our emulator follows an approach similar to the one adopted by TraceDroid [20]: It generates events that simulate user interaction, rebooting, in/out SMS or calls, etc. Aiming for comprehensive and precise user-activity simulation and anti evasion is out from our scope. From our experience, if the C&C server is active, in a few seconds the sniffer captures the data required to extract the threatening text, which is displayed almost immediately.

From the decoded application-layer traffic (e.g., HTTP), HELDROID parses printable strings. In addition to parsing plaintext protocols from network dumps, every modern sandbox (including the one that we are using) allows to extract strings passed as arguments to functions, which are another source of threatening text. Although we do not implement OCR-text extraction in our current version of HELDROID, we run a quick pilot study on the screenshots collected by TraceDroid. Using the default configuration of `tesseract` we were able to extract all the sentences displayed on the screenshots.

5.4   Static Code Analysis

We extract part of the features for the **Threatening Text Detector** by parsing the manifest and other configuration files found in the APK once uncompressed with `akptool`[7]. We compute the remaining ones by enumerating count, type or size of files contained in the same application package.

However, the most interesting data requires an analysis of the app's Dalvik code in its Smali[8] text representation generated by `apktool`. For the **Locking Detector**, instead of using *SAAF* [21], which we found unstable in multi-threaded scenarios, we wrote a simple emulator that "runs" Smali code, tailored for our needs. To keep it fast, we implemented the minimum subset of instructions required by our detector.

For the **Encryption Detector** we need precise flows information across the entire Smali instruction set. For this, we leveraged *FlowDroid* [22], a very robust, context-, flow-, field-, object-sensitive and lifecycle-aware static taint-analysis tool with great recall and precision. Source and sink APIs are configurable.

6   Experimental Validation

We tested HELDROID, running on server-grade hardware, against real-world datasets to verify if it detected known and new ransomware variants and samples. In summary, as discussed further in Sect. 8, it outperformed the state-of-the-art research tool for Android malware detection.

6.1   Datasets

We used a diverse set of datasets (Table 2), available at http://ransom.mobi.

---

[7] https://code.google.com/p/android-apktool/.
[8] https://code.google.com/p/smali/.

Table 2. Summary of our datasets. VT 5+ indicates that samples that are marked according to VirusTotal's positive results. VT top 400 are on Dec 24th, 2014.

Name	Size	Labelling	Apriori content	Use
AR	172,174	VT 5+	55.3 % malware + 44.7 % goodware	FP eval.
AT	12,842	VT 5+	68.2 % malware + 31.8 % goodware	FP eval.
MG	1,260	Implicit	100 % malware	FP eval.
R1	207	VT 5+	100 % ransomware + scareware	NLP training
R2	443	VT 5+	100 % ransomware + scareware	Detection
M1	400	VT top 400	100 % malware	FP eval.

Goodware and Generic Malware. We obtained access to the **AndRadar (AR)** [23] dataset, containing apps from independent markets (Blackmart, Opera, Camangi, PandaApp, Slideme, and GetJar) between Feb 2011 and Oct 2013. Moreover, we used the public **AndroTotal (AT)** API [24] to fetch the apps submitted in Jun 2014–Dec 2014. Also, we used the **MalGenome (MG)** [25] dataset, which contains malware appeared in Aug 2010–Oct 2011.

We labeled each sample using VirusTotal, flagging as *malware* those with 5+/56 positives. The **AR** and **AT** datasets do not contain any ransomware samples. The **MG** dataset contains only malware (not ransomware).

Last, the **Malware 1 (M1)** dataset contains the top 400 malicious Android applications as of Dec 2014, excluding those already present in the rest of our datasets and any known ransomware.

Known Ransomware (sentences for Text-Classifier Training). We need a small portion of sentences obtained from true ransomware samples. During the early stages of a malware campaign, samples are not always readily available for analysis or training. Interestingly, our text-classifier can be trained regardless of the availability of the sample: All it needs is the threatening text, which is usually easy to obtain (e.g., from early reports from victims).

We built the **Ransomware 1 (R1)** dataset through the VirusTotal Intelligence API by searching for positive (5+) Android samples labeled or tagged as *ransomware, koler, locker, fbilocker, scarepackage*, and similar, in Sep–Nov 2014. We manually verified that at least 5 distinct AV programs agreed on the same labels in **R1** (allowing slight lexical variations). In this way, we excluded outliers caused by naming inconsistencies, and could be reasonably safe that the resulting 207 samples were true ransomware. The training is performed only once, offline, but can be repeated over time as needed. We manually labeled sentences (e.g., threat, porn, copyright) from the **R1** dataset, totaling 51 English sentences and 31 Russian sentences.

Unknown Ransomware. Similarly, we built the **Ransomware 2 (R2)** dataset for samples appeared in Dec 2014–Jan 2015. This dataset is to evaluate HELDROID on an arbitrary, never-seen-before, dataset comprising ransomware — and possibly other categories of malware. Aposteriori, we discovered that this datasets contains interesting corner-case apps that resemble some of the typical ransomware features (e.g., screen locking, adult apps repackaged with *disarmed* ransomware payload), making this a particularly challenging test case.

6.2   Experiment 1: Detection Capability

HELDROID detected all of the 207 ransomware samples in **R1**: 194 with static text extraction, and the remaining 13 by extracting the text in live-captured web responses from the C&C server. However, this was expected, since we used **R1** for training. Thus, this experiment showed only the correctness of the approach.

We tested the true predictive capabilities of HELDROID on **R2**, which is disjoint from **R1**. Among the 443 total samples in **R2**, 375 were correctly detected as ransomware or scareware, and 49 were correctly flagged as neither. Precisely, the following ones were actually true negatives:

- 14 Badoink + 15 PornDroid clones (see below);
- 6 lock-screen applications to modify the system's look &feel;
- 14 benign, adware, spyware, or other non-ransomware threats.

Badoink and PornDroid are benign applications sometimes used as hosts of ransomware payload. HELDROID correctly only flagged the locking behavior. We installed and used such samples on a real device and verified that they were not performing any malicious operation apart from locking the device screen (behavior that was correctly detected). An analysis of network traffic revealed that the remote endpoint of all web requests issued during execution was unreachable, resulting in the application being unable to display the threatening web page.

The last 19 samples are known to AV companies as ransomware, but:

- 11 samples use languages on which HELDROID was not trained (see below).
- 4 samples contain no static or dynamically generated text, thus they were disarmed, bogus or simply incorrectly flagged by the commercial AVs.
- 4 failed downloading their threatening text because the C&C server was down. Strictly speaking, these samples can be safely considered as being disarmed. Manual analysis revealed that these samples belong to an unknown family (probably based on repackaged PornDroid versions).

False Negative Analysis. We focused on the samples that were not detected because of the missing language models. As a proof of concept we trained HELDROID on Spanish, by translating known threatening text from English to Spanish using Google Translator, adding known non-threatening Spanish text, and running the training procedure. The whole process took less than 30 min. After this, all previously undetected samples localized in Spanish were successfully flagged as ransomware.

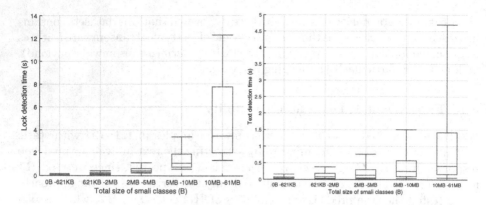

Fig. 2. Lock-detection (left) and text-classification (right) time as function of Smali class size (whiskers at the 9th and 91st percentiles).

6.3 Experiment 2: False Positive Evaluation

A false positive is a generic malware or a goodware sample flagged as ransomware. We first evaluated HELDROID on **M1** (generic malware, no ransomware). No sample in **M1** was flagged by HELDROID as ransomware.

We extended this experiment to the other datasets containing goodware and generic malware (i.e., **AR, AT, MG**). In the **AR** dataset, which contained both malware and goodware, HELDROID correctly reported zero ransomware samples, whereas in the **AT** dataset only 2 and 7 samples out of 12,842 were incorrectly flagged as ransomware and scareware, respectively. Manual investigation revealed that the 2 false ransomware samples were actually a benign sample and a generic trojan, respectively. Actually, both samples had a locking behavior that was correctly caught by HELDROID. The reason why these were flagged as ransomware is because they contained text localized in all major languages (most of which were different than those currently implemented in HELDROID), which brought the text classifier in a corner case. The 7 false scareware comprised 6 benign apps and 1 Leadbolt adware sample. In all cases, the source of error was an significant amount of text containing threatening-, porn-, law- or copyright-related keywords. Last, in the **MG** dataset, none of the malware samples was incorrectly flagged as ransomware or scareware.

However, we can conclude that the rate of false positives is minuscule compared to the size of the datasets. Moreover, the majority of false positives are actually known goodware, which can be pre-filtered easily with whitelisting.

6.4 Experiment 3: Detection Speed

We measured the speed of each detector component on 50 distinct random splits of **AR** with 1,000 samples each. Figure 2(a) and (b) show that text classification is extremely fast in all cases, while locking strategies detection is the main bottleneck, yet under 4 s on average. The encryption-detection module always took milliseconds.

If HELDROID must invoke the external sandbox to extract dynamically generated text, this takes up to 5 min in our implementation, but this is unavoidable for dynamic analysis. As we showed, however, this happens for a very limited number of samples.

7   Limitations and Future Work

Our results show that HELDROID has raised the bar for ransomware authors. However, there are limitations, which we describe in this section, that we hope will stimulate further research.

Portability. Although we focus on the mobile case, ransomware is a general problem. Porting the HELDROID *approach* to the non-mobile world is non-trivial but feasible. The **Threatening Text Detector** would be straightforward to port, as it only assumes the availability of text. For example, it could be applied *as it* is for filtering scareware emails. The toughest parts to port are those that assume the use of a well-defined API (e.g., for encryption or locking operations). Indeed, a malware author could evade our system by using native code or embedding cryptographic primitives, making porting much more complex. However, the progress on static program analysis (e.g., [26,27]) and reverse engineering (e.g., [28]) of native binary code have produced advanced analysis tools that would ease porting HELDROID to other settings, including the detection of cryptographic primitives in binary code [15,16]. The principles behind our detection modules do not change; only their implementation does.

One last discussion point regards the inspection site. For mobile applications, which are typically vetted prior or upon installation (e.g., by the distributing marketplace, on the device using call-home services such as Google App Verify), HELDROID works "as is." For non-mobile applications that do not follow this distribution model, HELDROID should be integrated into the operating system, in a trusted domain (e.g., kernel, driver). In this application scenario it is crucial that the system is allowed to block the currently executing code to prevent the malicious actions to continue. In HELDROID's terms, this means that the encryption and locking indicators of compromise should have high priority, to avoid cases in which the malware *first* silently encrypts every file and *then* displays the threatening text (when it is already too late).

Internationalization. As we proved in **Experiment 1** by quickly adding Spanish support, we designed HELDROID such that supporting other languages is a trivial task. Languages such as Chinese or Japanese, however, would be trickier than others to implement, due to significant differences in stemming and phrase structure. Fortunately, research prototypes such as Stanford's CoreNLP [29] that support (for instance) Chinese NLP makes this extension feasible with just some engineering work.

Evasion. In addition to the use of native machine code, which we already mentioned above, a simple yet naïve evasion to the static-analysis part of our approach (**Encryption Detector** and **Locking Detector**) consists of a benign APK that dynamically loads the code carrying out the actual attacks [30]. First, we note that this technique can be counter evaded by intercepting the loaded payload and analyzing it in a second round, as previous research have demonstrated [31]. Second, we note that this evasion mechanism is common to any static-based approach, and thus is not specific to HELDROID.

A more interesting discussion regards the threatening text. Text can be displayed via other means than strings (e.g., images, videos, audio), delivered out of band (e.g, e-mail) or obfuscated. A first mitigation, that we partially address, consists in using a sandbox that dumps dynamically allocated text, thus coping with obfuscated strings as well as encrypted application protocols (e.g., HTTPS). For example, Andrubis tracks decryption routines and allow the analyst to access the decrypted content.

Regarding image- or video-rendered text, state-of-the-art optical character recognition (OCR) techniques could be used. Although evasion techniques — such as those used in CAPTCHAs — can be mounted against OCR, the goal of the attacker is to make the text clear and easy to read for the victim, setting a limit to them; also, previous research demonstrated the fallacy of even the most extreme text-distortion techniques adopted by CAPTCHAs [32]. Regarding out-of-band text, our current implementation of HELDROID does not cope with it, although applying our text classifier to incoming email messages is trivial. In general, this strategy may be in contrast with the attacker's goal, that is to ensure that the victim receives the ransom-requesting message. Displaying this message synchronously is an advantage for the attacker, whereas out-of-band communication *alone* is ill suited to the task. For example, the victim may not read email or junk-mail filters could block such messages.

An even more interesting evasion technique is a mimicry attack on our text classifier, which we think is possible. In a nutshell, the attacker must be able to write a text containing a disproportionally large number of unknown words, unusual punctuation or many grammar errors. Unusual punctuation and grammar errors could be mitigated with some lexical pre-processing an advanced corrector. Interestingly, the most recent families (e.g., CBT-Locker) show that the attackers tend to write "perfect" messages, arguably prepared by native speakers, in order to sound more legitimate. After all, careful wording of threatening messages is essential to all social engineering-based attacks.

Future Work. In addition to addressing the aforementioned limitations, future research could focus on designing ransomware-resistant OSs. For example, in the case of Android, calls to encryption routines should be explicitly authorized by the users on a per-file basis. This is not trivial from a usability viewpoint, especially for long sequences of calls. Moreover, many applications may use encryption for benign purposes, making this goal even more challenging.

8   Related Work

Malware Detection. There exist several malware detection approaches, including static [8,33], dynamic [34], and hybrid [25] techniques. DREBIN [8] and MAST [33] are particularly related to our work. DREBIN aims at detecting malware statically, with a 94 % accuracy and 1 % false positives: It gathers features such as permissions, intents, used APIs, network addresses, etc., embeds them in a vector space and trains a support vector machine to recognize malware. MAST relies on multiple correspondence analysis and statically ranks applications by suspiciousness. Thanks to this ranking, it detects 95 % of malware at the cost of analyzing 13 % of goodware.

Unfortunately, generic approaches to malware detection seem unsuitable for ransomware. We tested DREBIN on our **R2** dataset of ransomware. Although DREBIN outperformed AVs, HELDROID outperformed DREBIN (which detected only 48.47 % of the ransomware samples). Even the authors of DREBIN, which we have contacted, in their paper state that their approach is vulnerable to mimicry attacks. Ransomware is a type of mimicry attack, because it composes benign actions (i.e., encryption, text rendering) toward a malicious goal.

Ransomware Detection. To the best of our knowledge, our paper is the first research work on mobile ransomware. The work by Kharraz et al. [35], published after the submission of HELDROID, is the first to present a thorough study on Windows ransomware. After analyzing 1,359 belonging to 15 distinct ransomware families, they present a series of indicators of compromise that characterize ransomware activity at the filesystem layer. This approach, in addition to being focused entirely on the Windows operating system, is complementary to ours. Indeed, we look at how ransomware behaves at the application level, whereas [35] focuses on the low level behavior.

Previous work focused on the malicious use of cryptography for implementing ransomware attacks [1,36]. However, no approaches exist for the explicit detection of this class of malware.

9   Conclusions

A single mobile ransomware family has already affected nearly one million of users [4] in one month. Judging by the most recent families [11] and their rapid evolution pace, this threat will arguably become more and more dangerous, and difficult to deal with. Before HELDROID, the only available tools were signature based, with all of the disadvantages this entails. Instead, we showed that our approach, after being trained on recent ransomware samples, is able to efficiently detect new variants and families. Even with mixed datasets including benign, malicious, scareware, and ransomware apps, HELDROID correctly recognized 99 % never-seen-before samples (375 + 11 + 4 over 394, in a dataset containing also 49 corner-case apps). Interestingly, the remainder 4 were incorrectly flagged by commercial AVs as ransomware. Thus, it is a first, significant step toward designing proactive detectors that provide an effective line of defense.

HELDROID could be integrated in mobile AVs, which would submit files to our JSON API, as recently proposed in [37]. Alternatively, HELDROID shall be deployed in one or more of the many checkpoints offered by modern app-distribution ecosystems. For instance, HELDROID could be part o the app-vetting processes performed by the online marketplaces, or upon installation (e.g., the Google App Verify service scans apps right before proceeding with installation).

Acknowledgments. We are thankful to the anonymous reviewers and our shepherd, Patrick Traynor, for the insightful comments, Steven Arzt, who helped us improving FlowDroid to track flows across threads, and Daniel Arp from the DREBIN project. This work has been supported by the MIUR FACE Project No. RBFR13AJFT.

References

1. Young, A., Yung, M.: Cryptovirology: extortion-based security threats and coun-termeasures. In: Proceedings of the IEEE Symposium on Security and Privacy, pp. 129–140, May 1996
2. McAfee Labs: Threats report, November 2014. McAfee Labs, November 2014
3. Ransomware on the rise, January 2015. http://www.fbi.gov/news/stories/2015/january/ransomware-on-the-rise
4. Perlroth, N.: Android phones hit by 'Ransomware', August 2014. http://bits.blogs.nytimes.com/2014/08/22/android-phones-hit-byransomware/
5. Lab. Koler - the police ransomware for android, June 2014. http://securelist.com/blog/research/65189/behind-the-android-oskoler-distribution-network/
6. SurfRight. HitmanPro.kickstart, March 2014. http://www.surfright.nl/en/kickstart
7. Avast Software. Avast ransomware removal, June 2014. https://play.google.com/store/apps/details?id=com.avast.android.malwareremoval
8. Arp, D., et al.: Drebin: effective and explainable detection of android malware in your pocket. In: Network and Distributed System Security (NDSS) Symposium, San Diego, California (2014)
9. Spagnuolo, M., Maggi, F., Zanero, S.: BitIodine: extracting intelligence from the bitcoin network. In: Financial Cryptography and Data Security, Barbados, 3 March 2014
10. Jarvis, K.: CryptoLocker ransomware, December 2013. http://www.secureworks.com/cyber-threat-intelligence/threats/cryptolockerransomware/
11. Chrysaidos, N.: Mobile crypto-ransomware simplocker now on steroids, February 2015. https://blog.avast.com/2015/02/10/mobile-cryptoransomware-simplocker-now-on-steroids/
12. Hamada, J.: Simplocker: first confirmed file-encrypting ransomware for android, June 2014. http://www.symantec.com/connect/blogs/simplocker-first-confirmed-file-encrypting-ransomware-android
13. Unuchek, R.: Latest version of svpeng targets users in US, June 2014. http://securelist.com/blog/incidents/63746/latest-version-ofsvpeng-targets-users-in-us/
14. Kelly, M.: US targeted by coercive mobile ransomware impersonating the FBI, July 2014. https://blog.lookout.com/blog/2014/07/16/scarepakage/

15. Gröbert, F., Willems, C., Holz, T.: Automated identification of cryptographic primitives in binary programs. In: Recent Advances in Intrusion Detection, pp. 41–60 (2011)
16. Lestringant, P., Guihéry, F., Fouque, P.-A.: Automated identification of cryptographic primitives in binary code with data flow graph isomorphism. In: Proceedings of the 10th ACM Symposium on Information, Computer and Communications Security, pp. 203–214, New York, NY, USA (2015)
17. Aggarwal, C.C., Zhai, C.: A survey of text classification algorithms. In: Aggarwal, C.C., Zhai, C. (eds.) Mining Text Data, pp. 163–222. Springer, US (2012)
18. The snowball language. http://snowball.tartarus.org/
19. Shuyo, N.: Language detection library for java (2010). http://code.google.com/p/language-detection/
20. van der Veen, V., Bos, H., Rossow, C.: Dynamic analysis of android malware. VU University Amsterdam, August 2013. http://tracedroid.few.vu.nl/
21. Hoffmann, J., et al.: Slicing droids: program slicing for smali code. In: Proceedings of the 28th Annual ACM Symposium on Applied Computing, pp. 1844–1851, New York, NY, USA (2013)
22. Arzt, S., et al.: FlowDroid: precise context, flow, field, object-sensitive and lifecycle-aware taint analysis for android apps. In: Proceedings of the 35th ACM SIGPLAN Conference on Programming Language Design and Implementation, pp. 259–269, New York, NY, USA (2014)
23. Lindorfer, M., Volanis, S., Sisto, A., Neugschwandtner, M., Athanasopoulos, E., Maggi, F., Platzer, C., Zanero, S., Ioannidis, S.: AndRadar: fast discovery of android applications in alternative markets. In: Dietrich, S. (ed.) DIMVA 2014. LNCS, vol. 8550, pp. 51–71. Springer, Heidelberg (2014)
24. Maggi, F., Valdi, A., Zanero, S.: AndroTotal: a flexible, scalable toolbox and service for testing mobile malware detectors. In: Proceedings of the Third ACM Workshop on Security and Privacy in Smartphones and Mobile Devices, pp. 49–54, New York, NY, USA (2013)
25. Zhou, Y., Jiang, X.: Dissecting android malware: characterization and evolution. In: Proceedings of the 33rd IEEE Symposium on Security and Privacy, San Francisco, CA, May 2012. http://www.malgenomeproject.org/
26. Song, D., Brumley, D., Yin, H., Caballero, J., Jager, I., Kang, M.G., Liang, Z., Newsome, J., Poosankam, P., Saxena, P.: BitBlaze: a new approach to computer security via binary analysis. In: Sekar, R., Pujari, A.K. (eds.) ICISS 2008. LNCS, vol. 5352, pp. 1–25. Springer, Heidelberg (2008)
27. Schwartz, E.J., et al.: Native x86 decompilation using semantics-preserving structural analysis and iterative control-flow structuring. In: USENIX security (2013)
28. Slowinska, A., Stancescu, T., Bos, H.: Howard: a dynamic excavator for reverse engineering data structures. In: Proceedings of the Network and Distributed System Security Symposium (NDSS), San Diego, CA (2011)
29. Manning, C.D., et al.: The stanford Core NLP natural language processing toolkit. In: Proceedings of 52nd Annual Meeting of the Association for Computational Linguistics: System Demonstrations, pp. 55–60 (2014). http://www.aclweb.org/anthology/P/P14/P14-5010
30. Poeplau, S., et al.: Execute this! analyzing unsafe and malicious dynamic code loading in android applications. In: Proceedings of the Network and Distributed System Security Symposium (NDSS), pp. 23–26 (2014)
31. Zhou, W., et al.: Fast, scalable detection of "piggybacked" mobile applications. In: Proceedings of the Third ACM Conference on Data and Application Security and Privacy, pp. 185–196, New York, NY, USA (2013)

32. Bursztein, E., Martin, M., Mitchell, J.: Text-based CAPTCHA strengths and weaknesses. In: Proceedings of the 18th ACM Conference on Computer and Communications Security, pp. 125–138, New York, NY, USA (2011)
33. Chakradeo, S., et al.: MAST: triage for market-scale mobile malware analysis. In: Proceedings of the Sixth ACM Conference on Security and Privacy in Wireless and Mobile Networks, pp. 13–24, New York, NY, USA (2013)
34. Shabtai, A., et al.: Andromaly: a behavioral malware detection framework for android devices. J. Intell. Inf. Syst. **38**(1), 161–190 (2012)
35. Kharraz, A., Robertson, W., Balzarotti, D., Bilge, L., Kirda, E.: Cutting the gordian knot: a look under the hood of ransomware attacks. In: Almgren, M., Gulisano, V., Maggi, F. (eds.) DIMVA 2015. LNCS, vol. 9148, pp. 3–24. Springer, Heidelberg (2015)
36. Young, A.: Cryptoviral extortion using microsoft's crypto API. Int. J. Inf. Secur. **5**(2), 67–76 (2006)
37. Jarabek, C., Barrera, D., Aycock, J.: ThinAV: truly lightweight mobile cloud-based anti-malware. In: Proceedings of the 28th Annual Computer Security Applications Conference, pp. 209–218, New York, NY, USA (2012)

Continuous Authentication on Mobile Devices Using Power Consumption, Touch Gestures and Physical Movement of Users

Rahul Murmuria[✉], Angelos Stavrou, Daniel Barbará, and Dan Fleck

Kryptowire LLC, Fairfax, VA 22030, USA
{rahul,angelos,dbarbara,dfleck}@kryptowire.com
http://www.kryptowire.com

Abstract. Handheld devices today do not continuously verify the identity of the user while sensitive activities are performed. This enables attackers, who can either compromise the initial password or grab the device after login, full access to sensitive data and applications on the device. To mitigate this risk, we propose continuous user monitoring using a machine learning based approach comprising of an ensemble of three distinct modalities: power consumption, touch gestures, and physical movement. Users perform different activities on different applications: we consider application context when we model user behavior. We employ anomaly detection algorithms for each modality and place a bound on the fraction of anomalous events that can be considered "normal" for any given user. We evaluated our system using data collected from 73 volunteer participants. We were able to verify that our system is functional in real-time while the end-user was utilizing popular mobile applications.

Keywords: Security · Anomaly detection · Noise-aware data mining · Continuous authentication · Behavioral models

1 Introduction

The amount of sensitive data stored on or processed by handheld devices has been on the rise. This is primarily due to a wealth of services that were made available over the last few years including access to emails, social media, banking, personal calendars, navigation and documents. Most commercially available devices employ the use of authentication techniques only at the "entry-point". They require the user to explicitly authenticate before every handheld device interaction but not necessarily when sensitive operations are performed. Thus, although users might be required to use their password often, sensitive data can be misused when an attacker gains physical access to a device immediately after authentication is completed.

There is a plethora of recent work that indicates that password authentication is not appropriate for mobile devices. For instance, Aviv et al. [1] demonstrated the feasibility of smudge attacks using residue oils on touch screen devices. Using

© Springer International Publishing Switzerland 2015
H. Bos et al. (Eds.): RAID 2015, LNCS 9404, pp. 405–424, 2015.
DOI: 10.1007/978-3-319-26362-5_19

this technique, the attackers could extract sensitive information about recent user input, which may include the legitimate user's successful authentication attempt. While intentional misuse of data is a concern, Muslukhov et al. [2] showed that users are also concerned about sharing mobile phones with guest users. Moreover, Karlson et al. [3] conducted interviews of smartphone users and concluded that the entry-point authentication model is too coarse-grained and the type of data that can be considered sensitive varies significantly depending upon the owner's relationship to the guest user. For example, the information that is considered sensitive in the presence of colleagues is different in nature from what is considered sensitive among business clients or competitors. However, protecting every piece of data with additional security mechanisms poses a usability hindrance.

In order to address the shortcomings of the entry-point authentication model, one of the approaches proposed in literature is called *continuous authentication* [4]. This is a process of verifying the identity of the user repeatedly while the handheld device is in use. Generally, continuous authentication methods assume that the process of authentication is unobtrusive. This is necessary as it is impractical to require users to explicitly authenticate themselves at recurring intervals.

In this paper, we propose a technique to authenticate users on handheld devices based on a diverse set of behavioral biometric modalities comprised of power consumption, touch gestures, and physical movement. We are one of the first research groups to propose the use of power measurements as a potential form of authentication for modern (Android) mobile devices. In addition to power behavior, we have implemented touch screen gestures and physical movement as modalities (both are independent behavioral traits in accordance with the survey paper on behavioral biometrics by Yampolskiy et al. [9]). These modalities use measurements from the touch input driver, and from a combination of accelerometer and gyroscope measurements respectively. In this paper, we show that the fusion of these three modalities can be used to corroborate the presence of a legitimate user while capturing long-term characteristics (power modality), short-term physical movement which includes hand vibrations (movement modality), as well as direct device interaction (touch modality).

The proposed approach includes a decision support process (see Fig. 1) where we build models based only on a set of measurements (system readings) for the legitimate user. To detect unauthorized access, we rely on those user-tailored models to provide us with evidence of deviation from the generated user envelope. The decision support process institutes a "test" that requires that no more than n readings within a window of events or time be anomalous, before the user's capabilities are diminished on the device. This threshold can be adjusted to obtain the desired False Reject Rate (FRR) and False Acceptance Rate (FAR), a trade-off that we explored in this paper. We show that every user is prone to infrequent anomalous behavior that is dispersed throughout the user's interaction with the mobile device and the rate at which these anomalies are expected varies for each user. As a result, the number of n readings that are allowed to be

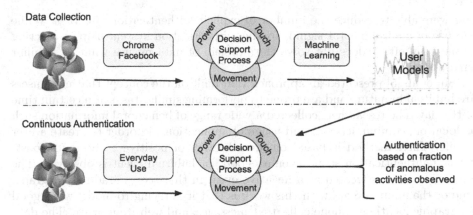

Fig. 1. General workflow

anomalous is part of a user's profile and we show that by using individualized thresholds, we improved performance of our authentication system.

We also show that authentication accuracy is affected by application context; any user's behavior differs from application to application. When a user is playing a game, the digital footprint that the user leaves behind in terms of power consumption, touch screen gestures or physical movement is expected to be significantly different from when the user is sending text messages. We present the performance of our system on two popular mobile applications – Google Chrome and Facebook – and show that by ignoring the application context, there is a clear degradation in identification accuracy.

The rest of this paper is organized as follows. Section 2 is a brief review of research publications that are related to the work done in this paper. Section 3 discusses the implementation details of our data collection architecture. Section 4 provides the experimental design and protocol used while collecting data from volunteers. Section 5 describes how the data was prepared for analysis. Section 6 identifies the algorithms employed for the task of continuous authentication of users in mobile devices. Section 7 presents a performance evaluation of the algorithms on the data collected. In Sects. 9 and 10, we suggest further research directions and conclude this paper.

2   Related Work

Riva et al. [6] presented an architecture that grants users access to any content on the device only when the authentication system evaluates the device operator's level of authenticity to be higher than what is required to access that content. Their system utilized face and voice recognition, location familiarity, and determining possession by sensing nearby electronic objects as signals to establish the legitimate user's level of authenticity. They motivated their work with a user study that explored models where there are at-least 3 levels of security: public, private, and confidential. With this framework, they tested nine users, and were able to reduce the number of explicit authentications by 42 %. While the use of environmental signals in the authentication system help in reacting to device theft, it does not solve the problem of data misuse while in familiar surroundings.

Shi et al. [5] presented an approach that built on the concept that most users are habitual in nature and are prone to performing similar tasks at a certain time of the day. The researchers collected a wide range of behavioral information such as location, communication, and usage of applications, in order to create a user profile. Their method is based on identification of positive events and boosting the authentication score when a "good" or habitual event is observed. The passage of time is treated as a negative event in that scores gradually degrade. One of the main caveats with this work is that it is trying to model what good geographic locations, phone calls, text messages, and website urls are. The data collected is highly intrusive in terms of privacy. They further model all good events as ones that are expected to be performed at a certain time of day, which is an assumption of habit that is not proven in the literature. However, if this works well, it can also be incorporated as another voter in our approach.

Kwapisz et al. [10] published a system to identify and authenticate users based on accelerometer data. They used a dataset of 36 users, labeled according to activities such as walking, jogging, and climbing stairs. These labels were used as context and the authors presented analysis with and without these labels. For feature extraction, the authors divided the 3 axes readings of the accelerometer into windows of 10 s, and for each window they extracted features such as mean, standard deviation, resultant, and binned distribution. For identification, the authors performed a 36-class classification, whereas for the task of authentication, the authors reduced the problem to a 2-class problem. They achieved a classification accuracy of 72.2 % for 10 s windows. While they concluded based on their results that it is not critical to know what activity the user is performing, their dataset was generated by users repeating a limited set of pre-defined activities. In contrast, instead of using real-world activities as context which requires manual labeling of the data, we consider the applications being used by the users as context which can be automated. We were able to show that user behavior is indeed subject to application context.

Frank et al. [7] performed a study where they collected touch screen behavior of 41 users and designed a proof-of-concept classification framework to examine the applicability of screen touches as a behavioral biometric. For their data collection, they designed a custom application that allowed users to swipe vertically and horizontally. Using this dataset as baseline, they matched users based on how they perform the same task in testing phase. For analyzing this data, they separated each type of stroke and matched 30 different features (such as mid-stroke area covered, 20 % pairwise velocity, and mid-stroke pressure) extracted for each stroke. Their study resulted in mis-classification error rates in the range of 0 % to 4 %. Although the researchers were able to demonstrate good performance while matching gestures in a controlled environment, they limited their analysis to vertical and horizontal swipes on their own application. The analysis depended on the concept that users are performing repetitive pre-defined tasks. In the real world, different users can perform a large variety of tasks that cannot be modelled individually. This technique clearly has a problem of scale that was not addressed in the paper.

Both Kwapisz et al. and Frank et al. created a two-class problem where the adversarial class had data points from other users. Contrastingly for traditional computing devices, Killourhy et al. [11] and Shen et al. [12] published a comparison of various anomaly-detection algorithms for keystroke dynamics and mouse dynamics respectively, limiting the discussion to 1-class verification due to lack of availability of imposter data in the real-world. In truth, the number of classes representing adversaries is unbounded. Modeling adversaries into a fixed number of classes leads to overfitting and lack of generalization, which results in poor performance of the deployed system.

Bo et al. [8] attempted to create a model to specifically identify transitions or change of hands between the device owner and a guest who may or may not be a known entity. The researchers model a user by leveraging her/his touch screen interactions as well as device feedback in form of vibrations into one single model. Though the device initially has only the owner's behavior data, and a one-class SVM model is trained to provide a judgment whether a new action belongs to the owner or not, the researchers quickly evolve this into a two-class SVM model by collecting guest user's data into a second class. They assign a confidence to this judgment, and the conclusion confidence increases with a continuous sequence of consistent judgments. When a change of user is detected, the sequence of consistent judgment is dissolved. While the authors demonstrate 100 % identification accuracy within a sequence of 5 to 10 observations, the analysis fails to show tolerance with anomalies, or in other words, the inherent noise. There is no detailed discussion about finding a new guest user verses anomalies committed by the device owner. Further, their model also does not consider different user behavior in different usage scenarios, such as the application context considered in our work.

Although we know of no other biometric systems based on power consumption as an identifier, there is widespread research in the area of power model generation on electronic devices. Zhang et al. [13] presented an automated power model construction technique that uses built-in battery voltage sensors and knowledge of battery discharge behavior to monitor power consumption of each application on an electronic device. They achieved an absolute average error rate of less than 10 %. Murmuria et al. [14] demonstrated that the power consumption by individual device drivers on a smartphone varies by state of operation of that particular device driver. Shye et al. [15] presented a power estimation model by leveraging real user behavior. They presented evidence that system power consumption patterns are highly correlated with user behavior patterns, but stopped short of trying to profile users on this basis.

3 Data Collection Architecture

The various hardware components available on a smartphone include: touch-screen, accelerometer, gyroscope, voltage sensor, current sensor, and battery. Each of the components has device drivers, which report sensory statistics to the kernel. The nature and frequency of this data depends on the individual hardware component. Some components require registering event listeners with the Android API, whereas other components require polling the system for data.

For the application context, the name of the application in focus was recorded using the Activity Manager API while users interacted with the mobile device. This is used to determine the context of the model.

For the power modality, in order to determine the power consumption result-ing from the activities performed by the user, we used the built-in voltage and current sensors available as part of the battery driver on smartphones. The power drained from battery is proportional to load. While the batteries decay nonlin-early (reflected directly in the voltage readings), the current readings offset this effect in order to deliver the required power. Therefore, in order to model power consumption, it is sufficient to capture voltage and current. The sensors report the voltage and current to the operating system's kernel in units micro-volts (μV) and micro-Ampere (μA) respectively. While the voltage reading depends on the battery charge and changes gradually between 4.35 V to 3.2 V, the current reading directly depends on the amount drawn by the Android Operating Sys-tem depending upon what activities are being performed. As a result, while we poll the voltage every 5 s, the current reading is polled every 1 s and we take an average of the recorded values every 5 s. Using these readings, we can calculate the average power consumption every 5 s.

For the movement modality, readings were recorded using the SensorEvent API, which is a part of the standard Android SDK. Depending upon which hardware sensors are present on the Android device, the API has the capability to report values from the following sensors: accelerometer, gyroscope, magnetic field, light, pressure, and proximity. For our analysis, we gathered movement readings from both accelerometer and gyroscope sensors. The accelerometer sen-sor measures acceleration in SI units (m/s^2) along the device's local [X, Y, Z] axes and the gyroscope sensor measures rate of rotation in SI units (rad/s) around the device's local axes.

For the touch modality, the user-level touchscreen gestures of key-press, pinch and zoom, swipe, and other gestures are all reported as multiple events to an input driver. The touch event interface exists as a character device under /dev/input and can be read by any program that has permissions to read it. For security reasons, this input driver is a protected interface. Only vendor programs are given this permission on any unmodified commercially available Android device. The device driver reports the following information: [X, Y] coordinates, number of fingers touching the screen, pressure of each finger, and touch area of each finger. We capture the events along with precise timing information directly from these low-level event streams and reconstruct it back to user-level gestures.

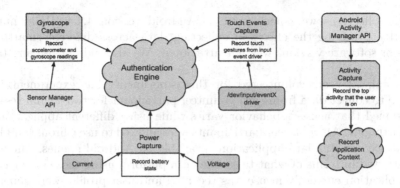

Fig. 2. Smartphone sensor data collection framework

Data Collection Tool. Figure 2 shows the smartphone sensor data collection architecture. There are 4 services running in our data collection application: PowerLogger, TouchLogger, GyroLogger, and ActivityLogger.

- Service 1 (PowerLogger): It collects the Voltage, Current and Battery Charge from the battery driver (via *sys* filesystem).
- Service 2 (TouchLogger): This service reads the input events driver to collect system-wide touchscreen events. The touch driver is protected by a system user group "input".
- Service 3 (GyroLogger): This uses the Android API to collect both gyroscope and accelerometer sensor data using a SensorEventListener.
- Service 4 (ActivityLogger): This service uses an Android API to record the user activity on the device. Specifically, we record the top running application, incoming and outgoing calls, and screen-off and screen-on events.

All these services are active during both training and testing, and the overall system power consumption is guided by user's behavior plus a constant from these services. Therefore, our measurement tool does not adversely impact the power profile we generate for a user. We took measures to make our services robust, such that we keep this constant noise in the power consumption readings small, regardless.

4   Experimental Design

When performing a study with volunteer participants, the results obtained depend strongly on the quality of the data collected. It is vital to understand any sources that can cause potential variance in the data for a specific user and to retain data in a uniform format using uniform devices. While our profile generation algorithms do not require such precautions, this step is needed in order to compare the datasets and evaluate the performance fairly.

To achieve uniformity of measurements, we used the same device (Google Nexus 5 Model:LG-D820) for all users who volunteered for this study. Further, all data collections were performed on Android version 4.4.4 (Build number KTU84P). Studying the effects of collecting data across different smartphone models or software versions was not attempted. We also did not use any tablet devices.

In total, 73 users volunteered for this experiment. The experiments were designed to collect data from each volunteer participant for two 45 min sessions. We assumed that a user's behavior varies while using different applications on the smartphone. All volunteer participants were allowed to use Chrome and Facebook, which are standard applications available on Android phones. They were not restricted in terms of what tasks they can perform using those applications. The application currently in use was recorded and user profiles were generated keeping separate data for each context.

We did not want environmental interference within our data and therefore, the user was restricted to remain within a room. Each user was asked to use the two pre-chosen applications for 20 min each with a break of 5 min for instructions. This session was repeated on two different days in order to capture the user's behavior effectively. This would total up to 80 min of actual smartphone usage data for each user. All tasks were performed while sitting down. Although no user walked or performed any other physical activity, the smartphones were subject to significant movement due to typical usage of the device.

Our experimental setup does not emulate real-world use of the chosen applications. However, related research on mobile authentication techniques relies solely on evaluating touch or movement patterns on custom designed applications or in much more restricted environments where users are asked to perform specific actions repeatedly (swiping or moving in a direction). One of the contributions of our work is the verification of the idea that the application itself plays a significant role and alters the user behavioral patterns. Our results indicate that previous results on active authentication are not applicable in real-world scenarios.

As part of our experimental protocol, we instructed the volunteers to login to Facebook first. No touch or other sensory data was collected during this first step. All other activities the volunteers performed on the smartphones did not involve entering a password of any nature. Each user was assigned a pseudonym with the convention Sxx, where the xx is a digit between 1 and 100. The real names of the users were not retained. We also did not record any user-generated content outside of the sensory data. No web traffic or URLs were recorded. No attempt was made to capture the content that a user saw on the screen. We recorded data from all the sensors concerned into files for each modality. These files were stored in the external storage directory of each smartphone. Upon completion of a user's session, we extracted that data out from the smartphone into our data store where we analyzed the data.

All our volunteer participants were aged between lower 20s and upper 40s, covering a variety of ethnicities and nationalities. Some of our participants were not regular smartphone users. We did not attempt to discriminate who volunteered, beyond requiring them to have an active Facebook account. Our research required behavioral data of human subjects and necessary approvals were acquired from the Institutional Review Board (IRB).

5 Data Preparation

5.1 Feature Engineering

After collecting the raw data, we performed feature extraction on the data from each modality. Currently, there are no universally accepted set of features that represent individual events for each of the modalities. For the purposes of this research, we selected our feature set based on our own experience with the data.

For the power modality, the activities performed by the user were represented in milliwatts (mW) using the voltage and current readings. These power consumption readings were used in our algorithm as a time-series.

For the movement modality, the recorded events were divided into small windows of time where we can measure properties related to the group of events. Let the size of this window of time be w units, then we employed the use of a sliding window technique that moved $w/2$ units in direction of increasing time for each subsequent record in our prepared movement dataset. As a result, every event in the raw data contributed to 2 windows in the movement dataset. We made this choice because it is difficult to determine the start and end of any particular movement gesture, and using non-overlapping windows would result in loss of precision. For the purposes of our analysis, the data associated within each window frame can be referred to as one movement gesture. Each movement gesture was encoded as a sequence of events; each event is a vector of sensory signals as described in Sect. 3. Fourteen features were extracted from each movement gesture. These features include mean and standard deviation along each axes and resultant magnitude of all axes, for both accelerometer and gyroscope readings.

For the touch modality, the recorded events were aggregated into touch gestures. Each gesture is a sequence of touch events that begins with touch down of the finger and ends with lifting the finger. Five features were extracted from each touch gesture. These include: duration, end-to-end distance, end-to-end direction, average pressure, and average touch area.

5.2 Data Cleaning and User Selection

Since each of the features we collected for touch and movement modalities had different units, we standardized the dataset using the mean and standard deviation of each feature over the entire dataset of all users.

After extracting features, the data was divided according to *application context*. The ActivityLogger in our data collection tool inserted place-markers in the data whenever the user switched from one application to another. As part of pre-processing the data, only those events were extracted, that were generated while using the application for which the user profiles are being created. As a result, multiple datasets were created, one for every combination of the users, applications, and modalities.

We then analyzed if a similar amount of data was collected for every user. As we mentioned in Sect. 4, every user was given a fixed amount of time to use the device. Users who generated very small datasets did not perform enough actions on the device for us to model. Further, users who generated too much data expectantly did not follow a normal use-case and would not match themselves under different circumstances. Therefore, any user who generated data of abnormally large or small sizes was discarded. In order to compute this, we first merged the data collected for each of the 73 users over the two days of experiments. The number of records was tabulated for each of the 6 datasets (2 applications and 3 modalities) for every user, and the means and standard deviations were computed. We then removed those users who had any dataset with sizes more than or less than 2 standard deviations from the corresponding mean. With this method, 59 users were selected who had comparable sizes of data. In order to prepare the baseline, 60 % of each user's dataset was used. The algorithms we used to train a model using this data are described in Sect. 6. As a result, users' profiles were created. The remaining 40 % of datasets for each user were used to test this model.

6   Analysis to Compute Authentication

We view the authentication task as one of determining whether the current stream of measurements of a given kind follows the same distribution as those obtained in a baseline session for a given user. As such, we employ algorithms that are capable of detecting outliers with respect to the baseline distribution and place a bound on how many outliers we can allow if we assume the test data follows the same distribution of the baseline. Exceeding this bound is an indication of the user being an impostor.

We separate the analysis techniques in two groups. The first, utilized for multivariate data (e.g., the data collected from touch and movement modalities), is an adaptation of an outlier detection algorithm first published by Barbara et al. [16] and described in Sect. 6.1. The second, utilized for univariate time-series data (e.g., power measurements) is based on a technique reported by Keogh et al. [17] and is explained in Sect. 6.2.

6.1   Strangeness-Based Outlier Detection

Strangeness-based Outlier Detection (StrOUD) algorithm, utilizing a machine learning technique called transduction, was devised by Barbara et al. [16] to detect outliers in datasets. Transduction is a machine learning technique based in the process of reasoning from specific (baseline) cases to specific (testing) cases. This is in contrast to induction which reasons from specific cases to rules that can be applied to test other cases. The method was invented by Vapnik et al. [18], motivated by his view that induction requires solving a more general

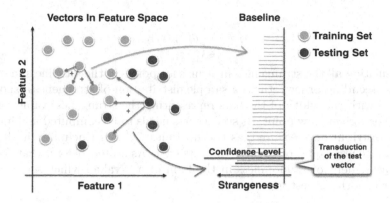

Fig. 3. Strangeness-based outlier detection

problem, while transduction requires solving a more specific problem, which is easier, and, in many cases, more accurate.

Transduction is carried out by placing a point in a known sample distribution of data and using hypothesis testing to determine whether it is a good fit or not. To that end, a measure of uniqueness, or strangeness is used for every point in the distribution, including the one we are trying to fit. Strangeness is defined by a function that measures the uniqueness of that point. Vapnik et al. utilized transduction in the context of classification, or supervised learning, to properly place new points in their rightful class. The technique is called Transductive Classification Machines or TCM. The transduction methodology does not build general models. The 'models' are captured in the distribution of uniqueness values for each class.

Statistical hypothesis testing which aims to prove or disprove one of the following hypotheses: the null hypothesis that says the test point is a good fit in the distribution (and in the case of TCMs, whether the point belongs to the class represented by that distribution), and the alternative hypothesis that says the point is not a good fit. The test is performed by computing a p-value (measure of randomness) as the fraction of the points in the sample distribution whose strangeness is greater or equal to that of the test point. If this p-value is less than the complement of the confidence level desired for the diagnosis, the alternative hypothesis is accepted.

StrOUD borrows the idea of TCM with an important change: nature of the strangeness function utilized. The goal in StrOUD is to find anomalies (not to classify points), so, the strangeness function should be a measure of how anomalous a point is within a distribution. Given a sample distribution, or baseline of observations, the strangeness of the jth point x_j can be computed as the sum of the distances to the k nearest points in the baseline data. Figure 3 presents an illustration of two sets of data (yellow and blue) in feature space. Strangeness calculation has been demonstrated in the figure for a point each from the training set and the testing set. Equation 1 shows the definition of strangeness utilized by Barbara et al. [16].

$$s_j = \sum_{i \in k} d(x_j, x_i). \qquad (1)$$

Calculating all the strangeness measures for points in the baseline and sorting them in ascending order returns a sample distribution of strangeness (shown in the Fig. 3 with the width of the bars representing the strangeness values of each point). For a given new point, its strangeness needs to be computed and its place on that distribution measured, as the fraction of points (including itself) that have strangeness equal or greater than its own. As stated before, that fraction is a measurement of randomness in the form of a p-value, which serves as the basis for hypothesis testing.

6.2   The Discord Algorithm

The power measurements are viewed as a time-series and for this modality an algorithm designed by Keogh et al. [17] that allows the discovery of *discords* on that kind of data was employed. A discord in a time series is a subsequence of the series whose distance to the closest subsequence (of the same size) is maximal. A discord is a particularly desirable indicator of anomaly, because it only requires a very intuitive parameter for its discovery: the size of the subsequence.

The discord idea is used with the power modality in two phases. In the first, the goal is to obtain a distribution of measures that represent the uniqueness of a time series, as a baseline distribution. To that end, the power baseline data collected for a user is divided in two parts. The first, of size m is used as a basis to find discords in chunks of the second part. In the Fig. 4, this step has been illustrated by using the training set time-series partitioned using the vertical line. Given a fixed size of the subsequence δ, we compare a subsequence from the second part with all subsequences in the first part, and the distance to its closest neighbor is returned. Doing this over the entire second part of the dataset results in a distribution of distances that can be sorted in ascending order (shown

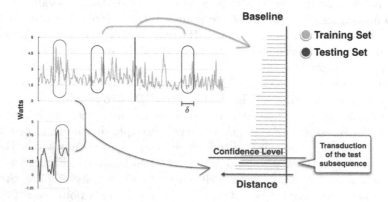

Fig. 4. Discord-based outlier detection

on the right side in the figure). This distribution is viewed as playing the role of the strangeness distribution.

When analyzing test data, after receiving δ observations, the algorithm computes the distance of that set of δ observations to the first part of the baseline time series (of size m). Doing so, the algorithm obtains a new distance to the test data's closest neighbor and proceeds to transduce that distance into the strangeness distribution, to analyze whether that subsequence is an anomaly or not. This is repeated for every new observation in the test data (always considering a window of size δ that spans the current observation).

6.3   User Diagnosis

After calculating the sorted distribution of strangeness any future incoming point is diagnosed using this distribution, which represents a user's profile. In an experimental setting, many datasets were tested against each user's baseline; some of these datasets came from the same user and some of them from users other than the one that generated the baseline. Such setting produces a matrix where each column and row represents one user. Every entry represents the probability of committing an anomaly for the corresponding pair of baseline/test user data set. This matrix is called the confusion matrix. The smaller the score, the better the testing data matched the baseline. Examples for this matrix are shown in Tables 3, 4, and 5 under Sect. 7.

The mere presence of an anomaly does not conclude presence of an imposter. The fraction of anomalies in the test dataset is an indication of whether the set belongs to the original distribution or not. Setting a threshold on the maximum probability that can be observed and still consider the data as coming from the same distribution of the baseline gives a way to diagnose a user as an impostor or not.

From this point onward, there are two ways to proceed while choosing thresholds. The first is to select a general threshold and diagnose as reject every matrix entry whose value is bigger than the threshold. If the reject occurs in a case for which the row and column are from the same user, it is a false reject (the model is saying the user is not who they say they are, while the truth says otherwise). If the reject occurs elsewhere, it is a true reject (the model is correctly saying this user is different than that of the baseline). After computing the rates at which these two events occur, False Reject Rate (FRR) and False Accept Rate (FAR) can be calculated as shown in Eq. 2.

$$FAR = 1 - \text{True Reject/Total Reject Cases}$$
$$FRR = \text{False Reject/Total Accept Cases.}$$

(2)

Varying the threshold for fraction of anomalies allows computing pairs of values for FRR and FAR for each threshold, and plotting the Receiving Operating Characteristic (ROC) curve. If a single column from the matrix is used to calculate the FRR and FAR, the ROC curve represents performance of the corresponding user's model. This requires having more than one test set that comes from the same user represented in the column (otherwise the computation of FRR is trivialized). If the entire matrix is used, the ROC curve represents overall performance of all the models for every user.

The second alternative is to utilize an individual threshold for each user. These thresholds are calculated using the fraction of anomalies of each user (which represent the rate of anomalies that are "normal" to every user). In this case, from the confusion matrix, the overall FRR and FAR are computed by varying threshold values per column (i.e., per user) and the ROC is reported with each FRR/FAR pair resulting from a vector of threshold values. Experiments show that selecting individual thresholds result in much improved ROC plots, and thus, better models.

Each modality produces its own confusion matrix. To calculate the overall result, we used two schemes to calculate the ensemble: *majority scheme* and *non-imposter consensus*. The majority scheme requires at least 2 out of the 3 modalities to vote for having found an imposter. The non-imposter consensus requires 3 out of the 3 modalities to vote for having found the same user and any other vote results in a declaration of imposter.

7   Results

We measured our system's performance in terms of the commonly used metrics: False Acceptance Rate (FAR), False Rejection Rate (FRR) and Receiver Operating Characteristic (ROC) curve. We defined these terms in Sect. 6.3 in the context of our analysis. Additionally, we make use of another metric called Equal Error Rate (EER), which is the rate at which the FAR and FRR are equal. EER is a widely used metric to determine the overall performance of an authentication system regardless of the choice of parameters.

The parameters we selected for the two algorithms discussed in Sect. 6 are shown in Table 1. The value of k in the StrOUD algorithm was selected to be 3. Other selections in the neighborhood of 3 did not result in a significant difference in the overall performance. The δ in the power consumption data was selected to be 12, which corresponds to time-series window of 1 min. Other window sizes of 30 s and 5 min performed poorly compared to the 1 min window. The parameter m splits the power data in two chunks during baseline generation phase of the discord algorithm. A split of 60-40 was considered appropriate, but other combinations can be explored in future. The confidence level determines how strictly the user diagnosis phase marks records as imposter. Different values between 85 % and 99 % were tested, and the best performing level was chosen.

Table 1. Parameters selected for our algorithms

Parameter	k	δ	m	$conf$
Value	3	12	60 %	90 %

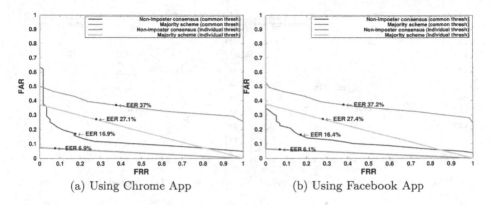

(a) Using Chrome App   (b) Using Facebook App

Fig. 5. ROC from ensemble model on all users

Our analysis of the experimental results demonstrate that our approach using the ensemble of modalities allow us to identify imposters with an Equal Error Rate between 6.1 % and 6.9 % for training times that vary between 20 and 60 min. The first response time to authenticate is as low as 2 s for the gyroscope modality, 1 gesture for the touch screen modality and 60 s for the power modality. Subsequently, each user action will produce a new authentication score in real-time.

We discussed our use of common thresholds and individualized thresholds in Sect. 6.3. Further, the voting schemes we used to create the ensembles is described in Sect. 6. Figure 5a shows the detection performance results for Chrome and Fig. 5b for Facebook. It is clear from the ensemble plots that for both voting schemes, the *individual thresholds* for each user gives a significant improvement to the predictions. Further, our voting scheme of *Non-imposter consensus* is consistently outperforming the *majority scheme*. By requiring the modalities to agree by consensus when a legitimate user is present, we placed a higher cost on acceptance and thereby improved the overall performance.

We examined the distribution of False Accept Rates (FAR) by 'clamping' the False Reject Rates (FRR) to 0.01 (i.e., 1 %). The results are tabulated in Table 2. The results follow intuition that we have very few users that can cause an FAR value to be higher than the average. We believe that this can be rectified with use of additional biometric modalities complementary to the three we have developed.

If used separately, each modality cannot generate models that offer good performance in terms of accuracy and classification results because each modality is a weak classifier. Put it simply, users can happen to closely resemble one of the

Table 2. Distribution of FAR of users at ≤1 % FRR

Range	0–2.5 %	2.5 %–7.5 %	7.5 %–12.5 %	12.5 %–50 %
Users (Chrome)	38	10	4	7
Users (Facebook)	45	7	0	7

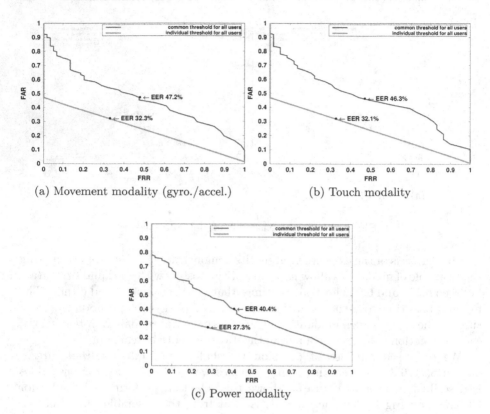

(a) Movement modality (gyro./accel.)   (b) Touch modality

(c) Power modality

Fig. 6. ROC for Chrome App captured on all users

modalities but it is extremely rare that they do so at the same time for all three modalities given our experimental results. As a result, because the modalities have non-overlapping weaknesses, together in an ensemble they form a strong identifier. We use ROC curves produced from the data of Chrome application as an example, to demonstrate that (see Fig. 6). The performance ranges in EER from 27.3 % to 32.3 % even with individual thresholds. Figure 5a is the corresponding ensemble plot that shows EER of 16.9 % for common thresholds and EER of 6.9 % with individual thresholds which are significant improvements. Modality plots for the Facebook application showed comparable performance and have been omitted here.

Results also depend on the Application context. See Tables 3, 4 and 5 that show the performance of the power modality for 5 randomly selected users. These confusion matrices have been created using the technique discussed in Sect. 6.3. The light gray color represents the rate of anomaly considered "normal" to the legitimate user. Using our per-user thresholds method, if any cell in the column happens to have a fraction of anomaly less than the value in the diagonal (colored light gray), then these would represent False Accepts, and we have colored them dark gray. It is clear from observation, that the number of dark gray boxes greatly

Table 3. Randomly selected 5 users from Chrome App for power modality

%	Baseline Users				
	A	B	C	D	E
Test Users A	3.6	15.6	19.2	10.7	28.5
B	30.1	12.2	14.8	8.5	32.5
C	17.1	4.2	2.5	5.0	35.8
D	42.1	2.7	21.0	12.1	47.8
E	19.8	8.5	8.9	0.8	6.7

Table 4. Randomly selected 5 users from Facebook App for power modality

%	Baseline Users				
	A	B	C	D	E
Test Users A	20.4	40.8	25.1	30.6	5.7
B	3.6	5.4	52.3	11.6	1.8
C	13.5	71.2	7.5	90.7	2.8
D	2.2	24.8	71.1	7.4	5.5
E	11.9	61.4	21.5	64.0	18.2

Table 5. Randomly selected 5 users from mixture of both apps for power modality

%	Baseline Users				
	A	B	C	D	E
Test Users A	10.8	11.3	11.3	5.4	16.3
B	8.8	18.3	17.1	2.7	13.3
C	7.8	3.3	15.8	2.0	15.3
D	10.6	3.2	17.0	41.6	22.3
E	3.9	4.5	4.7	0.5	16.0

increases in Table 5. User's behavior is not similar across Chrome and Facebook applications and thus the identification accuracy is dramatically reduced when we mix the datasets. In Fig. 7, we present the ROC curves for overall performance of the system on the combined data of Chrome and Facebook with the context removed. It can be observed that the overall performance has deteriorated.

8 Lessons Learned

It is not uncommon to encounter very noisy data when mining in the real-world. The same is the case with the behavioral biometrics dataset collected for this research. Despite moderately controlling the environment during data collection, the rate of anomalies due to noise is high, in comparison to misclassification error. Most research work in continuous authentication resort to one of two techniques: (1) Data cleansing by removing chunks of data whose class predictions contradict the ground truth during training, and (2) Assume the data to be clean, and consider the contradictions as misclassification error during testing. In truth, the nature of the data is changing so constantly that it is required to not only assume but explicitly model the noise. This research, therefore, considered the rate of anomalies generated by a user while testing against his own baseline to be a virtue of his own user profile. As seen in Tables 3 and 4, the rate of anomalies considered "normal" for different users cover a wide range of values. This indicates the assumption could be true, resulting in the need to build models that are error-aware.

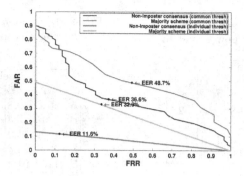

Fig. 7. ROC from ensemble model without application context

This research also showed that authentication accuracy is affected by application context; any user's behavior differs from application to application. The performance of the authentication engine therefore depends not only on which mobile application is being used (application context), but also on whether the mobile application can be modeled well or not. Different categories of applications can be identified, as described below, that will show high false accepts and false rejects depending upon how users are meant to interact with the application.

1. Randomized UI
   Mobile Applications that have completely randomized UI will have high false rejects. Some examples include Game applications that appear randomized on all of the modalities used in this research.
2. Static UI
   On the other hand, apps that have completely static UI can have very high false accepts. Some examples include Camera, Flashlight, Sound Recorder and Navigation. While these apps appear static from the point of view of the chosen biometric modalities, some of them can be incorporated into the system by introducing modalities such as voice recognition.
3. Mixed UI
   In general, apps that have a mix of UI inputs yield the best results for authentication. Chrome and Facebook were tested in this research, but other apps in this category include email and word processors.

Since different applications need different levels of security, it can be argued that some apps that need higher data security can employ the use of a rich set of user interactions in order to benefit from an overall improved authentication performance from their users.

9   Future Work

As discussed in Sect. 4, we presented results using a dataset that was generated while controlling environmental interference. One direct progression of this work is to study the impact on performance when allowing volunteers to perform their daily routine tasks. Such a test would warrant the need for much longer data collection sessions where the volunteer uses the mobile device over multiple days. In addition, we believe that further investigation of the scalability of the individualized parameters when we increase the number of users, apps, and modalities is warranted. The current testing was done to determine the efficacy of identifying users through their device interactions. Future work will assess the usability of the approach now that the efficacy has been established.

10   Conclusion

We have introduced a novel system that performs authentication on Android mobile devices by leveraging user behavior captured though three distinct modalities – power consumption, touch gestures, and physical movement (using both accelerometer and gyroscope). To the best of our knowledge, we are one of the first research groups to propose the use of mobile power measurements and leverage the application context in the authentication process. We further demonstrated that by using individualized thresholds for rate of anomalies expected from every user, we were able to improve performance significantly. To that end, we implemented a full set of algorithms and applications for the measurement, evaluation, and deployment of the framework to Nexus 5 Android phone and demonstrated our capability to perform continuous authentication in real time. By leveraging data collected from 73 volunteer participants, we evaluated our system while the end-user was utilizing two popular applications – Chrome and Facebook. We were able to achieve good performance with an equal error rate between 6.1 % and 6.9 % for 59 selected users who had generated sufficient data for evaluation. Given that the approach in this paper solves the problem of noise and context in very deployable ways, it is more viable as a real-world solution than other competing approaches in literature.

References

1. Aviv, A.J., Gibson, K., Mossop, E., Blaze, M., Smith, J.M.: Smudge attacks on smartphone touch screens. In: Proceedings of the 4th USENIX Conference on Offensive Technologies, pp. 1–7. USENIX Association (2010)
2. Muslukhov, I., Boshmaf, Y., Kuo, C., Lester, J., Beznosov, K.: Know your enemy: the risk of unauthorized access in smartphones by insiders. In: Proceedings of the 15th International Conference on Human-Computer Interaction with Mobile Devices and Services, pp. 271–280. ACM (2013)
3. Karlson, A.K., Brush, A.J., Schechter, S.: Can i borrow your phone?: understanding concerns when sharing mobile phones. In: Proceedings of the SIGCHI Conference on Human Factors in Computing Systems, pp. 1647–1650. ACM (2009)
4. Clarke, N.L., Furnell, S.M.: Advanced user authentication for mobile devices. Comput. Secur. 26, 109–119 (2007)
5. Shi, E., Niu, Y., Jakobsson, M., Chow, R.: Implicit authentication through learning user behavior. In: Burmester, M., Tsudik, G., Magliveras, S., Ilić, I. (eds.) ISC 2010. LNCS, vol. 6531, pp. 99–113. Springer, Heidelberg (2011)

6. Riva, O., Qin, C., Strauss, K., Lymberopoulos, D.: Progressive authentication: deciding when to authenticate on mobile phones. In: Proceedings of the 21st USENIX Security Symposium (2012)
7. Frank, M., Biedert, R., Ma, E., Martinovic, I., Song, D.: Touchalytics: on the applicability of touchscreen input as a behavioral biometric for continuous authentication. IEEE Trans. Inf. Forensics Secur. **8**, 136–148 (2013)
8. Bo, C., Zhang, L., Jung, T., Han, J., Li, X.-Y., Wang, Y.: Continuous user identification via touch and movement behavioral biometrics. In: 2014 IEEE International Conference on Performance Computing and Communications (IPCCC), pp. 1–8. IEEE (2014)
9. Yampolskiy, R.V., Govindaraju, V.: Behavioural biometrics: a survey and classification. Int. J. Biometrics **1**, 81–113 (2008)
10. Kwapisz, J.R., Weiss, G.M., Moore, S.A.: Cell phone-based biometric identification. In: 2010 Fourth IEEE International Conference on Biometrics: Theory Applications and Systems (BTAS), pp. 1–7. IEEE (2010)
11. Killourhy, K.S., Maxion, R.A.: Comparing anomaly-detection algorithms for keystroke dynamics. In: 2009 IEEE/IFIP International Conference on Dependable Systems and Networks, DSN 2009, pp. 125–134. IEEE (2009)
12. Shen, C., Cai, Z., Maxion, R.A., Xiang, G., Guan, X.: Comparing classification algorithm for mouse dynamics based user identification. In: 2012 IEEE Fifth International Conference on Biometrics: Theory, Applications and Systems (BTAS), pp. 61–66 (2012)
13. Zhang, L., Tiwana, B., Qian, Z., Wang, Z., Dick, R.P., Mao, Z.M., Yang, L.: Accurate online power estimation and automatic battery behavior based power model generation for smartphones. In: Proceedings of the Eighth IEEE/ACM/IFIP International Conference on Hardware/Software Codesign and System Synthesis, pp. 105–114. ACM (2010)
14. Murmuria, R., Medsger, J., Stavrou, A., Voas, J.M.: Mobile application and device power usage measurements. In: 2012 IEEE Sixth International Conference on Software Security and Reliability (SERE), pp. 147–156 (2012)
15. Shye, A., Scholbrock, B., Memik, G.: Into the wild: studying real user activity patterns to guide power optimizations for mobile architectures. In: Proceedings of the 42nd Annual IEEE/ACM International Symposium on Microarchitecture, pp. 168–178. ACM (2009)
16. Barbará, D., Domeniconi, C., Rogers, J.P.: Detecting outliers using transduction and statistical testing. In: Proceedings of the 12th ACM SIGKDD International Conference on Knowledge Discovery and Data Mining, pp. 55–64. ACM (2006)
17. Keogh, E., Lin, J., Fu, A.: Hot sax: efficiently finding the most unusual time series subsequence. In: Fifth IEEE International Conference on Data Mining. IEEE (2005)
18. Vovk, V., Gammerman, A., Saunders, C.: Machine-learning applications of algorithmic randomness. In: Proceedings of the Sixteenth International Conference on Machine Learning (ICML 1999), pp. 444–453 (1999)

Privacy

Privacy Risk Assessment on Online Photos

Haitao Xu[1,2]($\boxtimes$), Haining Wang[1], and Angelos Stavrou[3]

[1] University of Delaware, Newark, DE 19716, USA
{hxu,hnw}@udel.edu
[2] College of William and Mary, Williamsburg, VA 23187, USA
[3] George Mason University, Fairfax, VA 22030, USA
astavrou@gmu.edu

Abstract. With the rising popularity of cameras and people's increasing desire to share photos, an overwhelming number of photos have been posted all over the Web. A digital photo usually contains much information in its metadata. Once published online, a photo could disclose much more information beyond what is visually depicted in the photo and what the owner expects to share. The metadata contained in digital photos could pose significant privacy threats to their owners. Our work aims to raise public awareness of privacy risks resulting from sharing photos online and subsequent photo handling conducted by contemporary media sites. To this end, we investigated the prevalence of metadata information among digital photos and assessed the potential privacy risks arising from the metadata information. We also studied the policies adopted by online media sites on handling the metadata information embedded in the photos they host. We examined nearly 100,000 photos collected from over 600 top-ranked websites in seven categories and found that the photo handling policy adopted by a site largely varies depending on the category of the site. We demonstrated that some trivial looking metadata information suffices to mount real-world attacks against photo owners.

1 Introduction

With the proliferation of cameras, especially smartphone cameras, it is now very convenient for people to take photos whenever and wherever possible. Furthermore, the prevalence of online social networks and photo-sharing sites greatly facilitates people to share their digital photos with friends online. Every day, around 1.6 million photos are shared on Flickr [1], one of the largest online photo sharing sites. In their rush to share digital photos online, well-intentioned Internet users unwittingly expose much hidden metadata information contained in the digital photos. The metadata information such as camera serial number may seem relatively innocent and trivial but could pose privacy threats to photographers[1] and the people depicted in the photo. Unfortunately, one study [14] shows that up to 40 % of high-degree participants do not even know the term

---

[1] By photographer we mean the person who took the photo rather than who works as a professional photographer.

© Springer International Publishing Switzerland 2015
H. Bos et al. (Eds.): RAID 2015, LNCS 9404, pp. 427–447, 2015.
DOI: 10.1007/978-3-319-26362-5_20

metadata. The situation becomes worse concerning the fact that a photo could linger on the Web for many years.

During the spread of a digital photo, online social network (OSN) services and other media sites usually serve as the sink. Online media sites often compress and resize the photos they host for space saving. For instance, Instagram uses a resolution of 640*640 pixels for all its photos and automatically resizes any larger photos. Media sites may even remove the metadata information in their hosted photos. However, users usually do not know what online services will do with their uploaded photos [14]. Thus, it is important to raise public awareness of the potential privacy risks posed by metadata leakage and increase their knowledge of how online media sites handle the photos they upload.

Based on the life cycle and the propagation process, we create a taxonomy to classify digital photos into three different stages: "fresh," "intact," and "wild." "Fresh" photos are just freshly taken with a camera. "Intact" photos have been uploaded online but remain intact from the hosting sites. "Wild" photos may have been post-processed multiple times by the hosting sites. In this paper, we perform a data-driven assessment of privacy risks on contemporary digital photos. Specifically, we examine digital photos at the three stages in terms of metadata information contained and potential privacy risks, and we further explore the photo handling policies adopted by online media sites.

To obtain a representative dataset for our study, we collected nearly 200,000 photos in total in various ways including soliciting freshly taken photos through crowdsourcing, downloading original sized, intact photos from a major photo sharing site, and crawling "wild" photos from Google Images and over 600 top ranked websites. We examined the metadata information embedded in these photos and found that metadata was prevalent among photos at each of the three stages. We paid special attention to the metadata fields that may give rise to great privacy concerns. We found that about 10 % of "fresh" photos were tagged with GPS coordinates while 27 %–37 % of "intact" photos and only about 1 % of "wild" photos contained GPS information. We also measured the percentages of photos containing other sensitive metadata information including a photographer's name and modification history.

To understand how a photo is processed after being shared online, we also investigated online sites' policies on handling photos based on 97,664 photos crawled from 679 unique top sites in seven categories—"social networking," "news," "weblog," "college," "government," "shopping," and "classified"[2] sites. We found that photo handling policies adopted by online sites vary with different categories. The "college" and "government" sites hardly resize the photos they host or remove the embedded metadata information. However, the sites in the other categories are more likely to resize the photos and remove the metadata information.

In addition to the sensitive metadata information embedded in a photo, we demonstrated that some other trivial looking metadata information could be exploited to launch re-identification attacks against photo owners. For 62.6 % of

---

[2] "Classified" refers to the classified advertisements sites such as Craigslist.

Table 1. List of metadata information typically included in a digital photo.

Category	Information	Fields
When	Date Time	Create time, modify time
Where	Location	GPS coordinates, city/state/country
How	Device Info.	Camera make, model, serial number, light source, exposure mode, flash, aperture settings, ISO setting, shutter speed, focal length, color information
Who	People	Artist's name
What	Description	Title, headline, caption, by-line, keywords, copyright, special instructions
Modification	Modification History	Create tool, xmp toolkit, history action, history when, history software agent, history parameters

unique photographers, we were able to uncover their both online and real-world identities with just one photo they ever took and posted online.

The remainder of the paper is organized as follows. We provide background knowledge in Sect. 2. We describe data collection methods for "fresh" photos and characterize them in Sect. 3. We examine "intact" photos in Sect. 4. We characterize "wild" photos and investigate online sites' photo handling policies in Sect. 5. We demonstrate the re-identification attack in Sect. 6. We discuss the limitation of this work and propose our future work in Sect. 7. We survey the related work in Sect. 8 and conclude the paper in Sect. 9.

2 Background

In this section, we first give an overview of the metadata information typically contained in a digital photo, then discuss the potential privacy concerns, and finally illustrate the three stages we define for digital photos.

2.1 Metadata Information in a Photo

There are three most commonly used metadata standards for photos: EXIF, XMP, and IPTC. They often coexist in a photo and constitute the main part of the photo metadata. Table 1 lists the metadata fields typically included in a photo grouped by category.

A digital photo typically contains ample metadata information. When a shot is taken, the camera automatically embeds into the photo all the information it knows about the camera itself and the photo. In addition, users can add their own descriptive information with image processing software. Specifically, typical metadata information can be summarized as follows: (1) *when* – when the photo is created and modified if applicable, (2) *where* – the exact location (GPS coordinates and altitude) at which the photo is captured if a GPS receiver is equipped and enabled, or coarse-grained location information such as city/state/country, (3) *how* – the camera device used, its make, model, serial number, light circumstances (sunny or cloudy, flash on or off), exposure (auto or manual), and all other parameters used, (4) *who* – the photographer and the people depicted in the photo if manually added during post processing, (5) *what* – title, headline, caption, keywords, copyright restriction, and other detailed descriptions added for logging, organization or copyright protection, and (6) *modification* – if the photo is modified, on what date and time, by what software on what computer, and the specific actions done to the photo.

2.2   Potential Privacy Concerns Arising from Photo Metadata

Most metadata fields may look innocent and trivial. However, some could raise serious privacy concerns. We highlight several sensitive metadata fields below.

Geolocation. Contemporary cameras and smartphones are typically equipped with GPS functions. When taking photos with these GPS-enabled devices, geolocation information is automatically saved into the metadata. For a photo posted online, anybody able to access it could check the metadata information and may get the geolocation where the photo was taken. This definitely violates the privacy of the photographer and the people depicted. For instance, the time and location embedded in an online photo indicated that a public figure had been at an embarrassing location and not where he claimed to have been [5]. Moreover, a geo-located photo obviously taken at home and depicting high-value goods may give burglars incentives. In addition, young parents usually like to post many photos of their kids online, which may raise great concerns because the photos tagged with GPS coordinates could disclose the exact locations of where their kids live, play, or study.

Photographer's/Owner's Information. Some photos explicitly contain in the metadata the photographers' information, among which the name information is most commonly seen. No matter whether such information is embedded with or without the photographers' awareness, disclosing such information may cause identity leakage, especially given the availability of geolocation information in the metadata.

Modification History. When post processing a digital photo, an image processing software like Adobe Photoshop and Apple iPhoto often automatically embeds into the photo the detailed modification information, represented by three metadata fields: History When, History Software, and History Parameters. Table 2 presents an example of the embedded modification information in a photo. For the convenience of illustration, we add the photo's shot time in the table. It clearly shows that the photo has been processed twice in less than one month since it was taken on July 16, 2014. And two versions of Adobe Photoshop on one or two Macintosh computers were ever used for format conversion and save actions.

A photographer may not want to disclose such modification information, especially when such information may undermine what the photographer tries

Table 2. An example of modification information contained in a photo's metadata.

Create date	History when	History software	History parameters
2014:07:16 15:13:56	2014:07:19 01:30:03, 2014:08:08 21:17:25	Adobe Photoshop Lightroom 5.4 (Macintosh), Adobe Photoshop Lightroom 5.6 (Macintosh)	Converted from image/x-nikon-nef to image/dng, saved to new location, converted from image/dng to image/jpeg, saved to new location

to convey through the photo. For instance, the contained modification information may cast doubt on the legitimacy of a photo used as digital photographic evidence in court. In addition, celebrities may not like the public to know the photos they were depicted in are actually photoshopped.

2.3   Three Stages of Digital Photos

Based on their propagation process, contemporary digital photos fall into three stages: "fresh," "intact," and "wild." In the "fresh" stage, a photo is freshly taken, free from any post-processing manipulations and still stored in the local camera device. All the metadata information contained in a "fresh" photo is automatically embedded by the camera device, instead of being subsequently introduced by a post processing. In the "intact" stage, a photo has been uploaded online, but remains intact and has not yet been compressed or resized by the hosting media site. For a photo in the "wild" stage, it may have undergone resizing, cropping, and other editing actions conducted by the hosting site, which could change the hidden metadata too. By characterizing digital photos in these three different stages, we aim to depict the status of contemporary digital photos.

3   Fresh Photos

The photos in the "fresh" stage are just freshly created. We examine the metadata information, especially sensitive information, embedded in those freshly taken photos. In this section, we first describe the method used for collecting "fresh" photos and then characterize the collected photos.

3.1   Data Collection

The collection of "fresh" photos is not easy due to their inherent characteristics. We found that it is an effective way to solicit "fresh" photos through crowdsourcing. We posted tasks on a crowdsourcing platform. In each task, the required actions for a worker to take are two-fold: (1) pick up her smartphone, take a photo, and then send the photo to us directly via the instrumented email client application, and (2) take a short survey asking for her demographics information. In addition, to guarantee the unique origin of each photo, each worker is allowed to take our task only once.

Table 3. Demographic statistics of worker participants

Gender	Percent	Country	Percent	Age	Percent	Education	Percent	MobileOS	Percent
Male	71.7%	India	14.4%	<=17	2.3%	Graduate	17.7%	Android	72.8%
Female	28.3%	USA	13.7%	18–24	45.8%	Bachelor	47.0%	iOS	18.2%
NA	NA	Serbia	7.8%	25–34	36.3%	High Sch.	33.3%	WindowsP	5.2%
NA	NA	Nepal	5.3%	35–44	10.8%	Middle Sch.	1.7%	Blackberry	1.8%
NA	NA	Macedonia	4.4%	>=45	4.7%	Elementary	0.4%	Other	2.0%

For each received photo, we employed various methods to check if it is freshly taken with a smartphone rather than a photo randomly grabbed from the Internet. In addition, according to our tests, sending a photo via email does not affect its embedded metadata. Thus, our task requirements guarantee that the collected photos are freshly created and intact from any post-processing manipulation. The data collection lasts for two months and we collected 782 photos in total. We filtered out 170 photos that are either post-processed or created by other tools. We use the set of the remaining 612 photos for our study. We address potential ethical concerns on our data collection in Appendix A.

3.2 Characterizing "Fresh" Photos

Demographics. The 612 photos were collected from 612 unique workers from 76 countries. Table 3 lists the demographic statistics of the worker participants: (1) 71.7% of workers were male and the rest were female, (2) 45.5% of workers were from the top five countries, including India, United States, Serbia, Nepal, and Macedonia, (3) 82.1% of workers were between the ages of 18–34 and 10.8% between 35–44, (4) 47% of workers received the bachelor's degree, 33.3% with high school degree, and 17.7% with graduate degree, and (5) 72.8% of photos were taken with Android phones and 18.2% with iOS phones.

(Sensitive) Metadata Prevalence. Although Table 1 lists quite a few metadata fields typically embedded in a photo, a specific photo often has a large portion of its metadata information missing. According to our measurement results, we found that two metadata fields, camera make and model, are the most fundamental metadata information. That is, if they are missing in a photo, most other metadata fields are missing too. Thus, we decide whether a photo contains metadata information based on these two fields. A photo is regarded as containing metadata if either of the two fields has a non-empty value.

With the help of a third-party library [2], we examined the prevalence of metadata information among 612 "fresh" photos. We also examined if "fresh" photos contain any sensitive metadata fields, including geolocation, owner's information, and modification history, as mentioned in Sect. 2. Figure 1 shows the percentages of photos containing metadata and sensitive metadata fields. As high as 86.4% of "fresh" photos contain metadata, which demonstrates the prevalence of metadata information among freshly taken digital photos. As of the sensitive metadata fields, 15% of fresh photos are tagged with geolocation information. The results show that although nearly all smartphones are now

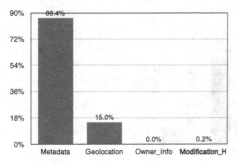

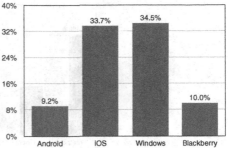

Fig. 1. Percentage of "fresh" photos containing metadata information.

Fig. 2. Percentage of "fresh" photos tagged with GPS for smartphone OS.

GPS-equipped, only some of them are GPS-enabled. The percentage is expected to be even lower if more people are aware that smartphones may automatically embed geolocation into photos and then choose to turn the GPS functionality off. None or hardly any of "fresh" photos contain photographers' information or modification history in their metadata. We speculate that it is due to (1) our strict task requirements and (2) the possibility that these two kinds of sensitive metadata fields may not be automatically embedded at the time of a photo shot.

Impact of Smartphone OS on Geolocation Metadata. It is interesting to examine which kind of smartphone OSes are more likely to automatically embed the sensitive geolocation information into photos. Figure 2 shows that about one third of iOS and Windows phones automatically embed geolocation into photos while only about 10 % of Android and Blackberry phones do this.

4   Intact Photos

In the "intact" stage, photos have been posted online while retaining intact metadata information. From this perspective, "intact photos" could reflect the status of metadata in digital photos at the time of being shared online. In this section, we describe our data collection method for "intact" photos and examine the embedded metadata information in them.

4.1   Data Collection

To collect such photos, we crawled photos from Flickr, a large photo-sharing website, using its API with the download option of "original size," which guarantees that the photos remain original and intact from the site. More specifically, we collected two sets of "intact" photos from Flickr. The first set denoted by *Flickr_p* contains 18,404 photos exclusively taken with smartphones. Those photos were crawled from the Flickr group "Smartphone Photography" where all photos were taken with smartphones. The other set denoted by *Flickr_6* contains 43,704 photos uploaded within six months from July 1, 2014 to December 31,

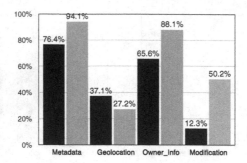

Fig. 3. Percentage of "intact" photos containing metadata information. In each of four pairs of columns, the left black column represents *Flick_p* while the right gray *Flick_6*.

2014. Our further examination shows that 94.3 % of the photos in *Flickr_6* were taken with digital cameras.

4.2 Metadata Information Embedded

Similarly, we examined the percentage of "intact" photos containing metadata information, especially sensitive metadata fields. Figure 3 shows the percentages of "intact" photos containing metadata and sensitive metadata fields.

It shows that intact photos in *Flickr_p* and *Flickr_6* have quite high percentages containing metadata information, 76.4 % and 94.1 %, respectively. The results indicate that most digital photos taken with either digital cameras or smartphones contain metadata when being uploaded online. In addition, 37.1 % *Flickr_p* and 27.2 % *Flickr_6* photos contain GPS information. Considering 15 % of "fresh" photos tagged with geolocation, we speculate that some photo owners may embed GPS information into photos during post processing to better show their photographic works on Flickr. Moreover, up to 65.6 % and 88.1 % *Flickr_p* and *Flickr_6* photos contain the photographer information, which could pose a great risk of identity leakage to photo owners. Additionally, about a half of *Flickr_6* photos contain modification information. Most photos in the set are taken with professional digital cameras and photo owners often show intense interest in refining their works with image processing software. By contrast, a much lower percentage of *Flickr_p* photos taken with smartphones are modified.

5   Wild Photos

In the "wild" stage, most online photos have lingered on the Internet for a while and may have experienced multiple modifications by the hosting sites. In this section, we attempt to figure out the metadata information remaining in the "wild" photos and explore how the top media sites handle the photos hosted on them.

5.1 Data Collection

We employed two methods to collect "wild" photos. The first method is to randomly collect photos by Google Images Search. In the custom search control panel, we set the image type as photo, file type as JPG/JPEG files, image size as larger than 400*300, and the date range from January 1, 2012 until January 1, 2015. Nearly all digital photos are in JPEG format. The specified image size can filter out most of graphs, drawings, and other non-photo images. In addition, we only focus on the photos posted online in the past three years. We totally collected 38,140 photos in this way and denoted them by *GoogleImage*.

Secondly, to investigate top media sites' policies on handling photos, we need to obtain a representative set of media sites. Alexa categorizes millions of sites and defines a list of site categories [4], from which we selected seven categories, which are "social networking," "weblog," "news," "college," "government," "classified," and "shopping". The reason why we chose them is that presumably the sites in these categories usually host large amounts of photos. Alexa provides for each category a list of the top 500 sites. We selected the top 100 sites for each category and thus we had 700 unique top ranked sites in total as our subject representative of online media sites.

Not every photo appearing on a site is hosted by the site. A photo is considered being hosted on a site only if its image URL has the same domain as the site URL. Only the photos hosted on a site are eligible to be used for studying the site's polices. During our photo collection from each site, we only crawled the photos hosted on that site. Specifically, for each of the 700 sites, we attempted to crawl 1,000 photos that appeared online after January 1, 2012. Those photos are expected to reflect the photo policy used by the hosting site under an assumption that the site has not made significant changes to its photo handling policy in the recent years. Due to unexpected factors including network connection failure and access permission denied, we were able to crawl 97,664 photos from 679 unique sites. To ensure the representativeness of these photos, we filtered out the sites from which less than 10 photos were collected. Finally, we had 97,403 photos for 611 unique sites as our dataset for the study, about 160 photos per site on average. This set of photos are denoted as *TopSitesPhoto*.

Figure 4 depicts the number of photos crawled from each site. It shows that about 80% of sites have over 60 photos crawled, about 35% of sites have over 120 photos crawled, and about 20% have over 300 photos crawled. We crawled a maximum number of 1,026 photos for one site[3].

5.2 Metadata Information Embedded

Figure 5 shows the percentages of "wild" photos containing metadata, especially those sensitive metadata fields. It shows that the percentages of "wild" photos containing metadata information in the sets *GoogleImage* and *TopSitesPhoto* are 41.5% and 40.4%, respectively, which are much smaller than that of "intact"

---

[3] We crawled the site twice and collected over 1,000 photos.

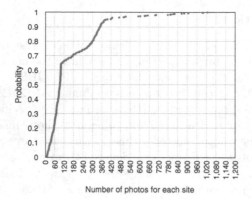

Fig. 4. CDF of number of photos crawled from each site.

photos (up to 94.1 %). In addition, very few "wild" photos are tagged with GPS coordinates. In *GoogleImage* and *TopSitesPhoto*, the percentages are 0.6 % and 1.8 %, respectively, smaller than those of "fresh" and "intact" photos. Moreover, only 13.2 % of *GoogleImage* photos and 8.7 % of *TopSitesPhoto* photos contain photographers' identification information. About 25.4 % of *GoogleImage* photos and 14.1 % of *TopSitesPhoto* photos contain modification history information. These results imply that compared to "fresh" and "intact" photos, a considerable proportion of "wild" photos have their embedded metadata stripped away.

5.3   Inferring Online Sites' Photo Handling Policies

Based on *TopSitesPhoto*, we have built a set of photos for each of the 611 unique sites. We attempt to infer a site's photo handling policy by characterizing the photos collected from the site. Specifically, we aim to answer two questions about a site's photo handling policy. One is whether the site resizes the photos it hosts,

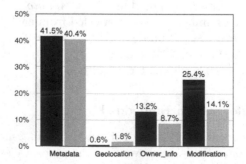

Fig. 5. Percentage of "wild" photos containing metadata information. In each of four pairs of columns, the left black column represents *GoogleImage* while the right gray *TopSitesPhoto*.

and the other is whether the site removes the metadata information embedded in those photos.

Whether a Site Resizes its Hosted Photos? After upload, a photo is typically compressed and resized by the hosting site in several sizes. For instance, Instagram uses an image size of 640 pixels in width and 640 pixels in height for nearly all its hosted photos. More commonly, an online site confines a photo's longest side length to a small set of values. Flickr resizes its photos in the following sizes: 100 pixels (on the longest side), 240 pixels, 800 pixels, 1600 pixels and so on [10]. Therefore, if the majority of photos hosted by a site have their longest side (width or height) lengths falling into a small set of numbers, then we speculate that the site does resize the photos it hosts.

For each photo in our dataset, we retrieved its longest side length from its file information. About 2 % of photos had no image size information available and were ruled out. Suppose "$DDDD$" is the longest side length value that is observed most frequently on a site. We calculated the proportion of the photos on the site with their longest side length of the value "$DDDD$". We then leveraged the proportion number to decide whether the site resizes its photos or not. If over 50 % of photos on the site have the longest side length of "$DDDD$", the site is considered to resize its photos. The argument is based on our observation that among more than 40,000 photos downloaded from Flickr with "original size" option, only 3.47 % have their longest side length of 1,600 pixels, while this length value occurs much more frequently for the photos that have been resized.

Figure 6 shows what percentage of sites that are regarded to resize the photos on their sites across the 7 categories. It is not surprising to see that only 3.0 % of "College" sites and 10.5 % "Government" sites have resized their photos, since colleges and governments usually have sufficient hosting resources to store high-resolution photos. About 36.7 % of "News" sites are estimated to resize the photos they host. A close examination reveals that news sites often resize their photos to many different sizes, which thereby lowers the percentage of photos with a unique longest side length size. In reality, there are probably

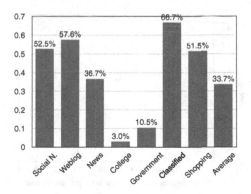

Fig. 6. Percentage of sites estimated to resize their photos across the seven categories.

much more news sites that resize their photos. In each of the other four categories, "Social networking," "Weblog," "Classified," and "Shopping," over 50 % of sites have resized the photos they host. The sites in those categories often contain large amounts of photos and resizing photos is an effective means to save valuable storage space. Irrespective of categories, at least one third of all sites in our dataset are regarded to resize the photos they host. Note that our results represent a lower bound of the percentage of sites that resize their photos.

Whether a Site Strips Out the Metadata Information Embedded in the Photos it Hosts? There is another issue people may be concerned about when they upload photos online. As mentioned before, we use two fields in the metadata—camera make and model—to determine if the metadata information exists or not. For each site in our dataset, we calculated the percentage of its photos containing metadata information. Note that a photo may have its metadata information erased by its owner before posted online. Thus, our estimated percentage of online sites that strip out the metadata information of the photos they host represents an upper bound.

Figure 7 shows the CDF of the percentage of photos containing metadata information on each of the 611 sites in the seven categories. About 16 % of sites have no photos containing metadata information. It is highly probable that those sites remove the metadata information from all hosted photos. About 45 % of total sites have at least half of their hosted photos containing metadata information. We determine that a site adopts a policy of removing photo metadata information if no photos hosted by the site contain metadata information; otherwise, the site is considered to preserve the metadata information of photos it hosts.

Figure 8 shows the percentage of sites in each category which are estimated to preserve the metadata information of photos they host. Again we found that the two categories "College" and "Government" present quite different statistical characteristics in preserving the photo metadata than the rest five categories. Specifically, 98 % of college sites and 93.7 % of government sites are estimated to

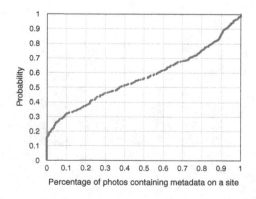

Fig. 7. CDF of the percentage of photos containing metadata information on each site.

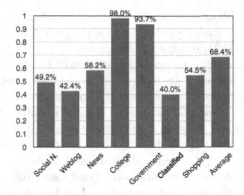

Fig. 8. Percentage of sites estimated to preserve the photo metadata information across the seven categories.

preserve the photo metadata information. Combined with the above estimation results on a site's photo resizing policy, we draw the conclusion that college and government sites seldom resize the photos they host or remove the embedded photo metadata information. In each of the other five categories, the proportions of the sites that preserve the photo metadata information are between 40 % and 60 %, much lower than those of college and government sites. On average, up to 68.4 % of the top sites in the seven categories preserve the photo metadata information, which suggests that a number of online photos may still have their metadata information open to public access for years.

6   Re-identification Attack

Except the sensitive metadata fields including geolocation, owner's information, and modification history, other metadata fields may appear relatively innocent. However, in this section, we demonstrate the feasibility of exploiting a trivial looking metadata field for re-identification attack.

Even without the photographer information explicitly included, a photographer can still be identified based on even only one photo she ever took. This can happen through a new attack vector—the camera serial number field in the photo metadata. A camera serial number can uniquely identify a camera most of the time.[4] All photos taken with a same digital camera are supposed to have the same serial number if provided.[5] In theory, a single photo with a camera serial number embedded could be used to trace other online photos taken with the same camera. Those photos together facilitate identifying the photographer.

We figured out that a public online database *stolencamerafinder* [3] could be leveraged to search for online photos tagged with a given camera serial number, although the online service was established to help find stolen cameras. For each

---

[4] A serial number is unique within a camera brand. Combined with camera make and model, a serial number can uniquely identify a camera.

[5] Smartphones typically do not store their serial numbers in their photos.

given serial number, *stolencamerafinder* returns a list of online photos taken with the same camera, and for each photo provides the page URL where the photo is posted and the image URL linking to the photo.

Next, we do experiments to prove it quite easy to identify a photo owner with only one photo she ever shared online in the case that the photo has a camera serial number embedded. About 12 % of the "wild" photos in the two sets *GoogleImage* and *TopSitesPhoto* were found to contain the serial number information. We randomly selected 2,000 unique serial numbers from them, then manually searched each serial number in the *stolencamerafinder*, and finally got back search results for 1,037 serial numbers in total. Note that not every camera serial number could get search results back. For those 1,037 serial numbers, by following the image URLs returned, we collected 38,140 photos that were posted on 4,712 unique websites. The photos collected for a specific serial number only represent a subset of all photos available online and tagged with the same serial number, due to the impossibility of finding all online photos with a given serial number.

Figure 9 shows the cumulative distribution function (CDF) of the number of photos that a single serial number links to. About 30 % of serial numbers link to over 25 photos and about 10 % link to over 100 photos. The average number of photos linked to a same serial number is 36.8, the median is 10, and the maximum is 923. With the considerable number of photos tagged with a same camera serial number, together with the page URLs where the photos are posted, and the photos already existing in the photo sets *GoogleImage* and *TopSitesPhoto*, we were able to set up a knowledge base for each serial number (tentatively a digital camera). The rich information available can evidently disclose much more privacy information about the camera owner than a single serial number itself. This demonstrates the potential of a camera serial number as an attractive attack vector for mounting privacy attacks.

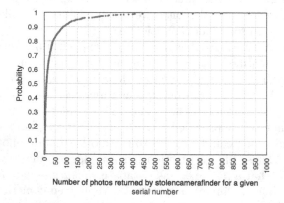

Fig. 9. CDF of the number of photos returned by *stolencamerafinder* for a given serial number.

Table 4. List of the information typically contained in an account profile in each of the five OSNs. Note that the listed information represents the maximum amount of information available with public permissions of an OSN account.

OSN	Account profile information
Flickr	Name, Occupation, Living City, Hometown, Gender, Personal Website(s), Email, Joined Time, Biography, Age, Religion
500px	Name, Biography, Living City, Contact, other OSN accounts
Google+	Name, Gender, Living City, Colleges Attended, Current Employer, Work Experience
Twitter	Name, Occupation, Living City, Telephone, Email, Personal Webpage(s), Joined Time, Photos and Videos, Tweets, Followings, Followers and Favorites
Facebook	Name, Living City, Gender, Education, Telephone, other OSN accounts, Life Events

Identifying a Photographer. The page URL and the page where a photo is posted can provide important clues to reveal a photographer's online identity. For instance, the URL https://plus.google.com/XYZ/photos suggests that the photographer should have a Google+ [8] account with the ID of "XYZ". Following the URL allows us to retrieve more information about the photographer, such as her real name, college attended, current employer, and photos posted on her account page. We have observed a great many such URL strings in our dataset with photographers' online social networks (OSNs) account IDs embedded. The involved OSNs include but not limited to Flickr, Facebook [6], Twitter [7], Google+, and 500px [9]. A photographer may have her multiple OSN accounts disclosed in this way. Table 4 lists the information typically contained in an account profile of the five social networks mentioned above. It shows that an account profile typically contains demographics and other sensitive information including age, gender, education, occupation, living city, other OSN accounts, and much more. Once one OSN account is identified, the true identity of the user in the real world can be readily disclosed.

Figure 10 shows the percentage of serial numbers from which we are able to identify the corresponding camera owners' IDs in one or more OSNs by scrutinizing the page URLs where the photos were posted. Among the 1,037 unique serial numbers in our dataset, 51.4 % (533) of the serial numbers have the camera owners' OSN accounts identified, and 9.0 % (93) have account IDs in two or more OSNs identified. And for one serial number we even identified the camera owner's four account IDs in four OSNs respectively.

As mentioned before, we were able to retrieve about 37 online photos on average for a given serial number. Those photos tagged with the same serial number may contain metadata information that could help identify the photographer. We closely examined the metadata information embedded in the related photos for each of the remaining 504 serial numbers without any OSN accounts

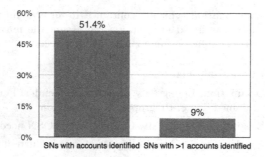

Fig. 10. Percentage of camera serial numbers (SNs) with camera owners' OSN accounts identified.

identified in the previous step. Among them, we successfully identified the photographers for 116 serial numbers. Compared to the photographers with their OSN accounts identified, the available information on those 116 photographers are restricted to the photo metadata embedded, mainly including their names, the processing softwares, and OSes used. However, more information could be collected online once a person's name is identified. Overall, 62.6 % (649) of serial numbers have had their photographers identified.

7   Discussion

One goal of this work is to track the propagation of the sensitive metadata information embedded in the digital photos at different stages. One ideal way is to monitor the process of creation, modification, and elimination of the metadata information contained in a same set of photos that sequentially experience three stages—"fresh," "intact," and "wild." However, it is very hard to obtain such an ideal photo set in large-scale. Instead, we employed different data collection methods and obtained three kinds of photo sets to represent the digital photos at the corresponding three stages.

We collected 612 valid "fresh" photos through crowdsourcing in a period of two months. Each photo collected was taken by a unique participant with a unique device, and participants from 76 countries contributed to this dataset. In addition, those photos were solicited directly from smartphones and no photos taken with digital cameras were collected in order to avoid data contamination. Therefore, although the dataset size of "fresh" photos is not comparable to those of "intact" and "wild" photos, its representativeness is high enough for this study.

To infer online media sites' policies on handling metadata information in the photos they host, we adopt a passive approach, that is, by examining the metadata information of the photos collected from the sites. Actually, we once considered to take an active approach to detect media sites' policies, by submitting (uploading) different types of photos to the sites, then re-downloading them, and comparing metadata fields. However, we had to abandon this approach because most of the 611 sites in the seven categories have specific user groups and are not open to public registration, not to mention photo uploading.

Table 5. Main functions of the browser extension prototype

Sensitive metadata	Potential threats	Website's policy
Geolocation	Location disclosure, house robbery	Metadata removing
Photographer's name	Identity disclosure	Photo resizing
Modification history	Undermining photo's authenticity	NA
Camera serial number	Re-identification attack	NA

Although it is known that a camera serial number can uniquely identify a camera to some extent, we are not aware of any previous research work revealing potential threats arising from this attribute in an empirical and systematic manner. We demonstrated the feasibility of re-identification attack by exploiting camera serial number. We were able to identify over 60 % of photo owners based on their camera serial numbers available in a public online database.

When a user shares a digital photo online, two questions about privacy issues are readily raised. One is whether sensitive hidden metadata information is embedded in the photo. The other concerning question is what the media site will do with the photo. According to our experiment results, a considerable proportion of digital photos contain sensitive metadata information, and many sites resize the photos they host or remove the embedded photo metadata information. In our future work, we will develop a browser extension to give users direct answers to these two questions.

The major functions that the tool should have are illustrated in Table 5. Specifically, once the sensitive metadata information in a photo being uploaded is detected, the browser extension should issue an alarm by popping up a window on the screen and provide customized alert information, including the sensitive metadata information embedded, the corresponding privacy risks, and the current visiting site's policy on photo handling. Note that the browser extension should display the alert information only when the privacy-related metadata information is detected, and thus it should not often interfere with normal photo upload workflows. Although there are already browser extensions for photo metadata visualization, we will focus on informing users of the sensitive metadata contained and customized privacy risks. Moreover, we will ensure users' right to know the actions that the hosting media sites will perform on their photos.

8   Related Work

Several previous works conduct user studies to understand users' privacy decisions during the photo sharing process and their privacy concerns on others' photo-sharing activities. Clark et al. [11] revealed the problem of unintended photo storage without users' awareness, which is mainly caused by the automatic features of cloud-based photo backup services. Ahern et al. [12] found that mobile users' decisions to post photos privately or publicly were determined more by identity or impression concerns than security concerns. Besmer et al. [13] made similar findings. They studied users' perception of being tagged in undesired photos uploaded by others. They found that a user's privacy concerns on that domain were mainly related to identity and impression management within her existing social circles. Henne et al. [14] showed in their survey results that among the information potentially disclosed by the tagged photos, personal references and location data raised most privacy concerns.

More related to our work, several researchers examined the privacy threat posed by the textual metadata information contained in online photos. Friedland and Sommer [15] focused on the privacy threats posed by the geolocation information available online. They showed that the geolocation data could be exploited to mount privacy attacks using three scenarios on Craigslist, Twitter, and YouTube, respectively. Pesce et al. [17] demonstrated that photo tagging on Facebook could be exploited to enhance prediction of users' information like gender, city, and country. Another work from Mahmood and Desmedt [16] discussed possible privacy violations from Google+'s policy that any users who access a photo can see its metadata online. While the above three works addressed the privacy issues with photos, we investigated the privacy issues with online photos on a much larger scale. We assessed the privacy risks arising from leakage of all possible sensitive metadata information rather than just geolocation data. Moreover, our study is not restricted to one media site. Instead, we collect our photo dataset from hundreds of top-ranked websites and through crowdsourcing platforms. Those photos cover various stages, i.e., "fresh," "intact," and "wild." In addition, we introduce a new attack vector and show its unexpected power in conducting a re-identification attack. We also performed a large-scale measurement of photo handling policies adopted by various categories of media sites.

Another large body of previous work has attempted to enhance people's privacy when sharing photos online. Besmer et al. [22] designed a privacy enhancement tool to improve the photo tagging process on Facebook. The tool allows tagged users to negotiate online with the photo uploaders about the permission settings on the photo. Fang and LeFevre [18] built a machine learning model for OSN users to configure privacy settings automatically with a limited number of rules provided. Zerr et al. [23] developed privacy classification models for users to search for private photos about themselves posted by others at an early stage. Henne et al. [21] proposed a watchdog service that allows users to keep track of potentially harmful photos uploaded by others at the expense of sharing their location data with the service. Ra et al. [19] presented a selective encryption algorithm that enables a photo to hide its "secret" part from the host photo-sharing site and the unauthorized viewers and only expose its "public" part. Ilia et al. [20] refined the access control mechanism currently used by OSNs on photo sharing. The new mechanism allows the depicted users in a photo to decide the exposure of their own face, and could present photos with the restricted faces blurred out to a visitor. Complementary to those works attempting to enhance privacy on the web server side, this study assesses the privacy risks arising from sensitive photo metadata and provides some guidelines for developing client-side privacy leakage prevention tools, which should be able to alert online users of potential privacy risks posed by uploading photos and also inform them of the photo handling policies adopted by the currently visiting website.

To the best of our knowledge, we have conducted the first large-scale empirical measurement study of the status of contemporary digital photos at the three different stages. In addition to examining the sensitive metadata information embedded, we inferred the photo handling policies used by hundreds of top-ranked sites, and proposed to exploit the camera identification number as an attack vector for re-identification attack. We are not aware of any previous work studying these topics.

9   Conclusion

In this paper, we performed a data-driven assessment of privacy risks on contemporary digital photos. We first collected from the Web nearly 200,000 digital photos at three different stages as our dataset. Then for photos at each stage, we measured the prevalence of metadata and assessed the privacy risks posed by metadata leakage. We found that metadata is quite prevalent among digital photos at each stage. In particular, 15 % of "fresh" photos, about 30 % "intact" photos, and about 1 % "wild" photos were tagged with GPS coordinates. The percentage of "wild" photos containing other sensitive metadata information is also much lower than that of "intact" photos. A possible reason is that online sites often remove the metadata information of the photos they host. Our speculation was confirmed by our investigation of photo handling policies based on nearly 100,000 photos crawled from 679 top sites in seven categories. We further found that photo policies used by a site vary with the category that the site belongs to. Finally, we proposed to use the camera serial number as a new attack vector towards privacy inference and demonstrated its power in deriving both online and real-world identities of a photographer with just one photo she ever took. In our future work, we will build a browser extension prototype to prevent users' photo privacy leakage and increase their knowledge of the online services' policies on photo handling.

Acknowledgement. We would like to thank our shepherd Chris Kanich and the anonymous reviewers for their insightful and detailed comments. This work was partially supported by ARO grant W911NF-15-1-0287 and ONR grant N00014-13-1-0088. Any opinions, findings, and conclusions or recommendations expressed in this material are those of the authors and do not necessarily reflect the views of the funding agencies.

A   Ethical Consideration

In our study, we leveraged several methods to collect photos, including: (1) soliciting "fresh" photos from crowdsourcing workers, (2) crawling photos from Flickr using its API, (3) random Google Image Search, and (4) crawling top websites for limited amounts of photos. Note that our crowdsourcing study has been vetted and approved by the Institutional Review Board (IRB) at our institution.

During our photo collection, we did not receive any concerns or get warnings from those involved sites and did not interfere with their normal operations. In addition, with the collected photos, we anonymized the metadata information embedded before using them for study. We strictly abide by the copyright licenses if present.

References

1. Number of photos uploaded to Flickr. https://www.flickr.com/photos/franckmichel/6855169886/
2. ExifTool library. http://www.sno.phy.queensu.ca/~phil/exiftool/
3. Site stolencamerafinder: Find your camera. http://www.stolencamerafinder.com/
4. Alexa top sites by category. http://www.alexa.com/topsites/category/Top
5. McAfee's location is leaked with photo metadata. http://www.wired.co.uk/news/archive/2012-12/04/vice-give-away-mcafee-location
6. Facebook: https://www.facebook.com/
7. Twitter: https://twitter.com/
8. Google+: https://plus.google.com/
9. 500px: https://500px.com/
10. Flickr file size limits. https://www.flickr.com/help/photos/
11. Clark, J.W., Snyder, P., McCoy, D., Kanich, C.: I saw images I didn't even know I had: understanding user perceptions of cloud storage privacy. In: Proceedings of the SIGCHI Conference on Human Factors in Computing Systems (CHI) (2015)
12. Ahern, S., Eckles, D., Good, N., King, S., Naaman, M., Nair, R.: Over-exposed? Privacy patterns and considerations in online and mobile photo sharing. In: Proceedings of the SIGCHI Conference on Human Factors in Computing Systems (CHI) (2007)
13. Besmer, A., Lipford, H.R.: Poster: privacy perceptions of photo sharing in facebook. In: Proceedings of the 4th Symposium on Usable Privacy and Security (SOUPS) (2008)
14. Henne, B., Smith, M.: Awareness about photos on the web and how privacy-privacy-tradeoffs could help. In: Adams, A.A., Brenner, M., Smith, M. (eds.) FC 2013. LNCS, vol. 7862, pp. 131–148. Springer, Heidelberg (2013)
15. Friedland, G., Sommer, R.: Cybercasing the joint: on the privacy implications of geo-tagging. In: Proceedings of the 5th USENIX Conference on Hot Topics in Security (HotSec) (2010)
16. Mahmood, S., Desmedt, Y.: Poster: preliminary analysis of Google+'s privacy. In: Proceedings of the 18th ACM Conference on Computer and Communications Security (CCS) (2011)
17. Pesce, J.P., Casas, D.L., Rauber, G., Almeida, V.: Privacy attacks in social media using photo tagging networks: a case study with Facebook. In: Proceedings of the 1st Workshop on Privacy and Security in Online Social Media (PSOSM) (2012)
18. Fang, L., LeFevre, K.: Privacy wizards for social networking sites. In: Proceedings of the 19th International Conference on World Wide Web (WWW) (2010)
19. Ra, M., Govindan, R., Ortega, A.: P3: toward privacy-preserving photo sharing. In: Proceedings of the 10th USENIX Symposium on Networked Systems Design and Implementation (NSDI) (2013)
20. Ilia, P., Polakis, I., Athanasopoulos, E., Maggi, F., Ioannidis, S.: Face/Off: preventing privacy leakage from photos in social networks. In: Proceedings of the 22nd ACM Conference on Computer and Communications Security (CCS) (2015)

21. Henne, B., Szongott, C., Smith, M.: SnapMe if you can: privacy threats of other peoples' geo-tagged media and what we can do about it. In: Proceedings of the 6th ACM Conference on Security and Privacy in Wireless and Mobile Networks (WiSec) (2013)
22. Besmer, A., Lipford, H.R.: Moving beyond untagging: photo privacy in a tagged world. In: Proceedings of the 28th SIGCHI Conference on Human Factors in Computing Systems (CHI) (2010)
23. Zerr, S., Siersdorfer, S., Hare, J., Demidova, E.: Privacy-aware image classification and search. In: Proceedings of the 35th International ACM Conference on Research and Development in Information Retrieval (SIGIR) (2012)

Privacy is Not an Option:
Attacking the IPv6 Privacy Extension

Johanna Ullrich[(✉)] and Edgar Weippl

SBA Research, Vienna, Austria
{jullrich,eweippl}@sba-research.org

Abstract. The IPv6 privacy extension introduces temporary addresses to protect against address-based correlation, i.e., the attribution of different transactions to the same origin using addresses, and is considered as state-of-the-art mechanism for privacy protection in IPv6. In this paper, we scrutinize the extension's capability for protection by analyzing its algorithm for temporary address generation in detail. We develop an attack that is based on two insights and shows that the notion of protection is false: First, randomization is scarce and future identifiers can be predicted once the algorithm's internal state is known. Second, a victim's temporary addresses form a side channel and allow an adversary to synchronize to this internal state. Finally, we highlight mitigation strategies, and recommend a revision of the extension's specification.

1 Introduction

Snowden's revelations on the National Security Agency's surveillance program startled the global public due to its sheer extent and sophistication. Practically everbody's Internet communication is collected. The gained data is filtered, analyzed, measured and finally stored for the purpose of compounding a precise picture of Internet users [1,2]. But other actors are also after massive amounts of user data: Western democracies, e.g., in the European Union or Australia, often introduce telecommunication data retention. Commercial enterprises spy on their customers on a massive scale to increase monetary revenue [3,4], and criminals may do so as well.

The power of such an approach lies in its capability of making sense from large amounts of data that seem unrelated to each other by combing countless pieces of information [5]. This means that a person's different activities on the Internet can be correlated to each other, and this condensed information typically exceeds what people believe can be found out about their lives. Addresses play a sensitive role in this: On the one hand, an address has to accurately identify the receiver so that traffic reaches its intended destination. On the other hand, address-based correlation enables the attribution of different transactions to the same origin and allows to gain insights into others' Internet behavior. General protection strategies against correlation like an attribute's removal or its encryption seem inadequate for addresses as intermediate nodes require access for appropriate data delivery.

© Springer International Publishing Switzerland 2015
H. Bos et al. (Eds.): RAID 2015, LNCS 9404, pp. 448–468, 2015.
DOI: 10.1007/978-3-319-26362-5_21

Addressing, in turn, is heavily dependent on the protocol, and IPv6 introduced new aspects in the matter of address-based correlation. Initially, all addresses of an interface were defined to include a globally unique identifier and thus allowed simplest address correlation over an interface's full lifetime [6]. In response, temporary addresses that change by default every 24 h were introduced. This mechanism is known as the privacy extension [7], and is considered as state-of-the-art privacy protection in IPv6 [8]. It is implemented in major desktop and mobile operating systems.

In this paper, we scrutinize the IPv6 privacy extension's capability of protecting against address-based correlation, and therefore focus on the algorithm for temporary address generation. We find that once the algorithm's state is known by an adversary, she is able to accurately predict a victim's future addresses. Beyond that, we develop a way that allows an adversary to synchronize to the victim's state by exploiting observed temporary addresses as a side channel, and appraise the attacker's effort to perform our attack with currently available technology. Our results yield 3.3 years of hashing but advances in technology are going to decrease this time period. We highlight mitigation strategies; however, our most important contribution may be the impetus for a revision of the extension's specification.

The remainder of the paper is structured as follows: Sect. 2 provides details on addressing in IPv6 and the privacy extension. Section 3 summarizes related work focusing on privacy implications of competing IPv6 addressing standards as well as known vulnerabilities of the privacy extension. Section 4 describes the assumed attack scenario and is followed by a security analysis of the extension's address generation algorithm that identifies four weaknesses in Sect. 5. Based on those insights, the development of our attack is described in Sect. 6. Its feasibility is discussed in Sect. 7, which is followed by an investigation of current operating systems' vulnerability in Sect. 8. Strategies for mitigation are presented in Sect. 9, and Sect. 10 concludes the paper.

2   Background

This section provides background on IPv6 addressing in general: the address structure, address assignment and their implications for address-based correlation. In a second step, we focus on the IPv6 privacy extension and describe its principal idea as well as its algorithm for temporary interface identifier generation.

IPv6 Addressing: IPv6 addresses have a length of 128 bit and are portioned into two distinct parts of equal size as depicted in Fig. 1. The first 64 bits form the network prefix, and are dependent on a host's location in the network. The remaining 64 bits form the interface identifier (IID) that enables a subscriber's identification on the link. Address configuration for clients is done via stateless address autoconfiguration [9] and does not require human intervention: Routers advertise the network prefix on the network, and hosts form their global IPv6 addresses by combining the announced prefix with a self-generated interface identifier.

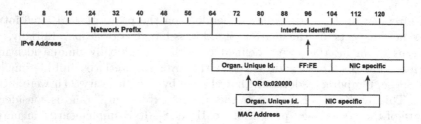

Fig. 1. IPv6 addresses using interface identifiers in modified EUI-64 format

The interface identifier was initially intended to follow the modified EUI-64 format [6] that infers an interface identifier from the 48 bit media access control (MAC) address, see also Fig. 1. The MAC address consists of a 24 bit organizationally unique identifier, and a network interface card (NIC)-specific part of equal size. A fixed pattern of two bytes is inserted between these parts and a universal/local bit is set to one in order to form the identifier.

The MAC address is globally unique and typically remains stable over a host's lifetime[1]. Consequently, the interface identifier that is included in every IPv6 address is globally unique and stable as well. All addresses of a certain host have the same second half, while their network prefix changes according to the visited location. An adversary is thus able to attribute various transactions to the same origin based on the identifier and trace a host's Internet behavior even beyond a certain sub-network. The adversary is further able to retrace a host's movement in the network as the included network prefixes allow localization.

The IPv6 Privacy Extension: The privacy extension is presented as a solution that impedes correlation *"when different addresses used in different transactions actually correspond to the same node"* [7]. Its basic principle are interface identifiers that change at a regular interval of typically 24 h. Hosts form temporary IPv6 addresses from the announced prefix in combination with the current interface identifier, and change the IPv6 address with every newly generated identifier. An expired address is considered deprecated and not used for new connections, but still serves already active transactions.

A host's successive interface identifiers have to be chosen in a way that appears random to outsiders and hinders them in attributing different identifiers to the same origin. Thus the IPv6 privacy extension defines an algorithm for a pseudo-random generation of these temporary identifiers as described in the following and depicted in Fig. 2:

1. A 64 bit history value is concatenated with the interface identifier in the modified EUI-64 format.
2. An MD5 digest is calculated over the concatenation of the previous step to gain a digest of 128 bit length.

---

[1] Technically speaking the MAC remains stable over the NIC's lifetime, but we suppose that personal computers, laptops, tablets and mobiles keep their NIC over their whole lifetime.

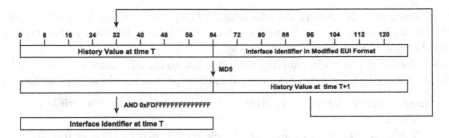

Fig. 2. Interface identifier generation according to the privacy extension

3. The digest's leftmost 64 bits are extracted and bit 6 is set to zero in order to form the temporary interface identifier.
4. The digest's rightmost 64 bits form the next iteration's history value and are stored.
5. In case the generated interface identifier is found to be used by other local devices or reserved, the process is restarted to gain another identifier.

The very first history value is initialized with a random value the first time a system boots. This algorithm is defined for systems with present stable storage, which is necessary to keep the history value across system restarts. Devices like stationary PCs, laptops, tablets and smart phones are typically considered to have such storage. However, in its absence, it is allowed to randomly re-initialize the history value after every system restart.

Temporary IPv6 addresses are assigned in addition to stable addresses in modified EUI-64 format, and do not replace them in order to prevent negative impacts on addressing. Temporary addresses are used in outgoing connections to stay private, while stable addresses make it possible to stay reachable for incoming requests.

3   Related Work

Our research has a two-pronged foundation: First, we discuss various IPv6 address structures with respect to privacy, and highlight the IPv6 privacy extension's outstanding positions due to its capability to protect against geographical as well as temporal address-based correlation. This further emphasizes why the extension's secure standardization and implementation is an important aspect of IPv6 privacy. Second, we summarize previously discovered vulnerabilities of the privacy extension, and illustrate their minor importance in comparison to the new attack that we present in this paper.

3.1   IPv6 Address Formats and Address Correlation

There are ways to form IPv6 interface identifiers for stateless address autoconfiguration beyond the modified EUI-64 format and the privacy extension: (1) manually configured stable identifiers, (2) semantically opaque identifiers [10] and

(3) cryptographically generated addresses (CGAs) [11]. CGAs, however, require authenticated messages as defined by Secure Neighbor Discovery (SeND) [12] instead of plain Neighbor Discovery [13].

We discussed these alternatives with respect to an adversary's capability for address correlation, and consider two distinct aspects of address correlation:

- Temporal correlation refers to address-based correlation over multiple sessions of a stationary host.
- Geographical correlation refers to address-based correlation over multiple sessions of a mobile node.

The difference is the network prefix: A stationary host stays in the same sub-network and includes the same network prefix in all its addresses. A mobile node wanders and changes the network prefix when moving.

Addresses using the modified EUI-64 format include the globally unique MAC address, and all of a host's addresses are equivalent in their second part. This fact allows the correlation of multiple sessions of a stationary or mobile node, i.e., this type of address is vulnerable to both forms of address correlation and, beyond that, also for active host tracking [14,15]. Apart from global uniqueness, the same is valid for (manually configured) interface identifiers that remain static.

Semantically opaque interface identifiers are generated by hashing the network prefix and a secret key among other parameters. As the hash calculation includes the address prefix, the interface identifier changes from subnet to subnet and prevents geographical correlation. The identifier, however, remains stable in a certain network, even when returning from another network, and allows temporal correlation over long periods of time. Due to their recent standardization their availability in current operating systems is limited.

Cryptographically generated addresses are generated by hashing the public key and other parameters and are bound to certain hosts. Ownership is verified by signing messages that originate from this address with the corresponding private key. The network prefix is included as a parameter into hashing, and a node's CGA changes from network to network, preventing geographical correlation of traffic. However, their generation comes at high computational costs, and prevents address changes as a means of protection against temporal correlation in practise [16]. An approach to overcome the limitation with respect to frequent address change has been proposed [17]. However, CGAs and SeND lack acceptance and are neither widely implemented nor deployed.

The discussion is summarized in Table 1, and is accompanied by the capabilities' native availability in the current client operating systems Mac OS X Yosemite, Ubuntu 14.10 (Utopic Unicorn) and Windows 8.1, see Table 2. The results emphasizes the unique position of the privacy extension: First, it is the only mechanism using stateless address autoconfiguration that is currently deployed at a larger scale that is intended to protect against traffic correlation. Second, it is the only mechanism that considers protection against temporal as well as geographical address correlation.

In this paper, we develop an attack that overcomes the belief that the privacy extension provides adequate protection against address correlation. The attack

Table 1. IPv6 address formats with respect to their capability of protecting against different forms of address correlation

	Modified EUI-64	Stable (Manual)	Sem. Opaque Id.	CGA	Privacy Extension
Temporal Correlation	-	-	-	-	✓
Geographical Correlation	-	-	✓	✓	✓

Table 2. IPv6 address formats with respect to their native availability in current client operating systems

Mac OS X Yosemite	✓	✓	-	-	✓
Ubuntu 14.10	✓	✓	-	-	✓
Windows 8.1	✓	✓	-	-	✓

leaves a gap that cannot be filled by another address mechanism, and highlights the importance of revisiting the extension's current definition.

3.3 Known Vulnerabilities of the Privacy Extension

Drawbacks of the IPv6 privacy extension were discussed before, and follow two principal directions. First, its design does not impede active tracking, e.g., by using ping. Temporary addresses are assigned in addition to stable ones, and an adversary can still actively probe multiple subnets for a certain interface identifier in order to trace a host's movement. The respective specification, however, explicitly states its intention to protect solely against passive eavesdroppers, and not against active adversaries [7].

Second, shortcomings in the extension's protection against address correlation are known. A node does not have to change its interface identifier when moving to a new network prefix. Thus, tracking a host's movement remains feasible within an identifier's lifetime of typically 24 h [14,18]. For mitigation, the inclusion of the network prefix into the interface identifier calculation was proposed [18]. The respective specification also allows the change of an identifier in such a situation [7]. Our attack supports the second direction, and highlights that adversaries are able to perform address correlation even when the privacy extension is used. In comparison to known attacks, our attack cannot be fully mitigated within the specification's limitations.

4   Attack Scenario

Our attack scenario is depicted in Fig. 3 and assumes full IPv6 deployment. We assume three stakeholders named Alice, Bob and Eve. Alice loves coffee, and regularly visits coffee shops. Then, she brings her laptop with her, and uses the offered Internet access to read mails or to chat. Bob and Eve each run a coffee shop, and provide Internet access to their guests. They deployed stateless address autoconfiguration, and their routers advertise the respective IPv6 network prefix so that customers are able to configure their global IPv6 addresses by connecting the prefix with their self-generated interface identifiers. Bob's router advertises the prefix P_{Bob}, Eve's router advertises P_{Eve}. Eve further runs a webserver to advertise current offers. She records her coffee shop's local traffic, and logs visits to her webserver.

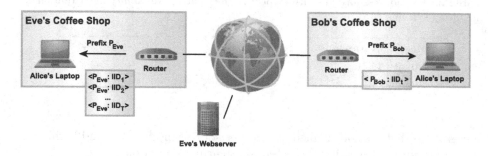

Fig. 3. Attack scenario

Alice visits Eve's coffee shop for T successive days[2], and connects her laptop to the coffee shop's local network. Eve's router advertises P_{Eve}, and Alice's laptop configures a stable IPv6 address from this prefix and the stable interface identifier. Alice has enabled the IPv6 privacy extension, and thus temporary addresses are created in addition to the stable address by combining the prefix with the interface identifier of the day. Alice's temporary addresses are $<P_{Eve} : IID_1>, <P_{Eve} : IID_2>, ..., <P_{Eve} : IID_T>$ for day $1, 2, ..., T$.

After T days, Alice stops going to Eve's coffee shop. On an arbitrary day t $(t > T)$, Alice visits Eve's competitor Bob. She connects her laptop to Bob's local network. Bob's router announces the prefix P_{Bob}, and Alice's laptop forms a stable identifier from this prefix. In addition, the privacy extension generates a temporary address $<P_{Bob} : IID_t>$. On this day, Alice visits Eve's website to check current offers and causes a respective log entry.

Eve is interested tracing her customers' activities, and wants to find out whether (1) Alice is still interested in her offers and visits the webserver, and whether (2) Alice is drinking coffee at a competitor.

---

[2] Although the T days do not necessarily have to be successive, we claim so here for better readability. In case days are missing, e.g., due to weekends, one simply has to consider these gaps when calculating the current state.

We refer to this scenario in the remainder of the paper for illustration of our attack. This scenario was developed due to its representativeness for day-to-day life, but we are sure that there are plenty of alternative scenarios. The preconditions for an adversary are moderate: She has to gain a victim's MAC address and T successive interface identifiers that have been generated by the privacy extension. The MAC address is gained from local traffic as in the presented scenario, or inferred from the stable IPv6 address in case the latter is in modified EUI-64 format. Interface identifiers are included in the temporary addresses, and are inferred from there.

5   Security Analysis

In this section, we perform a manual security analysis of the privacy extension's algorithm for temporary interface identifier generation as defined in [7] and presented in Sect. 2. Our analysis revealed four striking characteristics that facilitate the prediction of future interface identifiers. While some of them might seem minor in isolation, their combination forms a reasonable attack vector as described in Sect. 6. In this section, we consider each characteristic separately: First, we describe the characteristic and highlight the specification's argumentation in its favor. Next, we infer implications on security. Figure 4 contrasts the algorithm for temporary address generation with the discussed characteristics; the depicted numbers are consistent with the following paragraphs.

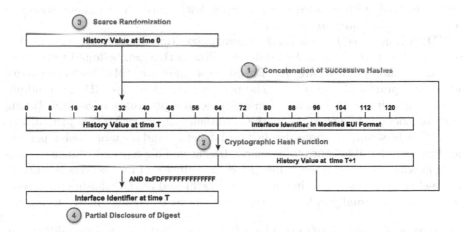

Fig. 4. The privacy extension's characteristics impacting its quality of protection

(1) Concatenation of Successive Hashes: Interface identifiers are based on MD5 digests that are chained with each other because an iteration's result is partly included into the next hash calculation. The RFC states that *"In theory, generating successive randomized interface identifiers using a history scheme [...]*

has no advantages over generating them at random," [7] but claims an advantage in case two hosts have the same flawed random number generators. Performing duplicate address detection would make both hosts recognize their identical identifiers and trigger the generation of new identifiers. However, the flawed random number generators would again provide identical numbers, leading to identical identifiers. The presented algorithm is said to avoid this as the inclusion of the (globally unique) interface identifier in modified EUI-64 format leads to different temporary interface identifiers in the next iteration.

It remains unclear why the inclusion of a globally unique identifier, e.g., in modified EUI-64 format, requires working with a history scheme, i.e., the concatenation of successive hashes. We believe that inclusion of a globally unique interface identifier and a random value into MD5 digest calculation is sufficient. It seems unlikely that sequences of equivalent random numbers result in successive collision in case a globally unique identifier is included into calculation.

The concatenation does not only appear dispensable with respect to the discussed aspect, but also negatively impacts the algorithm's quality of protection. Successive interface identifiers are dependent on each other, and today's state influences future identifiers. An adversary might exploit this to predict a victim's future identifiers.

(2) Cryptographic Hash Function: The privacy extension aims to create random-appearing interface identifiers, but states that pseudo-randomness suffices *"so long as the specific sequence cannot be determined by an outsider examining information that is readily available or easily determinable"* [7]. For the algorithm, MD5 with its adequate properties with respect to randomization has been *"chosen for convenience"* [7].

MD5 is considered broken, but a general dissolution would be an overshooting reaction: MD5 turned out to be prone to collisions that can be found within seconds on commodity hardware [19]. Pre-image attacks are still of high complexity and remain practically infeasible. The privacy extension uses MD5 for randomization, and neither relies on collision resistance nor pre-image resistance. Taking these considerations into account, the extension's choice of MD5 is justifiable.

MD5 is, however, a comparably fast hash function and the more hashes per second, the more feasible brute-force search becomes. This especially holds in combination with a limited input range. In 2012, a cluster of four servers hosting 25 off-the-shelf graphics processing units (GPU) achieved 180 Gigahashes per second [20], and time is usually in favor of the adversary as technology moves forward.

(3) Scarce Randomization: The RFC claims that *"To make it difficult to make educated guesses as to whether two different interface identifiers belong to the same node, the algorithm for generating alternate identifiers must include input that has an unpredictable component from the perspective of the outside entities that are collecting information"* [7].

Our analysis, however, identifies only scarce unpredictability in the algorithm for temporary address generation. Every iteration includes 128 bits into MD5 digest calculation:

- 64 bit of the former iteration's result, i.e., the remainder of the MD5 hash that was not used for the temporary interface identifier, and
- the 64 bit interface identifier in modified EUI-64 format. This identifier is not kept secret. An adversary might infer it from the stable IPv6 address that is assigned in addition to temporary addresses or from the MAC address. 17 bit of this identifier are fixed and thus the same for all nodes anyway.

In conclusion, there is no entropy added per iteration and this fact makes prediction of future identifiers easier as there are less possibilities. The only unpredictable component of the presented algorithm is the very first history value of 64 bit that should *"be generated using techniques that help ensure the initial value is hard to guess"* [7].

(4) Partial Disclosure of Digest: A temporary interface identifier is generated by taking *"the leftmost 64-bits of the MD5 digest and set bit 6 [...] to zero"* [7]. The gained interface identifier forms a temporary IPv6 address when combined with the current network prefix. The address is present in packets' address fields and accessible by others.

As a consequence, an eavesdropper gains 63 bit (one bit is overwritten with zero as mentioned above) of the calculated MD5 digest. This eavesdropped part does not present the algorithm's internal state, i.e., the history value, but both are part of the same MD5 digest. In conclusion, 63 bit of every iteration's MD5 digest is readily available to outsiders without any further processing effort and form a side channel of the algorithm's internal state. The algorithm leaks information but does not add entropy in an iteration.

6 Attack Design

We will now explain the steps of our attack in detail. We will include the characteristics that have been found in the security analysis of Sect. 5. In a first step, we will analyse the predictability of future addresses if the current state (history value) is known. As this turns out to be promising, we investigate methods to gain the current state. Finally, we summarize our full attack.

Predictability of Future Identifiers: For rather unambiguous prediction of future temporary identifiers, two requirements have to be met. First, future identifiers have to be dependent on the current state of the algorithm. Second, the calculation of the next identifier should include little randomness. The less random input, the better predictability.

We know from the previous section that both conditions apply to the IPv6 privacy extension: Interface identifiers are based on concatenated hashes. A part of the digest is used for the identifier, the other is called the history value and used as an input for the next calculation. An iteration's input is twofold – the mentioned history value and the interface identifier in modified EUI-64 format that is inferred from the MAC address. This means that there are no unpredictable components that are included. In conclusion, an adversary that is aware of the victim's history value and its MAC address is able to calculate the next temporary interface identifier according to the following recipe:

1. Infer the interface identifier in modified EUI-64 format from the victim's MAC address. This requires the insertion of a fixed pattern of two byte, and setting bit 6 as described in Sect. 2.
2. Concatenate the victim's current history value with the interface identifier in modified EUI-64 format generated in step 1.
3. Calculate the MD5 digest of the concatenation of step 2.
4. Extract the first 64 bits from the calculated digest and unset bit 6 to form the next temporary interface identifier.
5. Extract the remaining 64 bits from the digest and form the next history value.

This way an adversary is not only able to compute the next interface identifier, but all future identifiers by repeating the described steps. As a consequence, it seems worth developing methods to gain the algorithm's internal state.

Synchronization to the Current State: The internal state could be leaked, e.g., by means of malware, but this approach would imply an active adversary that does not simply eavesdrop. In the following paragraphs, we show that eavesdropping over a number of consecutive days is sufficient to gain the internal state: As described in Sect. 5, a temporary interface identifier that is included into an IPv6 address inherently discloses 63 bit of an iteration's MD5 digest. While the disclosed part is not the internal state, it is nevertheless related to the latter as both are clips of the same MD5 digest. The disclosed interface identifier can be considered a side channel of the internal state.

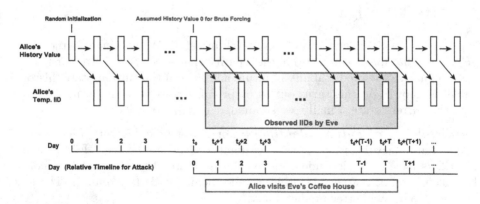

Fig. 5. Synchronization to current state

Figure 5 depicts a situation like our attack scenario from Sect. 4. The victim's very first history value is randomly initialized at day 0 and determines the history value and the temporary interface identifier of day 1; the history value of day 1 in turn determines history value and temporary interface identifier of day 2 and so on. The randomly assigned history value at day 0 determines one of 2^{64} deterministic sequences that the victim's interface identifiers follow.

An adversary might probe all possible values for this history value at day 0, and compare the first half of the MD5 digest with the interface identifier of day 1. If they are equal this value might represent an appropriate candidate. As it is only possible to compare 63 bit of the MD5 digest, it is likely that numerous candidates remain. The adversary thus extracts the second half of the digest as a candidate for the history value at day 1, includes it in another iteration containing an MD5 calculation, compares the result with the interface identifier at day 2 and further shrinks the candidate set until a single candidate remains. Then, the adversary has identified the internal state.

It is, however, unlikely that an adversary observes the very first temporary addresses that a victim generates after its installation; an adversary rather observes an arbitrary sequence of T successive addresses starting at day $t_0 + 1$ as indicated in Fig. 5. Due to the algorithm's structure, the adversary then assumes the history value at day t_0 to be randomly initialized without loss of generality. The adversary does not have to know the number of temporary addresses that the victim has generated before being recorded. For this reason, we added an relative time line for the attack in the figure for readability.

Composite Attack: Based on the attack scenario of Sect. 4, the gained insights of the previous paragraphs and Fig. 5, we summarize Eve's steps towards predicting Alice's future identifiers.

On Alice's first visit at Eve's coffee shop on day 1, Eve has to perform the following steps:

- *Data Extraction from Traffic Records:* Eve records the local traffic in her coffee shop, and is thus able to read Alice's MAC address from Ethernet headers as well as her temporary IPv6 address. From this temporary IPv6 address, Alice extracts the last 64 bits that are the interface identifier for the first day IID_1.
- *Generation of Modified EUI-64 Interface Identifier:* Eve infers Alice's interface identifier in modified EUI-64 Format from the MAC address by inserting a fixed pattern of two bytes and setting bit 6 as described in Sect. 2. Alternatively, she might read the identifier in modified EUI 64 format directly from Alice's stable IPv6 address.
- *Reduction of Candidate Set:* Eve probes all possible values for the assumed initial history value at day 0, concatenates the value with the stable identifier in modified EUI-64 format, and calculates the MD5 digest. If the first part of the MD5 digest equals Alice's current temporary address[3], the remainder of the digest forms a candidate for the next iteration's history value and is added to the candidate set of the first day C_1. In this step, Eve reduces the initial candidate set C_0 of 2^{64} alternative sequences to a smaller set C_1 that is stored for the next day.

---

[3] The comparison is done on 63 different bits (0–5 and 7–63); bit 6 is always set to zero in temporary addresses, see Sect. 2.

On every further visit of Alice at Eve's on subsequent days t with $1 < t \leq T$, Eve performs:

- *Data Extraction from Traffic Records:* Eve extracts today's temporary interface identifier IID_t from Alice by reading the traffic records.
- *Further Reduction of Candidate Set:* Eve probes all values for the history value that are present in yesterday's candidate set C_{t-1}, concatenates the values with the stable identifier in modified EUI-64 format, and calculates the MD5 digest. If the first part of the MD5 digest equals Alice's current temporary address IID_t, the remainder of the digest forms a candidate for the next iteration's history value and is added to the candidate set C_t. In this step, Eve further reduces the number of alternative sequences to a smaller set that is again stored for the next day.

This is performed whenever a new temporary address is available until a single candidate remains. This single candidate represents the algorithm's internal state, the history value, and allows to predict future addresses from now on.

On every further day t with $t > T$, Eve is able to anticipate Alice's temporary interface identifier for this day:

- *Anticipation of Current Temporary Address:* Eve concatenates the history value of day T with the stable identifier in modified EUI-64 format and calculates the MD5 digest. She extracts the history value, and repeats the calculation with the new history value. In total, $(t - T)$ MD5 digest calculation are performed.
- *Assemblage of the Interface Identifier:* Eve forms Alice's interface identifier IID_t from the first part of the last MD5 digest by setting bit 6 to zero.

With this knowledge, Eve is able to search her web server's logs for the calculated temporary identifier and attributes certain visits to Alice. At the same time, the prefix that the temporary identifier is concatenated with to form an IPv6 address provides information on the sub-network that Alice resided at the time of the page visit. If this is equivalent to Bob's assigned prefix, Eve is able to infer that Alice drank coffee at Bob's coffee shop.

7   Feasibility

In the previous sections, we identified weaknesses of the IPv6 privacy extension and developed an attack exploiting these characteristics. The question on the attack's practicability with respect to today's technology remains, and is discussed in this section. Three aspects have to be considered: (1) the minimum number of observed interface identifiers, i.e., the number of days that Alice has to visit Eve's coffee shop, (2) the expenditure of time for brute-forcing, and (3) the storage capacity to save the candidate set for the next day. Finally, a modified version of our attack for limited storage capabilities is presented.

Number of Address Observations: Alice has to visit Eve's coffee shop so often that Eve gains enough temporary identifiers for synchronization to the internal state. We assume that Alice generates one temporary address per day as recommended by the RFC [7], and an iteration of the attack corresponds to a day.

On the first day, Eve probes 2^{64} potential values for the history value and compares their MD5 digest to the observed interface identifier of Alice. The unequal ones are excluded, and the appropriate ones form the candidate set C_1 of potential values for the next day. The size of the candidate set is dependent on the ratio of candidates that Eve is able to reject per day. With p being this ratio, the size of the candidate set C_t for day t is calculated as follows

$$|C_t| = 2^{64} \cdot (1 - p)^t \tag{1}$$

Eve has to repeat the explained step until a single candidate remains, i.e., $|C_t| = 1$, and the minimum number of days T_{min} is calculated as follows

$$T_{min} = ceil \; \frac{log(2^{64})}{log(p - 1)} \tag{2}$$

The more candidates can be excluded per iteration, the less successive interface identifiers have to be known by Eve. If Eve is able to reduce the candidate set by only 50 % every day, the minimum number of days is 64. A reduction by 99 %, 99.99 %, 99.9999 % shortens this to 10, 5, 4 days.

Time Expenditure for Brute-Forcing: Every iteration requires brute-forcing the current candidate set C_t, and means an MD5 digest calculation for every candidate. Assuming a hash rate r indicating the number of calculated hashes per second, the total time T_{Brute} for brute-forcing is calculated as follows

$$T_{Brute} = \frac{1}{r} \sum_{i=0}^{T_{min}} |C_i| = \frac{2^{64}}{r} \sum_{i=0}^{T_{min}} (1 - p)^i \tag{3}$$

Assuming $1 - p < 1^4$, the equation is bounded as follows and allows an estimation of the total time expenditure for MD5 brute-forcing

$$T_{Brute} < \frac{2^{64}}{r} \sum_{i=0}^{\infty} (1 - p)^i = \frac{2^{64}}{r} \cdot \frac{1}{p} \tag{4}$$

A hash rate of 180 G/s with MD5 is feasible [20]. The more candidates can be excluded, the less time is required. If Eve is able to reduce the candidate set on average by only 50 % every day, the time for brute-forcing remains 6.5 years, a reduction by 99 % shortens this to 3.3 years. Time expenditure appears high at the first sight, but time plays for the adversary, and advances in technology are likely to decrease this effort. It is likely that faster hashing is already feasible

---

[4] p is the portion of candidates that can be excluded per iteration.

today as the given hash rate was measured at a cluster of 25 consumer GPUs back in the year 2012 and GPUs have recently experienced extensive advancement.

Storage of Candidate Set: Appropriate candidates for the history value have to be stored for the next iteration. The history value size is 8 byte, and the storage demand S_t is dependent on the size of the candidate set.

$$S_t = |C_t| \cdot 8\,byte = 2^{64} \cdot (1-p)^t \cdot 8\,byte \tag{5}$$

The following calculation considers the first iteration due to its worst case character[5]: If Eve is able to reduce the candidate set on average by only 50 % every day, the storage demand for the first iteration is 74 Exabyte, a reduction of 99 %, 99.99 %, 99.9999 % reduces the storage demand to 1.5 Exabyte, 15 Petabyte, 148 Terabyte.

This storage demand, however, can be circumvented by a modification of the attack. In our initial design of Sect. 6, Eve synchronized to Alice's state simultaneously to her coffee shop visits, but Eve might alternatively perform the attack retroactively. Therefore, she stores Alice's successive interface identifiers for T_{min} days before starting the attack. Instead of storing an appropriate candidate after the first iteration, she performs the second, third, etc. iteration with this candidate as long as it appears appropriate. Otherwise, it is rejected. This way the storage demand is reduced to a few bytes for execution of the algorithm for temporary interface identifier generation.

8   Implementation in Operating Systems

In this section, we assess current operating systems that support the IPv6 privacy extension with respect to their individual vulnerability. We tested Mac OS X Yosemite, Ubuntu 14.10 (Utopic Unicorn) and Windows 8.1 Enterprise as representatives of the three major ecosystems on clients. In doing so, we faced the challenge that we cannot access the respective sources of all operating systems, and had to rely on the externally observable pattern of successively generated interface identifiers. A machine running an operating systems that implemented the privacy extension as described in the respective RFC has to generate the same sequence of successive interface identifiers whenever originating from a defined initial state. The sequence appears unchanged when faced with some external factors, while changing in dependence of other factors. The specific influencing factors are discussed later in this section.

For checking the stated premise, we created a setup of two virtual machines running in VMWare Workstation 11 and Fusion Pro 7. The machines were virtually connected for networking. One ran the tested operating system; we refer to this machine as the testee. To save time, we decreased the preferred lifetime on all operating systems and forced the generation of a new temporary address at an interval of twelve minutes. We finally created a snapshot of the testee that

---

[5] The candidate set C_0 does not have to be stored as it contains all 2^{64} possible values.

made it possible to return it to the initial state after every test. The testee generated temporary addresses after a router's announcement of a network prefix. The second virtual machine thus ran Ubuntu 14.10 simulating this router; to send ICMPv6 Router Advertisements the tool fake_router6 from the thc-ipv6 toolkit [21] was used. We recorded the temporary addresses of the testee by means of local scripts.

Using the above premise, we tested the operating systems for five criteria. First, repeating the test without any changes multiple times has to result in the same sequence of successive interface identifiers due to the algorithm's determinism. If this holds, the sequence is checked for their dependence on various influencing factors. The algorithm has to be invariant to time, the announced prefix as well as system restarts and provide the same sequence of identifiers, while it has to be variant to a change of the MAC address. These conditions are inferred from the algorithm's definition in the respective RFC: Neither the point in time of address generation is included into the calculation nor the identifier's lifetime. Thus, a later repetition of the experiment or a change in the interval may not have an impact on the identifiers. The same holds for the announced network prefix. The algorithm has to be invariant to system restarts as the current state has to be stored in stable storage; all the tested operating systems require the availability of such a storage. In contrast, the MAC address is included into the calculation, and its change should result in different identifiers. These are necessary criteria, and are not sufficient criteria. The results of our tests are shown in Table 3.

Table 3. Temporary address characteristics wrt to different operating systems

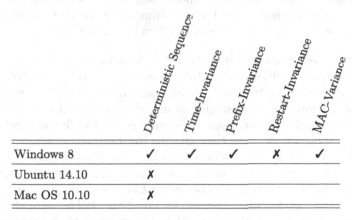

	Deterministic Sequence	Time-Invariance	Prefix-Invariance	Restart-Invariance	MAC-Variance
Windows 8	✓	✓	✓	✗	✓
Ubuntu 14.10	✗				
Mac OS 10.10	✗				

Ubuntu 14.10 does not generate deterministic sequences, and its temporary interface identifiers appear to be assigned by a random number generator without following the defined algorithm. A review of the source code[6] supports this. Mac OS X Yosemite showed the same behavior.

---

[6] Kernel 3.16.0, /net/ipv6/addrconf.c, line 1898.

Windows 8.1 provides the same sequence whenever originating from the same state, and further fulfills the conditions of time and prefix invariance as well as MAC variance. Restarting the machine or the interface, however, influences the sequence. Thus, we assume that Windows 8.1 implements the privacy extension's version for systems without presence of stable storage. In such a case, the first history value after a restart is randomly assigned. This assumption coincides with the fact that we could not find any appropriate history value in the Windows Registry analysing Registry diffs. Further signs supporting our assumption are the collaboration of Microsoft in the definition of the RFC, as well as the algorithm's description in older TechNet Library articles [22].

The gained insights lead to the following conclusion: While Ubuntu 14.10 and Mac OS X Yosemite seem to be immune to our attack, Windows 8.1 appears to be vulnerable – admittedly to a decreased extent as reinitialization of the history value is performed with every restart. However, systems that are continuously running for longer periods or using sleep mode remain vulnerable; and sleep mode is widely used for laptops. For interest, the operating systems' protection to our attack is gained by disobeying the privacy extension's standard. Ubuntu and Mac OS seem to totally ignore the proposed generation algorithm, while Windows 8.1 appears to implement the alternative for systems without stable storage albeit it assumes such storage according to its system requirements.

9   Mitigation

In this section, we recommend changes to the address generation mechanism for mitigation of our attack. We propose two kinds of strategy: The first aims at impeding synchronization to the algorithm's current state, while the other removes the predictability of future identifiers in general.

Restraint of Synchronization: Our attack is based on the fact that an adversary is able to learn a victim's state by observating them over multiple days, and one might hamper an adversary's synchronization to the algorithm's internal state for mitigation. These strategies do not offer protection in case the state is leaked. The following explanations are supported by Fig. 6; the numbers in the figure match those provided in the following paragraphs.

(1) An increased history value would imply improved randomization and increase the size of the initial candidate set C_0, see Eq. 1. As a consequence, the adversary has to observe more successive identifiers according to Eq. 2, and time expenditure for brute-forcing increases, see Eqs. 3 and 4. The algorithm's current design, however, does not allow an isolated increase of the history value. The MD5 digest's first half forms the temporary interface identifier and its second the current history value. Beyond, there are no bits available that could serve as additional bits for an increased history value. Thus, this strategy would require the replacement of MD5 by another hash function.

(2) MD5 is considered insecure, and its replacement by a state-of-the-art hash function seems tempting. MD5 is vulnerable to collision attacks, and insecure

Fig. 6. Mitigation strategies for generation of temporary IIDs

for applications that rely on collision resistance, e.g., as necessary for certificates [23]. The IPv6 privacy extension, however, exploits a hash function's randomization, and replacing MD5 with the currently used SHA-265 would only modestly increase brute-force effort [24].

Removal of Identifiers' Predictability: Another precondition of our attack is the dependency of future identifiers on the current state and predictable inputs only. The following mitigation approaches tackle this issue by removing the predictability of future identifiers in different ways.

(3) Including a random value in every iteration makes the digest dependent on more inputs, and adds unpredictability with every new interface identifier. This is the major difference to an increased history value as mentioned above that solely increases randomization at the algorithm's initialization. Even if the current state is leaked, it is impossible to accurately predict future interface identifiers. Moreover, this measure does not require a dissolution of MD5.

(4) A removal of the concatenation would result in successive addresses that are not related to each other; instead, the history value could be randomly initialized for every new address. A similar but more limited approach is defined by the privacy extension's standard, but only for devices without stable storage [7]. As such systems are not able to store the history value across system restarts, they are allowed to randomly initialize the first history value after a reboot. Their vulnerability is thus dependent on their typical restart intervals in comparison to the temporary addresses' lifetime. Nevertheless, it seems curious that an alternative algorithm for specific devices is more secure than the standard algorithm.

Alternatively, temporary interface identifiers could be randomly assigned without such a complex algorithm. A host's vulnerability to address correlation is then dependent on the quality of its random number generator. We see advantages in this approach because high-quality random number generators are necessary in modern operating systems on personal computers, laptops and mobiles anyway. The privacy extension would benefit from this quality and further be updated automatically with every improvement of the number generator. For systems without an appropriate random number generator, an alternative would have to be available. This practice is opposed to today's standard that defines a rather complex algorithm *"to avoid the particular scenario where two nodes generate the same randomized interface identifier, both detect the situation via DAD, but then proceed to generate identical randomized interface identifiers via the same (flawed) random number generation algorithm"* [7] and lowers security for all systems that implement the privacy extension.

Finally, we considered the question which mitigation strategies are in accordance with the current specification, and have drawn the following conclusions: (1) It is allowed to use another hash function instead of MD5. The brute-force effort would, however, increase only modestly, and a replacement brings only limited protection. (2) The history value is allowed to be randomly re-initialized after every system restart, but this behavior is restricted to systems without stable storage. However, a variety of systems that implement the privacy extension like personal computers, laptops, tablets or mobiles do not lack stable storage, and have to follow the standard variety of the algorithm. (3) The privacy extension is considered more secure the shorter the temporary addresses' lifetime. This inherent belief has to be revised with respect to the presented attack because more addresses are provided to the adversary within the same time interval, making synchronization to the current state easier.

10   Conclusions

The IPv6 privacy extension aims to protect privacy by regularly changing the address, and defines an algorithm for the generation of interface identifiers that are combined with the advertised network prefix to form temporary IPv6 addresses. In this paper, we presented an attack that questions the extension's capability of protection: An adversary is able to predict future temporary interface identifiers once the internal state is known, and is further able to synchronize to this internal state by observing the victim's previous interface identifiers. In consequence, an adversary knows interface identifiers belonging to the same host; in turn, she is able to perform address-based correlation of different transactions and infer (private) details about people's Internet behavior. Moreover, an adversary might even retrace a host's movement in the network based on the network prefixes that are included in the respective addresses.

The presented attack is worthwhile as it does not solely identify a privacy vulnerability but questions a whole measure for privacy protection. The privacy extension was developed with the intention to impede address-based correlation, and our attack shows that it does not meet its goal. Nevertheless, we believe that the general idea of temporary addresses is valuable, and recommend a revision of the algorithm for interface identifier generation. We want to highlight the fact that merely replacing MD5 does not solve the problem, as the vulnerability arises from the concatenation of successive interface identifiers, scarce randomization and information leakage via a side channel. MD5 just makes the attack easier due to its fast nature. Proper mitigation within the current definition appears impractical, and we want to stress the importance of strategies beyond today's specification.

Operating systems appeared less vulnerable than originally assumed. This does not, however, oppose a revision, as their robustness is gained by silently disobeying the standard and should not be held as a virtue. The standard in its current form can tempt developers to implement a vulnerable version of the privacy extension, and should be adapted soon. This utmost concern is further emphasized by the fact that the privacy extension is the only widely deployed IPv6 mechanism using stateless address autoconfiguration that is intended to protect against temporal as well as geographical address correlation.

Acknowledgments. The authors thank Peter Wurzinger, Dimitris E. Simos, Georg Merzdovnik and Adrian Dabrowski for many fruitful discussions. This research was funded by P 842485 and COMET K1, both FFG - Austrian Research Promotion Agency.

References

1. Landau, S.: Making sense from snowden: what's significant in the NSA surveillance relevations. IEEE Secur. Priv. Mag. **4**, 54–63 (2013)
2. Landau, S.: Making sense from snowden, part II: what's significant in the NSA surveillance relevations. IEEE Secur. Priv. Mag **1**, 62–64 (2014)
3. Leber, J.: Amazon Woos Advertisers with What It Knows about Consumers, January 2013. http://www.technologyreview.com/news/509471/amazon-woos-advertisers-with-what-it-knows-about-consumers/
4. Blue, V.: Facebook turns user tracking 'bug' into data mining 'feature' for advertisers, June 2014. http://www.technologyreview.com/news/509471/amazon-woos-advertisers-with-what-it-knows-about-consumers/
5. Cooper, A., Tschofenig, H., Aboba, B., Peterson, J., Morris, J., Hansen, M., Smith, R.: Privacy Considerations for Internet Protocols, RFC 6973, July 2013
6. Hinden, R., Deering, S.: IP Version 6 Addressing Architecture, RFC 4291, February 2006
7. Narten, T., Draves, R., Krishnan, S.: Privacy Extensions for Stateless Address Autoconfiguration in IPv6, RFC 4941, September 2007
8. Ullrich, J., Krombholz, K., Hobel, H., Dabrowski, A., Weippl, E.: IPv6 security: attacks and countermeasures in a nutshell. In: USENIX Workshop on Offensive Technologies (WOOT). USENIX Association, San Diego, CA, August 2014. https://www.usenix.org/conference/woot14/workshop-program/presentation/ullrich
9. Thomson, S., Narten, T., Jinmei, T.: IPv6 Stateless Address Autoconfiguration, RFC 4862, September 2007
10. Gont, F.: A Method for Generating Semantically Opaque Interface Identifiers with IPv6 Stateless Address Autoconfiguration (SLAAC), RFC 7217, April 2014
11. Aura, T.: Cryptographically Generated Addresses (CGA), RFC 3972, March 2005
12. Arkko, J., Kempf, J., Zill, B., Nikander, P.: SEcure Neighbor Discovery (SEND), RFC 3971, March 2005
13. Narten, T., Nordmark, E., Simpson, W., Soliman, H.: Neighbor Discovery for IP version 6 (IPv6), RFC 4861, September 2007
14. Dunlop, M., Groat, S., Marchany, R., Tront, J.: IPv6: now you see me, now you don't'. In: International Conference on Networks (ICN), pp. 18–23 (2011)

15. Groat, S., Dunlop, M., Marchany, R., Tront, J.: IPv6: nowhere to run, nowhere to hide. In: Hawaii International Conference on System Sciences (HICSS) (2011)
16. Alsadeh, A., Rafiee, H., Meinel, C.: Cryptographically generated addresses (CGAs): possible attacks and proposed mitigation approaches. In: IEEE International Conference on Computer and Information Technology (CIT) (2012)
17. AlSadeh, A., Rafiee, H., Meinel, C.: IPv6 stateless address autoconfiguration: balancing between security, privacy and usability. In: Garcia-Alfaro, J., Cuppens, F., Cuppens-Boulahia, N., Miri, A., Tawbi, N. (eds.) FPS 2012. LNCS, vol. 7743, pp. 149–161. Springer, Heidelberg (2013)
18. Barrera, D., Wurster, G., Van Oorschot, P.C.: Back to the future: revisiting IPv6 privacy extensions. USENIX Mag. **36**(1), 16–26 (2011). LOGIN
19. Turner, S., Chen, L.: Updated Security Consideration for the MD5 Message-Digest and the HMAC-MD5 Algorithms, RFC 6151, March 2011
20. Gosney, J.M.: Password cracking HPC. In: Passwords Security Conference (2012)
21. Heuse, M.: Thc-ipv6 toolkit v2.7, April 2015. https://www.thc.org/thc-ipv6/
22. TechNet: IPv6 Addressing (Tech Ref), April 2011. https://technet.microsoft.com/en-us/library/dd392266(v=ws.10).aspx
23. Stevens, M., Sotirov, A., Appelbaum, J., Lenstra, A., Molnar, D., Osvik, D.A., de Weger, B.: Short chosen-prefix collisions for MD5 and the creation of a rogue CA certificate. In: Halevi, S. (ed.) CRYPTO 2009. LNCS, vol. 5677, pp. 55–69. Springer, Heidelberg (2009)
24. eBASH (ECRYPT Benchmarking of All Submitted Hashes), March 2015. http://bench.cr.yp.to/results-hash.html

Evaluating Solutions

Evaluation of Intrusion Detection Systems in Virtualized Environments Using Attack Injection

Aleksandar Milenkoski[1]([✉]), Bryan D. Payne[2], Nuno Antunes[3], Marco Vieira[3], Samuel Kounev[1], Alberto Avritzer[4], and Matthias Luft[5]

[1] University of Würzburg, Würzburg, Germany
{milenkoski,skounev}@acm.org
[2] Netflix Inc., Los Gatos, CA, USA
bdpayne@acm.org
[3] University of Coimbra, Coimbra, Portugal
{nmsa,mvieira}@dei.uc.pt
[4] Siemens Corporation, Corporate Technology, Princeton, NJ, USA
alberto.avritzer@siemens.com
[5] Enno Rey Netzwerke GmbH, Heidelberg, Germany
mluft@ernw.de

Abstract. The evaluation of intrusion detection systems (IDSes) is an active research area with many open challenges, one of which is the generation of representative workloads that contain attacks. In this paper, we propose a novel approach for the rigorous evaluation of IDSes in virtualized environments, with a focus on IDSes designed to detect attacks leveraging or targeting the hypervisor via its hypercall interface. We present *hInjector*, a tool for generating IDS evaluation workloads by injecting such attacks during regular operation of a virtualized environment. We demonstrate the application of our approach and show its practical usefulness by evaluating a representative IDS designed to operate in virtualized environments. The virtualized environment of the industry-standard benchmark SPECvirt_sc2013 is used as a testbed, whose drivers generate workloads representative of workloads seen in production environments. This work enables for the first time the injection of attacks in virtualized environments for the purpose of generating representative IDS evaluation workloads.

Keywords: Intrusion detection systems · Virtualization · Evaluation · Attack injection

1 Introduction

Virtualization has been receiving increasing interest as a way to reduce costs through server consolidation and to enhance the flexibility of physical infrastructures. It allows the creation of virtual instances of physical devices, such as network and processing units. In a virtualized system, governed by a hypervisor, resources are shared among virtual machines (VMs).

© Springer International Publishing Switzerland 2015
H. Bos et al. (Eds.): RAID 2015, LNCS 9404, pp. 471–492, 2015.
DOI: 10.1007/978-3-319-26362-5_22

Although virtualization provides many benefits, it introduces new security challenges; that is, the introduction of a hypervisor introduces new threats. Hypervisors expose several attack surfaces such as device drivers, VM exit events, or hypercalls. Hypercalls are software traps from a kernel of a partially or fully paravirtualized VM to the hypervisor. They enable the execution of severe attacks. For instance, triggering a vulnerability of a hypercall handler (i.e., a hypercall vulnerability) may lead to crash of the hypervisor or to altering the hypervisor's memory (see, for example, [1,2]).

The research and industry communities have developed security mechanisms that can detect hypercall attacks. These include intrusion detection systems (IDSes), such as Xenini [3] and the de-facto standard host-based IDS OSSEC (Open Source SECurity),[1] as well as access control systems, such as XSM-FLASK (Xen Security Modules - FLux Advanced Security Kernel), which is distributed with the Xen hypervisor, and McAfee's VM protection system.[2] Under hypercall attack, we understand any malicious hypercall activity, for example, triggering a hypercall vulnerability or covert channel operations [4].

The rigorous evaluation of IDSes designed to detect hypercall attacks is crucial for preventing breaches in virtualized environments. For instance, one may compare multiple IDSes in terms of their attack detection accuracy in order to identify the optimal IDS. Workloads that contain hypercall attacks are a key requirement for evaluating the attack detection accuracy of IDSes designed to detect hypercall attacks. However, the generation of such workloads is challenging since publicly available scripts that demonstrate hypercall attacks are very rare [5,6]. An approach towards addressing this issue is attack injection, which enables the generation of representative IDS evaluation workloads. Attack injection is controlled execution of attacks during regular operation of the environment where an IDS under test is deployed. The injection of attacks is performed with respect to attack models constructed by analysing realistic attacks. Attack models are systematized activities of attackers targeting a given attack surface.

In this paper, we propose an approach for evaluating IDSes using attack injection. As part of the proposed approach, we present *hInjector*, a tool for injecting hypercall attacks. We designed hInjector to achieve the challenging goal of satisfying the key criteria for the rigorous, representative, and practically feasible evaluation of an IDS using attack injection: injection of realistic attacks, injection during regular system operation, and non-disruptive attack injection (e.g., prevention of potential crashes due to injected attacks). The approach we propose may be conceptually applied not only for evaluating IDSes designed to detect hypercall attacks, but also attacks involving the execution of operations that are functionally similar to hypercalls. Such operations are, for example, the ioctl (input/output control) calls that the KVM hypervisor supports.

Our approach uses live IDS testing, since existing IDSes designed to detect hypercall attacks perform on-line monitoring. Further, it enables the evaluation

---

[1] http://www.ossec.net/; OSSEC can be configured to analyze in real-time log files that contain information on executed hypercalls.

[2] http://www.google.com/patents/US8381284.

of IDSes that do and do not require training (i.e., it involves IDS training, which is needed for evaluating IDSes that require training). We demonstrate the application and practical usefulness of the approach by evaluating Xenini [3], a representative IDS designed to detect hypercall attacks. We inject realistic attacks triggering publicly disclosed hypercall vulnerabilities and specifically crafted evasive attacks. We extensively evaluate Xenini considering multiple configurations of the IDS. Such an extensive evaluation would not have been possible before due to the previously mentioned issues.

This paper is organized as follows: in Sect. 2, we provide the essential background and discuss related work; in Sect. 3, we present an approach for evaluating IDSes; in Sect. 4, we introduce the hInjector tool; in Sect. 5, we demonstrate the application of the proposed approach; in Sect. 6, we discuss future work and conclude this paper.

2   Background and Related Work

Paravirtualization and Hypercalls. Paravirtualization, an alternative to full (native) virtualization, is a virtualization mode that enables the performance-efficient virtualization of VM components based on collaboration between VMs and the hypervisor. VM components that may be paravirtualized include disk and network devices, interrupts and timers, emulated platform components (e.g., motherboards and device buses), privileged instructions, and pagetables.

With recent advances in hardware design, paravirtualizing privileged instructions and pagetables often does not provide performance benefits over full virtualization. However, paravirtualizing the other VM components mentioned above is beneficial. As a result, multiple virtualization modes have emerged, many of which involve paravirtualizing VM components of fully virtualized VMs. Hypercalls are operations that VMs use for working with paravirtualized components. They are software traps from a kernel of a VM to the underlying hypervisor.

The Hypercall Attack Surface. The hypercall interface is an attack surface that can be used for executing attacks targeting the hypervisor or breaking the boundaries set by it. This may result in unauthorized information flow between VMs or executing malicious code with hypervisor privilege (see [1,2]).

In a previous work [5], we have analyzed 35 publicly disclosed hypercall vulnerabilities and identified patterns of activities for triggering the considered vulnerabilities. We categorized the identified patterns into the following attack models: *setup phase* (optional) — execution of one or multiple regular hypercalls (i.e., hypercalls with regular parameter value(s) that may be executed during regular system operation) setting up the virtualized environment as necessary for triggering a given hypercall vulnerability; *attack phase* — execution of a single regular hypercall, or a hypercall with specifically crafted parameter value(s); or, execution of a series of regular hypercalls in a given order. In this work, we use these models for injecting hypercall attacks.

Intrusion Detection. Given the high severity of hypercall attacks, the research and industry communities have developed IDSes that can detect such attacks.

Examples are Collabra [7], Xenini [3], C^2(Covert Channel) Detector [4], Wizard [8], MAC/HAT (Mandatory Access Control/Hypercall Access Table) [6], RandHyp [9], and OSSEC. Most of these IDSes have the following characteristics in common:

- *monitoring method* and *attack detection technique* — they perform on-line (i.e., real-time) monitoring of VMs' hypercall activities and use a variety of anomaly-based attack detection techniques, which require training using benign (i.e., regular) hypercall activities;
- *architecture* — they have a module integrated into the hypervisor, intercepting invoked hypercalls and sending information relevant for intrusion detection to an analysis module deployed in a designated VM.

Current IDSes designed to detect hypercall attacks analyze the following properties of VMs' hypercall activities, which we refer to as *detection-relevant properties*: (i) hypercall identification numbers (IDs) and values of parameters of individual, or sequences of, hypercalls, and (ii) hypercall call sites (i.e., memory addresses from where hypercalls have been executed).

IDS Evaluation and Attack Injection. The accurate and rigorous evaluation of IDSes is crucial for preventing security breaches. IDS evaluation workloads that contain realistic attacks are a key requirement for such an evaluation. In Sect. 1, we stated that IDSes designed to detect hypercall attacks currently cannot be evaluated in a rigorous manner due to the lack of publicly available attack scripts that demonstrate hypercall attacks. Attack injection is a method addressing this issue, which is in the focus of this work.

To the best of our knowledge, we are the first to focus on evaluating IDSes designed to operate in virtualized environments, such as IDSes designed to detect hypercall attacks. Further, we are the first to consider the injection of hypercall attacks and of attacks targeting hypervisors in general. Pham et al. [10] and Le et al. [11] focus on injecting generic software faults directly into hypervisors. This is not suitable for evaluating IDSes — IDSes do not monitor states of hypervisors since they are not relevant for detecting attacks in a proactive manner.

Fonseca et al. [12] present an approach for evaluating network-based IDSes, which involves injection of attacks. They built Vulnerability Injector, a mechanism that injects vulnerabilities in the source code of web applications, and an Attack Injector, a mechanism that generates attacks triggering injected vulnerabilities. There are fundamental differences between our work and the work of Fonseca et al. [12], which is focussing on attack injection at application level. This includes the characteristics of the IDSes in focus, the required attack models, and the criteria for designing procedures and tools for injecting attacks.

3 Approach

Figure 1a shows our approach, which has two phases: planning and testing. The planning phase consists of: (i) specification of an IDS monitoring landscape

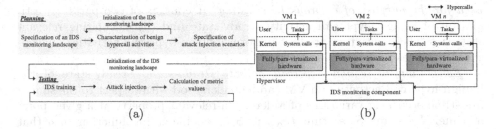

Fig. 1. (a) Approach for evaluating IDSes; (b) IDS monitoring landscape

(i.e., specifying a virtualized environment where the IDS under test is to be deployed), (ii) characterization of benign hypercall activities (i.e., making relevant observations about the benign hypercall activities), and (iii) specification of attack injection scenarios (Sect. 3.1). The testing phase consists of: (i) IDS training, (ii) attack injection, and (iii) calculation of metric values (Sect. 3.2). The activities of the testing phase are performed based on observations made in the planning phase. IDS training needs to be performed only when evaluating an IDS that requires training (i.e., an anomaly-based IDS).

3.1   Planning

Specification of an IDS Monitoring Landscape. A typical IDS designed to detect hypercall attacks monitors the hypercall activity of one or multiple VMs at the same time. VM characteristics influence the hypercall activity:

- *virtualization mode* influences which hypercalls can be executed,
- *workloads* influence which system calls can be executed, many of which map to hypercalls, and
- *system architecture and hardware* influence the VM's interface, and the type and frequency of hypercalls needed (e.g., page table update operations, which take place when page swapping occurs due to insufficient memory).

The aggregate of these characteristics across all VMs on a hypervisor is the *monitoring landscape* of an IDS designed to detect hypercall attacks. Figure 1b depicts an IDS monitoring landscape. The first activity of the planning phase of our approach is to specify an IDS monitoring landscape by defining the characteristics above for the test system. By defining workloads, we mean specifying drivers generating workloads in an automated and repeatable manner. By defining hardware, we mean allocating an amount of hardware resources to VMs that is fixed over time (i.e., disabling CPU or memory ballooning). We discuss more on the importance of specifying an IDS monitoring landscape in Sect. 3.2.

Characterization of Benign Hypercall Activities. Characterization of a VM's benign hypercall activity is crucial for answering two major questions: *How long should the IDS under test be trained?* and *What injected attacks should be* *used for the purpose of rigorous IDS testing?* It consists of two parts: (i) estimation of benign hypercall activity steady-state and (ii) calculating relevant statistics. These activities are best performed when hypercall activities are captured in traces for processing off-line.

Estimation of benign hypercall activity steady-state: Steady-state of the benign hypercall activity of a VM can be understood with respect to the sum of first-time occurring variations of a detection-relevant property at a given point in time. We define S_t at time t where S_t is an increasing function such that $\lim_{t\to\infty} S_t = const$. The estimation of steady-state is crucial for determining an optimal length of the period during which an IDS under test should be trained in the testing phase (i.e., for avoiding IDS under-training).

In order to estimate steady-state, an IDS evaluator should first *initialize the IDS monitoring landscape*; that is, bring the VMs in the landscape to the state after their creation and start workloads in the VMs. Then the steady-state of the benign hypercall activities of a VM may be estimated by setting a target for the slope of a growth curve depicting S_t until a given time t_{max}. The slope of such a curve, when observed over a given period, indicates the rate of first-time occurring variations of the detection-relevant property in the period. Letting σ be a target for the slope of a growth curve over a period $t_s = t_{s2} - t_{s1}$, we have $0 <= \frac{S_{t_{s2}} - S_{t_{s1}}}{t_s} <= \sigma$. This process may be repeated multiple times for different values of t_{max} to experimentally determine σ for each VM.[3] Attacks should be injected from a VM until time t_{max}, but only after the VM's hypercall activity has reached steady-state.

The IDS under test should operate in learning mode when steady-state is estimated. This helps to create operating conditions of the overall virtualized environment, which are (almost) equivalent to those when the IDS will be trained in the testing phase. Note that an IDS may have an impact on the time needed for hypercall activities to reach steady-state due to incurred monitoring overhead.

Calculating relevant statistics: Two key statistics need to be calculated: (i) the average rate of occurrence of the detection-relevant property — this statistic should be calculated using data collected between t_{s1} and t_{max}, and (ii) the number of occurrences of each variation of the detection-relevant property — this statistic should be calculated using data collected while the system is progressing towards a steady state. These statistics help calculate metric values in the testing phase and create realistic attack injection scenarios as discussed next.

Specification of Attack Injection Scenarios. Two characteristics distinguish each attack injection scenario: *attack content* and *attack injection time*.

Attack content is the detection-relevant property of a hypercall attack in the context of a given IDS evaluation study (e.g., a specific sequence of hypercalls). Specification of attack content enables the injection of attacks that conform to representative attack models (see Sect. 2). In addition, it enables the injection of evasive attacks, for example, attacks that closely resemble common regular

---

[3] This raises the question whether hypercall activities are repeatable. We discuss this topic in Sect. 3.2.

activities — these attacks may be highly effective "mimicry" attacks. Crafting "mimicry" attacks is done based on knowledge on what, and how frequently, detection-relevant properties occur during regular operation of the IDS monitoring landscape (i.e., during IDS training); this is the statistic 'number of occurrences of each variation of the detection-relevant property'.

Attack injection time is the point(s) in time when a hypercall attack consisting of one or more hypercalls is injected. This allows for the specification of arbitrary temporal distributions of attack injection actions. It also allows for the specification of the following relevant temporal properties of malicious activities:

- *Base rate*: Base rate is the prior probability of an intrusion (attack). The error occurring when the attack detection accuracy of an IDS is assessed without taking the base rate into account is known as the *base rate fallacy* [13]. The specification of attack injection times provides a close estimation of the actual base rate in the testing phase. As we demonstrate in Sect. 5, base rate can be estimated by considering the number of injected attacks and the number of variations of the detection-relevant property that have occurred during attack injection. The latter is estimated based on the statistic 'average rate of occurrence of the detection-relevant property'.
- *IDS evasive properties*: Specification of the attack injection time enables the injection of "smoke screen" evasive attacks. In the context of this work, the "smoke screen" technique consists of delaying the invocation of the hypercalls comprising an attack such that a given amount of benign hypercall activity occurs between each hypercall invocation. This is an important test since some IDSes have been shown to be vulnerable to such attacks (e.g., Xenini; see [14]).

3.2   Testing

IDS Training. IDS training is the first activity of the testing phase. We require reinitialization of the IDS monitoring landscape between the planning and testing phases (see Fig. 1a). The rationale behind this is practical: many parameters of the existing IDSes designed to detect hypercall attacks (e.g., length of IDS training period, attack detection threshold) require a priori configuration. These parameters are tuned based on observations made in the planning phase (see Sect. 3.1). This raises concerns related to the non-determinism of hypercall activities, a topic that we discuss in paragraph 'on repeatability concerns'.

Attack Injection. For this critical step, we developed a new tool called *hInjector*. Section 4 introduces this tool and describes how it is used.

Calculation of Metric Values. After attack injection is performed, values of relevant metrics can be calculated (e.g., true and false positive rate). This also raises concerns related to the non-determinism of hypercall activities, which we discuss next.

On Repeatability Concerns. Observations and decisions made in the planning phase might be irrelevant if hypercall activities are highly non-deterministic and therefore not repeatable. For example, the benign hypercall activities occurring in the testing phase may not reach steady-state at a point in time close to the estimated one in the planning phase.

In addition, metric values reported as end-results of an evaluation study, where workloads that are not fully deterministic are used, have to be statistically accurate. This is crucial for credible evaluation. Principles of statistical theory impose metric values to be repeatedly calculated and their means to be reported as end-results. Therefore, we require repeated execution of the testing phase (see Fig. 1a). However, this may be time-consuming if the number of needed repetitions is high due to high non-determinism of hypercall activities.

Specifying an IDS monitoring landscape as we define it (see Sect. 3.1) alleviates the above concerns; that is, it helps to reduce the non-determinism of hypercall activities by removing major sources of non-determinism, such as non-repeatable workloads. This is in line with Burtsev [15], who observes that, given repeatability of execution of VMs' user tasks is preserved, VMs always invoke the same hypercalls. We acknowledge that achieving complete repeatability of hypercall activities by specifying VM characteristics is infeasible. This is mainly due to the complexity of the architectures and operating principles of kernels.

In Sect. 5, we empirically show that, provided an IDS monitoring landscape is specified, a VM's hypercall activities exhibit repeatability to an extent sufficient to conclude that: (i) the decisions and observations made in the planning phase are of practical relevance when it comes to IDS testing, and (ii) the number of measurement repetitions needed to calculate statistically accurate metric values is small. This is in favor of the practical feasibility of our approach, which involves repeated initialization of an IDS monitoring landscape.

4   hInjector

hInjector is a tool for injecting hypercall attacks. It realizes the attack injection scenarios specified in the planning phase (see Sect. 3.1). The current implementation of hInjector is for the Xen hypervisor, but the techniques are not Xen-specific and can be ported to other hypervisors.

hInjector supports the injection of attacks crafted with respect to the attack models that we developed (see Sect. 2). We extend these attack models with a model involving different hypercall call sites. Hypercall call sites are one of the detection-relevant properties that existing IDSes designed to detect hypercall attacks analyze. We consider that hypercalls can be executed from *regular* or *irregular* call sites. The latter is typically a hacker's loadable kernel module (LKM) used to mount hypercall attacks.

Our design criteria for hInjector are *injection of realistic attacks*, *injection during regular system operation*, and *non-disruptive attack injection*. These criteria are crucial for the representative, rigorous, and practically feasible IDS evaluation. We discuss more in Sect. 4.2.

Availability. hInjector is publicly available at https://github.com/hinj/hInj.

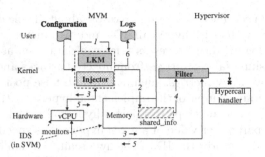

Fig. 2. The architecture of hInjector

4.1 hInjector Architecture

Figure 2 depicts the architecture of hInjector. It shows the primary components: *Injector*, *LKM*, *Filter*, *Configuration*, and *Logs*. We refer to the VM from where hypercall attacks are injected as the malicious VM (MVM). We also depict a typical IDS designed to detect hypercall attacks, with components in the hypervisor and a secured VM (SVM), co-located with MVM (see Sect. 2). The IDS monitors the MVM's hypercall activity by monitoring virtual CPU registers and the virtual memory of MVM using its hypervisor component.

The *Injector* component, deployed in the MVM's kernel, intercepts at a given rate hypercalls invoked by the kernel and modifies hypercall parameter values on-the-fly (i) making them specifically crafted for triggering a vulnerability, or (ii) replacing them with random, irregular values that an IDS may label as anomalous. The Injector injects hypercalls invoked from a regular call site (i.e., from the kernel address space). We discuss more on Injector in Sect. 4.3.

The *LKM* component, a module in MVM's kernel, invokes hypercalls with regular or specifically crafted parameter value(s), including a series of hypercalls in a given order. The LKM injects hypercalls invoked from an irregular call site (i.e., from a loadable kernel module).

The *Filter* component, deployed in the hypervisor's hypercall handlers, identifies hypercalls injected by the Injector or the LKM, blocks the execution of the respective hypercall handlers, and returns valid error codes. The Filter identifies injected hypercalls based on information stored by the Injector/LKM in the *shared_info* structure, a memory region shared between a VM and the hypervisor. To this end, we extended *shared_info* with a string field named *hid* (hypercall identification), which contains identification information on injected hypercalls. We discuss more about the Filter when we discuss the design criterion 'non-disruptive attack injection' in Sect. 4.2.

The *Configuration* component is a set of user files in XML containing configuration parameters for managing the operation of the Injector and the LKM. It allows specifying, for example, parameter values for a given hypercall (relevant to the Injector and the LKM), ordering of a series of hypercalls (relevant to the LKM), and temporal distribution of injection actions.

The *Logs* are user files containing records about invoked hypercalls that are part of attacks; that is, hypercall IDs and parameter values, as well as timestamps. The logged data serves as reference data (i.e., as "ground truth") used for distinguishing false positives from injected attacks and calculating IDS attack detection accuracy metrics, such as true and false positive rate.

We now present an example of the implemented hypercall attack injection procedure. Figure 2 depicts the steps to inject a hypercall attack by the LKM: *(1)* the LKM crafts a parameter value of a given hypercall as specified in the configuration; *(2)* the LKM stores the ID of the hypercall, the number of the crafted parameter, and the parameter value in *hid*; *(3)* the LKM passes the hypercall to MVM's vCPU, which then passes control to hypervisor; *(4)* the Filter, using the data stored in *hid*, identifies the injected hypercall when the respective hypercall handler is executed; *(5)* the Filter updates *hid* indicating that it has intercepted the injected hypercall, then returns a valid error code to block execution of the handler; *(6)* after the error code arrives at MVM's kernel, the LKM first verifies whether *hid* has been updated by the Filter and then logs the ID and parameter values of the injected hypercall.

4.2   hInjector Design Criteria

Injection of Realistic Attacks. The injection of realistic attacks is crucial for the representative IDS evaluation. In order to inject realistic hypercall attacks, hInjector requires representative hypercall attack models. hInjector supports the injection of attacks crafted with respect to arbitrary attack models, for example, the models that we developed [5] (see Sect. 2).

We developed proof-of-concept code for triggering the hypercall vulnerabilities that we analyzed [5].[4] The proof-of-concept code enables granularization of the attack models. For example, we can specify specific parameter values or the order of a series of hypercalls that trigger a hypercall vulnerability. This enables the injection of realistic hypercall attacks, crafted to trigger publicly disclosed hypercall vulnerabilities. In Fig. 3a, we show how we triggered the vulnerability CVE-2012-3495 of the Xen hypervisor in a testbed environment. In Fig. 3b, we present the configuration of hInjector for injecting an attack triggering CVE-2012-3495. Configuration files for injecting attacks that trigger publicly disclosed hypercall vulnerabilities are distributed with hInjector.

Injection During Regular System Operation. Benign activities, mixed with attacks, are needed to subject an IDS under test to realistic attack scenarios. hInjector is designed to inject hypercall attacks *during* regular operation of guest VMs. Thus, provided that during an IDS evaluation experiment representative user tasks run in the VMs in the IDS monitoring landscape, the presence of representative benign hypercall activities is guaranteed.

---

[4] We developed proof-of-concept code based on reverse-engineering the released patches fixing the considered vulnerabilities.

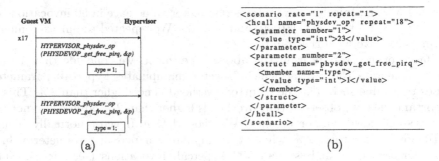

```
<scenario rate="1" repeat="1">
  <hcall name="physdev_op" repeat="18">
    <parameter number="1">
      <value type="int">23</value>
    <parameter number="2">
      <struct name="physdev_get_free_pirq">
        <member name="type">
          <value type="int">1</value>
        </member>
      </struct>
  </hcall>
</scenario>
```

(a)   (b)

Fig. 3. (a) Triggering CVE-2012-3495 [the hypercall *physdev_op* is executed 18 times: the value of its first parameter is 23 (*PHYSDEVOP_get_free_pirq*); the value of the field *type* of its second parameter (struct *physdev_get_free_pirq*) is 1]; (b) Configuration of hInjector for injecting an attack triggering CVE-2012-3495

Non-disruptive Attack Injection. The state of the hypervisor or the VM(s) from where attacks are injected may be altered by the attacks injected by hInjector. This may cause crashes obstructing the execution of the IDS evaluation process. Filter prevents crashes by blocking the execution of the hypervisor's handlers that handle the injected hypercalls. This preserves the states of the hypervisor and of the VM(s) from where attacks are injected, and, in addition, it ensures that injected attacks do not impact the operation of the IDS under test, which normally has components in the hypervisor and in a VM (see Sect. 2). After blocking the execution of hypervisor's handlers, Filter returns valid error codes. This allows the control flow of the kernel of the VM from where hypercall attacks are injected to properly handle failed hypercalls that have been executed by it and have been modified by the Injector on-the-fly.

4.3   Injector: Performance Overhead

The rate at which the kernel invokes hypercalls is high (i.e., in some cases more than 30000 hypercalls per second, see Sect. 5). Therefore, Injector, which manipulates hypercalls on-the-fly, can easily incur intolerable system performance overhead. We made the following observation when developing Injector: manipulating orders of series of hypercalls is very performance-expensive; therefore, Injector can manipulate only hypercall parameter values. Further, we measured the overhead incurred by Injector on the execution rate of hypercalls, relative to this rate when Injector is inactive, when replacing regular hypercall parameter values with random, irregular values. In Fig. 4, we depict this overhead, which we measured as follows. We deployed Injector in the kernel of a Debian 8.0 operating system running on top of Xen 4.4.5. We invoked the *mmuext_op* hypercall 40000 times using a loadable kernel module. We measured the time, in microseconds (μs), needed for the invoked hypercalls to complete their operation ('Execution time' in Fig. 4) in scenarios where: (i) Injector is inactive ('Base' in Fig. 4), and (ii) Injector manipulates the value of the second parameter of *mmuext_op* at the

rate of 1:50 (i.e., Injector manipulates parameter value once in 50 invocations of
mmuext_op), 1:100, 1:500, 1:1000, and 1:10000. We repeated the measurements
30 times and averaged the results.

Based on the results from the above experiment, we conclude that a user
should constrain the rate at which Injector manipulates hypercall parameter
values to a value such that the incurred overhead is not higher than 2%. This is
important since we observed that overheads higher than 2% often cause noticeable system slowdowns or crashes. We showed that Injector normally incurs
overheads higher than 2% when it manipulates hypercall parameter values
approximately once in less than 500 hypercall invocations (see Fig. 4). Note
that overheads incurred by Injector for hypercalls other than *mmuext_op* do
not significantly differ from those depicted in Fig. 4 since the implementation of
Injector is the same for all hypercalls.

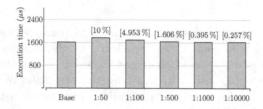

Fig. 4. Overhead incurred by Injector [measurements of the incurred overhead are
depicted in square brackets]

5   Case Study

We now demonstrate the application of our approach by evaluating Xenini [3]
following the steps presented in Sect. 3. Xenini is a representative anomaly-based
IDS. It uses the popular Stide [16] method. Xenini slides a window of size k over
a sequence of n hypercalls and identifies mismatches (anomalies) by comparing
each k-length sequence with regular patterns learned during IDS training. Xenini
records the number of mismatches as a percentage of the total possible number
of pairwise mismatches for a sequence of n hypercalls (i.e., $(k-1)(n-k/2)$).
We call this percentage *anomaly score*. When the anomaly score exceeds a given
threshold $th \in [0;1]$, Xenini fires an alert. For the purpose of this study, we configured Xenini such that its detection-relevant property is sequences of hypercall
IDs of length 4 (i.e., $k = 4$; $n = 10$).

It is important to emphasize that we focus on demonstrating the feasibility
of attack injection in virtualized environments for IDS testing purposes and not
on discussing the behavior of Xenini in detail or comparing it with other IDSes.
We specify arbitrary attack injection scenarios and evaluate Xenini with the sole
purpose of demonstrating all steps and functionalities of the proposed approach.
We refer the reader to Sect. 5.3 for an overview of further application scenarios.

5.1 Case Study: Planning

Specification of an IDS Monitoring Landscape. We use the SPECvirt_sc2013 benchmark to specify an IDS monitoring landscape.[5] SPECvirt_sc2013 is an industry-standard virtualization benchmark developed by SPEC (Standard Performance Evaluation Corporation). Its complex architecture matches a typical server consolidation scenario in a datacenter — it consists of 6 co-located front- and back-end server VMs (i.e., web, network file, mail, batch, application, and database server VM) and 4 workload drivers that act as clients generating workloads for the front-end servers. The workload drivers are heavily modified versions of the drivers of the SPECweb 2005, SPECimap, SPECjAppServer2004, and SPECbatch (i.e., SPEC CPU 2006) benchmarks. They generate workloads representative of workloads seen in production virtualized environments.

In Fig. 5, we depict the deployment of SPECvirt_sc2013 as an IDS monitoring landscape. The workload drivers generate workloads that map to hypercalls. We used Xen 4.4.1 as hypervisor and we virtualized the VMs using full paravirtualization.[6] To each server VM, we allocated 8 virtual CPUs pinned to separate physical CPU cores of 2 GHz, 3 GB of main memory, and 100 GB of hard disk memory. In Fig. 5, we depict the operating systems and architectures of the server VMs, and the server software we deployed in the VMs.[7]

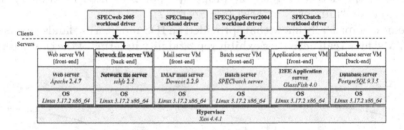

Fig. 5. SPECvirt_sc2013 as an IDS monitoring landscape [IMAP stands for Internet Message Access Protocol; J2EE stands for Java 2 Enterprise Edition]

Characterization of Benign Hypercall Activities. We now estimate steady-states of the benign hypercall activities of the server VMs and calculate the relevant statistics (see Sect. 3.1). We initialized the IDS monitoring landscape and deployed Xenini before the characterization. We used *xentrace*, the tracing facility of the Xen hypervisor, to capture hypercall activities in trace files.

---

[5] http://www.spec.org/virt_sc2013/.

[6] We did not use any other virtualization mode because of a technical limitation; that is, the *xentrace* tool, which we use to capture benign hypercall activities in files for processing off-line, currently supports only full paravirtualization. However, support for other virtualization modes is currently being implemented.

[7] An overview of the software and hardware requirements for deploying and running SPECvirt_sc2013 is available at https://www.spec.org/virt_sc2013/docs/SPECvirt_UserGuide.html.

Table 1. Benign workload characterization

	Run 1		Run 2	
Server VM	t_s (sec.)	r (occ./sec.)	t_s (sec.)	r (occ./sec.)
Web	5350	19644.5	5357	19627.3
Network file	5343	10204.9	5360	10231.3
Mail	5391	3141.5	5382	3148.7
Batch	5315	633.4	5330	623.8
Application	5367	31415.9	5377	31437.5
Database	5285	27294.9	5273	27292.3

Figure 6 a–f show growth curves depicting S_t until time $t_{max} = 5500$ s for each
server VM (see the curves entitled 'Run 1'). We set the target σ to 15 over a time
period of 100 s for the slope of each growth curve. In Table 1, column 'Run 1',
we present t_s (in seconds – sec.), which is the time at which the VMs' hypercall
activities reach steady-state. We also present r (in number of occurrences per
second – occ./sec.), which is the average rate of occurrence of the detection-
relevant property. We also calculated the statistic 'number of occurrences of each
variation of the detection-relevant property' (not presented in Table 1), which
we use to craft "mimicry" attacks (see Sect. 5.2).

We now empirically show that, provided an IDS monitoring landscape is specified, VMs' hypercall activities exhibit repeatability in terms of the characteristics

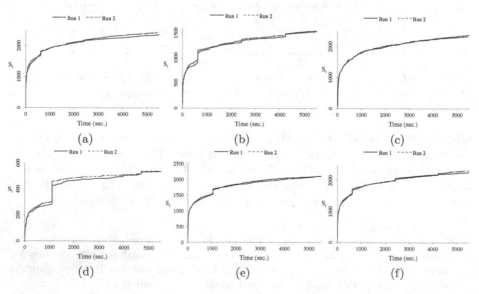

Fig. 6. Growth curves: (a) web (b) network file (c) mail (d) batch (e) application
(f) database server VM.

of interest to an extent sufficient for accurate IDS testing (see Sect. 3.2). We performed the above characterization campaign twice and compared the results. In Fig. 6 a–f, we depict the obtained growth curves (see the curves entitled 'Run 1' and 'Run 2'). These curves are very similar, which indicates that the characteristics of the VMs' hypercall activities of interest are also similar. In Table 1, we present t_s and r for each server VM (see column 'Run 1' and 'Run 2'). We observe a maximum difference of only 17 $sec.$ for t_s and 26.4 $occ./sec.$ for r. We repeated this process over 30 times and calculated maximum standard deviation of only 8.036 for t_s and 15.95 for r. These small deviations indicate that benign hypercall activities exhibit non-repeatability to such a small extent that it has no significant impact on metric values, which we repeatedly calculate for statistical accuracy (see Sect. 3.2).

Specification of Attack Injection Scenarios. We now specify attack injection scenarios that we will realize in separate testing phases. We focus on injecting attacks triggering publicly disclosed hypercall vulnerabilities. However, the injection of any malicious hypercall activity using hInjector is possible (e.g., covert channel operations as described in [4]), in which case an IDS evaluation study would be performed following the same process we demonstrate here.

Scenario #1: We will first evaluate the attack coverage of Xenini when configured such that $th = 0.3$. We will evaluate Xenini's ability to detect attacks triggering the vulnerabilities CVE-2012-5525, CVE-2012-3495, CVE-2012-5513, CVE-2012-5510, CVE-2013-4494, and CVE-2013-1964. We thus demonstrate injecting realistic attacks that conform to the attack models that we constructed [5]. We will inject attacks from the web and mail server VM using the LKM component of hInjector.

Attack contents: In Fig. 7 (a)–(e), we depict the contents of the considered attacks (the content of the attack triggering CVE-2012-3495 is depicted in Fig. 3a; we will inject this attack from the web server VM). The semantics of these figures is the same as that of Fig. 3a — we depict the hypercalls executed as part of an attack and relevant hypercall parameters; that is, integer parameters defining the semantics of the executed hypercalls (e.g., *XENMEM_exchange*), and, where applicable, parameters with values specifically crafted for triggering a vulnerability, which are marked in bold.

Attack injection times: After the hypercall activities of both the web and mail server VM have reached a steady state, we will inject the considered attacks, with 10 s of separation between each attack, and, where applicable, with no delays between the invocation of the hypercalls comprising an attack.

Scenario #2: We will investigate the accuracy of Xenini at detecting the attacks considered in *Scenario #1*, however, modified such that they have IDS evasive characteristics (i.e., they are "mimicry" and "smoke-screen" attacks). We will inject from the database server VM, using the LKM component of hInjector, both the unmodified attacks that consist of multiple hypercalls (i.e., we exclude the attack triggering CVE-2012-5525) and their modified counterparts as part of three separate testing phases. Therefore, we will observe how successful the modified attacks are at evading Xenini.

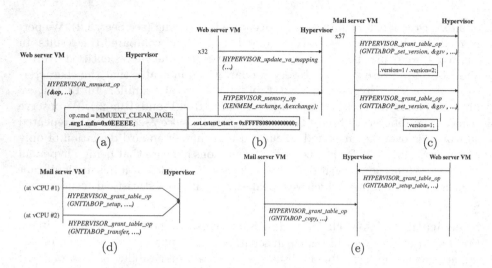

Fig. 7. Injecting attacks that trigger: (a) CVE-2012-5525; (b) CVE-2012-5513; (c) CVE-2012-5510; (d) CVE-2013-4494 [invoking hypercalls from two virtual CPUs (vCPUs)]; (e) CVE-2013-1964 [this vulnerability can also be triggered by invoking hypercalls from one VM]

Attack contents: The contents of the unmodified attacks and the "smoke-screen" attacks we will inject are depicted in Figs. 3a and 7 (b)–(e). To craft "mimicry" attacks, we place each individual hypercall that is part of an attack in the middle of a sequence of 20 injected hypercalls (i.e., at position 10). We built this sequence by starting with the most common detection-relevant property we observed in the planning phase — *iret, iret, iret, iret*. We then added 16 hypercalls such that sliding a window of size 4 over the sequence provides common detection-relevant properties seen during IDS training (i.e., while the hypercall activity of the database server VM has been progressing towards a steady state); we were able to perform this because we calculated the statistic 'number of occurrences of each variation of the detection-relevant property' (see Sect. 3.1). Therefore, we obscure attack patterns making them similar to regular patterns. For example, in Fig. 8a, we depict the content of the "mimicry" attack triggering CVE-2013-1964.

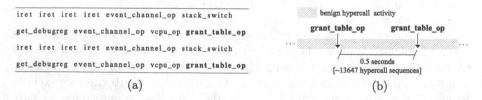

Fig. 8. Injecting IDS evasive attacks triggering CVE-2013-1964: (a) "mimicry" attack; (b) "smoke screen" attack [the hypercalls triggering CVE-2013-1964 are marked in bold]

Attack injection times: We craft "smoke screen" attacks by specifying attack injection times (see Sect. 3.1). We will inject a "smoke screen" attack by delaying for 0.5 s the invocation of the hypercalls comprising the attack. Since the average rate of occurrence of the detection-relevant property for the database server VM is 27294.9 occ./sec. (see Table 1, column 'Run 1'), we obscure attack patterns by making Xenini analyze approximately 13647 benign occurences of the detection-relevant property before encountering a hypercall that is part of an attack. For example, in Fig. 8b, we depict the "smoke screen" attack triggering CVE-2013-1964.

After the hypercall activities of the database server VM have reached a steady state, we begin three separate attack injection campaigns: unmodified attacks, "mimicry" attacks, and "smoke screen" attacks. Each campaign injects 6 attacks, with 10 s of separation between each attack.

5.2   Case Study: Testing

We now test Xenini with respect to the scenarios presented in Sect. 5.1.

Scenario #1

IDS Training. We deployed and configured Xenini and hInjector. We initalized the IDS monitoring landscape and we trained Xenini until time $t_s = 5391$ s. This is the time period needed for the hypercall activities of both the web and mail server VM to reach steady-state (see Table 1, column 'Run 1').

Attack Injection and Calculation of Metric Values. We injected the considered attacks over a period of $t_{max} - ts = 109$ s and then calculated metric values, that is, true and false positive rate. These are calculated as ratios between the number of true, or of false, alerts issued by Xenini, and the total number of injected attacks, or of benign variations of the detection-relevant property occuring during attack injection, respectively. We estimate the latter based on the statistic 'average rate of occurrence of the detection-relevant property'. We repeated the testing phase only 3 times in order to calculate statistically accurate metric values with a relative precision of 2 % and 95 % confidence level.[8]

Performing repeated measurements is important for calculating a statistically accurate value of the false positive rate. This is because the number of issued false alerts and the total number of benign variations of the detection-relevant property occuring during attack injection vary between measurements due to the non-determinism of benign hypercall activities. We observed that the true positive rate normally does not vary, since the number and properties of injected attacks (i.e., the attacks' contents and attack injection times) are fixed.

---

[8] In addition, we repeated the testing phase over 30 times observing that the obtained metric values negligibly differ from those we present here. This is primarily because of the high repeatability of hypercall activities and it indicates that only a small number of repetitions is needed to calculate statistically accurate metric values.

In Table 2, we present Xenini's attack detection score. It can be concluded that Xenini exhibited a true positive rate of 0.5 when configured such that $th = 0.3$. We now consider multiple IDS operating points (i.e., IDS configurations which yield given values of the false and true positive rate). In Fig. 9, we depict a ROC (Receiver Operating Characteristic) curve, which plots operating points for different values of th. We executed separate testing phases to quantify the false and true positive rate exhibited by Xenini for each value of th. We quantified these rates by comparing the output of Xenini with the "ground truth" information recorded by hInjector. We considered the total number of true and false alerts issued by Xenini (i.e., 6 and 6), injected attacks, and occurences of the detection-relevant property during attack injection, originating from both the web and mail server VM. The results depicted in Fig. 9 match the expected behavior of Xenini (i.e., the lesser the value of th, the more sensitive the IDS, which results in higher true and false positive rates; see [3]). This shows the practical usefulness of our approach.

Table 2. Detection score of Xenini [✓: detected/x: not detected, $th = 0.3$]

Targeted vulnerability (CVE ID)	Detected
CVE-2012-3495	✓
CVE-2012-5525	x
CVE-2012-5513	✓
CVE-2012-5510	✓
CVE-2013-4494	x
CVE-2013-1964	x

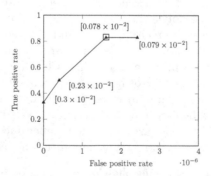

Fig. 9. Attack detection accuracy of Xenini [$th = 0.1$: $(2.42 \times 10^{-6}; 0.83)$ • $th = 0.2$: $(1.61 \times 10^{-6}; 0.83)$ • $th = 0.3/th = 0.4$: $(0.4 \times 10^{-6}, 0.5)$ • $th=0.5$: $(0, 0.33)$ • □ marks the optimal operating point]

We now calculate values of the 'expected cost' metric (C_{exp}) developed by Gaffney and Ulvila [17], which expresses the impact of the base rate (see Sect. 3.1). This metric combines ROC curve analysis with cost estimation by associating an estimated cost with each IDS operating point. The measure of cost is relevant in scenarios where a response that may be costly is taken when an IDS issues an alert. Gaffney and Ulvila introduce a cost ratio $C = C_\beta/C_\alpha$, where C_α is the cost of an alert when an intrusion has not occured, and C_β is the cost of not detecting an intrusion when it has occurred. To calculate values of C_{exp}, we set C to 10 (i.e., the cost of not responding to an attack is 10 times higher than the cost of responding to a false alert; see [17]).

We estimate the base rate as follows. We have injected 6 attacks consisting of 115 hypercalls over 109 s. Further, the average rate of occurence of the detection relevant property originating from the web and mail server VM during attack injection is estimated at $19644.5 + 3141.5 = 22786$ occ./sec. (see Table 1, column 'Run 1'). Therefore, the base rate is $\frac{115}{(22786 \times 109 + 3)} = 0.5 \times 10^{-4}$.

We calculated the actual base rate by calculating the actual average rate of occurence of the detection relevant property during attack injection. We observed that the difference between the actual and estimated base rate is negligible and has no impact on values of C_{exp}. This is primarily because the difference between the actual and estimated value of the average rate of occurence of the detection relevant property is small. Further, the ratio between the number of injected attacks and the number of occurences of the detection-relevant property during attack injection is very low due to the typical high value of the latter. This indicates the practical relevance of the planning phase.

In Fig. 9, we depict in square brackets values of C_{exp} associated with each IDS operating point. The 'expected cost' metric enables the identification of an optimal IDS operating point. An IDS operating point is considered optimal if it has the lowest C_{exp} associated with it compared to the other operating points. We mark in Fig. 9 the optimal operating point of Xenini.

Scenario #2

IDS Training. We deployed and configured Xenini and hInjector. We initalized the IDS monitoring landscape and, since we will inject attacks from the database server VM, we trained Xenini over a period of 5285 s.

Attack Injection and Calculation of Metric Values. We injected the unmodified, the "mimicry", and the "smoke screen" attacks as part of three separate testing phases. In Table 3, we present the anomaly scores reported by Xenini for the injected attacks. We thus quantify the success of the "mimicry" and "smoke screen" attacks at evading Xenini. Their evasive capabilities are especially evident in the case of the attacks triggering CVE-2012-3495 and CVE-2012-5510. That is, these attacks, when unmodified, can be very easily detected by Xenini (see the high anomaly scores of 1.0 in Table 3). However, when transformed into "mimicry" attacks, the detection of these attacks is significantly challenging (see the low anomaly scores of 0.17 and 0.14 in Table 3).

Table 3. Anomaly scores for the injected non-evasive and evasive attacks

Targeted vulnerability (CVE ID)	Anomaly scores		
	Unmodified	"Mimicry"	"Smoke screen"
CVE-2012-3495	1.0	0.17	0.25
CVE-2012-5513	0.32	0.107	0.28
CVE-2012-5510	1.0	0.14	0.31
CVE-2013-4494	0.21	0.14	0.14
CVE-2013-1964	0.25	0.14	0.14

The results presented in Table 3 match the expected behavior of Xenini when subjected to evasive attacks (i.e., Xenini reports lower anomaly scores for the evasive attacks than for the unmodified attacks; see [14]). This shows the practical usefulness of our approach and the relevance of the observations made in the planning phase, which we used to craft evasive attacks.

5.3 Further Application Scenarios

Besides evaluating typical anomaly-based IDSes, such as Xenini, our approach, or hInjector in particular, can be used for:

- *evaluating hypercall access control (AC) systems* — an example of such a system is XSM-FLASK. By evaluating AC systems, we mean verifying AC policies for correctness. This is performed by first executing hypercalls whose execution in hypervisor context should be prohibited and then verifying whether their execution has indeed been prohibited. hInjector can greatly simplify this process since it allows for executing arbitrary hypercall activities and recording relevant information (e.g., information on whether invoked hypercalls have been executed in hypervisor context, see Sect. 4.1);
- *evaluating whitelisting IDSes* — by whitelisting IDS, we mean IDS that fires an alarm when it observes an activity that has not been whitelisted, either by an user or by the IDS itself while being trained. For example, OSSEC can be configured to whitelist the hypercall activities it observes during training — our approach involves both rigorous IDS training and execution of arbitrary hypercall activities (see Sect. 3); RandHyp [9] and MAC/HAT [6] detect and block the execution of hypercall invocations that originate from untrusted locations (e.g., a loadable kernel module) — hInjector supports the injection of hypercall attacks both from the kernel and a kernel module (see Sect. 4.1).

6 Conclusion and Future Work

We presented an approach for the live evaluation of IDSes in virtualized environments using attack injection. We presented *hInjector*, a tool for generating IDS evaluation workloads that contain virtualization-specific attacks (i.e., attacks leveraging or targeting the hypervisor via its hypercall interface — hypercall attacks). Such workloads are currently not available, which significantly hinders IDS evaluation efforts. We designed hInjector with respect to three main criteria: injection of realistic attacks, injection during regular system operation, and non-disruptive attack injection. These criteria are crucial for the representative, rigorous, and practically feasible evaluation of IDSes. We demonstrated the application of our approach and showed its practical usefulness by evaluating a representative IDS designed to detect hypercall attacks. We used hInjector to inject attacks that trigger real vulnerabilities as well as IDS evasive attacks.

Our work can be continued in several directions:

- We plan to explore the integration of VM replay mechanisms (e.g., XenTT [15]) in our approach. This may help to further alleviate concerns related to the repeatability of VMs' hypercall activities;
- We intend to establish a continuous effort on analyzing publicly disclosed hypercall vulnerabilities in order to regularly update hInjector's attack library (see Sect. 4.2). This is an important contribution since the lack of up-to-date workloads is a major issue in the field of IDS evaluation;
- We plan to extensively evaluate a variety of security mechanisms (see Sect. 5.3) and work on applying our approach for injecting attacks involving operations that are functionally similar to hypercalls, such as KVM ioctl calls.

We stress that robust IDS evaluation techniques are essential not only to evaluate specific IDSes, but also as a driver of innovation in the field of intrusion detection by enabling the identification of issues and the improvement of existing intrusion detection techniques and systems.

Acknowledgments. This research has been supported by the Research Group of the Standard Performance Evaluation Corporation (SPEC; http://www.spec.org, http:// research.spec.org).

References

1. Rutkowska, J., Wojtczuk, R.: Xen Owning Trilogy: Part Two. http:// invisiblethingslab.com/resources/bh08/part2.pdf
2. Wilhelm, F., Luft, M., Rey, E.: Compromise-as-a-Service. https://www.ernw.de/ download/ERNW_HITBAMS14_HyperV_fwilhelm_mluft_erey.pdf
3. Maiero, C., Miculan, M.: Unobservable intrusion detection based on call traces in paravirtualized systems. In: Proceedings of the International Conference on Security and Cryptography (2011)
4. Wu, J.Z., Ding, L., Wu, Y., Min-Allah, N., Khan, S.U., Wang, Y.: C^2Detector: a covert channel detection framework in cloud computing. Secur. Commun. Netw. **7**(3), 544–557 (2014)
5. Milenkoski, A., Payne, B.D., Antunes, N., Vieira, M., Kounev, S.: Experience report: an analysis of hypercall handler vulnerabilities. In: Proceedings of the 25th IEEE International Symposium on Software Reliability Engineering. IEEE (2014)

6. Le, C.H.: Protecting Xen Hypercalls. Master's thesis, UBC (2009)
7. Bharadwaja, S., Sun, W., Niamat, M., Shen, F.: A Xen hypervisor based collaborative intrusion detection system. In: Proceedings of the 8th International Conference on Information Technology, pp. 695–700. IEEE (2011)
8. Srivastava, A., Singh, K., Giffin, J.: Secure observation of kernel behavior (2008). http://hdl.handle.net/1853/25464
9. Wang, F., Chen, P., Mao, B., Xie, L.: RandHyp: preventing attacks via Xen hypercall interface. In: Gritzalis, D., Furnell, S., Theoharidou, M. (eds.) SEC 2012. IFIP AICT, vol. 376, pp. 138–149. Springer, Heidelberg (2012)
10. Pham, C., Chen, D., Kalbarczyk, Z., Iyer, R.: CloudVal: a framework for validation of virtualization environment in cloud infrastructure. In: Proceedings of DSN 2011, pp. 189–196 (2011)
11. Le, M., Gallagher, A., Tamir, Y.: Challenges and opportunities with fault injection in virtualized systems. In: VPACT (2008)
12. Fonseca, J., Vieira, M., Madeira, H.: Evaluation of web security mechanisms using vulnerability and attack injection. IEEE Trans. Dependable Secure Comput. 11(5), 440–453 (2014)
13. Axelsson, S.: The base-rate fallacy and its implications for the difficulty of intrusion detection. ACM Trans. Inf. Syst. Secur. 3(3), 186–205 (2000)
14. Wagner, D., Soto, P.: Mimicry attacks on host-based intrusion detection systems. In: Proceedings of the 9th ACM Conference on Computer and Communications Security, pp. 255–264 (2002)
15. Burtsev, A.: Deterministic systems analysis. Ph.D. thesis, University of Utah (2013)
16. Forrest, S., Hofmeyr, S., Somayaji, A., Longstaff, T.: A sense of self for Unix processes. In: IEEE Symposium on Security and Privacy, pp. 120–128, May 1996
17. Gaffney, J.E., Ulvila, J.W.: Evaluation of intrusion detectors: a decision theory approach. In: Proceedings of the 2001 IEEE Symposium on Security and Privacy, pp. 50–61 (2001)

Security Analysis
of PHP Bytecode Protection Mechanisms

Dario Weißer, Johannes Dahse$^{(\boxtimes)}$, and Thorsten Holz

Horst Görtz Institute for IT-Security (HGI), Ruhr-University Bochum,
Bochum, Germany
{dario.weisser,johannes.dahse,thorsten.holz}@rub.de

Abstract. PHP is the most popular scripting language for web applications. Because no native solution to compile or protect PHP scripts exists, PHP applications are usually shipped as plain source code which is easily understood or copied by an adversary. In order to prevent such attacks, commercial products such as *ionCube*, *Zend Guard*, and *Source Guardian* promise a source code protection.

In this paper, we analyze the inner working and security of these tools and propose a method to recover the source code by leveraging static and dynamic analysis techniques. We introduce a generic approach for decompilation of obfuscated bytecode and show that it is possible to automatically recover the original source code of protected software. As a result, we discovered previously unknown vulnerabilities and backdoors in 1 million lines of recovered source code of 10 protected applications.

Keywords: Security · Reverse engineering · Obfuscation · PHP · Bytecode

1 Introduction

Protecting intellectual property (IP) in software systems, such as algorithms, cryptographic keys, serial numbers, or copyright banners, is a challenging problem: an adversary can study the program with static or dynamic analysis methods [7,13,19] and attempt to deduce the sensitive information. To impede such an analysis, many different types of obfuscation techniques for binary executables were developed (e.g., [3,11,15,21]). Although the semantics of the program can be reconstructed with different (automated) reverse engineering methods [4,16,20,29], obfuscation provides at least some protection of the source code and hampers an adversary to a certain extent.

IP protection is more challenging in the web context: PHP, the most popular server-side scripting language on the web, is an interpreted language. This implies that an interpreter transforms the PHP source code on demand into bytecode that is then executed. As such, an adversary who can obtain access to the source code (e.g., via software bugs or a legitimate trial version) can directly study or modify the code and reveal sensitive information. To remedy such attacks, different tools are available that offer code protection: commercial products like *ionCube*, *Zend Guard*, and *Source Guardian* promise to

© Springer International Publishing Switzerland 2015
H. Bos et al. (Eds.): RAID 2015, LNCS 9404, pp. 493–514, 2015.
DOI: 10.1007/978-3-319-26362-5_23

"prevent unlicensed use and reverse engineering and to safeguard intellectual property" [30].

All these tools follow the same methodology: They pre-compile PHP source code into obfuscated bytecode that can then be shipped without the original source code. On the server side, these tools require a PHP extension that allows to run the bytecode. Popular PHP software such as *NagiosFusion*, *WHMCS*, and *xt:Commerce* ship certain files protected with such tools to safeguard their IP. As a result, an adversary can at most access the pre-compiled bytecode and cannot directly access the source code. Unfortunately, it is not documented how these products work internally and what security guarantees they provide.

In this paper, we address this gap. We study the three most popular commercial PHP code protection products in detail and analyze their security properties. We find that all share the same limitation that enables an adversary to reconstruct the semantics of the original code. More specifically, we introduce methods to recover the code by statically and dynamically analyzing the interpretation of the bytecode. Since the interpreter needs to transform the encrypted/obfuscated bytecode back to machine code, we can recover the semantic information during this phase. We found that all tools can be circumvented by an adversary and we are able to successfully reconstruct the PHP source code. In this paper, we first present our findings from manually reverse engineering the different PHP code protection tools. Based on these findings, we introduce our method to break the encryption and obfuscation layers using dynamic analysis techniques, and show how to build a generic decompiler. Note that our techniques can be used against all PHP bytecode protectors that rely on bytecode interpretation and our method is not limited to the three analyzed products.

To evaluate our decompiler, we studied several popular protected software programs. We uncovered critical vulnerabilities and backdoors in some of these protected programs that would have remained invisible without decompilation since the identified flaws were hidden in obfuscated/encrypted bytecode. Furthermore, we detected critical security vulnerabilities in the products themselves that weaken the encrypted application's server security. In conclusion, our results indicate that PHP source code protection tools are not as strong as claimed by the vendors and such tools might even lead to an increased attack surface.

In summary, we make the following contributions in this paper:

- We analyze and document in detail the inner working of the three most popular PHP bytecode protectors.
- We propose a method to generically circumvent such protectors based on the insight that we can recover the semantics of the original code during the interpretation phase. We present an automated approach to reconstruct protected PHP source code and implemented a prototype of a decompiler.
- We evaluate our prototype with 10 protected, real-world applications and show that it is possible to reconstruct the original source code from the protected bytecode.

Last but not least, we would like to raise awareness about the usage of PHP bytecode protectors and their effectiveness on protecting sensitive data. We hope that our research can guide future work on protecting interpreted languages and that it offers new insights into the limitations of obfuscation techniques.

2   Background

In order to analyze PHP source code protectors, we first take a look at several PHP internals. We provide a brief introduction to PHP's interpreter, virtual machine, and instructions. Then, we outline the general concept of PHP source code protectors and introduce the three most popular tools on the market.

2.1   PHP Interpreter

PHP is a platform independent scripting language that is parsed by the PHP interpreter. The PHP interpreter is written in C and can be compiled cross-platform. Unlike low-level languages such as C, no manual compilation into an executable file is performed for PHP code. Instead, an application's code is compiled to *PHP bytecode* on every execution by the Zend engine. The Zend Engine [25] is a core part of PHP and is responsible for the code interpretation.

During the compilation process, a PHP file's code is split into tokens by a tokenizer. The process is initiated by PHP's core function `zend_compile_file()`. After tokenizing the code, the compiler uses the tokens to compile them into bytecode. Similarly, the core function `zend_compile_string()` compiles a string and is used, for example, to run code within `eval()`. As we will see in Sect. 4, PHP core functions play an important role for the dynamic analysis of bytecode protectors. An overview of the PHP interpreter's structure is given in Fig. 1.

After the engine parsed and compiled the PHP code into bytecode, its instructions (*opcodes*) are executed by PHP's virtual machine (VM) that comes with the Zend Engine. It has a *virtual CPU* and its own set of instructions. These instructions are more high level than regular machine code and are not executed by the CPU directly. Instead, the virtual machine provides a handler for each instruction that parses the VM command and runs native CPU code.

The execution process is initiated by passing the *opcode array* to the function `zend_execute()`. It iterates over the opcodes and executes one after another.

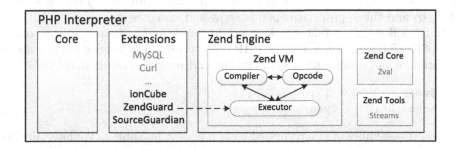

Fig. 1. The PHP interpreter with its core, extensions, and the Zend Engine.

Calls to user-defined functions are handled recursively and return to the call site's opcode. The function terminates when a *return* opcode in the *main* opcode array is found. In the next section, we look at opcodes in detail.

2.2 PHP Bytecode

The register-based bytecode of PHP consists of opcodes, constants, variables, and meta information. PHP has around 150 different opcodes that cover all existing language constructs [26]. Basically, each opcode has an *opcode number* that is used to find the corresponding opcode handler in a lookup table, two *parameter* operands, and a *result* operand to store return values. The parameter operands of an opcode store the values that are processed in the operation. These operands can have five different types and there is a variety of use cases. For example, an operand can be a constant or a variable. Temporary variables are used for auxiliary calculations or results that are not assigned to a variable.

Since there are different operand types, there are multiple instances of opcode handlers as there are 25 possible operand combinations for each instruction. For example, the handler function for adding two variables is different to the one for adding two constants. The overall number of handler functions is less than 150*25 because some combinations are redundant or invalid. The index to retrieve the handler address from the handler table is calculated using the following formula:

$$index = opcode\_number * 25 + op1\_type * 5 + op2\_type \tag{1}$$

Every operand combination for each opcode is stored within this table and links to the appropriate handler that performs the operation. Invalid combinations terminate the PHP process with a corresponding error message.

Next to the opcodes, the bytecode contains structures. These hold constant values, such as numbers or strings, and variable names which are referenced in operands with a key. Furthermore, meta information, such as line numbers and doc comments, is available as well as a *reserved* variable that allows extensions to store additional information. The bytecode of user-defined functions and methods is stored similarly in opcode arrays. Here, the name and argument information is stored additionally. A global function table links to the corresponding opcode array by function name. Classes have their own method table that links to the methods. When a method or function call is initiated, PHP uses these tables to find the appropriate opcode array and executes it.

In the following, we take a look at a code sample and its bytecode after compilation. The following three lines of PHP code perform a mathematical operation, concatenate the result with a static string, and print the result *RAID2015*.

```
$year = 2000 + 15;
echo "RAID" . $year;
```

The disassembly of the compiled code is shown in Table 1. We have already mapped the opcode numbers to the corresponding handler names as well as variable names to operands. The compilation process converted the script into four

Table 1. Exemplary bytecode.

#	Opcode	Operand 1	Operand 2	Result
1	ADD	2000	15	TMP:1
2	ASSIGN	$year	TMP:1	
3	CONCAT	'RAID'	$year	TMP:2
4	ECHO	TMP:2		

operations. First, the ADD opcode handler adds the two constants 2000 and 15 and stores the result in the temporary variable TMP:1. Second, the ASSIGN opcode handler assigns the temporary variable TMP:1 to the variable $year. Third, the CONCAT opcode handler concatenates the string 'RAID' with the variable $year and stores the result in the temporary variable TMP:2. Fourth, the ECHO opcode handler prints the value of the temporary variable TMP:2.

2.3   PHP Bytecode Encoder

The general idea to create a *closed-source* PHP application is to compile a PHP script once and to dump all opcode arrays. This data can then be directly deployed to PHP's executor without another compilation of the source code. Because PHP has no native solution for this, a custom PHP extension can be implemented that dumps the bytecode into a file before it is executed (*encoder*). A second extension (*loader*) then parses the dumpfile and deploys the bytecode to the PHP engine. The process is depicted in Fig. 1 with a dashed arrow. As a drawback, PHP version specific extensions have to be provided if the bytecode format changes with different PHP releases.

However, as we have seen in Sect. 2.2, PHP bytecode is still readable, thus, additional protection mechanisms are reasonable. For example, it is possible to add several encryption layers around the bytecode. Furthermore, the execution of the encrypted bytecode can be limited to a specific user license or hardware environment by the loader extension. While such mechanisms can increase the security (or obscurity), the performance of an application might suffer. In the following, we introduce the three most popular commercial PHP bytecode protection tools. For all three, the loader extension is available for free, while the encoder extension is commercial. All three products promise bytecode protection by offering encryption, environment restriction, prevention of file tampering, as well as symbol name obfuscation (except for SourceGuardian).

ionCube is probably the most popular and most used software that obfuscates PHP scripts since 2003. The vendor describes its product as "the ideal and only serious no-compromise solution for protecting PHP" [9]. A single-user license for the latest version 8.3 costs $ 199.

Zend Guard has been developed by Zend Technologies in order to protect scripts from software pirates. The currently available version 7.0 costs $ 600 annually and is the most expensive solution. The vendor's online shop claims "to prevent unlicensed use and reverse engineering and to safeguard your intellectual property through encryption and obfuscation" [30]. However, during our analysis, no encryption process was identified.

SourceGuardian exists since 2002 [14] and was merged with phpShield in 2006. Both products are similar with the difference that SourceGuardian includes environment restriction features. Encoded files can be compatible with different versions of PHP at once. The product is advertised as "the most advanced PHP Encoder on the market" [22]. The latest version 10.1.3 is available for $159.

3   Static Analysis of Loader Extensions

In order to reveal the inner working of the introduced tools, we reverse engineered the corresponding loader extensions. In approximately four weeks, we analyzed the encoders for PHP version 5.4 which was the only common supported PHP version for the encoders at the time of our analysis. As a result, we were able to identify protection mechanisms, algorithms, and security vulnerabilities. Although new versions of the encoders were released in the meantime, no significant changes in the inner working were introduced to the best of our knowledge. In this section, we first provide a brief overview of the encoder similarities and then go into product-specific details. Due to space limitation and ethical considerations (see Sect. 8), we focus on our key findings.

3.1   Overview

Although all analyzed encoders use different methods for data encoding and encryption, the overall structure of a protected file and its binary data is similar. We depicted the general workflow in Fig. 2. First, each protected file identifies itself as encoded (1). Then, native PHP code provides a fallback routine in case no loader extension was found (2b). It informs the user about the missing extension and terminates the execution. If the loader is available, the binary data is parsed (2a) that hides the PHP bytecode in a proprietary binary format. A first unencrypted header is extracted that specifies the PHP and encoder version. The following second header is encoded or encrypted and stores more detailed

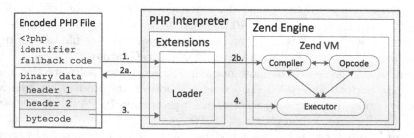

Fig. 2. Workflow of a loader extension: it parses the binary data of a protected file and extracts the PHP bytecode that is then executed.

Table 2. Overview of the loader extensions' internals.

File format	ionCube	Zend Guard	SourceGuardian
identifier	`<?php`	`<?php`	`<?php`
fallback length	`//004ff` (hex)	`@Zend;` `4147;` (octal)	`@"SourceGuardian";`
fallback code	try to load extension		try to load extension
	print message	print message	print message
data	`?>`	`?>`	`sg_load('binary data')`
	binary data	binary data	`?>`
fallback check	Adler32	n/a	32 bit BSD
data encoding	custom Base64/raw	n/a	Base64
header 1	ionCube	Zend Guard	SourceGuardian
header info	version, PRNG seed	version	version, protection flags
header 2	ionCube	Zend Guard	SourceGuardian
encryption	XOR with PRNG	n/a	Blowfish CBC mode
encoding		custom GZIP	Lempel Ziv (lzo1x)
checksum	MD4, custom Adler32	n/a	32 bit BSD
header info	license info	license info	license info
	restriction rules	restriction rules	restriction rules
	fallback checksum	license checksum	fallback checksum
bytecode	ionCube	Zend Guard	SourceGuardian
encryption	XOR with PRNG	n/a	Blowfish CBC mode
encoding	GZIP	custom GZIP	Lempel Ziv (lzo1x)
checksum	custom Adler32	n/a	32 bit BSD
obfuscation	forged opcode nr	forged opcode nr	n/a
license file	XOR, Blowfish	DSA signature	Blowfish encryption

information regarding license information, expiry time and environment restrictions. Some of these information can be outsourced to an external license file. In this case, the second header also stores information regarding this file's protection. Finally, the PHP bytecode follows in a proprietary format (3). If the license is not expired and the runtime environment matches the restriction rules, the PHP bytecode is executed by passing it to the PHP VM (4). In the following, we introduce product specific details. We reverse engineered each loader extension's process of extracting the bytecode from the binary data step by step. Surprisingly, very little obfuscation is used within the extensions itself. This would at least hinder the reverse engineering process and require more effort, but not prevent it. An overview of the identified core features is given in Table 2.

3.2 IonCube

The ionCube loader is compiled with multiple optimizations and without debug symbols. All internal function names are obfuscated. Internal strings, such as error messages, are XOR'ed with a static 16 bytes key, while a prefixed character in the string denotes the offset for the XOR operation to start. Other protection mechanisms against reverse engineering are not present.

The loader hooks `zend_compile_file()` and tests for the string `<?php //` at the beginning of an executed PHP file. The then following hexadecimal number denotes the size of the native PHP fallback code. If the ionCube extension is loaded, the fallback code is skipped and the loader begins to parse the binary data at the end of the file.

IonCube ships the binary data either raw or encoded with a custom base64 encoding (default). The base64 character set is slightly modified so that numbers occur first in the set. Once the data is decoded, a binary stream is used to parse it. The first four byte specify the ionCube version used for encoding. Because ionCube's format changed over time, different parsing routines are used. For example, `0x4FF571B7` is the identifier for version 8.3. The version identifier is followed by three integers: the file size, header size, and a header key. This key is used to decrypt the header size and file size, using the following calculation:

```
header_size = header_key ^ ((header_size ^ 0x184FF593) - 0xC21672E)
file_size = (file_size ^ header_key ^ 0x23958cde) - 12321
```

While the `file_size` is used for debugging, the `header_size` indicates the length of the second header. The second header is XOR'ed with a pseudo random byte stream. For this purpose, a *SuperKISS*-like PRNG is seeded with the `header_key` from the first header. The last 16 bytes of the encrypted second header represent the MD4 checksum of the decrypted second header's data. An Adler32 checksum follows that is used to verify the integrity of the first and second header, as well as its MD4 checksum. Within the modified Adler32 algorithm, the sum of all bytes is initialized to 17 instead of 1. The MD4 checksum is unscrambled first using the following pseudo algorithm.

```
md4_sum = substr(header, -16);
for(i=0; i<16; i++) {
    md4_sum[i] = ((md4_sum[i] >> 5) | (md4_sum[i] << 3));
}
```

Here, every byte of the checksum is rotated by 5 bits. Then, the PRNG is initialized and pseudo-random bytes and parts of the MD4 checksum are used as decryption key. The following pseudo algorithm is used to decrypt the second header byte-wise.

```
prng = new ion_prng(header_key);
for(i=0; i < header_size - 16; i++) {
    raw_header[i] ^= md4_sum[i & 15] ^ (prng->next() & 0xFF);
}
```

At the end, the integrity of the header's data is verified by calculating and comparing its MD4 checksum. The second header contains the configuration values of the ionCube protection. For example, a version number allows the loader to determine if the file's PHP version matches the system's PHP version and to find the corresponding decoding routine. A checksum of the native fallback code allows to validate its integrity. Furthermore, licensing information and environment restriction rules are found. For optional name obfuscation, a salt is found that is used to hash names of variables, functions, and classes with MD4. If the restriction rules are outsourced to a license file, the file path and decryption key is provided.

After the second header and its checksum, two integers and the encrypted PHP data follow. The first integer seeds a PRNG in order to generate a byte sequence that is the XOR key for the encrypted PHP data. After successful decryption, the data is decompressed using GZIP. At this point, the opcode numbers within the bytecode are still encrypted. A new PRNG is seeded with the second integer. In combination with a static value from the second header, a new byte sequence is generated in order to decrypt the opcode numbers and to perform a runtime obfuscation. We explain this process in Sect. 4.2 in detail.

In contrast to Zend Guard and SourceGuardian, ionCube does not send the bytecode to PHP's native execution function in order to run the code. Instead, slightly modified parts of the native PHP interpreter are compiled into the loader extension and are used as a proprietary VM with further obfuscation.

3.3   Zend Guard

Zend Guard's loader extension is not protected against reverse engineering, except for the obfuscation of its verbose error messages. These are XOR'ed using the four bytes \xF8\x43\x69\x2E. Moreover, Zend Guard leaks its compile information which helps to exclude library code from reverse engineering, while the latest loader version even includes debug symbols.

In order to detected encoded files, Zend Guard replaces PHP VM's function zend_compile_file(). If the string <?php @Zend; is not found at the beginning of the file, it will be passed back to the original compile function. Otherwise, the file is processed by Zend Guard. It reads the octal number in the second line and skips the amount of bytes of the fallback routine in order to reach the raw binary data at the end of the file.

To retrieve the data, a parser iterates over the byte stream. The data blocks are stored using a simple binary format which basically consists of four different data types: bytes, bools, numbers, and strings. When a single byte or bool is requested from the stream, the parser reads one character. Numeric values consist of a single byte which defines the length of the number followed by the actual integer (e. g., [\x05][2015\x00]). Strings extend the integer type with a byte sequence and its length (e. g., [\x02][5\x00][RAID\x00]). Both, numbers and strings, are terminated with a null byte.

The binary data consists of two parts: a minimalistic header followed by compressed data. There are four values stored within the first header. The first value indicates the version of Zend Guard and the second value identifies the PHP version the script was compiled for. Then, two numeric values specify the size of the compressed and the uncompressed data. The then following data is compressed using *GZIP* and a custom compression dictionary. This dictionary lists words that occur frequently in PHP code in order to improve the compression rate. It is required to decompress the data and stored within the Zend Guard loader. The decompressed data contains a second header and the PHP bytecode.

In the second header, license information, such as the license owner's name, and configuration flags, such as if the license is attached as a file, is stored. It also provides an expiration timestamp. If the current time is ahead of the timestamp, or if the license is invalid, Zend Guard denies executing the file. The license is validated by calculating an Adler32 checksum of the owner's name and comparing it to a checksum in the header. For this purpose, a slightly modified Adler32 algorithm is used that lacks the modulo operation.

Once the second header is completely decoded and verified, the compiled PHP data is parsed. For this purpose, Zend Guard uses the previously introduced stream format to parse the data. Opcodes, literals, and variables are the main part of this structure but also meta information, such as line numbers or comments, is available if it was not explicitly disabled during encoding. Moreover, Zend Guard scrambles the opcode numbers. For recovery, a substitution table is created using constant values from two arrays and the license owner checksum from the second header. With the help of the substitution table and the current opcode index, the original opcode number can be calculated.

Furthermore, Zend Guard is able to obfuscate function and variable names. Here, the lowercased name is XOR'ed with the MD5 hash of the name, such that the original name is lost. However, the name can be brute-forced with a dictionary. Also, the key space is reduced because the original name is lowercased first and the obfuscated name has the same length as the original one.

3.4   SourceGuardian

The process of reverse engineering SourceGuardian is comforted by available debug symbols within its loader extension. Almost all function and symbol names are intact and ease the understanding of internal processes. A PHP file's protection is indicated in the first line with the identifier @"SourceGuardian" (or @"phpSHIELD" for older versions). Instead of hooking the zend_compile_file() function, SourceGuardian adds a new native function sg_load() to the PHP core which parses a proprietary binary format.

```
<?php @"SourceGuardian";
if(!function_exists('sg_load')){ // fallback code
} return sg_load('12345678CHECKSUM/BASE64/BASE64/BASE64/BASE64=');
```

The argument of sg_load() is a concatenation of 16 hexadecimal characters and *base64* encoded binary data. First, a checksum is calculated over the characters ranging from the opening PHP tag <?php to the 8th character of

the `sg_load()` argument. This checksum is then compared to the next eight characters of the argument in order to verify the fallback code's integrity. The checksum algorithm appears to be a 32bit version of the BSD checksum.

The *base64* encoded binary data is decoded and reveals a binary format with four data types. The type `char` is used to represent single characters, small numbers, and boolean values. Integers are stored using four bytes in little endian format (type `int`) and strings can either be zero terminated (type `zstr`) or have a prefixed length (type `lstr`).

At the beginning, a first header is parsed that contains a version number and protection settings, in case the file is locked to a specific IP address or hostname. The first byte of a data block in the first header decides upon the purpose of the upcoming bytes, until a `0xFF` byte is found. For example, the value *0x2* indicates that execution is restricted to a hostname and the value *0x4* indicates that the length of the second header follows.

Once the offset of the encrypted second header is obtained from the first header, it is decrypted using the block cipher *Blowfish* in CBC mode. For this purpose, SourceGuardian's loader comes with multiple static keys that belong to three different groups. Depending on the file version, it iterates over the appropriate group's keys until the decryption succeeds (checksum matches). Multiple keys exist because of backwards compatibility and the *phpShield* aggregation:

```
NTdkNGQ1ZGQxNWYOZjZhMjc5OGVmNjhiOGMzMjQ5YWY=  // public key
MmU1NDRkMGYyNDc1Y2YOMjU5OTlmZDExNDYwMzcwZDk=  // public key
NzkxNThhZDhkOThjYTk3ZDE5NzY4OTRkYzZkYzM3MzU=  // license file key
ODIOYzI2YmMyODQ2MWE4MDY3YjgzODQ2YjNjZWJiMzY=  // phpShield pub key
YTJmNjc2MDQ3MWU5YzAxMjkxNTkxZGEzMzk2ZWI1ZTE=  // phpShield pub key
```

In case the execution of the protected file is restricted to a server's IP address or hostname, this value is appended to the decryption key of the second header and body. Hence, the loader will not be able to decrypt the binary block in other environments and the execution fails. By default, an attacker can perform decryption by using the static keys. We believe that the additional key data (IP or hostname) does not add any further security because the origin of a stolen source code file is most likely known to the attacker or can be brute-forced.

Each successfully decrypted block contains three integers and the actual data. The first integer is a checksum calculated over the plain data. The second integer contains the length of the unencrypted data and the third integer is the size of the data after decompression. The checksums are calculated with the previously mentioned 32bit BSD checksum. If the first integer matches the calculated checksum, the decryption was successful.

At this point the data is decrypted, but still compressed with the Lempel Ziv algorithm. SourceGuardian uses the *lzo1x* implementation and *lzss* for files encoded with an older version of SourceGuardian. The second header and the PHP data blocks are compressed and encrypted using this technique.

Similar to the first header, a parser iterates over the data and retrieves the values of the second header. It contains information about the environment restrictions, such as the license owner, license number, file creation, and file expiration date. After the second header, the PHP data follows. SourceGuardian is able to store multiple versions of it for compatibility with different PHP versions. One data block is used for each version. Each block consists of two integers that note the compatible PHP version and the size of the encrypted data, as well as the actual PHP data. If a compatible data block for the currently running PHP version is found, the block is decrypted. No further obfuscation, such as of variable names, is performed and the deobfuscated opcode array is passed to zend_execute().

3.5   Security Vulnerabilities in Loader Extensions

Protecting a PHP application can prevent intellectual property theft and modification when shipped to a customer. At the same time, however, it prohibits that the customer can review the code before it is deployed and run on his server. In order to mitigate risks, PHP mechanisms such as safe_mode and disable_functions can be activated that can forbid OS interaction, such as executing system commands, when running unknown protected PHP code.

During the process of reverse engineering, we detected memory corruption vulnerabilities in each of the loader extension. By crafting a malicious PHP file, it is possible to corrupt the loader's parser and to inject shellcode. While these vulnerabilities are not remotely exploitable, they allow a protected application to bypass PHP's security mechanisms and to execute arbitrary system commands with user privileges of the web server. We informed ionCube, Zend Guard, and SourceGuardian about these issues.

Furthermore, we detected an undocumented feature in SourceGuardian which allows to leak the license information. By sending the HTTP GET parameter __sginfo__ to a protected application, it responds with the encoder version, registration date, license owner, and date of encoding.

4   Generic Deobfuscation via Dynamic Analysis

We now introduce two *dynamic* approaches to analyze protected PHP applications. Our goal is to retrieve information about the original code by circumventing deployed encryption or obfuscation layers at runtime. We tested both approaches against ionCube, Zend Guard, and SourceGuardian and found all tools to be vulnerable against both attacks.

4.1   Debugging

A straight-forward approach to analyze protected PHP code is to include it into the context of own code that uses PHP's built-in debug functions to leak information about the current runtime environment. For example, the functions get_defined_vars(), get_defined_functions(), get_declared_classes(), and get_class_methods(), as well as PHP's built-in ReflectionClass allow to retrieve a list of all variables, user-defined functions, classes, and methods. Once obtained, variables can be dumped and functions can be called as a blackbox with different input in order to obtain further information. All three tested tools have an option to prevent the inclusion of compiled code within an untrusted context to prevent this analysis, but this is disabled by default.

4.2 Hooking

A more sophisticated approach is to hook [10] internal PHP functions in order to retrieve the complete bytecode before it is executed. As explained in Sect. 3, Zend Guard and ionCube replaces the zend_compile_file() function. It returns the decoded and decrypted bytecode of a given file. We can use these functions as a black box in order to retrieve the deobfuscated opcode arrays without knowledge of the loaders' inner working. Bytecode from SourceGuardian files cannot be obtained this way because it does not replace zend_compile_file().

However, every product passes the deobfuscated opcode arrays as an argument to zend_execute() (see Fig. 1, dashed arrow). By hooking this function, we can interrupt the execution and obtain the main opcode array. Opcode arrays of methods and functions can be located with the help of PHP's internal compiler_globals structure. This way, the raw PHP bytecode of applications protected with SourceGuardian can be retrieved directly. For ionCube and Zend Guard, further obfuscation has to be removed (see Sects. 3.2 and 3.3).

ionCube. To avoid opcode dumping, ionCube implements a runtime obfuscation that XOR's single opcodes before execution and XOR's them again afterwards. This ensures that only one opcode is deobfuscated at a time. Furthermore, ionCube contains a copy of the native PHP engine and bytecode is processed within the loader instead of the PHP VM. Consequently, the last step in Fig. 2 is omitted and ionCube's internal zend_execute() function needs to be hooked for dynamic analysis.

The executed instructions are obfuscated with two techniques. First, the opcode number, the handler address, and the operands of all opcodes are encrypted with XOR. Second, numeric operands of assignments are obfuscated by mathematical operations with constants. The *reserved* variable of the opcode array references to an ionCube structure which contains the keys for opcode decryption (see Sect. 3.2) and assignment deobfuscation. Each opcode is XOR'ed with a different key which is referenced by the opcode index. Then, the opcode is executed and obfuscated again using the same XOR operation. By retrieving all keys from the ionCube structure, we are able to deobfuscate all opcodes.

Zend Guard. When a PHP file is parsed, the opcode number is used by the PHP interpreter to resolve the handler's address. As noted in Sect. 3.3, Zend Guard removes the opcode number before passing the bytecode to zend_execute(). In order to recover the opcode number again, we can search the present handler address in the opcode lookup table. This is achieved by calculating the index of all existent opcodes (see Formula 1 in Sect. 2.2) and comparing it to the index of the current address.

5   Decompiler for Obfuscated PHP Bytecode

Using the insights introduced in Sect. 3 and the techniques presented in Sect. 4.2, we implemented a decompiler. For this purpose, we set up a PHP environment with the three loader extensions as well as a custom PHP extension. The decompilation is performed in three steps. First, we hook PHP's executor in order to access the bytecode. Second, we remove all remaining obfuscation and dump the bytecode to a file. Third, the dumped bytecode is decompiled into PHP syntax. It is also possible to statically recover the PHP bytecode from the protected PHP file without execution by using the insights presented in Sect. 3. However, the implementation of a version-specific parser for each loader extension is required, while the dynamic approach can be applied generically.

5.1   Hooking

Our PHP extension hooks the `zend_execute()` function by replacing it with our own implementation. Then, we execute each file of a protected PHP application in our PHP environment. As explained in Sect. 3, the corresponding loader extension now hooks `zend_compile_file()` and extracts the PHP bytecode from the proprietary binary format. When the bytecode is passed to `zend_execute()`, our extension terminates the execution. Because SourceGuardian does not hook `zend_compile_file()` and implements the native PHP function `sg_load()`, we here intercept only the second invocation of `zend_execute()`. This way, we allow the initial execution of `sg_load()` that performs the initial decryption and deobfuscation of the bytecode, before it is passed to `zend_execute()` again.

5.2   Dumping

For ionCube and Zend Guard, we perform further bytecode deobfuscation as described in Sect. 4.2. Then, the bytecode is free of any encoder-specific modifications. Each opcode array contains several data structures which are referred by the operands (see also Sect. 2.2). Operands of type VAR and CV refer to variables with a name which is stored within the vars structure. Constants are used by operands of type CONST and can be found within the literals structure. Opcodes themselves are stored in the opcodes structure. If the opcode array represents a function, the parameters are available in the structure arg_info. We begin dumping the main opcode array and continue with user defined functions. Classes are stored in an own structure that basically contain information about member variables and the method table. After dumping the bytecode into a file, it can be deployed to our decompiler for further processing.

5.3 Decompilation

Next, each instruction is inspected and transformed into the corresponding source code representation. The opcodes can be grouped into one of three different types of instructions:

1. **Expressions** are instructions which produce temporary values that are used as operands by other instructions, for example, a mathematical operation.
2. **Statements** are instructions that cannot be used as an expression and do not have a return value, for example an echo or break statement.
3. **Jumps** are special cases of statements. They defer the execution by a jump and represent a loop or conditional code.

In general, the best way of decompiling bytecode back into source code is to create a graph by connecting separated basic blocks such that each part of the code can be converted separately [1, 2, 12]. However, this approach is out of scope for this paper. For our proof of concept, we follow a simpler approach: our decompiler is based on a pattern recognition approach that finds jump and loop structures. Empirically we found that this approach is already sufficient to recover most PHP source code.

Our approach consists of two steps. First, we iterate over all opcodes in order to reconstruct expressions and statements. During this process, ternary operators and arrays are rebuilt and coherent conditions are merged. Afterwards, we remain with PHP source code and jump instructions. Finally, we try to find patterns of commonly used jump and loop structures in order to reassemble the control flow.

The code in Table 3 provides an example of PHP bytecode. Here, we first buffer the PHP syntax of the ADD expression stored in TMP:1 (op1+op2). Next, the first line of code is recovered by resolving the operand TMP:1 in the assignment of variable $test. Further, we construct the *greater-than* constraint created from the variable $test and the constant value 500 (op1>op2). Then, the operand TMP:2 can be resolved in line 4. In the next line, we create the echo statement. We ignore the JMP for now and finish with the transformation of the return

Table 3. Exemplary bytecode with decompiled syntax.

#	Opcode	Operand1	Operand2	Result	Code
1	ADD	222	333	TMP:1	
2	ASSIGN	$test	TMP:1		`$test = 222 + 333;`
3	IS_GREATER	$test	500	TMP:2	
4	JMPZ	TMP:2	JMP:7		`if ($test>500) {`
5	ECHO	$test			`echo $test;`
6	JMP	JMP:7			`}`
7	RETURN	1			`return 1;`

statement. When all expressions and statements are processed, we begin with finding patterns by processing the jump operands. In our example, we recognize the JMPZ in line 4 that jumps to the same location as the following JMP in line 6 as an if construct.

Similarly, we can recognize more complex if/else constructs. As shown previously, a single if block without an else branch is identified by a conditional jump instruction that skips upcoming statements in case the condition fails. Unoptimized bytecode has a JMP instruction inside the if block that jumps to the next instruction after the if block. In this particular case, the second jump is unnecessary for execution but helps to recognize the pattern. If this JMP instruction would skip upcoming statements instead, these statements would be assigned to an elseif/else block.

In PHP bytecode, for loops have an unique pattern. The overall layout comprises a loop constraint, a JMPZNZ, an iteration expression, a JMP, followed by the loop body and a final JMP. The JMPZNZ operation has two jump locations stored in its operands. The first jump is taken in case of a zero value, and the second one otherwise. The second location points behind the loop body. The interpreter jumps to this location when the condition of the JMPZNZ instruction does not match. The bytecode at the first location represents the start of the loop body. The JMP instruction at the body's end jumps back to the loop's constraint.

Similarly, while loops can be detected. Here, a constraint is followed by a JMPZ instruction that points behind the loop's body. Then, the loop's body follows which ends with a JMP instruction that points back to the loop's constraint.

More convenient is the recognition of foreach loops. Here, the rare opcode FE_RESET is used to reset an array's pointer and then a FE_FETCH opcode follows to fetch the current array's element. Then, the loop body follows that ends with a JMP instruction. The initial FE_ opcodes both have a jump location stored in their second operand. This location points behind the last JMP instruction in the loop's body and it is accessed when the loop is finished. The JMP instruction itself points back to the FE_FETCH opcode.

In order to resolve nested constructs, our algorithm uses an inside out approach in several iterations. We mark sustained patterns as resolved and repeat our pattern matching algorithm until no new patterns are detected. This way, in a nested construct, the most inner pattern is resolved first, followed by the identification of the outer pattern in the next iteration.

Our pattern matching approach works very well on unoptimized bytecode since PHP adds redundant opcodes that ease the recognition process. Unfortunately, these patterns can change when bytecode optimization is enabled. Here, redundant operations are removed, structures are compressed, and targets of jump operations are pre-resolved. This makes it significantly harder to find and decompile structures. To overcome such limitations, a more elaborated decompiler design could be implemented in the future [2].

Parts of our approach for reconstructing expressions and statements into source code could be adopted for other register-based virtual machines. While simple opcodes, such as for addition or concatenation, can be compared to other languages, complex opcodes, such as for the access of arrays, are very PHP specific. For stack-based bytecode, as used in Java, Python, or Perl, the operands have to be resolved from the stack first. Our pattern matching approach for the evaluation of code structures bases on artifacts found in PHP bytecode and thus is not directly applicable to other languages.

6 Evaluation

We evaluate our decompiler in two steps. First, we try to quantify our decompilation results by encoding a set of known source code and comparing the decompiled code to the original version. Then, we test our decompiler against 10 protected real-world applications and try to recover unknown source code.

6.1 Source Code Reconstruction

Measuring the quality of decompiled PHP code is hard and, to the best of our knowledge, no code similarity algorithm for PHP exists. While the code's semantic remains after decompilation, the syntax changes due to PHP's native and the encoders' additional bytecode optimization. Due to limitations of our proof of concept implementation (see Sect. 5.3), our prototype does not always produce syntactically correct code and a comparison of successful unit tests of a decompiled application is not applicable. Hence, we developed a basic metric based on PHP tokens [23]. We categorized all tokens into one of seven groups:

1. **DATA:** tokens of literals, constants, and variables (T_VARIABLE)
2. **EQUAL:** tokens of assignment operators, such as T_PLUS_EQUAL
3. **COMP:** tokens of comparison operators, such as T_EQUAL and T_ISSET
4. **CAST:** tokens of type casts, such as T_INT_CAST and T_STRING_CAST
5. **INCL:** tokens of include statements, such as T_INCLUDE and T_REQUIRE
6. **PROC:** tokens of procedural code, such as T_FUNCTION and T_NEW
7. **FLOW:** tokens of jump and loop statements, such as T_IF and T_WHILE

Tokens that do not fall into one of these categories were ignored. We also ignored encapsulated variables and constants, comments, whitespaces, logical operators, and inline HTML. Next, we compiled the three most popular PHP projects *Wordpress*, *Drupal*, and *Joomla* with the most complex encoder ionCube with default optimization level. Then, we used our prototype for decompiling the protected code again. We used PHP's built-in tokenizer [24] to collect the number of tokens in all PHP files of the original and the recovered source code and calculated the individual success rate for each token. In Table 4, we list the average similarity of each token category that was weighted by token popularity in each group. We observed a very similar amount for tokens that are not part of optimization. As expected, the number of tokens for optimized instructions or loops (FLOW) vary more significantly. Based on our results, we estimate a successful reconstruction rate of about 96 %.

Table 4. Average token similarity (in %) for three compiled/decompiled applications.

Software	Version	EQUAL	DATA	COMP	CAST	INCL	FLOW	PROC
Wordpress	4.2.2	95.83	95.13	98.52	99.77	99.85	84.17	96.83
Joomla	3.4.1	96.45	95.33	99.76	99.53	99.77	82.33	97.36
Drupal	7.37	98.81	92.81	98.64	98.45	98.78	89.00	98.34

6.2 Protected Real-World Applications

In order to inspect protected code in real-world applications, we selected 10 popular encoded PHP applications. Our corpus is presented in Table 5. The number of evaluated software per encoder was chosen by the encoder's popularity. In total, we were able to recover more than 1 million lines of actual code (RELOC) in 3 942 protected PHP files. Bytecode optimization was enabled for some of the applications which led to errors when decoding optimized structures. These errors are very specific to the optimized code and cannot be generalized. Here, our prototype implementation requires improvement for a more precise reconstruction. However, errors in code nesting, such as the misplacement of curly braces, does not hinder to fully understand the recovered source code and to retrieve sensitive information, such as cryptographic keys, or to detect security vulnerabilities. In the following, we present our findings. Note that due to the large corpus, only a fraction of code could be analyzed.

License Systems. In all 10 analyzed applications, the protection is primarily used to hide a license system. It can limit the application's use to a specific time (7), number of users (5), domain or MAC address (4), software version (3),

Table 5. Corpus of selected real-world applications that apply an encoder.

Software	Version	Category	Encoder	Files		RELOC
				Total	Protected	
WHMCS	5.3.13	hosting	ionCube	946	688	157 651
HelpSpot	3.2.12	helpdesk	ionCube	493	163	41 033
xt:Commerce	4.1	webshop	ionCube	4 090	118	35 864
PHP-Cart	4.11.4	webshop	ionCube	271	3	2 762
Precurio	4	intranet	ionCube	2 985	5	579
XT-CMS	1.8.1	CMS	SourceGuardian	320	87	21 653
Mailboarder	4.1.5	email	SourceGuardian	110	110	16 365
NagiosFusion	2014R1.0	monitoring	SourceGuardian	294	15	3 337
Scriptcase	8.0.047	development	Zend Guard	3 751	2 676	726 552
gSales	rev1092	billing	Zend Guard	206	77	34 012

or restrict software features of a demo version (5). By decompiling the protected sources, we can reveal the keys and algorithms used. For example, we could recover the static secret in PHP-Cart (MD5 salt), HelpSpot (RC4), gSales (SHA1 salt) and Mailborder (AES 128bit) that is used to validate or decrypt the license data. In NagiosFusion, we discovered a custom decoding algorithm that is used to infer the installation's restrictions from the license key. The decompilation of these sensitive sources does not only allow to fake a valid runtime environment and license, but also to remove these checks completely.

Vulnerabilities. Furthermore, we detected critical security vulnerabilities in the decompiled source codes which could be confirmed against the original protected applications. For example, we detected multiple *path traversal* vulnerabilities in HelpSpot and scriptcase which allow to remotely retrieve any file from the server, and multiple *SQL injection* vulnerabilities in HelpSpot, xt:Commerce, and gSales which allow to extract sensitive data from the database. We believe that these vulnerabilities remained previously undetected for the reason of unavailable source code. It is controversial whether this is more helpful for the vendor or the attackers [18,28]. Arguably, some vulnerabilities could be also detected without the source code. However, some vulnerabilties are hard to exploit in a blackbox scenario, for example, a detected *second-order file inclusion* vulnerability [5] in Mailborder or *PHP object injection* vulnerabilities [6] in xt:Commerce, PHP-Cart, and HelpSpot. Clearly, a vendor should not rely on source code protectors to assume security issues remain undetected. We reported all identified issues responsibly to the corresponding vendor.

Pingbacks and Backdoors. Next to vulnerabilities, we looked for suspicious functionalities of the protected applications. We found rather harmless pingback features, for example in xt:Commerce, that send information about the installation environment and license to a SOAP-based web service. While this can be used to check for updates, it is also a good way to observe active installations. More severe is that xt:Commerce also sends the user's PayPal API credentials in plaintext to its server via HTTP. Precurio collects information about the application's server and owner and sends it via CURL request to the Precurio website, in case the ionCube license does not match to the server or is expired.

However, we also detected an odd vulnerability in Precurio. The following three lines of code determine if the request path is a file and in that case output its content. Thus, by requesting for example the URL /index.php/index.php from the server, the PHP source code of the index file is leaked.

```
$filename = $root . '/public/' . $_SERVER['PATH_INFO'];
if ( is_file($filename) )
    echo file_get_contents($filename);
```

Moreover, the code allows to retrieve any file from Precurio's web directory, including user files and the license file. Additionally, we found that the

`ErrorController` in Precurio implements a `downloadAction`. Thus, the URL `/error/download` allows the Precurio team, as well as any other remote user, to download the log file of the Precurio installation which leaks detailed stack traces and exceptions. We informed Precurio about both issues.

7   Related Work

Obfuscation of software systems is used in practice to increase the costs of reverse engineering, for example in the context of digital rights management systems [27] or IP protection. As a result, many different types of obfuscation techniques were developed in the past years and most of them focus on binary executables (e.g., [3,11,15,21]). So called *executable packers* implement different obfuscation and encryption strategies to protect a given binary. Note that obfuscation is also commonly used by adversaries to hamper analysis of malicious software samples. To counter such tactics, several methods for automated deobfuscation were developed [4,16,20,29], and we observe an ongoing arms race.

Similar obfuscation strategies are used to protect PHP source code and commercial tools are available to implement such strategies. To the best of our knowledge, there is no academic work on PHP obfuscation. Our work is most closely related to a talk by Esser [8], who provided an overview of PHP source code encryption and ideas on how source code could be recovered. Saher presented in a talk some reverse engineering details for ionCube [17]. We reverse engineered the three most popular PHP code protection products and provide detailed information about their internals, together with a decompiler approach.

Static and dynamic code analysis techniques can detect security vulnerabilities and are an important research topic. We complement this field by demonstrating how to access protected PHP code such that an analysis can be performed. In other areas, obfuscation/protection mechanisms have been broken by reverse engineering and binary instrumentation techniques (e.g., [27]) and we show that such attacks are also viable against PHP obfuscation tools.

8   Conclusion

In this paper, we evaluated and documented the level of protection provided by current IP protection tools available for PHP source code. We studied the internals of the three most popular encoder and demonstrated an attack against a shared weakness by a proof-of-concept implementation. As a result, we showed that our decompiler is able to recover 96 % of the protected PHP code which would enable an attacker to crack license systems and identify previously unknown vulnerabilities and backdoors. Therefore, we argue that currently available encoder products are no appropriate solutions for intellectual property protection and more elaborated obfuscation approaches are necessary to better protect PHP source code.

Ethical Considerations: We would like to clarify that our work was not motivated by the intention to perform illegal activities, such as copyright violation or server compromise, nor to ease these activities for others. For this reason, we do not publish our decompilation tool and we reported all detected vulnerabilities responsibly to the vendors. Moreover, we presented only key insights of the analyzed products and specific details are intentionally left out, while presented keys and constants are likely subject of change. Thus, we feel that an attacker is still left with a high reverse engineering effort in order to reproduce our attacks for the latest encoders. Rather, we hope that our research helps in building better encoders that do not suffer from our attacks and to advance the state-of-the-art.

References

1. Brumley, D., Lee, J., Schwartz, E.J., Woo, M.: A native x86 decompilation using semantics-preserving structural analysis and iterative control-flow structuring. In: USENIX Security Symposium (2013)
2. Cifuentes, C.: Reverse compilation techniques. Ph.D. thesis, Queensland University of Technology (1994)
3. Collberg, C., Thomborson, C., Low, D.: A taxonomy of obfuscating transformations. Technical report, University of Auckland, New Zealand (1997)
4. Coogan, K., Lu, G., Debray, S.: Deobfuscation of virtualization-obfuscated software: a semantics-based approach. In: ACM Conference on Computer and Communications Security (CCS), pp. 275–284 (2011)
5. Dahse, J., Holz, T.: Static detection of second-order vulnerabilities in web applications. In: USENIX Security Symposium (2014)
6. Dahse, J., Krein, N., Holz, T.: Code reuse attacks in PHP: automated POP chain generation. In: ACM Conference on Computer and Communications Security (CCS) (2014)
7. Egele, M., Scholte, T., Kirda, E., Kruegel, C.: A survey on automated dynamic malware analysis techniques and tools. ACM Comput. Surv. 44(2), 1–42 (2008)
8. Esser, S.: Vulnerability Discovery in Closed Source/Bytecode Encrypted PHP Applications. Power of Community (2008)
9. ionCube Ltd. ionCube PHP Encoder. https://www.ioncube.com/php_encoder.php?page=features, May 2015
10. Ivanov, I.: API Hooking Revealed. The Code Project (2002)
11. Linn, C., Debray, S.: Obfuscation of executable code to improve resistance to static disassembly. In: ACM Conference on Computer and Communications Security (CCS) (2003)
12. Miecznikowski, J., Hendren, L.: Decompiling Java bytecode: problems, traps and pitfalls. In: Nigel Horspool, R. (ed.) CC 2002. LNCS, vol. 2304, pp. 111–127. Springer, Heidelberg (2002)
13. Nielson, F., Nielson, H.R., Hankin, C.: Principles of Program Analysis. Springer, New York (1999)
14. phpSHIELD. About phpSHIELD. PHP Encoder by SourceGuardian. https://www.phpshield.com/about.html, May 2015
15. Popov, I.V., Debray, S.K., Andrews, G.R.: Binary obfuscation using signals. In: USENIX Security Symposium (2007)
16. Royal, P., Halpin, M., Dagon, D., Edmonds, R., Lee, W.: PolyUnpack: automating the hidden-code extraction of unpack-executing malware. In: Annual Computer Security Applications Conference (ACSAC) (2006)

17. Saher, M.: Stealing from thieves: breaking IonCube VM to RE exploit kits. Black-Hat Abu Dhabi (2012)
18. Schryen, G., Kadura, R.: Open source vs. closed source software: towards measuring security. In: ACM Symposium on Applied Computing (SAC) (2009)
19. Schwartz, E.J., Avgerinos, T., Brumley, D.: All you ever wanted to know about dynamic taint analysis and forward symbolic execution (but might have been afraid to ask). In: IEEE Symposium on Security and Privacy (S&P) (2010)
20. Sharif, M., Lanzi, A., Giffin, J., Lee, W.: Automatic reverse engineering of malware emulators. In: IEEE Symposium on Security and Privacy (S&P) (2009)
21. Sharif, M.I., Lanzi, A., Giffin, J.T., Lee, W.: Impeding malware analysis using conditional code obfuscation. In: Symposium on Network and Distributed System Security (NDSS) (2008)
22. SourceGuardian Ltd. PHP Encoder Features. https://www.sourceguardian.com/protect_php_features.html, May 2015
23. The PHP Group. List of Parser Tokens. http://php.net/tokens, May 2015
24. The PHP Group. Tokenizer. http://php.net/tokenizer, May 2015
25. The PHP Group. Zend API: Hacking the Core of PHP. http://php.net/manual/en/internals2.ze1.zendapi.php, May 2015
26. The PHP Group. Zend Engine 2 Opcodes. http://php.net/manual/internals2.opcodes.php, May 2015
27. Wang, R., Shoshitaishvili, Y., Kruegel, C., Vigna, G.: Steal this movie: automatically bypassing DRM protection in streaming media services. In: USENIX Security Symposium (2013)
28. Witten, B., Landwehr, C., Caloyannides, M.: Does open source improve system security? IEEE Softw. 18(5), 57–61 (2001)
29. Yadegari, B., Johannesmeyer, B., Whitely, B., Debray, S.: A generic approach to automatic deobfuscation of executable code. In: IEEE Symposium on Security and Privacy (S&P) (2015)
30. Zend Technologies Ltd. PHP Obfuscator, PHP Encoder & PHP Encryptionfrom Zend Guard. http://www.zend.com/products/guard, May 2015

Radmin: Early Detection of Application-Level Resource Exhaustion and Starvation Attacks

Mohamed Elsabagh[✉], Daniel Barbará, Dan Fleck, and Angelos Stavrou

George Mason University, Fairfax, USA
{melsabag,dbarbara,dfleck,astavrou}@gmu.edu

Abstract. Software systems are often engineered and tested for functionality under normal rather than worst-case conditions. This makes the systems vulnerable to denial of service attacks, where attackers engineer conditions that result in overconsumption of resources or starvation and stalling of execution. While the security community is well familiar with volumetric resource exhaustion attacks at the network and transport layers, application-specific attacks pose a challenging threat. In this paper, we present Radmin, a novel system for early detection of application-level resource exhaustion and starvation attacks. Radmin works directly on compiled binaries. It learns and executes multiple probabilistic finite automata from benign runs of target programs. Radmin confines the resource usage of target programs to the learned automata, and detects resource usage anomalies at their early stages. We demonstrate the effectiveness of Radmin by testing it over a variety of resource exhaustion and starvation weaknesses on commodity off-the-shelf software.

Keywords: Resource exhaustion · Starvation · Early detection · Probabilistic finite automata

1 Introduction

Availability of services plays a major – if not the greatest – role in the survivability and success of businesses. Recent surveys [2,5] have shown that IT managers and customers alike tend to prefer systems that are more often in an operable state, than systems that may offer higher levels of security at the expense of more failures. This means that any disruption to the availability of a service is directly translated into loss of productivity and profit. Businesses invest in deploying redundant hardware and replicas to increase the availability of the services they offer. However, as software designers often overlook Saltzer-Schroeder's "conservative design" principle [32], systems are often engineered and tested for functionality under normal rather than worst-case conditions. As a result, worst-case scenarios are often engineered by the attackers to overconsume needed resources (resource exhaustion), or to starve target processes of resources (resource starvation), effectively resulting in partial or complete denial of service (DoS) to legitimate users.

© Springer International Publishing Switzerland 2015
H. Bos et al. (Eds.): RAID 2015, LNCS 9404, pp. 515–537, 2015.
DOI: 10.1007/978-3-319-26362-5_24

A system is exposed to resource exhaustion and starvation if it fails to properly restrict the amount of resources used or influenced by an actor [3]. This includes, but is not limited to, infrastructure resources, such as bandwidth and connection pools, and computational resources such as memory and cpu time. The attacks can operate at the network and transport layers [37], or at the application layer such as algorithmic and starvation attacks [17,18]. The asymmetric nature of communication protocols, design and coding mistakes, and inherently expensive tasks all contribute to the susceptibility of programs to resource exhaustion and starvation attacks. Attacks targeting the network and transport layers have attracted considerable research attention [21,23,31]. Meanwhile, attacks have become more sophisticated and attackers have moved to higher layers of the protocol stack. Since 2010, resource exhaustion attacks that target the application layer have become more prevalent [1,17] than attacks at the network layer and transport layer.

In this paper, we present Radmin, a system for automatic *early* detection of application-level resource exhaustion and starvation attacks. By application-level attacks we refer to the classes of DoS attacks that utilize small, specially crafted, malicious inputs that cause uncontrolled resource consumption in victim applications. To this end, Radmin traces the resource consumption of a target program in both the user and kernel spaces (see Sect. 3), builds and executes multiple state machines that model the consumption of the target program.

The key observation is that attacks result in *abnormal* sequences of transitions between the different resource consumption levels of a program, when compared to normal conditions. By modeling the resource consumption levels as multiple realizations of a random variable, one can estimate a conditional distribution of the current consumption level given the history (context) of measurements. Consequently, the statistical properties of the resulting stochastic process can be used to detect anomalous sequences.[1]

Radmin operates in two phases: offline and online. In the offline phase, the monitored programs are executed on benign inputs, and Radmin builds multiple Probabilistic Finite Automata (PFA) models that capture the temporal and spatial information in the measurements. The PFA model is a finite state machine model with a probabilistic transition function (see Sect. 4). Both the time of holding a resource, and the amount used of that resource are mapped to states in the PFA, while changes in the states over the time are mapped to transitions.

In the online phase, Radmin executes the PFAs as shadow resource consumption state machines, where it uses the transition probabilities from the PFAs to detect anomalous consumption. Additionally, Radmin uses a heartbeat signal to *time out* transitions of the PFAs. Together with the transition probabilities, this enables Radmin to detect both exhaustion and starvation attacks.

Radmin aims at detecting attacks as early as possible, i.e., *before* resources are wasted either due to exhaustion or starvation. Radmin does *not* use any

---

[1] Unless stated otherwise, we use "measurements" and "sequences" interchangeably in the rest of this paper.

static resource consumption thresholds. Instead, the PFAs capture the transitions between the different consumption levels of different program states, and statistics of the PFAs are used to detect anomalies. The PFAs allow Radmin to *implicitly* map different program states, i.e., program behavior at some execution point given some input, to *dynamic* upper and lower resource consumption bounds.

We quantified the earliness of detection as the ratio of resources that Radmin can save, to the maximum amounts of resources that were consumed in benign conditions (see Sect. 5). This corresponds to the tightest *static* threshold that traditional defenses can set, without causing false alarms. Radmin has an advantage over all existing defenses that use static thresholds (see Sect. 7), since exhaustion and starvation attacks can evade those defenses. Exhaustion attacks can consume the highest amounts of resources possible, just below the static threshold [1,17]. Additionally, starvation attacks, by design, do not aim at directly consuming resources such as attacks that trigger deadlocks or livelocks [17].

To summarize, this study makes the following contributions:

- **Radmin.** A novel system that can detect both resource exhaustion and starvation attacks in their early stages. Radmin employs a novel detection algorithm that uses PFAs and a heartbeat signal to detect both exhaustion and starvation attacks. Radmin takes both temporal and spatial resource consumption information into account and adds minimal overhead.
- **Working Prototype**[2]. We implement a prototype that uses kernel event tracing and user space instrumentation to efficiently and accurately monitor resource consumption of target processes.
- **Evaluation.** We demonstrate the effectiveness of Radmin using a wide range of synthetic attacks against a number of common Linux programs. We show that Radmin can efficiently detect both types of anomalies, in their early stages, with low overhead and high accuracy.

The rest of the paper is organized as follows. Section 2 discusses the assumptions and threat model. Section 3 presents the technical details of Radmin and its implementation. Section 4 describes the models used in Radmin and the detection algorithm. Section 5 evaluates Radmin. Section 6 provides a discussion of different aspects of Radmin and possible improvements. We discuss related work in Sect. 7, and conclude in Sect. 8.

2   Assumptions and Threat Model

Radmin's main goal is early detection of application-level resource exhaustion and starvation, which may result in full or partial depletion of available resources (CPU time, memory, file descriptors, threads and processes) or in starvation and stalling. We assume that actors can be local or remote, with no privilege to overwrite system binaries or modify the kernel.

We consider the following types of exhaustion and starvation attacks. First, attacks that result in a sudden surprisingly high or low consumption of resources

---

[2] Source code available under GPLv3 at: https://github.com/melsabagh/radmin.

(e.g., an attacker controlled value that is passed to a `malloc` call). Second, attacks that result in atypical resource consumption sequences such as algorithmic and protocol-specific attacks that aim at maximizing (flattening) the amounts of consumed resources. Third, attacks that result in stalling of execution, including triggering livelocks or prolonged locking of resources.

Although, in our experiments, we considered only programs running on x86 Linux systems and following the Executable and Linkable Format (ELF), the proposed approach places no restrictions on the microarchitecture, the binary format, or the runtime environment.

3   System Architecture

The major components of Radmin are a kernel space tracing module (Kernel Tracer), a user space tracing library (User Tracer), and a daemon process (Guard) where the bulk of processing takes place. The tracing modules monitor and control a target program by binding checkpoints to events of interest, in the execution context of the target. Checkpoints are functions in the tracing modules that are called when an event of interest is triggered. Each checkpoint communicates measurements and control information to the Guard. We refer to a code site at which an event was triggered as a checkpoint site. Figure 1 shows the system architecture of Radmin.

Radmin takes a target program binary as input, and operates in two phases: offline and online. In the offline phase, Radmin instruments the target binary by injecting calls to the User Tracer into the binary, and writes the instrumented binary to disk. The instrumented program is then executed over benign inputs, while Radmin monitors its execution in both the user and kernel spaces, using the User Tracer and the Kernel Tracer modules, respectively. During that stage, the Guard receives the measurements from the tracers and learns multiple PFAs

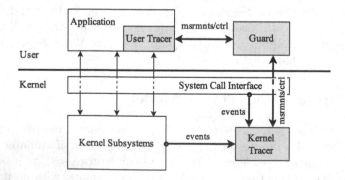

Fig. 1. Architecture of Radmin. The User Tracer, and Kernel Tracer, monitor and collect measurements from a target program by binding checkpoints to events of interest in both the user and kernel spaces. They send the measurements to the Guard, where the bulk of processing takes places.

Table 1. Checkpoint sites monitored by the tracing modules. Checkpoint sites used by the Kernel Tracer are given in the SystemTap probes notation.

Checkpoint Site	User/Kernel	Resource Type
`vm.brk`, `vm.mmap`, `vm.munmap`	Kernel	Memory
`kernel.do_sys_open`, `syscall.close`	Kernel	File descriptors
Recursive sites Sites that manipulate the stack pointer	User	Stack
`scheduler.ctxswitch`, `perf.sw.cpu_clock` Heartbeat every 500 ms	Kernel Both	CPU
`scheduler.wakeup_new`, `kprocess.exec_complete` `kprocess.exit`	Kernel	Child tasks

that capture the resource consumption behavior of the target program. Finally, in the online phase, the Guard executes the PFAs along with the target program, and raises an alarm if a deviation of the normal behavior is detected (see Sect. 4).

Each measurement is a vector of ⟨*consumed kernel time, consumed user time, consumed resource amount*⟩ associated with a resource type and a task[3] ID. Here, "consumed resource amount" accounts for the total amount of a resource that would be in consumption if the allocation or deallocation request is granted. We tracked parent-child task relationships by recording both the parent and current task IDs, in addition to the process ID. The measurement vectors accurately capture the resource consumption behavior of a process, as they map out both the sequences of resource consumption changes and the time for each change, which effectively captures both the temporal and spacial information in the resource consumption behavior of the process.

We developed the user space components in C/C++, using the Dyninst [4] library for static binary rewriting. The kernel tracer was developed using SystemTap [8]. A number of coordination scripts and a command line interface were also developed in Shell Script.

A summary of the checkpoint sites and the associated resource types is shown in Table 1, which we discuss in the following sections.

3.1   Kernel Tracer

The Kernel Tracer binds checkpoints to various kernel events by binding probes to the corresponding kernel tracepoints. Kernel tracepoints provide hooks to various points in the kernel code by calling functions (probes) that are provided at runtime by kernel modules [20]. Binding to the centralized, well-defined, kernel tracepoints associated with resource (de)allocation is more robust than attempting to enumerate and trace, from user space, *all* possible ways a program can

---

[3] Unless stated otherwise, we use "task" to indistinguishably refer to child processes and threads spawned by a monitored program.

(de)allocate resources through library calls. Additionally, kernel tracing gives maximum visibility into the target process, allows for low-penalty monitoring and control of the target.

The Kernel Tracer keeps track of task creation by binding to the kernel scheduler wakeup tracepoint (scheduler.wakeup_new), which is triggered when a task is being scheduled for the first time. It monitors task destruction by binding to the task exit tracepoint (kprocess.exit). The tracer also monitors processes overlaid by the exec call family by binding to the exec completion tracepoint (kprocess.exec_complete).

For memory monitoring, the Kernel Tracer install probes for the tracepoints that are triggered upon the allocation of contiguous memory (vm.brk), memory regions (vm.mmap), and the release of memory to the kernel (vm.munmap). For file monitoring, probes are installed for tracepoints that are triggered when file descriptors are allocated (kernel.do_sys_open) or released (syscall.close). For CPU monitoring, the Kernel Tracer keeps track of the consumed clock ticks by binding to the scheduler tracepoints that trigger when monitored tasks context switch (scheduler.ctxswitch), and when the kernel clock ticks (perf.sw.cpu_clock) inside the context of a monitored task. The reason for monitoring only those two events is to minimize the overhead of profiling the CPU time.

It is important to note that even though memory is monitored from the kernel module, user space processes can exhaust their stack space without interfacing with the kernel. Therefore, we decided to include additional checkpoints for monitoring the stack in user space.

3.2   User Tracer

The User Tracer consists of a user space library, where calls to that library are injected in the target binary at assembly sites of interest. The User Tracer is injected as follows. First, Radmin statically parses the input binary and extracts a Control Flow Graph (CFG) using the Dyninst ParseAPI library. It then analyzes the CFG to identify assembly sites that dynamically operate on the stack such as recursive calls (direct and indirect) and variable length arrays. Radmin injects calls to the tracer library at the marked sites in the binary, and saves the modified binary to disk.

To calculate the stack size consumed by recursive call sites, we first experimented with two options: (a) parse the process memory maps from /proc/pid/smaps, and (b) unwinding the stack. Both options proved unreliable. The obtained values from smaps were too coarse to reflect actual stack consumption. Unwinding the stack was very expensive, and required special arrangements at compilation time, such as the usage of frame pointers, that were not feasible to attain since we are directly working with compiled programs. Instead, Radmin implements a workaround by tagging (marking) the stack inside the *caller* function site, at a point directly before the recursive call, then calculating the distance from the entry point of the recursive *callee* function site to the tag. The tag is injected *only* in non-recursive caller function sites, which avoids mistakenly overwriting the tag due to indirect recursion.

Additionally, the User Tracer spawns a *heartbeat* thread that periodically consumes 1 clock tick then switches out. Consequently, the heartbeat tick is captured by the Kernel Tracer whenever the heartbeat thread is scheduled out. It delivers a clock signal from the monitored process to the Guard, which we use to detect starvation attacks by testing if the transitions between the PFA states have timed out (see Sect. 4).

3.3 Radmin Guard

Figure 2 shows the underlying architecture of the Guard. In the offline phase, the Guard learns a codebook over a finite alphabet Σ, and encodes the incoming measurements over Σ. Encoding the measurements serves two purposes: (1) it discretizes the continuous measurements, making them useful for estimating the conditional probabilities using the PFAs; and (2) it reduces the dimensionality (lossy compression) of the measurements by mapping them to a finite alphabet of a much smaller size. The Guard then builds multiple PFAs over the encoded sequences, one for each monitored resource type. In the online phase, the Guard encodes the incoming stream of measurements, executes the PFAs (per task, per resource type), runs the detection algorithm, and raises an alarm if an anomaly is detected. In our experiments, we only terminated the violating process. However, more advanced recovery can be used such as resource throttling or execution rollback [35].

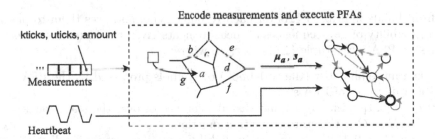

Fig. 2. Overview of Radmin Guard.

In the following section, we discuss in more depth how the Guard encodes the measurements, learns and executes the PFAs, and detects attacks.

4   Learning and Detection

4.1   Encoding

Radmin learns each codebook, used by the encoder, by running a k-means quantizer over the raw vectors of measurements, where $k = |\Sigma|$ is the number of desired codewords. In our implementation, we used k-means++ [10,13], which

is guaranteed to find a codebook (clusters) that is $O(\lg k)$-competitive with
the optimal k-means solution [13]. To build the codebook, each measurement
(consumed kernel and user time, and resource value) is treated as a point in
a three-dimensional space. k-means++ starts by selecting one center point at
random, from among all measurement points. Then, the distance $d(x)$ between
each measurement point x and the *nearest* center point is computed. Next, one
more center point is chosen with probability proportional to $d^2(x)$. This seeding process repeats until k centers are chosen. After which, standard k-means
clustering is performed resulting in k point clusters, the centers of which are
the codewords. We refer the interested reader to [13] for a detailed discussion of
k-means++.

Each codebook Σ (one codebook per resource type) stores an indexed list
of codewords. Each codeword σ is represented by three-dimensional centers μ_σ
and spreads s_σ, where each dimension corresponds to one dimension of the raw
measurement vector. The number $|\Sigma|$ of codewords is determined such that each
dimension gets at least 1 degree of freedom (level), constrained by a total of 64
degrees of freedom per codeword, i.e., $|\Sigma| \in [3 \dots 64]$. This setup allows at most
4 degrees of freedom per dimension (4^3 total), in case that *all* dimensions have
the same amount of variance. Finally, encoding is done by mapping a given measurement vector to the *index* of its nearest codeword. If a measurement vector
falls outside the coverage of all codewords, an empty codeword $\emptyset$ is returned.

4.2   Learning the PFAs

Radmin builds multiple PFAs for each resource type, and uses them to predict
the probability of new sequences of measurements given the history of measurements. A PFA is a 5-tuple $(\Sigma, Q, \pi, \tau, \gamma)$, where:

- Σ is a finite alphabet (the codebook) of symbols processed by the PFA.
- Q is a finite set of PFA states.
- $\pi \colon Q \to [0, 1]$ is the probability distribution vector over the start states.
- $\tau \colon Q \times \Sigma \to Q$ is the state transition function.
- $\gamma \colon Q \times \Sigma \to [0, 1]$ is the *emitted* probability function (predictive distribution)
  when making a transition.

The subclass of PFA used in Radmin is constructed from their equivalent
Probabilistic Suffix Tree (PST) model [30], which is a *bounded* variable-order
Markov model where the history length *varies* based on the context (statistical
information) of the subsequences of measurements, and the tree does not grow
beyond a given depth L. In other words, the PST captures all statistically significant *paths* between resource consumption levels (encoded measurements), where
the path length is at most L. In the construction of the PST, a subsequence of
encoded measurements $s \in \Sigma^*$ is added to the PST *only if*:

1. s has a significant prediction probability, i.e., there is some symbol $\sigma \in \Sigma$
   such that $P(\sigma|s) \geq \gamma_{min}$, where γ_{min} is the *minimum prediction probability*
   of the model.

2. And, s makes a contribution, i.e., the prediction probability is significantly *different* from the probability of observing σ after the parent node of s, i.e., $\frac{P(\sigma|s)}{P(\sigma|\texttt{Parent}(s))} \geq r_{min}$ or $\leq \frac{1}{r_{min}}$, where r_{min} is the minimum difference ratio.

The PFA model provides tight time and space guarantees since it has a bounded order, and *only* the current state and the transition symbol determine the next state. Those are desirable properties for Radmin since (1) we construct the PFAs without prior knowledge of the dependencies order (the length of statistical history in the measurements produced by target programs); and (2) we want to minimize the execution overhead of Radmin by maintaining a minimal amount of state-keeping information for the PFAs, and calculating the prediction probability for each measurement as fast as possible. For a sequence of n measurements, the PFA model allows us to compute the prediction probability in $O(n)$ time and $O(1)$ space. Due to space constraints, we refer the reader to [14,19,30] for detailed discussions of various construction algorithms.

In the subclass of PFA used in Radmin, each state $q \in Q$ has a unique ID corresponding to the subsequence captured by that state, and the PFA has a *single* start state q°, where $\pi(q^\circ) = 1$. Given a PFA M and a string of encoded measurements $s = s_1 \ldots s_l$, we walk M (for each $s_i \in s$) where each transition $q^{i+1} = \tau(q^i, s_i)$ emits the transition probability $\gamma(q^i, s_i)$. The *prediction probability* of s by M is given by:

$$P(s) = \prod_{i=1}^{l} \gamma\left(q^{i-1}, s_i\right). \tag{1}$$

For example, given the PFA in Fig. 3, the prediction probability of the sequence of encoded measurements "abca" is given by:

$$
\begin{aligned}
P(abca) &= \gamma(\phi, a) \times \gamma(a, b) \times \gamma(ab, c) \times \gamma(c, a) \\
&= 3/8 \times 2/3 \times 1 \times 1/2 \\
&= 1/8.
\end{aligned}
$$

Learning the PFAs, for a target program, requires running the target program over benign inputs. The following are some possible ways to handle this:

- **Dry runs and collected benign traffic.** Radmin can be trained through dry runs over benign inputs. This is typical in internal acceptance and pre-release testing. Radmin can also be trained using traffic that has already been processed by applications and shown to be benign. This is arguably the easiest approach to train Radmin if it is deployed to protect a web-server.
- **Functionality tests.** Radmin can be trained using positive functionality tests. Testing is integral to the software development lifecycle, and Radmin can integrate with the test harness at development time. The main disadvantage is the additional effort needed for integration and debugging.
- **Endusers.** Radmin can be trained by endusers. Even though this causes an increased risk of learning bad behavior, the resulting PFAs can be compared

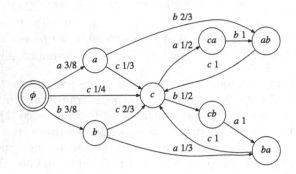

Fig. 3. Example of a PFA over the alphabet $\Sigma = \{a, b, c\}$. ϕ is the start state. Every edge is labeled by the transition symbol and transition probability. Transition symbols correspond to encoded measurements. Note, transition probabilities were rounded, and low probability transitions were removed for simplicity.

or averaged based on the type and privileges given to each class of users. The PFAs can be averaged, for example, based on the distance between their transition functions. Additionally, the learning algorithm can be modified such that the PFA learns new behavior if the new behavior is statistically similar to old behavior, by using statistics over the frequency of minimum probability transitions.

Once trained, Radmin can continue learning or be locked down, based on the system policy. For example, system administrators may desire to limit guest users to what Radmin already knows, while PFAs for sudoers can still adjust and add to what they learned. The PFAs can also be locked after some time of no change, which can be an effective strategy for preventing future attacks from compromised users.

4.3 Anomaly Detection

In the online phase, the Guard operates by encoding the received sequences over Σ, and executing the corresponding PFAs as shadow automata, where each sequence results in a transition in one or more PFA. In addition to the measurements, the Guard uses the received heartbeat signal to *timeout* the transitions of the PFAs.

Algorithm 1 outlines the detection algorithm. Radmin raises an alarm if *any* of the following conditions is satisfied:

1. A foreign symbol is detected (lines 2–4). In this case, the program is requesting some resource amount that is *not* within the spread of *any* of the codewords in the codebook. This typically indicates an overshoot or undershoot signal. A very common example is DoS attacks that use data poisoning to pass a huge value to a `malloc` call, resulting in immediate crashing.

Algorithm 1. AcceptMeasurement

input : Measurement vector $\mathbf{v}$, heartbeat signal t,
              PFA M, Current state $q_i \in M$, Current path probability p
output: Accept or Reject

1 $c \leftarrow \texttt{Encode}(\mathbf{v})$;

2 **if** $c = \emptyset$ **then**
3 | Reject   ▷ Foreign value
4 **end**

5 **if** $p \cdot \gamma(q_i, c) < \gamma_{min}(M)$ **then**
6 | Reject   ▷ Low probability transition or path
7 **end**

8 $timedout \leftarrow 1$;
9 **foreach** $outgoing\ edge\ e_i\ from\ q_i$ **do**
10 | **if** Timedout(e_i, t) **then**
11 | | $timedout \leftarrow timedout \wedge 0$;
12 | **end**
13 **end**
14 **if** $timedout = 1$ **then**
15 | Reject   ▷ All transitions timed out
16 **end**

17 Accept   ▷ take the transition

- $\gamma_{min}(M)$ is the minimum prediction probability of M.
- Timedout(e_i, t) tests if the time signal t lies outside the spread of the time dimensions of the codeword corresponding to transition e_i.

---

2. The program is requesting a transition that has a very low probability (lines 5–7). This case captures scenarios where attackers craft input that consumes (or locks) resources at program states that differ from benign runs. A common example is attacks that aim at maximizing the amounts of resources consumed by the program.
3. One or more PFAs time out (lines 8–16). In this case, the program has *not* transitioned to any of the next states within an acceptable time, with respect to one or more resource types. This, for example, could indicate the presence of a livelock.

The algorithm takes $O(|\Sigma|)$ time in the worst case, since the number of outgoing edges from any state is at most $|\Sigma|$.

5 Empirical Evaluation

We conducted a series of experiments to evaluate the effectiveness of Radmin. The first set of experiments evaluate the effectiveness of Radmin in detecting attacks that trigger uncontrolled resource consumption. The first experiment

uses a web server and a browser, with sufficient input coverage. We then conducted a second experiment using common Linux programs, and only using the
functionality tests that shipped with them as a representation of normal inputs.
Finally, we conducted a third experiment to evaluate the effectiveness of Radmin
in detecting starvation, using starvation and livelock cases that are common in
the literature.

We refer to test cases that trigger abnormal behavior by *positive* (malicious),
and those that do not by *negative* (benign). Each positive test case can either
be correctly detected or missed, giving a true positive (TP) or a false negative
(FN), respectively. Each negative test case can either be detected as such or
incorrectly detected as an attack, giving a true negative (TN) or a false positive
(FP), respectively.

5.1   Procedure and Metrics

For every target program, we proceeded as follows. We executed two thirds of the
negative test cases to collect benign measurements and build the PFAs. Then,
we executed the remaining one third to measure the false positive rate. Finally,
we executed all positive test cases to measure the detection rate and earliness of
the detection.

We trained the PFAs, and optimized their hyperparameters, using 5-fold
cross-validation (CV) over the training sequences (measurements from the two-
thirds of negative test cases used in training). For each resource type, we build
a PFA and select its hyperparameters from a cross product of all possible values
(see Appendix A). Training sequences were divided into five roughly equal segments. Each fold in the CV used the sequences in one such segment for testing,
and a concatenation of the rest for training. CV testing is performed by calculating the average log-loss of the prediction probability of sequences, given by
$-\frac{1}{T}\sum_{i=1}^{T} \lg P(s_i)$, where $P(s_i)$ is the prediction probability of test sequence s_i
and T is the total number of test sequences. This is done for each fold, resulting
in five average log-loss values per hyperparameters vector. Finally, the hyperparameter vector with the best median log-loss over the five folds is used for
building the PFA over the entire training sequences.

We used the following metrics in our evaluation: False Positive Rate (FPR),
True Positive Rate (TPR), and Earliness (Erl.). Earliness is calculated as the
percentage of the amount of resources that Radmin *saved* under an attack, to
the *maximum* resources used by negative runs. We use Erl. to quantify how quick
Radmin detected the attacks. For example, if a program consumed a maximum of
40 MB under benign conditions, and an attack consumed 30 MB before Radmin
detected it, the earliness of detecting the attack would be $\frac{40-30}{40} = 25\%$. Erl.
reaches its best value at 100 and its worst at 0.

For resource exhaustion detection, we used synthetic attacks (which we discuss in the following section). In the case of starvation and livelocks, we used
a number of common cases that appeared in prior livelock detection studies
[6,7,22,27]. Note, since the attacks aimed at exhausting system resources, they
were always detected once consumed resources more than the maximum of

benign runs. Therefore, Radmin always achieved a TPR of 1. The same applies to starvation and livelock test cases.

5.2   Synthetic Exhaustion Attacks

One approach to evaluate Radmin against resource exhaustion attacks would be to test it with several known attacks. While such an approach is common in the literature, it suffers from two major drawbacks. First, it is very challenging to identify real exhaustion attacks that exploit different weaknesses, different resource types, and exercise different code paths for each target program. That means the produced results could be biased, because the number of attacks would have little to no correlation with the *variety* of attacks that can be detected. Second, evaluating a defense system against only known attacks limits the scope of the evaluation and the results to *only* the known attacks. As we have seen in the past [15,25,29], this may establish a false sense of security against attacks that are possible in practice but have not yet been seen in the wild. Therefore, we decided against using the only few known attacks, and instead opted for generating synthetic attacks that resemble, and even surpass in sophistication and variety, the attacks seen in the wild. Our ultimate goal is to stress the system and find out its limits on a much richer set of attack entries.

To achieve that, we assume that the attacker has successfully identified some exhaustion vulnerability in the target program, and has crafted malicious input that successfully triggers the vulnerability. The nature of the exploit by which the vulnerability is triggered is not pertinent to our evaluation, since we are only concerned about the scope of the exploit (in our case, resource exhaustion) rather than its cause. Therefore, the malicious input that caused the exhaustion can be substituted by attack code that executes to the same effect at some vulnerable code site in the context of the process. Therefore, we generated synthetic attack datasets by separately collecting measurements for exhaustion attack samples, and injecting those measurements in the trace of negative (benign) measurements. The attack measurements are injected once per trace file at a randomly selected location. To account for differences in the total amount of the attacked resource at the injection point, we adjust the injected measurements by adding (summing) the last benign measurement vector of the same resource type to each attack vector in the rest of the trace. Being able to inject the attacks at *any* point in the trace allows us to accurately capture attacks seen in the wild, and even cover more sophisticated cases, including exhaustion attacks at very early or very late stages in the execution of the process. For example, exhaustion may be possible through attacker controlled environment variables that are used by dynamic libraries during process creation or termination.

The attack snippets were designed to enable the attacks to execute stealthily (by slowly harvesting resources) and avoid early detection. This is a worst-case scenario that is much more conservative than current attacks seen in the wild. For attacks that targeted memory, file descriptors, and tasks, we allocated 10 memory pages, 1 file descriptor, and 1 task per each iteration of the attack, respectively. For stack attacks, we used uncontrolled recursion where each stack frame is approximately 512 bytes. CPU attacks were infinite loops that compute sqrt and pow operations, where each iteration consumed 4 clock ticks on average. In general, the attacks covered the following CWE classes[4]: 400, 401, 404, 674, 770, 771, 772, 773, 774, 775, and 834. Note that the choice of the parameters does not bias our results because they do not, by themselves, alter the outcome of the attack or the pattern at which it occurs.

5.3 Resource Exhaustion Results

Experiment 1. The first experiment replayed a dataset of ∼60 K *unique* benign URLs of incoming HTTP GET requests to our school servers. We used the w3m browser on the xterm terminal, and the host domains were mirrored and served using apache. On xterm, w3m renders tables, frames, colors, links, and images. Radmin monitored both apache and w3m. In the case of apache, the monitoring was performed per each request handler.

Table 2 shows the results for this experiment. Radmin achieved a FPR of only 11 out of 10,000 requests in the case of w3m. For apache, the number further decreases to only 4 out of 10,000 requests. In the case of apache, Radmin saved more than 85 % of the file descriptors (the maximum of negative runs was 10 file descriptors). The memory saving for apache is only 5 %, which is due to the highly centralized distribution of memory consumption of apache during negative runs (1.19 GB mean, 1.22 GB median, 1.28 GB mode). In the case of w3m, the maximum saving achieved was 87 % for CPU time (maximum of benign runs was 56 ticks). Overall, the results show that Radmin can effectively save resources with very high accuracy.

Table 2. Detection performance for Experiment 1.

Prog	TP	FP	TN	FPR	%Erl. (mean ± std.)			
					CPU	File	Task	Mem
apache-2.4.7	6064	5	12167	0.0004	40 ± 23	85 ± 19	12 ± 10	05 ± 03
w3m-0.5.3	14245	20	18684	0.0011	87 ± 08	49 ± 40	25 ± 23	51 ± 27

Experiment 2. The second experiment used 10 common Linux programs. The functionality test packages that shipped with the programs were used to train Radmin. The major difference between this experiment and Experiment 1 is the lack of input coverage. In Experiment 1, we had sufficient input to build a profile of benign behavior with high confidence. In Experiment 2, the functionality tests were few, and some of the consumption subsequences were not significant to be learned by the model (see Sects. 4.2 and 5.1), resulting in a higher FPR.

---

[4] For details and code samples, please refer to the CWE project at http://cwe.mitre. org.

Table 3. Detection performance for Experiment 2.

Prog	TP	FP	TN	FPR	%Erl. (mean ± std.)			
					CPU	File	Task	Mem
cmp-3.3	9	0	14	0	98 ± 01	62 ± 32	-	54 ± 39
cpio-2.11	24	0	17	0	99 ± 01	49 ± 35	-	99 ± 03
diff-3.3	56	0	109	0	90 ± 01	65 ± 32	-	55 ± 41
gawk-4.0.1	223	2	389	0.0051	81 ± 03	50 ± 29	76 ± 15	28 ± 21
gzip-1.6	109	2	201	0.0099	77 ± 28	53 ± 35	-	39 ± 48
openssl-1.0.1f	380	0	594	0	94 ± 01	77 ± 25	-	28 ± 38
rhash-1.3.1	22	1	35	0.0278	47 ± 40	62 ± 33	-	57 ± 33
sed-4.2.2	108	6	194	0.0300	70 ± 30	62 ± 33	-	80 ± 16
tar-1.27.1	480	3	980	0.0031	98 ± 02	82 ± 24	25 ± 24	70 ± 19
wget-1.5	55	0	79	0	95 ± 01	79 ± 21	-	50 ± 32

The selected programs cover critical infrastructure services that are often utilized by desktop and web applications — namely, compression, text processing
(pattern matching and comparison), hashing, encryption, and remote downloads.
Attacks on compression programs can involve highly-recursive compressed files
(zip bombs), where decompressing the files would result in uncontrolled consumption of CPU time and file descriptors. Attacks on text processing applications typically use specially crafted regular expressions or data blocks that
result in CPU and memory exhaustion. Hashing and encryption are notorious
for CPU and memory exhaustion through specially crafted or erroneous messages. Download managers often suffer from exhaustion of file descriptors and
CPU time.

Table 3 shows the results of this experiment. As expected, the FPR is higher
than Experiment 1. Nevertheless, Radmin achieved a low FPR in most of the
cases. For earliness, Radmin achieved high savings for all resources, saving more
than 90 % of CPU time in most cases. This is mainly due to the high skewness
of the CPU time (in clock ticks) distribution of those programs (e.g., 374 mean,
120 median, and 1987 mode for tar). Overall, the results demonstrate the effectiveness of our approach, and the feasibility of using functionality tests to train
Radmin.

We emphasize that the FPR of Radmin is inverse proportional to input coverage. As higher input coverage is achieved, the PFA models used in Radmin
become more complete and the FPR decreases. We discuss this in Sect. 6.1, along
with ways to further increase the earliness of detection.

5.4   Starvation and Livelock Results

In this experiment, we used a number of common resource starvation samples
[6,7,22,27]. Simplified snippets of the test cases are provided in Appendix B.

The test cases spanned the two major resource starvation causes: (1) starvation due to prolonged holding of resources by other processes, and (2) livelocks due to busy-wait locking.

The first test case, `filelock`, is a multi-process program that manages exclusive access to resources by holding a lock on an external file. In this case, starvation can happen when a process holds the lock for a prolonged time, preventing other processes from making progress. In the second test case, `twolocks`, two threads try to acquire two locks, in reversed order, and release any acquired locks if the two locks were not both acquired. This is a fundamental livelock case due to unordered busy-wait locking of resources. Finally, the third test case is a rare bug in `sqlite`, when two or more threads fail, at the same time, to acquire a lock.

In this experiment, we ran each test case a 1000 times, and timed out each run after 20 s. Runs that finished before the 20 s deadline were considered negative samples, and runs that did not finish by the deadline were considered positive. Table 4 shows the results for this experiment.

Radmin detected the positive samples with high earliness. For `filelock`, Radmin saved 59 % of the maximum (8 ticks) of negative `filelock` runs. In the case of `twolocks`, Radmin saved more than 93 % of 12 ticks. For `sqlite`, Radmin saved 76 % of 19 clock ticks. Additionally, Radmin achieved 0 FPs and 0 FNs, indicating that none of the negative samples spent time in a PFA state more than the spread of the codewords corresponding to all outgoing transitions from that state. This means that the negative runs showed a set of similar timing behaviors that were fully learned by the model. Due to the external factors involved, such as internal parameters of the kernel scheduler, further studies are needed in order to reach a conclusive understanding of such behavior. Overall, the results show the promise of our approach, even in starvation situations that involved multiple processes and threads.

Table 4. Starvation detection performance.

Prog	TP	FN	FP	TN	TPR	FPR	%Erl. (mean $\pm$ std.)[†]
`filelock`	570	0	0	143	1	0	59 ± 26
`twolocks`	705	0	0	98	1	0	93 ± 04
`sqlite`	460	0	0	180	1	0	76 ± 13

5.5 Overhead

We report the overhead incurred by Radmin, in the online phase, for the programs used in our experiments as well as for the UnixBench [9] benchmark. We chose UnixBench because it tests various aspects of the system performance and uses well-understood and consistent benchmarks. Note, Radmin generated no false positives for UnixBench. All experiments were executed on machines running Ubuntu Server 14.04, quad-core 2.83 GHz (base) Intel Xeon X3363 processor and 8 GB of memory. The overhead is summarized in Fig. 4. Radmin incurred less than 16 % overhead, with mean overhead (geometric) of 3.1 %. The runtime overhead is more pronounced in CPU bound programs that were more frequently interrupted by the heartbeat thread. Overall, since Radmin avoids sampling, uses static rewriting, and selectively traces a particular set of events, the overhead incurred is significantly less than generic dynamic instrumentation and profiling tools (more than 200 % runtime increase [36,39]).

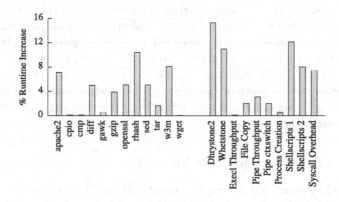

Fig. 4. Runtime overhead incurred by Radmin, in the online phase, for theprograms used in Experiments 1 and 2 (left), and the UnixBench benchmark (right).

6 Discussion and Limitations

6.1 Higher Accuracy and Earliness

The PFA model used in Radmin learns *only* the subsequences that have significant prediction probability (see Sect. 4.2), which means that some *benign but rare* subsequences may *not* be learned by the PFA. Such subsequences would be erroneously flagged as attacks (false positives), since they traverse low probability paths in the PFA. Although it is straightforward to force the inclusion of such subsequences in the PFA by adjusting the transition probabilities of their corresponding paths, we decided against doing so in order to give a clear and realistic view of the efficacy of the system. However, Radmin has the nice property that the FPR is inverse proportional to input coverage, i.e., as benign input coverage increases, the number of benign rare subsequences decreases and the PFAs become eventually complete.

Leveraging more information about the target process can allow Radmin to achieve higher earliness. For example, we can associate input values and attributes with paths in the PFAs. The challenges here are reaching a reliable model for representing and matching various input vectors, such as command line arguments, file IO, environment variables, and succinctly associating the input with paths in the PFAs. Given such a model, we can traverse the PFAs without actually executing the program. That would give the *near*-optimum earliness, since traversing the PFAs is much cheaper than running the target program itself. Also, one can synthesize static input filters from the PFAs. We plan to explore these ideas in more details in our future work.

6.2 Behavior Confinement

Radmin can be used to confine the behavior of processes to users rather than only detecting anomalous usage. Depending on how each user uses a program, Radmin will learn different behavior that is specific to the user. This can help defend unknown attacks by detecting anomalous, but valid, consumption of resources. Radmin can be easily extended to seal off paths of infrequent or undesired resource usage in protected programs by adjusting the conditional distributions in the PFAs. Similarly, Radmin can be used to construct a profile of specific behavioral aspects of target programs, such as sequences of executed events or files accessed. It can also confine the behavior of protocols, which is currently in our future work.

6.3 Attacker Knowledge of Radmin

Attackers could potentially attempt to employ Radmin to learn the PFAs for a target program, then craft input that maximizes the consumption of the program by steering the execution to paths of high resource consumption. We argue that such an attack is not a resource exhaustion attack per se. The reason is that if the PFA contains a path of high resource consumption, that means some typical benign input to the program does exercise that path, and the subsequences of the path are statistically significant. Therefore, the consumed resources cannot amount to an exhaustion, otherwise the input should have not been accepted (as benign) by the program in the first place. In this case, rate limiting techniques can be employed to throttle the rate of requests (whether benign or not) that exercise such paths. Nevertheless, Radmin still limits the potential of the attacks to cause *actual* resource exhaustion damage, by confining them to *only* high probability paths in the PFAs. In other words, the attacker has to identify a PFA path that exhibits high resource consumption, but such path might not be present in many of the programs.

6.4 Accuracy of Recursive Sites Identification

Dyninst ParseAPI uses recursive traversal parsing to construct the CFG, and employs heuristics to identify functions that are reached only through indirect flows. The resulting CFG may be incomplete, which might cause the User Tracer to miss some recursive code sites if the recursion is chained using indirect calls that ParseAPI could not resolve. While we argue that such construct is rare in practice, it can be addressed by dynamically tracing indirect calls using a shadow call stack, at the expense of increased runtime overhead. We plan on exploring this option as part of our future work.

6.5   Exhaustion Through Separate Runs

The current monitoring approach monitors consumption that lives only within individual processes. This does not allow detection of attacks that span multiple runs of some target program. For example, if a program creates a new file every time it runs, excessively running the program can exhaust the storage space. Extending Radmin to monitor consumption of system resources across separate runs is straightforward.

7   Related Work

Modern operating systems offer a number of threshold-based facilities to limit the resource consumption of processes (e.g., `setrlimit`, `ulimit`, `AppArmor`). Those facilities, while widely available, fall short of detecting or mitigating resource exhaustion and starvation attacks, for two reasons. First, the limits are set irrespective of the actual consumption of different program segments for different inputs or users. This enables attackers to exhaust resources by crafting input that consumes the highest possible resources, for prolonged times [17,18,26]. Second, the facilities cannot detect starvation attacks, since only an upper bound is used in detection.

Antunes et al. [12] proposed a system for testing server programs for exhaustion vulnerabilities. The system depended on a user supplied specifications of the server protocol, and automatically generated (fuzzed) test cases and launched them against the server. In [23], Groza et al. formalized DoS attacks using a set of protocol cost-based rules. Aiello et al. [11] formalized a set of specifications that a protocol has to meet to be resilient to DoS attacks. While the idea is promising, the specifications need explicit cost calculation of required computational resources, which is often not feasible in practice [37].

Chang et al. [16] proposed a static analysis system was for identifying source code sites that may result in uncontrolled CPU time and stack consumption. The authors used taint and control-dependency analysis to automatically identify high complexity control structures in the source code, whose execution can be influenced by untrusted input. Similar approaches that required manual source code annotation were also developed [24,38]. Radmin substantially differs from those systems in that it a dynamic solution, does not require access to the source code or any side information, and it covers different types of resources rather than only CPU and stack consumption.

In [33,34], Sekar et al. introduced approaches for detecting abnormal program behavior by building automata from system calls and executing the automata at runtime, flagging invalid transitions as anomalies. Mazeroff et al. [28] described methods for inferring and using probabilistic models for detecting anomalous sequences of system calls. They built a baseline model of sequences of system calls executed by benign programs, a test model of a target program, and compared the distance between the two models to detect anomalies. While approaches based on system call monitoring are easy to deploy, they are prone to mimicry attacks [25,29]. Additionally, they either completely ignore call arguments, which makes them inapplicable for exhaustion detection; or they model the arguments using point estimates, which is insufficient for early exhaustion detection.

Radmin is fundamentally different from all these systems in that it captures both program code and input dependencies of resource consumption, by modeling both the temporal and spatial information in resource consumption behavior of the program. Radmin detects both exhaustion and starvation attacks, and does not use static thresholds. By leveraging temporal information, Radmin also detects when target programs are starving of resources. Additionally, Radmin monitors the target programs by hooking into the kernel tracing facilities, which allows for maximum visibility into the target process and allows for low-penalty monitoring.

8   Conclusion

The paper presented Radmin, a system for early detection of resource exhaustion and starvation attacks. Unlike existing solutions, Radmin does not use static limits and utilizes both temporal and spatial resource usage information. Radmin reduces the monitoring overhead by hooking into kernel tracepoints. The Radmin user space library keeps track of stack usage used by target processes, and provides a heartbeat signal that enables Radmin to detect starvation. We showed that Radmin can detect resource exhaustion and starvation attacks with high earliness and accuracy, and low overhead. The implementation of Radmin was discussed along with its limitations and possible areas for improvements.

Acknowledgements. We thank Konstantinos Kolias, the anonymous reviewers, and our shepherd Andrei Sabelfeld for their insightful comments and suggestions. We thank Sharath Hiremagalore for technical assistance. This work is supported by the National Science Foundation Grant No. CNS 1421747 and II-NEW 1205453. Opinions, findings, conclusions, and recommendations expressed in this material are those of the authors and do not necessarily reflect the views of the NSF or the US Government.

A   PST Hyperparameters Grid

See Table 5.

Table 5. Hyperparameter values used in training the PSTs.

Param	Possible values	Chosen (median)
γ_{min}	$\{10^{-5}, 10^{-7}, 10^{-11}, 10^{-13}\}$	10^{-11}
r_{min}	$\{1.05\}$	1.05
L	$\{30, 40, 50, 60\}$	40

B   Starvation and Livelock Snippets

Listing 1.1. `filelock`

```
1  void filelock() {
2    fork()
3    ...
4    system("lockfile lockfile.lock");
5    ...
6    // do some work
7    ...
8    system("rm -f lockfile.lock");
9  }
```

Listing 1.2. `sqlite-lock`

```
1  void execute(char *s) {
2    ...
3    while (sqlite3_step(stmt) == SQLITE_BUSY)
4      sleep(1);
5    sqlite3_finalize(stmt);
6  }
7
8  void thread2() {
9    open_db();
10   execute("UPDATE foo SET ...");
11   ...
12 }
13
14 void thread1() {
15   open_db();
16   ...
17   sqlite3_prepare_v2("SELECT id FROM foo", ...);
18   sqlite3_step(stmt);
19   ...
20   start_thread(thread2, ...);
21   ...
22   // livelock if interrupted thread2
23   execute("INSERT INTO foo VALUES(100)");
24   ...
25 }
```

Listing 1.3. twolocks

```
1  void thread1() {
2    while (true) {
3      ...
4      lock lock_x(resource_x);
5      ...
6      try_lock lock_y(resource_y);
7      if (!lock_y) continue;
8      ...
9    }
10 }
11
12 void thread2() {
13   while (true) {
14     ...
15     lock lock_y(resource_y);
16     ...
17     try_lock lock_x(resource_x);
18     if (!lock_x) continue;
19     ...
20   }
21 }
```

References

1. Myths of DDoS attacks. http://blog.radware.com/security/2012/02/4-massive-myths-of-ddos/
2. Availability overrides security concerns. http://www.hrfuture.net/performance-and-productivity/availability-over-rides-cloud-security-concerns.php?Itemid=169
3. CWE-400: Uncontrolled resource consumption. http://cwe.mitre.org/data/definitions/400.html
4. Dyninst API. http://www.dyninst.org/dyninst
5. Mobile users favor productivity over security. http://www.infoworld.com/article/2686762/security/mobile-users-favor-productivity-over-security-as-they-should.html
6. Pthread livelock. http://www.paulbridger.com/livelock/
7. Sqlite livelock. http://www.mail-archive.com/sqlite-users@sqlite.org/msg54618.html
8. Systemtap. https://sourceware.org/systemtap/

9. Unixbench. https://github.com/kdlucas/byte-unixbench
10. Vectorized implementation of k-means++. https://github.com/michaelchughes/KMeansRex
11. Aiello, W., Bellovin, S.M., Blaze, M., Ioannidis, J., Reingold, O., Canetti, R., Keromytis, A.D.: Efficient, DoS-resistant, Secure Key Exchange for Internet Protocols. In: Proceedings of the 9th ACM Conference on Computer and Communications Security, pp. 48–58. CCS 2002. ACM, New York (2002)
12. Antunes, J., Neves, N.F., Veríssimo, P.J.: Detection and prediction of resource-exhaustion vulnerabilities. In: ISSRE 2008, 19th International Symposium on Software Reliability Engineering, 2008, pp. 87–96. IEEE (2008)
13. Arthur, D., Vassilvitskii, S.: k-means++: The advantages of careful seeding. In: Proceedings of the Eighteenth annual ACM-SIAM Symposium on Discrete Algorithms, pp. 1027–1035. Society for Industrial and Applied Mathematics (2007)
14. Bejerano, G., Yona, G.: Variations on probabilistic suffix trees: statistical modeling and prediction of protein families. Bioinformatics 17(1), 23–43 (2001)
15. Carlini, N., Wagner, D.: Rop is still dangerous: Breaking modern defenses. In: USENIX Security Symposium (2014)
16. Chang, R.M., Jiang, G., Ivancic, F., Sankaranarayanan, S., Shmatikov, V.: Inputs of coma: Static detection of denial-of-service vulnerabilities. In: Proceedings of the 22nd IEEE Computer Security Foundations Symposium, CSF 2009, Port Jefferson, New York, USA, July 8–10, 2009, pp. 186–199. IEEE Computer Society (2009)
17. Chee, W.O., Brennan, T.: Layer-7 DDoS (2010)
18. Crosby, S., Wallach, D.: Algorithmic DoS. In: Encyclopedia of Cryptography and Security, pp. 32–33. Springer (2011)
19. Dekel, O., Shalev-Shwartz, S., Singer, Y.: The power of selective memory: self-bounded learning of prediction suffix trees. In: Advances in Neural Information Processing Systems, pp. 345–352 (2004)
20. Desnoyers, M.: Using the linux kernel tracepoints. https://www.kernel.org/doc/Documentation/trace/tracepoints.txt
21. Fu, S.: Performance metric selection for autonomic anomaly detection on cloud computing systems. In: Global Telecommunications Conference (GLOBECOM 2011), 2011 IEEE, pp. 1–5. IEEE (2011)
22. Ganai, M.K.: Dynamic livelock analysis of multi-threaded programs. In: Qadeer, S., Tasiran, S. (eds.) RV 2012. LNCS, vol. 7687, pp. 3–18. Springer, Heidelberg (2013)
23. Groza, B., Minea, M.: Formal modelling and automatic detection of resource exhaustion attacks. In: Proceedings of the 6th ACM Symposium on Information, Computer and Communications Security, pp. 326–333. ACM (2011)
24. Gulavani, B.S., Gulwani, S.: A numerical abstract domain based on *expression abstraction* and *max operator* with application in timing analysis. In: Gupta, A., Malik, S. (eds.) CAV 2008. LNCS, vol. 5123, pp. 370–384. Springer, Heidelberg (2008)
25. Kayacik, H.G., et al.: Mimicry attacks demystified: What can attackers do to evade detection? In: Sixth Annual Conference on Privacy, Security and Trust, PST 2008, pp. 213–223. IEEE (2008)
26. Kostadinov, D.: Layer-7 DDoS attacks: detection and mitigation - infosec institute (2013). http://resources.infosecinstitute.com/layer-7-ddos-attacks-detection-mitigation/
27. Lin, Y., Kulkarni, S.S.: Automatic repair for multi-threaded programs with deadlock/livelock using maximum satisfiability. In: Proceedings of the 2014 International Symposium on Software Testing and Analysis, pp. 237–247. ACM (2014)

28. Mazeroff, G., Gregor, J., Thomason, M., Ford, R.: Probabilistic suffix models for API sequence analysis of Windows XP applications. Pattern Recogn. **41**(1), 90–101 (2008)
29. Parampalli, C., Sekar, R., Johnson, R.: A practical mimicry attack against powerful system-call monitors. In: Proceedings of the 2008 ACM symposium on Information, computer and communications security, pp. 156–167. ACM (2008)
30. Ron, D., Singer, Y., Tishby, N.: The power of amnesia: learning probabilistic automata with variable memory length. Mach. Learn. **25**(2–3), 117–149 (1996)
31. Rutar, N., Hollingsworth, J.: Data centric techniques for mapping performance measurements. In: 2011 IEEE International Symposium on Parallel and Distributed Processing Workshops and Phd Forum (IPDPSW), pp. 1274–1281, May 2011
32. Saltzer, J., Schroeder, M.: The protection of information in computer systems. Proc. IEEE **63**(9), 1278–1308 (1975)
33. Sekar, R., Bendre, M., Dhurjati, D., Bollineni, P.: A fast automaton-based method for detecting anomalous program behaviors. In: Proceedings 2001 IEEE Symposium on Security and Privacy, 2001, S&P 2001, pp. 144–155. IEEE (2001)
34. Sekar, R., Venkatakrishnan, V., Basu, S., Bhatkar, S., DuVarney, D.C.: Model-carrying code: a practical approach for safe execution of untrusted applications. ACM SIGOPS Operating Syst. Rev. **37**(5), 15–28 (2003)
35. Sidiroglou, S., Laadan, O., Perez, C., Viennot, N., Nieh, J., Keromytis, A.D.: Assure: automatic software self-healing using rescue points. ACM SIGARCH Comput. Archit. News **37**(1), 37–48 (2009)
36. Uh, G.R., Cohn, R., Yadavalli, B., Peri, R., Ayyagari, R.: Analyzing dynamic binary instrumentation overhead. In: Workshop on Binary Instrumentation and Application (2007)
37. Zargar, S.T., Joshi, J., Tipper, D.: A survey of defense mechanisms against distributed denial of service (DDoS) flooding attacks. IEEE Commun. Surv. Tutorials **15**(4), 2046–2069 (2013)
38. Zheng, L., Myers, A.C.: End-to-end availability policies and noninterference. In: 18th IEEE Workshop Computer Security Foundations, CSFW-18 2005, pp. 272–286. IEEE (2005)
39. Zinke, J.: System call tracing overhead. In: The International Linux System Technology Conference (Linux Kongress) (2009)

Towards Automatic Inference of Kernel Object Semantics from Binary Code

Junyuan Zeng and Zhiqiang Lin[✉]

The University of Texas at Dallas, 800 W. Campbell Rd,
Richardson, TX 75080, USA
{junyuan.zeng,zhiqiang.lin}@utdallas.edu

Abstract. This paper presents ARGOS, the first system that can automatically uncover the semantics of kernel objects directly from a kernel
binary. Based on the principle of data use reveals data semantics, it
starts from the execution of system calls (i.e., the user level application
interface) and exported kernel APIs (i.e., the kernel module development
interface), and automatically tracks how an instruction accesses the kernel object and assigns a bit-vector for each observed kernel object. This
bit-vector encodes which system call accesses the object and how the
object is accessed (e.g., read, write, create, destroy), from which we derive
the meaning of the kernel object based on a set of rules developed according to the general understanding of OS kernels. The experimental results
with Linux kernels show that ARGOS is able to recognize the semantics of
kernel objects of our interest, and can even directly pinpoint the important kernel data structures such as the process descriptor and memory
descriptor across different kernels. We have applied ARGOS to recognize
internal kernel functions by using the kernel objects we inferred, and we
demonstrate that with ARGOS we can build a more precise kernel event
tracking system by hooking these internal functions.

1 Introduction

Uncovering the semantics (i.e., the meanings) of kernel objects is important
to a wide range of security applications, such as virtual machine introspection
(VMI) [11], memory forensics (e.g., [13,24]), and kernel internal function inference. For example, knowing the meaning of the task_struct kernel object in
the Linux kernel can allow VMI tools to detect hidden processes by tracking the
creation and deletion of this data structure. In addition, knowing the semantics of task_struct enables security analysts to understand the set of functions
(e.g., the functions that are responsible for the creation, deletion, and traversal
of task_struct) that operate on this particular data structure.

However, uncovering the semantics of kernel objects is challenging for a couple of reasons. First, an OS kernel tends to have a large number of objects
(up to tens of thousands of dynamically created ones with hundreds of different
semantic types). It is difficult to associate the meanings to each kernel object
when given such a large number. Second, semantics are often related to meaning,

© Springer International Publishing Switzerland 2015
H. Bos et al. (Eds.): RAID 2015, LNCS 9404, pp. 538–561, 2015.
DOI: 10.1007/978-3-319-26362-5_25

which is very vague even to human beings. It is consequently difficult to precisely define semantics that can be reasoned by a machine. In light of these challenges, current practice is to merely rely on human beings to *manually* inspect kernel source code, kernel symbols, or kernel APIs to derive and annotate the semantics of the kernel objects.

To advance the state-of-the-art, this paper presents ARGOS, the first system for *A*utomatic *R*everse en*G*ineering of kernel *O*bject *S*emantics. To have a wider applicability and practicality, ARGOS works directly on the kernel binary code without looking at any kernel source code or debugging symbols. Similar to many other data structure (or network protocol) reverse engineering systems (e.g., [4,5,7,17,18,23]), it is based on the principle of *data uses tell data types*. Specifically, it uses a dynamic binary code analysis approach with the kernel binary code and the test suites as input, and outputs the semantics for each observed kernel object based on how the object is used.

There are two key insights behind ARGOS. One is that different kernel objects are usually accessed in different kernel execution contexts (otherwise, they should be classified into the same type of object). Consequently, we can use different kernel execution contexts to classify each object. The other is that we can further derive the semantics by using well-accepted public knowledge, such as the user level system call (syscall for brevity henceforth) interface, which is used when developing user level applications; the kernel level exported API interface, which is used when developing kernel modules; and the different memory operations such as memory read and write, which we can use to track and associate the execution context with each kernel object.

To address the challenge of precisely defining the kernel object semantics, we introduce a bit vector to each kernel object. This bit vector encodes which syscalls accessed the object (one syscall per bit), and using what kind of access (e.g., create, read, write, and destroy). In total, given an N number of syscalls for a given OS kernel, our bit vector has $4N$ bits in length for each distinctive kernel object. This $4N$ bit vector captures all the involved syscalls during the lifetime of a particular kernel object, which can be understood as a piece of information contributed by the accessing syscalls. Consequently, the meaning for each object is represented by the syscalls that accessed it and the different ways that it was accessed. Such information can uniquely represent each kernel object and its meaning.

Since syscalls are usually compatible across different kernels for the same OS family, this would allow ARGOS to directly reason about the kernel objects for a large set of OSes. More importantly, it would also allow ARGOS to interpret the meaning of kernel objects in a unified way. For instance, there could be different names for certain kernel objects even though they have the same semantic type. By using the same encoding across different OSes, we can uniformly identify the common important data structures such as process descriptor, memory descriptor, file descriptor, etc., regardless of their symbol names.

There will be many valuable applications enabled by ARGOS. One use case, as we will demonstrate in this paper, is that we can use the uncovered object semantics to infer the internal kernel functions. The knowledge of the internal kernel functions is extremely useful for kernel malware defense. Other applications include kernel data structure reverse engineering, virtual machine introspection, and memory forensics. In particular, ARGOS will complement the existing data structure reverse engineering work that previously only focused on recovering the syntactic information (i.e., the layout and shape) of data structures by adding the semantic information.

In summary, we make the following contributions in this paper:

- We present ARGOS, the first system that is able to automatically uncover the semantics of kernel objects from kernel binary code.
- We introduce a bit-vector representation to encode the kernel object semantics. Such representation separates the semantic encoding and semantic presentation, and makes ARGOS work for a variety of syscall compatible OSes.
- We have built a proof-of-concept prototype of ARGOS. Our evaluation results show that our system can directly recognize a number of important kernel data structures with correct semantics, even across different kernels.
- We show a new application by applying ARGOS to discover the internal kernel functions, and demonstrate that a better kernel event tracking system can be built by hooking these internal kernel functions.

2   System Overview

While the principle of *"data uses tell data types"* is simple, we still face several challenges when applying it for the reverse engineering of kernel object semantics. In this section, we walk through these challenges and give an overview of our system.

Challenges. Since ARGOS aims to uncover kernel object semantics, we have to first define what the semantics are and how a machine can represent and reason about them. Unfortunately, this is challenging not just because the semantics themselves are vague but also because it is hard to encode.

Second, where should we start from? Given kernel binary code, we can inspect all of its instructions (using static analysis) or the execution traces (using dynamic analysis). While static analysis is complete, it is often an over approximation and may lead to imprecise results. Dynamic analysis is the opposite. Therefore, we have to make a balance and select an appropriate approach.

Third, there are various ways and heuristics to perform the reverse engineering, e.g., blackbox approaches by feeding different inputs and observing the output differences, or whitebox approaches by comparing the instruction level differences (e.g., [14]). It is unclear which approach we should use, and we have to select an appropriate one for our problem.

Insights. To address these challenges, we propose the following key ideas to reverse engineer the kernel object semantics:

- **Starting from Well-Known Public Knowledge.** Similar to many other reverse engineering systems, ARGOS must start from a well-known knowledge base to infer unknown knowledge. For a given OS kernel, there are two pieces of well-known public knowledge: (1) the syscall specification that is used by application programmers when developing user level programs, and (2) the public exported kernel API specification that is used by kernel module programmers when developing kernel drivers. Therefore, in addition to the kernel test cases, ARGOS will take syscall and kernel API specifications as input to infer the kernel object semantics.
- **Using Execution Context Differencing.** In general, different kernel objects are usually accessed in different execution contexts (otherwise, they should be classified as the same object). Consequently, we can use different execution contexts to classify each object, and we call this approach execution context differencing.
- **Encoding the Semantics with a Bit-Vector.** To keep a record of the different accesses by different syscalls, we use a bit-vector associated with each distinctive object. This bit-vector captures which syscall, under what kind of context, accessed the object. Through this approach, we can separate the semantic encoding and presentation.

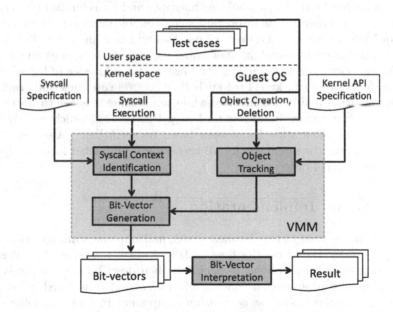

Fig. 1. An Overview of ARGOS.

Overview. To make ARGOS work with a variety of OS kernels, we design it atop a virtual machine monitor (VMM), through which we observe and trace each kernel instruction execution. As shown in Fig. 1, there are four key components

inside ARGOS: *object tracking, syscall context identification, bit-vector generation,* and *bit-vector interpretation.* They work as follows: starting from kernel
object creation, *object tracking* tracks the dynamically created kernel objects
and indexes them based on the calling context during object creation; whenever
there is an access, which is defined as a 4-tuple (create, read, write, destroy),
syscall context identification resolves the current context and tracks which syscall
is accessing the object and under what kind of context. This information will be
recorded by *bit-vector generation* during the lifetime for each observed object.
Finally, we use *bit-vector interpretation* to interpret the final semantics based on
the encoded bit vector.

Scope and Assumptions. We focus on the reverse engineering of the object
semantics of the OS kernels that are executed atop the 32-bit x86 architecture.
To validate our experimental results with the ground truth, we use open source
Linux kernels as the testing software. Note that even though the source code of
Linux kernel is open, it is actually non-trivial to retrieve the semantic information for each kernel object. Currently, we use a manual approach to reconstruct
the semantic knowledge based on our best understanding of Linux kernels, and
compare with the results generated by ARGOS.

While we can integrate other techniques (e.g., REWARDS [18] and Howard
[23]) to recover the kernel object syntax (i.e., the fields and layout information),
we treat each kernel object as a whole in this paper and focus on the uncovering of
the kernel object semantics, an important step to enable many other applications.

In addition, we assume the users of our tool will provide a syscall specification that includes each syscall number and syscall name, as well as an exported
kernel API specification that includes the instruction addresses of kernel object
allocation functions (e.g., `kmalloc`) such that ARGOS can hook and track kernel object creation and deletion. Meanwhile, since ARGOS needs to watch each
instruction execution, we build our tool atop PEMU [26], which is a dynamic
binary code instrumentation framework based on QEMU [2]. Also, we do not
attempt to uncover the semantics for all kernel data, but rather focus on dynamically accessed kernel objects.

3   Design and Implementation

In this section, we present the detailed design and implementation of each component of ARGOS. Based on the flow of how ARGOS works, we first describe
how we track each kernel object in Sect. 3.1; then describe how we resolve the
corresponding syscall execution context when an object is accessed in Sect. 3.2;
next, we present the *bit-vector generation* component in Sect. 3.3, followed by
the *bit-vector interpretation* component in Sect. 3.4.

3.1   Object Tracking

Since the key idea of ARGOS is based on the object use to infer the object semantics
and kernel objects are usually dynamically allocated, we have to (1) track object

allocation/deallocation, (2) track the size of each object, and (3) index each object such that when given a dynamic access of the kernel object, we are able to know to which object the address belongs. In the following, we describe how we achieve these goals.

(1). Tracking the Object Allocation and Deallocation. A widely used approach to track a kernel object is to hook its creation and deletion APIs. These APIs are usually publicly accessible for kernel developers (even in closed source OSes such as Microsoft Windows). In our implementation, we just hook the kernel object allocation and deallocation functions such as kmem_cache_alloc/kmem_cache_free, kmalloc/kfree, vmalloc/vfree at the VMM layer for the Linux kernel. To support efficient look up, we use a red-black (RB) tree indexed by their starting address and size to track the allocated object.

(2). Tracking the Object Size. Unlike at user level, we can intercept the argument to malloc-family functions to identify the object size (while this is still true for kmalloc), but there is no size argument to many other kernel object allocation functions (e.g., kmem_cache_alloc). The reason is that the kernel memory allocator (e.g., the slab or slub allocator) usually caches similar size type objects and organizes them into clusters. For example, when allocating a kernel object (e.g., task_struct), kernel developers will just pass a flag argument and a pointer argument that points to kmem_cache structure, which is the descriptor of the cluster that contains the objects with similar size. This descriptor is created by the kernel API kmem_cache_create and the size of the object is passed to this descriptor's creation function. Then one may wonder why the size argument passed to kmem_cache_create cannot be used as the object size. This is because this size is actually an over approximation and the size of the real kernel object can be smaller than the one specified in the descriptor. Meanwhile, the pointer argument of kmem_cache_alloc can point to the kmem_cache that has entirely different types of objects. For instance, our trace with the slab allocator in Linux 2.6.32 shows that the kernel objects of the file and vfs_mount data structures are stored in the same kmem_cache even though they have different types and different sizes.

Therefore, we have to look for new techniques to recognize the kernel object size. Since we use dynamic analysis, we can in fact track the allocated object size at run time based on the object use. While this is still an approximate approach, it is at least sound and we will not make any mistakes when determining to which object a given virtual address belongs. Specifically, to access any dynamically created object, there must be a base address. Right after executing a kernel object allocation function, a base address is returned, which we shall refer to as v. Any further access to the field of the object must start from v, or the propagation of v. As such, we can infer the object size by monitoring the instruction execution and checking whether there is any memory address that is derived from the virtual address v as well as its propagation.

Without loss of generality, as shown in Fig. 2(a), when an object O_i is created, we will have its starting (i.e., base) address v (suppose it is stored in eax). To access the fields of O_i, there must be a data arithmetic operation of the base pointer (or its derivations), and we can therefore infer the size based on the offset of the access. For instance, as shown in Fig. 2(a), assume the kernel uses eax+m

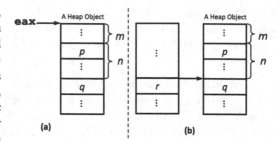

Fig. 2. An Example Illustrating How to Track the Object Size. Note that Taint (eax) = Taint (p) = Taint (q) = Taint (*r) = T_i, and Taint (r) = T_j.

to access a field p of O_i, then we can get the size of O_i as $m + 4$ from this particular operation. Then, assume the kernel inserts O_i to some other data structures (e.g., a linked list); it must compute a dereferenced address of O_i such that traversing other objects can reach O_i. Assume this address is q, which is computed from $p + n$, then we can infer the $Size(O_i)$ as $(m + n + 4)$ according to the execution of these accesses. Next, assume we assign the address of q to r (Fig. 2(b)). Then all future dereferences will use $*r$ as a base address to access O_i (instead of v, the starting address), and we can similarly derive the size based on the pointer arithmetic. Note that when dereferencing a kernel object, the kernel can start from its middle instead of the starting address, which is very common in both the Windows and Linux kernels.

Therefore, in order to resolve the size, we have to know that eax, p, q, and $*r$ actually all reference the same allocated object (i.e., they belong to the same closure). If we assign a unique taint tag for each O_i using T_i, namely Taint(eax) = Taint(v) = T_i, then we can propagate T_i to $p, q, *r$ based on the pointer data movement and arithmetic operations. Thus, this eventually leads to a dynamic taint analysis [19] approach to decide whether eax, p, q, and $*r$ belong to the same T_i. Since taint analysis is a well established approach, we omit its details for brevity in this paper. Basically, in our taint analysis, we capture how a memory access address is computed from the base address v and its propagations (e.g., eax), from which we resolve the object size. This size is the one being observed at run time.

Meanwhile, kernel objects usually point to each other. Looking at the point-to graph can facilitate the inference of the important kernel data structures based on their relations. Since we have assigned a unique taint tag T_i for each kernel object, we can now track the dependence between kernel objects by looking at their taint tags during memory write operations. Specifically, whenever there is a memory write, we will check the taint tags of both its source and destination operand. If they belong to our tracked objects, we will connect these two objects using their point-to relation and store this information in their static object types. The particular offset for the two objects of the point-to relation will also be resolved. This information, namely object O_i at offset k points to O_j at offset l, will be recorded.

(3). Indexing the Dynamic Kernel Objects with Static Representation. Since kernel data structure semantics are static attributes, they should be applied to all of the same type of a kernel object. However, when we use dynamic analysis, what we observe is instances of kernel objects. Therefore, we need to translate these dynamic instances into static representations such that our bit-vector can just associate with the static representation instead of the dynamic object instances.

In general, there are two basic approaches when converting dynamic object instances into static forms: (1) using the concatenation of all the call-site addresses from the top callers to the callee, or (2) using the program counter of the instruction that calls a kernel object allocation function. The first approach can capture all the distinctive object allocations, but it may over classify the object types since the same type can be allocated in different program calling contexts. While the second approach mitigates this problem, it cannot handle the case where an allocation function is wrapped. Therefore, the solution is always domain-specific and somewhere in-between of these two approaches.

In our design, we adopt the second approach because we observe that a single kernel object can often be allocated in different calling contexts (e.g., we observe that the `task_struct` in Linux can be allocated in syscalls such as `vfork`, `clone`, etc.). If we assign the call-site chain as the static type, we could over classify the kernel object (having an N-to-one mapping). Also, our analysis with a ground-truth labeled Linux kernel 2.6.32 shows that when we use the call site PC of the allocation function (denoted as $PC_{kmalloc}$) to assign the static type, 80.3 % of the kernel objects have a one-to-one mapping. In contrast, when we tried the call-site chain approach, we found 97.5 % of the objects had N-to-one mapping. Therefore, eventually, in our current design, we decided to take the second approach.

Summary. In short, our *object tracking* component will track the lifetime of the dynamically allocated object using an RB-tree, which we call an RB_{type} tree. It is used to store $< v, s, T_i, PC_{kmalloc} >$, which is indexed by v, where v is the starting address, s is the current resolved size (subject to be updated during run-time), T_i is the taint tag for O_i, and $PC_{kmalloc}$ is the static type of the allocated object. The reason to use the RB_{type}-tree is to speed up locating the static type (encoded by $PC_{kmalloc}$) when given a virtual address, and we maintain an RB_{type}-tree to track these dynamically allocated objects. The basic algorithm is to check whether a given virtual address α falls into $[v, v+s]$ of our RB-tree node; if so, we return its $PC_{kmalloc}$ as the type. Also, we maintain a hash table (HT) that uses $PC_{kmalloc}$ as the index key. This HT will be used to store the bit-vectors of the kernel objects based on their assigned static types as well as the point-to relations between objects.

3.2   Syscall Context Identification

To associate the execution context with each dynamically accessed kernel object, we must resolve the execution context when an instruction is accessing our monitored object. The execution context in this paper is defined as *the information that captures how and when a piece of data gets accessed*. More specifically, as our starting point of the known knowledge is the syscall, we need to first resolve which syscall is currently accessing a given piece of data. Also, since we need to capture the different data accesses in order to identify the internal functions (e.g., the internal function that creates the process descriptor structure), we have to further classify the data access into different categories such as whether it is a read access or a write access.

Precisely Identifying the Syscall Execution Context. When a given kernel object is accessed, we need to first determine which syscall is accessing it. Since an execution context must involve a stack (to track the return addresses for instance), we can use each kernel stack to differentiate each execution context. Whenever there is a kernel stack change, there must be an execution context change.

Then how many kernel stacks are inside an OS kernel at any given moment? This depends on how many user level processes and kernel level threads are running. In particular, each user level process (including user level threads) will have a corresponding kernel stack. This kernel stack is used to store the local variables and return addresses when a particular syscall is executed inside the kernel. Besides the kernel stack for user level processes to execute syscalls, there are also kernel threads that are responsible for handling background tasks such as asynchronous event daemons (e.g., `ksoftirqd`) or worker threads (e.g., `pdflush`, which flushes dirty pages from the page cache). The difference between kernel threads and user level processes is that kernel threads do not have any user level process context and will not use the syscall interface to request kernel services (instead they can directly access all kernel functions and data structures).

Therefore, by tracking each syscall entry and exit (e.g., `sysenter`/`sysexit`, `int 0x80`/`iret`) and stack change (e.g., `mov stack_pointer, %esp`), we can identify the syscall execution context, as demonstrated in our earlier work VMST [10]. Note that the execution of the top half of an interrupt handler may use the current process' or kernel thread's kernel stack, and we have to exclude this interrupt handler's execution context. Fortunately, the starting of the interrupt handler's execution can be observed by our VMM, and these handlers always exit via `iret`. As such, we can precisely identify the interrupt execution contexts and exclude them from the syscall context.

To resolve to which syscall the current execution context belongs, we will track the syscall number based on the `eax` value when the syscall traps to the kernel for this particular process. The corresponding process is indexed by the base address of each kernel stack (not the CR3 approach as suggested by Antfarm [15] because threads can share the same CR3). We use the 19 most significant bits (MSB) of the kernel `esp`, i.e., the base address of the stack pointer (note that the size of Linux kernel stack is $8192 = 2^{13}$ bytes), to uniquely identify a process. The base address of the stack pointer is computed by monitoring the memory write to the kernel esp. We also use an RB-tree, which we call RB_{sys} tree, to dynamically keep the MSB19(esp) and the syscall number from eax for this process such that we can quickly return the syscall number when given a kernel esp.

Tracking Syscall Arguments of Interest. The majority of syscalls are designed for a single semantic goal such as to return a pid (getpid) or to close a file descriptor. However, there are syscalls that have rich semantics—namely having different behaviors according to their arguments. One such a syscall is sys_socketcall, which is a common kernel entry point for the socket syscall. Its detailed argument decides which particular socket function to be executed (e.g., socket, bind, listen, setsockopt, etc.). Therefore, we have to parse its arguments and associate the arguments to the syscall context such that we can infer the exercised kernel object semantics under this syscall.

Besides sys_socketcall, in which we have to track its arguments, we find two other syscalls (sys_clone and sys_ unshare) that also have strong argument controlled behavior. In particular, sys_clone can associate certain important kernel objects with the new child process when certain flags are set (e.g., CLONE_FS flag will make the caller and the child process share the same file system information), and sys_unshare can reverse the effect of sys_clone by disassociating parts of the process execution context (e.g., when CLONE_FS is set, it will unshare file system attributes such that the calling process no longer shares its root directory, current directory, or umask attributes with any other processes). Therefore, we will track these three syscalls, and associate their arguments with the exercised kernel objects, because these arguments specify the distinctive kernel behavior of the corresponding syscall.

3.3 Bit-Vector Generation

Having tracked all dynamically allocated objects that are executed under each specific syscall execution context, we will then attach this context using a bit-vector to the object type we resolved in *object tracking*. The length of our bit-vector is $4*N$ bits, where N is the number of syscalls provided by the guest OS kernel. Meanwhile, for each syscall, we will track and assign the following bits in the bit-vector to 1 or 0 based on:

- C-**bit**: whether this syscall created the object;
- R-**bit**: whether this syscall read the object;
- W-**bit**: whether this syscall wrote the object;
- D-**bit**: whether this syscall destroyed the object.

These bits together form an entropy of how a syscall uses the object, from which we can derive the meanings.

Since our *bit-vector generation* is the core component in our system and it connects the *object tracking* and *syscall context identification* components, in the following we present a detailed algorithm to illustrate how it exactly works. At a high level, we use an online algorithm to resolve the object's static type, syscall context, and different ways of access, and generate the bit vector, which is stored in a hash table indexed by the object's static type (i.e., $PC_{kmalloc}$). As presented in Algorithm 1, each kernel instruction execution is monitored in order to resolve and generate our bit vector.

In particular, before beginning our analysis, we will first create a hash table (HT) at line 2 that stores the bit vector of the accessed kernel object. Then we iterate through each kernel instruction (line 3–43). We first check whether the current instruction involves pointer data arithmetic (line 5–6), if so, we will track the dependences of the involved pointers and infer their sizes. Next, we check if the instruction is `sysenter/int0x80` (line 8–10). If so, we update the syscall context tracking data structure RB_{sys}-tree that stores the syscall number for the current process, which is determined by variable Ex. This Ex is a global variable, which keeps the MSB19(esp) and gets updated when kernel stack switches (line 13–15). The node of the

---

Algorithm 1: Bit-vector Generation

```
1  Procedure BvG () :
   Output: Hash Table HT that contains bit vector of the
   observed kernel object type and their point-to relations.
2  HT ← CreatSemanticTypeBitVectorHashTable() ;
3  for each executed instruction I do
4      op ← Operand(I);
5      if PointerArithmeticOrPropagation(op) then
6          └ TaintOPAndUpdateTrackedSize(op);
7      switch I do
8          case sysenter/int0x80
9              │ UpdateRBsysNode(Ex, eax)  ;
10             └ // Ex represents the process context
11         case syscall(exit_group) SUCCESS
12             └ RemoveRBsysNode(Ex)
13         case mov op, esp
14             │ Ex ← MSB19(esp);
15             └ InsertRBsysNodeIfNotExist(Ex)
16         case PC_kmalloc: eax ← call {kmalloc}
17             │ t ← PC_kmalloc;
18             │ T_i ← GetUniqueTaintTag();
19             │ InsertRBtypeNode(eax, 4, T_i, t);
20             │ InsertHTifNotExist(t);
21             │ if I ∈ SyscallContext then
22             │     sysnum ← QueryRBsysNum(Ex);
23             └     └ HT[t][sysnum][C-bit] ← 1;
24         case PC_kfree: call {kfree}(v)
25             │ t ← QueryRBtype(v);
26             │ RemoveRBtypeNode(v);
27             │ if I ∈ SyscallContext then
28             │     sysnum ← QueryRBsysNum(Ex);
29             └     └ HT[t][sysnum][D-bit] ← 1;
30         case MemoryAccess(op)
31             │ if I ∉ SyscallContext then
32             │     └ continue;
33             │ switch access do
34             │     src ← Source(op);
35             │     t ← QueryRBtype(src);
36             │     sysnum ← QueryRBsysNum(Ex);
37             │ case READ
38             │     └ HT[t][sysnum][R-bit] ← 1;
39             │ case WRITE
40             │     │ HT[t][sysnum][W-bit] ← 1;
41             │     │ dst ← Destination(op);
42             │     │ TrackingObjectPointToRelation(HT,
43             └     └                           src, dst);
44 return HT;
```

RB_{sys}-tree will be deleted when the process exits (line 11–12).

Next, when the kernel execution is to create an object (line 16–23), we then insert the created instance into the RB_{type}-tree that keeps the type and size information about the object (line 19). We also insert the static type assigned for this object (namely $PC_{kmalloc}$) into the HT if this type has not been inserted before (line 20). In addition, we update the bit vector with a C-bit for this particular object if the object is created under the syscall execution context (line 21–23), neither in top-half nor bottom-half. Similarly, we remove the dynamic instance from the RB_{type}-tree, and update the D-bit in the corresponding HT entry if the necessary, when the object is deallocated (line 24–29). Then, if the instruction is accessing the memory address that belongs to our tracked kernel object (line 30) and is under a syscall execution context (line 31–42), we update the corresponding R-bit and W-bit based on the access (line 38, 40). We also track the object point-to relation if there is a memory write that involves two monitored kernel objects (line 42). All the involved data structures are presented in Fig. 3.

3.4 Bit-Vector Interpretation

Having generated the bit-vector for each observed object type, ARGOS is then ready to finally output the meanings (i.e., semantics) of the observed objects. Since our bit-vector has $4*N$ bits in length, it contains a very large amount of information, sufficiently distinguishing each different semantic type. In particular, our bit-vector captures how a syscall accessed the object during the life time of the object. Such an access denotes the connection between the object and the syscall. At a high level, we can view the bit-vector

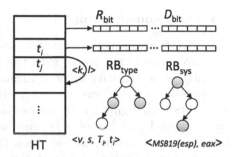

Fig. 3. The Data Structures Used in ARGOS.

as representing (1) which of the syscalls have contributed to the meaning of the object, (2) how these syscalls contributed (recorded in our R, W, C, D-bits). Given such rich information, there could be many different approaches to derive the semantics and interpret the meanings.

One possible approach is to simply transform the bit-vector to a large integer value (using a deterministic algorithm), and map the integer value to a kernel object acquired from the ground truth. If there is always a one-to-one mapping, then this approach would work. For instance, from the general OS kernel knowledge, we know that a process descriptor (i.e., task_struct in Linux), is usually the root of the kernel data structure when accessing all other objects inside OS kernel for a particular process. Many of the syscalls would have accessed this object. Therefore, a process descriptor would have a larger value than many other data structures when translating these bits into integers. Based on such values, we could possibly determine the semantic types.

In our current ARGOS design, we present another simple approach: instead of checking all bit-vectors (normalizing them to an integer value), we check certain syscalls for the object of our interest from the bit-vector, by using the manually derived rules based on general syscall and kernel knowledge. Again, taking task_struct as an example, we know that this data structure must be created by a fork-family syscall, and destroyed by a exit_group syscall. When there is a getpid syscall executed, it must first fetch this data structure, from which to traverse other data structures to reach the pid field. Therefore, we can develop data structure specific rules to derive the semantics by checking the bit-vectors. We have developed a number of such rules to recognize the important kernel data structures as presented in Sect. 4.

4   Evaluation

In this section, we present how we evaluate ARGOS to uncover the object semantics. We first describe how we set up the experiment in Sect. 4.1, and then present our detailed results in Sect. 4.2.

4.1   Experiment Setup

Since we focus on the reverse engineering of the kernel object semantics, we have to compare our result with the ground truth. To this end, we took two recently released Linux kernels: Linux-2.6.32 and Linux-3.2.58, running in debian-6.0 and debian-7, respectively, as the guest OS for ARGOS to test. Each guest OS is configured with 2G physical memory. The main reason to use the open source Linux kernel is because we can have the ground truth. Therefore, in our object tracking, we also keep the truth type when the object is created in our object tracking. The truth type is acquired through a manual analysis of the corresponding kernel source code. The host OS is ubuntu-12.04 with kernel 3.5.0-51-generic. The evaluation was performed on a machine with an Intel Core i-7 CPU and 8 GB physical memory.

An end user needs to provide three pieces of information to ARGOS as input: a syscall specification, a kernel API specification, and the test cases.

- **Syscall Specification.** Basically, it just needs the syscall number and the corresponding syscall name. In addition, it also requires an understanding of the arguments and corresponding semantic behavior of three syscalls (sys_socketcall, sys_clone and sys_unshare), which are used to derive the semantics of the objects accessed in these syscalls.
- **Kernel API Specification.** To track the dynamic object creation and deletion, we need the Kernel API specification of the kmalloc family of functions. Similar to the syscall specification, we just need the name of each function, its starting virtual address, and its arguments such that we can intercept these function executions.
- **Test Cases.** ARGOS is a dynamic analysis based system. We need to drive the kernel execution through running the test cases. Ideally, we would like to use existing test cases. To this end, we collected several user level benchmarks including ltp-20140115 and lmbench-2alpha8. We also used all the test cases from the Linux-test-project [1].

4.2   Detailed Result

In total, it took ARGOS 14 hours[1] each to run all the test programs (the most time consuming part is the LTP test cases) for the testing guest OS, with a peak memory overhead of 4.5G at the host level for the 2G guest OS. Specifically, we

---

[1] Note that ARGOS is an *automated* offline system. Performance is not a big issue as long as we produce the result in a reasonable amount of time.

observed 105 static types for `Linux-2.6.32`, and 125 for `Linux-3.2.58`. Due to space limitations, we cannot present the detailed representation of the bit-vectors for all these objects, and instead we just present the statistics of their bit vectors.

We first categorized the syscalls into groups based on the different type of resources (e.g., processes, files, memory, etc.) that the syscalls aim to manage. The classification result is presented in Table 1. We can notice that these two kernels do not have the exact same number of syscalls, and `Linux-3.2.58` introduces 11 additional syscalls to `Linux-2.6.32`. Consequently, the length of their bit-vectors are different. We present a number of bit-vector statistics in the last 10 columns of Table 3. The statistics of these bit vectors show the distributions of the sycalls that have read and write access of each corresponding object. For instance, for the `pid` data structure presented in the first row, its $P=25$ means there are 25 process related syscalls that have accessed this object.

Table 1. Syscall Classification

Syscall Type	Short Name	#Syscalls	
		Linux-2.6.32	Linux-3.2.58
Process	P	90	92
File	F	152	156
Memory	M	19	21
Time	T	13	13
Signal	G	25	25
Security	S	3	3
Network	N	2	4
IPC	I	7	7
Module	D	4	4
Other	O	3	3
Total	-	317	328

Table 2. The Inference Rules We Developed to Recognize The Semantics of Important Kernel Data Structures.

Rule Num	Detailed Rules	Data Structure
I	sys_clone[C] ∩ sys_getpid[R]	task_struct, pid
II	((sys_clone[C] - sys_vfork[C]) ∩ sys_brk[RW]) ∩ sys_munmap[D]	vm_area_struct
III	((sys_clone[C] - sys_vfork[C]) ∩ sys_brk[RW]) - sys_munmap[D]	mm_struct
IV	sys_open[C] ∩ sys_lseek[W] ∩ sys_dup[R]	file
V	sys_clone[C] - sys_clone[C](CLONE_FS)	fs_struct
VI	sys_clone[C] - sys_clone[C](CLONE_FILES)	files_struct
VII	sys_mount[C] ∩ sys_umount[D]	vfs_mount
VIII	sys_socketcall[C](SYS_SOCKET) ∩ sys_socketcall[W] (SYS_SETSOCKOPT)	sock
IX	sys_clone[C] - sys_clone[C](CLONE_SIGHAND)	sighand_struct
X	sys_capget[R] ∩ sys_capset[W]	credential

Next, we present how we would discover the semantics of each kernel object. As discussed in Sect. 3.4, there could be several different ways of identifying the kernel objects and their semantics. In the following, we demonstrate a general way of identifying the kernel objects that are of security interest (such as process descriptor, memory descriptor, etc.) by manually developing rules based on the semantics of the syscalls (which is generally known to the public) and also using execution context differencing. In total we developed 10 rules, which are presented in Table 2.

We tested our rules against both Linux-2.6.32 and Linux-3.2.58, for which we have the manually obtained ground truth. We show that we can successfully pinpoint 11 kernel objects (presented in the 3rd-column with the ground truth shown in the 4th-column in Table 3) and their meanings. By using the rules we derived, there is not even a need to train for each kernel and we just use them to scan the bit-vector. In the following, we describe how we derived these rules, and how we applied them in finding the semantics of kernel objects of our interest.

Table 3. The Inference of the Selected Kernel Data Structures and The Statistics of Their Bit-Vector.

Rule Num	Kernel Version	Static Type	Symbol Name	Traced Size	Statistics of the R/W Bit Vector									
					P	F	M	T	G	S	N	I	D	O
I	2.6.32	c10414e8	pid	44	25	16	4	0	3	0	1	3	1	0
		c102db48	task_struct	1072	47	48	5	0	12	0	1	1	2	0
	3.2.58	c104bb18	pid	64	28	24	3	0	3	0	1	3	1	0
		c10371e3	task_struct	1072	73	109	13	6	19	1	2	7	2	0
II	2.6.32	c102d8af	vm_area_struct	88	4	17	12	0	3	0	0	1	1	0
	3.2.58	c1036f6a	vm_area_struct	88	3	5	12	0	0	0	1	1	1	0
III	2.6.32	c102d762	mm_struct	420	15	6	5	0	0	0	0	1	1	0
	3.2.58	c1036dc8	mm_struct	448	15	9	6	0	0	0	1	1	1	0
IV	2.6.32	c10b23ae	file	128	41	93	12	0	10	0	1	7	2	0
	3.2.58	c10ceea4	file	160	35	97	12	0	11	0	1	7	2	0
V	2.6.32	c10cac66	fs_struct	32	4	50	0	0	0	0	1	1	1	0
	3.2.58	c10eaad7	fs_struct	64	4	51	0	0	0	0	1	1	1	0
VI	2.6.32	c10c185c	files_struct	224	11	73	3	0	4	0	1	6	1	0
	3.2.58	c10df2cd	files_struct	256	39	84	5	0	6	0	1	6	1	0
VII	2.6.32	c10c3a4c	vfs_mount	128	1	17	0	0	0	0	0	0	1	0
	3.2.58	c10dfd37	vfs_mount	160	3	4	0	0	0	0	0	0	1	0
VIII	2.6.32	c11cd7c8	sock	1216	19	55	8	0	9	1	6	6	2	0
	3.2.58	c11cd7c8	sock	1248	28	74	7	0	9	1	1	6	2	0
IX	2.6.32	c102dfd8	sighand_struct	1288	15	5	0	0	12	0	1	1	1	0
	3.2.58	c10376a7	sighand_struct	1312	15	7	0	0	12	0	1	1	1	0
X	2.6.32	c1047938	cred	128	51	72	8	3	3	1	2	4	2	0
	3.2.58	c1052611	cred	128	53	75	7	3	2	1	2	4	2	0

Process Related. The most important process related data structure is the *process descriptor* (i.e., task_struct in Linux), which keeps a lot of information regarding the resources a process is using, and how to reach these resources. Surprisingly, by looking at the bit-vectors of all the kernel objects, it is actually quite simple to identify the process descriptor.

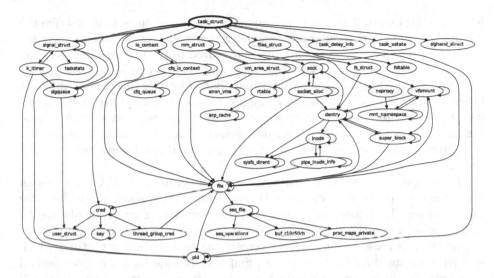

Fig. 4. The reverse engineered data structure type graph with task_struct as the root of Linux Kernel 2.6.32. Each node represents a reverse engineered data structure (the symbol name is just for better readability), and each edge represents the point-to relation between the data structures. There can be multiple point-to edges between two nodes at different offsets. They are merged for better readability.

Specifically, since task_struct must be created by process creation related syscalls (e.g., sys_clone, sys_vfork), we can in fact scan the C-bit of the objects and check the ones that are created under these syscalls (e.g.,sys_clone[C]); task_struct must exist in this set. However, during the process creation, it will also create many other data structures such as the *memory descriptor* for this process. Consequently, we have to exclude these data structures. Our insight is that we can perform a set intersection (basically execution context differencing) to identify the desired object. Back to the process descriptor example, from a general understanding of the syscall semantics, we know that sys_getpid must access the task_struct in order to get the pid. As such, we can then check the sys_getpid[R] bit.

Therefore, through the intersection of sys_clone[C] ∩ sys_getpid[R] (as illustrated in the first rule of Table 2), we can get two objects with static types of c10414e8 and c102db48. Then the next question is how to get the task_struct. In fact, we can look at the relation between the data structure (i.e., the type graph we extracted). As illustrated in Fig. 4, we can see clearly that c10414e8[2] is reached from c102db48. Therefore, we can conclude that c102db48 is the task_struct based on general OS kernel knowledge, and c10414e8 is the pid descriptor. This rule also applies to Linux-3.2.58, and we can correctly recognize its task_struct and pid descriptor without any training.

---

[2] Note that we show the symbol name instead of the address in Fig. 4 just for the readability of the type graph.

Memory Related. There are two important data structures that describe the memory usage for a particular process. One is the *memory descriptor* (mm_struct in Linux) that contains all the information related to the process address space, such as the base address of the page table and the starting address of process code and data. Also, since memory is often divided into regions to store different types of process data (e.g., memory mapped files, stacks, heaps, etc.), the kernel uses the other important data structure called *virtual memory area descriptor* (vm_area_struct) to describe a single memory area over a contiguous interval in a given address space. Certainly, vm_area_struct can be reached from the mm_struct.

To recognize these two data structures, we again use general OS and syscall knowledge. In particular, we know that all the child threads share the same virtual space. Therefore, mm_struct and some vm_area_struct should not be created when a new thread is forked. We can then scan the C-bit of the object bit-vector of sys_clone, which is used to create the process, and sys_vfork, which is used to create threads. Then we can find a set of objects. Then, from general knowledge we know sys_brk (which changes program data segment size) will access mm_struct and some vm_ area_struct. Meanwhile, sys_munmap, which aims to delete a memory region, will certainly delete vm_area_struct (then we look at its D-bit). As such, we have developed Rule-II and Rule-III presented in Table 2 to successfully identify vm_area_ struct and mm_struct, respectively. Meanwhile, as illustrated in Fig. 4, we can also observe the type graph to infer the vm_area_struct because it has to be reached from mm_struct when we only look at these two data structures, which are in $\{$(sys_ clone$[C]$ - sys_vfork$[C]$) $\cap$ sys_brk$[RW]\}$.

File Related. There are several important file related data structures of our interest. Specifically, we are interested in the (1) *file descriptor* (file structure in Linux) that describes a file's properties, such as its opening mode, the position of the current file cursor, etc., (2) *file system descriptor* (fs_struct) that describes the file system related information including such as the root path of the file system, and the current working directory, (3) files_struct that describes the opening file table (e.g., the file descriptor array), (4) vfs_mount that describes the mounted file systems, and (5) sock structure that describes a network communication point in the OS kernel. In the following, we discuss how we recognize these data structures.

- *File Descriptor.* From general OS knowledge, we know that a file descriptor is created by the open syscall. However, open will create many other objects as well (e.g., we found 43 different types of objects by scanning sys_open$[C]$ bits). Fortunately, we also know that lseek will definitely modify file (i.e., sys_lseek$[W]$ will be set). Meanwhile, sys_dup will also absolutely read and write to the file structure. Therefore, we developed our Rule-IV by using sys_open$[C]$ $\cap$ sys_lseek$[W]$ $\cap$ sys_dup$[R]$ to directly pinpoint the file structure.

- *File System Data Structure.* From the syscall specification, we know that when a child process is created, it will inherit many important kernel objects from its parent process. File system structure is definitely one of them. Also, sys_clone will provide flags to allow programmers to control whether to inherit or not. Recall in Sect. 3.2, we have tracked the flag of sys_clone, and we can therefore trivially identify the fs_struct. In particular, flag CLONE_FS will let the child process clone from its parent FS (it means no new fs_struct will be created). By performing sys_clone [C] - sys_clone[C](CLONE_FS), we directly pinpoint fs_struct.
- *Open File Table Structure.* Each process has its own opened file set. This is maintained by its files_struct in the Linux kernel. Similar to fs_struct identification, we check the flag CLONE_FILES of sys_clone to identify this structure, as presented in the Rule-VI in Table 2.
- *Mounting Point Descriptor.* When a file system is mounted, the OS uses a mounting point descriptor to track the mounted file system. There are two syscalls (sys_mount and sys_umount) involved in the mouting and unmouting operation. Basically, sys_mount creates a mouting structure and sys_umount removes it. To identify vfs_mount is actually quite simple, and we just perform a sys_mount [C] ∩ sys_umount[D], which directly produces the desired data structure.
- *Socket.* By associating the argument with the syscall context for sys_socket call, we can easily identify the socket data structure in the OS kernel. For instance, we can check the created object in sys_socketcall[C](SYS_SOCKET), and check the updated object in sys_socketcall[W][SYS_SETSOCKOPT]. An intersection of these two sets will directly identify the socket data structure.

Signal Related. Among the signal related data structures, the signal handler is of our interest since it can be subverted. To identify this data structure, it is also quite simple, especially if we check the flags of sys_clone. In particular, there is a CLONE_ SIGHAND flag, and if it is set, the calling process and the child process will share the same table of signal handlers. Thus, sys_clone[C] - sys_clone[C](CLONE_ SIGHAND) directly identifies the signal handler data structure. There are also other ways to identify this data structure. For instance, sys_alarm will set an alarm clock for delivery of a signal, which will modify the signal handler. By looking at sys_alarm[W] as well as the type graph, we can also easily tell the sighand_struct.

Credential Related. Each process in a modern OS has certain credentials, such as its uid, gid, euid, and capabilities used for access control. The Linux kernel uses a cred data structure to store this information. To identify this data structure, we found that sys_capget and sys_capset will set and get the cred field of a process. Both syscalls will read and write the credential objects and we can use set intersection to find this data structure (i.e., sys_capget[R] ∩ sys_capset[W]). Also, this data structure is reachable from task_struct as well.

5   Applications

Uncovering the semantics of kernel objects will be useful in many applications. For example, it allows us to understand what the created objects are in an OS kernel when performing introspection, and we can also use data structure knowledge to recognize the internal kernel functions. In the following, we demonstrate how we can use ARGOS to identify the internal kernel functions, especially the object creation and deletion functions, which is important to both kernel rootkit offense and defense.

Recently, kernel malware has been increasingly using internal functions to perform malicious actions. This is no surprise since kernel malware can call any internal kernel function because they share the same address space. For instance, prior studies have shown that instead of calling NtCreateProcess, kernel malware will directly call PspCreateProcess. Therefore, hooking these internal functions is very important to detect malware attacks. Note that PspCreateProcess is for the Windows kernel; the corresponding one in Linux is actually copy_process [9]. Then can we automatically identify these internal functions, such as copy_process?

Fortunately, it is quite straightforward to identify some of the internal functions given the semantics of the identified kernel data structure. Take task_struct as an example: once we have understood a dynamically allocated object is a task_struct, we can check which function calls the object allocation for task_struct, and the caller is usually the one that is responsible for the object creation. Interestingly, while this is a simple heuristic, we tested with the two kernels and found it works well. Therefore, for this experiment, we also instrumented the kernel execution and tracked the call-stacks such that we can identify the parent function of our interest.

Based on the above heuristic, we have applied ARGOS to recognize the creation and deletion functions for the objects we identified in Table 3. This result is presented in Table 4. Again, there is no false positive while using this very simple caller-callee heuristic, and we correctly identified these functions when compared with the ground truth result in the kernel source code. For readability, we present the corresponding symbols of these functions, in addition to the PCs that denote their starting addresses.

For proof-of-concept, we then developed a virtual machine introspection [11] tool atop QEMU to track and interpret the kernel object creation and deletion events related to the object we reverse engineered by hooking the internal kernel functions listed in Table 4. Without any surprise, our tool can successfully track the corresponding events for all process creations, including even a hidden process that is created with the internal function by a rootkit we developed.

Table 4. Internal Kernel Function Recognization for the Testing Linux Kernels.

Type	Version	Creation Function		Deletion Function	
		PC	Symbol	PC	Symbol
pid	2.6.32	c10414d0	alloc_pid	c10413de	put_pid
	3.2.58	c104bb02	alloc_pid	c104b969	put_pid
task_struct	2.6.32	c102daaf	copy_process	c102da55	free_task
	3.2.58	c103719d	copy_process	c10368a7	free_task
vm_area_struct	2.6.32	c102d730	dup_mm	c109d387	remove_vma
	3.2.58	c1036d97	dup_mm	c10b13d7	remove_vma
mm_struct	2.6.32	c102d730	dup_mm	c102d3dc	__mmdrop
	3.2.58	c1036d97	dup_mm	c1036a58	__mmdrop
file	2.6.32	c10b230d	get_empty_filp	c10b2030	file_free_rcu
	3.2.58	c10cee78	get_empty_filp	c10ceba0	file_free_rcu
fs_struct	2.6.32	c10cac50	copy_fs_struct	c10cae5b	free_fs_struct
	3.2.58	c10eaac4	copy_fs_struct	c10eaa55	free_fs_struct
files_struct	2.6.32	c10c1839	dup_fd	c1030a32	put_files_struct
	3.2.58	c10df2ab	dup_fd	c103b16d	put_files_struct
vfs_mount	2.6.32	c10c3a35	alloc_vfsmnt	c10c30ba	free_vfsmnt
	3.2.58	c10dfd23	alloc_vfsmnt	c10dfe36	free_vfsmnt
sighand_struct	2.6.32	c102daaf	copy_process	c102d148	__cleanup_sighand
	3.2.58	c103719d	copy_process	c103717b	__cleanup_sighand
sock	2.6.32	c11cd7a5	sk_prot_alloc	c11cc884	__sk_free
	3.2.58	c12146e5	sk_prot_alloc	c1214d46	__sk_free
cred	2.6.32	c1047923	prepare_creds	c1047d00	put_cred_rcu
	3.2.58	c10525fe	prepare_creds	c105230b	put_cred_rcu

6 Limitations and Future Work

While we have demonstrated we can infer the kernel object semantics from the object use, there are still a number of avenues to improve our techniques. In the following, we discuss each of the limitations of our system and shed light on our future work.

First and foremost, we need to develop more rules or other approaches to derive the kernel object semantics based on the bit-vectors. Currently, we just illustrated we can recognize some of the kernel data structures through syscall execution context diffing and general OS knowledge. As discussed earlier in Sect. 3.4, there could be many other alternatives, such as assigning different weights to the bit of interest and then converting the bit-vector into a numeric value, from which semantics could be mapped. Meanwhile, there might also be an interesting solution of only tracking a certain number of syscalls instead all of them. We leave the validation of these alternative approaches to one of our future works.

Second, currently ARGOS only aims to reveal the semantics of the kernel data structures; it does not make any effort to reveal the syntax (especially the layout of each data structure) or meaning for each field of each data structure. Since there are several existing efforts (e.g., [16,18,23,27]) focusing on user level data structure reverse engineering, especially on field layout and syntax, we plan to integrate these techniques into ARGOS to give it more capabilities.

Third, ARGOS will have false negatives because of the nature of dynamic analysis. In addition, it will not be able to track an object if its allocation functions are inlined since it uses the dynamic hooking mechanism to intercept `kmalloc` family functions. To identify these inlined kernel object allocation and deallocation functions would require a static analysis of the kernel binary code, and we leave it to another of our future works. Also, our current design uses $PC_{kmalloc}$ to type the kernel object, but there are still a number of kernel objects (e.g., 20 % in Linux 2.6.32) with an N-to-one mapping. We plan to address this issue in our future work as well.

Forth, there might be some execution contexts that are asynchronized. Consequently, we might miss the exact syscall context for the objects that are accessed in the asynchronized code. We have encountered a few cases in Linux (e.g., kernel worker threads, which are processed usually in the bottom-half of the interrupt context), and our current solution is to ignore tracking the context for these objects. Thus, an immediate future effort is to propose techniques that can also resolve the execution context of asynchronized execution code.

Finally, while we have demonstrated our techniques working for the Linux kernel, we would like to validate the generality of ARGOS with other kernels. We plan to extend our analysis to FreeBSD, since it is also open source and we can compare our result with its ground truth. Eventually, we would like to test our system with closed source OSes such as Microsoft Windows.

7   Related Work

Our work is closely related to data structure reverse engineering. More broadly, it is also related to virtual machine introspection and memory forensics. In this section, we compare ARGOS with the most closely related work—data structure reverse engineering.

Being an important component of a program, data structures play a significant role in many aspects of modern computing, such as software design and implementation, program analysis, program understanding [20], and computer security. However, once a program has been compiled, the definition of the data structure is gone. In the past decade, a considerable amount of research has been carried out to recover data structure knowledge from binary code, and they are all based on the same principle of *"from data use infer the data types"*. In general, these existing approaches can be classified into two categories: static analysis based and dynamic analysis based.

Static Analysis. An early attempt of using static analysis to recover data structure is aggregate structure identification (ASI) [21]. Basically, it leverages the program's access patterns and the type information from well-known functions to recover the structural information about the data structures. While it focused on Cobol programs, its concepts can be applied to program binary code. By statically walking through the binary code, value set analysis (VSA) [3,22] tracks the possible values of data objects, from which it can build the point-to relation among addresses (which can help with shape analysis), and also reason about the integer values an object can hold at each program point. Most recently, TIE [16] infers both the primitive types and aggregate types of the program's variables from its binary code using the instruction type sinks and a constraint solving approach.

Dynamic Analysis. Guo et al. [12] propose an algorithm for inferring the variables' abstract types by partitioning them into equivalence classes through a data flow based analysis. However, this approach requires the program to be compiled with debugging symbols. A number of protocol reverse engineering efforts have been developed (e.g., [5,7,17,25]) to infer the format of network protocol messages—essentially the data structure type information of network packets—from program execution. The key idea of these approaches is to monitor the execution of network programs and use the instruction access patterns (i.e., the data use) to infer the data structure layout and size.

Rather than focusing on the data structure of network packets, REWARDS [18] shows an algorithm that can resolve the program's internal data structures through type recovery and type unification. Howard [23] recovers data structures and arrays using pointer stride analysis. PointerScope [27] infers pointer and non-pointer types using a constrained type unification [8]. Also, Laika [6] uses a machine learning approach to identify data structures in a memory snapshot and cluster those of the same type, with the applications of using data structures as program signatures.

Compared to all these existing works, ARGOS is the first system that focuses on the semantic reverse engineering of data structures. Also, nearly all of the existing work focused on the reverse engineering of user level data structures, and ARGOS makes the first step towards reverse engineering of kernel data structures.

8   Conclusion

We have presented ARGOS, the first system that can automatically uncover the semantics of kernel objects from kernel execution traces. Similar to many other data structure reverse engineering systems, it is based on the very simple principle of data-use implying data-semantics. Specifically, starting from the system call and the exported kernel APIs, ARGOS automatically tracks the instruction execution and assigns a bit vector for each observed kernel object. The bit vector encodes which syscall accesses this object and how the object is accessed (e.g., whether the object is created, accessed, updated, or destroyed under the execution of this syscall), and from this we derive the meaning of the kernel object. The experimental results with Linux kernels show that ARGOS can effectively recognize the semantics for a number of kernel objects that are of security interest. We have applied ARGOS to recognize the internal kernel functions, and we show that with ARGOS we can build a more precise kernel event tracking system by hooking these internal functions.

Acknowledgement. We thank our shepherd William Robertson and other anonymous reviewers for their insightful comments. This research was partially supported by an AFOSR grant FA9550-14-1-0119, and an NSF grant 1453011. Any opinions, findings, conclusions, or recommendations expressed are those of the authors and not necessarily of the AFOSR and NSF.

References

1. Linux test project. https://github.com/linux-test-project
2. QEMU: an open source processor emulator. http://www.qemu.org/
3. Balakrishnan, G., Reps, T.: Analyzing memory accesses in x86 executables. In: Duesterwald, E. (ed.) CC 2004. LNCS, vol. 2985, pp. 5–23. Springer, Heidelberg (2004)
4. Caballero, J., Poosankam, P., Kreibich, C., Song, D.: Dispatcher: enabling active botnet infiltration using automatic protocol reverse-engineering. In: Proceedings of the 16th ACM Conference on Computer and and Communications Security (CCS 2009), pp. 621–634, Chicago, Illinois, USA (2009)
5. Caballero, J., Song, D.: Polyglot: automatic extraction of protocol format using dynamic binary analysis. In: Proceedings of the 14th ACM Conference on Computer and and Communications Security (CCS 2007), pp. 317–329, Alexandria, Virginia, USA (2007)
6. Cozzie, A., Stratton, F., Xue, H., King, S.T.: Digging for data structures. In: Proceeding of 8th Symposium on Operating System Design and Implementation (OSDI 2008), pp. 231–244, San Diego, CA, December 2008
7. Cui, W., Peinado, M., Chen, K., Wang, H.J., Irun-Briz, L.: Tupni: automatic reverse engineering of input formats. In: Proceedings of the 15th ACM Conference on Computer and Communications Security (CCS 2008), pp. 391–402, Alexandria, Virginia, USA, October 2008
8. Damas, L., Milner, R.: Principal type-schemes for functional programs. In: Proceedings of the 9th ACM SIGPLAN-SIGACT Symposium on Principles of Programming Languages, pp. 207–212, January 1982
9. Deng, Z., Zhang, X., Xu, D.: Spider: stealthy binary program instrumentation and debugging via hardware virtualization. In: Proceedings of the 29th Annual Computer Security Applications Conference, ACSAC 2013, pp. 289–298, New Orleans, Louisiana (2013)
10. Fu, Y., Lin, Z.: Space traveling across VM: automatically bridging the semantic gap in virtual machine introspection via online kernel data redirection. In: Proceedings of 33rd IEEE Symposium on Security and Privacy, May 2012
11. Garfinkel, T., Rosenblum, M.: A virtual machine introspection based architecture for intrusion detection. In: Proceedings Network and Distributed Systems Security Symposium (NDSS 2003), pp. 38–53, February 2003
12. Guo, P.J., Perkins, J.H., McCamant, S., Ernst, M.D.: Dynamic inference of abstract types. In: ISSTA, pp. 255–265, July 2006

13. Hay, B., Nance, K.: Forensics examination of volatile system data using virtual introspection. SIGOPS Oper. Syst. Rev. **42**, 74–82 (2008)
14. Johnson, N., Caballero, J., Chen, K., McCamant, S., Poosankam, P., Reynaud, D., Song, D.: Differential slicing: identifying causal execution differences for security applications. In: Proceedings of 32nd IEEE Symposium on Security and Privacy, pp. 347–362, May 2011
15. Jones, S.T., Arpaci-Dusseau, A.C., Arpaci-Dusseau, R.H.: Antfarm: tracking processes in a virtual machine environment. In: Proceedings of the Annual Conference on USENIX 2006 Annual Technical Conference. USENIX Association, Boston (2006)
16. Lee, J., Avgerinos, T., Brumley, D.: Tie: principled reverse engineering of types in binary programs. In: Proceedings of the 18th Annual Network and Distributed System Security Symposium (NDSS 2011), San Diego, CA, February 2011
17. Lin, Z., Jiang, X., Xu, D., Zhang, X.: Automatic protocol format reverse engineering through context-aware monitored execution. In: Proceedings of the 15th Annual Network and Distributed System Security Symposium (NDSS 2008), San Diego, CA, February 2008
18. Lin, Z., Zhang, X., Xu, D.: Automatic reverse engineering of data structures from binary execution. In: Proceedings of the 17th Annual Network and Distributed System Security Symposium (NDSS 2010), San Diego, CA, February 2010
19. Newsome, J., Song, D.: Dynamic taint analysis for automatic detection, analysis, and signature generation of exploits on commodity software. In: Proceedings of the 14th Annual Network and Distributed System Security Symposium (NDSS 2005), San Diego, CA, February 2005
20. O'Callahan, R., Jackson, D.: Lackwit: a program understanding tool based on type inference. In Proceedings of the 19th International Conference on Software Engineering, ICSE 1997, pp. 338–348, Boston, Massachusetts, USA (1997)
21. Ramalingom, G., Field, J., Tip, F.: Aggregate structure identification and its application to program analysis. In: Proceedings of the 26th ACM SIGPLAN-SIGACT Symposium on Principles of programming languages (POPL 1999), San Antonio, Texas, pp. 119–132. ACM (1999)
22. Reps, T., Balakrishnan, G.: Improved memory-access analysis for x86 executables. In: Hendren, L. (ed.) CC 2008. LNCS, vol. 4959, pp. 16–35. Springer, Heidelberg (2008)
23. Slowinska, A., Stancescu, T., Bos, H.: Howard: a dynamic excavator for reverse engineering data structures. In: Proceedings of the 18th Annual Network and Distributed System Security Symposium (NDSS 2011), San Diego, CA, February 2011
24. Walters, A.: The volatility framework: volatile memory artifact extraction utility framework. https://www.volatilesystems.com/default/volatility
25. Wondracek, G., Milani, P., Kruegel, C., Kirda, E.: Automatic network protocol analysis. In: Proceedings of the 15th Annual Network and Distributed System Security Symposium (NDSS 2008), San Diego, CA, February 2008
26. Zeng, J., Fu, Y., Lin, Z.: Pemu: a pin highly compatible out-of-VM dynamic binary instrumentation framework. In: Proceedings of the 11th Annual International Conference on Virtual Execution Environments, pp. 147–160, Istanbul, Turkey, March 2015
27. Zhang, M., Prakash, A., Li, X., Liang, Z., Yin, H.: Identifying and analyzing pointer misuses for sophisticated memory-corruption exploit diagnosis. In: Proceedings of the 19th Annual Network and Distributed System Security Symposium (NDSS 2012), San Diego, CA, February 2012

Attack Detection II

BotWatcher
Transparent and Generic Botnet Tracking

Thomas Barabosch[1]([✉]), Adrian Dombeck[1], Khaled Yakdan[1,2],
and Elmar Gerhards-Padilla[1]

[1] Fraunhofer FKIE, Bonn, Germany
{thomas.barabosch,adrian.dombeck,
elmar.gerhards-padilla}@fkie.fraunhofer.de
[2] University of Bonn, Bonn, Germany
yakdan@cs.uni-bonn.de

Abstract. Botnets are one of the most serious threats to Internet security today. Modern botnets have complex infrastructures consisting of multiple components, which can be dynamically installed, updated, and removed at any time during the botnet operation. Tracking botnets is essential for understanding the current threat landscape. However, state-of-the-art analysis approaches have several limitations. Many malware analysis systems like sandboxes have a very limited analysis time-out, and thus only allow limited insights into the long-time behavior of a botnet. In contrast, customized tracking systems are botnet-specific and need to be adopted to each malware family, which requires tedious manual reverse engineering.

In this paper, we present BotWatcher, a novel approach for transparent and generic botnet tracking. To this end, we leverage dynamic analysis and memory forensics techniques to execute the initial malware sample and later installed modules in a controlled environment and regularly obtain insights into the state of the analysis system. The key idea behind BotWatcher is that by reasoning about the evolution of system state over time, we can reconstruct a high-level overview of the botnet lifecycle, i.e., the sequence of botnet actions that caused this evolution. Our approach is generic since it relies neither on previous knowledge of the botnet nor on OS-specific features. Transparency is achieved by performing outside-OS monitoring and not installing any analysis tools in the analysis environment. We implemented BotWatcher for Microsoft Windows and Mac OS X (both 32- and 64-bit architectures), and applied it to monitor four botnets targeting Microsoft Windows. To the best of our knowledge, we are the first to present a generic, transparent, and fully automated botnet tracking system.

Keywords: Botnet tracking · Memory forensics · Malware analysis

1 Introduction

Botnets are a major threat to today's Internet security. They are used for a wide range of malicious purposes, e.g., launching of denial-of-service attacks on

© Springer International Publishing Switzerland 2015
H. Bos et al. (Eds.): RAID 2015, LNCS 9404, pp. 565–587, 2015.
DOI: 10.1007/978-3-319-26362-5_26

networked computers, committing click-fraud, sending spam, and distributing malware. Recent studies estimated that some botnets contain in the order of a million infected systems [25], illustrating the magnitude of the botnet threat. Modern botnets are increasingly complex and comprise several modules that can be installed, removed, and updated on the infected system at run time. This complex and modular structure helps to achieve a high resilience against takedown attempts by security researchers and law enforcement [25]. Also, it hampers the time-critical and difficult task of timely botnet analysis.

Tracking botnets is essential for understanding the current threat landscape. It provides valuable information about the botnet lifecycle, i.e., the botnet infrastructure, its malicious actions, and the distributed malware. Understanding the botnet lifecycle is an important building block for developing effective countermeasures and performing successful takedowns. Previous work presented customized tracking systems for specific botnets [15,17]. These solutions are highly manual and require knowledge of the inner workings of the tracked botnet. For this reason, they cannot cope with the dynamic nature of modern botnets, which may install new and previously unknown components at any time. Moreover, these solutions must be adopted to each malware family, and thus do not scale well when analyzing unknown botnets, i.e., botnets whose infrastructure and lifecycle are not yet known. Existing malware analysis systems like sandboxes have a very limited analysis time-out (often five minutes or less). For this reason, they can only provide limited insights into the long-time behaviour of a botnet. Moreover, evasive malware leverages the fact that dynamic analysis systems monitor execution for a limited amount of time, and employ several timing attacks to delay execution of suspicious functionality and evade sandbox analysis [21]. While modern sandboxes can detect several evasion techniques and patch them to elicit the malicious behavior, they cannot influence timing attacks on the server side. A C&C server may delay the delivery of actual botnet components several hours or days when a new bot joins the botnet, which will be missed by analysis sandboxes. Rossow et al. [26] presented an approach for generic and long-term botnet monitoring. They used this system to characterize several Windows-based malware downloaders concerning their communication architectures, carrier protocols and encryption schemes. However, this approach is based on a kernel rootkit and does not follow the transparency goal.

In this paper, we present BOTWATCHER, a novel approach for generic and transparent tracking of botnets. The main intuition behind our approach is that program execution and interaction with the operating system (OS) affect the system state. By observing the evolution of this state over time, we can reconstruct a high-level overview about the series of high-level actions that caused this evolution. To this end, BOTWATCHER executes an initial malware sample in a controlled analysis environment (virtual machine) and continuously takes snapshots of the system state. We then compare subsequent system states to extract *low-level events* that caused the state change (e.g., connection establishment or thread termination). By reasoning about the evolution of these low-level events over time, BOTWATCHER infers the corresponding high-level behaviour such as malware downloads and DDoS attacks. For example, the sequence of establishing a network connection, downloading a file from the Internet, and starting a new process is inferred as a MALWAREDOWNLOAD event. As transparency is a key requirement to avoid detection from malware, we do not introduce any malware analysis tools in the analysis environment and perform outside-OS monitoring, i.e., monitoring the analysis environment from the outside. BOTWATCHER is a generic approach. First, no previous knowledge about the botnet is required and thus it can be used to analyze unknown botnets. Second, BOTWATCHER represents the system state using a set of concepts that are shared among most modern operating systems, e.g., threads, processes, and files. Therefore, it can be applied to a wide range of operating systems. We extract system state information from two sources: the main memory of the analysis environment and the network traffic. To this end, we leverage memory forensic techniques to extract state-related information from the main memory. This serves as abstraction layer and enables us to implement our analyses in an OS-independent way.

In summary, we make the following contributions:

- We present a novel approach – called BOTWATCHER – for transparent and generic botnet tracking. Our approach reconstructs the series of botnet actions by reasoning about the evolution of the system state. To this end, we leverage dynamic analysis and memory forensics techniques to periodically record the state of the analysis system.
- We present a set of inference rules to reconstruct high-level malware behaviors based on the observed differences between two consequent system states.
- We evaluated a prototype of BOTWATCHER on Microsoft Windows and Mac OS X (both 32- and 64-bit architectures). We demonstrate the applicability and efficacy of BOTWATCHER by using it to track four current botnets from the families Upatre, Gamarue, Emotet and Necurs. Our experiments reveal a trend in modern botnets to move evasion techniques to the server side, which renders client-side anti-evasion techniques employed by analysis sandboxes ineffective.

2   BOTWATCHER

In this section, we introduce our design goals and then describe our approach BOTWATCHER in detail.

2.1   Objectives

The focal point of this paper is on *generic* and *transparent* botnet tracking. In our context, we aim to gain insights into the behaviour of the botnet under investigation and identify its *life-cycle*. We define the *life-cycle* of a botnet as the sequence of its actions over time, such as participating in DDoS attacks, sending spam, and installing new malware, etc.

The main goal of our work is to design a botnet tracking system that fulfils two key requirements: First, the tracking method must be *generic*. That is, it must not assume any previous knowledge about the botnet under investigation. This is essential for having a scalable solution that can automatically track new and previously unknown botnets. Due to the diversification of operating systems, a second important aspect of this requirement is that the tracking logic should be applicable to many operating systems. This implies that it should not rely on OS-specific features.

The second requirement is that the tracking method must be *transparent*. That is, it must be impossible (or very difficult) for a malware to detect that it is running in an analysis environment. Otherwise, a malware can easily refrain from executing its malicious payload. This requires that (1) no analysis tools are installed in the analysis environment; and (2) the tracking approach should operate on a more privileged level than the observed malware.

We strive to fill the gap and address the shortcomings of current approaches. Customized tracking approaches are too specific and cannot be easily adapted to track new botnets. Traditional malware analysis systems only observe the malware during a very short period of time. We argue that a trade-off between both approaches is possible to have a botnet tracking system that fulfills the above mentioned requirements.

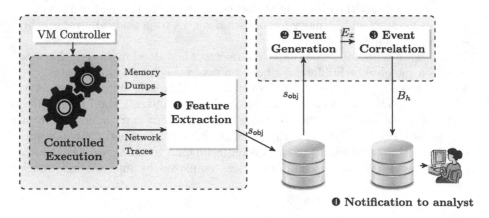

Fig. 1. Architecture of BotWatcher. BotWatcher executes an initial sample in a controlled environment and then periodically takes a snapshot of the system state of the analysis environment (❶). By comparing subsequent state snapshots, we identify the set of execution events that represent the state transition E_{ex} (e.g., process creation) (❷). By reasoning about the evolution of these events, BotWatcher infers the corresponding high-level behaviour B_h (e.g. MalwareDownload) (❸). Finally, the analyst is notified (❹).

2.2 General Overview

A high-level overview of BotWatcher is given in Fig. 1. First, we execute an initial malware sample in a controlled analysis environment (virtual machine [5]) with Internet connectivity. The initial malware is typically a dropper that serves as an entry point to the botnet. Second, BotWatcher takes a snapshot of the system state at regular intervals (Sect. 2.3). This system state includes information such as the list of running processes or active network connections. Third, we compare the current and last snapshots to infer the set of events that caused the state transition (Sect. 2.4). We denote these events by *execution events*, which include starting a new process and closing a network connection. Finally, BotWatcher reasons about the execution events to infer more complex and interesting events related to the botnet life-cycle (Sect. 2.5). For example, the sequence opening a network connection, downloading a file, and then starting a new process is inferred as a MalwareDownload event.

To address the genericity requirement, BotWatcher represents the system state as a set of concepts that are shared by most modern operating systems such as processes, threads, and files. We leverage memory forensic techniques to extract this information from the main memory of the analysis environment. Additionally, we extract relevant information from the network traffic passing through the analysis environment. This serves as abstraction layer that allows to build subsequent analysis steps independently from the target operating system. Moreover, the reliance on such generic features enables BotWatcher to monitor new and unknown botnets since no previous knowledge is needed.

Extracting system state information from the main memory and network activity of the virtual analysis environment helps to fulfill the transparency requirement since it allows to perform outside-OS monitoring. Moreover, we do not introduce any analysis tools into the virtual analysis environment. This makes it difficult for malware to detect that it is being analyzed by fingerprinting the execution environment. A key motivation for developing our system is that it is very difficult for malware to hide the artifacts left in memory as a result of its execution. They are therefore reliable and robust sources of information about the behavior of the malware.

2.3 Phase I: Feature Extraction

The first phase of BotWatcher is to record the system state of the analysis environment at regular intervals. We define the system state at given point in time t, denoted by $S(t)$, as the set of *execution features* that exist in the system at that time. Execution features represent system properties that are created, changed, and removed as a result of program execution, e.g., running processes, ongoing network connections, or opened files.

A key property of BotWatcher is that it performs outside-OS monitoring. That is, it does not extract any information from inside the analysis environment. It rather observes the analysis environment from the outside so as to remain transparent to the running malware. To this end, we use two reliable sources of information to extract execution features; the main memory of the analysis environment and the network traffic it sends or receives. This approach has two advantages: first, no modifications are introduced into the analysis environment, making it extremely difficult for the malware to detect that it is running in an analysis system. Second, memory and network traffic are reliable sources of information that provide host-based and network-based views into the system state.

The main memory is the primary source of information used by BOTWATCHER. Operating systems maintain several data structures in memory to manage many aspects of their operation. This provides a wealth of information about the system state at any given point in time such as the list of running processes, open files, kernel modules etc. Program execution and interaction with the operating system result in several changes to the contents of the main memory. In our case, we use the intuition that by monitoring these changes, we can reconstruct the sequence of actions that caused them. To extract execution features from the main memory, BOTWATCHER uses Volatility [8]. Volatility is a mature framework that supports investigating memory images of operating systems and helps to bridge the semantic gap encountered in a raw memory dump. BOTWATCHER creates memory dumps of the virtual analysis environment periodically. We conducted several experiments and found that a period T_d of three minutes is sufficient for our purpose.

Note that we do not take traditional VM snapshots to extract the system state. This would stall the VM for several seconds, making BOTWATCHER easy to detect. Alternatively, we leverage the hypervisor features to efficiently create memory dumps. In our implementation, we use the command line tool *VBoxManage debugvm dumpvmcore* in order to dump the memory of a VM. This first copies the VM's memory into another memory location and then writes the copied data to hard disk. To ensure a consistent and atomic read of the VM's memory, the VM is only paused during the first step. The amount of time depends on the memory throughput of the hypervisor. Current memory modules have a very high throughput of more than 10 GB [16]. The copying of memory leads to a short time frame in which the VM is unresponsive. Since many normal operations cause a similar effect, e.g., waiting for an interrupt of some hardware device, this should be hard to detect by malware. Though, we plan to evaluate this in the future (see Sect. 7).

Network traffic is the second source of information that we use to gain insights into the role a bot plays in the botnet infrastructure. Bots use the network to communicate with their C&C server or other peers as well as to perform malicious actions such as sending spam or participating in DDoS attacks. BOTWATCHER captures network traffic that passes by the virtual network interface of the analysis environment and extracts features like IP addresses, transport protocols, port numbers. We use the network security monitor Bro [6] for analyzing the network traffic. Network-related features collected in the time interval $[t_k, t_k + T_d]$, where t_k is time of the last period, are attributed to the point in time $t_k + T_d$.

2.4 Phase II: Execution Events Extraction

After having extracted the system state $S(t_k)$ of the analysis machine, we identify the state transition relative to the previous state $S(t_{k-1})$. More specifically, we identify the set of newly created execution features since that last snapshot $F^+ = S(t_k) \setminus S(t_{k-1})$. Similarly, we identify the set of terminated execution features since the last snapshot $F^- = S(t_{k-1}) \setminus S(t_k)$. The fact that a feature is created or terminated at a given point in time is denoted as *execution event*. Each execution event is assigned a timestamp and characteristic meta data to fully describe it. For example, for process creation events, we record the corresponding process identifier. Table 1 shows the execution events extracted by BOTWATCHER. In the following, we discuss the extracted events in detail and explain our motivation behind tracking them.

Table 1. Execution events

Event	Description
$\mathcal{P}[p_{id}, \tau, ts]$	*Process* event of type $\tau \in \{\tau_{\text{create}}, \tau_{\text{terminate}}\}$ that represents the creation or termination of a process with identifier p_{id} at time ts
$\mathcal{T}[t_{id}, p_{id}, \tau, ts]$	*Thread* event of type $\tau \in \{\tau_{\text{create}}, \tau_{\text{terminate}}\}$ that represents the creation or termination of a thread with identifier t_{id} from process p_{id} at time ts
$\mathcal{M}[a_s, a_e, p_{id}, ts]$	*Memory* event represents the allocation of a memory block with a start address a_s and an end address a_e in the address space of process p_{id} at time ts
$\mathcal{F}[f, ts]$	*File* event that represents opening and closing a file f at time ts
$\mathcal{C}[k, v, ts]$	*Configuration* event that represents storing a configuration information k with value v at time ts
$\mathcal{K}[\tau, ts]$	*Kernel* event of type $\tau \in \{\tau_{\text{module}}, \tau_{\text{timer}}, \tau_{\text{callback}}\}$ at time ts that represents starting a new kernel module m
$\mathcal{N}[s, p_{id}, \tau, ts]$	*Network* event of type $\tau \in \{\tau_{\text{TCP}}, \tau_{\text{UDP}}\}$ that corresponds to the socket s owned by process p_{id} at time ts

Processes. Malware often installs new modules on the infected system. This can be a new version of the malware sent by its C&C server or a new malware to install [15]. BOTWATCHER extracts a list of running processes from every memory dump to keep track of active programs. In order to remain stealthy, rootkits often manipulate OS-internal data structures to hide processes. For example, Windows maintains a double-linked list of EPROCESS structures. A rootkit can hide a specific process by unlinking the corresponding entry in this list. For this reason, BOTWATCHER uses several sources of information in order to detect all running processes including the hidden ones.

Threads. Modern malware often employs code injections, a technique to execute code in the context of a remote process without having to create a new process. This helps malware to operate covertly and gain higher privileges [13]. A common way to achieve that is to copy code into the address space of a benign process space and then start a new thread to execute its malicious code in the context of the benign process. For this reason, BOTWATCHER monitors all threads on the analysis system.

Memory. Malware needs to have its code in main memory in order to be executed. We assume that this code resides in its own memory region (leaving methods like return oriented programming aside). The allocation of new memory blocks is therefore a valuable source of information. For example, it is usually the first step of a code injection. For this reason, BOTWATCHER keeps track of allocated memory blocks and their assigned access rights for each process.

Files. Malware interacts with files on a system for several purposes, e.g., information stealing, installing new modules, ransomware. BOTWATCHER monitors file handles and detects that files are opened or closed.

Configurations. Malware alters system configurations for several reasons such as achieving persistence to survive system reboots, disabling firewalls and other security tools, and manipulating network routes. In order to capture interesting modifications of system configurations, BOTWATCHER keeps track of those configurations as a set of key and value pairs.

Kernel events. Today's malware uses rootkit components in order to operate stealthy in the infected system. For example, these components can hide malware modules that operate in user space. Malware typically registers its rootkit component as a new kernel module that can modify sensitive kernel data structures such as the system call table. For this reason, BOTWATCHER observes kernel modules and kernel data structure modifications.

Network traffic. Bots use the network to communicate with their botmaster and participate in malicious activities such as sending spam and taking part in DDoS attacks. Network communication provides valuable information about the bot's behavior and the role it plays in the botnet. BOTWATCHER monitors network traffic of both stateful (TCP) and stateless (UDP) transport protocols. Also, meta information from application-level protocols such as HTTP, FTP, and DNS is extracted.

An important aspect is to be able to distinguish between the source of activities observed in the analysis environment. This is particularly important to avoid mixing behaviors in case malware starts to download/drop other malware. For this reason, we extract the process and thread identifiers for several execution events, which enables us to attribute observed activities to the corresponding process and thread. However, for some events, Volatility does not extract the process/thread identifiers. In these cases, we cannot attribute this event to a specific malicious process.

2.5   Phase III: Events Correlation

The final phase of BOTWATCHER monitors the evolution of execution events over time and infers the corresponding high-level complex malware-related actions.

For example, the sequence of starting a network connection, downloading a file, and starting a new process is inferred as a malware download event. Those high-level events represent characteristic stages of the botnet life-cycle.

Inference rules. At the core of BotWatcher's correlation logic are inference rules represented by the form:

$$\frac{P_1 \; P_2 \; \ldots \; P_n}{C}$$

The top of the inference rule bar contains the premises $P_1, P_2, \ldots, P_n$. If all premises are satisfied, then we can conclude the statement below the bar C. Inference rules provide a formal and compact notation for single step inference and implicitly specify an inference algorithm by recursively applying rules on premises until a fixed point is reached. BotWatcher uses an extensible set of rules that cover a wide spectrum of malware-related actions. A subset of the inference rules is shown in Fig. 2. Due to space constraints, we cannot present the complete set of our inference rules. For this reason, we provide a supplemental document on our website [12]. In the following, we explain some of the high-level behaviors that can be inferred by BotWatcher.

$$(1) \quad \frac{\mathcal{M}\,[a_s, a_e, p_{id}, ts_1] \quad \mathcal{T}\,[t_{id}, p_{id}, a_t, \tau_{\text{create}}, ts_2] \quad ts_2 \geq ts_1 \quad a_t \in [a_s, a_e]}{\textsc{CodeInjection}\,[p_{id}, ts_2]}$$

$$(2) \quad \frac{\mathcal{N}\,[s, p_{id}, \tau_{\text{start}}, -, ts_1] \quad \mathcal{N}\,[s, p_{id}, \tau_{\text{stop}}, -, ts_2] \quad ts_2 \geq ts_1}{\textsc{Download}\,[p_{id}, ts_2]}$$

$$(3) \quad \frac{\textsc{Download}[pp_{id}, ts_1] \quad \mathcal{P}\,[p_{id}, pp_{id}, \tau_{\text{create}}, ts_2] \quad ts_2 \geq ts_1}{\textsc{MalwareDownload}\,[p_{id}, ts_2]}$$

$$(4) \quad \frac{\mathcal{N}\,[s, p_{id}, \tau_{\text{start}}, -, ts_1] \quad s.\text{dest} \in PM}{\textsc{Spamming}\,[p_{id}, ts_2]} \qquad (5) \quad \frac{\mathcal{C}\,[ts, k, v] \quad k \in K}{\textsc{Persistence}\,[p_{id}, ts_2]}$$

Fig. 2. Exemplary inference rules. Premises are execution events and as conclusion malicious behavior is inferred.

CodeInjection. We infer code injection attacks when the allocation of a memory page in a running process is followed by starting a thread whose starting address is located inside this page (rule (1) in Fig. 2).

MalwareDownload. We use three rules to infer MalwareDownload events. First, a binary is downloaded and later executed resulting in creating a new process (rule (3) in Fig. 2). The second rule detects hot patches, i.e., dynamically updating a program at runtime without the need for restart. To this end, the rule checks for a download of a binary, followed by the manipulation of a memory page that hosts malicious code. The third rule detects the execution of a binary within another process space. This is inferred when a binary is downloaded and then a code injection event is detected.

Spamming. Botnets often send spam emails to distribute new malware and infect new systems. BOTWATCHER detects sending spam when an outgoing network connection to a mail server is established (rule (4) in Fig. 2). An example is establishing a connection to port 25 (SMTP). This allows to extract spam templates from the network traffic.

Persistence. Once malware gains access to a system, often its goal it to operate there for a long time. This behavior is known as persistence and enables the malware to survive reboots of the infected machine. We detect two persistence mechanisms; first copying a file to a system folder, and second modifying the system configurations to ensure automatic start of the malware at system start (rule (5) in Fig. 2).

CCInfrastructure. Any network activity that cannot be classified otherwise is inferred as communication between the bot and the botnet infrastructure. BOT-WATCHER follows the same intuition of the honeypot paradigm. This means that it assumes that any observable behavior is caused by a malicious process and tries to attribute them to malware actions. Although our experiments showed satisfactory results, it is conceivable that the C&C inference rule is overly simplified.

Rootkit. The installation of rootkit components is detected by one of the following two methods. First, the appearance of a new module in the list of loaded kernel modules is inferred as rootkit event. The second method is through kernel callbacks. Certain kernel callbacks are associated with kernel rootkits and include notifications about the creation of new threads and processes or the loading of new user-mode modules. For example, ZeroAccess registers a driver-supplied callback that is subsequently notified whenever an image is loaded for execution.

MassiveFileAccess. This event is inferred when a large amount of files is opened by the malware ($n > 1000$). The intuition behind detecting this type of events is that it characteristic for several malicious activities; first, ransomware may encrypt certain types of files using public-key cryptography, with the private key stored only on the malware's control servers. The malware then offers to decrypt the data if a payment is made by a stated deadline, and threatens to delete the private key if the deadline passes. A second scenario is when malware tries to replicate itself by infecting other executable files in the system. These activities share the property that a large amount of files is opened, which is detected by BOTWATCHER.

Finding the optimal value of such thresholds is quite difficult: a too high value results in several events being missed. On the other hand, a too low value results in benign file activities being mistakenly marked as malicious. The values presented in this paper were sufficient for our experiments. However, these values are not hard coded and the inference rules are configurable. This is done to avoid making it easy to evade detection of events whose inference rules rely on such thresholds. Moreover, we store the extracted execution events so that the inference analysis can be repeated offline if one decided to insert new rules or modify existing ones.

DGA. Modern botnets employ domain generation algorithms (DGA) to periodically generate domain names that can be used as rendezvous points with their C&C servers. This helps the botnet to achieve resilience against takedown attempts and evasion against protection systems that rely upon blacklists. When using a DGA, the bot often generates a large number of domain names and attempts to randomly contact one from the generated domains until it succeeds. BOTWATCHER detects the use of DGAs by leveraging the fact that using DGAs often results in a high failure rate of DNS responses [14].

2.6 Containment

We run each new executable under containment using netfilter/iptables [7]. We confine each piece of malware in its execution by a custom, manually created containment policy that allows us to decide per-flow whether to allow traffic to interact with the outside, drop it, rewrite it, or reroute it. In our scenario, the malware family and behavior is completely unknown when we run a sample. Thus, we create a containment policy that allows us to run our samples safely, and to extract relevant features from their network traffic.

The main challenge is that blocking network connections or redirecting them to internal servers would interfere with the inner workings of the botnet and cause interesting behaviors to go missed. This contradicts with our goal to monitor botnets and identify their lifecycle. On the other hand, running unknown malware completely unsupervised may result in our analysis system participating in malicious actions. We opt for a trade-off between tracking quality and execution containment. Our containment policy blocks SMTP to avoid prevent sending spam. Reverse shells and SOCKS connections are also blocked. Future work includes improving our containment strategy and employ more sophisticated approaches like [22].

3 Evaluation

This section describes the experiments we have performed to demonstrate that our approach is effective for botnet tracking. We first describe our experiment setup, and then present the results of using BOTWATCHER to monitor four current botnets. Finally, we also apply BOTWATCHER to another OS in order to show its genericity. The detailed results of our experiments including the concrete output generated by BOTWATCHER can be found in a supplementary document [12].

3.1 Setup of the Analysis Environment

We conducted our experiments using a PC with a 3.4 GHz Intel Core i7-2600 CPU and 16 GB of main memory. This PC ran Ubuntu 14.04 x86-64. We used

VirtualBox [5] to create three virtual analysis environments running Windows XP SP3 (32-bits, used in Case Study 1 and 4), Windows 8.1 (32-bits, used in Case Study 2 and 3), and Mac OS X 10.9.5 Mavericks (64-bits, used in Case Study 5). The virtual machine was connected to its own private virtual network, which was connected via network address translation to the Internet.

3.2   Case Study 1: Upatre

Upatre is a Trojan downloader that operates at least since August 2013 [10]. It is spread either via drive-by-downloads or spam. We executed Upatre[1] on 2015-01-15 at 12:06 PM and tracked the botnet until 2015-01-22 at 12:15 PM.

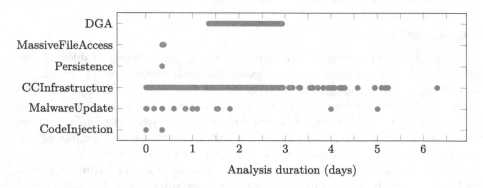

Fig. 3. Upatre case study

Results. Figure 3 shows the inferred behavior of the botnet. Initially, Upatre contacted its C&C server and downloaded an additional binary that was later executed. This binary injected itself into the already running process svchost. exe. Our manual analysis reveals that the new binary is a banking Trojan called Dyzap (also known as Dyre) [3]. BOTWATCHER detected several malware downloads within the first 24 h. Later manual analysis revealed the following: five of these downloads are updates of Dyzap. Some of these updates that occurred in the first six hours were especially interesting; first, the rootkit Pushdo (also known as Cutwail) was downloaded and executed. BOTWATCHER observed then how Pushdo created a registry entry under a key that is often used for surviving system reboots. The second interesting malware update was Pushdo downloading the credential stealer Kegotip. We determined this in a later analysis. BOTWATCHER detected that Kegotip was injected into a newly created process named svchost.exe. Kegotip enumerates all files on the hard disk and checks for online credentials like FTP credentials [1]. After having started, Kegotip began opening and closing a large amount of files, which BOTWATCHER inferred as MASSIVEFILEACCESS behavior. Pushdo began 24 h later resolving many different domain names which failed to resolve. BOTWATCHER inferred that the malware is executing a domain generation algorithm.

---

[1] MD5 sum Upatre: D4A999B1314CFE152774F709BB4EC94B.

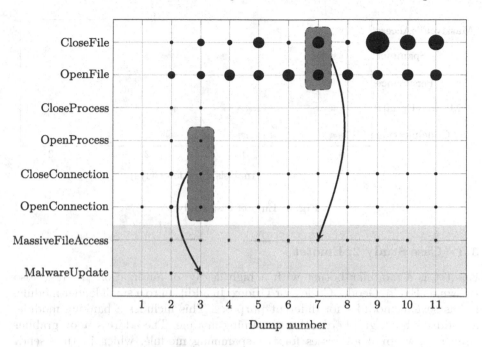

Fig. 4. Example for BOTWATCHER's inference rules. BOTWATCHER infers a malware update (download of Kegotip by Pushdo) in the third dump. Also, a massive file access (enumerating local files to look for credentials) is inferred in the seventh dump.

Figure 4 illustrates how BOTWATCHER inferred the MALWAREDOWNLOAD event corresponding to the download of Kegotip as well as the enumeration of local files that it performed subsequently. The figure shows selected events for eleven consecutive memory dumps. The area of plotted dots is proportional to the number of corresponding events observed in a given dump. At the third dump, BOTWATCHER inferred the sequence of opening a connection, closing the same connection, and starting a new process as a MALWAREDOWNLOAD event. Also, the fact that many files were opened and closed in the seventh dump is inferred as a massive file access event and that corresponds to the enumeration of local files performed by Kegotip.

In total, BOTWATCHER observed four different malware families (Upatre, Dyzap, Pushdo, Kegotip) that form part of this botnet. In the course of the case study BOTWATCHER collected eighteen malware downloads.

Discussion. In this case study, BOTWATCHER illuminated the different components of an Upatre-based botnet. BOTWATCHER was able to extract several artifacts like executable files. Further investigations can be based on these artifacts. We would like to stress that a quick dynamic analysis would have only given a shallow overview of this complex, multi-component botnet. In contrary, BOTWATCHER monitors such botnets for a long time and is capable of detecting various behaviors and dynamically loaded components that would otherwise be missed.

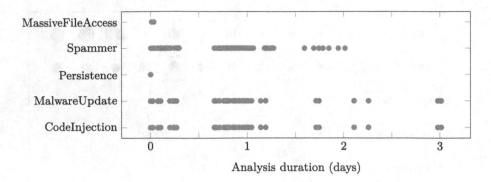

Fig. 5. Emotet case study.

3.3   Case Study 2: Emotet

Emotet is a modular botnet with a high degree of automation [2]. It is also known as Feodo, Geodo, Cridex, or Dridex. In addition to a small loader module, it has several modules for different purposes. This includes a banking module, an address book grabber, and a spamming module. The address book grabber collects new email addresses for the spamming module, which in turn sends emails with the loader module attached. The banking module ensures a steady cash flow [2]. We executed Emotet[2] on 2015-05-19 at 3:56 PM and tracked the botnet until 2015-05-22 at 4:19 PM.

Results. Immediately after execution, Emotet persisted in the system and after thirty minutes it downloaded another binary (`cr_mss3.exe`). As it can be seen in Fig. 5, BOTWATCHER observed that the bot continuously tried to contact several mail servers. By manually reverse engineering the binary, we could confirm that it is in fact a spamming module of Emotet. While the spamming continued, further binaries were downloaded; after three hours BOTWATCHER detected the download and execution of another binary that performed a code injection. Directly after that, BOTWATCHER observed massive access of files performed by the process targeted by code injection. Our manual analysis shows that the downloaded binary is an information stealer malware. The spamming stopped after eight hours. After some period of inactivity, BOTWATCHER observed several downloads of binaries combined with spamming activity that lasted for roughly two thirds of a day. BOTWATCHER collected 48 binaries in total during this case study. All these binaries injected code in other processes, which was correctly detected by BOTWATCHER. 37 of these 48 binaries have unique MD5 hashes and correspond only to a couple of modules that were rehashed periodically.

Discussion. Emotet showed a very high degree of automation during the case study. BOTWATCHER observed periods of spamming, information exfiltration

---

[2] MD5 sum Emotet: `06B92478CB19FDE2665038CBDD0B1420`.

and execution of further binaries. The insights provided by BotWatcher into the botnet life-cycle and the collected binaries during the previous stages of the botnet tracking facilitated our manual investigation of the various modules involved. This allowed us to deduce key aspects of the botnet operation. First, spamming occurs in periods that last several hours. Second, the botnet's modules are frequently rehashed in order to evade AV products. Third, this rehashing occurs more often during spamming periods.

3.4   Case Study 3: Gamarue

Gamarue is a malware downloader that is also known as Andromeda, which is often distributed via spam. For this case study, we took a Gamarue sample from a spam email related to a hotel booking confirmation. We executed this sample[3] on 2015-04-27 at 2:55 PM and tracked the botnet until 2015-05-06 at 7:08 AM.

Results. Initially, BotWatcher detected that Gamarue created a new process – the system process `msiexec.exe` – and injected code into it. Then, Gamarue terminated its dropper process. For the next three days BotWatcher detected continuous HTTP-based C&C-server communication carried out by `msiexec.exe`. On 2015-04-30 at 7:00 PM, BotWatcher observed a download performed by `msiexec.exe` that is followed by the creation of a new process. Subsequently, BotWatcher detected that this process created an autostart registry key in order to persist in the system. Furthermore, BotWatcher noticed that another system process – `svchost.exe` – was started and that code was injected into it. This system process then contacted a C&C-server for further instructions. A manual inspection of the downloaded executable revealed that Gamarue downloaded the bootkit Rovnix. For the rest of this case study, both samples stayed active and continuously contacted their C&C-server.

Discussion. The C&C-server of Gamarue delayed the delivery of Rovnix for around three days. There might be two possible explanations for this behavior. First, the operators of this botnet were very cautious. In this scenario, it took three days until the C&C-server trusted our bot and decided to send further modules to the infected system. Second, the C&C-server had no commands during this period of time and therefore let the bot wait.

The downloaded malware – Rovnix – is also used as infrastructure building malware. Unfortunately, we could not observe further downloads within the last four days of this case study. This case study shows that static analysis and short-time dynamic analysis cannot cope with these kinds of operators. It shows also the importance of tracking botnets for longer than the average sandbox execution time in order to get a full overview about a botnet's activities.

---

[3] MD5 sum Gamarue: `28E01A0E29155E5B993DFF915ACEA976`.

Case Study 4: Necurs. Necurs is a complex botnet that performs several malicious actions like sending spam and distributing additional malware [4]. In order to remain stealthy and avoid detection from security tools, it is equipped with a rootkit component to hide its userland components. We executed Necurs[4] on 2015-01-23 at 8:59 AM and tracked the botnet until 2015-01-26 at 7:32 AM.

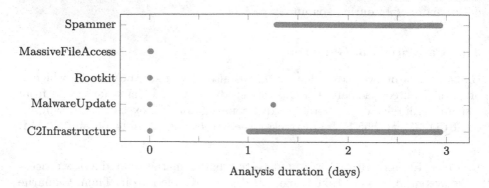

Fig. 6. Necurs case study.

Results. Figure 6 shows the behavior of the botnet as inferred by BOTWATCHER. Necurs started by installing a kernel module and searching through all files on the hard disk. Subsequently, it did not show any interesting activity for 24 h. After that, the bot contacted the C&C server and initiated a download of an additional module. BOTWATCHER detected this as malware update behavior. After 30 h, the analysis environment's hostname was resolved and a connectivity test conducted. Further manual analysis revealed that Necurs checked if its host IP has been already blacklisted on blocking lists. Afterwards, BOT-WATCHER detected continuous C&C communication with two IP addresses. A manual analysis showed that the first IP address was contacted to report back to its C&C server. The second IP was contacted in order to request new spam templates. While continuously contacting its C&C serverand spam template server, it also contacted various mail servers for sending spam. The latter behavior was identified by BOTWATCHER as spamming behavior. This behavior lasted for two days.

Discussion. BOTWATCHER detected all significant behaviors such as malware installation and update, rootkit installation and spamming. The detection of these events pointed us directly to interesting spots so that we could further analyze the detected behavior manually. This case study shows that execution stalling on the client-side in combination with delaying on the server-side are an effective combination for evading short-term dynamic analyses.

---

[4] MD5 sum Necurs: C39FBB4B968C882705F3DACAEF3F51C5.

3.5 Observing Mac OS X: OSX/VidInstaller

Malware also targets new platforms like Mac OS X due to an ongoing diversification of operating systems. However, there are only a few Mac OS X-based botnets at the moment. Unfortunately, we could not find a live botnet for this platform during our experiments. C&C infrastructures of botnets like WireLurker were already sinkholed or taken down. We decided to run BotWatcher with an adware in order to show BotWatcher's capacity to monitor other platforms besides of Microsoft Windows. We chose the adware OSX/VidInstaller. This adware might download and install further software. It comes disguised as a codec, font or key generator. We executed OSX/VidInstaller[5] on 2015-06-03 at 8:57 AM and observed it until 2015-06-03 at 1:13 PM. The guest system was Mac OS X Mavericks (64 bits).

Observation and Discussion. After the execution of OSX/VidInstaller, BotWatcher detected a new process. This process asked the user to agree to its installation. We simulated a user and accepted this request. Subsequently, BotWatcher observed several HTTP-requests to shady-looking domains. Also the browser Safari was started presenting the user a webpage advertising a program called MacKeeper. Once again we simulated a user and installed this program. BotWatcher detected the creation of two MacKeeper-related processes. For the remaining time no further activities occurred.

Foremost, we showed that our approach is also capable of analysing other platforms that are increasingly targeted by cyber criminals. This platform agnosticism is valuable to malware researchers. With the former primary malware target Microsoft Windows in continuous decline, malware authors target other popular platforms such as Mac OS X and Android.

4 Time-Based Evasion Techniques

Malware employs several techniques in order to evade dynamic analysis. A prominent example is execution stalling to delay the execution of the actual malicious payload. This technique exploits the fact that sandboxes analyze the malware for a very limited period of time. Modern analysis approaches can circumvent client-side execution stalling to elicit the malicious behavior (e.g. Hasten [21]). However, command and control servers can also delay delivering modules or commands to their bots. Given the fact that analysis tools cannot manipulate the code on the server side, this is a powerful technique to stall the execution in order to hinder dynamic analysis. Moreover, this serves as mechanism to establish a trust relationship with the recently joined bots. For a botmaster, it is utterly important that a bot can be trusted so as to prevent being infiltrated by malware analysts. Our experiments show that modern botnets move some of these stalling techniques to the server side. This way they can achieve more

---

[5] MD5 sum OSX/VidInstaller: 4ddf5d89249c58c5f0f9b38300b49b91.

resilience against current anti-evasion approaches. We strongly believe that this kind of evasion can only be circumvented by tracking over an extended period of time as performed by BOTWATCHER.

Table 2. Resilience to time-based evasion techniques.

Evasion Technique	BotWatcher	Hasten	Sandboxes
Client-side	✓	✓	✗
Server-side	✓	✗	✗
Both	✓	✗	✗

Our experiments show that there are three types of time-based evasion techniques. These are listed in Table 2. The classic technique is performed by the malware on the client side. This includes calling an API function to sleep or by performing time-consuming computations before actually executing the malicious payload (e.g. Sect. 3.2 Dyzap). The second technique is to delay the execution on the server side (e.g. Sect. 3.2 Gamarue). A combination of these can also be used (e.g. Sect. 3.4 Necurs). Classical sandboxes cannot cope with these techniques. The research community proposed several techniques to overcome time-based evasion techniques on the client side [21]. However, they remain ineffective against server-based techniques. Since we perform monitoring over an extended period of time, we are less likely to be affected by client-side and server-side time-based evasion technique.

5   Limitations

This section discusses limitations of BOTWATCHER. These limitations are memory dump frequency and analysis environment detection.

5.1   Memory Dump Frequency

BOTWATCHER does not monitor every change of the virtual analysis environment's memory. Execution events that start and terminate between two consecutive memory dumps might go missed by BOTWATCHER. However, the corresponding artifacts usually stay for a longer period of time in memory. Therefore, BOTWATCHER finds these data structures and can still detect the corresponding short-living execution events.

5.2   Analysis Environment Detection

BOTWATCHER analyzes malware in a non invasive fashion. However, the malware is run in a virtual analysis environment. Like any dynamic analysis system,

BotWatcher can be detected by malware [11]. As a result the malware might refuse to work properly. However, this is increasingly unlikely since today several productive systems run in virtual machines. We also try to minimize the chance that malware detects our analysis environment by hardening it. For example, we assign real vendor names to virtual hardware devices instead of the default names that are used to fingerprint virtual machines.

An alternative approach would be using bare-metal machines instead of virtual machines [20]. When deploying BotWatcher on bare-metal machines additional challenges have to be faced. BotWatcher's analysis steps are based on memory dumps and network traffic. We could implement the interception of network traffic at networking switches (e.g. mirror port). However, the creation of memory dumps would be a little bit more demanding. A possible way would be direct memory access (DMA). DMA allows hardware devices such as network cards or hard disks to directly read and write the main memory [29]. For example, a specially crafted PCI device would be needed. With it, we could create continuously memory dumps. Unfortunately, it would not be possible to read out all the system's memory at once with DMA. This means that we would have to soften the notion of an exact memory dump at point in time t since the creation of a memory dump would last up to several seconds. However, Volatility can also work with these memory dumps. Please note that the remaining analysis steps of BotWatcher remain unchanged in the bare-metal case.

6   Related Work

This section discusses related work in the fields of botnet tracking and automated dynamic malware analysis.

6.1   Botnet Tracking

Freiling et al. [17] are the first to describe the tracking of botnets in a detailed and scientific manner. Caballero et al. [15] performed a measurement study of Pay-per-Install services. They infiltrated several of these services by implementing milkers. A milker is a hand-crafted replica of a malware downloader that only downloads the malicious payload but does not execute it. Several publications and projects focus on tracking one single malware component of one botnet instance. Plohmann et al. [24] tracked the Miner botnet for four months. The public project ZeuS Tracker tracks Zeus botnet instances [9]. Rossow et. al [25] propose several attack methods for P2P botnets. Their paper features also the tracking of several P2P botnets like ZeusP2P over six weeks. BotWatcher is different from these works. Our approach focuses on generic tracking of multi-component botnets in an automated fashion. We provide a global overview of these botnets without assuming any previous knowledge about the tracked botnet.

Rossow et al. performed a large-scale and long-term analysis for malware downloaders [26]. They analyzed 32 Windows-based malware downloader over two years. They used the Sandnet [27] to execute and dynamically analyze down-loaders' communication architectures, carrier protocols and encryption schemes. While this work presents a generic long-term botnet monitoring system, it does not follow the transparency goal. For example, the system is based on kernel-based Windows system driver that records the file images whenever new processes are forked or system drivers are loaded.

6.2   Botnet Infiltration and Takeover

We aim to generically and transparently analyze unknown botnets. Orthogonal related work monitors previously-known botnets. These approaches leverage knowledge about the functionality and structure of botnets to gain detailed information about several aspects of the botnet operation. For example, Kanich et al. infiltrated the Storm botnet by impersonating proxy peers in the overlay network [19]. They used this approach to analyze two spam campaigns. Stone-Gross et al. took over the Torpig botnet C&C infrastructure and performed a live analysis [28]. This enabled the authors to provide estimates on the botnet size and statistics about the stolen data. Rossow et al. presented several generic attacks against P2P botnets and used them to evaluate the resilience of eleven active P2P botnets [25]. Using these attacks, the authors provide estimation of botnet sizes. The approaches provide more detailed and accurate insights than BotWatcher. However, they rely on previous knowledge and are difficult to adapt to new and previously-unknown botnets.

6.3   Automated Dynamic Malware Analysis

Willems *et al.* [30] present CWSandbox, one of the first dynamic malware system for collecting behavioral information. To achieve this, CWSandbox injects a library into every process space and hooks several APIs. The sandbox is intended for quick behavior-analysis of a large number of samples. Lengyel *et al.* [23] present DRAKVUF, a system that uses active virtual machine introspection by injecting breakpoints into the monitored guest. Each malware sample is run for sixty seconds and behavior information is extracted. Even though they claim their system to be transparent, the injected breakpoints can be easily found by self-hashing [18]. Their system is also vulnerable to time-based evasion techniques. Kirat *et al.* [20] propose BareCloud, a dynamic analysis system based on bare metal machines. This system does not introduce in-guest monitoring components and it is therefore transparent. Although BareCloud focuses on the detection of evasive malware and not on botnet tracking, it can be extended to support our techniques. By periodically providing memory dumps and network traffic, our techniques can be directly applied on top of bare-metal systems like BareCloud. A bare-metal solution of BOTWATCHER might be built on top of BareCloud (see Sect. 5.2).

BOTWATCHER is different from these systems. Our approach does not focus on quickly processing as much malware samples as possible, but rather it focuses on investigating the life-cycle of complex botnets. These botnets consists of several components that can be dynamically downloaded at any point during the botnet operation.

7   Conclusion and Future Work

BOTWATCHER is a novel approach for transparent and generic botnet tracking. It works in a non-invasive way and offers a host-based (memory dumps) as well as network-based (network traffic) view of the botnet life-cycle. To this end, BOTWATCHER analyses the evolution of the analysis environment's state and reconstructs the actions that caused this evolution. Our monitoring approach is less likely to be affected by time-based evasion techniques – on the client and the server side – since BOTWATCHER tracks botnets for a longer period of time than typical sandboxes.

We implemented BOTWATCHER for Microsoft Windows and Mac OS X for both 32- and 64-bits. Our experiments show that BOTWATCHER provided valuable insights into the behavior of the observed botnets. These insights would allow security researchers and law enforcement to better understand the modus operandi of the botnets in order to take further actions.

Future work includes extending the set of inference rules and long-term investigations of botnets. It will also focus on porting BOTWATCHER to further platforms like Android in order to cope with future threats. We also intend to extend the source of information from which we extract the system state to include the hard disk. Furthermore, we will evaluate the current way of creating memory dumps and other possible solutions in order to minimize the time during which the VM is unresponsive.

Acknowledgments. We would like to thank our shepherd Christian Rossow for his assistance to improve the quality of this paper. We also want to express our gratitude toward the reviewers for their helpful feedback, valuable comments and suggestions.

References

1. Blue Coat Labs, CryptoLocker, Kegotip, Medfos Malware Triple-Threat, 26 September 2015. http://bluecoat.com/security-blog/2013-10-11/cryptolocker-kegotip-medfos-malware-triple-threat
2. Kaspersky Lab ZAO, The Banking Trojan Emotet: Detailed Analysis, 26 September 2015. http://securelist.com/analysis/publications/69560/the-banking-trojan-emotet-detailed-analysis
3. Microsoft Malware Protection Center, MSRT January 2015 - Dyzap, 26 September 2015. http://blogs.technet.com/b/mmpc/archive/2015/01/13/msrt-january-2015-dyzap.aspx
4. Microsoft Malware Protection Center, Unexpected reboot: Necurs, 26 September 2015. http://blogs.technet.com/b/mmpc/archive/2012/12/07/unexpected-reboot-necurs.aspx

5. Oracle VirtualBox, 26 September 2015. www.virtualbox.org
6. The Bro Network Security Monitor, 26 September 2015. www.bro.org
7. The netfilter project (1999). www.netfilter.org
8. The Volatility Foundation, 26 September 2015. www.volatilityfoundation.org
9. ZeuS Tracker, 26 September 2015. www.zeustracker.abuse.ch
10. Zscaler Research, Evolution of Upatre Trojan Downloader, 26 September 2015. www.research.zscaler.com/2014/11/evolution-of-upatre-trojan-downloader.html
11. Balzarotti, D., Cova, M., Karlberger, C., Kirda, E., Kruegel, C., Vigna, G.: Efficient detection of split personalities in malware. In: Network and Distributed System Security Symposium (NDSS) (2010)
12. Barabosch, T.: Complementary material used in Botwatcher: Transparent and Generic Botnet Tracking, 26 September 2015. http://net.cs.uni-bonn.de/wg/cs/staff/thomas-barabosch/
13. Barabosch, T., Eschweiler, S., Gerhards-Padilla, E.: Bee master: detecting host-based code injection attacks. In: Dietrich, S. (ed.) DIMVA 2014. LNCS, vol. 8550, pp. 235–254. Springer, Heidelberg (2014)
14. Bilge, L., Kirda, E., Kruegel, C., Balduzzi, M.: EXPOSURE: finding malicious domains using passive DNS analysis. In: Network and Distributed System Security Symposium (NDSS) (2011)
15. Caballero, J., Grier, C., Kreibich, C., Paxson, V.: Measuring pay-per-install: the commoditization of malware distribution. In: USENIX Security Symposium (2011)
16. Denneman, F.: Memory Deep Dive - Optimizing for Performance, 26 September 2015. http://frankdenneman.nl/2015/02/20/memory-deep-dive/
17. Freiling, F.C., Holz, T., Wicherski, G.: Botnet tracking: exploring a root-cause methodology to prevent distributed denial-of-service attacks. In: di Vimercati, S.C., Syverson, P.F., Gollmann, D. (eds.) ESORICS 2005. LNCS, vol. 3679, pp. 319–335. Springer, Heidelberg (2005)
18. Horne, B., Matheson, L.R., Sheehan, C., Tarjan, R.E.: Dynamic self-checking techniques for improved tamper resistance. In: Sander, T. (ed.) DRM 2001. LNCS, vol. 2320, pp. 141–159. Springer, Heidelberg (2002)
19. Kanich, C., Kreibich, C., Levchenko, K., Enright, B., Voelker, G.M., Paxson, V., Savage, S.: Spamalytics: an empirical analysis of spam marketing conversion. In: Proceedings of the 15th ACM Conference on Computer and Communications Security (CCS) (2008)
20. Kirat, D., Vigna, G., Kruegel, C.: BareCloud: bare-metal analysis-based evasive malware detection. In: USENIX Security Symposium (2014)
21. Kolbitsch, C., Kirda, E., Kruegel, C.: The power of procrastination: detection and mitigation of execution-stalling malicious code. In: ACM Conference on Computer and Communications Security (CCS) (2011)
22. Kreibich, C., Weaver, N., Kanich, C., Cui, W., Paxson, V.: GQ: practical containment for measuring modern malware systems. In: ACM SIGCOMM Internet Measurement Conference (IMC) (2011)
23. Lengyel, T.K., Maresca, S., Payne, B.D., Webster, G.D., Vogl, S., Kiayias, A.: Scalability, fidelity and stealth in the DRAKVUF dynamic malware analysis system. In: Annual Computer Security Applications Conference (ACSAC) (2014)
24. Plohmann, D., Gerhards-Padilla, E.: Case study of the Miner Botnet. In: International Conference on Cyber Conflict (CYCON) (2012)
25. Rossow, C., Andriesse, D., Werner, T., Stone-Gross, B., Plohmann, D., Dietrich, C.J., Bos, H.: P2PWNED: modeling and evaluating the resilience of peer-to-peer botnets. In: IEEE Symposium on Security and Privacy (S&P) (2013)

26. Rossow, C., Dietrich, C., Bos, H.: Large-scale analysis of malware downloaders. In: Flegel, U., Markatos, E., Robertson, W. (eds.) DIMVA 2012. LNCS, vol. 7591, pp. 42–61. Springer, Heidelberg (2013)
27. Rossow, C., Dietrich, C.J., Bos, H., Cavallaro, L., van Steen, M., Freiling, F.C., Pohlmann, N.: Sandnet: network traffic analysis of malicious software. In: Proceedings of Building Analysis Datasets and Gathering Experience Returns for Security (BADGERS) (2011)
28. Stone-Gross, B., Cova, M., Cavallaro, L., Gilbert, B., Szydlowski, M., Kemmerer, R., Kruegel, C., Vigna, G.: Your Botnet is My Botnet: analysis of a Botnet takeover. In: Proceedings of the 16th ACM Conference on Computer and Communications Security (CCS) (2009)
29. Weis, S.: Protecting data in use from firmware and physical attacks. In: BlackHat (2014)
30. Willems, C., Holz, T., Freiling, F.: Toward automated dynamic malware analysis using CWSandbox. In: IEEE Symposium on Security and Privacy (S&P) (2007)

Elite: Automatic Orchestration of Elastic Detection Services to Secure Cloud Hosting

Yangyi Chen[1][✉], Vincent Bindschaedler[2], XiaoFeng Wang[1], Stefan Berger[3], and Dimitrios Pendarakis[3]

[1] Indiana University Bloomington, Bloomington, USA
{yangchen,xw7}@indiana.edu
[2] University of Illinois Urbana-Champaign, Champaign, USA
bindsch2@illinois.edu
[3] IBM Thomas J. Watson Research Center, Yorktown Heights, USA
{stefanb,dimitris}@us.ibm.com

Abstract. Intrusion detection on today's cloud is challenging: a user's application is automatically deployed through new *cloud orchestration* tools (e.g., OpenStack Heat, Amazon CloudFormation, etc.), and its computing resources (i.e., virtual machine instances) come and go dynamically during its runtime, depending on its workloads and configurations. Under such a dynamic environment, a centralized detection service needs to keep track of the state of the whole deployment (a *cloud stack*), size up and down its own computing power and dynamically allocate its existing resources and configure new resources to catch up with what happens in the application. Particularly in the case of anomaly detection, new application instances created at runtime are expected to be protected instantly, without going through conventional profile learning, which disrupts the operations of the application.

To address those challenges, we developed *Elite*, a new elastic computing framework, to support high-performance detection services on the cloud. Our techniques are designed to be fully integrated into today's cloud orchestration mechanisms, allowing an o rdinary cloud user to requ est a detection service and specify its parameters conveniently, through the cloud-formation file she submits for deploying her application. Such a detection service is supported by a high-performance stream-processing engine, and optimized for concurrent analysis of a large amount of data streamed from application instances and automatic adaptation to different computing scales. It is linked to the cloud orchestration engine through a communication mechanism, which provides the runtime information of the application (e.g., the types of new instances created) necessary for the service to dynamically configure its resources. To avoid profile learning, we further studied a set of techniques that enable reuse of normal behavior profiles across different instances within one user's cloud stack, and across different users (in a privacy-preserving way). We evaluated our implementation of Elite on popular web applications deployed over 60 instances. Our study shows that Elite efficiently shares profiles without losing their accuracy and effectively handles dynamic, intensive workloads incurred by these applications.

© Springer International Publishing Switzerland 2015
H. Bos et al. (Eds.): RAID 2015, LNCS 9404, pp. 588–614, 2015.
DOI: 10.1007/978-3-319-26362-5_27

1 Introduction

Cloud computing has emerged as the mainstay of cost-effective, high-performance platforms for hosting personal and organizational information assets and computing tasks. This thriving computing paradigm, however, also comes with security perils. Recent years have seen a rising trend of security breaches in the cloud. Examples include the high-impact attacks on Amazon AWS [1] and Dropbox [2]. Countering those threats requires effective security protection, which today mainly relies upon the virtual-machine (VM) instances with assorted protection mechanisms (firewalls, intrusion detection systems, malware scanners, etc.) pre-installed. Prominent examples include McAfee, Trend-Micro and Alert Logic [3–5], all of which provide such instances with embedded security agents to their customers for running their cloud applications.

A fundamental issue for this solution is that each instance has to allocate resources for accommodating a complete security system, even when it cannot make full use of the system most of the time. This goes against the resource-sharing, on-demand service design of the cloud. As a result, the same security functionalities are duplicated across all the instances when running a cloud application, even for those temporarily rented to handle the burst of workloads. Resources are squandered in this way when some instances do not have enough workloads to merit the cost of operating the whole set of security mechanisms (e.g., loading a large number of signatures into memory for malware scanning). This inevitably interferes with the operations of the user application running within the same instance. Further, security systems hosted in different instances work independently, which fails to leverage cross-instance information to better protect the cloud.

All these problems can be addressed by a centralized detection framework that concurrently serves different application instances, for example, through inspecting audit trails from those instances to detect cloud-wide malicious activities. Deployment of such a service, however, faces significant challenges in a dynamic cloud environment, where different instances are generated and their connections with assorted computing resources (storages, other instances) are established during runtime. Management of this environment is complicated enough to justify the use of an *orchestration* mechanism, such as OpenStack *Heat* [6] and Amazon *CloudFormation* [7], which automatically creates different types of cloud instances in response to changes to an application's workload, links them to each other and other cloud resources, and further configures the *software stack* (a set of software packages for performing a task) within individual instances according to the cloud user's specifications (called *template*). Clearly, to protect those instances, the detection service needs to work closely with the orchestration process.

Challenges. To better understand the challenges for the detection service to work in the cloud environment, let us look at a simple system with three *auto-scaling* groups, whose resource level, such as the number of instances, goes up or down automatically according to conditions set by the cloud user. These groups are assigned to host load balancers, web servers, and database servers respectively. Effective protection of all their instances needs a high-performance detection engine capable of auto-scaling. More specifically, during runtime, some of the groups may expand, adding in more instances to help manage extra workload. This puts the detection service protecting them under pressure, which may also need to scale up its capability to handle new tasks so that it can timely respond to malicious events. This process is actually much more complicated than it appears to be, involving re-arrangement of tasks, for example, connecting a new detector instance to a set of application instances, and configuring the detector properly according to the contexts of those instances, e.g., whether they are load balancers, web servers or database servers.

Further, in the case of anomaly detection, where the intrusion detection system (IDS) is supposed to catch an application instance's deviation from its normal behavior, the detector needs to instantly create a normal behavior profile for every instance generated in an auto-scaling process, based upon its context information such as its software stack and configurations. Note that this needs to be done in the most efficient way possible: given the large scale of the computation the cloud undertakes and timely responses it needs to make to workload changes, we cannot directly adopt conventional approaches, such as profile learning, which could take a long time to build up an instance's behavior model. Those issues can only be addressed by new techniques that incorporate the detection service into the orchestration mechanism, making the service work seamlessly within the cloud work-flow and tuning it to meet the high performance demands from the cloud. However, except for some attempts to directly deploy secure instances (just like ordinary instances) through CloudFormation, as TrendMicro [4] does, so far, little has been done to understand how to automatically arrange, coordinate and manage centralized security services and their resources through cloud orchestration.

Our Approach. To this end, we developed a new *elastic intrusion detection framework*, called *Elite*, as an extension of the cloud orchestration mechanism. Elite is designed to support parallel detection systems, automatically scheduling them on-demand, provisioning their resources and allocating their tasks. A cloud user can conveniently require detection services through her template when she specifies the infrastructure for her cloud application using the file. Based upon the template, an orchestration mechanism enhanced with Elite automatically creates detector instances, configures them based upon their context information, connects them to cloud resources and scales their number up and down according to the application's workload. Also as part of the framework, those instances accommodate a high-performance distributed stream-processing engine to support different detection techniques.

Elite also includes a novel technique that quickly builds up a normal profile for each newly-created application instance, through adjusting the profiles of other instances within the same auto-scaling group. The idea here is that since those instances accommodate an identical software stack with identical configurations, and are tasked to process the same datasets, their behaviors should be very similar (but not identical). More specifically, our approach first generalizes the profiles from multiple instances within the same group into a *profile template*, and then specializes it using the parameters (e.g., temporary file names) of a new instance automatically identified. In this way, instances acquired by the cloud application during its runtime are automatically profiled and protected. We further developed a technique that enables profile reuse across different auto-scaling groups, particularly when a cloud user wants to take advantage of existing profiles (from other users) associated with a similar software configuration to avoid training her detector instance from scratch. This profile sharing needs to be done in a privacy-preserving manner, given the sensitivity of individual users' system configurations. Our approach is built upon a simple security protocol that helps one user retrieve the profile from another party when their configurations are close enough, without exposing their sensitive information to each other and the cloud.

We implemented Elite on Openstack's Heat orchestration engine and utilized *Apache Storm*, a high-performance stream processing system, to build detection services. Our implementation was evaluated using a cloud application capable of scaling up to 60 instances. During our experiments, Elite ran anomaly detection and the profiles it automatically created were found to work effectively, without any negative impact on the effectiveness of the underlying detection technique. Also, our stress test shows that Elite introduced negligible overheads and was well adapted to dynamic workloads.

Contributions. The contributions of the paper are summarized below:

- *New framework for elastic detection services.* We designed a new framework to support high-performance auto-scaling detection services. This framework has been fully integrated into the existing cloud orchestration mechanism, which enables a user to conveniently specify the parameters for detector instances together with other cloud resources she requests for her application. The cloud then acts on such specifications to automatically structure and restructure the infrastructure of the detection service and scale its capability in accordance with the application's workload. Our framework also utilizes a high-performance stream processing engine to accommodate different detection techniques.
- *Profile reuse techniques.* We developed a suite of new techniques to reuse normal behavior profiles within one auto-scaling groups and across different groups. Our approach leverages the similarity among different cloud instances' software configurations to generate accurate profiles for the instances dynamically created during runtime. Also, sharing of profiles between different users is supported by a security mechanism that preserves the privacy of the parties involved.
- *Implementation and evaluation.* We implemented our design on OpenStack and evaluated it using 60 cloud instances. Our study shows that our framework and techniques work effectively in practice, incurring negligible overheads.

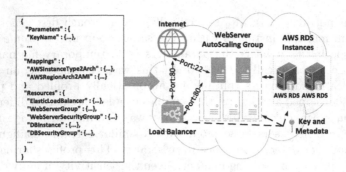

Fig. 1. Cloud orchestration example

2 Background

In this section, we provide background information for our research, including brief introductions to cloud orchestration techniques, IDS systems and the stream processing engine that supports our high-performance detection service.

Cloud Orchestration. The orchestration mechanism, also known as *orchestrator*, is a critical cloud service that automates arrangement, coordination and management of the cloud resources for a complicated application the user deploys on the cloud. To use the service, the user is supposed to describe the infrastructure of the application in a text file (a template) and submit it to the orchestrator. Within the template are the specifications of types of cloud instances, their software stacks and their relationships with other resources, for example, how an Amazon EC2 instance is connected to an Amazon RDS database instance. For each instance, one can utilize the configuration management tools integrated with the template to define how its software should be configured. Also various services provided by the orchestrator, such as auto-scaling, can also be requested as a resource within the template. Figure 1 shows a simplified template file and the application infrastructure it defines.

Using the template, the orchestrator automatically manages the whole life-cycle of the user's application, acquiring new resources from the cloud, configuring them, re-arranging tasks for different instances when new workloads come up and deleting resources when a job is done. The whole infrastructure can be conveniently adjusted by the user through updating her template. Such functionalities are supported by mainstream orchestration products, including Openstack Heat [6] and Amazon CloudFormation [7]. Also well-specified templates are extensively reused and customized by cloud users to quickly deploy their applications.

In our research, we incorporate a high-performance parallel IDS service into the orchestration mechanism as a cloud resource, which can be conveniently specified in a template. To provide the service with context information necessary for its operations, we further modified the orchestrator, adding a new channel for it to communicate with the IDS resource. Also, we constructed a template with necessary configurations to enable auto-scaling and configuration of detector instances, which can be customized by a cloud user to integrate the service into her application infrastructure.

Intrusion Detection. Intrusion detection techniques have served as the backbone of organizational security protection for decades. An IDS detects malicious activities either through identifying a set of signatures (signature-based detection) or through monitoring a system's deviations from its normal behavior profile (anomaly detection). Examples for the former include network intrusion detectors like snort, which screens network traffic flows for the patterns of known threats (e.g., propagation of Internet worms), and host-based scanners that inspect the code of suspicious programs or their behaviors (e.g., system calls) [8–11] to catch malware. Anomaly detection, on the other hand, typically looks at a legitimate program's operations to find out whether it is doing something that it normally does not do, based on its behavior profile. Such a profile can be system-call sequences [12–14], or just a white list of system calls (with parameters) the program is supposed to make when it is not compromised, as many host-based detectors (e.g., *systrace* [15]) do. In our research, we implemented a simple signature-based detector and a white-list based anomaly detector for inspecting audit trails submitted by application instances. Note that our framework is also capable of supporting more complicated techniques, like call-sequence based anomaly detection.

Such conventional detection techniques, particularly those host-based, are not designed to serve a large number of cloud instances and process a large amount of data at a high speed. To move them into a cloud service, we need to incorporate them into a parallel, high-performance computing platform. What was adopted in our design is a stream processing engine, as elaborated below.

Stream Processing. A stream processing engine is a distributed computing system for analyzing unbounded streams of data in real time. This capability is crucial to the mission of the cloud detection service, which receives a large amount of data streamed from different instances. Examples of such systems include IBM InfoSphere Streams [16], Apache Storm [17] etc. In our research, we built our distributed detection service on top of Storm.

Storm is an open-source system known for its fast speed and ease of use [18]. A typical Storm system is deployed as a *cluster*, which includes a *Nimbus node*, a *Zookeeper* [19] node and a set of *Supervisor* nodes. The Nimbus node is the master of the whole cluster, in charge of managing the interaction topology of the cluster as well as task allocation and tracking. Zookeeper helps coordinate Nimbus and Supervisors, which run a group of *worker* processes to do the real job. Among the workers, a set of *sprout* processes receive streaming data from other cloud instances and route it to *bolts*, which perform the user's computation task on the data (e.g., filtering, aggregating, database access, etc.). The interconnections among sprouts and bolts form a topology managed by the Nimbus and predefined by the Storm user.

Over the Storm platform, we specified a topology and implemented detection algorithms into bolts, together with a mechanism for interacting with the Heat engine for getting context information of newly-created instances. The details of this parallel detection service are explicated in Sect. 3.2.

3 Design and Implementation

In this section, we present the design of Elite, which is meant to achieve the following goals:

- *High performance*. The detection service should work in parallel, concurrently processing a large number of streams, and also auto-scaling, dynamically extending and shrinking its computing resources in response to changes to its workload.
- *Context information support*. The framework should be able to effectively communicate with the detection service a cloud application's state information. Particularly when new resources are added into the application's infrastructure, the detection service needs their context information to determine how to protect the resources.
- *Ease of use*. Through our framework, we expect that a cloud user can directly require the detection service and set its parameters, including the amount of computing resources she is willing to rent for the service and detection algorithms, without going through a complicated process of configuring individual instances that host the service.

This design was implemented over the open-source OpenStack Heat orchestration system and the Apache Storm engine. Here we first describe Elite at a high level and then elaborate on its technical details.

3.1 Overview

Architecture. The architecture of Elite is illustrated in Fig. 2. This detection framework has been built around the cloud orchestration system. It includes an extension to the *cloud formation language* used to describe an application's infrastructure for automatic configuration of our detection service, a communication mechanism built into the orchestration system for collecting the contexts of the application's runtime and dispatching such information to the detector instances, and a set of VM images for different types of parallel detection mechanisms (signature-based or anomaly detection) implemented over a stream-processing engine.

How it Works. Consider a cloud user who requests a detection service from the cloud to protect her application. All she needs to do is to state the detection image (associated with different detection techniques) and auto-scaling conditions (e.g., creating a new instance when the processing time of the detection service goes above a threshold) within the template she submits to the cloud for running her application. The specifications are then parsed by the orchestration system, which runs a template we built to automatically configure the whole

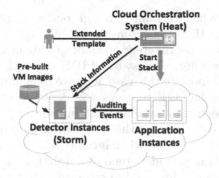

Fig. 2. System architecture

detection infrastructure, setting parameters for individual detector instances and connecting them to application instances. During the application's runtime, the auditing daemons(which can be pre-configured and incorporated into the application image) within its instances stream audit trails to the detectors. Also, the orchestrator continuously updates the detectors the state of the application, particularly context information of any auto-scaling groups or new instances dynamically generated. In the case of anomaly detection, the orchestrator can run a few "training" instances that generate input traffic to application instances for building up their normal behavior profiles and bootstrapping a whole auto-scaling group. When this happens, the detector needs to be informed that the system operates in a "training mode[1]".

All the detector instances are created from a selected detection image. They work concurrently on a large number of streams from application instances. Those detectors can go through all the audit trails to look for attack signatures or any deviations from the application's normal behaviors. When it comes to anomaly detection, the detectors also need to find out whether the system runs in a training mode, in which they automatically build up profiles for different instances (e.g., a list of system calls and their parameters) and further generalize them into a profile template within each auto-scaling group. During the normal operation of the application, such profile templates are specialized automatically to provide instant protection for every new instance. Also, profiles are reused across different auto-scaling groups and even different users to shorten or even remove the whole training stage. Such reuse needs to happen in a privacy-preserving way, given the sensitivity of the user's system configurations. This is achieved in our system through a simple security mechanism.

---

[1] How long the detector needs to stay in "training mode" depends on many factors such as the nature of the service provided by the application instances, the quality of training inputs, and to what extent the cloud user can tolerate the false positives. Precise tuning of the training time and the trade-offs involved is not the focus of this paper.

Adversary Model. What we built is a high-performance, auto-scaling cloud platform for supporting IDS. Depending on specific IDS techniques running on top of Elite, we need to make different assumptions about the adversary's capabilities. Specifically, for a normal host-based IDS, the sensor for collecting audit trails runs as an OS daemon. In this case, we have to assume that the OS kernel is sound. On the other hand, if the sensor is deployed at the level of virtual machine monitor, the detection system operating within Elite can catch kernel-level attacks. Also, we consider that the orchestrator has not been compromised and the cloud is honest but curious when it comes to cloud users' data privacy. In practice, commercial cloud providers tend to refrain from inspecting the content of their customers' instances for liability concerns. All we want to avoid here is to expose more data than the customer is willing to share to the cloud.

3.2   Detection Service Orchestration

As described before, Elite supports a convenient set-up of a high-performance detection service and automatic orchestration of the service in response to the states of the user's cloud application. Here we elaborate the techniques behind this elastic, scalable detection platform, including the extension made to the template language, a stream-based IDS platform and a high-performance detection system built on top of it, and the mechanism for coordinating the cloud orchestrator and our detector instances.

Detection Service Specification. To integrate our detection service into the cloud orchestrator, we extended the template language to allow the user to conveniently set up the detection service. Specifically, our extension includes a new group of cloud resources "AWS::IDS::ENGINE_NAME", which describes a special auto-scaling group for detectors, whose type (ENGINE_NAME) is specified by the user. Each detector type is associated with a pre-built VM image that hosts a parallel, stream-based detection algorithm. As an example, we implemented in our research a concurrent anomaly detector running Systrace-like profile based detection [15]. The detector was constructed in a way that it can easily incorporate other detection mechanisms and also support attack path analysis, which we discuss later.

Using this new statement, the user can request the detection service from the cloud and further describes auto-scaling conditions for the service. For example, the user can specify a fixed auto-scaling ratio or let the detection service auto-scale based on conditions like `message processing delay` or `CPU usage` of the detector instances. After Heat parses the statement and its related settings, it automatically creates detector instances from the image the user chooses and builds an auto-scaling group to accommodate the instances. Within each instance, Heat further invokes a script we built to configure the IDS engine with a set of default parameters. For example, `NumFileBolts` defines how many bolts the user wants Storm Engine to start for processing file-related system calls. The user can also change the default value of those parameters when submitting the template for stack creation through Heat API. We further developed configuration scripts to run inside each instance generated by the user's application to set up an auditing daemon that streams out the instance's audit trails during its runtime.

Stream-Based IDS Platform. At the receiving end of the audit-trail streams are the detector instances. In our research, those instances were all built on top of the Storm stream-processing engine. As described before, a Storm cluster includes two types of worker nodes, sprouts and bolts, which connect to each other to form a network structure as part of the system's configuration. For simplicity, our implementation just utilizes one sprout node to receive streams from application instances and dispatch them to different bolt nodes. The latter can be added at the system's runtime to handle extra workload brought in by the application during its auto-scaling process. When this happens, each new bolt is dynamically connected to the sprout. A direct use of this stream-based IDS platform is just to let the stream from each application instance be taken care of by one bolt. For this purpose, the bolt was built to gather context information from a database maintained by Heat and upload data such as intrusion signatures or normal behavior patterns of the application from Storm's internal database to its memory, which we elaborate later. With such supports, a classic signature-based or anomaly IDS can directly run within the bolt to process the audit trails from application instances.

A problem for this design is the lack of cooperations among bolts. Such cooperations can potentially improve the performance and flexibility of the whole detection service. In our research, we implemented a simple Systrace-like system-call inspection system, which is designed to concurrently process audit trails from hundreds of application instances, each containing a large number of calls. Those calls are checked one by one against the behavior profile of each instance, including the names and parameter patterns of the calls considered to be normal for the instance. Those profiles are maintained within the detector database. A small set of them are created offline when the whole template stack (the cloud application and the detection service) runs in a training mode. Most of them, however, are generated online through profile reuse within an auto-scaling group or across different groups, which we describe in Sect. 3.3.

The operations of an application often generate a huge amount of auditing data. For example, opening Firefox and using it to perform a Google search can produce as many as 36936 system calls. To avoid the performance overheads on both the application instance and the detector, our system-call inspector only focuses on several categories of calls considered to be inevitable for an intrusion to succeed. More specifically, what are currently inspected in our detector include those for operating on file systems (e.g., open), networking (e.g., connect) and generating a remote shell (e.g., execve)[2]. For the Firefox example, this means the inspector needs to check only 44 (instead of 36936) system calls. We further designed the detection service in a way that a group of bolts were tuned to processing a single category of calls only. This allows the bolts to work more

---

[2] Those calls need to happen on almost all intrusion vectors (as evidenced by our false negative evaluation in Sect. 4.2). Also our design can be easily extended to accommodate other types of calls.

efficiently on the data, helps better balance the workload across different bolts and most importantly makes it possible to integrate other detection mechanisms into the system. Specifically, bolts working on the same category only need to maintain the profiles of the system calls in that category across all auto-scaling groups, instead of complete profiles of those groups in the case that one bolt is assigned with the whole stream from a random application instance within the template stack. Also, depending on the number of calls observed in each category, the system can dynamically increase or decrease the number of bolts associated with the category to better allocate the resources of the detection service. Further, this treatment automatically organizes the outputs of our detector into categories: all file operations are assigned to one set of bolts and network activities are given to the other set, etc. As a result, we can conveniently let those bolts stream their outputs to another set of bolts that run other detection mechanisms. Particularly, in our implementation, we added a group of bolts that run Snort on the content produced by network calls, which are transmitted from the workers associated with the network category.

Our implementation serving this purpose is illustrated in Fig. 3. We built two layers of bolts. On the first layer are *dispatchers* that parse streams, extract system calls, group them into vectors with various lengths depending on the category of the calls. A simplified form of such a vector is (mac, ID, program, name, parameters), which describes the MAC address of the instance from which the call was initiated, its identifier within the cloud (including the number of its stack and the name of its auto-scaling group), the program that made the call, the name of the system function called and its parameters. Note that the identifier ID is left blank by the dispatchers, which cannot directly observe them. Based upon name (the call type it is associated with), the vectors are regrouped. Those within the same category (file operations, networking, etc.) are streamed to the same group of worker bolts on the second layer. The worker bolts maintain the profiles of different instances within their memory, which only include the functions in the category and their parameters. During its runtime, each worker uses a vector's mac to locate the profile for a specific instance and checks whether other elements of the vector, such as program, name and parameters, are in compliance with it. These workers also retrieve the identifier for each MAC address from the orchestrator, which is used for profile sharing. Behind those bolts, our implementation can accommodate other layers of bolts in the user's request, for the purpose of signature-based detection and attack graph reconstruction.

Automated Orchestration and Scaling. Although the detection service is configured by Heat and automatically scales through Heat, the communication between them is quite limited during runtime. Particularly, the service does not know what happens in the user's cloud application, for example, when a new instance is created and which auto-scaling group the instance belongs to. Without such information, it is almost impossible for the service to properly configure new detector instances in response to the dynamics within the application. To address this issue, we built into Heat a mechanism to facilitate its communication

Fig. 3. Detector Storm topology

Fig. 4. Automated Orchestration and Scaling

with the detection service at runtime, through its OpenStack Heat database and Storm's internal database. Figure 4 illustrates how the mechanism works.

Specifically, we modified Heat's database, adding in three tables (ids_stack, ids_autoscaling and ids_instance) for a user's stack, auto-scaling groups and application instances respectively. Among them, ids_stack is for profile reuse across different stacks, ids_autoscaling maintains all the auto-scaling groups within the same stack and ids_instance keeps all instances within the same group. Those tables are utilized by Heat when building up the whole stack and dynamically adjusting its infrastructure, adding or removing instances from different auto-scaling groups. In this way, the orchestrator keeps record of the provenance for each instance, i.e., the stack and auto-scaling group it belongs to. Such information is saved to the role attribute of the instance. In our implementation, we instrumented Heat engine functions EngineService.create_stack, resources.AutoScalingGroup._handle_create, StackResource.create_with _template and resources.instance.check_create_complete to operate on those tables and track the provenance of each instance

Through the instance table, the Heat orchestrator can mark the status of a stack as "training" or "enforcement". This mark is then passed to the detector that queries the Heat database for instance information. Such a query needs to go through proper authentication, which in our research is based upon the cloud user's credential, as the database is shared among different users. With the state information from the orchestrator, the detection service will decide whether to learn a behavior profile (which is kept within Storm's internal database) of an instance or go ahead to detect its suspicious behaviors using the existing profile or malicious activities by looking for known signatures. When the application adds in new instances within its auto-scaling group, the detection service will notice that new MAC addresses show up, whose profiles and other information are not present in the internal database. In this case, the service will query the instance table in the Heat database for a newly observed MAC address to get the role of its instance. This attribute, as elaborated before, contains the provenance of the instance, which enables the detector to figure out how to reuse existing profiles for protecting the instance in an anomaly detection.

3.3   Context-Aware Profile Configuration

Challenges in Anomaly Detection on the Cloud. As mentioned before, the high-performance IDS platform within Elite can support different kinds of detection techniques. For signature-based detection, all we need to do is just running the existing mechanism within the bolts tasked to process the whole streams of individual application instances. When it comes to anomaly detection, however, we have to consider the complexity introduced by profile learning. Specifically, there should be an off-line learning stage during which training traffic is used to drive the operations of the user's application. The audit trails produced thereby are analyzed by the detection service for constructing different instances' profiles. More challenging here is profiling a newly created instance during the application's runtime, which needs to happen in real-time. Although it is conceivable that the new instance will behave in a similar way as others within the same auto-scaling group, subtle differences can still exist in their profiles. The problem we faced in our research is how to automatically construct an accurate profile without going through the learning stage, both for the instances within an existing auto-scaling group and for those in a newly created stack. Following we elaborate a set of techniques that facilitate reuse of profiles within one group and cross users.

Profile Generation and Reuse. Profile learning is fully supported by Elite. Once a user selects an anomaly detection image when building her template, the Elite components within Heat automatically set the application's execution mode to "training" as soon as the stack is deployed. Through Heat, our implementation creates a set of instances, based upon the user's specification, to run scripts[3] that generate training traffic for the whole stack. For example, these instances can produce HTTP traffic to a web application running on top of Apache servers deployed in application instances. In the meantime, the detection service learns from individual instances' audit trails invariants in their behaviors and save such profiles to the detector's database. Also, all the profiles from different instances within the same auto-scaling group are generalized into a profile template. During the system's runtime, whenever a new instance is created for a group, its template signature is then specialized according to the unique feature of the new instance to provide it immediate protection.

For the Storm-based system call inspector implemented in our research, its learning phase involves 2 to 5 instances per auto-scaling group. Each of these instances is monitored by a set of concurrently running detector instances. As discussed before, those detectors extract from the application instance's audit trail system-call vectors and classify them into different categories according to the types of the calls (e.g., all those related to file operations). The recipients of the vector stream within one category, the worker bolts, further group all the vectors using their MAC addresses, program names, specific system call names and others, and removes duplicated ones. For example, all the system calls **open**

---

[3] An example here is JMeter Script Recorder, which can be provided by the cloud and customized by the user.

from a given `mac` and a specific program are placed inside one group and for each vector within the group, others with the exactly same parameters are dropped. The worker bolts further attempt to generalize call parameters across the vectors within the group. Particularly, for each outgoing network call, they contact the Heat orchestrator to find out whether the call is made to another auto-scaling group: for example, a web server instance accesses an instance within the auto-scaling group of database servers. Note that such connections are typical for a cloud application, which actually describe the topology of its whole stack. What our approach does here is to replace the IP address within the parameters for such a network call (e.g., `connect`) with the identifier (e.g. `102-DBServerGroup`, where 102 is the number of the stack and the rest part is the group name) of the target auto-scaling group. This step is necessary for reducing the false positives of the profile generated by the bolts, which comprises all those generalized vectors for a specific MAC address and is stored under the identifer of the application instance or its auto-scaling group.

The detection service further compares the profiles from multiple instances within the same auto-scaling group to generate a profile template. Specifically, the vectors that appear across all profiles are directly moved to the template. For other vectors, our approach inspects them one by one, across the profiles, looking for the invariants in the parameters of the same system call (from the same program) and the strings that match a set of predetermined patterns (e.g., the instance's identifier). For example, consider the call `open(/var/lib/cloud/i-0000010a/config)` in one profile and `open (/var/lib/cloud/i-0000010b/config)` in another. The vector (`mac`, ID, `program`, `open`, `/var/lib/cloud/(instance_id)/config`) will be added to the template. Note that `mac` is left blank here, which needs to be filled with the MAC address of a new instance and the content "`(instance_id)`" matches the instance's ID and is therefore annotated for the specialization purpose.

During the system's runtime, whenever a new instance within the same auto-scaling group is created, the detection service specializes the profile template to generate one for the instance. The idea here is to replace wildcards with the concrete value observed from the new instance's operation, once the call name, related parameter invariants and other elements (e.g., `program`) are matched. In the above example, as soon as the service finds that the new instance makes a call `open(/var/lib/cloud/i-0000010c/config)`, the aforementioned vector is immediately specialized into (`mac`, ID, `program`, `open`, `/var/lib/cloud/i-0000010c/config`) and added into the instance's profile. Note that in the case that no invariant can be found in the parameters of the same calls across all instances, the whole parameter part of the vector within a profile template is replaced with a wildcard "*". This notifies the detection service that for a new instance, if it makes the call within the vector, any parameter of the call will be acceptable.

Reuse Across Users. The above profile-sharing technique makes it possible to run anomaly detection on an auto-scaling cloud application. What is also desired here is to shorten or even completely remove the learning phase that bootstraps the detection mechanism. To this end, we investigated the technique that supports profile reuse across auto-scaling groups, even across different cloud users.

A key observation is that whenever two application instances run an identical software stack (e.g., OS/web server/web application) with identical configurations, their behavior profiles should be very similar. Indeed, in Sect. 4.2, we present our study on popular stacks, which shows that they produced the same set of system calls with very similar parameters. Further, even in the presence of small discrepancies in the configurations, as long as critical components remain unchanged (such as plug-in settings for `Joomla!`), the profiles from those instances often still come close to each other. In these cases, we can reuse the profile template from one auto-scaling group on the other one to avoid the off-line learning stage[4], and instead adjust the template and the profiles derived from it during the new group's runtime whenever false positives show up. Also, given that people tend to make minor customizations on popular software stacks with default settings, there are lot of chances to reuse profiles even across different cloud users.

What stands in the way of such a reuse, however, is privacy concerns. Specifically, cloud users may not be willing to expose all her software settings to the cloud, which may reveal potential security weaknesses in her system [20]. In this case, the template file one submits to the orchestrator may only describe part of her software stack and some configurations can happen within each application instance using the scripts provided by the user. Note that even though the cloud service provider can figure out such information by inspecting the content of the user's VM instances, they are reluctant to do so and afraid of legal liabilities. In our research, we designed a simple mechanism that facilitates the reuse of profiles across users without leaking out configuration information to either the cloud or the parties who adopt different settings, and also the identities of the parties involved.

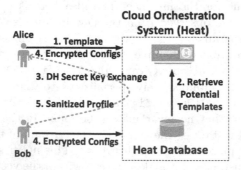

Fig. 5. Privacy-preserving profile-sharing

---

[4] False positives incurred by such profile sharing can be further adjusted during the system's online operation.

Figure 5 illustrates the way the mechanism works. As soon as a user submits her template file to the orchestrator to deploy a stack with the detection service, the Elite component within Heat searches the table `ids_stack` for other template files that contain auto-scaling groups or instances with identical software stacks and configurations. For each of such template files discovered, which may not document the full configurations made by its owner, the cloud contacts the owner to further compare her configurations with those of the new user in a privacy-preserving way. Specifically, both users, without knowing each other, exchange a secret key through the cloud using the classic Diffie-Hellman (DH) key exchange protocol. The DH protocol is designed to establish a secret between strangers over an insecure channel, as long as the party eavesdropping on the channel (the cloud) is considered to be honest but curious, never inserting its own messages into the channel to play a man-in-the-middle. Using the exchanged secret, these two users can compute keyed hash values for the value part of each key-value pair within their system configuration files for an instance and submit them to the cloud for a comparison. If the cloud finds that their configurations are identical or very similar, one party can anonymously share her profile template for the instance to the other through the cloud. Specifically, the party first searches for the occurrences of instance IDs within the profiles, and removes them but sets indicators there to let the recipient fill in his own IDs. Then, she continues to sanitize other content of her profile template, replacing confidential information with the indicators for the types of data that should be in place. This template is then encrypted using the shared secret key and delivered to the recipient through the cloud. This way, profiles are reused anonymously, without disclosing sensitive information to the cloud and the party with different settings.

For example, Alice joins a community organized by the cloud, in which every user is committed to sharing her profiles to others when needed in a privacy-preserving way, and also benefits from other profiles in accelerating her deployment of cloud applications. In this case, Alice wants to create a website using a WordPress CloudFormation template [21]. After the template is submitted, the cloud orchestrator first compares it with other templates in its database: if another user, say Bob, has utilized a very similar template file before, Alice might be able to reuse his profile. To further assess the possibility of reuse, Alice and Bob need to compare the configurations for their software such as Apache HTTP server and WordPress. Because their configurations may contain sensitive data like passwords (WordPress involving MySQL password), Alice and Bob cannot do this in plaintext. Instead, they exchange a secret key K using the DH protocol through the cloud, and then encrypt their software configurations. Specifically, for each key-value pair within their configuration files, the value part is encrypted using K. The ciphertext here is sent to the cloud, which compares them to find out how similar these two configurations are. If they are identical except for some minor keys (e.g., WordPress Database Table prefix), Alice and Bob are instructed by the cloud that the profile can be reused. Then Bob sanitizes his profile automatically by removing the content of private items, including secrets such as passwords, unique identifiers like instance IDs, host names and

IP addresses, and other information like installation path, but annotates each item with its content type (e.g., password, host name, etc.). The profile is then encrypted under K and handed over to Alice through the cloud. The recipient here, Alice, fills in the blanks (sanitized items) with her information before running the profile to protect her website.

As we can see from the example, at the end of this procedure, Alice and Bob do not know each others' identities. They do not have exact information about the overlap of their configuration files, not to mention the parts that differ from each other. The cloud knows the identity of both parties but has no idea about the values of their configuration settings (other than how similar the two configurations are).

4   Evaluation

To understand how Elite performs in practice, we tested our prototype against real-world security threats and heavy computing tasks. What we want to find out includes the impacts of our profile reuse approach on the effectiveness of the detectors running on top of Elite, and the performance of the framework in protecting the cloud application with a dynamic,intensive workload. In this section, we report the results of the study.

4.1   Settings

Our evaluation study was conducted under the following system settings:

The Cloud and Orchestrator. The cloud used in our study includes 22 workstations, each equipped with a 4-core 3.10 GHz Intel i5-2400, 8 GB memory and an 80 GB local disk. On those workstations, we deployed an OpenStack (Icehouse) cluster with 1 controller node and 21 compute nodes. The Heat orchestration service within OpenStack was modified to accommodate the Elite components we implemented. The instance used in our experiments was typically configured with 1 core, 2 GB memory and 10 GB storage and ran Fedora 17 with heat-cfntools [22] to support cloud orchestration.

Cloud Applications. Multiple applications were run on top of this cloud infrastructure to evaluate the effectiveness and performance of our techniques. Specifically, three popular content-management systems, WordPress, Drupal and Joomla!, were used to understand the effectiveness of profile reuse (see Table 1). Also serving this purpose were two prominent penetration testing platforms: Kali Linux and Metasploitable2. WordPress was further utilized in our performance evaluation.

The Detection Service. The detection service was built within a Storm 0.9.1 engine, with a default configuration, in which a single sprout node was connected to multiple bolts. Each detector node was hosted within a typical VM instance (1 core, 2 GB memory and 10 GB disk). The whole service was set to be able to automatically scale in the presence of dynamic workloads.

Table 1. Workloads for false positive evaluation.

Stack Application	Automatic (1000 Users)	Manual
WordPress	Create User, User Login, Browse Blog, Post/Comment Blog, Reply Comment	Change Theme, Activate Widgets, Change User Role, Add/Edit Media in Library
Joomla!	User Registration, User Login, Create/Browse/Edit Article	Enable/Activate User, Add Menu, Enable/Disable Plug-ins, Edit/Publish/Unpublish Modules
Drupal	User Registration, User Login, Browse/Add Article, Add Comments	Unblock User, Install/Enable/Disable Theme, Add Role, View Reports, Enable/Disable Module, Change Site Config/Structure

4.2 Effectiveness

For anomaly detection in general and our prototype service in particular, the most important issue we want to understand is the effectiveness of profile reuse through Elite. To this end, we measured in our study the false positive and negative rates of the profile derived from a profile template, as described in Sect. 3.3, under different web traffic and real-world exploits. The results show that our approach does not undermine the accuracy of a detection system, and instead, makes it convenient to use in a cloud environment through swiftly deploying profiles for new instances acquired by a cloud application.

False Positive. We ran WordPress, Drupal and Joomla! on Apache 2.2.23 under the Elite-enhanced orchestrator to find out whether the new profile automatically reused causes more false alarms than the one constructed through profile learning. In the experiments, all those web services were configured using sample templates provided by the AWS CloudFormation website [23].

Once deployed under Elite, the cloud stack running these applications first operated in learning mode. To generate a workload as realistic as possible for the study, we leveraged one of the most wildly used load testing tool, JMeter, to simulate 1000 users who produced random requests to explore common functionalities of those web applications (e.g., browsing blogs). To complement those requests, we further performed administrative operations manually on a set of application instances. The complete list of the activities can be found in Table 1.

The learning stage ended up creating profile templates for the auto-scaling groups hosting those applications, which are used to generate new profiles for new instances added to the groups. Direct testing on the new instances is complicated, since the traffic is automatically distributed to all the instances within an auto-scaling group, including existing ones. What we did in our research is to create a new stack using the same template file for the old one and apply the profile templates (from the old cloud orchestration stack) to their corresponding groups

Table 2. False Positive Results

Stack Application	Profile			Auditing Events	False Positives
	File	Exe	Net		
WordPress	4313	245	45	˜271120	11
Joomla!	7427	306	41	˜577040	8
Drupal	4945	334	40	˜190400	9

on the new stack, which were specialized automatically during the operation of the new stack[5]. This new stack was directly set to the enforcement mode, in the presence of requests (which were different from those used in learning stage) from JMeter, for a false-positive measurement.

Table 2 shows the experiment results. The false positive rates for all these three web applications were found to be exceedingly low, around 10 over hundreds of thousands of auditing events. Most importantly, comparing the profile learnt (on the old stack) and the one derived (on the new stack), the false positives observed are identical: all caused by network-related system calls. For example, one false alarm from WordPress came from the connection of httpd to a different IP address than the one observed during the learning phase, which all belong to WordPress.org.

Interestingly, we found that all the MYSQL database server instances across the stacks for WordPress, Drupal and Joomla! had very similar profiles, allowing the profile template from one stack to be automatically specialized to protect the instance in the corresponding auto-scaling group within another stack. This also happened to the load balancers across these stacks. All these instances (database servers or load balancers) were installed with identical software stacks and configured in the same way across the stacks. However, they are working on completely different types of data, serving different web applications. Our findings show that it is realistic to share profiles between the instances within different stacks and belonging to different users, as long as they all have the same software stacks and configurations.

Note that such profile sharing cannot be achieved by directly applying a profile learnt from one instance to another, even when both instances belong to the same auto-scaling group. We actually found the presence of significant differences within some vectors in different instances' profiles, which were automatically identified and specialized. An example is the open call made to a random file under the directory /var/lib/mysql/, as illustrated in Fig. 6. This file name is within the profile learnt but varies across different instances. Our approach automatically identified its invariant patterns (highlighted in Fig. 6), which were used to specialize the profile. Should such a profile be directly reused without specialization, much more false alarms would be produced.

---

[5] In addition to the contents with wildcards, those profile templates were also specialized according to the ID of the stack.

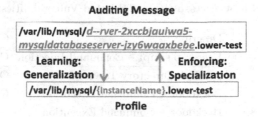

Fig. 6. An example of profile generalization/specialization.

False Negative. To study whether profile reuse could cause the detector to miss the attacks it should be able to catch, we utilized two well-known penetration testing platforms: `Kali Linux` and `Metasploitable2`. Kali Linux is a Linux distribution built for advanced and versatile penetration testing. It integrates more than 300 tools, including the `Metasploit framework`, a tool for developing and executing security exploits. `Metasploitable2` is an intentionally vulnerable Linux VM image (based on Ubuntu 8). It contains a collection of outdated vulnerable and improperly configured software and services for testing security tools.

In our experiments, we deployed `Metasploitable2` over a cloud stack and again, ran the stack first in learning mode. During this process, a script was used to generate requests, causing the application instance (hosting Metasploitable2) to perform different operations. For example, for Samba (SMB) and FTP, the script made connections to their service daemons, listed files, and uploaded/downloaded a set of files. For Apache 2, the script ran two crawlers (a python crawler and a wget based crawler) to crawl its web content. To gener-

Table 3. False Negative Results.('rev' is a shortcut for 'reverse')

Exploit	Payload	Detection	
		Baseline	Elite
Samba usermap script	cmd/unix/reverse	Yes	Yes
	cmd/unix/rev_netcat	Yes	Yes
Samba Symlink Traversal	-	No	No
vsftpd 2.3.4 Backdoor	-	Yes	Yes
UnrealIRCd 3.2.8.1 Backdoor	cmd/unix/reverse	Yes	Yes
PHP-CGI Arg Injection	generic/shell_rev_tcp	Yes	Yes
dRuby Code Exec	cmd/unix/reverse	Yes	Yes
	cmd/unix/rev_netcat	Yes	Yes
Java RMI Server Code Exec	java/shell/rev_tcp	Yes	Yes
	linux/x86/shell_rev_tcp	Yes	Yes
DistCCd Command Exec	cmd/unix/reverse	Yes	Yes
Detection Rates		11/12	11/12

Table 4. Metasploitable2 Selected Vulnerabilities.

Target	Description	CVE / OSVDB
Samba	Usermap script − Command Injection	CVE-2007-2447
Samba	Symlink Directory Traversal	OSVDB-62145
vsftpd 2.3.4	Backdoor − Command Execution	CVE-2011-2523
UnrealIRCd 3.2.8.1	Backdoor − Command Execution	CVE-2010-2075
PHP-CGI	Argument Injection	CVE-2012-1823
dRuby [24]	DRB Remote Code Execution	-
Java RMI Server [25]	Java Remote Code Execution	-
DistCCd	Command Execution	CVE-2004-2687

ate a realistic workload for DistCCd, a distributed compilation tool, the script requested a Metasploitable2 instance to compile the source code of sqlite3 [26].

The profile templates created in learning stage were then specialized for the instances within a new Heat stack generated from the same orchestration template file. Again, this new stack operated in enforcement mode and ran Metasploitable2 in the presence of exploit attempts made from Kali. Table 4 lists 12 exploits tested in our study, including 8 attacks with different payloads, which will cause a compromised system to behave differently (e.g., spawning a shell). All of them led to successful attacks. Using the original profile ("Baseline" in Table 3), which is the one built up during the learning stage, the detector caught 11 of these exploits, all except Samba symlink traversal. After replacing the original profile with the derived one (specialized from a shared profile template), we observed that Elite detected the exactly same set of exploits (11 out of 12). Note that the Samba symlink traversal exploit [27,28], which provides access to the victim's file system, was missed in both cases, due to the incomplete set of system calls monitored in our prototype. We emphasize that this problem is caused by the underlying detection mechanism, not by the reuse of profiles. The results actually strongly indicate that our profile-reuse approach will not affect the accuracy of a detector.

4.3   Performance

We further studied the performance of the Elite-enhanced orchestration in terms of its consumption of computing resources and its impacts on the cloud user's experience. Specifically, we measured the overheads incurred by our implementation when collecting audit trails from individual application instances and streaming them out to the detection service. Then we evaluated how our elastic detectors help control the time for processing audit trails and the amount of resources required for this purpose.

Overheads. The only overheads brought in by Elite to individual application instances come from 3 audit-related processes for generating, dispatching and streaming out auditing events. These processes are auditd, audispd and

Table 5. Overheads of Audit Processes.

Process	Peak Memory (KB)			Peak %CPU
	Virtual (VSZ)	Physical (RSS)	%MEM	
auditd	91768	524	0.03	1
audispd	80692	556	0.03	1
audisp-remote	6876	492	0.02	0.33

audisp-remote. To measure this cost, we set up an instance with WordPress installed and ran JMeter to simulate 100 concurrent users, automatically generating workloads as described in Table 1. We can see that the CPU and memory usages of the processes are very low from Table 5.

The communication cost for running Elite was mainly caused by streaming out the audit trails to detectors. For example, on one WordPress instance, during the process of installing WordPress and handling 100 concurrent users' requests for around 30 min, audit dispatcher needs to stream out ~10 MB of auditing events. Given the average bandwidth between instances in our OpenStack setup is ~2.5 MB/s and bandwidths provided by public clouds are even higher [29], so this level of bandwidth consumption is rather low for a cloud application and does not affect its normal operation. For the Heat orchestrator, the performance impact of our approach is unobservable, due to a large workload it already undertakes to build up the whole stack and coordinate its operations.

Elastic Detection. To understand the important support Elite provides to the intrusion detection on the cloud, we compared the performance of detection with and without the elastic service offered by Elite. Here we measured the performance in terms of the average delay in processing an auditing event (called *Average Message Complete Latency* or AMCL). This latency describes the average duration from the moment a detector receives an auditing event to the time when this event is fully analyzed. To get AMCL, we set up two stacks using the standard WordPress CloudFormation template (with and without Elite) and gradually increased their runtime workloads. For the stack with elastic detection, we utilized a simple yet conservative policy that set the auto-scaling ratio to 1:5, e.g., there were 12 detector instances when the number of application instances grew to 60. Note that our design can also support other auto-scaling policies based on CloudWatch's alarm mechanism, for example those based upon CPU usages. As we can see from Fig. 7, in the absence of the elastic detection service, the AMCL became prohibitively large when the number of application instances went up to 30 (which were all served by a single detector instance). This basically means that system administrator can only find out an attack event more than 10 min after it actually happens on an application instance. We tried twice to scale the stack to 60 application instances without elastic detection, unfortunately Storm IDS engine inside the single detector crushed simply because it just can't handle events from so many application instances. By comparison, Elite automatically added in more resources for detection when large workloads

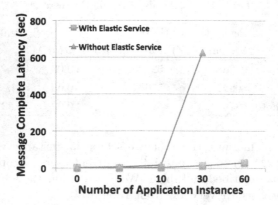

Fig. 7. Average message complete latency with and without elite.

Table 6. Performance of privacy-preserving configuration matching. The elapsed time is reported in seconds.

DH Key Exchange Derivation		Key-Value Pairs Matching	
DH Generation	DH Shared Key	82 Pairs	1000 Pairs
0.05	1.36	0.41	1.46

came in, which results in a relatively stable AMCL: even in the presence of 60 application instances, the latency observed in our study is still below 30 s.

Reuse Across Users. We built a prototype implementation of our privacy-preserving profile sharing subsystem with the goal of evaluating the performance of two key components: DH key exchange and privacy-preserving configuration matching. The results are shown in Table 6. As we can see from the table, the whole operation is very efficient, which is always done within 2 s.

5   Discussion

Our evaluation study shows that Elite works effectively against dynamic and intensive workloads from the popular applications it protects, without undermining the accuracy of detection. On the other hand, our current design and implementation are still preliminary. Much needs to be done to further improve its capabilities, which we discuss as follows.

Platform. Our design extends the cloud-formation language to allow the user to request a detection service to be set up according to a set of parameters. What can be done next is to further enrich the language for configuration of a complicated security service, including not only a single type of intrusion detectors and their combination but also other protection mechanisms, like integrity checker and a forensic analysis mechanism. Also, to support those new security components, changes need to be made to the orchestration engine to provide the components stack-wide information, particularly interactions between different instances.

Protection Service. The prototype we implemented just includes a parallel detection service. Follow-up research could build other aforementioned protection mechanisms on top of the stream processing engine. Also in addition to serving individual users, the security service offered by the cloud can leverage its global view to help detect malicious code or activities and prevent them from propagating to other cloud users. Such a service becomes increasingly important under the current trend in moving organizational infrastructures to commercial clouds.

Profile Reuse. As a very preliminary step toward leveraging stack-wide or even cloud-wide information for security protection, we developed a suite of techniques for sharing normal behavior profiles across auto-scaling groups and different users. However, the effectiveness of those techniques need to be further evaluated against different types of detection systems. Also likely the design itself needs to be adjusted to make profile-reuse work on those systems.

Instance Migration. Due to regular infrastructure maintenance, cloud providers may need to migrate instances across physical machines. A concern is that such migration could interrupt the executions of detector and application instances. However, with new technologies like live migration [30] being adopted by cloud providers today, such an infrastructure maintenance can be transparent to instances and therefore will not affect Elite's normal operations.

6 Related Work

Traditional Intrusion Detection. Intrusion detection has been studied for decades. Numerous approaches have been proposed for signature-based and anomaly detection. Techniques are developed for host-based [31,32] and network-based IDS [33], using various machine learning [34] and data mining [35,36] algorithms. Moving those conventional techniques to the cloud faces great challenges, due to the dynamics in the cloud environment. Elite is designed to address those challenges, offering a high-performance platform to support those detection techniques on the cloud.

Cloud-Based Intrusion Detection and Prevention. Cloud-based IDS can leverage the information collected outside VM instances. For example, detection systems [37,38] were built to run on the hypervisor to support no-intrusive inspections of events that happen inside VM instances. Such detectors can also be accommodated by the Elite platform, which can operate a centralized service to analyze all the events of individual instances gathered at hypervisor level.

Most related to our work is CIDS [39], which constructs a peer-to-peer (P2P) network on top of application instances with embedded detectors. Through this P2P infrastructure, detectors collaborate with each other, sharing resources and balancing their workloads. Also, a few conceptual designs of centralized detectors have been reviewed in [40,41]. Virtual middleboxes framework like Stratos [42] has also been proposed for hosting IDS in an elastic way. However, to our knowledge, no effort has ever been made to integrate a centralized detection service into the cloud orchestration mechanism, which is crucial for protecting a highly dynamic, auto-scaling computing system.

System Call Based Host Protection. The anomaly detector implemented in our prototype is a parallelized version of system-call-policy based protection. Examples for this type of detection techniques include Systrace [15], Blue-Box [43], SELinux [44], AppArmor [45] and TOMOYO Linux [46]. An extension of these approaches, which largely enforce security policies at individual calls, is call-sequence based anomaly detection [12,47]. Such techniques can also be conveniently supported by our elastic detection platform to protect cloud applications in a large scale.

7   Conclusion

The dynamics of the cloud-computing environment makes it extremely challenging to protect a cloud user's application. A detection service designed for the cloud is expected to continuously monitor the state of the application, dynamically adapt its computing scale to workloads and reallocate its existing resources and configure new resources at runtime. This requirement can only be met through close interactions with cloud orchestrators. In this paper, we describe Elite, the first elastic detection platform designed for this purpose. Elite is developed to enhance existing cloud orchestrators, enabling the user to conveniently request a detection service and specify its parameters through her cloud-formation template. Such a detection service is built upon a high-performance stream-processing engine, capable of concurrently analyzing a large number of audit streams and automatically adjusting its computing scale. The service is further supported by the Elite components within the orchestrator, which timely updates the application's state information. To avoid learning a new instance's behavior profile for anomaly detection, which is unrealistic during the application's runtime, we studied a set of new techniques to facilitate profile reuse within an auto-scaling group, and also across users in a privacy-preserving way. Our evaluation shows that such profile sharing does not undermine the accuracy of detection, and also the whole system effectively handles heavy workloads produced by popular web applications.

Acknowledgments. The project is supported in part by National Science Foundation CNS-1117106, 1223477, 1223495, 1223967, 1330491, and 1408944. Yangyi Chen was also supported in part by IBM internship program. The views and conclusions contained herein are those of the authors only and do not necessarily reflect those of the NSF or IBM.

References

1. Somorovsky, J., Heiderich, M., Jensen, M., Schwenk, J., Gruschka, N., Lo Iacono, L.: All your clouds are belong to us: Security analysis of cloud management interfaces. In: CCSW (2011)
2. Mulazzani, M., Schrittwieser, S., Leithner, M., Huber, M., Weippl, E.: Dark clouds on the horizon: using cloud storage as attack vector and online slack space. In: USENIX Security (2011)
3. McAfee SaaS Endpoint Protection Suite. http://www.mcafee.com/us/products/saas-endpoint-protection-suite.aspx
4. Trend Micro Deep Security as a Service. http://www.trendmicro.com/us/business/saas/deep-security-as-a-service/index.html
5. Alerg Logic Public Cloud Security. https://www.alertlogic.com/products-services/public-cloud-security/
6. Heat - OpenStack. https://wiki.openstack.org/wiki/Heat
7. AWS CloudFormation. https://aws.amazon.com/cloudformation/
8. Sung, A.H., Xu, J., Chavez, P., Mukkamala, S.: Static analyzer of vicious executables (save). In: ACSAC, Washington, DC, USA (2004)
9. Kirda, E., Kruegel, C., Banks, G., Vigna, G., Kemmerer, R.A.: Behavior-based spyware detection. In: USENIX Security, Berkeley, CA, USA (2006)
10. Kolbitsch, C., Comparetti, P.M., Kruegel, C., Kirda, E., Zhou, X., Wang, X.: Effective and efficient malware detection at the end host. In: USENIX Security (2009)
11. Yin, H., Song, D., Egele, M., Kruegel, C., Kirda, E.: Panorama: Capturing system-wide information flow for malware detection and analysis. In: CCS, New York, USA (2007)
12. Hofmeyr, S.A., Forrest, S., Somayaji, A.: Intrusion detection using sequences of system calls. J. Comput. Secur. 6, 151–180 (1998)
13. Forrest, S., Hofmeyr, S.A., Somayaji, A., Longstaff, T.A.: A sense of self for unix processes. In: IEEE S&P (1006)
14. Michael, C.C., Ghosh, A.: Simple, state-based approaches to program-based anomaly detection. ACM Trans. Inf. Syst. Secur. 5, 203–237 (2002). http://doi.acm.org/10.1145/545186.545187
15. Provos, N.: Improving host security with system call policies. In: USENIX Security (2002)
16. IBM InfoSphere Streams. http://www-03.ibm.com/software/products/en/infosphere-streams
17. Storm - The Apache Software Foundation! http://storm.incubator.apache.org/
18. Apache Storm - A system for processing streaming data in real time. http://hortonworks.com/hadoop/storm/
19. Apache ZooKeeper. http://zookeeper.apache.org/
20. Google Hacking Database. http://www.exploit-db.com/google-dorks/
21. AWS CloudFormation Sample Template WordPressMultiAZ. https://s3-us-west-2.amazonaws.com/cloudformation-templates-us-west-2/WordPress_Multi_AZ.template
22. Heat API Instance Tools. https://launchpad.net/heat-cfntools
23. AWS CloudFormation Templates. https://aws.amazon.com/cloudformation/aws-cloudformation-templates/
24. Distributed Ruby Send instance eval/syscall Code Execution. https://www.rapid7.com/db/modules/exploit/linux/misc/drb_remote_codeexec

25. Java RMI Server Insecure Default Configuration Java Code Execution. https://www.rapid7.com/db/modules/exploit/multi/misc/java_rmi_server
26. SQLite Home Page. http://www.sqlite.org/
27. Samba Guest Account Symlink Traversal Arbitrary File Access. http://www.osvdb.org/62145
28. Samba Symlink Directory Traversal. https://www.rapid7.com/db/modules/auxiliary/admin/smb/samba_symlink_traversal
29. Need for speed: Testing the networking performance of the top 4 cloud providers. http://gigaom.com/2014/04/12/need-for-speed-testing-the-networking-performance-of-the-top-4-cloud-providers/
30. Google Compute Engine: Transparent maintenance. https://developers.google.com/compute/docs/zones#maintenance
31. Kim, G.H., Spafford, E.H.: The design and implementation of tripwire: a file system integrity checker. In: CCS, New York, USA (1994)
32. Vigna, G., Kruegel, C.: Host-based intrusion detection (2005)
33. Roesch, M.: Snort - lightweight intrusion detection for networks. In: USENIX System Administration, Berkeley, CA, USA (1999)
34. Tsai, C.-F., Hsu, Y.-F., Lin, C.-Y., Lin, W.-Y.: Intrusion detection by machine learning: a review. Expert Syst. Appl. **36**, 11994–12000 (2009)
35. Lee, W., Stolfo, S.J., Mok, K.W.: A data mining framework for building intrusion detection models. In: S&P (1999)
36. Lee, W., Stolfo, S.J., Mok, K.W.: Adaptive intrusion detection: a data mining approach. Artif. Intell. Rev. **14**, 533–567 (2000)
37. Azmandian, F., Moffie, M., Alshawabkeh, M., Dy, J., Aslam, J., Kaeli, D.: Virtual machine monitor-based lightweight intrusion detection. ACM SIGOPS **45**, 38–53 (2011)
38. Garfinkel, T., Rosenblum, M., et al.: A virtual machine introspection based architecture for intrusion detection. In: NDSS (2003)
39. Kholidy, H.A., Baiardi, F.: CIDS: a framework for intrusion detection in cloud systems. In: ITNG (2012)
40. Modi, C., Patel, D., Borisaniya, B., Patel, H., Patel, A., Rajarajan, M.: A survey of intrusion detection techniques in cloud. JNCA **36**, 42–57 (2013)
41. Patel, A., Taghavi, M., Bakhtiyari, K., Celestino Jr., J.: Review: an intrusion detection and prevention system in cloud computing: a systematic review. JNCA **36**, 25–41 (2013)
42. Gember, A., Krishnamurthy, A., John, S.S., Grandl, R., Gao, X., Anand, A.: Stratos: a network-aware orchestration layer for virtual middleboxes in clouds. arXiv (2013)
43. Chari, S.N., Cheng, P.-C.: Bluebox: A policy-driven, host-based intrusion detection system. ACM TISSEC **6**, 173–200 (2003)
44. Smalley, S., Vance, C., Salamon, W.: Implementing selinux as a linux security module. NAI Labs Rep. **1**, 43 (2001)
45. SUSE AppArmor. https://www.suse.com/support/security/apparmor/
46. Harada, T., Horie, T., Tanaka, K.: Task oriented management obviates your onus on linux. In: Linux Conference (2004)
47. Forrest, S., Hofmeyr, S., Somayaji, A.: The evolution of system-call monitoring. In: ACSAC (2008)

AmpPot: Monitoring and Defending Against Amplification DDoS Attacks

Lukas Krämer[1], Johannes Krupp[1], Daisuke Makita[2,3], Tomomi Nishizoe[2], Takashi Koide[2], Katsunari Yoshioka[2], and Christian Rossow[1(✉)]

[1] CISPA, Saarland University, Saarbrücken, Germany
crossow@mmci.uni-saarland.de
[2] Yokohama National University, Yokohama, Japan
[3] National Institute of Information and Communications Technology, Koganei, Japan

Abstract. The recent amplification DDoS attacks have swamped victims with huge loads of undesired traffic, sometimes even exceeding hundreds of Gbps attack bandwidth. We analyze these amplification attacks in more detail. First, we inspect the reconnaissance step, i.e., how both researchers and attackers scan for amplifiers that are open for abuse. Second, we design AMPPOT, a novel honeypot that tracks amplification attacks. We deploy 21 honeypots to reveal previously-undocumented insights about the attacks. We find that the vast majority of attacks are short-lived and most victims are attacked only once. Furthermore, 96 % of the attacks stem from single sources, which is also confirmed by our detailed analysis of four popular Linux-based DDoS botnets.

1 Introduction

Distributed denial-of-service (DDoS) attacks have threatened critical Internet infrastructures for many years [1–3]. Recently, in particular amplification DDoS attacks [4] have gained increasing popularity. In such amplification attacks, an attacker abuses so called *amplifiers* (or *reflectors*) to exhaust the bandwidth of a victim. Instead of directing the attack traffic to the victim directly, the adversary sends requests to reflectors and spoofs the source IP address, so that the reflectors' responses are directed to the victim. An attacker may abuse any public server that is vulnerable to reflection attacks, such as open DNS resolvers or NTP servers. Worse, these protocols are known to amplify the bandwidth significantly, easily allowing an attacker to launch Gbps-scale attacks with a much smaller uplink. In fact, amplification attacks have caused the largest DDoS attack volume ever observed, e.g., against Spamhaus in 03/2013 (≈ 300 Gpbs) and OVH in 02/2014 (≈ 400 Gbps).

The rise of amplification attacks raises many research questions. How frequent are such attacks, and whom do they target? Are individual sources spoofing traffic to trigger attack traffic, or do distributed botnets cause the DDoS attacks? Which software do adversaries use to launch the attacks, and how do they identify amplifiers? Can network-based filtering methods be used to detect

© Springer International Publishing Switzerland 2015
H. Bos et al. (Eds.): RAID 2015, LNCS 9404, pp. 615–636, 2015.
DOI: 10.1007/978-3-319-26362-5_28

amplification attacks? All these questions help to improve our understanding of the threat, to learn attack motivations, and to devise effective countermeasures.

In this paper, we will close this gap by studying in-the-wild activities of attackers preparing and launching amplification DDoS attacks. We first leverage a /16 IPv4 darknet to identify scans for amplifiers, revealing that over 5,000 hosts scanned for DDoS-related services. We observe the scans over time, and monitor a sudden increase of scans caused by whitehats in early 2014. Further analyses reveal that scans are widely distributed, and large parts of the scans rely on Zmap [5] for their reconnaissance.

We then perform a longitudinal study of amplification attacks. To this end, we introduce AMPPOT, a novel open-source honeypot specifically designed to monitor amplification attacks. AMPPOT can mimic services that are known to be vulnerable to amplification attacks, such as DNS and NTP. To make them attractive to attackers, our honeypots send back legitimate responses. Attackers, in turn, will abuse these honeypots as amplifiers, which allows us to observe ongoing attacks, their victims, and the DDoS techniques. To prevent damage caused by our honeypots, we limit the response rate. This way, while attackers can still find these rate-limited honeypots, the honeypots stop replying in the face of attacks.

We deployed 21 globally-distributed AMPPOT instances, which observed more than 1.5 million attacks between Feb. and May 2015. Analyzing the attacks more closely, we find that more than 96 % of the attacks stem from single sources, such as booter services. We show that most attacks are relatively short-lived, and victims are rarely attacked multiple times—giving interesting insights into the motivation behind the attacks. We conclude that amplification DDoS attacks are a global problem, with most victims being located in the US (32 %) and China (14 %).

To foster attack mitigation, we further devise reactive countermeasures against amplification attacks. First, we provide a live feed of amplification attacks. Second, we derive and present a list of domains that are abused in DNS-based amplification attacks. Finally, to study the root cause of amplification attacks, we analyze the new trend of Linux-based DDoS botnets. We inspect over 200 DDoS malware samples and classify most of them into four families. We manually reverse-engineer these samples to analyze their attack techniques, revealing amplification capabilities in all families. In an attempt to map attacks to DDoS botnets, we fingerprint the traffic of these families and link it to the attacks observed at the honeypots. This analysis reveals little overlap, showing that DDoS botnets are not the main source of amplification attacks.

To summarize, the contributions of this paper are as follows:

1. We design AMPPOT, a novel honeypot to capture amplification DDoS attacks. We evaluate various response modes and, based on our collected attacks, devise best practices for deploying such honeypots.
2. We leverage a /16 darknet and the data collected by 21 AMPPOT instances to shed light on the current state of in-the-wild amplification attacks. We use these results to derive honeypot-assisted defense mechanisms.

3. We analyze the recent threat of Linux-based DDoS bots. We show that these bots offer amplification DDoS capabilities, but using traffic fingerprinting, we also reveal that their overall share in the amplification attacks is negligible.

2   AmpPot

This section starts with background information on amplification DDoS attacks. We then describe AMPPOT, our novel honeypot that monitors amplification DDoS attacks.

2.1   Background

Amplification DDoS attacks aim to congest the network bandwidth of attack targets [4]. Attackers use two main techniques to launch amplification attacks. First, they abuse UDP-based Internet services that reflect traffic. For example, attackers may abuse open DNS resolvers to trigger responses to DNS lookups. By choosing particular DNS queries, attackers can even ensure that the responses are much larger than the requests—therefore triggering traffic amplification. Second, attackers spoof the source IP address of the traffic so that the responses flood a victim, instead of going back to the attacker. Such attacks inherently require *amplifiers*, i.e., hosts offering services that are vulnerable to amplification DDoS. Rossow documented 14 UDP-based protocols that can be abused for DDoS attacks, such as DNS, NTP or SNMP [4]. For many of these protocols, adversaries simply use Internet-wide scans to identify millions of amplifiers. Once discovered, attackers will abuse a subset of the discovered amplifiers as part of their attacks.

2.2   Honeypot Design

In the following, we will describe AMPPOT, which acts as fake amplifier. Based on the above observations, we can use this honeypot to (i) monitor reconnaissance steps performed by potential attackers, and (ii) monitor amplification attacks. AMPPOT mimics services having amplification attack vectors by listening on UDP ports that are likely to be abused. In particular, AMPPOT supports all protocols that are said to be vulnerable [4]: QOTD (17), CharGen (19), DNS (53), NTP (123), NetBIOS (137), SNMP (161) and SSDP (1900), plus MSSQL (1434) and SIP (5060/5061). To serve these protocols, AMPPOT listens on the according ports for incoming UDP packets.

Modes: Whenever AMPPOT receives a request, it will respond. We use three "modes" that influence the type of response we send back:

- **Emulated:** In this mode, we use protocol-specific parsers. If a request is valid, we reply with a response, which is randomly chosen from a pre-generated set of protocol-specific responses. For a few protocols such as DNS, which requires dynamically-generated responses that are specific to the request (e.g., the queried domain name), we recursively resolve the requested resource before responding.

- **Proxied:** The proxy mode turns AMPPOT into a proxy that forwards requests to internal servers that actually operate the vulnerable protocol. The responses, in turn, are sent back to the client. While this mode requires configuring servers (such as a DNS resolver, or NTP time server), it has the advantage that no emulation is needed.
- **Agnostic:** Finally, when run in the agnostic mode, AMPPOT responds regardless of the validity of the request. In fact, even the response is invalid: AMPPOT replies with a large response that contains random bytes (either 100x the size of the requests, or with the maximum MTU). This mode assumes that the attacker does not really care about the validity of the responses, but instead just aims to find hosts that send back large replies.

Section 4 will compare these three modes in terms of their effectiveness.

Responses: AMPPOT is most attractive for attackers if its responses result in amplification. To be attractive, we carefully designed protocol-specific responses (emulated mode) or configured servers that send back attractive payloads (proxy mode). For example, for DNS we resolve the request that the client sent, and respond with the entire response, in particular also following the EDNS extensions to support large payloads. Furthermore, we trigger responses that are both vulnerable to NTP's `monlist` request and many other amplifying responses (e.g., version info). We gained this knowledge by (a) inspecting known vulnerability reports, (b) passively observing requests targeting a darknet (see Sect. 3), and (c) scanning the Internet to find typical large responses. Except for the agnostic mode, we made sure that popular client software for each protocol can successfully parse the responses.

Rate Limiting: By mimicking services that have amplification vulnerabilities, AMPPOT runs a risk of becoming involved in actual DDoS attacks. On the other hand, in order to attract attackers, the honeypots need to respond as if they were vulnerable. We have thus added a rate-limiting mechanism to AMPPOT that helps to distinguish between scans (to which we would like to reply) and attacks (in which we do not want to participate). In particular, we block a client IP address (and its corresponding /24 network), if the client sends more than 10 requests per minute. Once a network is blocked, no requests from this network range will be answered. After an hour, we re-evaluate the blacklist and remove a network from the blacklist when it has ceased sending requests. In our later deployment of the honeypots, we received only four emails from attack victims, which we responsibly answered. After our clarification, none of the victims claimed that we caused damage.

Data Collection: One of the core components of AMPPOT is data collection. We collect data in two ways: raw requests and filtered data. Raw requests are simply recorded as .pcap files. However, as the raw data becomes large and difficult to handle quickly, we also record a filtered dataset. For this, each honeypot records the first 100 requests per source IP address and stores them in a *sqlite* database. The relational database eases analysis and data sharing.

Tool Sharing: AMPPOT is implemented in Python and follows a modular design. We will share AMPPOT with trusted parties and make it accessible to fellow researchers, assuming that we can use the derived data as input for the attack portal. Please contact Christian Rossow to obtain access to the source code.

2.3 Honeypot Deployment

We deployed 21 AMPPOT instances to collect attack information. Table 1 summarizes our farm: eleven emulated, seven proxying and three agnostic honeypots. The emulated honeypots are scattered across countries, whereas the other honeypots are all located at Japanese ISPs.

In an attempt to make the honeypots popular, we tried to host the honeypots at ISPs providing static IP addresses. In a few cases, the honeypots have semi-dynamic IP addresses. That is, the addresses change every 3–10 weeks on average, as indicated by the braces in the *IP Addr.* column. Most honeypots were deployed in 2014 and have been continuously operated since then.

The honeypots support a variety of protocols. The proxy honeypots support CharGen, QOTD, DNS, NTP, SNMP and SSDP. In a continuous effort to support more protocols, we gradually added SNMP and SSDP after an initial deployment with the remaining subset of four protocols only. P02 support DNS only. The emulated honeypots support three additional protocols (NetBIOS, MSSQL, SIP). Finally, two of the agnostic honeypots listen on all UDP ports with varying response strategy settings. *Agnostic F* denotes that the honeypot always replied with 1472 bytes UDP payload. In contrast, *Agnostic M* multiplies the length of the request payload by 100 to create a response that is relative in length to the request. Either way, the responses contained random UDP payload that is not valid for the scanned protocol. Section 4 will analyze the effects of the varying settings of the agnostic honeypots.

3   Amplification Reconnaissance

Before analyzing the amplification attacks in more detail, we first want to understand how amplifiers are found. To launch effective amplification DDoS attacks, attackers have to actively search for amplifiers on the Internet. For many services, the easiest way to find amplifiers is an Internet-wide scan. Identifying scanners is also important in the later step of analyzing traffic at our honeypots (Sect. 4), to avoid falsely flagging scans as attacks. Therefore, in this section, we analyze scans performed for amplification reconnaissance. To grasp the trends

Table 1. Overview of honeypot deployments.

HP	Type	Location	Deployed	IP Addr.	Services
E01	Emulated	Australia	2014-11-14	Static	9
E02	Emulated	Brazil	2014-11-14	Static	9
E03	Emulated	US West	2014-11-14	Static	9
E04	Emulated	Ireland	2014-11-14	Static	9
E05	Emulated	Japan	2014-11-14	Static	9
E06	Emulated	US West	2014-11-14	Static	9
E07	Emulated	US West	2014-11-14	Static	9
E08	Emulated	US East	2014-11-14	Static	9
E09	Emulated	Greece	2014-12-10	Static	9
E10	Emulated	Iceland	2014-12-10	Static	9
E11	Emulated	Netherlands	2014-12-10	Static	9
P01	Proxy	Japan	2012-10-07	Dyn. (27d)	6
P02	Proxy	Japan	2013-05-13	Dyn. (22d)	1
P03	Proxy	Japan	2014-05-13	Dyn. (71d)	6
P04	Proxy	Japan	2014-05-13	Dyn. (33d)	6
P05	Proxy	Japan	2014-05-10	Static	6
P06	Proxy	Japan	2014-05-10	Static	6
P07	Proxy	Japan	2014-05-10	Static	6
A01	Agnostic F	Japan	2014-10-14	Dyn. (51d)	7
A02	Agnostic F	Japan	2014-10-24	Static	any
A03	Agnostic M	Japan	2014-11-23	Static	any

and characteristics of the reconnaissance activities, we analyze a *darknet*, i.e.,
traffic observed at unused IPv4 addresses. By definition, a darknet has no hosts
in its network, meaning that all traffic can be regarded as backscatter communication or scan traffic. In this paper, we analyze traffic of a /16 darknet (i.e.,
65,536 successive unused IPs) that is operated by NICTER [6].

Past 10 Years' Scans: To grasp the overall trend of the reconnaissance, we
investigated the hosts that scanned the DDoS-related protocols listed in [4] for
the past 10 years. To this end, we first had to drop traffic that is not related to
scans. In a best-effort approach, we only consider traffic from hosts that scanned
at least 64 addresses of the darknet on the same port in a day. We defined these
hosts as *scanners*.

Figure 1 shows the number of scanners from Sept. 2006 to Mar. 2015. The
graph plots a 30-day moving average to smooth daily fluctuations. Before 2012,
the number of scanners is small, with the notable exception of NetBIOS scans.
In 2012, scanning for DNS became more popular, peaking at 55 hosts per day. In

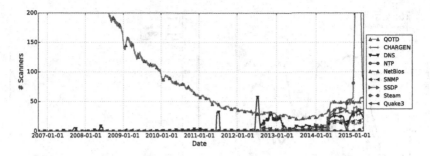

Fig. 1. Number of scanners per protocol and day.

2014, the number of scanners for all protocols increased dramatically, possibly an effect of the public release of amplification vulnerabilities in Feb. 2014 [4]. As we will show in the following paragraph, most of the new scanners come from security organizations (such as ShadowServer.org, Team Cymru, and Mauch's OpenNTPProject and the like). The popularity of NetBIOS constantly decreased although the negative trend similarly stopped in 2014. We speculate that most NetBIOS scanners are actually not related to amplification attacks, but are name lookups done by regular Windows-based systems that are directly connected to the Internet (i.e., not NATed). The obvious spike of NTP scanners at the end of 2014 is caused by a heavily-distributed scan by a single security company.

Attribution of Scanners: Next, we aim to measure (a) which scanning tool was used and (b) which organization performed the scans.

Both whitehats and adversaries can use off-the-shelf scanning tools, e.g., open-source scanners such as ZMap [5] and Masscan [7], to find amplifiers on the Internet. To measure the use of these scanners, we estimate the incoming packets generated by these scanners based on traffic fingerprints. In ZMap, the identification field of the IP header is hardcoded to 54321, which we use as ZMap's fingerprint.

In Masscan, the ID in the IP header is derived by XORing the destination address, the destination port of the UDP header and the ID field of the application header (such as the DNS message ID).

Figure 2 shows the percentage of probes identified by these fingerprints from Jan. 2014 to Mar. 2015. While Masscan is not frequently seen, Zmap's popularity increased since Apr. 2014 and holds a share of up to 60 % of all scan probes.

Furthermore, we examined the scanning sources using Reverse DNS and WHOIS information. We found that about 70 % of the scanning hosts using Zmap are hosted by universities and security organizations. We cannot determine the motivation and origin of the other scanning hosts, and found sources spread among many countries globally.

Scanners' Characteristics: Next, we aim to understand the scanning behaviors in more detail. We conduct statistical analyses to analyze the reconnaissance

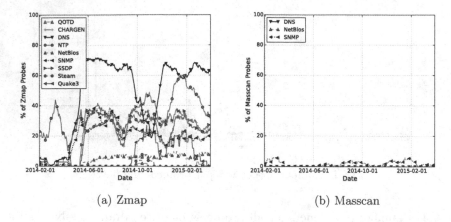

(a) Zmap   (b) Masscan

Fig. 2. Percentage of ZMap and Masscan probes

activities, focusing on the top 4 services that are abused for amplification most frequently: CharGen, DNS, NTP and SSDP. Using the methodology defined above, we identified 5,269 scanners in the 27 month period from Jan. 2013 to Mar. 2015. We then analyzed the scanning activities in detail:

- **Scan Coverage:** We analyze how complete the scans are (i.e., the percentage of the darknet that is covered by a scanner). Figure 3a illustrates the CDF of the scan coverage per protocol. The coverage by the scanners, regardless of the protocol, is surprisingly low. About 64 % of the scanners probed less than 10 % of the darknet and only 10 % of the scanners cover more than the 90 % of the darknet. Therefore, we checked the low-coverage scanners and found that some scanners conducted distributed scanning. For instance, a security company conducted scans using about 240 hosts in the same /24 network. Each scanner scanned only for about 260 hosts of our darknet, but as a whole the scanners covered 97 % of our darknet.
- **Scan Probes:** We count how many packets the scanners send per destination IP address. Figure 3b shows the CDF of the number of probes per IP address, scanner and day. About the 94 % of the scanners send less than two packets per IP address on average. Surprisingly, 5.7 % of the scanners send multiple (i.e., two or more than two) identical packets for the same service, presumably to mitigate packet loss. Identifying such scanners is also important to clean up our dataset of potentials attacks (cf. Sect. 4).
- **Scan Ports:** Finally, we analyzed how many services each scanner searches for. We found that 90 % of the scanners search for a single protocol only (i.e., one port); just a few scanners send probes for multiple services. The most popular service was DNS (36 %), followed by the equally-popular other three protocols (each 20 %–22 %).

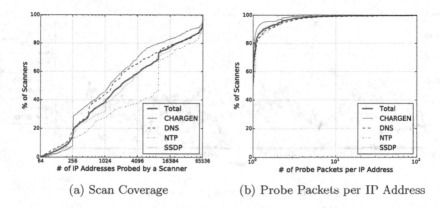

(a) Scan Coverage   (b) Probe Packets per IP Address

Fig. 3. CDFs of scan coverage (left) and probe packets per IP address (right).

4 Amplification Attacks

After shedding light on the reconnaissance part, we will now turn to the actual amplification attacks. We define an attack, then give an overview of attacks, and finally analyze the attacks in more detail.

Attack Definition: When considering traffic at the honeypots, we have to separate actual attacks from random packets such as scans or backscatter before further analyses. To do so, we filter on those sources that sent at least 100 *consecutive* requests to our honeypots, whereas consecutive means that there was no gap of an hour or more between two packets. This conservative threshold discards most scanners, while it clearly also captures all powerful attacks. We chose this threshold given the lack of ground truth of labeled data on attacks/backscatter/scanners. We further discard all hosts that have been identified as scanners to obtain a dataset that consists purely of attacks.

We aggregate attacks based on the source IP address (i.e., the attack victim) and destination port (i.e., the protocol being abused). We group attacks seen by multiple honeypots into one combined attack, as long as the source IP address and the abused protocol match. If an attack pauses for an hour, and then resumes, we separate the traffic into two attacks.

Attack Overview: Figure 4 summarizes the attacks our honeypots monitored over the period from Jan. 2015 to May 2015. In these five months, we monitored 1,535,322 amplification attacks.

The graph shows that some protocols are clearly more popular than others. In fact, QOTD, MSSQL, NetBIOS and SNMP attacks sum up to less than 0.3 % of all attacks. Most popular are NTP (37.0 %), DNS (28.5 %), SSDP (27.3 %) and CharGen (7.0 %), with a combined share of over 99 %. The graph also shows that attacks are relatively constant over time.

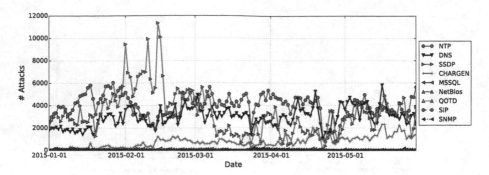

Fig. 4. Number of attacks per protocol and day.

Honeypot Convergence: We next assess the completeness of our data by measuring whether the observed attacks converge. In other words, did we deploy sufficiently many honeypots to detect all attacks? For this, we measure how many previously-unknown attacks an additional honeypot observes. We focus only on those six protocols that all honeypots (with the exception of P02) support. Figure 5 shows the convergence graph, ordered by honeypot mode and honeypot name. The lower dark part of the bars indicates the percentage of attacks that a honeypot observed and were not yet been observed by the prior honeypots (i.e., the ratio of new attacks). For example, consider the eleven emulated honeypots. While the first honeypots (E01–E07) contributed many new attacks, the ratio of new attacks converges to small percentages at the later honeypots (E08–E11). This shows that—per mode—we had enough honeypots to cover most attacks out there.

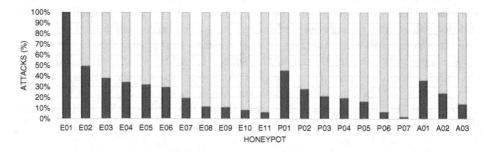

Fig. 5. Ratio of new (dark gray) vs. known (light gray) attacks per honeypot.

Comparing the data across the honeypot modes reveals further interesting insights. First, the proxied honeypots (P01–P07) contributed many new attacks, showing that the protocol emulation was good, but not complete. Similarly, the agnostic honeypots discovered new attacks that the other honeypots had not seen, most of which abused protocols that neither of the other honeypots supported. For example, the agnostic honeypots attracted 9600 attacks abusing TeamSpeak servers, which offer about 5-fold amplification. In addition, we observed 9700 attacks abusing Quake game servers. We noted a few attacks against other protocols (including Sun RPC, ASF-RMCP, UT game servers, and more), but none of them was abused frequently.

Finally, we aim to answer the question of which honeypot mode was most effective. To this end, we drew convergence graphs with swapped orders of the honeypot modes (figures omitted for brevity), one with proxied honeypots first, and one with agnostic honeypots first. The share of attacks that are missed by the agnostic honeypots is significant, meaning that not all attackers blindly accept any large response. While this shows that agnostic honeypots alone are not sufficient for complete analysis, they are still helpful to capture new attacks—not only those abusing previously unseen protocols. We speculate that some attackers may favor the agnostic responses, as they are sometimes even larger than proxied or emulated responses. A good rule of thumb is to run agnostic honeypots in parallel to others. Similarly, the proxied honeypots missed attacks, particularly for unsupported protocols. But even for supported protocols, the proxied honeypots missed a significant proportion of attacks that the emulated honeypots did see—possibly as the number of proxied honeypots with static IP addresses was too low to converge towards a complete set of attacks. Summarizing, we cannot conclude that proxied honeypots are ultimately the best choice.

Deployment to Abuse: Next, we analyze the time span between deploying a honeypot and the time it gets abused. In fact, all honeypots were already abused within 24 h after deployment. However, the number of initial attacks was quite low, and we saw an increasing number of attacks as days passed after deployment. On average, the attacks observed at the honeypots reach a steady level after five days. While this may seem short, note that amplifiers in general are ephemeral in nature, and attackers constantly need to refresh their set of amplifiers. With the exception of NTP, Kührer et al. have shown that 42 % 53 % of the amplifiers vanish after one week due to IP address churn [8].

Attack Sources: Due to IP address spoofing, it is not straightforward to attribute the attack traffic back to its true origin. Instead, the honeypots reveal the attack victim (i.e., based on the source IP address). However, we still aim to address an important question: Are amplification DDoS attacks caused by single sources (such as booter services), or do multiple hosts cause an attack (such as DDoS botnets)?

We aim to approach the analysis by leveraging the Time-To-Live (TTL) field in the IP header. Generally, the TTL field is decremented by every hop that forwards an IP packet. For the following analysis, we leverage the fact that our honeypots would observe varying TTL values for an attack if multiple attack sources are used. In contrast, if there is a single source, we would see a fixed (or at most a few) TTL values, assuming that the route from attacker to amplifier does not frequently change, and assuming that the initial TTL value is not randomized.

Therefore, we measured for which attacks the majority of honeypots saw at most two distinct TTL values. We use this small conservative threshold and a majority vote to counter potential route changes for individual (*attacker, honeypot*) pairs. Using this method, we find that 96.3 % of the attacks stem from a single source. This is an important observation, indicating that booter services cause more attacks than DDoS botnets.

For the other 3.7 %, we cannot tell with certainty if they stem from DDoS botnets. Unfortunately, an attacker may fool us by randomizing the initial TTL value. In other words, even if we see multiple TTL values, this could be caused by a single source. Still, our analysis gives a lower bound, showing that the vast majority of attacks are not distributed.

Attack Duration and Repetition: Our honeypots also reveal how long a victim is being attacked. For these analyses, we were interested in the victim, rather than the protocol used to attack the victim. Therefore, we have grouped the attacks by source IP address, and regarded attacks abusing multiple protocols towards the same victim as a single combined attack.

Figure 6a shows the cumulative distribution of attack durations, i.e., the time between the first and the last packet monitored in an attack on a particular victim. Similar to the observations of DDoS botnets [9], amplification attacks also seem to be short-lived: 62 % of the attacks are shorter than 15 min, and 90 % of the attacks last at most one hour. Only 1.4 % of the attacks last longer than 4 h. This shows that attackers quickly move on to attack other victims. This is also in line with observations done on booter services [10], indicating that many clients run attacks in parallel.

This is also confirmed by the high number of concurrent attacks: on average, we monitored 125.7 simultaneous attacks abusing our honeypots.

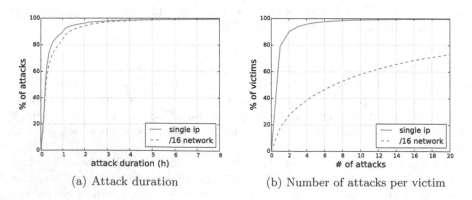

(a) Attack duration   (b) Number of attacks per victim

Fig. 6. CDFs of attack duration (left) and attacks per victim IP (right).

We further investigated *how often* a victim (i.e., an IP address) was attacked, as shown in Fig. 6b. 79 % of the victims were attacked only once; a further 11 % were attacked twice. 0.81 % of the victims were attacked more than 10 times. This may be counter-intuitive, especially as anecdotes claim that extortion is the main motivation for DDoS attacks. However, the vast majority of attacks are one-off operations, showing that in many cases the extortion—if any—is a non-persistent threat.

These observations may be biased due to our fine-grained definition of a victim, so we have repeated the measurements with a looser definition of an attack victim. Instead of measuring the attacks per IP address, we measured the attacks per victim network, aggregating per /16 (i.e., class B) network. Figure 6 includes this comparison (dashed lines). Interestingly, while the number of attacks per network significantly increases, the attack duration does not. Following basic intuition, entire networks indeed attract more attacks than single IP addresses. However, the individual attacks are likely not linked to each other, as otherwise one would expect to see ongoing and consecutive attacks targeting the same network.

Instead, the time span between two attacks (i.e., the time between two attacks during which there was no attack) is 9.6 days on average.

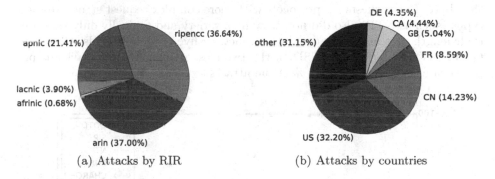

(a) Attacks by RIR   (b) Attacks by countries

Fig. 7. Geolocation of victims and their share of the overall attacks.

Victim Analysis: In an attempt to understand the motivation of the attacks, we inspected the targets of the amplification attacks. To this end, we resolved GeoIP data for all attacked IP addresses, queried their reverse DNS record, and mapped the IP addresses to autonomous systems (ASes). Figures 7a and b show the distribution of countries and Regional Internet Registry (RIR) of the victims, respectively. Victims that belong to ARIN and RIPE each attract 37 % of the attacks and APNIC attracts another 21 %. Providers in Central- and South America (LACNIC) or Africa (AfriNIC) face relatively few attacks.

When looking at countries, the US stands out, hosting one-third of the victims. There are also many victims in China (14 %) and France (8.6 %), whereas all other victims form a long-tail distribution of 192 affected countries. Of those,

28 countries faced over 1000 attacks, showing the wide geographical distribution and global threat of amplification attacks. In addition, the destination port may reveal what type of service is attacked. 35 % of the attacks target UDP port 80, possibly to pass misconfigured firewalls that allow port 80 in general (i.e., not only TCP). However, in a few cases, the attacks are actually directed at UDP-based services. In descending order, 2.6 % of the attacks target Xbox Live, 2.0 % DNS servers, 0.9 % Minecraft game servers and 0.6 % each Steam game servers and TeamSpeak VoIP servers. The majority of attacks is scattered in a long-tail distribution over other ports. The less popular services include MSSQL servers, NTP servers, MMORPG servers, and further VoIP systems. All remaining requests seem to randomize the source port.

Request Entropy: In an attempt to understand the attack techniques, we next inspected how much variety we see in the request payloads. That is, we measure how many different request payloads (i.e., *excluding* UDP and IP headers) we observe per protocol. The less adversaries vary their requests, the easier it will be to filter their requests (see Sect. 5).

Figure 8 shows a CDF of the request variety among all honeypots and attacks. The request variety is quite low for most protocols. For CharGen and QOTD, 99.66 % and 99.34 % of the requests are one byte long, with a low variety in that byte. But requests for protocols with more complex request structures and types (such as NTP) also did not show high variety and typically only varied in their length (not in type or content). In fact, for five of the protocols (CharGen, QOTD, NTP, MSSQL and SSDP), the two most popular request payloads per protocol caused more than 98 % of the attacks.

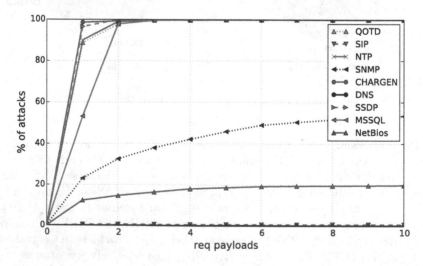

Fig. 8. CDF of the number of UDP payloads over all attacks.

DNS is at the other end of the scale, attributed to the fact that adversaries (a) change the DNS headers (such as the DNS message ID), and (b) change the domain name being queried. Similarly, the SNMP requests varied, as the attackers (a) varied the Object Identifiers (OIDs) and transaction IDs, and (b) also varied the request type (`getBulkRequest` and `GetRequest` being most prominent). But NetBIOS (randomized 2-byte-wide transaction ID) and SIP (random session ID) requests have also shown a higher variety. In any of these protocols, detecting the traffic towards the amplifiers is not as trivial as incorporating the most popular request payloads into network-based filters. However, one can still define payload signatures over static, non-randomized packet headers.

Finally, we also measure the request entropy within individual attacks. Following the observation from above, most attacks based on protocols with low request variety were caused by only a single request payload. However, even for DNS, which offers a high request variety, most attacks use very few different payloads. For example, 45.3 % of the DNS-based attacks used a single request payload, and more than 80 % of the DNS attacks had at most 3 request payloads. Interestingly, though, NetBIOS, SNMP and SIP still have a high request entropy (less than 30 % of the attacks have only a single payload). This shows that one cannot conclude that the request payloads are static within individual attacks.

5   Honeypot-Assisted Defenses

Honeypots are powerful as early-warning systems. In this section, we describe how we can leverage our honeypots to create valuable inputs for both proactive and reactive DDoS defenses.

5.1   Real-Time Attack Monitoring

We have published a live feed of attacks based on the data obtained by our honeypots. We use a web portal[1] to share information about incidents (such as attack start and end times) with registered service providers and trusted individuals. Providers can use the attack information to inform their customers or to filter attack traffic based on IP and port information. We chose to require registration only to prevent attackers misusing the data (e.g., to fingerprint or to evade our honeypots).

To test the usefulness of the honeypot data to detect DDoS attacks, we have cooperated with a large Japanese ISP. We compared the honeypot-based DDoS detection with a flow-based detection system that ISP had already deployed [11]. To this end, our honeypots generated an alert as soon as a potential victim (i.e., a single IP address) sent more than ten packets in a ten-second interval (i.e.,

---

[1] Note that we intentionally do not publish the address of the web portal, as the portal contains potentially sensitive information. If you are interested in obtaining access, please request an account from Christian Rossow via email.

more than 1 pps on average). In contrast, the ISP's detection mechanism raises an alert based on a threshold of packets per destination for DDoS-related ports.

We compared both systems in the time span from August 1st to November 30th, 2014. Our honeypots detected 75 potential attacks towards the ISP's networks. Of these, the ISP detected 56 alerts.

43 of the 56 alerts (77 %) were detected first by our honeypot, and then by the ISP, with an average delay of 39 s. The honeypots detected 13 attacks later than the ISP, indicating that in these the attackers rotated the set of amplifiers. We hypothesize that deploying more honeypots would further improve the reaction times.

5.2   DNS Abuse Domain List

DNS stands out when it comes to amplification attacks. Most other protocols can be filtered, as they have little benign use on the Internet (e.g., CharGen, QOTD, or even typical LAN protocols such as NetBIOS and SSDP). In addition, unlike for management protocols like SNMP, DNS communication may involve different and distant endpoints (e.g., authoritative name servers). Finally, bad DNS filters would cause malfunctions for Internet users.

In any case, as we have seen in Sect. 4, DNS remains one of the typical attack protocols. Thus, to support better filtering, we derive a list of domains that have been abused for amplification attacks. Table 2 lists the 10 most popular attack domains since Feb. 2015, in descending order of the number of requests recorded at the honeypots. In the following, we will draw four observations from the table.

Table 2. DNS domains, ordered by the number of requests seen at the honeypot.

FQDN	Type	First Seen	Last Seen	Days	Victims
067.cz	ANY	2015-02-21	2015-05-31	47	15804
mg1.pw	ANY	2015-04-12	2015-05-31	49	71357
isc.org	ANY	2015-02-01	2015-05-31	106	12228
psg.com	ANY	2015-04-05	2015-05-28	51	25986
vizit.spb.ru	ANY	2015-03-23	2015-05-31	45	99543
mg1.pw	A	2015-04-12	2015-05-31	36	1606
pidarastik.ru	ANY	2015-02-11	2015-05-31	80	14431
dhs.gov	ANY	2015-02-24	2015-05-03	64	41857
r3a.es	ANY	2015-03-25	2015-04-16	23	23943
ironmen-style.ru	ANY	2015-04-22	2015-05-29	15	120595

First, in some cases it is not possible to use this list as a blacklist to filter bad traffic, as benign domains are also in the dataset (e.g., isc.org or dhs.gov). This is largely due to domains that deploy RRSIG or DNSKEY resource records, which are required for DNSSEC. For example, an `ANY` request for isc.org results in an approximately 1500-byte response, containing two `DNSKEY` and four `RRSIG` records—both of which are required for DNSSEC. The problem of potential false positives may be resolved by combining the request type (e.g., `ANY`) with the requested domain. However, without evaluating this further, our suggestion is not to blindly use the abuse list as input for filters.

Second, attackers register domains only for the purpose of DDoS attacks. For example, according to web archives, mg1.pw never hosted real content. Furthermore, Passive DNS analysis (using dnsdb.info) shows that the domain was first ever used only 30 h before we noticed its abuse.

Third, each domain keeps being abused for a long time: The average time for abuse in the top 10 domains is 8 weeks (i.e., the time span from the first to the last attack). Even when considering all attack domains, the time span is still 7.5 weeks. We presume that attackers keep abusing the same domain to limit the overhead for registering new domains and setting up authoritative name servers.

Defenders can use these insights on domains that are popular in amplification attacks, for example, to aid existing detection mechanisms (see Sect. 5). Similarly, collecting evidence on attacks via honeypots can help law enforcement to take down purely malicious domains.

6 DDoS Bot Analysis

We now turn our analysis to explore a potential source of amplification attacks: DDoS botnets. Botnets span multiple hosts that are instructed by the botmaster and have already been known to launch DDoS attacks in general [9,12]. The TTL analyses in Sect. 4 have already indicated that the majority of attacks stem from a single source. In this section, we seek to test this hypothesis by analyzing DDoS botnets in more detail.

Recently, adversaries have started to compromise insecure or vulnerable embedded devices, leading to a sudden increase in Linux-based DDoS bots. Embedded devices that are directly connected to the Internet (e.g., home routers) are an attractive platform to launch amplification attacks, as they are not filtered by firewalls or NAT gateways. Therefore, we will study these botnets in particular detail.

Analysis Methodology: We analyzed a set of Linux-based bots that are known to provide DDoS services. We obtained these binaries using Telnet- and SSH-based honeypots and via keyword searches on VirusTotal. Our dataset of Linux-based DDoS bots consists of 247 binaries that we collected between Jan. 2014 and May 2015. Our particular interest is to understand the DDoS attack functionality of the bots. To this end, we dynamically analyzed the samples in a sandbox and traced the C&C communication. Furthermore, using static analysis, we classified our samples into families, assigning names to the families based on characteristic strings.

Table 3. Attack capabilites

	IptabLes	XorDoS	BackdoorA/M	BillGates
DNS Amplification	✓	✓	✓	✓
• Fixed query type	A	A	ANY	
• EDNS payload size		4096	4096	8192
• DNSSEC OK				✓
• Random domain	✓			✓
SYN	✓	✓	✓	✓
SYN+ACK	✓			
SYN with payload			✓	
ICMP PING				✓
Auth NS		✓		✓
Generic TCP				✓
Generic UDP				✓
HTTP GET			✓	✓
TCP connections			✓	✓

Analyzed Families: Our analysis has revealed four popular Linux-enabled and DDoS-capable bot families. While Windows-based DDoS bots are well-explored, to the best of our knowledge, we are the first to inspect Linux-based malware of this type. An overview of the attack capabilities of each family is given in Table 3. The two families *IptabLes* and *XorDoS* have only limited attack capabilites, whereas *BackdoorA/M* and *BillGates* offer a wide range of different attacks.

All four families abuse DNS for amplification attacks. Interestingly, *IptabLes* and *XorDoS* support only A lookups, which were less prominent in the attack domains (cf. Sect. 5). Three out of four families use EDNS to expand the maximum UDP-based response size to at least 4096 bytes, and *BillGates* bots specifically also ask for DNSSEC records. None of the families supports any amplification protocols other than DNS. However, *BillGates* also features generic UDP and TCP attacks, where headers, flags and the payload are taken as input via a C&C command. *BillGates* could thus be used for amplification attacks with any protocol.

For completeness, note that all bots also support non-amplification attacks. These span ICMP and TCP SYN floods, HTTP GET floods or TCP connection exhaustion. Two bots also support DNS-based "random domain" attacks, in which the bots randomize the FQDN of the lookup request. These requests are not abusing amplification, but presumably aim to flood authoritative name servers instead.

Attack Fingerprints: Seeing the potential for amplification attacks, we wondered how large the impact of these botnets is in the attacks we are observing with AMPPOT. We derived attack fingerprints for the botnets by identifying artifacts in their attack traffic. Much to our surprise, this was possible for all families, as the malware authors re-used randomly generated values for various header fields. *IptabLes* sets the UDP source port to a value that is derived from the IP packet ID. *BillGates* uses the same value for DNS message ID and IP packet ID, and randomizes the TTL to five initial values. Similarly, *XorDos* equalizes both DNS message ID and IP packet ID, and also derives the source port from these values. Finally, *BackdoorA/M* uses a specific source port range and randomly draws an initial TTL value from four distinct groups.

We then searched for DNS-based amplification attacks that satisfy these filters at our honeypots. The above-mentioned filters were simple enough so that we could use SQL queries to search for matching packets in our attack database. For each attack, we computed the ratio of the number of packets that matched the filters compared to all packets belonging to this attack. While we found individual packets to match, presumably caused by accidental value pairs that just happen to match our filters, the ratio of "attributed" packets per attack never exceeded 1%. This indicates that these DDoS bots are not frequently used in amplification attacks, although they remain a lingering threat.

7   Discussion

This section raises a few aspects left over for discussions about the implementation and deployment of AMPPOT.

Ethics: With AMPPOT, we provide valuable insights into amplification attacks that otherwise could not be observed on such large scale. Unfortunately, we face a dilemma, as these insights can only be revealed if AMPPOT participates in the attacks to some extent. To minimize the harm by AMPPOT, we have included a rate limiting mechanism. Still, this leaves a small number of attack packets. Content-based classifiers to distinguish between scan and attack traffic are unfeasible, as attackers typically use the same kind of requests for both activities.

Seeing this risk, we considered to clearly mark AMPPOT's responses as such, e.g., by embedding an info text explaining the traffic. However, first, this would enable attackers to trivially detect AMPPOT deployments. Second, attack victims usually do not inspect the payload of each and every attack packet, but rely on flow-based information instead. Looking at the flows, however, would hide any note that we add to the responses.

Summarizing, we concluded that an effective rate-limiting module is the most reliable and practical option to prevent abuse of the honeypots. Each AMP-POT deployment can configure the rate-limiting thresholds on their own, possibly resorting to an overly conservative threshold (e.g., only a single request is answered per IP address and hour).

Rate Limiting: In our experiments, we chose an arbitrary rate-limiting threshold that seemed reasonable to us. However, choosing the threshold may have consequences on the number of scanners that discover AMPPOT. In future work, we plan to evaluate varying rate-limiting thresholds and their effects on the attacks that are observed subsequently.

Furthermore, our current rate-limiting implementation treats all protocols equal. This may be unsuitable for protocols that have comparatively chatty responses, such as the `monlist` reply in the NTP protocol implementation, which consists of dozens of response packets. An alternative might be to include dynamic thresholds for rate-limiting, which vary depending on the response size and aggressiveness of the requests.

Honeypot Detection: Although we have not witnessed concrete attempts of doing so, an attacker can identify AMPPOT instances to exclude them from any attacks she launches. AMPPOT offers services on many UDP ports, and as such can be identified relatively easily. However, detection becomes more tricky if the honeypot is configured to listen on a single UDP port only. Still, an attacker may inspect artifacts, such as the response payloads, or observations of dropped requests due to rate-limiting. We leave it open to future work to explore how we could increase the stealthiness of AMPPOT.

8 Related Work

This section summarizes related work, which we group by topic.

DDoS: Works on reflective DDoS attacks date back to early observations by Paxson in 2001 [3]. But while theoretically known, amplification attacks have not played a big role until recently. Instead, research analyzing the DDoS threats focused on analyzing DDoS attacks in general. Büscher and Holz monitored the C&C servers of DDoS botnets to analyze the attacks and their targets and documented TCP- and HTTP-based attacks [12]. Similarly, Welzel et al. tracked commands of two DDoS botnet families and monitored whether victims of DDoS botnets were actually affected by the attacks [9]. Thus, DDoS botnets are a well-explored area, although none of the existing analyses inspected Linux-based bots.

With the recent increase of amplification attacks, which we believe is an orthogonal problem to DDoS botnets, researchers started to explore the new threat. Rossow provided an overview of 14 protocols that are vulnerable to amplification attacks [4]. As a follow-up, Kührer et al. have shed light on the amplifiers landscape, revealing their fingerprints and observing their lifetime [8]. These works inspect concrete amplification vulnerabilities in protocols, propose defense mechanisms and survey amplifiers, while giving only anecdotal evidence on actual attacks.

Others devoted their research to particular amplification protocols. Czyz et al. explored NTP in great detail, exploring all amplification vulnerabilities and inspecting attack victims based on artifacts in the NTP `monlist` feature [13]. Van Rijswijk-Deij et al. analyzed how DNS (and in particular DNSSEC) can be abused for amplification attacks [14], observations many of which confirm the trend of DNS attacks we observe. Our work adds to this in that we give insights on how the protocols actually are abused in DDoS attacks.

Closest to our work, researchers inspected *booters*, which are services that offer DDoS attacks on a pay-per-use basis. Karami and McCoy were the first to monitor such booter services, studying the adversarial DDoS-As-a-Service concept [15]. They observed booters launching amplification attacks, however, but did not reveal more details. Similarly, Santanna et al. analyze the databases and payment of 15 booters [10]. In contrast to using honeypots, analyzing booter services is a forensic challenge, and requires gaining access to the booter systems (or obtaining an image thereof). Our dataset is more complete in that we monitor attacks regardless of the specifics of particular booter services. Thus, the scale of our recorded dataset exceeds other observations by orders of magnitude.

Honeypots: Honeypots have been used in many other contexts [16], such as for collecting malware [17], creating automated network signatures [18], or finding malicious websites [19]. To the best of our knowledge, AMPPOT is the first honeypot to track amplification DDoS attacks. The idea of using vulnerable services to observe DDoS attacks was already known [4], whereas—due to the short deployment time of these "baits"—the dataset under analysis spanned only eight attacks. We revise this result by longitudinal, broad deployment of 21 honeypots, revealing that honeypots actually *are* useful to gain attack intelligence.

Scan Analysis: Durumeric et al. have also analyzed a darknet to explore scanning behaviors [20]. They inspected scans for NTP, and we extend their analyses by considering all amplification-related ports.

9 Conclusion

Amplification attacks continue to be a dangerous threat to millions of users. We have shown that one can passively monitor attacks, and insights into these attacks can help to derive helpful countermeasures. However, our research has also identified new research directions, such as trying to understand the attackers' motives and actual origins. We have shown that DDoS botnets are likely not the main source for amplification attacks, shifting focus to other potential attack sources such as booter services. AMPPOT assists in analyzing the amplification threats in more detail, and the web portal can help operational security operators to become informed about or to defend against attacks.

References

1. Mirkovic, J., Reiher, P.: A taxonomy of DDoS attack and DDoS defense mechanisms. ACM SIGCOMM Comput. Commun. Rev. **34**, 39–53 (2004)

2. Specht, S.M., Lee, R.B.: Distributed denial of service: taxonomies of attacks, tools, and countermeasures. In: Proceedings of the International Conference on Parallel and Distributed Computing (and Communications) Systems (ISCA PDCS), San Francisco, CA (2004)
3. Paxson, V.: An analysis of using reflectors for distributed denial-of-service attacks. ACM SIGCOMM Comput. Commun. Rev. **31**(3), 38–47 (2001)
4. Rossow, C.: Amplification hell: revisiting network protocols for DDoS abuse. In: Proceedings of the 2014 Network and Distributed System Security (NDSS) Symposium (2014)
5. Durumeric, Z., Wustrow, E., Halderman, J.A.: ZMap: fast internet-wide scanning and its security applications. In: Proceedings of the 22nd USENIX Security Symposium, Washington, D.C., USA (2013)
6. NICTER (http://www.nicter.jp/)
7. Graham, R.D.: MASSCAN: mass IP port scanner (2014). https://github.com/robertdavidgraham/masscan
8. Kührer, M., Hupperich, T., Rossow, C., Holz, T.: Exit from hell? Reducing the impact of amplification DDoS attacks. In: Proceedings of the 23rd USENIX Security Symposium (2014)
9. Welzel, A., Rossow, C., Bos, H.: On measuring the impact of DDoS botnets. In: Proceedings of the 7th European Workshop on Systems Security (EuroSec) (2014)
10. Santanna, J., Durban, R., Sperotto, A., Pras, A.: Inside booters: an analysis on operational databases. In: 14th IFIP/IEEE International Symposium on Integrated Network Management (IM) (2015)
11. Urakawa, J., Sawaya, Y., Yamada, A., Kubota, A., Makita, D., Yoshioka, K., Matsumoto, T.: An early scale estimation of DRDoS attack monitoring honeypot traffic. In: Proceedings of the 32nd Symposium on Cryptography and Information Security (2015)
12. Büscher, A., Holz, T.: Tracking DDoS attacks: insights into the business of disrupting the web. In: Proceedings of the 5th USENIX LEET, San Jose, CA, USA (2012)
13. Czyz, J., Kallitsis, M., Gharaibeh, M., Papadopoulos, C., Bailey, M., Karir, M.: Taming the 800 pound gorilla: the rise and decline of NTP DDoS attacks. In: Proceedings of the 2014 Conference on Internet Measurement Conference, pp. 435–448. ACM (2014)
14. van Rijswijk-Deij, R., Sperotto, A., Pras, A.: DNSSEC and its potential for DDoS attacks - a comprehensive measurement study. In: Proceedings of the Internet Measurement Conference 2014, Vancouver, BC, Canada. ACM Press (2014)
15. Karami, M., McCoy, D.: Understanding the emerging threat of DDoS-as-a-service. In: Presented as part of the 6th USENIX Workshop on Large-Scale Exploits and Emergent Threats (2013)
16. Provos, N., Holz, T.: Virtual Honeypots: From Botnet Tracking to Intrusion Detection. Pearson Education, New Delhi (2007)
17. Baecher, P., Koetter, M., Holz, T., Dornseif, M., Freiling, F.C.: The nepenthes platform: an efficient approach to collect malware. In: Zamboni, D., Kruegel, C. (eds.) RAID 2006. LNCS, vol. 4219, pp. 165–184. Springer, Heidelberg (2006)
18. Kreibich, C., Crowcroft, J.: Honeycomb: creating intrusion detection signatures using honeypots. ACM SIGCOMM Comput. Commun. Rev. **34**, 51–56 (2004)
19. Nazario, J.: PhoneyC: A virtual client honeypot. In: Proceedings of USENIX Workshop on Large-scale Exploits and Emergent Threats (LEET) (2009)
20. Durumeric, Z., Bailey, M., Halderman, J.A.: An internet-wide view of internet-wide scanning. In: USENIX Security Symposium (2014)

Author Index

Abu-Ghazaleh, Nael   3
Amann, Johanna   133
Andronio, Nicoló   382
Antunes, Nuno   471
Avritzer, Alberto   471

Barabosch, Thomas   565
Barbará, Daniel   405, 515
Berger, Stefan   588
Biersack, Ernst   111
Bindschaedler, Vincent   588
Bodden, Eric   295

Cai, Zhongmin   155
Chen, Yangyi   588
Cheng, Liang   247
Choi, Byungkwon   89

Dahse, Johannes   493
Damopoulos, Dimitrios   317
Deng, Yi   247
Ding, Xuhua   66
Dombeck, Adrian   565
Donovick, Caleb   3

Eckert, Claudia   177
Elsabagh, Mohamed   515

Fong, Dengguo   198, 247
Fleck, Dan   405, 515
Francillon, Aurélien   48
Fu, Yu   247

Gerdes, Ryan M.   26
Gerhards-Padilla, Elmar   565
Gu, Dawu   359
Guan, Xiaohong   155

Han, Dongsu   89
Heen, Olivier   48
Holz, Thorsten   339, 493

Hu, Jinlong   198
Hu, Wenjun   359

Jacquemart, Quentin   111
Jamshed, Muhammad   89

Khasawneh, Khaled N.   3
Kirsch, Julian   177
Kittel, Thomas   177
Koide, Takashi   615
Kounev, Samuel   471
Krämer, Lukas   615
Krupp, Johannes   615

Le Scouarnec, Nicolas   48
Li, Bodong   359
Li, Juanru   359
Li, Qi   198
Lin, Zhiqiang   538
Luft, Matthias   471

Maggi, Federico   382
Makita, Daisuke   615
Mallick, Saptarshi   26
Mao, Weixuan   155
Maurice, Clémentine   48
Milenkoski, Aleksandar   471
Murmuria, Rahul   405

Nam, Jachyun   89
Neumann, Christoph   48
Nie, Meining   198
Nishizoe, Tomomi   615

Ozsoy, Meltem   3

Park, KyoungSoo   89
Payne, Bryan D.   471
Pellegrino, Giancarlo   295
Pendarakis, Dimitrios   588
Ponomarev, Dmitry   3
Portokalidis, Georgios   317

Röpke, Christian   339
Rossow, Christian   295, 615
Ryder, Barbara G.   270

Shu, Junliang   359
Shu, Xiaokui   270
Smutz, Charles   225
Sommer, Robin   133
Stavrou, Angelos   225, 405, 427, 515
Su, Purui   198
Sun, Xiaoshan   247

Towsley, Don   155
Tschürtz, Constantin   295

Ullrich, Johanna   448
Urvoy-Keller, Guillaume   111

Vervier, Pierre-Antoine   111
Vieira, Marco   471
Vogl, Sebastian   177

Wang, Haining   427
Wang, XiaoFeng   588
Wang, Zhi   198
Weißer, Dario   493
Weippl, Edgar   448

Xu, Haitao   427

Yakdan, Khaled   565
Yang, Qilang   317
Yang, Wenbo   359
Yao, Danfeng (Daphne)   270
Ying, Lingyun   198
Yoshioka, Katsunari   615
Yuan, Pinghai   66

Zanero, Stefano   382
Zeng, Junyuan   538
Zeng, Qingkai   66
Zeng, Shuke   247
Zhang, Yang   247
Zhang, Yuanyuan   359